AN
INCOMPLETE
EDUCATION

AN
INCOMPLETE
EDUCATION

3,684 Things You Should Have Learned but Probably Didn't

Judy Jones and William Wilson

Third Edition

 BALLANTINE BOOKS
NEW YORK

Published in the United States by Ballantine Books, an imprint of The Random House Publishing Group, a division of Penguin Random House LLC, New York. This work was originally published in 1987 and a revised edition was published in 1995 by Ballantine Books, an imprint of The Random House Publishing Group, a division of Penguin Random House LLC.

BALLANTINE and colophon are registered trademarks of Penguin Random House LLC.

Portions of this book originally appeared in *Esquire.*

Grateful acknowledgment is made to the following for permission to reprint previously published material.

City Lights Books, Inc.: Excerpt from "The Day Lady Died" from *Lunch Poems* by Frank O'Hara, copyright © 1964 by Frank O'Hara. Reprinted by permission of City Lights Books, Inc.

Farrar, Straus & Giroux LLC and Faber & Faber Ltd.: Excerpt from "For the Union Dead" from *For the Union Dead* by Robert Lowell, copyright © 1960, 1964 by Robert Lowell. Rights in Great Britain administered by Faber & Faber Ltd., London. Reprinted by permission of Farrar, Straus & Giroux LLC and Faber & Faber Ltd.

Henry Holt and Company LLC and Jonathan Cape Ltd., an imprint of The Random House Group Ltd.: "Nothing Gold Can Stay" and excerpt from "Directive" from *The Poetry of Robert Frost,* edited by Edward Connery Lathem, copyright © 1923, 1947, 1969 by Henry Holt and Company, copyright © 1975 by Lesley Frost Ballantine, copyright © 1951 by Robert Frost. Rights in Great Britain administered by Jonathan Cape Ltd., an imprint of The Random House Group Ltd., London. Reprinted by permission of Henry Holt and Company LLC and Jonathan Cape Ltd., an imprint of The Random House Group Ltd.

HarperCollins Publishers, Inc.: Excerpt from "Daddy" from *The Collected Poems of Sylvia Plath,* edited by Ted Hughes, copyright © 1963 by Ted Hughes. Reprinted by permission of HarperCollins Publishers, Inc.

Maps by Mapping Specialists Ltd.

Page 702 constitutes a continuation of the copyright page.

Library of Congress Cataloging-in-Publication Data

Jones, Judy.
An incomplete education.
Includes index.
1. Handbook, vade-mecums, etc.   I. Wilson, William, 1948–1999.   II. Title.
AG105.J64   1987   031'.02   86-91572
ISBN: 0-345-46890-2

This edition printed in the United States of America

Proprietary ISBN: 978-0-525-61509-5

www.ballantinebooks.com

9   8   7   6   5   4   3   2   1

Text design by Beth Tondreau
Photo editor: Cheryl Moch

Cover drawings © David Levine
Reprinted with permission from *The New York Review of Books*

Cover design by Andrew M. Newman

Third Edition

ACKNOWLEDGMENTS

The authors would like to thank the following, all of whom contributed their energies, insights, and expertise (even if only three of them know the meaning of the word "deadline") to the sections that bear their names:

Owen Edwards, Helen Epstein, Karen Houppert, Douglas Jones, David Martin, Stephen Nunns, Jon Pareles, Karen Pennar, Henry Popkin, Michael Sorkin, Judith Stone, James Trefil, Ronald Varney, Barbara Waxenberg, Alan Webber, and Mark Zussman.

CONTENTS

INTRODUCTION TO THE FIRST REVISED EDITION, JULY 1994

W hen this book was first published in the spring of 1987, literacy was in the air. Well, not literacy itself—almost everyone we knew was still misusing "lie" and "lay" and seemed resigned to never getting beyond the first hundred pages of *Remembrance of Things Past*. Rather, literacy as a concept, a cover story, an idea to rant, fret, and, of course, Do Something about. Allan Bloom's snarling denunciation of Americans' decadent philistinism in *The Closing of the American Mind*, followed closely by E. D. Hirsch's laundry list, in *Cultural Literacy*, of names, dates, and concepts—famous if often annoying touchstones, five thousand of them in the first volume alone—fueled discussion groups and call-in talk shows and spawned a whole mini-industry of varyingly comprehensive, competent, and clever guides to American history, say, or geography, or science, which most people not only hadn't retained but also didn't feel they'd understood to begin with. At the same time, there was that rancorous debate over expanding the academic "canon," or core curriculum, to include more than the standard works by Dead White European Males, plus Jane Austen and W. E. B. Du Bois, a worthy but humorless brouhaha characterized—and this was the high point—by mobs of Stanford students chanting, "Hey hey ho ho, Western Civ has got to go." Emerging from our rooms, where we'd been holed up with our portable typewriters and the working manuscript of *An Incomplete Education* for most of the decade, we blinked, looked around, and remarked thoughtfully, "Boy, this ought to sell a few books."

Now, back to revise the book for a second edition, we're astonished at how much the old 'hood has changed in just a few years. We thought life was moving at warp speed in the 1980s, yet we never had to worry, in those days, that what we wrote on Friday might be outdated by the following Monday (although we did stop to consider whether "Sean and Madonna" would still be a recognizable reference on the Monday after that). When we wrote the original edition, psychology was, if not exactly a comer, at least a legitimate topic of conversation—this was, remember, in the days before Freud's reputation had been trashed beyond repair and when plenty of people apparently still felt they could afford to spend eleven years and several hundred thousand dollars lying on a couch, free-associating their way from hysterical misery to ordinary unhappiness. Film, as distinct from movies, likewise still had intellectual appeal (and it made money, too), until that appeal dissolved somewhere between the demise of the European auteur theory and the rise of the video-rental store. We can actually remember a time—and so can you, if you're old enough to be reading this book—when a new film by Truffaut or Bergman or Fellini was considered as much of an event as the release of another Disney animation is today. And political science, while always more of a paranoiac's game than a bona fide academic discipline, at least had well-defined opposing teams (the Free World vs. the Communist one), familiar playing pieces (all those countries that were perpetually being manipulated by one side or the other), and a global game board whose markings weren't constantly being redrawn.

One thing hasn't changed, however, to judge by the couples standing in line behind us at the multiplex or the kids in the next booth at the diner: Nobody's gotten so much as a hair more literate. In fact, we seem to have actually become dopier, with someone like Norman Mailer superseded as our national interpreter of current events by someone like Larry King.

But then, why would it have turned out differently? If literacy was ever really—as all those literacy-anxiety books implied and as we, too, believed, for about five minutes back in 1979, when we first conceived of writing this one—about amassing information for the purpose of passing some imaginary standardized test, whether administered by a cranky professor, a snob at a dinner party, or your own conscience, it isn't anymore. Most of us have more databases, cable stations, CDs, telephone messages, e-mail, books, newspapers, and Post-its than we can possibly sort through in one lifetime; we don't need any additional information we don't know what to do with, thanks.

What we do need, more than ever, in our opinion, is the opportunity to have up-close-and-personal relationships, to be intimately if temporarily connected, with the right stuff, past and present. As nation-states devolve into family feuds and every crackpot with an urge to vent is awarded fifteen minutes of airtime, it seems less like bourgeois indulgence and more like preventive medicine to spend quality time with the books, music, art, philosophy, and discoveries that have, for one reason or another, managed to endure. What lasts? What works? What's the difference between good and evil? What, if anything, can we trust? It's not that we can't, in some roundabout way, extract clues from the testimony of the pregnant twelve-year-olds, the mothers of serial killers, and the couples who have sex with their rottweilers, who've become standard fare on Oprah and Maury and Sally Jessy, it's just that it's nice, when vertigo sets in, to be able to turn for a second opinion to Tolstoy or Melville or even Susan Sontag. And it helps restore one's equilibrium to revisit history and see for oneself whether, in fact, life was always this weird.

Consequently, what we've set out to provide in *An Incomplete Education* is not so much data as access; not a Cliffs Notes substitute or a cribsheet for cultural-literacy slackers but an invitation to the ball, a *way in* to material that has thrilled, inspired, and comforted, sure, but also embarrassed, upset, and/or confused us over the years, and which, we've assumed with our customary arrogance, may have stumped you too on occasion. In this edition, as in the first, we've endeavored—at times with more goodwill than good grace—to make introductions, uncover connections, facilitate communication, and generally lubricate the relationship between the reader (insofar as the reader thinks more or less along the same lines we do) and various aspects of Western Civ's "core curriculum," since the latter, whatever its shortfalls, still provides a frame of reference we can share without having to regret it in the morning, one that doesn't depend for its existence on market forces or for its appeal on mere prurient interest, and one that reminds us that we're capable of grappling with questions of more enduring—even, if you think about it, more immediate—import than whether or not O.J. really did it.

Finally, a note to those (mercifully few) readers who wrote to us complaining that the first edition of *An Incomplete Education* failed, despite their high hopes and urgent needs, to complete their educations: Don't hold your breath this time around, either. We'll refrain from referring you, snidely, to the book's title (but for goodness' sake, don't you even *look* before you march off to the cash register?), but we will permit ourselves to wonder what a "complete" education might consist of, and why, if such a thing existed, you would want it anyway. What, know it all? No gaps to fill, no new territory to explore, nothing left to learn, education over? (And no need for third and fourth revised editions of this book?) Please, write to us again and tell us you were just kidding.

INTRODUCTION TO THE ORIGINAL EDITION, MARCH 1986

It's like this: You're reading the Sunday book section and there, in a review of a book that isn't even about physics but about how to write a screenplay, you're confronted by that word again: *quark*. You have been confronted by it at least twenty-five times, beginning in at least 1978, but you have not managed to retain the definition (something about building blocks), and the resonances (something about threesomes, something about birdshit) are even more of a problem. You're feeling stymied. You worry that you may not use spare time to maximum advantage, that the world is passing you by, that maybe it *would* make sense to subscribe to a third newsweekly. Your coffee's getting cold. The phone rings. You can't bring yourself to answer it.

Or it's like this: You *do* know what a quark is. You can answer the phone. It is an attractive person you have recently met. How are you? How are you? The person is calling to wonder if you feel like seeing a movie both of you missed the first time around. It's *The Year of Living Dangerously*, with Mel Gibson and that very tall actress. Also, that very short actress. "Plus," the person says, "it's set in Indonesia, which, next to India, is probably the most fascinating of all Third World nations. It's like the political scientists say, 'The labyrinth that is India, the mosaic that is Indonesia.' Right?" Silence at your end of the phone. Clearly this person is into overkill, but that doesn't mean you don't have to say something back. India you could field. But Indonesia? Fortunately, you have cable—and a Stouffer's lasagna in the freezer.

Or it's like *this*: You know what a quark is. Also something about Indonesia. The two of you enjoy the movie. The new person agrees to go with you to a dinner party one of your best friends is giving at her country place. You arrive, pulling into a driveway full of BMWs. You go inside. Introductions are made. Along about the second margarita, the talk turns to World War II. Specifically, the causes of World War II. More specifically, Hitler. Already this is not easy. But it is interesting. "Well," says another guest, flicking an imaginary piece of lint from the sleeve of a double-breasted navy blazer, "you really can't disregard the impact Nietzsche had, not only on Hitler, but on a prostrate Germany. You know: The will to power. The Übermensch. The transvaluation of values. Don't you agree, old bean?" Fortunately, you have cable—and a Stouffer's lasagna in the freezer.

So what's your problem? Weren't you supposed to have learned all this stuff back in college? Sure you were, but then, as now, you had your good days and your bad days. Ditto your teachers. Maybe you were in the infirmary with the flu the week your Philosophy 101 class was slogging through *Zarathustra*. Maybe your poli-sci prof was served with divorce papers right about the time the class hit the nonaligned nations. Maybe you failed to see the relevance of subatomic particles given your desperate need to get a date for Homecoming. Maybe you actually *had* all the answers—for a few glorious hours before the No-Doz (or whatever it was) wore off. No matter. The upshot is that you've got some serious educational gaps. And that, old bean, is what this book is all about.

Now we'll grant you that educational gaps today don't signify in quite the way they did even ten years ago. In fact, when we first got the idea for this book, sitting around *Esquire* magazine's research department, we envisioned a kind of intellectual *Dress for Success*, a guidebook to help reasonably literate, reasonably ambitious types like ourselves preserve an upwardly mobile image and make an impression at cocktail parties by getting off a few good quotes from Dr. Johnson—or, for that matter, by not referring to Evelyn Waugh as "she."

Yup, times have changed since then. (You didn't think we were still sitting around the *Esquire* research department, did you?) And the more we heard people's party conversation turning from literary matters to money-market accounts and condo closings, the more we worried that the book we were working on wasn't noble (or uplifting, or profound; also long) enough. Is it just another of those bluffers' handbooks? we wondered. Is its guiding spirit not insight at all, but rather the brashest kind of one-upmanship? Is trying to reduce the complexities of culture, politics, and science to a couple hundred words each so very different from trying to fill in all the wedges of one's pie in a game of Trivial Pursuit? (And why hadn't *we* thought up Trivial Pursuit? But that's another story.)

Then we realized something. We realized that what we were really going for here had less to do with competition and power positions than with context and perspective. In a world of bits and bytes, of reruns and fast forwards, of information overloads and significance shortfalls (and of Donald Trump and bagpersons no older than one is, but that's another story) it feels good to be grounded. It feels good to be able to bring to the wire-service story about Reagan's dream of packing the Supreme Court a sense of what the Supreme Court is (and the knowledge that people have been trying to pack it from the day it opened), to be able to buttress one's comparison of Steven Spielberg and D. W. Griffith with a knowledge of the going critical line on the latter. In short, we found that we were casting our vote for grounding, as opposed to grooming. Also that grounding, not endless, mindless mobility, turns out to be the real power position.

And then something really strange happened. Setting out to discover what conceivable appeal a Verdi, say, could have on a planet that was clearly—and, it seemed at the time, rightly—dominated by the Rolling Stones, we stumbled into a nineteenth-century landscape where the name of the game was grandeur, not grandiosity; where romanticism had no trashy connotations; where music and spectacle could elicit overwhelming emotions without, at the same time, threatening to fry one's brains. No kidding, we actually *liked* this stuff! What's more, coming of age in a world of T-shirts and jeans and groovy R & B riffs apparently didn't make one ineligible for a passport to the other place. One just needed a few key pieces of information and a willingness to travel.

And speaking of travel, let's face it: Bumping along over the potholes of your mind day after day can't be doing much for your self-esteem. Which is the third thing, along with power and enrichment, this book is all about. Don't you think you'll feel better about yourself once all those gaps have been filled? Everything from the mortifying (how to tell Keats from Shelley) to the merely pesky (how to tell a nave from a narthex)? Imagine. Nothing but you and the open road.

Before you take off, though, we ought to say something about the book's structure. Basically, it's divided into chapters corresponding to the disciplines and departments you remember from college (you were paying *that* much attention, weren't you?). Not that everything in the book is stuff you'd necessarily study in college, but it's all well within the limits of what an "educated" person is expected to know. In those areas where our own roads weren't in such great repair, we've called on specialist friends and colleagues to help us out. Even so, we don't claim to have covered everything; we simply went after what struck us as the biggest trouble spots.

Now, our advice for using this book: Don't feel you have to read all of any given chapter on a single tank of gas. And don't feel you have to get from point A to point B by lunchtime; better to slow down and enjoy the scenery. Do, however, try to stay alert. Even with the potholes fixed, you'll want to be braced for hairpin turns (and the occasional five-car collision) up ahead.

AN
INCOMPLETE
EDUCATION

AMERICAN STUDIES

Contents

Flag drill, farmworkers' camp, Caldwell, Idaho, 1941

American Literature 101

A FIRST-SEMESTER SYLLABUS

You signed up for it thinking it would be a breeze. After all, you'd read most of the stuff back in high school, hadn't you?

Or had you? As it turned out, the thing you remembered best about *Moby-Dick* was the expression on Gregory Peck's face as he and the whale went down for the last time. And was it really *The Scarlet Letter* you liked so much? Or was it the Classics Illustrated version of *The Scarlet Letter*? Of course, you weren't the only one who overestimated your familiarity with your literary heritage; your professor was busy making the same mistake.

Then there was the material itself, much of it so bad it made you wish you'd signed up for The Nineteenth Century French Novel: Stendhal to Zola instead. Now that you're older, though, you may be willing to make allowances. After all, the literary figures you were most likely to encounter the first semester were by and large only moonlighting as writers. They had to spend the bulk of their time building a nation, framing a constitution, carving a civilization out of the wilderness, or simply busting their chops trying to make a living. In those days, no one was about to fork over six figures so some Puritan could lie around Malibu polishing a screenplay.

Try, then, to think only kind and patriotic thoughts as, with the help of this chart, you refresh your memory on all those things you were asked to face—or to face again—in your freshman introduction to American Lit.

JONATHAN EDWARDS (1703–1758)

Product of:

Northampton, Massachusetts, where he ruled from the pulpit for thirty years; Stockbridge, Massachusetts, where he became an Indian missionary after the townspeople of Northampton got fed up with him.

Earned a Living as a:

Clergyman, theologian.

High-School Reading List:

The sermon, "Sinners in the Hands of an Angry God" (1741), the most famous example of "the preaching of terror."

Jonathan Edwards' church, Northampton, Massachusetts

College Reading List:

Any number of sermons, notably "God Glorified in the Work of Redemption by the Greatness of Man's Dependence on Him in the Whole of It" (1731), Edwards' first sermon, in which he pinpoints the moral failings of New Englanders; and "A Faithful Narrative of the Surprising Work of God" (1737), describing various types and stages of religious conversion. Also, if your college professor was a fundamentalist, a New Englander, or simply sadistic, one or two of the treatises, e.g., "A Careful and Strict Enquiry into the Freedom of the Will" (1754), or the "Great Christian Doctrine of Original Sin Defended" (1758). Not to be missed: a dip into Edwards' *Personal Narrative*, which suggests the psychological connection between being America's number-one Puritan clergyman and the only son in a family with eleven children.

What You Were Supposed to Have Learned in High School:

Edwards' historical importance as quintessential Puritan thinker and hero of the Great Awakening, the religious revival that swept New England from the late 1730s to 1750.

Twain's frontier humor; the essays "Fenimore Cooper's Literary Offenses" (1895, 1897) and "The United States of Lyncherdom" (1901), as examples of his scathing wit and increasing disillusionment with America; and the short novel, *The Mysterious Stranger* (published posthumously, 1916), for the late, bleak, embittered Twain.

What You Were Supposed to Have Learned in High School:

That *Huckleberry Finn* is the great mock-epic of American democracy, marking the beginning of a caste-free literature that owed nothing to European tradition. That this was the first time the American vernacular had made it into a serious literary work. That the book profoundly influenced the development of the modern American prose style. And that you should have been paying more attention to Twain's brilliant manipulation of language and less to whether or not Huck, Tom, and Jim made it out of the lean-to alive. Also, that Mark Twain, which was river parlance for "two fathoms deep," was the pseudonym of Samuel Langhorne Clemens.

What You Didn't Find Out Until College:

That Twain grew more and more pessimistic about America—and about humanity in general—as he, and the country, grew older, eventually turning into a bona fide misanthrope. And that he was stylistically tone-deaf, producing equal amounts of brilliant prose and overwritten trash without ever seeming to notice the difference.

The Beat Goes On

A HUNDRED YEARS' WORTH OF MODERN AMERICAN POETRY

So much of what we've all been committing to memory over the past lifetime or so—the words to "Help Me, Rhonda" typify the genre—eventually stops paying the same dividends. Sure, the beat's as catchy as ever. But once the old gang's less worried about what to do on Saturday night than about meeting

What You Didn't Find Out Until College:

What Edwards thought *about*, namely, the need to get back to the old-fashioned Calvinist belief in man's basic depravity and in his total dependence on God's goodwill for salvation. (Forget about the "covenant" theory of Protestantism; according to Edwards, God doesn't bother cutting deals with humans.) Also, his insistence that faith and conversion be emotional, not just intellectual.

BENJAMIN FRANKLIN (1706–1790)

Product of:

Philadelphia, Pennsylvania.

Earned a Living as a:

Printer, promoter, inventor, diplomat, statesman.

High-School Reading List:

The *Declaration of Independence* (1776), which he helped draft.

College Reading List:

The Autobiography of Benjamin Franklin (1771–1788), considered one of the greatest autobiographies ever written; sample maxims from *Poor Richard's Almanack* (1732–1757), mostly on how to make money or keep from spending it; any number of articles and essays on topics of historical interest, ranging from "Rules by Which a Great Empire May Be Reduced to a Small One," and "An Edict by the King of Prussia" (both 1773), about the colonies' Great Britain problem, to "Experiments and Observations on Electricity" (1751), all of which are quite painless.

What You Were Supposed to Have Learned in High School:

Not a thing. But back in grade school you presumably learned that Franklin invented a stove, bifocal glasses, and the lightning rod; that he established the first, or almost the first, library, fire department, hospital, and insurance company; that he helped negotiate the treaty with France that allowed America to win independence; that he was a member of the Constitutional Convention; that he was the most famous American of the eighteenth century (after George Washington) and the closest thing we've ever had to a Renaissance man.

What You Didn't Find Out Until College:

That Franklin had as many detractors as admirers, for whom his shrewdness, pettiness, hypocrisy, and nonstop philandering embodied all the worst traits of the American character, of American capitalism, and of the Protestant ethic.

WASHINGTON IRVING (1783–1859)

Washington Irving's house, Tarrytown, New York

Product of: New York City and Tarrytown, New York.

Earned a Living as a: Writer; also, briefly, a diplomat.

High-School Reading List: "Rip Van Winkle" and "The Legend of Sleepy Hollow," both contained in *The Sketch Book* (1820).

College Reading List: Other more or less interchangeable selections from *The Sketch Book*, *Bracebridge Hall* (1822), *Tales of a Traveller* (1824), or *The Legends of the*

Alhambra (1832), none of which stuck in anyone's memory for more than ten minutes.

What You Were Supposed to Have Learned in High School:

That Irving was the first to prove that Americans could write as well as Europeans; that Ichabod Crane and Rip Van Winkle's wife both got what they deserved.

What You Didn't Find Out Until College:

That Irving's grace as a stylist didn't quite make up for his utter lack of originality, insight, or depth.

JAMES FENIMORE COOPER (1789–1851)

Product of:

Cooperstown, New York.

Earned a Living as a:

Gentleman farmer.

High-School Reading List:

Probably none; *The Leatherstocking Tales*, i.e., *The Pioneers* (1823), *The Last of the Mohicans* (1826), *The Prairie* (1827), *The Pathfinder* (1840), and *The Deerslayer* (1841) are considered grade-school material.

College Reading List:

Social criticism, such as *Notions of the Americans* (1828), a defense of America against the sniping of foreign visitors; or "Letter to his Countrymen" (1834), a diatribe written in response to bad reviews of his latest novel.

What You Were Supposed to Have Learned in High School:

That Cooper was America's first successful novelist and that Natty Bumppo was one of the all-time most popular characters in world literature. Also that *The Leatherstocking Tales* portrayed the conflicting values of the vanishing wilderness and encroaching civilization.

What You Didn't Find Out Until College:

That the closest Cooper ever got to the vanishing wilderness was Scarsdale, and that, in his day, he was considered an insufferable snob, a reactionary, a grouch, and a troublemaker known for defending slavery and opposing suffrage for everyone but male landowners. That eventually, everyone decided the writing in *The Leatherstocking Tales* was abominable, but that during the 1920s Cooper's social criticism began to seem important and his thinking pretty much representative of American conservatism.

RALPH WALDO EMERSON (1803–1882)

Product of: Concord, Massachusetts.

Earned a Living as a: Unitarian minister, lecturer.

High-School Reading List: A few passages from *Nature* (1836), Emerson's paean to individualism, and a couple of the *Essays* (1841), one of which was undoubtedly the early, optimistic "Self-Reliance." If you were spending a few days on Transcendentalism, you probably also had to read "The Over-Soul." If, on the other hand, your English teacher swung toward an essay like "The Poet," it was, no doubt, accompanied by a snatch of Emersonian verse— most likely "Brahma" or "Days." (You already knew Emerson's "Concord Hymn" from grade-school history lessons, although you probably didn't know who wrote it.)

College Reading List: Essays and more essays, including "Experience," a tough one. Also the lecture "The American Scholar," in which Emerson called for a proper American literature, freed from European domination.

What You Were Supposed to Have Learned in High School: That Emerson was the most important figure of the Transcendentalist movement, whatever that was, the friend and benefactor of Thoreau, and a legend in his own time; also, that he was a great thinker, a staunch individualist, an unshakable optimist, and a first-class human being, even if you wouldn't have wanted to know him yourself.

What You Didn't Find Out Until College:

That you'd probably be a better person if you *had* known him yourself and that almost any one of his essays could see you through an identity crisis, if not a nervous breakdown.

NATHANIEL HAWTHORNE (1804–1864)

Nathaniel Hawthorne

Hawthorne's house, Concord, Massachusetts

Product of:

Salem and Concord, Massachusetts.

Earned a Living as a:

Writer, surveyor, American consul in Liverpool.

High-School Reading List:

The Scarlet Letter (1850) or *The House of the Seven Gables* (1851); plus one or two tales, among which was probably "Young Goodman Brown" (1846) because your teacher hoped a story about witchcraft would hold your attention long enough to get you through it.

College Reading List:

None, since you were expected to have done the reading back in high school. One possible exception: *The Blithedale Romance* (1852) if your prof was into Brook Farm and the Transcendentalists;

another: *The Marble Faun* (1860) for its explicit fall-of-man philosophizing.

What You Were Supposed to Have Learned in High School: What the letter *A* embroidered on someone's dress means.

What You Didn't Find Out Until College: That Hawthorne marked a turning point in American morality and a break from our Puritan past, despite the fact that he, like his ancestors, never stopped obsessing about sin and guilt. Also, that he's considered something of an underachiever.

EDGAR ALLAN POE (1809–1849)

Edgar Allan Poe's cottage, New York City

Product of: Richmond, Virginia; New York City; Baltimore, Maryland.

Earned a Living as a: Hack journalist and reviewer.

High-School Reading List: "The Raven" (1845), "Ulalume" (1847), "Annabel Lee" (1848), and a few other poems, probably read aloud in class; a detective story: "The Murders in the Rue Morgue" (1841) or "The Purloined Letter" (1845), either of which you could skip if you'd seen the movie; one or two of the supernatural-death stories, say, "The Fall of the House of Usher" (1839) or "The Masque of the Red Death" (1842), either of which you could skip if you'd seen the movie; a couple of the psychotic-murderer stories, e.g., "The Tell-Tale Heart" or "The Black Cat" (both 1843), either of which you could skip if you'd seen the movie; and a pure Poe horror number like "The Pit and the Pendulum" (1842), which you could skip if you'd seen the movie. Sorry, but as far as we know, they still haven't made a movie of "The Cask of Amontillado" (1846), although somebody once wrote to us, claiming to have seen it.

College Reading List:

None; remedial reading only, unless you chose to write your dissertation on "The Gothic Element in American Fiction."

What You Were Supposed to Have Learned in High School:

That Poe invented the detective story and formulated the short story more or less as we know it. That maybe poetry wasn't so bad, after all. Also, that Poe was a poverty-stricken alcoholic who did drugs and who married his thirteen-year-old cousin, just like Jerry Lee Lewis did.

What You Didn't Find Out Until College:

That once you're over seventeen, you don't ever admit to liking Poe's poetry, except maybe to your closest friend who's a math major; that while Poe seemed puerile to American critics, he was a cult hero to European writers from Baudelaire to Shaw; and that, in spite of his subject matter, Poe still gets credit—even in America—for being a great technician.

HARRIET BEECHER STOWE (1811–1896)

Product of:

Litchfield and Hartford, Connecticut; Cincinnati, Ohio; Brunswick, Maine.

Earned a Living as a:

Housewife.

High-School Reading List:

Uncle Tom's Cabin (1851–1852).

Harriet Beecher Stowe

| College Reading List: | *The Pearl of Orr's Island* (1862) and *Old Town Folks* (1869), if your professor was determined to make a case for Stowe as a novelist. Both are considered superior to *Uncle Tom's Cabin.* |

What You Were Supposed to Have Learned in High School:

What happened to Uncle Tom, Topsy, and Little Eva. That the novel was one of the catalysts of the Civil War.

What You Didn't Find Out Until College:

That you'd have done better to spend your time reading the real story of slavery in *My Life and Times* by Frederick Douglass. That the fact that you didn't was just one more proof, dammit, of the racism rampant in our educational system.

HENRY DAVID THOREAU (1817–1862)

Product of:

Concord, Massachusetts, and nearby Walden Pond.

Earned a Living as a:

Schoolteacher, pencil maker, surveyor, handyman, naturalist.

High-School Reading List:

Walden (1854), inspired by the two years he spent communing with himself and Nature in a log cabin on Walden Pond.

College Reading List:

"Civil Disobedience" (1849), the essay inspired by the night he spent in jail for refusing to pay a poll tax; *A Week on the Concord and Merrimack Rivers* (1849), inspired by a few weeks spent on same with his brother John, and considered a literary warm-up for *Walden*; parts of the *Journal*, inspired by virtually everything, which Thoreau not only kept but polished and rewrote for almost twenty-five years—you had fourteen volumes to choose from, including the famous "lost journal" which was rediscovered in 1958.

What You Were Supposed to Have Learned in High School:

That Thoreau was one of the great American eccentrics and the farthest out of the Transcendentalists, and that he believed you should spend your life breaking bread with the birds and the woodchucks instead of going for a killing in the futures market like your old man.

What You Didn't Find Out Until College:

That *Walden* was not just a spiritualized *Boy Scout Handbook* but, according to twentieth-century authorities, a carefully composed literary masterpiece. That, according to these same authorities, Thoreau *did* have a sense of humor. That Tolstoy was mightily impressed with "Civil Disobedience" and Gandhi used it as the inspiration for his *satyagraha*. That despite his reputation as a loner and pacifist, Thoreau became the friend and defender of the radical abolitionist John Brown. And that, heavy as you were into Thoreau's principles of purity, simplicity, and spirituality, you still had to figure out how to hit your parents up for plane fare to Goa.

Henry David Thoreau's house, Concord, Massachusetts

HERMAN MELVILLE (1819–1891)

Product of: New York City; Albany and Troy, New York; various South Sea islands.

Earned a Living as a: Schoolteacher, bank clerk, sailor, harpooner, customs inspector.

High-School Reading List: *Moby-Dick* (1851; abridged version, or you just skipped the parts about the whaling industry); *Typee* (1846), the early bestseller, which was, your teacher hoped, sufficiently exotic and action-packed to get you hooked on Melville. For extra credit, the novella *Billy Budd* (published posthumously, 1924).

College Reading List: *Moby-Dick* (unabridged version), *The Piazza Tales* (1856), especially "Bartleby the Scrivener" and "Benito Cereno"; and the much-discussed, extremely tedious *The Confidence Man* (1857).

What You Were Supposed to Have Learned in High School: That *Moby-Dick* is allegorical (the whale = Nature/God/the Implacable Universe; Ahab = Man's Conflicted Identity/Civilization/Human Will; Ishmael = the Poet/Philosopher) and should be read as a debate between Ahab and Ishmael.

Herman Melville's house, Albany, New York

What You Didn't Find Out Until College:

That Melville didn't know *Moby-Dick* was allegorical until somebody pointed it out to him. That his work prefigured some of Freud's theories of the unconscious. That, like Lord Byron, Norman Mailer, and Bob Dylan, Melville spent most of his life struggling to keep up with the name he'd made for himself (with the bestselling *Typee*) before he turned thirty. And that if, historically, he was caught between nineteenth-century Romanticism and modern alienation, personally he was pretty unbalanced as well. He may or may not have been gay, as some biographers assert (if he was, he almost certainly didn't know it), but whatever he was, Nathaniel Hawthorne eventually stopped taking his calls.

MARK TWAIN (1835–1910)

The Clemens family

Product of:

Hannibal, Missouri; various Nevada mining towns; Hartford, Connecticut.

Earned a Living as a:

Printer, river pilot, newspaper reporter, lecturer, storyteller.

High-School Reading List:

The Adventures of Huckleberry Finn (1884). Also, if you took remedial English, *The Adventures of Tom Sawyer* (1876).

College Reading List:

The short story "The Celebrated Jumping Frog of Calaveras County" (1865), as an example of

child-support payments and stemming periodontal disease, it's nice to have something more in the way of consolation, perspective, and uplift to fall back on. Good news: All the time you were glued to the car radio, a few people with a little more foresight were writing—and what's more, printing—poetry, some of which is as about as Zeitgeisty as things get.

It is, however, a little trickier than the Beach Boys. For one thing, it's modern, which means you're up against alienation and artificiality. For another, it's poetry, which means nobody's just going to come out and say what's on his mind. Put them together and you've got modern poetry. Read on and you've got modern poetry's brightest lights and biggest guns, arranged in convenient categories for those pressed for time and/or an ordering principle of their own.

THE FIVE BIG DEALS

EZRA POUND (1885–1972)

Profile: Old Granddad . . . most influential figure (and most headline-making career) in modern poetry . . . made poets write modern, editors publish modern, and readers read modern . . . part archaeologist, part refugee, he scavenged past eras (medieval Provence, Confucian China) with a mind to overhauling his own . . . in so doing, masterminded a cultural revolution, complete with doctrines, ideology, and propaganda . . . though expatriated to London and Italy, remained at heart an American, rough-and-ready, even vulgar, as he put it, "a plymouth-rock conscience landed on a predilection for the arts" . . . responsive and rigorous: helped Eliot (whose *The Waste Land* he pared down to half its original length), Yeats, Joyce, Frost, and plenty of lesser poets and writers . . . reputation colored by his anti-Semitism, his hookup with Mussolini, the ensuing charges of treason brought by the U.S. government, and the years in a mental institution.

Motto: "Make it new."

A colleague begs to differ: "Mr. Pound is a village explainer—excellent if you were
a village, but, if you were not, not."—Gertrude Stein

Favorite colors: Purple, ivory, jade.

Latest Books read: Confucius, Stendhal, the songs of the troubadours, the memoirs of Thomas Jefferson.

The easy (and eminently quotable) Pound:

> There died a myriad,
> And of the best, among them,
> For an old bitch gone in the teeth,
> For a botched civilization,
>
> Charm, smiling at the good mouth,
> Quick eyes gone under earth's lid,
>
> For two gross of broken statues,
> For a few thousand battered books.
>
> from *Hugh Selwyn Mauberley*

The prestige Pound (for extra credit):

> Zeus lies in Ceres' bosom
> Taishan is attended of loves
>   under Cythera, before sunrise
> and he said: "Hay aquí mucho catolicismo—(sounded catoli*th*ismo)
>   y muy poco reliHión"
> and he said: "Yo creo que los reyes desaparecen"
> (Kings will, I think, disappear)
> That was Padre José Elizondo
>   in 1906 and 1917
> or about 1917
>   and Dolores said "Come pan, niño," (eat bread, me lad)
> Sargent had painted her
>   before he descended
> (i.e., if he descended)
>   but in those days he did thumb sketches,
> impressions of the Velásquez in the Museo del Prado
> and books cost a peseta,
>   brass candlesticks in proportion,
> hot wind came from the marshes
>   and death-chill from the mountains. . . .

from *Cantos,* LXXXI (one of the Pisan Cantos, written after World War II while
Pound was on display in a cage in Pisa)

T. S. (THOMAS STERNS) ELIOT (1888–1965)

Profile: Tied with Yeats for most famous poet of the century . . . his masterpiece *The Waste Land* (1922), which gets at the fragmentation, horror, and ennui of modern times through a collage of literary, religious, and pop allusions . . . erudition for days: a page of Eliot's poetry can consist of more footnotes and scholarly references than text . . . born in Missouri, educated at Harvard, but from the late 1910s (during which he worked as a bank clerk) on, lived in London and adopted the ways of an Englishman . . . tried in his early poetry to reunite wit and passion, which, in English poetry, had been going their separate ways since Donne and the Metaphysicals (see page 190) . . . his later poetry usually put down for its religiosity (Eliot had, in the meantime, found God); likewise, with the exception of *Murder in the Cathedral*, his plays . . . had a history of nervous breakdowns; some critics see his poetry in terms not of tradition and classicism, but of compulsion and craziness.

Motto: "Genuine poetry can communicate before it is understood."

A colleague begs to differ: "A subtle conformist," according to William Carlos Williams, who called *The Waste Land* "the great catastrophe."

Favorite colors: Eggplant, sable, mustard.

Latest books read: Dante, Hesiod, the *Bhagavad Gita*, Hesse's *A Glimpse into Chaos*, St. Augustine, Jessie L. Weston's *From Ritual to Romance*, Frazer's *The Golden Bough*, Baudelaire, the Old Testament books of Ezekiel, Isaiah, and Ecclesiastes, Joyce's *Ulysses*, *Antony and Cleopatra*, "The Rape of the Lock," and that's just *this* week.

The easy (and eminently quotable) Eliot: The opening lines of "The Love Song of J. Alfred Prufrock," the let-us-go-then-you-and-I, patient-etherised-upon-a-table, women-talking-of-Michelangelo lead-in to a poem that these days seems as faux-melodramatic and faggy—and as unforgettable—as a John Waters movie. (We'd have printed these lines for you here, but the Eliot estate has a thing about excerpting.)

The prestige Eliot (for extra credit): Something from the middle of the *The Waste Land*, just to show you've made it through the whole 434 lines. Try, for example, the second stanza of the third book ("The Fire Sermon"), in the course of which a rat scurries along a river bank, the narrator muses on the death of "the king my father," Mrs. Sweeney and her daughter "wash their feet in soda water," and Eliot's own footnotes refer you to *The Tempest*, an Elizabethan poem called *Parliament of Bees*, the World War I ballad in which Mrs. Sweeney makes her first appearance (ditto her daughter), and a sonnet by Verlaine.

WILLIAM CARLOS WILLIAMS
(1883–1963)

Profile: Uncle Bill . . . at the center of postwar poetry, the man whom younger poets used to look to for direction and inspiration . . . smack-dab in the American grain . . . determined to write poetry based on the language as spoken *here*, the language he heard "in the mouths of Polish mothers" . . . avoided traditional stanza, rhyme, and line patterns, preferring a jumble of images and rhythms . . . spent his entire life in New Jersey, a small-town doctor, specializing in pediatrics . . . played homebody to Pound's and Eliot's gadabouts, regular guy to their *artistes*—the former a lifelong friend, with whom he disagreed loudly and often . . . wanted to make "contact," which he took to mean "man with nothing but the thing and the feeling of that thing" . . . not taken seriously by critics and intellectuals, who tended, until the Fifties, to treat him like a literary Grandma Moses . . . *Paterson* is his *The Waste Land*.

Motto: "No ideas but in things."
A colleague begs to differ: "A poet of some local interest, perhaps."—Eliot. "Antipoetic."—Wallace Stevens.
Favorite colors: Blue, yellow, tan.
Latest books read: Keats, Pound's *Cantos*, Allen Ginsberg's *Howl*.

The easy (and eminently quotable) Williams:

> so much depends
> upon
>
> a red wheel
> barrow
>
> glazed with rain
> water
>
> beside the white
> chickens.

"The Red Wheelbarrow"

The prestige Williams (for extra credit):

> The descent beckons
>   as the ascent beckoned
>   Memory is a kind
> of accomplishment
>   a sort of renewal
>   even
> an initiation, since the spaces it opens are new
> places
>   inhabited by hordes
>   heretofore unrealized,
> of new kinds—
>   since their movements
>   are towards new objectives
> (even though formerly they were abandoned)
>
> No defeat is made up entirely of defeat—since
> the world it opens is always a place
>   formerly
>   unsuspected. A
> world lost,
>   a world unsuspected
>   beckons to new places
> and no whiteness (lost) is so white as the memory
> of whiteness

from *Paterson*, Book 2 ("Sunday in the Park"), Section 2

ROBERT FROST (1874–1963)

Profile: The one who got stuck being popular with readers outside college English departments . . . but not just the "miles-to-go-before-I-sleep" poet; as one critic said, "sees the skull beneath the flesh" . . . born in California, where he spent his boyhood: The New England accent just a bit of a fraud . . . re-created, in his poems, the rhythms of actual speech, the actions of ordinary men . . . "got" nature, tradition, and anxiety . . . his tone sad, wry, and a little narcissistic . . . eventually carved out an elder-statesman role for himself in official American culture . . . isolation, limitation, and extinction were favorite themes . . . said to have been a creep to his wife and son (who committed suicide) . . . for better or worse, hard not to memorize.

Motto: "We play the words as we find them."

A colleague begs to differ: "His work is full (or said to be full) of humanity."—Wallace Stevens.

Favorite colors: Teal blue, slate gray, blood red.

Latest books read: The King James Bible, Thoreau's *Walden*, Hardy's *Tess of the D'Urbervilles*.

The easy (and eminently quotable) Frost:

> Nature's first green is gold,
> Her hardest hue to hold.
> Her early leaf's a flower;
> But only so an hour.
> Then leaf subsides to leaf.
> So Eden sank to grief,
> So dawn goes down to day.
> Nothing gold can stay.

> "Nothing Gold Can Stay"

The prestige Frost (for extra credit):

> . . . Make yourself up a cheering song of how
> Someone's road home from work this once was,
> Who may be just ahead of you on foot
> Or creaking with a buggy load of grain.
> The height of the adventure is the height
> Of country where two village cultures faded
> Into each other. Both of them are lost.

And if you're lost enough to find yourself
By now, pull in your ladder road behind you
And put a sign up CLOSED to all but me.
Then make yourself at home. The only field
Now left's no bigger than a harness gall.
First there's the children's house of make-believe,
Some shattered dishes underneath a pine,
The playthings in the playhouse of the children.
Weep for what little things could make them glad. . . .

from "Directive"

WALLACE STEVENS (1879–1955)

Profile: With Yeats and Eliot, billed as a great "imaginative force" in modern poetry . . . self-effacing insurance executive who spent a lifetime at the Hartford Accident and Indemnity Company, writing poetry nights and weekends . . . didn't travel in literary circles (and was on a first-name basis with almost no other writers); did, however, manage to get into a famous fistfight with Ernest Hemingway while vacationing in Key West . . . believed in "the essential gaudiness of poetry" . . . his own verse marked by flair, self-mockery, virtuoso touches, aggressive art-for-art's-sakeishness . . . in it, he portrayed himself as the aesthete, the dandy, the hedonist . . . held that, since religion could no longer satisfy people, poetry would have to . . . had the sensuousness and brilliance of a Keats (cf., as the critics do, Frost's "Wordsworthian plainness").

Motto: "Poetry is the supreme fiction, madame."

A colleague begs to differ: "A bric-a-brac poet."—Robert Frost.

Favorite colors: Vermilion, chartreuse, wine.

Latest books read: A Midsummer Night's Dream, the poetry of Verlaine, Mallarmé, and Yeats, Henri Bergson's *On Laughter*.

The easy (and eminently quotable) Stevens:

I placed a jar in Tennessee,
And round it was, upon a hill.
It made the slovenly wilderness
Surround that hill.

The wilderness rose up to it,
And sprawled around, no longer wild.
The jar was round upon the ground.
And tall and of a port in air.

It took dominion everywhere.
The jar was gray and bare.
It did not give of bird or bush,
Like nothing else in Tennessee.

"Anecdote of the Jar"

The prestige Stevens (for extra credit):

Ramon Fernandez, tell me, if you know,
Why, when the singing ended and we turned
Toward the town, tell why the glassy lights,
The lights in the fishing boats at anchor there,
As the night descended, tilting in the air,
Mastered the night and portioned out the sea,
Fixing emblazoned zones and fiery poles,
Arranging, deepening, enchanting night.

Oh! Blessed rage for order, pale Ramon,
The maker's rage to order words of the sea,
Words of the fragrant portals, dimly-starred,
And of ourselves and our origins,
In ghostlier demarcations, keener sounds.

from "The Idea of Order at Key West"

THE FIVE RUNNERS-UP

MARIANNE MOORE (1887–1972)

If "compression is the first grace of style,"
you have it.

from "To a Snail"

Has been called "the poet's poet" and compared to "a solo harpsichord in a concerto" in which all other American poets are the orchestra . . . has also been called, by Hart Crane, "a hysterical virgin" . . . in either case, was notorious for staring at animals (pangolins, frigate pelicans, arctic oxen), steamrollers, and the Brooklyn Dodgers, then holding forth on what she saw . . . believed in "predilection" rather than "passion" and wanted to achieve an "unbearable accuracy," a "precision" that had both "impact and exactitude, as with surgery" . . . watch for her quotes from history books, encyclopedias, and travel brochures . . . original, alert, and neat . . . appealed to fellow poets, including young ones, with her matter-of-fact tone, her ability to make poetry read as easily as prose.

JOHN CROWE RANSOM (1888–1974)

—I am a gentleman in a dustcoat trying
To make you hear. Your ears are soft and small
And listen to an old man not at all. . . .

from "Piazza Piece"

Finest of the Southern poets (he beats out Allen Tate and Robert Penn Warren), and the center of the literary group called the Fugitives (mention tradition, agrarianism, and the New Criticism and they'll read you some of their own verse) . . . liked the mythic, the courtly, the antique, and flirted with the pedantic . . . small poetic output: only three books, all written between 1919 and 1927 . . . founder and editor, for over twenty years, of the *Kenyon Review*, arguably the top American literary magazine of its day . . . at his worst, can be a little stilted, a little sentimental; at his best, devastatingly stilted and wonderfully ironical . . . worth reading on mortality and the mind/body dichotomy.

E. E. (EDWARD ESTLIN) CUMMINGS (1894–1962)

. . . the Cambridge ladies do not care, above
Cambridge if sometimes in its box of
sky lavender and cornerless, the
moon rattles like a fragment of angry candy

from "[the Cambridge ladies who live in furnished souls]"

Innovative in a small and subversive way . . . the one who used capital letters, punctuation, and conventional typography only when he felt like it, which helped him convince a considerable readership that what they were getting was wisdom . . . the son of a minister (about whom he'd write "my father / moved through dooms of love"), he sided with the little guy, the fellow down on his luck, the protester . . . has been likened to Robin Hood (the anarchist), Mickey Spillane (the tough guy), and Peter Pan (the boy who wouldn't grow up) . . . wrote love poems marked by childlike wonder and great good humor.

HART CRANE (1899–1932)

The photographs of hades in the brain
Are tunnels that re-wind themselves, and love
A burnt match skating in a urinal.

from *The Bridge* ("The Tunnel")

Wanted, like Whitman, to embrace the whole country, and was only egged on by the fact that he couldn't get his arms around it . . . his major poem *The Bridge* (that's the Brooklyn Bridge, a symbol of the heights to which modern man aspires), an epic about, as Crane put it, "a mystical synthesis of 'America' "; in it you can hear not just Whitman, but Woody Guthrie . . . as somebody said, found apocalypse under rocks and in bureau drawers . . . "through all sounds of gaiety and quest," Crane claims he hears "a kitten crying in the wilderness" . . . a homosexual who, at thirty-three, committed suicide by jumping overboard into the Gulf of Mexico.

ROBERT LOWELL (1917–1977)

The Aquarium is gone. Everywhere
giant-finned cars move forward like fish;
a savage servility
slides by on grease.

from "For the Union Dead"

One of the New England Lowells (like James Russell and Amy) . . . discussed the intricacies of the Puritan conscience, then converted to Catholicism . . . his principle subject the flux, struggle, and agony of experience . . . was interested in "the dark and against the grain" . . . lived a high-profile personal life (political stress, marital strain, organized protest, mental illness) . . . even so, managed to outlive and outwork such equally troubled colleagues and intimates as Delmore Schwartz, Randall Jarrell, Theodore Roethke, and John Berryman . . . gave poetry a new autobiographical aspect and a renewed sense of social responsibility . . . aroused greater admiration and jealousy, for the space of twenty years, than any other contemporary American poet.

ROOTS: FOUR PRIMARY INFLUENCES

THE ROMANTICS: Wordsworth, Shelley, et al. (see pages 192–93 and 195–96). The line of descent starts here, with all that talk about the importance of the imagination and the self. Don't tell your modern-poet friends this, though; they probably follow Yeats and Eliot in repudiating the early nineteenth century and would rather date things from Whitman and/or the Symbolists.

THE SYMBOLISTS: Rimbaud, Verlaine, Mallarmé, and the rest of the Frogs, plus the young Yeats. (Poe and Baudelaire were forerunners.) Believed there was another world beyond the visual one, a world of secret connections and private references, all of which just might, if you gave them a shove, form a pattern of some kind. Thus drunken boats and "fragrances fresh as the flesh of children." Gets a little lugubrious, but don't we all? Anyway, they made poetry even more an affair of the senses than the Romantics had done.

WALT WHITMAN: Founding father of American poetry. Charged with the poetic mission ("I speak the password primeval"), he raised all the issues that modern poetry is about: experimentation with language and form; revelation of self; the assumption that the poet, the reader, and the idea are all in the same room together and that a poem could make something happen. Hyperventilated a lot, but people on the side of freedom and variety are like that.

EMILY DICKINSON: Founding mother of American poetry; as William Carlos Williams put it, "patron saint" and "a real good guy." Reticent and soft-spoken where Whitman is aggressive and amped. Short lines to Whitman's long ones, microcosm to his macrocosm: "The brain is wider than the sea." Gets you to see how infinity can mean infinitely small as well as infinitely big.

HOOTS: FOUR TWENTIETH-CENTURY POETS NOT TO TOUCH WITH A TEN-FOOT STROPHE

First, Edna St. Vincent Millay, Our Lady of the Sonnets, who, in 1923, beat out—with three slender volumes, including one titled *A Few Figs from Thistles*—T. S. Eliot's *The Waste Land* for the Pulitzer Prize; but who, subsequently, despite former boyfriend Edmund Wilson's efforts to save her, began to seem, "ah, my foes, and oh, my friends," very silly. Also, Amy Lowell, dragon to Millay's

Clockwise from top left: Edna St. Vincent Millay, Amy Lowell, Edwin Arlington Robinson, Carl Sandburg

sylph, whom Eliot called "the demon saleswoman of poetry" and whom Pound accused of reducing the tenets of Imagism to "Amy-gism"; you may remember, from tenth-grade English, her musings on squills and ribbons and garden walks. Now she doesn't even make the anthologies.

Then, Carl Sandburg, who catalogued so memorably the pleasures of Chicago, his hometown ("City of the Big Shoulders," and so forth), who almost certainly liked ketchup on his eggs, but who was, even back then, accused—by Robert Frost, hardly an innocent himself—of fraud; better to go with Will Rogers here, or Whitman (whom Sandburg consciously imitated). Finally, Edwin Arlington Robinson, whose "Richard Cory" and "Miniver Cheevy" we can recite whole stanzas of, too, which is precisely the problem. Picture yourself in a room full of well-groomed young adults, all of whom, if they chose, could swing into "Miniver loved the Medici, / Albeit he had never seen one; / He would have sinned incessantly / Could he have been one."

OFFSHOOTS: FIVE CULT FIGURES

Five poets, no longer young (or even, in a couple of cases, alive), who are nevertheless as edgy, angry, and/or stoned as you are.

ALLEN GINSBERG: Dropout, prophet, and "Buddhist Jew," not necessarily in that order. "America I'm putting my queer shoulder to the wheel." His most famous works, *Howl* (about the beat culture of the Fifties, the second part of which was written during a peyote vision) and "Kaddish" (about his dead mother, this one written on amphetamines). Some critics see him in the tradition of William Blake: A spiritual adventurer with a taste for apocalypse, who saw no difference between religion and poetry. As William Carlos Williams said in his intro to *Howl*, "Hold back the edges of your gowns, Ladies, we are going through hell."

FRANK O'HARA: Cool—but approachable, also gay. At the center of the New York School of poets (others were John Ashbery, James Schuyler, and Kenneth Koch), and a bridge between artists and writers of the Sixties. Objected to abstraction and philosophy in poetry, preferring a spur-of-the-moment specificity he called "personism." Had a thing about the movies, James Dean, pop culture in general; his poems prefigure pop art. Thus, in "The Day Lady Died," lines like, "I go on to the bank / and Miss Stillwagon (first name Linda I once heard) / doesn't even look up my balance for once in her life. . . ." Killed by a dune buggy on Fire Island when he was only forty.

ROBERT CREELEY: One of the Black Mountain poets, out of the experimental backwoods college in North Carolina where, back in the Fifties, the idea of a "counterculture" got started. Kept his poems short and intimate, with titles such as "For No Clear Reason" and "Somewhere." His most famous utterance: "Form is never more than an extension of content." (Stay away from the prose, though, which reads like Justice Department doublespeak.) The consummate dropout: from Harvard—twice, once to India, once to Cape Cod—with additional stints in Majorca, Guatemala, and, of course, Black Mountain. "If you were going to get a pet / what kind of animal would you get."

SYLVIA PLATH: Her past is your past: report cards, scholarships (in her case, to Smith), summers at the beach. In short, banality American-style, on which she goes to town. May tell you more about herself than you wanted to know (along with Robert Lowell, she's the model of the confessional poet); watch especially for references to her father ("marble-heavy, a bag full of God, / Ghastly statue with one grey toe / Big as a Frisco seal . . ."). Wrote *The Bell Jar*, autobiographical—and satirical—novel of an adolescent's breakdown and attempted suicide. Married to English poet Ted Hughes, she later committed suicide herself. The new style of woman poet (along with Anne Sexton and Adrienne Rich), a cross between victim and rebel.

IMAMU AMIRI BARAKA (The poet and activist formerly known as Leroi Jones): Started off mellow, doing graduate work at Columbia and hanging out with his first wife (who, as it happened, was white) in Greenwich Village. Subsequently turned from bohemian to militant: "We must make our own / World, man, our own world, and we can not do this unless the white man / is dead. Let's get together and kill him, my man, let's get to gather the fruit / of the sun." Moved first to Harlem, then back to Newark, where he'd grown up; took up wearing dashikis and speaking Swahili. Likewise to be noted: his plays, especially *Dutchman* (1964); his most famous coinages, "tokenism" and "up against the wall." In 2002 he was named poet laureate of New Jersey—stop laughing—and proved he was still capable of raising hackles with the public reading of his poem "Somebody Blew Up America," in which he sided with conspiracy theorists who suggested that the Israeli and U.S. governments knew in advance that the September 11 attacks were going to take place: "Who told 4000 Israeli workers at the Twin Towers / To stay home that day / Why did Sharon stay away?" Was New Jersey's last poet laureate.

American Intellectual History, and Stop That Snickering

EIGHT AMERICAN INTELLECTUALS

The French have them, the Germans have them, even the Russians have them, so by God why shouldn't we? Admittedly, in a country that defines "scholarship" as free tuition for quarterbacks, intellectuals tend to be a marginal lot. Jewish, for the most part, and New York Jewish at that, they are accustomed to being viewed as vaguely *un*-American and to talking mainly to each other—or to themselves. (The notable exception is Norman Mailer, an oddball as intellectuals go, but a solid American who managed to capture the popular imagination by thinking, as often as not, with his fists.) The problem is precisely this business of incessant thinking. Intellectuals don't think up a nifty idea, then sell it to the movies; they just keep thinking up more ideas, as if that were the point.

GERTRUDE STEIN (1874–1946)

Our man in Paris, so to speak, Stein was one of those rare expatriates who wasn't ashamed to be an American. In fact, for forty-odd years after she'd bid adieu to Radcliffe, medical school, and her rich relatives in Baltimore, she was positively thrilled to be an American, probably because her exposure to her compatriots was pretty much limited to the innumerable doughboys and GIs she befriended (and wrote about) during two world wars—all of whom, to hear her tell it, adored her—and to the struggling-but-stylish young writers for whom she coined the phrase "The Lost Generation" (Hemingway, Sherwood Anderson, et al.), who were happy to pay homage to her genuine wit and fearless intellect while scarfing up hors d'oeuvres at the Saturday soirées at 27 rue de Fleurus (an address, by the way, that's as much to be remembered as anything Stein wrote). True, Hemingway later insisted that, although he'd learned a lot from Gert, he hadn't learned as much as she kept telling everyone he had. True, too, that if she hadn't been so tight with Hemingway and Picasso (whom she claimed to have "discovered"), the name Gertrude Stein might today be no more memorable than "Rooms," "Objects," or "Food," three pieces of experimental writing that more or less sum up the Gertrude Stein problem. The mysterious aura that still surrounds her name has less to do with her eccentricity or her lesbianism (this was Paris, after all) than with the fact that most of what she wrote is simply unreadable. Straining to come up with the exact literary equivalent of Cubist painting, the "Mama of Dada" was often so pointlessly cerebral that once the bohemian chic wore off, she seemed merely numbing.

RECOMMENDED READING: *Three Lives* (1909), three short novels centered on three serving women; an early work in which Stein's experiments with repetition, scrambled syntax, and lack of punctuation still managed to evoke her subjects instead of burying them. *The Autobiography of Alice B. Toklas* (1933), the *succès de scandale* in which Stein, adopting the persona of her long-time secretary and companion, disseminated her opinions on the famous artists of her day with great good humor and, the critics said, an outrageous lack of sense. Also, give a listen to *Four Saints in Three Acts* (1934), an opera collaboration with Virgil Thomson that still gets good notices.

EDMUND WILSON (1895–1972)

A squire trapped in the body of a bulldog. Or do we mean a bulldog trapped in the body of a squire? Anyhoo, America's foremost man of letters, decade after decade, from the Twenties until the day of his death. Erudite and cantankerous, Wilson largely steered clear of the teaching positions and institutional involvements that all other literary critics and social historians seemed to take refuge in, preferring to wing it as a reviewer and journalist. The life makes good reading: quasi-aristocratic New Jersey boyhood, Princeton education (and start of lifelong friendship with F. Scott Fitzgerald), several marriages, including one to Mary McCarthy (whom he persuaded to write fiction), robust sex life, complete with a fairly well-documented foot fetish, running battles with the IRS (over unpaid income taxes) and Vladimir Nabokov (over Russian verse forms), the nickname "Bunny." Plus, who else went out and studied Hebrew in order to decipher the Dead Sea Scrolls (Wilson's single biggest scoop) or ploughed through a thousand musty volumes because he wanted to figure out the Civil War for himself? Bunny, you see, was determined to get to the bottom of things, make connections, monitor the progress of the Republic, and explain the world to Americans and Americans to themselves, all with the understanding that it could be as much fun to dissect—and hold forth on—Emily Post as T. S. Eliot.

RECOMMENDED READING: *Axel's Castle* (1931), a book-length study of the symbolist tradition in Europe and a good general introduction to Yeats, Eliot, Proust, Joyce, et al. *To the Finland Station* (1940), a book-length study of the radical tradition in Europe and a good general introduction to Vico, Michelet, Lenin, Trotsky, et al. *Upstate* (1972), an old man's meditation on himself, his life, and his imminent death.

LIONEL TRILLING (1905–1975)

Self, society, mind, will, history, and, needless to say, culture. It can be a bit of a yawn, frankly, especially when you really only wanted him to explain what Jane Austen was up to in *Mansfield Park*, but at least you'll find out what liberalism—of the intellectual as opposed to the merely political variety—is all about. A big Freudian, also a big Marxist, and affiliated with Columbia University for his entire professional life, Trilling worries about things like "the contemporary ideology of irrationalism" (this in the Sixties, when the view from Morningside Heights wouldn't hold still, and when Trilling himself was beginning to seem a little, uh, over the hill); "our disaffection from history"; and, more than anything else, the tensions between self and society, literature and politics, aesthetics and morality. A touch rueful, a little low-key, Trilling wasn't constantly breaking out the port and the bon mots like Wilson, but his heart was in the right place: He cared about the nature and quality of life on the planet, and probably would have lent you the guest room if, as one of his undergraduates, you'd gotten locked out of the dorm.

RECOMMENDED READING: *The Liberal Imagination* (1950), the single most widely read "New York" critical work, which, under the guise of discussing literature, actually aimed, as Trilling said, to put liberal assumptions "under some degree of pressure." *The Middle of the Journey* (1947), his one novel, about political issues (read Stalinism) confronting American intellectuals of the day; loosely based on the life of Whittaker Chambers. *Sincerity and Authenticity* (1972), late Trilling, especially the concluding examination of "the doctrine that madness is health."

HANNAH ARENDT (1906–1974)

Back in the Fifties she seemed like an absolute god-send—a bona fide German intellectual come to roost in the American university system at a time when intellectuals had the kind of clout that real estate developers have today. Not only did Arendt actually condescend to *talk* to her students at Princeton (where she was the first woman professor ever), and Columbia, and Berkeley, and so on, but she saw nothing demeaning in writing about current events, bringing to bear the kind of Old World erudition and untranslated Latin and Greek phrases that made Mr. and Mrs. America feel they could stand tall. She wasn't afraid to take on the looming postwar bogeymen—war crimes, revolution, genocide—and, as it seemed at the time, wrestle them to the ground with the sheer force of her Teutonic aloofness, her faith in the power of the rational, her ability to place unspeakable events in the context of a worldview and a history that, inevitably, brought us home to Plato and the moderation-minded Greeks. Granted, she was a little too undiscriminating about her audience, a little too arbitrary in her assertions, and a little too sweeping in her generalizations for many of her fellow political philosophers. And she was a little too intent on forging order out of chaos for our taste: When it came to distinguishing among "labor," "work," and "action," or reading 258 pages on the nature of "thinking," we decided we'd rather merengue. Still, who else dispensed so much intellectual chicken soup to so many febrile minds? Who else thought to point out, amid the hysteria of the Nuremberg trials, that perhaps Adolf Eichmann had not acted alone? And when Arendt had an insight, it was usually a lulu—like the notion that even nice middle-class folks were capable of monstrous acts of destruction. The latter idea gave rise not only to her now-famous phrase, "the banality of evil," but, it is generally agreed, to the New Left—which, of course, later disowned Arendt as a flabby bourgeois.

RECOMMENDED READING: *The Origins of Totalitarianism* (1951), a dense, sometimes meandering study of the evolution of nineteenth-century anti-Semitism and imperialism into twentieth-century Nazism and Communism; still the classic treatise on the subject, it was, surprisingly enough, a bestseller in its day. *Eichmann in Jerusalem: The Banality of Evil* (1963), with which she made a lot of enemies by insisting not only that Eichmann didn't vomit green slime and speak in tongues, but that he didn't even get a fair trial. *The Life of the Mind* (1977), her unfinished magnum opus, two volumes of which were published posthumously; as one critic pointed out, it may fall short of chronicling the life of the mind, but it does a bang-up job of chronicling the life of Arendt's mind.

PAUL GOODMAN (1911–1972)

True, he was an anarchist, draft dodger, sexual liberationist (and confirmed bisexual), as well as den father to the New Left, but Paul Goodman still comes off sounding an awful lot like Mr. Chips. Talk about soft-spokenness, talk about lending a hand, talk about talking it out: Goodman is *there* for the "kids," as he calls them, including the "resigned" beats and the "fatalistic" hoods, plus everybody else who's going to wind up either dropping out or making Chevy tail fins on an assembly line. Humankind is innocent, loving, and creative, you dig? It's the bureaucracies that create the evil, that make Honor and Community impossible, and it's the kids who really take it in the groin. Thus goes the indictment of the American social and educational systems in Goodman's *Growing Up Absurd* (1960), the book that made him more than just another underground hero. But to get the whole picture, you'll also have to plow through his poems, plays, novels, magazine pieces, and confessions; his treatises on linguistics, constitutional law, Gestalt therapy, Noh theater, and, with his brother, city planning; plus listen to him tell you about his analysis and all those sit-ins. A Renaissance man in an era that favored specialization, Goodman never lost his sense of wonder—or of outrage. And one more thing: If your parents used to try to get you to watch them "making love," it may well have been on Goodman's say-so.

RECOMMENDED READING: *Growing Up Absurd*, of course. And, if you liked that, *The Empire City* (1959), a novel with a hero perversely named Horatio Alger and a lambasting of the Thirties, Forties, and Fifties. *Five Years: Thoughts in a Useless Time* (1967), his journal of late-Fifties despair. And "May Pamphlet" (1945), a modern counterpart to Thoreau's "Civil Disobedience."

NORMAN MAILER (1923–)

Although he probably wouldn't have wowed them at the Deux Magots, Mailer, in the American intellectual arena, is at least a middleweight. Beginning in the mid-Fifties, when he took time off from his pursuit of the Great American Novelist prize to write a weekly column for *The Village Voice* (which he co-founded), he was, for decades, our most visible social critic, purveyor of trends, attacker of ideologies, and promoter of the concept of the artist as public figure. Operating as a sort of superjournalist—even Mailer has never claimed to be a man of letters—he proceeded to define new waves of consciousness, from "hip" to the peace movement to feminism, just as (though never, as his detractors point out, before) they hit the cultural mainstream. Like a true New Journalist, he was forever jumping into the action, taking risks, playing with the language, and making sociological connections. Unlike other New Journalists, however, he came equipped with a liberal Jewish background, a Harvard education, considerable talent as a novelist, and enough ambition to make him emperor, if only he'd been a little less cerebral and a lot less self-destructive. By the late Sixties, he'd hit on the strategy (soon to become an MO) of using narcissism as a tool for observation and commentary, a device that seemed both to validate a decade or so of personal excess (drugs, drink, fistfights, and the much-publicized stabbing of his second wife) and to set him up as the intellectual successor to Henry Adams. Later, he got himself into debt, wrote second-rate coffee-table books, launched an unsuccessful campaign for the mayoralty of New York City, married too many women, sired too many children, made too many belligerent remarks on TV talk shows, got behind one of the worst causes célèbres ever (Jack Abbott), spent a decade writing a "masterpiece" no one could read (*Ancient Evenings*) and another decade writing a spy story no one had *time* to read (*Harlot's*

Ghost, 1,310 pages, and that's only part one), and generally exhausted everyone's patience—and that goes double for anyone even remotely connected with the women's movement. Still, it's worth remembering that, as *Time* magazine put it, "for a heady period, no major event in U.S. life seemed quite complete until Mailer had observed himself observing it." Plus, he did marry that nice redhead and finally started behaving himself at parties. Most important, it's hard to think of anyone who managed to explore the nature of celebrity in the media age from so many different angles—and lived to tell the tale.

RECOMMENDED READING: *Advertisements for Myself* (1959), a collection of combative essays and mean-spirited criticism of fellow writers, which marked the beginning of Mailer's notoriety; read it for the two acknowledged masterpieces: "The White Negro" and "The Time of Her Time." *Armies of the Night* (1968), Mailer's account of the anti–Vietnam War march on Washington; his most widely read nonfiction book and the debut of the narrator-as-center-of-the-universe format. *Miami and the Siege of Chicago* (1969), more of the same, only different; an attempt to penetrate to the heart—or lack thereof—of the Republican and Democratic conventions. *The Executioner's Song* (1979), the Pulitzer Prize–winning saga of convinced murderer Gary Gilmore; Mailer's comeback after all those coffee-table books and, as one critic suggested, his single foray into punk literature.

NOAM CHOMSKY (1928–)

For the better part of two decades served as the conscience of a nation. From the earliest days of the Vietnam War, he spearheaded resistance against the American presence in Southeast Asia, chiding the fancy, amoral policy makers in Washington, the technocrats of the military-industrial complex, and the "liberal intelligentsia," especially those members of it charged with making sense of what was really happening, at the Pentagon as in the Mekong Delta. (It was the media's failure to tell the whole story—and its implications, including the racism and arrogance inherent in First World imperialism—that arguably annoyed him most.) No

shrinking violet, he maintained, for instance, back when Henry Kissinger was up for a Columbia professorship, that the former secretary of state and professional *éminence grise* was fit to head only a "Department of Death." And he wasn't just talk: In peace march after peace march you could count on spotting him in the front lines.

Meanwhile, he somehow managed to function as an MIT linguistics professor, and, in fairly short order, became indisputably the most influential linguist of the second half of the century. Chomsky's most famous theory concerns something he called generative—a.k.a.

transformational—grammar, in which he argued that the degree of grammatical similarity manifested by the languages of the world, coupled with the ease with which little children learn to speak them, suggested that man's capacity for language, and especially for grammatical structure, is innate, as genetically determined as eye color or left-handedness. The proof: All of us constantly (and painlessly) use sequences and combinations of words that we've never heard before, much less consciously learned. Chomsky singlehandedly managed to bring linguistics front and center, transforming it—you should pardon the expression—from an academic specialty practiced among moribund Indian tribes and sleepy college sophomores into the subject of heated debate among epistemologists, behavioral psychologists, and the French. Naturally, he accumulated his share of detractors in the process. Some complained that he made the human consciousness sound suspiciously like a home computer; others noted that he never really defined what he meant by "deep structure," the psychic system from which our spoken language is generated and of which any sentence or group of sentences is in some way a map.

Chomsky's influence on political life seemed to peak, at least in the United States, in the early Seventies, after which, we can't help noting, the threat of being drafted and sent to Vietnam ended for many of his most ardent campus-radical supporters. (It probably hadn't helped that he'd spoken up for the Khmer Rouge over in Cambodia and for the Palestinians back when the Israelis were still the guys in the white hats, then turned around and defended a book, which he later admitted he hadn't read, that denied the historical reality of the Holocaust.) And there was the problem of Chomsky's own prose style, a flat, humorless affair that left many readers hankering for Gary Trudeau and *Doonesbury*. But Chomsky kept writing—and writing and writing. By the 1990s some publishers were savvy enough to publish his political essays as short, reader-friendly paperbacks, making him more accessible to a mainstream audience. Then came the attack on the World Trade Center and the Bush administration's response, which apparently caused some people to feel they needed an alternative to the daily media spin. Suddenly Chomsky was no longer a figure on the radical fringe. His fierce denunciations of U.S. foreign policy (he views America as the mother of all "rogue states" and the Bush administration's "grand imperial design" as an out-of-the-closet version of the kind of global aggression and disregard for international law we've been guilty of since the end of World War II) resonated with many people who did not consider themselves radicals, or even leftists. Chomsky's *9-11* (2001), *Power and Terror: Post 9-11 Talks and Interviews* (2003), and *Hegemony or Survival* (2004) all made the bestseller lists, and his backlisted political books have sold millions of copies.

RECOMMENDED READING: Aforementioned bestsellers, plus you might want to try *Language and Mind*, a series of three lectures Chomsky gave at Berkeley in 1967, for his clearest statement on the relations between his theory of language and his theory of human nature; follow with *Topics in the Theory of Generative Grammar* (1966), an easy-to-understand reprise of his basic linguistic beliefs. *Aspects of the Theory of Syntax* (1965) is the classic working out of Chomsky's mature theory, but if you stood even the slimmest chance of being able to read it, you wouldn't be reading *this*. Many of the early political essays are collected in *American Power and the New Mandarins* (1969); a more recent collection is *Deterring Democracy* (1991).

SUSAN SONTAG (1933–2004)

She delineated a new aesthetic, heavy on style, sensation, and immediacy. For Sontag (the Sontag of the Sixties, that is) art and morality had no common ground and it didn't matter what an artist was trying to say as long as the result turned you on. For everyone from the *Partisan Review* crowd to the kids down at the Fillmore, she seemed like a godsend; she not only knew where it was at, she *was* where it was at. A serious thinker with a frame of reference to beat the band, a hard-nosed analytical style, and subscriptions to all the latest European journals, she would emerge from her book-lined study (where she had, presumably, been immersed in a scholarly comparison of Hegel's philosophical vocabulary, Schoenberg's twelve-tone theory, and the use of the quick cut in the films of Godard), clad in jeans, sneakers, and an old cardigan, to tell the world it was OK to listen to the Supremes. Maybe you never *did* understand what Godard was getting at— at least you knew that if Sontag took him on, he, too, was where it was at. Ditto Bergman, Genet, Warhol, Artaud, John Cage, Roland Barthes, Claude Lévi-Strauss, Norman O. Brown, and the government of North Vietnam. Eclecticism was the hallmark of Sontag's modernist (today, read postmodernist) sensibility. A writer who had, at the time, all the grace and charm of a guerrilla commando issuing proclamations to a hostile government, she came under heavy attack from her critics for her political naïveté (and revisionism); for the uncompromising vehemence of her assertions; and for suffering, as one writer put it, "from the recurring delusion that life is art." Over the years, however, as life came more to resemble bad television—and after Sontag herself survived breast cancer—she changed her mind about a lot of things, denouncing Soviet-style communism as just another form of fascism and insisting that style wasn't everything after all, that the content of a work of art counted, too. In a culture increasingly enamored of simple-minded stereotypes and special effects, Sontag crusaded for conscience, seriousness, and moral complexity. She also branched out: writing theater and film scripts, directing plays (notably, a production of *Waiting for Godot* in war-torn Sarajevo in 1993), and trying her hand at fiction—she produced a self-proclaimed "romance" (*The Volcano Lover*, 1992) that managed to get some rave reviews. Still, throughout her life she remained outspoken about politics. For example, she made plenty of enemies after September 11, 2001, when she wrote in the *New Yorker*, "Whatever may be said of the perpetrators . . . they were not cowards." Her last piece, "Regarding the Torture of Others," published in 2004, the same year that she was to die of cancer (after fighting the disease, on and off, for more than thirty years), reflected on the photographs of Iraqi prisoners tortured at Abu Ghraib. In it she declared, that, as representing both the fundamental corruption of any foreign occupation and the signature style of the U.S. administration of George W. Bush, "The photographs are us."

RECOMMENDED READING: *Against Interpretation* (1966), a collection of essays that includes some of her best-known works, e.g., the title piece, "On Style," and "Notes on Camp." *Styles of Radical Will* (1966), another nonfiction grab bag whose high points are a defense of pornography ("The Pornographic Imagination"), a lengthy discussion of Godard ("Godard"), and one of her most famous—and certainly most readable—essays, "Trip to Hanoi." *On Photography* (1977), the book that won her a large lay audience and innumerable enemies among photographers (and that helped a lot of people feel they finally knew what to make of Diane Arbus). *Illness as Metaphor* (1978), written during her own fight against cancer, dissected the language used to describe diseases and challenged the blame-the-victim attitudes behind society's cancer metaphors. *AIDS and Its Metaphors* (1988), a kind of sequel to the above, exposed the racism and homophobia that colored public discussion of the epidemic.

AND EIGHT PEOPLE WHO, AMERICAN OR NOT, HAD IDEAS WHOSE TIME, IT SEEMED AT THE TIME, HAD COME

MARSHALL McLUHAN (1911–1980)

"The medium is the message," of course. That is, the way we acquire information affects us more than the information itself. The medium is also, as a later version of the aphorism had it, "the massage": Far from being neutral, a medium "does something to people; it takes hold of them, bumps them around." Case in point—television, with its mosaic of tiny dots of light, its lack of clarification, its motion and sound, and its relentless projection of all of the above straight at the viewer, thereby guaranteeing that viewer an experience as aural and tactile as it is visual. And high time, too. Ever since Gutenberg and his printing press, spewing out those endless lines of bits of print, the eye had gotten despotic, thinking linear, and life fragmented; with the advent of the age of electronics man was at last returning to certain of his tribal ways—and the world was becoming a "global village." There were those who dismissed McLuhan (for the record, a Canadian) as less a communications theorist cum college professor than a phrase-mongering charlatan, but even they couldn't ignore entirely his distinction between "hot" and "cool" media (it's the latter that, as with TV or comic books or talking on the phone, tend to involve you so much that you're late for supper). Besides, McLuhan had sort of beaten his critics to the punch: Of his own work, he liked to remark, "I don't pretend to understand it. After all, my stuff is very difficult."

R. BUCKMINSTER FULLER (1895–1983)

"An engineer, inventor, mathematician, architect, cartographer, philosopher, poet, cosmogonist, comprehensive designer, and choreographer" was how Fuller described himself; for a few other people "crackpot," "megalomaniac," "enfant terrible," or "Gyro Gearloose" did as good a job more economically. Convinced that man, through technology and planning, could become superman and "save the world from itself"; that "Spaceship Earth" was a large mechanical device that needed periodic tuning; that "the entire population" of that earth "could live compactly on a properly designed Haiti and comfortably on the British Isles"; that the geodesic dome, a sphere composed of much smaller tetrahedrons, was the most rigorously logical structure around; and that he himself had "a blind date with principle," "Bucky" flew tens of thousands of miles annually, visiting Khrushchev's Moscow and everybody else's college campus with equal élan, waving excitedly from behind Coke-bottle glasses for up to six hours at a time. (Annually, that is, except for the year during which he refused to speak at all, to anybody, including his wife.) His ultimate conclusion: The universe is governed by relatively few principles and its essence is not matter but design. P.S. He may have been right. In 1985, scientists discovered a spherical carbon molecule, which, because it's reminiscent in its structure of a geodesic dome, they dubbed a "buckyball"—or, more formally, a buckminster fullerene—and which has subsequently spawned a whole new heavy-breathing branch of chemistry.

KATE MILLETT (1934–)

Whatever their personal feelings about women in combat boots, you'd have thought men would be open-minded enough to admit that, for a chick, Millet had guts. An academic turned activist, and one of those unstoppable Catholics-in-revolt, she was always willing to walk it like she talked it. While Betty Friedan, the supply-sider of sisterhood, was still dressing for success and biting her nails over whether or not it was OK to have lesbians as friends, Millett was out in full drag, holding the Statue of Liberty hostage, chronicling her affairs in vivid—not to say tedious—detail, and telling women it was time to get out from underneath, not just figuratively but literally. But it all paid off eventually: *Sexual Politics* became a bestseller, its once-revolutionary thesis was accepted as basic feminist canon, men started having trouble getting it up, and Betty Friedan began to wonder if having your own corner office and your own coronary was really all it was cracked up to be.

Not that Millet herself necessarily got to spend much time gloating over her ideological ascendency; diagnosed as manic-depressive in 1973, she rebelled against her lithium regimen seven years later and spent the early Eighties being chased around by men in white coats, an interlude she chronicled in her 1991 memoir, *The Loony Bin Trip*. Today, older, wiser, and presumably back on lithium, she runs a women's artist collective on her Christmas-tree farm in Poughkeepsie, New York.

MALCOLM X (1925–1965)

The Last Angry Negro, before he got everybody to stop saying Negro, Brother Malcolm (né Malcolm Little and a.k.a. Red, Satan, Homeboy, and El-Hajj Malick El-Shabazz) was one of the first to come right out and tell the world what he *really* thought of honkies. Although in his days as a radical—which, in what was to become a trend, followed closely on his days as a dealer/pimp/burglar/convict/Muslim convert—Malcolm never actually *did* much, he managed, through sheer spleen, to scare the socks off Whitey, make Martin Luther King Jr. reach for the Excedrin, and provide a role model for a generation of black activists who were ready to put their muscle where Malcolm's mouth had been. Whatever folks thought of his politics, everyone had to admit that Malcolm had charisma: At one point, the *New York Times* rated him the country's second most popular campus speaker, after Barry Goldwater. Malcolm mellowed considerably after Elijah Muhammad booted him out of the Black Muslims (and Muhammad Ali dropped him as his personal spiritual advisor). Unfortunately, it wasn't long after that that he was gunned down by an informal firing squad hired, various rumors had it, by the Muslims, the U.S. government, or the Red Chinese. Whatever—he was immortalized by the bestselling autobiography coauthored with Alex "Roots" Haley. A symbol of black manhood and righteous anger for the next three decades (and, some social observers have suggested, a direct progenitor of "gangsta" rap), Malcolm briefly became a matinee idol—and barely escaped being reduced to a fashion statement—when director Spike Lee based a movie on the autobiography in 1992.

ERNESTO "CHE" GUEVARA (1928–1967)

The peripatetic Argentine revolutionary who became a model of radical style and, along with Huey Newton, one of the seminal dorm posters of the Sixties. Although he did have a catchy nickname (it translates, roughly, as "Hey, you") and a way with a beret, the main points to remember are that he was the number two man, chief ideologue, and resident purist of the Cuban revolution, and that he wrote *the* book on guerrilla warfare. He also showed all the kids back in Great Neck that a nice middle-class boy from Buenos Aires, with a medical degree, no less, could make good defending the downtrodden in the jungles of the Third World. His split with Fidel over the latter's cop-out to Soviet-style materialism (Che was holding out for the purity of Chinese Marxism) didn't hurt his reputation, either; nor did going underground for a couple of years, during which, it later turned out, he was in all the right places—North Vietnam, the Congo, various Latin American hot spots. Unfortunately, his revolutionary theories were a little half-baked, and when he tried to implement them down in Bolivia, he ran smack into the Bolivian army—a colonel of which summarily executed him, thereby creating an instant martyr.

HUNTER S. THOMPSON (1939–2005)

The one journalist you could trust back when you were a sophomore at the University of Colorado. A sportswriter by training and temperament (he was Raoul Duke in *Rolling Stone* magazine, although you may know him better as Uncle Duke in *Doonesbury*), Hunter, as we all called him, became a media star by inventing "gonzo journalism," a reportorial style that was one step beyond New Journalism and two steps over the edge of the pool. Gonzo journalism revolved around drugs, violence, and the patent impossibility of Hunter's ever meeting his deadlines, given the condition he was in. It assumed that all global events were engineered to make you laugh, make you famous, or kill you. For the record, Hunter really did fear and loathe Richard Nixon, with whom he shared the rampant paranoia of the day; once he'd finished cataloguing the various controlled substances he'd supposedly ingested to ease the pain of the 1972 presidential campaign, he was a shoo-in as the Walter Cronkite of the Haight-Ashbury set. By the end of the decade, however, the joyride was over. Dr. Gonzo, arriving in Saigon to cover the evacuation, learned that he'd just lost his job as top gonzo journalist and with it his medical insurance. Failing to convince the North Vietnamese that he'd be a major asset to their cause, he filed his expenses and caught the next plane home. It wasn't long after that that college kids started thinking that maybe there *was* life outside Hunter's hotel room; worse, history rounded a bend and they discovered John Belushi. For over a decade it was hard to think about Hunter at all, much less care what he might be freaking out over—or on—this week. But he turned out to be smarter or luckier than his copy had led us to believe; he resurfaced in the early Nineties, along with bell-bottoms and platform shoes, as the subject of three, count 'em, three, biographies, which, he pointed out, was more than Faulkner had had during *his* lifetime. True, he was often portrayed as a drug-addled shell, cut off from the rest of the world and mired in the past (or, as he once referred to himself, "an elderly dope fiend living out in the wilderness"). And he certainly didn't appear to be enjoying his golden years; even his voluntary exile in a small Colorado town was disrupted by baby boomers—the very people Hunter referred to as the "Generation of Swine"—who invaded nearby Aspen, building million-dollar homes and complaining bitterly about Dr. Gonzo's tendency to shoot firearms and set off explosives while under the influence, which he was at least daily. But when Thompson died in 2005, from a self-inflicted gunshot wound to the head, an awful lot of people seemed to take the loss personally. Loyal supporters, including many high-profile writers and journalists, mourned the passing of an icon and, with it, a healthy sense of outrage over the hypocrisies of American life.

WILHELM REICH (1897–1957)

Brilliant but dumb, if you know what we mean, and certainly, by the end, not playing with a full deck. His early Marxist-Freudian notions made some sense, such as the idea that you can't revolutionize politics without revolutionizing the people who make them, or that thinking about yourself constantly can make you neurotic. And we'll lay dollars to doughnuts trauma really *does* eventually show up as tight muscles and shallow breathing, although, frankly, his emphasis on the regenerative powers of the orgasm seemed a little simple-minded even at the time. But it wasn't until his discovery of orgone energy—the life force which he found to be bluish green in color—that some of us got up and moved to the other end of the bus. Before you could say "deadly orgone energy," Reich was babbling about cosmic orgone engineers—"CORE men"—from other planets and comparing himself to such historic martyrs as Jesus, Socrates, Nietzsche, and Woodrow Wilson (that "great, warm person"). He died in a federal penitentiary in 1957, having been hounded for years by the FBI and convicted, finally, of transporting empty orgone boxes across state lines.

GEORGE IVANOVITCH GURDJIEFF
(1874–1949)

The Paul Bunyan of mystics, Gurdjieff spent twenty years pursuing "truth" through the wilds of Asia and North Africa, crossing the Gobi on stilts, navigating the River Kabul on a raft, clambering blindfolded through vertiginous mountain passes, chatting up dervishes and seers, unearthing a map of "presand" Egypt, digging through ruins, hanging out in a secret monastery, and soaking up ancient wisdom and esoteric knowledge. If you're wondering what he learned, we suggest you do the same, as Gurdjieff certainly isn't going to tell you: His summa, *All and Everything*, is 1,266 pages in search of an editor. You could try wading through the explications of P. D. Ouspensky, the Russian mathematician who was Gurdjieff's top disciple for a while, remembering, however, that Gurdjieff thought Ouspensky was an ass for trying to explicate him. Never mind. Just ask yourself, "Would I really buy spiritual guidance from a man who once raised cash by dyeing sparrows yellow and selling them as canaries?" If your answer is no, you probably would have missed the point anyway.

Family Feud

A BRIEF HISTORY OF AMERICAN
POLITICAL PARTIES

The symbology (donkey and elephant, Daniel Patrick Moynihan and Strom Thurmond) seems carved in stone and the structure (wards and precincts, national committees and electoral colleges) as intrinsically American as a BLT. Imagine your surprise, then, when we remind you of something you learned for the first time back in fifth grade, namely, that this nation of ours, purple mountain majesties and all, began its life without any political parties whatsoever. George Washington—whose election in 1788 had been unanimous and unopposed, and who at one point found himself being addressed as "Your Highness the President"—was above even thinking in terms of party loyalty. The rest of the Founding Fathers considered "factions," as they put it, straightening their periwigs, to be unscrupulous gangs hell-bent on picking the public pocket. James Madison, for instance, while an old hand at lining up votes and establishing majorities on specific issues, assumed that those majorities would (and should) fall away once the issue in question had been resolved.

But then there was Alexander Hamilton, who, having managed to dictate foreign policy to Washington and domestic policy to Congress for the better part of two administrations, finally gave Madison and Jefferson no choice but to take action against him. Hamilton was a Northerner, a federalist (as opposed to a state's rightser), an industrialist, a venture capitalist, and a power broker. Jefferson you know about: Southerner, agrarian, progressive, and all-around Renaissance man. Thus began the power struggle that would result, by 1796, in the formation of two rival parties—Hamilton's Federalists and Jefferson's Democratic Republicans, ancestors of our Republicans and Democrats, respectively.

The blow-by-blow (including how Jefferson bested Hamilton and what the difference between Jeffersonian and Jacksonian democracy is) we'll save for another time. In the meantime, take a look at this chart for the big picture:

	DEMOCRATIC REPUBLICANS*	FEDERALISTS
Round 1	(1796, Jefferson, Madison, et al.— the South and landowning interests)	(1792, Hamilton, John Adams, et al.— the North and commercial interests; gone by 1816)

TIME OUT: Monroe's factionless "Era of Good Feelings," 1817–1824

	DEMOCRATS*	NATIONAL REPUBLICANS
Round 2	(1832, Andrew Jackson—as above, plus small farmers, backwoods types, "little guys" in general)	(1828, J. Q. Adams, Henry Clay—as above, plus border-states residents; gone by 1832)
		WHIGS (as above, plus anti-Jackson Democrats)
Round 3		REPUBLICANS (1856, Abraham Lincoln—Northerners, urbanites, business types, factory workers, blacks)

	DEMOCRATS*	REPUBLICANS
Round 4	(FDR—dominant 1932 through 1960s, Northeasterners and, in the old days, Southerners, city dwellers, blue-collar workers, Catholics, liberals, ethnics)	(Midwesterners, businessmen, farmers, white-collar workers, Protestants, the "Establishment," plus right-to-lifers, religious fundamentalists, and social conservatives in general)

*Dominant party.

Note that for almost two hundred years the same two parties, variously named, have been lined up against each other; third parties—Teddy Roosevelt's Bull Moose, Robert LaFollette's Progressive Action, Strom Thurmond's Dixiecrats, and, more recently, George Wallace's American Independence—while a godsend for political commentators trying to fill column inches, have had little success with the electorate. (By contrast, H. Ross Perot had surprising success in the 1992 presidential election, but don't get too excited: Perot's United We Stand America was technically not a political party at all, just a not-for-profit "civic league.") Nor is this a country where we think much of, or where most of us could define, coalition as a political form.

As to how you can distinguish Republicans from Democrats today, we'll content ourselves with quoting from a letter from a friend: "Republicans hire exterminators to kill their bugs; Democrats step on them. . . . Democrats buy most of the books that have been banned somewhere; Republicans form censorship committees and read the books as a group. . . . Democrats eat the fish they catch; Republicans hang theirs on the wall. . . . Republicans tend to keep their shades drawn, although there is seldom any reason why they should; Democrats ought to and don't."

Back to you, George.

American Mischief

FIVE TALES OF AMBITION, GREED, PARANOIA, AND MIND-BOGGLING INCOMPETENCE THAT TOOK PLACE LONG BEFORE THE INVASION OF IRAQ

THE TWEED RING: The gang of crooked politicians that ran New York City like a private kingdom throughout the mid-1800s. Led by William Marcy "Boss" Tweed and operating through Tammany, New York's powerful Democratic political machine, these boys were the stuff old gangster movies are made of. Although the "boss" system was widespread in those days and political machines were always, by their very nature, corrupt (essentially, they provided politicians with votes in return for favors), none could match the Tweed Ring for sheer political clout and uninhibited criminality. During its reign, the group bilked the city out of at least $30 million (a conservative estimate); Tweed himself got $40,000 in stock as a bribe for getting the Brooklyn Bridge project approved and

TWEED-LE-DEE AND TILDEN-DUM.

REFORM TWEED. "If all the people want is to have somebody arrested, I'll have you plunderers convicted. You will be allowed to escape; nobody will be hurt; and then TILDEN will go to the White House, and I to Albany as Governor."

a lot more for manipulating the sale of the land that is now Central Park. He also got himself elected to the state senate. The ring was finally broken in the 1870s through the dogged efforts of the *New York Times*, *Harper's Weekly* cartoonist Thomas Nast (whose caricatures helped demolish Tweed's gangster-with-a-heart-of-gold public image), and Samuel Tilden, a Democratic reformer with his eye on the presidency. Tweed died in prison; though his name is now synonymous with political corruption, some commentators point out that without crooks like him, there never would have been enough incentive to get this country built.

CRÉDIT MOBILIER: One of the worst pre-Enron financial scandals on record, this tacky affair took place during the notoriously incompetent presidency of Ulysses S. Grant and revolved around the building of the Union Pacific Railroad. Its most visible villain was Oakes Ames, a director of the railroad and a member of the House of Representatives. When Congress agreed to pick up the tab for building the Union Pacific, Ames, who knew the job could be done for much less than the amount granted, got together with some other stockholders to form the Crédit Mobilier, a dummy construction corporation. They used the company to divert excess funds into their pockets. By the time the project was completed in 1869, it was heavily in debt and Ames and his friends had skimmed about $23 million in profits. To be on the safe side, Ames passed out Crédit Mobilier stock to some of his favorite congressmen. Then, in one of those priceless moves that make history, he wrote a letter to a friend telling him he'd distributed the stock "where it would do the most good" and listing the names of the lucky recipients. Naturally, the newspapers got hold of the letter, and you can guess the rest. Note, however, that although the list implicated officials as high up as the vice president, none was ever prosecuted. In fact, some historians now wonder what the big fuss was about. After all, they say, what's a few million dollars in the nation's history? They got the job done, didn't they? Yes, but on the other hand, who rides the Union Pacific anymore?

TEAPOT DOME: An oil scandal that took place during the administration of Warren G. Harding, generally acknowledged to have been one of the most worthless presidents ever. Secretary of the Interior Albert B. Fall persuaded Harding to give him control of the U.S. naval oil reserves at Elk Hill, California, and Teapot Dome, Wyoming. A year later, Fall secretly leased the reserves to the owners of two private oil companies, one in exchange for a personal "loan" of $100,000, the other for $85,000 cash, some shares of stock, and a herd of cattle. It wasn't long before the secret leaked and everybody was up before a Senate investigating com-

JUGGERNAUT.

mittee. In yet another remarkable verdict, all three men were acquitted, although Fall was later tried on lesser charges and became the first cabinet member ever to go to prison. Meanwhile, the public was outraged that the Senate had prosecuted at all; this was, as you'll recall, the Roaring Twenties, when everyone was busy doing the Charleston or making shady deals themselves. Even the New York newspapers accused the Senate of character assassination, mudslinging, and generally acting in poor taste.

THE SACCO-VANZETTI CASE: People still seem to take this one personally. Nicola Sacco and Bartolomeo Vanzetti were Italian immigrants accused of murdering two people during an armed robbery in Massachusetts in 1920. The trial, which took place in the wake of the wave of national hysteria known as the "Red Scare," was a joke; the public was paranoid about immigrants and the presiding judge made it clear that *he* knew what to expect from people who talked funny. To make matters worse, Sacco and Vanzetti were avowed anarchists who both owned guns. Although there was no hard evidence against them, they were convicted and sentenced to death. The case became an international cause célèbre, and people like Felix Frankfurter, John Dos Passos, and Edna St. Vincent Millay spent years pressing for a retrial. When Sacco and Vanzetti were finally electrocuted in 1927, everyone was convinced that the whole liberal cause had collapsed. In the end, liberalism didn't die, of course, and Sacco and Vanzetti became martyrs, with poems and plays written about them. Unfortunately, modern ballistics tests conducted in 1961 seemed to prove conclusively that the fatal bullet used in the robbery did indeed come from Sacco's gun. Never mind, it still looks like Vanzetti might have been innocent.

THE PUMPKIN PAPERS: A misnomer, referring to the Alger Hiss case. It is essentially another story of Red-baiting and questionable goings-on in the courtroom, but nobody feels all that bad about this one; they just love to argue about it. In 1948 Alger Hiss, a former high official in the State Department, was accused by Whittaker Chambers, a senior editor at *Time* magazine and a former spy, of helping him deliver secret information to the Russians. Nobody believed Chambers until Richard Nixon, then an ambitious young lawyer out to make a name for himself, took on his case. Soon afterward, Chambers suddenly produced five rolls of incriminating microfilm (not "papers" at all) that he claimed to have hidden inside a pumpkin on his Maryland farm. These, along with an old typewriter supposedly belonging to Hiss, were the famous props on which the case against him rested. Nixon pushed hard, and the government bent the law in order to try Hiss after the statute of limitations on the alleged crime had run out. He was convicted and served almost four years in jail; Nixon's fortunes were—or seemed to be—made. The case just won't die, however; new evidence and new theories keep popping up like ghosts in an Edgar Allan Poe story. The most recent appeared in October 1992, when a Russian general named Volkogonov, chairman of Russia's military-intelligence archives, declared that in examining the newly opened KGB files, he'd found nothing to incriminate Hiss. He concluded that the charges against Hiss were "completely groundless." Hiss fans celebrated, and the news media headlined the story for days. Then Volkogonov recanted, saying, well, he hadn't actually gone through all the files himself, it was more like he'd chatted with a couple of former KGB agents for a few minutes. Hiss foes celebrated, while at least one pro-Hiss political commentator suggested that Nixon may have had a word with Russian president Boris Yeltsin, who happened to be Volkogonov's boss. The upshot: To this day, nobody quite believes that Hiss was entirely innocent; on the other hand, they're *sure* Nixon wasn't.

Famous Last Words

TWELVE SUPREME COURT DECISIONS WORTH KNOWING BY NAME

W hy worth knowing? Because in a country with a two-hundred-year-old constitution that was never very nuts-and-bolts in the first place, executive and legislative powers that cancel each other out, and a couple hundred million people all talking at once, it can be mighty tricky to tell our rights from our wrongs, much less make either stand up in court. In the end, none of us can be sure of what's a freedom and what's a felony until nine cantankerous justices have smoothed their robes, scratched their heads, and made up their minds. And lately, given how rarely the justices are able to agree on anything, even *that* doesn't seem to help.

The Supreme Court in 1921. That's Justice Brandeis in the back row, far left; Oliver Wendell Holmes is seated second from right.

MARBURY v. MADISON (1803)

You may know this one only by name, given the catchy alliteration and the fact that we've all had a lot on our minds since 1803. Nevertheless, this was the single most important decision ever handed down by the Court because it established the right of judicial review, without which there wouldn't *be* any Supreme Court decisions worth knowing by name.

The plot gets complicated, but it's worth the effort. John Marbury had been appointed a district-court judge by outgoing president John Adams. In the hubbub of changing administrations, however, the commission—the actual piece of paper—never got delivered. When the new secretary of state, James Madison, refused to honor the appointment, Marbury appealed to the Supreme Court to issue a writ of mandamus, which would force the new administration to give him his commission. Now forget Marbury, Madison, and the meaning of the word "mandamus" for the moment; what was *really* going on was a power struggle between John Marshall, newly appointed chief justice of the Court and an unshakable Federalist, and Thomas Jefferson, newly elected president of the United States and our most determined anti-Federalist. Marbury's had been only one of innumerable last-minute judgeships handed out by the lame-duck Federalists in an effort to "pack the courts" before the anti-Federalists, who had just won the elections by a landslide, swept them into permanent oblivion. Understandably, the anti-Federalists were furious at what they considered a dirty trick. To make matters even worse, Marshall himself was one of these so called midnight judges, appointed just before Jefferson's inauguration; and, as it happened, it was Marshall's brother who had neglected to deliver Marbury's commission in the first place.

By all standards of propriety, Marshall should have been vacationing in Acapulco while this case was being argued. Instead, he wrote the opinion himself, managing to turn it into the classic mix of law and politics that approaches art. First, he declared that Marbury was theoretically entitled to his commission. Second—and here's the twister—he *denied* Marbury's petition on the grounds that the part of the law that allowed the Supreme Court to issue writs of mandamus in this sort of case was unconstitutional, and therefore null and void.

The results: (1) Marbury got to keep his dignity, if nothing else; (2) Jefferson was appeased because Marbury didn't get the job; (3) the Court avoided a confrontation with the president it would certainly have lost, since it didn't have the power to enforce a writ of mandamus even if it had had the power to issue one; and (4) most important, the Court officially established itself as the final arbiter of the constitutionality of any law passed by Congress, and it did so by righteously *denying* itself a power. This last point made the Court the effective equal—in a checks-and-balances sort of way—of both Congress and the president. And let's not forget that (5) Marshall came away from the case looking like the soul of judicial integrity, not only because he'd rejected a Federalist place-seeker, but because the law he'd overturned was a Federalist law. This left him free to spend the next thirty-five years interpreting the Constitution and shaping American history according to his own brilliant, but decidedly Federalist, views.

McCULLOCH v. MARYLAND (1819)

Why should you care about a case that prevented the state of Maryland from tax-ing notes issued by the Second Bank of the United States? Because what was re-ally in question was the constitutionality of the Bank itself, and the Bank brouhaha was symbolic of the major preoccupation of the day: Who was going to run this show, the federal government or the individual states? Had John Mar-shall not had his way, we might have ended up as a loose confederation of states that couldn't see eye-to-eye on anything, and that certainly wouldn't have had a prayer of pooling their resources to produce a Miss America pageant.

The controversy over the establishment of the First Bank of the United States was still smoldering in the hearts of states' rights advocates when this new out-rage came along. They argued that by incorporating the Second Bank, Congress had exceeded its constitutional powers and that, in any event, the states could tax whatever they wanted to as long as it was on their turf.

Marshall, who, as you'll recall, was an ardent Federalist with a vision of a strong Union, scored the biggest win of his career with this one. In upholding the constitutionality of the Bank's incorporation, he managed to fire off several state-ments that subsequently became classics of American law. For instance, he deftly worked the opposition's argument—that nowhere in the constitution was Con-gress specifically empowered to charter a bank—into the premise that the Con-stitution speaks in a broad language so that it can be "adapted to the various crises of human affairs." He also claimed that the sovereign people had made the cen-tral government supreme over all rivals within the sphere of its powers, and con-cluded that the Maryland tax was invalid because "the power to tax is the power to destroy," and it just wouldn't make sense to let a supreme power be destroyed by an inferior one. He neatly summed up the whole thing:

> Let the end be legitimate, let it be within the scope of the Constitution, and all means which are appropriate, which are plainly adapted to that end, which are not prohibited but consist with the letter and spirit of the Con-stitution are constitutional.

Thus, with a few well-chosen words, Marshall not only proclaimed, once and for all, the supremacy of national over state government (well, there was still the Civil War to come, but the theory, at least, was now down on paper), but also established both the federal government's—and, by extension, the Court's—right to make what was henceforth to be known as a "loose construction" of the Constitution. Which, of course, is another way of saying it's anybody's ball game.

DRED SCOTT v. SANFORD (1857)

Yes, Dred Scott was a slave; no, he had nothing to do with John Brown or Harpers Ferry. Nearly everyone seems to have a mental block here, so let's get the story straight, even if it is a bit of a downer. Dred Scott was a Missouri black man who sued his master, claiming that he had been automatically freed by having been taken first to Illinois, a free state, then to the Minnesota Territory, where slavery had been forbidden by the Missouri Compromise.

The case was a real cliff-hanger; not only did the Court take forever to decide, but, given the year, there was, naturally, a lot more at stake than one man and a few legal loopholes. The whole country was waiting to see who would ultimately get control of the new western territories. If the slave states succeeded in institutionalizing slavery there, it would mean more votes and political power for the agrarian South. If the antislavery states got their way, it would mean an even greater concentration of power for the industrial North; in which case, the South threatened, it would secede.

Finally, Chief Justice Roger Taney delivered the opinion for a predominantly Southern Court. First, he ruled, Negroes were not citizens of the United States (they had, as he put it, "no rights any white man was bound to respect") and were not, therefore, entitled to go around suing people. Petition denied. The Court could have stopped there, but it chose to go for the extra point: Scott, it declared, couldn't possibly have been freed by his stay in the Minnesota Territory because Minnesota wasn't free territory. In fact, Congress had no right to create free territory since, in so doing, it had violated the Fifth Amendment by depriving Southerners of their right to property. Ergo, the Missouri Compromise was unconstitutional, null, and void. The South, naturally, saw this as the Supreme Court's shining hour, while Northerners began to mutter that maybe there was a higher law than the Constitution, after all.

HAMMER v. DAGENHART (1918)

Once the Civil War had dispatched the federal/state power struggle, the Court turned its attention to the country's latest concern: getting rich. Making America wealthy involved yet another wrestling match, this time between government and business. Now the justices leapt into the ring, headed straight for the big-money corner, and spent the remainder of the Gilded Age utilizing their now-considerable repertoire of judicial maneuvers to defend vested wealth against government interference. From Reconstruction through the Depression, they handed down a series of decisions that succeeded in blocking federal and state regulations, promoting the principle of laissez-faire, and generally helping the rich get richer. By the early twentieth century, the Court found itself pitted not only against government, but against what it saw as the menace of socialism (the growing labor movement) and the clamor of the masses (social reform).

Hammer v. Dagenhart was one of the more memorable illustrations of the spirit of the age. In it, the Court overturned a congressional act designed to limit child labor. The act prohibited interstate or foreign commerce of commodities produced in factories employing children under fourteen and in mines employing children under sixteen. (If the legislation seems a bit roundabout, it's because the Court had already ruled it unconstitutional for Congress to interfere in the manufacture of goods in any way.) The suit, by the way, was brought by Dagenhart, who had two sons working in a North Carolina cotton mill and who was determined to keep them there. Describing himself as "a man of small means" with a large family to feed, Dagenhart claimed that he needed the boys' pay "for their comfortable support and maintenance." The Court's unshakable conservatism and consistent success in such cases blocked social legislation for years and finally led to Franklin Roosevelt's notorious efforts to "pack the court" with justices friendly to the New Deal. The Court did eventually bow to public pressure for reform, of course, so feel free to hold it responsible (along with the Democrats) for the development of the "welfare state."

SCHENCK v. UNITED STATES (1919)

The case that set the bottom line on freedom of speech and, in so doing, gave Justice Oliver Wendell Holmes the opportunity to make one of the Supreme Court's most historic statements:

> The most stringent protection of free speech would not protect a man falsely shouting fire in a theatre and causing panic. . . . The question in every case is whether the words are used in such circumstances and are of such a nature as to create a clear and present danger that will bring about the substantive evils that Congress has a right to prevent. It is a question of proximity and degree. . . . When a nation is at war many things that might be said in time of peace are such a hindrance to its effort that their utterance will not be endured so long as men fight and that no Court could regard them as being protected by any constitutional right.

The principle of "clear and present danger" became one of the rare justifications for restraining freedom of speech (until the 1990s, that is, when political correctness seemed like reason enough to some folks). In the case at hand, it was used to deny the petition of John Schenck, a young man arrested for distributing pamphlets arguing against the legality of the draft. In the Thirties and Forties, it became the basis for prosecuting many people whom the government considered politically subversive.

BROWN v. BOARD OF EDUCATION OF TOPEKA (1954)

The decision that, theoretically at least, ended school segregation, although Little Rock was still three years down the road. *Brown*, which was the umbrella for five separate segregation cases from five different states, was the petition brought on behalf of eight-year-old Linda Brown, whose father was tired of watching her take the school bus to a blacks-only Topeka school every day when there was a whites-only school within spitting distance—so to speak—of their home. The Court's decision overturned the principle of "separate but equal" facilities it had established with *Plessy v. Ferguson* back in 1896. Separate but equal was the doctrine that had, for sixty years, allowed segregationists to insist that they weren't implying that Negroes were inferior just because they didn't want to eat, wash up, or share a bus seat with one. Only slightly less controversial than the Scopes trial, *Brown* attracted friend-of-the-court briefs from everyone from the American Jewish Congress to the AFL-CIO, but the main characters to remember are:

1. Thurgood Marshall, the NAACP lawyer who argued for the petitioners and who later became the Supreme Court's first black justice.
2. Dr. Kenneth B. Clark, the New York psychologist who made the courts safe for psychosociology by introducing as evidence his now-famous "dolls experiment." Clark had shown a group of black children two dolls, one black and one white, asking them to choose the doll they found prettiest and would most like to play with, and the doll they thought looked "bad." The children's overwhelming preference for the white doll was seen as proof that segregation was psychologically damaging to black children.
3. Chief Justice Earl Warren, who proved his talents as an orchestrator by herding eight feisty justices and nine more or less dissimilar viewpoints together to form one unanimous opinion; to wit, that "separate educational facilities are inherently unequal."
4. President Dwight D. Eisenhower, who was so unsympathetic to the cause of desegregation that the Court, knowing it couldn't count on him

to enforce its decision, put off elucidating the how-tos of the opinion for a whole year. At that point, in *Brown II*, it made the cautious, and ultimately disastrous, declaration that the Southern school districts must undertake desegregation measures "with all deliberate speed," a phrase which many Southern school districts chose to interpret as sometime in the afterlife.

BAKER *v.* CARR (1962)

All about reapportionment, but don't go away, we won't bore you with the details (unless of course, you'd *like* to know that Baker was the disgruntled voter, Carr the election official, and the setting was Tennessee). Besides, Earl Warren claimed that this was the most important decision of his not unremarkable tenure as chief justice. What you need to grasp: That the country's demographics had changed over the years but its election districts hadn't, so that small towns and rural areas were consistently overrepresented while cities were underrepresented. This put power firmly in the hands of minority and special-interest groups, who were determined to keep it there. The Court had long refused to get involved in the "political thicket" of voting rights, but with *Baker v. Carr*, it plunged in and decided that unequal election districts were discriminatory and violated the Fourteenth Amendment. This, and the armload of reapportionment cases that followed, not only gave us the phrase "one man, one vote" (or, as more progressive historians would have it, "one person, one vote"), it also shifted the country's center of gravity from the hinterlands to the cities. Paradoxically, the decision helped open the can of worms that was the Voting Rights Act of 1965, which, with its 1982 revision and various related court rulings, legitimized gerrymanders created for the specific purpose of giving African Americans a chance at political power in states notorious for racial discrimination. In 1993, however, a much more conservative Supreme Court suddenly got fed up and declared unconstitutional a particularly eye-catching racial gerrymander in North Carolina, a snakelike critter 160 miles long and, in some spots, no wider than the two-lane highway running through it.

MIRANDA *v.* ARIZONA (1966)

The rights of the accused, especially the right to counsel, the right to remain silent when taken into custody, and the right to be informed of one's rights, were at stake here. But you already know this if you've ever watched network television. You may also know that the Miranda rule makes cops snarl and gives the DA ulcers. Miranda was the culmination of a series of decisions designed to protect the accused before trial, all of which got their muscle from the exclusionary rule (i.e., throwing out evidence that doesn't conform to tight judicial standards) and none of which won the Warren Court much popularity with law-and-order fans.

The issue is, in fact, a sticky one. Consider it, for instance, from the point of view of Barbara Ann Johnson. One day in 1963, Johnson, an eighteen-year-old candy-counter clerk at a movie theater in Phoenix, was forcibly shoved into the backseat of a car, tied up, and driven to the desert, where she was raped. The rapist then drove her back to town, asked her to say a prayer for him, and let her go. Soon afterward, the police arrested twenty-three-year-old Ernesto Miranda, a high school dropout with a criminal record dating back to the time he was fourteen. Miranda had already been convicted of rape in the past. Johnson identified him in a lineup. Miranda then wrote out a confession, stating that it was made with full knowledge to his rights. He was convicted and sentenced to forty to fifty-five years in prison, despite his court-appointed lawyer's contention that his client had been ignorant of his right to counsel. An appeal to the state supreme court failed, but the Supreme Court's decision set Miranda free. Miranda and the ACLU were naturally appreciative of the Court's libertarian stance, Barbara Ann Johnson less so. But not to worry. Miranda was later reconvicted on new evidence. He served time in prison, was released on parole, and was stabbed to death in a Phoenix bar ten years after the Court's landmark decision. Although the Burger Court didn't really make chopped meat of this and most of the other Warren Court rights-of-the-accused provisions, as conservatives had hoped, the Rehnquist Court did.

A BOOK NAMED JOHN CLELAND'S "MEMOIRS OF A WOMAN OF PLEASURE" v. MASSACHUSETTS (1966)

Fanny Hill goes to Washington, there to help clarify the hopelessly vague three-pronged definition of obscenity the Court had formulated nearly a decade earlier in *Roth v. U.S.* Since Roth, the burden had been on the censors to prove that a work under scrutiny (1) appealed to prurient interest; (2) was patently offensive; and (3) was utterly without redeeming social value. But every small-town PTA seemed to have its own idea of what all that meant, and whatever it was, it usually involved harassing the manager of the local bookstore or movie theater. In *Fanny Hill*, which was decided in a single day, along with two other obscenity cases, the court took great pains to speak slowly and enunciate carefully: Even when there was no question that a work fit the first two criteria, it could not be declared obscene unless it was *utterly* without redeeming social value—not a shred, not a smidgen. And *Fanny Hill* didn't fit that criterion. Of course, the judgment went on, that doesn't necessarily mean that the book *couldn't* be ruled obscene under certain circumstances, say, if the publishers marketed it solely on the basis of its prurient appeal. That helped. Pornographers took to making "medical films" prefaced by passages from Shakespeare, and the Court continued to be deluged by obscenity cases for years, until it finally threw up its hands and turned the whole mess into a question of "community standards" and local zoning laws.

FURMAN v. GEORGIA (1972)

Capital punishment outlawed, in one of the longest (243 pages) and most tortured (a 5–4 split and nine separate opinions) decisions in the Court's history. Never mind the gory details of *Furman*, which was only the lead case among five involving rapes, murders, and rape-murders. More to the point are the four separate arguments the Court was asked to consider as bases for declaring the death penalty unconstitutional:

1. The death penalty was imposed in a discriminatory manner; statistics showed that it was usually black and poor people who died, whereas middle-class whites simply hired the kind of lawyers who could get them off.
2. The death penalty was imposed in an arbitrary manner, with no clear criteria for deciding who would live and who would die.
3. Because it was so seldom used, the death penalty never really functioned as an effective deterrent.
4. Society's standards had evolved to the point where the death penalty, like branding and the cutting off of hands, constituted "cruel and unusual punishment."

To make matters more painful, there had already been an informal moratorium on executions in 1967, so that six hundred people now sat on death row, awaiting the final decision. Even those justices who favored capital punishment squirmed at the idea of having *that* much blood on their hands.

In the end, the Court took the wishy-washy stance that capital punishment was unconstitutional *at that time* because it was arbitrarily and capriciously imposed. Only two justices out of the five-man majority thought the death penalty was cruel and unusual punishment. The Court's decision left everyone confused as to what to do next—but not for long. Within three years, thirty-five states had redesigned their death-penalty laws to get around the Court's restrictions, and public-opinion polls showed Americans to be overwhelmingly in favor of capital punishment, thereby disproving at least one of the petitioners' arguments: that society had evolved beyond the death penalty. In 1975, the Court ruled on the existing laws in five states and found only one (North Carolina's) to be unconstitutional. In 1976, it reversed its stand altogether; ruling on a batch of five cases, it found that the death penalty was not cruel and unusual punishment per se. Still, no one wanted to cut off the first head. It wasn't until 1977, when Gary Gilmore broke the ice by insisting that the state of Utah stand him in front of a firing squad, that anyone was actually executed. The first involuntary execution took place in 1979, with the electrocution of John Spenkelink, who had been reprieved by the *Furman* decision seven years earlier. Since then there have been around one thousand executions nationwide, most by lethal injection. Texas leads the country with the highest number of executions per capita. Why aren't you surprised?

ROE v. WADE (1973)

The decision that legalized abortion as part of a woman's right to privacy (although Justice Blackmun, who wrote the majority opinion, spent many months trying to prove that abortion was part of the doctor's right to privacy). According to the opinion, the state only has the right to intervene when it can prove it has a "compelling interest," such as the health of the mother. As for the fetus, its rights can begin to be considered only after the twenty-sixth week of pregnancy. The Court thus tiptoed around the quagmire of moral and religious disputes raging over the abortion issue and based its decision on the relatively neutral ground of medicine. However, this was not the most airtight of Supreme Court opinions, and it came under constant, ferocious attack for the next twenty years. The state of Texas, for instance, filed a petition for rehearing, comparing the Court's assertion that a fetus was not a person before the third semester of pregnancy to the Court's 1857 decision that Dred Scott was not a person (see page 55). In speeches and articles preceding her ascension to the Supreme Court, Justice Ruth Bader Ginsburg publicly opined that the Court might have avoided a lot of headaches if it had simply based its decision on the grounds of equality instead of privacy and had refrained from getting enmeshed in the gory medical details. Still, by 1993 the court had reaffirmed women's basic right to abortion so many times that the storm center had shifted from the issue of abortion itself to questions like who should pay for it. Meanwhile, some radical antiabortionists had given up on legal challenges altogether and, in the spirit of the times, just started shooting doctors. Under Presidents Bill Clinton and George W. Bush, abortion opponents shifted tactics to focus on teenagers. By 2005, forty-four states had laws on the books requiring teens either to notify or get consent from their parents before getting an abortion. Most states allow adolescents to go to court for a waiver if they can show that their parents are, say, alcoholics or abusive. So for the moment, any fifteen-year-old who's savvy enough to go to court on her own and persuade a judge of the merits of her case can still consider abortion an option.

UNIVERSITY OF CALIFORNIA REGENTS
v. ALLAN BAKKE (1978)

The clearest thing to come out of this, the Court's first affirmative-action case, was that it probably was not a good idea to try to stage a media event around a Burger Court decision.

The story line, in case you lost it in all the confusion, was as follows: Allan Bakke, a thirty-eight-year-old white engineer, had twice been refused admission to the University of California's medical school at Davis, despite a 3.5 college grade-point average, which was well above the 2.5 required for white applicants and the 2.1 required for minorities. Concluding that he'd been passed over because of Davis' strict minority admissions quota, Bakke took his case to the Supreme Court, charging reverse discrimination. The media jumped all over *Bakke*, in part because it was the first time affirmative action had been tested in the courts, and everyone was anxious to see how much the mood of the country had changed—for better or worse—since the Sixties; in part because the Burger Court's somewhat shoddy civil-rights record promised to lend an edge to the whole affair.

The outcome, however, was a two-part decision that merely left most people scratching their heads. The Court declared itself firmly behind the principle of affirmative action, but just as firmly behind Bakke's right to get into medical school. In effect, it said: Principles, yes; quota systems, no. Some civil-rights groups decided to take this as a resounding success, others as a crushing blow; ditto for the opposition. Some said it left the door open for future affirmative-action measures (there are other ways to promote racial balance besides quota systems, the Court pointed out, and no one was ruling out an institution's right to take race into account as one factor among many when deciding on an applicant's qualifications). Others insisted it left an even wider margin for businesses and universities to discriminate against minorities. Some legal scholars pointed out inconsistencies and downright lapses of reason in the justices' opposing opinions (the Court was split 5–4); others declared the everyone-gets-to-take-home-half-a-baby decision a fine example of judicial wisdom.

Although the haziness of *Bakke* pretty much ensured that the courts would be gnawing on affirmative-action cases for years to come, it was the press that was really left holding the bag. Screaming headlines that contradicted each other

("Court Votes 'Yes' to Bakke"; "Court Votes 'Yes' to Affirmative Action") just made a lot of newspapers look silly and, after a couple of frustrating go-nowhere specials, TV reporters had to conclude that legal ambiguities did not make for optimum prime-time fare. The rest of us got a taste of how unsatisfying Supreme Court decisions would be for at least the next fifteen years.

RT HISTORY

T   W   O

Contents

Marcel Duchamp's L.H.O.O.Q. *(a cheap French pun translating roughly to "she's got a hot ass"), a.k.a.* Mona Lisa with a Moustache

Ten Old Masters

In a way, we're sorry. What we had really wanted to do was talk about our ten *favorite* painters. Then we got to thinking that it should be the ten painters whose stock is currently highest, who are most in vogue in a crudités-and-hired-bartenders way. (Whichever, you'd have heard about Piero della Francesca, Caravaggio, Velásquez, and Manet, all notably absent here.) Then we realized that, if you were anything like us, what you really needed was remedial work, not a pajama party or a year in finishing school. So, here they are, the ten greatest—we suppose that means something like "most seminal"—painters of all time.

GIOTTO (GIOTTO DI BONDONE)
(c. 1266–c. 1337)

Giotto's Deposition

As the little girl said in *Poltergeist*: "They're heeere!" By which we mean artists who sign their work, travel in packs, and live lives about which something, and sometimes too much, is known. Before Giotto (that's pronounced "JOT-to"), the artist hadn't counted for any more than the stonemason or the glassblower; from here on in, he'd be accorded a degree of respect, authority, and press unknown since ancient Greece. Also in abeyance since the Greeks: the human body, about which the courtly and rigid Byzantines—Giotto's only available role models—had felt some combination of deeply ashamed and not all that interested anyway. Giotto, out of the blue (and we're waist-deep in the Middle Ages, remember), turned mannequins into people, dry Christian doctrine into vivid you-are-there narrative, mere colored shapes into objects that seemed to have weight and volume, and his native Florence into the art world's red-hot center for the next 250 years. No painter would prove either as revolutionary or as influential as Giotto for six centuries, at which point Cézanne opined that eyewitness-style reporting on life might not be the ultimate artistic high.

KEY WORKS: The Arena Chapel frescoes in Padua, thirty-three scenes from the lives of Christ and the Virgin Mary and her folks.

COLLEAGUES AND RIVALS: Duccio, from neighboring Siena, where life was conservative, aristocratic, and refined, and where ballots were cast for beauty rather than truth.

MASACCIO
(TOMMASO DI SER GIOVANNI DI MONE)
(1401–1428?)

Played Elvis Presley to Giotto's Frank Sinatra. That is, Masaccio took his predecessor's three-dimensional realism and put some meat on it, encouraged it to flex its muscles and swivel its hips, enlarged the stage it was playing on, and generally shook the last vestiges of middle age(s) out of the whole performance. Thus begins the Renaissance, the era that rediscovered Greece and Rome; that posed the questions "Why?" "How?" and "So what?"; that promoted such novelties as humanism, freedom, and the idea of leading a full life; and that—casting its gaze on the lot of the artist—came up with a support system of studios, patrons, and apprentices. With Masaccio (a nickname that equates roughly with "Pigpen"), we're at that Renaissance's heroic beginnings, smack-dab in the middle of boomtown, no-holds-barred Florence, and we're watching as the new sciences of perspective and anatomy encourage painters to paint things as they appear to the eye. That doesn't, however, mean you're going to get off on Masaccio the way your parents or grandparents got off on Elvis. For one thing, Masaccio died at twenty-seven, before he'd really done all that much. For another, until recently most of his extant work was in rough shape or badly lit (those darned Italian churches) or both. Most important, few of us these days are wowed by perspective and anatomy. As a result, Masaccio is what art historians call a "scholar's painter." But it was his stuff and nobody else's that Leonardo, Michelangelo, et al., back in the mid-fifteenth century, were ankling over to the Brancacci Chapel to take a long hard look at.

Masaccio's The Expulsion from Paradise

KEY WORKS: *The Holy Trinity with the Virgin, St. John, and Donors* (Sta. Maria Novella, Florence), *The Tribute Money* and *The Expulsion from Paradise* (both Brancacci Chapel, Sta. Maria del Carmine, Florence).

COLLEAGUES AND RIVALS: In this case, not fellow painters, but an architect, Brunelleschi, and a sculptor, Donatello. Together, the three ushered in the Renaissance in the visual arts.

RAPHAEL (RAFFAELLO SANZIO)
(1483–1520)

Button up your overcoat. That chill you're feeling, coupled with the fact that, if you took History of Art 101, he was the one you got hit with the week before Christmas vacation, means that it's impossible to smile brightly when the name Raphael comes up, the way you do with Leonardo da Vinci and Michelangelo—the two contemporaries with whom he forms a trinity that is to the High Renaissance what turkey, ham, and Swiss are to a chef's salad. That said, the thing about Raphael is—and has always been—that he never makes mistakes, fails to

Raphael's The School of Athens

achieve desired effects, or forgets what it is, exactly, he's supposed to be doing next Thursday morning. He *perfected* picture painting, the way engineers perfected bridge building or canal digging or satellite launching; each of his canvases is an exercise in balance, in organization, in clarity and harmony, in coherence and gracefulness. For four hundred years, right through the nineteenth century, Raphael was every painter's idol; lately, though, he's begun to seem a little bland, as well as a lot sticky-fingered, absorbing and assimilating and extracting from other artists (especially Michelangelo) rather than trying to figure things out for himself. Note: With the High Renaissance, painting packs its bags and moves from Florence to Rome, where the papacy will take over the Medicis' old Daddy Warbucks role, and where Raphael—handsome, tactful, and possessed of a good sense of timing—will earn his reputation as the courtier among painters, a fixture at the dinner parties of popes and princes.

KEY WORKS: The early Madonnas (e.g., *Madonna of the Goldfinch*, Uffizi, Florence), the portrait of Pope Leo X (Pitti Palace, Florence), the murals in the Stanza della Segnatura (Rome), then the Pope's private library, especially the one entitled *The School of Athens*.

COLLEAGUES AND RIVALS: Michelangelo and, to a lesser extent (at least they weren't constantly at each other's throats), Leonardo.

TITIAN (TIZIANO VECELLIO)
(1477–1576)

Welcome to Venice—opulent, voluptuous, pagan, on the profitable trade route to the Orient, given to both civic propaganda and conspicuous consumption—where light and color (as opposed to Florence's structure and balance) are the name of the game. With Titian, the most important of the Venetians, painting becomes a dog-eat-dog profession with agents and PR people and client mailings, a business in which religious and political demands are nothing next to those of the carriage—make that gondola—trade. Titian was versatile (he did everything an oil painter could do, from altarpieces to erotica, from straight portraits to complex mythologies) and obscenely long-lived (it took the plague to bring him down, at something like ninety-nine), and he dominated the art scene for seventy-five years, with his flesh-and-blood, high-wide-and-handsome ways. He presided at the divorce of painting from architecture and its remarriage to the easel, and assured that the primary medium of the new union would be oil on canvas. Don't expect rigor or even real imagination from the man, though; what's

Titian's
Venus of Urbino

on display here are energy and expansiveness. Prestige point: In his old age, Titian, whose eyes weren't what they used to be, began painting in overbold strokes and fudged contours, encouraging modern critics to praise his newfound profundity and cite him as the first Impressionist, a man who painted how he *saw* things, not how he knew them to be.

KEY WORKS: It's the corpus, not the individual canvas, that counts. Right up there, though: *Madonna with Members of the Pesaro Family* (Frari, Venice), *Rape of Europa* (Gardner Museum, Boston), *Venus of Urbino* (Pitti Palace, Florence), and *Christ Crowned with Thorns* (Alte Pinakothek, Munich).

COLLEAGUES AND RIVALS: Giorgione, who played sensualist, die-young Keats to Titian's long-lived, Spirit-of-the-Age Wordsworth.

EL GRECO
(DOMENICOS THEOTOCOPOULOS)
(1541–1614)

He was, in the words of Manet, "the great alternative." Though of late El Greco's been positioned as the seasoned thinker, rather than the God-happy wild man, either way he was too much of an anomaly to have real impact on his contemporaries—or to found a school of Spanish painting. (Both of those would have to wait for Velázquez to come along, a few years later.) In fact, it was the twentieth century that made El Greco's reputation, applauding his distortions—especially those gaunt, tense, strung-out figures—and his creation of an inward, fire-and-ice world, complete with angst and hallucination. From Van Gogh through the young Picasso and the German Expressionists, up to the American Abstract Expressionists of the Forties and Fifties, all of whom had a big I-gotta-be-me streak, El Greco has served as a patron saint. A little history: "El Greco" was the nickname given to this footloose Greek ("Greco," get it?) by the citizens of rarefied, decaying Toledo, Spain, when he arrived there after a boyhood spent among Byzantine icons, followed by stints in Venice (where he glanced at the

El Greco's Toledo in a Storm

Titians) and Rome (where he offered to redo Michelangelo's Sistine Ceiling). Which is funny, inasmuch as we tend to think of his vision as more Spanish than anybody's but Cervantes'. For art historians, he holds two records: "Last of the Mannerists" (those anticlassical eccentrics who knew you couldn't top Raphael at the perfection game, and decided to put all their chips on weirdness instead) and "most disturbingly personal painter ever." Critics go into raptures over his "incandescent"—some prefer "phosphorescent"—spirituality. Whatever: Here's a painter you'll always be able to recognize on any wall in any museum in the world.

KEY WORKS: First and foremost, *Burial of Count Orgaz* (Santo Tomé, Toledo), the largest and most resplendent El Greco. Also: *Toledo in a Storm* and *Cardinal Niño de Guevara* (both at the Metropolitan, New York), the latter a portrait of Spain's menacing, utterly unholy-looking Grand Inquisitor.

COLLEAGUES AND RIVALS: Like we say, none among his contemporaries. But forms, with Velázquez and Goya, the trinity of Great Spanish Painters.

PETER PAUL RUBENS (1577–1640)

Not an anal retentive. From factory headquarters in Antwerp (now Belgium, then still the Spanish Netherlands), Rubens, the "prince of painters," purveyed his billowy, opulent, robust, and sensual portraits, altarpieces, landscapes, historical tableaux, and mythological treatments to the Church, the town fathers, private patrons, and virtually every royal household in Europe. (It helped that he was as much a diplomat as an artist, entrusted with secrets of state by, among others, the Infanta of Spain, and hence provided with entrée to all the best palaces.) To be associated with the name Rubens: First, success beyond anybody's wildest dreams: financial, professional, and personal. Second, Flemish painting, which began with the restrained van Eyck, proceeded through Bosch and Brueghel, and reached its culmination now, an art that was drumming up a full-tilt Catholic sumptuousness even as its north-of-the-border Dutch cousin was becoming more and more Protestant and bourgeois. Third, the concept of the baroque, the organizing principle behind all seventeenth-century art—dynamic, emotional, exuberant, and asymmetrical in all those places where the classicism of the High Renaissance had been static, poised, and balanced; a principle that, among other things, decreed that the work of art was greater than the sum of its parts. Anyway, Rubens created and created and created, and if his

Rubens'
The Judgment
of Paris

altarpieces didn't seem particularly mystical or his bacchanals all that wild and crazy, still, there was enough sheer activity in each of them that you couldn't really squawk. For the conscientious: There's always the chance that you'll forget which painting is Rubens' and which is Titian's (and anyone who tells you that's impossible because the two men are separated by a hundred years and half of Europe is lying). Just remember that Titian subordinated the whole of his painting to its parts, Rubens the parts to the whole; that Titian valued serenity, even in an orgy scene, Rubens tumult; and that Titian painted the equivalent of Vassar coeds, Rubens Ziegfeld showgirls.

KEY WORKS: As with Titian, it's the shooting match, not the individual shot. However, *The Judgment of Paris* (National Gallery, London; that's his second wife in the middle); the Marie de' Medici series (Louvre, Paris; thirty-six panels' worth of commemoration); and the late landscapes (various museums), with the Rubens family chateau in the background, will give you a sense of his range.

COLLEAGUES AND RIVALS: A rung down the ladder, Anthony van Dyck, the portraitist of aristocrats, especially English ones, and Rubens' one-time assistant.

REMBRANDT VAN RIJN (1606–1669)

Rembrandt's
Self-Portrait

The son of a miller and a baker's daughter, with a face—famous from over a hundred self-portraits—much likened to a loaf of bread. But, as Miss Piggy, herself every inch a Rubens gal, might say, *quel* loaf of bread. The man who manipulated tonality (lights and darks, to you) and eschewed contour better than anybody ever, Rembrandt was also the painter who realized, first and most fully, that the eye could take in a human figure, the floor it was standing on, the wall behind it, plus the flock of pigeons visible through the window in that wall, without having to make any conscious adjustments. (If we were talking automotive rather than art history, Rembrandt would be the advent of the automatic transmission.) More than *that*, even, Rembrandt was the very model of the sensitive and perceptive person, as some of us used to say sophomore year, taking the sober, commonplace Dutch panorama—guildhall and slum, merchant and beggar—and portraying it in all its poignancy and detail; even Christianity, the inspiration for the other half of the Rembrandtian output, becomes, in his hands and for the first time since Giotto, an affair for ordinary men and women. And if all that's not enough, Rembrandt's still the answer most game-show contestants would come up with when asked to name a famous painter. Historical generalization: Rembrandt (and the rest of the seventeenth-century Dutch, who had no popes or patrons farming out commissions) turned out the first art to be consumed exclusively by us mere-mortal types, paintings that were to be tucked under your arm, carried home, and hung over the living-room sofa.

KEY WORKS: Many. The ones that come up over and over are *The Night Watch* and *The Syndics of the Cloth Guild* (the latter adopted by the Dutch Masters cigars folks; both, Rijksmuseum, Amsterdam) and a pair of late self-portraits (1659, National Gallery, London; 1660, Kenwood, London). And you'll need one of the religious paintings, perhaps *Return of the Prodigal Son* (Hermitage, Leningrad). But beware: Since 1968, the Rembrandt Research Project, based in Amsterdam, has been reassessing the authenticity of the entire Rembrandt corpus. Among the casualties: *The Polish Rider, The Man in the Golden Helmet,* and *The Girl at the Door,* each now attributed to a different student of Rembrandt's.

COLLEAGUES AND RIVALS: Lots of them; painting and painters were as much in evidence in seventeenth-century Holland as they'd been in fifteenth-century Florence. You should know Frans Hals (impulsive, with a predilection for people hanging out and getting drunk) and Jan Vermeer (intimate, with a predilection for people opening mail and pouring milk). Everybody else is categorized as a "Little Dutchman," a genre painter specializing in landscapes, still lifes, portraits, or interiors.

CLAUDE MONET (1840–1926)

The problem is, you're dealing with two legendary reputations (and that's not counting M*a*net, Monet's hip contemporary). The first Monet is the Father of Impressionism. You remember Impressionism: the mid-nineteenth-century movement that grabbed an easel and a handful of paintbrushes and announced it was going outdoors; that attempted to capture the spontaneous and transitory effects of light and color by painting with the eye (and what it saw), rather than with the mind (and what it knew to be true); that couldn't have cared less about form, in the sense of either composition or solidity; that was initially reviled by the conservative French critics and artgoing public; and that wound up becoming, in our time, the most popular, most cooed-over style of painting ever. The second Monet is the great-uncle of Modernism, the man who—getting progressively blinder and more obsessed with reducing the visible world to terms of pure light—eventually gave up form altogether and took out the first patent on ab-

Monet's Terrace at Sainte-Adresse

straction; it's this Monet the avant-garde has tended to prefer. Note to those wondering what happened to the eighteenth century: You shouldn't exactly forget about it, but any hundred-year period whose biggest box-office draw is Watteau is strictly optional.

KEY WORKS: For the Impressionist Monet: at your discretion. Try *Terrace at Sainte-Adresse* (1866, Metropolitan, New York) or *Impression—Sunrise* (1872, Musée Marmottan, Paris). For the proto-Modernist Monet: The touchstones are the Rouen Cathedral series (1894, Metropolitan, New York, and Museum of Fine Arts, Boston, among others) and the water lilies series (1899, 1904–1925, Museum of Modern Art, New York, and Carnegie Institute Art Museum, Pittsburgh, among others).

COLLEAGUES AND RIVALS: The only "true" Impressionists besides Monet are Pissarro and Sisley. Manet is a proto-Impressionist, among other things. Degas and Renoir are quasi-Impressionists. Cézanne, Seurat, Van Gogh, and Gauguin are post-Impressionists. And Toulouse-Lautrec is played by José Ferrer, on his knees, with his feet strapped to his buttocks.

PAUL CÉZANNE (1839–1906)

This is a test. Pass it—that is, "get" what Cézanne was up to, maybe even like it—and chances are you'll have no trouble with "modern" art, abstraction, alienation, and all. Flunk it—that is, wonder what the fuss is about and move immediately on to Van Gogh and/or Gauguin—and you've got big problems ahead of you. As to what Cézanne *was* up to, exactly: First, he was rejecting Impressionism (note that he's an exact contemporary of Monet), not only its commitment to transience and to truth-as-what-the-eye-sees, but its affiliation with the bourgeoisie and the boulevards; Cézanne wanted to infuse some gravity, even grandeur, back into painting. Second, he was refuting classical "one-point" perspective, which makes the viewer the person on whom everything converges and for whom everything is done. For Cézanne "seeing" was a process, a weighing of choices, not a product. (He also decreed color, not line, to be the definer of form; geometry, not the needs of composition, to be its basis; and the laws of representation to be revokable at will.) Third, he was single-handedly reversing the pendulum swing toward representational "accuracy" that Giotto had set in motion six hundred years before; from here on in, *how* you perceive is going to count for more than *what* you perceive, the artist's modus operandi for more than the illusions he can bring off. Granted, this is pretty heavy stuff, but at least the paintings are sensuous, inviting, and still of the world as we know it. The sledding gets rougher with Picasso and the Cubists, up next.

KEY WORKS: Any still life. Ditto, any view of Mont Sainte-Victoire, in Cézanne's native Provence, *the* mountain in art history. Ditto, any and all scenes of card players. And the portraits of his wife and himself. In general, the later a Cézanne, the bigger a deal it's likely to be—also the more abstract. A lot of people consider *Bathers* (1898–1905, Philadelphia Museum of Art) the painter's summa, but follow his example and come to it last.

COLLEAGUES AND RIVALS: The other three Post-Impressionists: Seurat (the one with the thousands of little dots), Van Gogh (him you know), and Gauguin (of Brittany and Tahiti).

Cézanne's Still Life with Apples

PABLO PICASSO (1881–1973)

Try to rise to the occasion. God knows, the critics and commentators try, labeling Picasso, among other things, "the charging bull of modern art," "that Nietzschean monster from Málaga," and "the walking scrotum, the inexhaustible old stud of the Côte d'Azur." Be all that as it may, you've got to understand something about Cubism (which has nothing to do with actual cubes, and everything to do with seeing things in relationship to one another, simultaneously, and from more than one vantage point at a time, with the result that you may find yourself looking at a teacup, say, or a birdcage, both head on and from the air). And something about celebrity (Picasso, toward the end, enjoyed a fame no painter, not even worldlings like Raphael and Rubens, had ever known, complete with bastard heirs, sycophantic dealers, and *Life* magazine covers). Beyond those two basics there's the energy, the fecundity, the frankness, the no-flies-on-me penchant for metamorphosis and the consequent welter of styles (one critic counted eighty of them, and that was back in the early Fifties), the mythologizing (watch for Minotaurs, nymphs, and river gods), and, in a personal vein, the womanizing (he was notorious for classifying his lady friends as either "goddesses" or "doormats"). You should know that Cézanne and the primitive sculpture of Africa and pre-Christian Spain were big influences and El Greco

Picasso's
Les Demoiselles d'Avignon

a lesser one; that the "pathetic" Blue and "wistful" Rose periods predate Cubism per se; that the appeal of collage—literally, "gluing"—was that it got scraps of modern life right inside the picture frame; that Picasso claimed to "paint forms as I think them, not as I see them" (let alone as they looked); and that the painting after 1950 (not the sculpture, however) was once judged to be lacking in intensity.

KEY WORKS: *Les Demoiselles d'Avignon* (1907, Museum of Modern Art, New York), arguably the most "radical" of all paintings, and *Guernica* (1937, Prado), last of the great "political" paintings. Also, a sculpture; try *The Guitar* (1912, Museum of Modern Art), all metal sheets and empty spaces.

COLLEAGUES AND RIVALS: Georges Braque, who once commented that he and Picasso were "roped together like mountaineers," but who wound up playing Ashley Wilkes to his friend's Rhett Butler. For the record: Juan Gris and Fernand Léger are the two other ranking Cubists; Henri Matisse (see under "Fauvism"), the other great painter of the century; Marcel Duchamp, the alternative role model (see under "Dada") for young—and subversive—artists; Salvador Dalí (see under "Surrealism"), the fellow Spaniard who valued publicity and the high life even more than Picasso did.

The Leonardo/ Michelangelo Crib Sheet

	Leonardo da Vinci	Michelangelo Buonarroti
Full Name	Leonardo da Vinci	Michelangelo Buonarroti
Dates	1452–1519	1475–1564
Address	Florence, then Milan, finally Paris	Florence, then Rome
Nickname	"The First Modern Man"	"Il Divino"
Quote	"Intellectual passion drives out sensuality."	"The more the marble wastes, the more the statue grows."
Mind-set	Universal and diffuse, enigmatic and elusive	Narrow and single-minded, passionate and thorny
The Italian Word for the Above, Approximately	*Misteriosità*	*Terribilità*
At Heart Not a Painter So Much as a . . .	Scientist and philosopher	Sculptor and architect
He Most Wanted to . . .	Understand	Create
The Work Celebrated the World Over	*Mona Lisa, The Last Supper*	The Sistine Ceiling (especially *The Creation of Man*), the statue of David

The Leonardo/Michelangelo Crib Sheet

The Works You Can Get Points for Knowing About	One of the scientific drawings from the *Notebooks*, as below	One of the lesser sculptures, like an unfinished *Slave*, or something architectural, like Rome's Campidoglio

Italian Art Term Most Likely to Crop Up in a Discussion of His Work	*Sfumato* (see page 83)	*Contrapposto* (see page 81)
When He Wrote, He . . .	Jotted down descriptions of his experiments	Composed sonnets to his lovers
Gay?	Yup; major boyfriend a hustler who stole his drawings and then sold them, ditto the outfits Leonardo bought him	Yup; major boyfriend handsome, learned, thoughtful, and from a good family; affair said to have been "platonic," however
Beard?	Right, like the one on the bag person in the Penn Station men's room	Sure, like the one on the pot dealer in Washington Square

Practical Italian for the Gallery-Goer

Artwise, New York may have recently had a field day, but it's Italy that had a High Renaissance. Which means that if it's snob appeal you're after, you're going to have to learn to roll your *r*s a bit. Here's your basic lesson.

CHIAROSCURO (kee-ahr-e-SKEWR-o): Literally means "bright-dark" in Italian and describes the technique, in painting or drawing, of modeling three-dimensional figures by contrasting or gradating areas of light and dark. Leonardo da Vinci was among the first to use chiaroscuro to break out of the tradition of flat, one-dimensional outlining of figures. One of the great achievements of the Renaissance, chiaroscuro soon became part and parcel of painting. Rembrandt is the acknowledged master of the technique; if you want a more recherché example, try Caravaggio.

Chiaroscuro: Caravaggio's The Musicians

CONTRAPPOSTO (kohn-tra-POH-stoe): In sculptures of the human form, the pose in which the upper body faces in a slightly different direction from the lower, with the weight resting on one leg. Contrapposto was originally the Greeks' solution to the problem of balancing the weight of the body in sculpture. The earlier formula had been the frontal, static pose, in which the legs were treated like two columns with the torso set squarely on top of them and the head balancing on top of that. The Greeks, rightly, found this boring and stupid. Renaissance sculptors revived the Greek formula, renamed it, and added dynamic tension by making the placement of body parts more extreme

Contrapposto: Cristofano da Bracciano's Orpheus

and contrasting. This may seem like picky technical stuff to you, but it was a watershed in the history of art. Contrapposto is all over the place in Renaissance sculpture, but the example you can't get away with ignoring is Michelangelo's *David.*

FRESCO: This was *the* method for painting indoor murals, from the days of the Minoan civilization in Crete right up to the seventeenth century. It involves brushing water-based pigments onto fresh, moist lime plaster (*fresco* means "fresh" in Italian), so that the pigment is absorbed by the plaster as it dries and becomes part of the wall. Fresco painting reached its peak during the Renaissance, when artists had the backing—and the backup crews—to allow them to undertake the kind of monumental works the technique is best suited to. Today, it's also referred to as "buon fresco" or "true fresco," to distinguish it from "secco" or "mezzo" fresco, a later method of painting on dry plaster that allowed artists to get similar results with less trouble. Frescoes abound in European art history, but some of the most famous are Michelangelo's, in the Sistine Chapel; Raphael's, in the Stanza della Segnatura and the Loggia of the Vatican; and Giotto's, at the Arena Chapel in Padua. During the 1930s and 1940s, the WPA Federal Arts Project commissioned a couple thousand frescoes, mostly for municipal buildings and mostly forgettable.

IMPASTO: The technique of applying thick layers or strokes of oil paint, so that they stand out from the surface of a canvas or panel: also called "loaded

Impasto:
Van Gogh's
Self-Portrait

brush." Such seventeenth-century painters as Rubens, Rembrandt, Velázquez, and Frans Hals used impasto to emphasize pictorial highlights; in the nineteenth century, Manet, Cézanne, Van Gogh, and others used it more extensively for texture and variety. Some modern painters, including de Kooning and Dubuffet, took to laying the paint on with a palette knife or simply squeezing it directly from the tube. (One does not, it should be clear, create impasto with water colors.)

MORBIDEZZA (MOR-buh-DETZ-uh): Literally, "softness," "tenderness." Used to describe the soft blending of tones in painting—by Correggio, for instance— or rounding of edges in sculpture, especially in the rendering of human flesh. On a bad day, could seem to degenerate into effeminacy and sickliness.

PENTIMENTO: A painter's term (and Lillian Hellman's) derived from the Italian word for "repentance," and referring to the evidence that an artist changed his mind, or made a mistake, and tried to conceal it by painting over it. As time goes by, the top layer of paint may become transparent, and the artist's original statement begins to show through. Pentimento can often be found in seventeenth-century Dutch paintings, in which the artists commonly used thin layers of paint to obliterate an element of a composition—one of the children, say, in an interior—only to have its ghost reappear behind a lady's dress or a piece of furniture a couple hundred years later. One of the most famous examples of pentimento is the double hat brim in Rembrandt's portrait *Flora*.

Pentimento: Rembrandt's Flora

PUTTO (POO-toe): Putti (note the plural) are those naked, chubby babies that cavort through Italian paintings, especially from the fifteenth century on. "Putto" means "little boy" in Italian, and originally the figure was derived from personifications of Eros in early Greek and Roman art; by extension, the term came to apply to any naked child in a painting. Putti were very popular in Renaissance and Baroque paintings, where they stood for anything from Cupid, to the pagan attendants of a god or goddess, to cherubim celebrating the Madonna and child.

Putti in Veronese's Mars and Venus United by Love

QUATTROCENTO; CINQUECENTO (KWA-tro-CHEN-toe; CHINGK-weh-CHEN-toe): Literally, "the four hundred" and "the five hundred"; to art buffs, the fifteenth and sixteenth centuries, respectively. In other words, the Early and the High Renaissances.

SFUMATO (sfoo-MAH-toe): Comes from the Italian word for "smoke" and describes a method of fusing areas of color or tone to create a soft, hazy, atmospheric effect, not unlike the soft focus in old Hollywood movies. Sfumato is most often mentioned in connection with Leonardo and his followers.

SOTTO IN SU (soh-toe-in-SOO): This one is good for a few brownie points; it means, approximately, "under on up," and describes the trick of painting figures in perspective on a ceiling so that they are extremely foreshortened, giving the impression, when viewed from directly underneath, that they're floating high overhead instead of lying flat in a picture plane. Sotto in su was especially popular in Italy during the Baroque and Rococo periods (seventeenth and eighteenth centuries), when lots of people were painting ceilings and trying to create elaborate visual illusions. The names to drop: Tiepolo, Correggio, Mantegna.

VEDUTA (veh-DOO-tah): Means "view"; in this case, a detailed, graphic, and more or less factual view of a town, city, or landscape. Vedute (note the plural) were in vogue during the seventeenth and eighteenth centuries, when the artists who painted, drew, or etched them were known as *vedutisti*. A variation of the veduta was the veduta *ideata* ("idealized"), in which the realistic elements were juxtaposed in such a way as to produce a scene that was positively bizarre (e.g., Canaletto's drawing of St. Peter's in Rome rising above the Doge's Palace in Venice). The *vedutisti* to remember: Canaletto, the Guardi family, Piranesi.

Six –isms, One –ijl, and Dada

YOUR PERSONAL GUIDE TO EUROPEAN ART MOVEMENTS BETWEEN 1900 AND HITLER

Be grateful we edited out Orphism, Vorticism, Suprematism, and the Scuola Metafisica at the last minute.

FAUVISM

Henri Matisse,
Blue Nude
(1907)

Headquarters:	Paris and the South of France.
Life Span:	1905–1908.
Quote:	*"Donatello chez les fauves!"* ("Donatello among the wild beasts!"), uttered at the Salon d'Automne by an anonymous art critic upon catching sight of an old-fashioned Italianate bust in a roomful of Matisses.
Central Figures:	Henri Matisse, André Derain, Maurice de Vlaminck, all painters.
Spiritual Fathers:	Paul Gauguin, Henri "Le Douanier" Rousseau.
Salient Features:	Raw, vibrant-to-strident color within bold black outlines; moderately distorted perspective; an assault on the Frenchman's traditional love of order and harmony that today reads as both joyous and elegant; healthiest metabolism this side of soft-drink commercials.
Keepers of the Flame:	None (though Matisse is a big, and ongoing, influence on everybody).

EXPRESSIONISM

Ernst Ludwig Kirchner,
Street, Dresden *(1908)*

Wassily Kandinsky, Black Lines
(1913)

Headquarters:	Germany.
Life Span:	1905–1920s.
Quotes:	"He who renders his inner convictions as he knows he must, and does so with spontaneity and sincerity, is one of us."—Ernst Kirchner.
	"Something like a necktie or a carpet."—Wassily Kandinsky, of what he feared abstract art might degenerate into.
Central Figures:	In Dresden (in "The Bridge"): Kirchner, Emil Nolde, Karl Schmidt-Rottluff, painters. In Munich (in "The Blue Rider"): Kandinsky, Paul Klee, Franz Marc, painters. Under the banner "New Objectivity": George Grosz, Otto Dix, Max Beckmann, painters. Confrères and honorary members: Arnold Schoenberg, composer; Bertolt Brecht, dramatist; Franz Kafka, writer.
Spiritual Fathers:	Vincent van Gogh, Edvard Munch, Friedrich Nietzsche.
Salient Features:	A tendency to let it all—pathos, violence, morbidity, rage—hang out; distortion, fragmentation, Gothic angularity, and lots of deliberately crude woodcuts; the determination to shake the viewer up and to declare Germany's artistic independence from France. Down in Munich, under Kandinsky—a Russian with a tendency to sound like a scout for a California religious cult—abstraction, and a bit less morbidity.
Keepers of the Flame:	The abstract expressionists of the Forties and Fifties, the neo-expressionists of the Eighties, and a barrioful of graffiti artists.

CUBISM

Georges Braque,
Soda *(1911)*

Headquarters: Paris.

Life Span: 1907–1920s.

Quote: Anonymous tasteful lady to Pablo Picasso: "Since you can draw so beautifully, why do you spend your time making those queer things?" Picasso: "That's why."

Central Figures: Picasso, of course, and Georges Braque. Also, Juan Gris and Fernand Léger, all painters. Guillaume Apollinaire, poet.

Spiritual Father: Cézanne.

Salient Features: The demise of perspective, shading, and the rest of the standard amenities; dislocation and dismemberment; the importance of memory as an adjunct to vision, so that one painted what one knew a thing to be; collage; analytic (dull in color, intricate in form, intellectual in appeal), then synthetic (brighter colors, simpler forms, "natural" appeal); the successful break with visual realism.

Keepers of the Flame: Few; this half century has gone not with Picasso but with antiartist and master debunker Marcel Duchamp.

FUTURISM

Umberto Boccioni,
Unique Forms of
Continuity in Space
(1913)

Headquarters: Milan.

Life Span: 1909–1918.

Quotes: "A screaming automobile is more beautiful than the *Victory of Samothrace.*" "Burn the museums! Drain the canals of Venice!" —Filippo Tommaso Marinetti.

Central Figures: Marinetti, poet and propagandist; Giacomo Balla and Gino Severini, painters; Umberto Boccioni, sculptor and painter; Antonio Sant'Elia, architect.

Spiritual Fathers: Georges Seurat, Henry Ford.

Salient Features: Dynamism, simultaneity, lines of force; vibration and rhythm more important than form; exuberant, optimistic, anarchic, human behavior as art. Had an immediate impact bigger than Cubism's—on Constructivism, Dada, and Fascism.

Keepers of the Flame: Performance artists (who likewise stress the theatrical and the evanescent), conceptualists.

CONSTRUCTIVISM

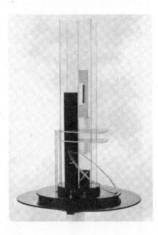

Naum Gabo, Column
(1923)

Headquarters: Moscow.

Life Span: 1913–1932.

Quotes: "Engineers create new forms."—Vladimir Tatlin.

"Constructivism is the Socialism of vision."—László Moholy-Nagy.

Central Figures: Tatlin, sculptor and architect; Aleksandr Rodchenko, painter and typographer; El Lissitzky, painter and designer; Naum Gabo and Antoine Pevsner, sculptors.

Spiritual Fathers: Kasimir Malevich, Lenin, Marinetti.

Salient Features: Art as production, rather than elitist imaginings, and squarely in the service of the Left; abstract forms wedded to utilitarian simplicity; rivets, celluloid, and airplane wings; the State as a total work of Art.

Keepers of the Flame: None: The State ultimately squashed it.

DE STIJL ("THE STYLE")

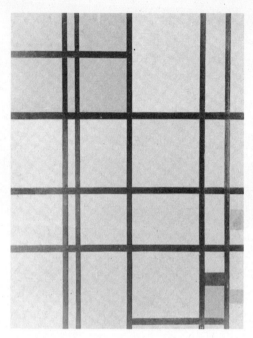

Piet Mondrian, Composition 7
(1937–1942)

Gerrit Rietveld, armchair (c. 1917)

Headquarters:	Amsterdam.
Life Span:	1917–1931.
Quote:	"The square is to us as the cross was to the early Christians."—Theo van Doesburg.
Central Figures:	Van Doesburg and Piet Mondrian, painters; Gerrit Rietveld and J. J. P. Oud, architects.
Spiritual Father:	Kandinsky.
Salient Features:	Vertical and horizontal lines and primary colors, applied with a sense of spiritual mission; Calvinist purity, harmony, and sobriety; purest of the abstract movements (and Mondrian the single most important new artist of the between-the-wars period); say "style," by the way, not "steel."
Keepers of the Flame:	Minimalists.

DADA

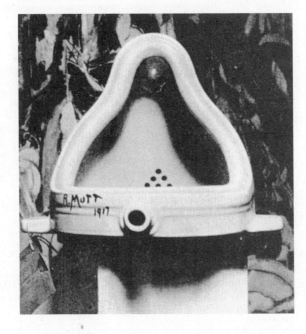

Marcel Duchamp, Fountain *(1917)*

Headquarters:	Zurich (later Berlin, New York, and Paris).
Life Span:	1916–1922.
Quotes:	"Like everything in life, Dada is useless." "Anti-art for anti-art's sake."—Tristan Tzara.
Central Figures:	Zurich: Tzara, poet, and Jean Arp, painter and sculptor. New York and Paris: Marcel Duchamp, artist; Francis Picabia, painter; Man Ray, photographer. Berlin: Max Ernst, George Grosz, Kurt Schwitters.
Spiritual Father:	Marinetti.
Salient Features:	Anarchic, nihilistic, and disruptive; childhood and chance its two most important sources of inspiration; the name itself a nonsense, baby-talk word; born of disillusionment, a cult of nonart that became, in Berlin, overtly political.
Keepers of the Flame:	Performance artists, "happenings" and "assemblages" people, conceptualists.

SURREALISM

Salvador Dalí,
The Persistence of
Memory *(1931)*

Headquarters:	Paris (later, New York).
Life Span:	1924–World War II.
Quote:	"As beautiful as the chance meeting on a dissecting table of a sewing machine and an umbrella."—Comte du Lautréamont.
Central Figures:	André Breton, intellectual; Louis Aragon, Paul Eluard, writers; Jean Cocteau, writer and filmmaker; Luis Buñuel, filmmaker. Abstract wing: Joan Miró, painter. Explicit wing: Salvador Dalí, Yves Tanguy, Max Ernst, René Magritte, painters.
Spiritual Fathers:	Sigmund Freud, Giorgio de Chirico, Leon Trotsky.
Salient Features:	Antibourgeois, but without Dada's spontaneity; committed to the omnipotence of the dream and the unconscious; favored associations, juxtapositions, concrete imagery, the more bizarre the better.
Keepers of the Flame:	Abstract expressionists, "happenings" people.

Thirteen Young Turks

Well, not all that young. And certainly not Turks. In fact, the Old World has nothing to do with it. For the last forty years, it's America—specifically, New York—that's been serving as the clubhouse of the art world. Now shake hands with a dozen of its most illustrious members. That's Jackson Pollock in the Stetson and Laurie Anderson in the Converse All Stars.

JACKSON POLLOCK (1912–1956)

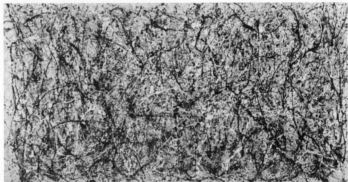

Jackson Pollock's One *(1950)*

Don't settle for the "cowboy" legend, in which Pollock—the most talked-about artist of the last half century years—blows into New York City from Cody, Wyoming, riding his canvases like broncos and packing his frontier image like a six-gun. The man had a rowdy streak, it's true, spattering, flinging, and dripping paint by day and picking fights in artists' bars by night, but his friends always insisted that he was a sensitive soul; inspired by the lyricism of Kandinsky and steeped in the myths of Jung, all he wanted was to be "a part of the painting," in this case "all-over" painting, with no beginning, no end, and no center of interest. Some nomenclature: "Action painting" is what Pollock (alias "Jack the Dripper") did, a particularly splashy, "gestural" variant of Abstract Expressionism, the better-not-hang-this-upside-down art turned out by the so called New York School.

MARK ROTHKO (1903–1970)

Declaring that he painted "tragedy, ecstasy, doom, and so on," Rothko was pleased when people broke down and cried in front of The Work—and withdrew from an important mural commission for New York's Four Seasons restaurant because he couldn't stand the idea of them eating in front of it. Here we're in the presence of Abstract Expressionism's so called theological wing (which also sheltered Barnett Newman and Clyfford Still), typified by—in addition to a fondness for monasticism and bombast—large, fuzzy-edged rectangles of color, floating horizontally in a vertical field. Renunciation is the keyword. In a sense, minimalism begins here, with Rothko.

WILLEM DE KOONING (1904–1997)

The *other* "action" painter, and the most famous New York School artist (even if he was born in Holland) after his Wyoming colleague. De Kooning never totally lost faith in recognizable imagery—most notably, a gang of big-breasted middle-aged women (of whom he later said, "I didn't mean to make them such monsters")—and never tossed out his brushes. But he did paint in the same hotter-than-a-pepper-sprout fever, allowing paint to dribble down the canvas, as soup down a chin, and he did reach beyond where he could be sure of feeling comfortable.

DAVID SMITH (1906–1965)

Was to postwar sculpture what Jackson Pollock was to postwar painting (and, like Pollock, was killed at his peak in an automobile accident). Influenced by the work of Picasso and by a summer vacation he'd spent as a welder in a Studebaker factory, and intent on glorifying, rather than apologizing for, the workaday world, Smith constructed his work instead of casting or molding it. The result: shapes that are "ready-made" rather than solid, arrangements that look provisional instead of stately, and a mood that is anything but monumental. Whereas the Englishman Henry Moore (the other "sculptor of our time") always seemed to be making things for museum foyers and urban plazas, Smith's work is more likely to rise, oil-well-style, from a spot nobody could have guessed would be home to a work of art.

ANDREW WYETH (1917–)

Of course, not everybody was really ready to deal with de Kooning's *Woman II* or Smith's *Cubi XVIII*, and they almost certainly hadn't given a thought to owning one of them. For those thus resistant to Art, but still desirous of a bona fide art acquisition, there was Andrew Wyeth, working in the American realist tradition of Grant "American Gothic" Wood and Edward "All-Night Diner" Hopper, and given to painting in a manner middlebrow critics liked to call "hauntingly evocative," as with the much-reproduced *Christina's World*. As to whether Christina is trying to get away from the house (à la *Texas Chainsaw Massacre*) or back to it (à la *Lassie, Come Home*), don't look at us. Don't look at Wyeth for too long, either: You'll lose all credibility as intellectual, aesthete, and cosmopolite.

ROBERT RAUSCHENBERG (1925–)
JASPER JOHNS (1930–)

Counts as one selection: Not only were Rauschenberg and Johns contemporaries, not only did they together depose, without really meaning to, the reigning abstract expressionists, they also, for a time, lived together. However, they couldn't have been less alike, temperamentally and philosophically. Think of them as a vinaigrette dressing. Rauschenberg is the oil: applied lavishly, sticking to everything, rich, slippery, viscous. Probably best known for his so called combines (like this freestanding angora goat, with a tire around its belly), he scoured the streets and store windows of downtown Manhattan for junk; believed that art

Monogram *and Robert Rauschenberg (1955–1959)*

could exist for any length of time, in any material, and to any end; and, as one critic said, "didn't seem house-trained."

Johns, by contrast, is the vinegar; poured stintingly, cutting through everything, sharp, stinging, thin. In his paintings of flags, targets, stenciled words and numbers, and rulers—all as familiar, abstract, simple, and flat as objects get—he endowed the pop icons of the twentieth century with an "old master" surface, reduced painting to the one-dimensionality it had been hankering after for a generation, and got to seem sensuous, ironic, difficult, and unavailable—all those hipper-than-hip things—in a single breath. Together, Rauschenberg and Johns

Three Flags *and Jasper Johns (1958)*

did for art (whose public, such as it was, had been getting tired of not being able to groove on the stuff Rothko, de Kooning, et al. were turning out) what the Beatles did for music. Note: Rauschenberg and Johns are usually billed as proto-pop artists; the former is not to be confused with pop artists Roy Lichtenstein (the one who does the paintings based on comic-book panels), Claes Oldenburg (the one who does the sculptures of cheeseburgers and clothespins), and James Rosenquist (the one who does mural-sized canvases full of F-111 fighter-bombers and Franco-American spaghetti).

ANDY WARHOL (1928–1987)

Needs no introduction here. But forget for a minute Andy, the albino in the silver fright wig, the guy who painted the Campbell's soup cans and the Brillo boxes, Liz and Marilyn; who made underground movies like *The Chelsea Girls* and *Flesh*; who founded *Interview* and took Studio 54 as his anteroom; and who got shot in the gut by Valerie what's-her-name. Concentrate instead on Warhol, the tyrant and entrepreneur, the man who taught the art world about the advantages of bulk (a few hundred was a *small* edition of his prints, and the two hundredth of them was presented, promoted, and, inevitably, purchased, as if it were the original) and who persuaded the middle class that hanging a wall-sized picture of a race riot, or an electric chair, or an automobile accident, or Chairman Mao, over the couch in the family room not only was chic, but made some kind of sense. More recently, there were the commissioned portraits: Not since Goya's renditions of the Spanish royal family, it's been observed, has a group of people who should have known better so reveled in being made to look silly.

FRANK STELLA (1936–)

"All I want anyone to get out of my paintings . . . is the fact that you can see the whole *idea* without any confusion. What you see is what you see." Thus spake Frank Stella, who'd learned something from Jasper Johns, and who would go on, while still in his twenties, to help launch the movement known as Minimalism, according to some the most self-consciously American of all the -isms (and according to others the last, wheezy gasp of modernism itself). The idea was to get away from the how-often-have-you-seen-this-one-before literalness of pop and back to abstraction—a new abstraction that was fast, hard, flat, and hauntingly unevocative. Key words here are "self-referentiality" and "reduction"; the former meant that a painting (preferably unframed and on a canvas the shape of a lozenge or a kite) had no business acknowledging the existence of anything but itself, the latter that the more air you could suck out of art's bell jar the better. By the 1970s, Stella would be making wall sculptures of corrugated aluminum and other junk, cut by machine then crudely and freely painted, that relate to his early work approximately as Francis Ford Coppola's *Dracula* relates to *The Godfather*.

CHRISTO AND JEANNE-CLAUDE
(1935–, 1935–)

It started as an obsession with wrapping. The Bulgarian-born artist Christo spent years swaddling bicycles, trees, storefronts, and women friends before moving on to wrap a section of the Roman Wall, part of the Australian coastline, and eventually all twelve arches, plus the parapets, sidewalks, streetlamps, vertical embankment, and esplanade, of Paris' Pont Neuf. And yes, together they did wrap the Reichstag. But Christo and his wife/manager/collaborator Jeanne-Claude are quick to insist that wrappings form only a small percentage of their total oeuvre. There were, for instance, those twenty-four and a half miles of white nylon, eighteen feet high, they hung from a steel cable north of San Francisco; the eleven islands in Biscayne Bay, Florida, they "surrounded"—not wrapped, mind you—with pink polypropylene fabric; and the 3,100 enormous blue and yellow "umbrellas" they erected in two corresponding valleys in California and Japan. Not to mention their 2005 blockbuster, "The Gates," 7,503 sixteen-foot-tall saffron panels they suspended, to the delight of almost everybody, over twenty-three miles of footpaths in New York's Central Park.

So, what's their point? Rest assured, you're not the first to ask. And no one is more eager to tell you than the artist formerly known as Christo (now, officially, "Christo and Jeanne-Claude") whose art is nothing if not Open to the Public. In fact, taking art public—that is, taking it away from the Uptown Museum-Gallery Complex by making it too big to fit in studios, museums, or galleries—was part of the original idea. Now that lots of artists have adopted what critics once dubbed the "New Scale," Christo and Jeanne-Claude will tell you that their point is, literally, to rock your world. By temporarily disrupting one part of an environment, they hope to get you to "perceive the whole environment with new eyes and a new consciousness." Along the way, it's been nice to get tons of media attention, make buckets of money (Christo's been known to issue stock in himself, redeemable in working drawings), and, as with so much that went before it, *épater les bourgeois*.

LAURIE ANDERSON (1947–)

"Our plan is to drop a lot of odd objects onto your country from the air. And some of these objects will be useful. And some will just be . . . odd. Proving that these oddities were produced by a people free enough to think of making them in the first place." That's Laurie Anderson speaking, NASA's first—and almost certainly last—artist-in-residence. She of the trademark red socks and white high-top sneakers, the seven-hour performance pieces, the lights-up-in-the-dark electric violin, the movie clip of an American flag going through the fluff-dry cycle. Anderson has spent the last quarter-century as a performance artist, yoking music with visuals, cliché with poetry, electronics with sentiment, slide shows with outrage, the intimate with the elephantine. Like Christo, performance artists do what they can to take art out of the institution; they also tend to quote that indefatigable old avant-gardist John Cage, who years ago declared art to be a way "simply" to make us "wake up to the very life we're living."

Over the years, performance art has tended to move farther and farther from its visual-arts roots to embrace, especially, theater and dance. In the process, it has more than once drifted toward the self-indulgent and the soporific, leaving some of us wondering what, exactly, the payoff was for sitting through another six-hour Robert Wilson piece on Stalin or Queen Victoria or for witnessing Karen Finley cover herself in melted chocolate, alfalfa sprouts, and tinsel in protest against society's treatment of women.

Still, it has survived. Stripped down (Anderson, for instance, now wears mostly black, creates ninety-minute shows, and relies, for special effects, on what she can produce with her violin and a laptop), hitched more or less firmly to technology (you'll find most emerging performance artists on the Internet), and straddling so many of postmodernism's fault lines—where feminism grinds against male-bonding rituals, where stand-up comics hold forth on First Amendment freedoms, where multiculturalism vies for attention with simple autobiography, Dadaist absurdity with vaudeville pratfalls—performance art shows no signs of going quietly up to bed.

JULIAN SCHNABEL (1951–)

Julian Schnabel and St. Francis in Ecstasy *(1980)*

He was arguably the most ambitious painter since Jackson Pollock, and for a time no American artist loomed larger or used up more oxygen. Schnabel specialized in Ping-Pong-table-sized canvases covered with entire cupboards' worth of broken crockery, yards of cheap velvet, lots of thick, gucky paint, and the occasional pair of antlers. Also, as Mark Rothko might say, in "tragedy, ecstasy, doom, and so on"—or what passed for same in the supply-side art world of the 1980s, where dealers such as Mary Boone frequently got higher billing than their artists. Schnabel's work was everywhere and sold like crazy—until one day the Eighties were over and the critics began to refer to his mammoth neo-expressionist smorgasbords as leftovers from yesterday's bender. Schnabel himself proved unstoppable, however; he's since made a successful comeback, not as a painter but as the writer/director of critically respected—and surprisingly viewer-friendly— feature films, such as *Basquiat* (1996) and *Before Night Falls* (2000).

MATTHEW BARNEY (1967–)

Worked his way through Yale modeling for Ralph Lauren and J. Crew, and had barely arrived in New York when his sculptures (especially the weightlifter's bench made of petroleum jelly) and videos (particularly the one that featured the artist using ice screws to haul himself, naked, across the ceiling and down the walls of the gallery in which it was being shown) turned him, at twenty-four, into the art scene's Next Big Thing. To date, Barney is best known for the *Cremaster Cycle,* a series of five lavishly surreal films made between 1993 and 2001, which attracted huge, mostly young, audiences; garnered wildly enthusiastic, if slightly bewildered, reviews; and taught museum-goers a new vocabulary word ("cremaster," the muscle that raises and lowers the testicles in response to temperature and fear). The *Cremaster* films, which were made and released out of order, range from a forty-minute 1930s-style musical featuring elaborately costumed chorus girls, an Idaho football field, and two Goodyear blimps (*Cremaster 1*) to a three-hour allegory starring the Chrysler Building, in which the sculptor Richard Serra, playing the role of the Master Architect, and Barney, playing the Entered Apprentice, reenact elaborate Masonic rituals; a paraplegic fashion model pares potatoes with blades fastened to her prosthetic feet; and a bunch of Chryslers stage a demolition derby in the lobby of the building (*Cremaster 3*). The series, which we're told has something to do with pregenital sexuality as a metaphor for pure potential and something to do with violence sublimated into pure form, is thickly layered with mythological references, historical details, and arcane symbolism and is, in Barney's words, "somewhat autobiographical." Before you could say "captures the Zeitgeist," critics were hailing Barney as "the most important American artist of his generation" and comparing *Cremaster* to Richard Wagner's *Ring* cycle. We'd love to weigh in ourselves, but we have a hair appointment.

Raiders of the Lost Architecture

A SPRINTER'S GUIDE TO THE GREEK TEMPLE AND THE GOTHIC CATHEDRAL

You don't have to be standing in front of the Parthenon to be suffused with all those old doubts about what's Doric and what's Ionic and where to look, approximately, when somebody calls your attention to the frieze; almost any big-city post office can make you feel just as stupid. Ditto, Chartres, naves and narthexes, and even a moderately grandiose Catholic—or Episcopal—church. In fact, a little practice here at home isn't such a bad idea *before* you hit Athens, Paris, and points in between.

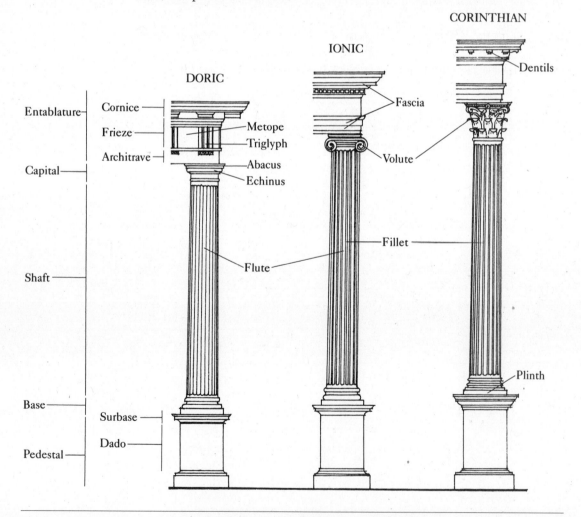

GOTHIC ELEVATION

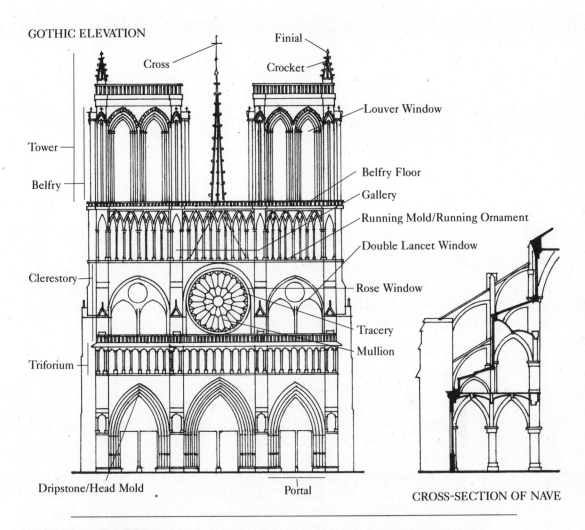

Cross

Finial

Crocket

Louver Window

Tower

Belfry

Belfry Floor

Gallery

Running Mold/Running Ornament

Double Lancet Window

Clerestory

Rose Window

Tracery

Mullion

Triforium

Dripstone/Head Mold

Portal

CROSS-SECTION OF NAVE

GOTHIC FLOOR PLAN

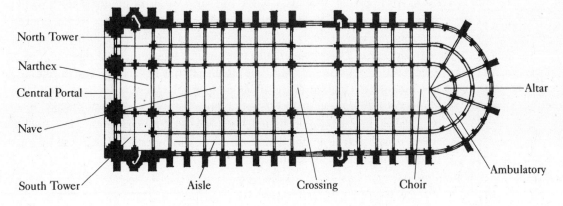

North Tower

Narthex

Central Portal

Nave

South Tower

Aisle

Crossing

Choir

Altar

Ambulatory

Real-Estate Investment for the Aesthete

Contributor **Michael Sorkin** assesses the choicest styles, hottest architects, primest buildings, and pithiest sayings of modern architecture. And then we add our two cents' worth.

FIVE MODERN STYLES

Architectural fashion is like any other: It changes. The difference is that architects are forever looking for a Universal Style, something suitable for every occasion. This is hardly a new impulse. The folks who brought you the Doric order and the Gothic cathedral had something similar in mind. However, while it may have taken hundreds of years to put up Chartres, a smart-looking Hamptons beach house can get done practically overnight.

The International Style

A coinage of the early 1930s, this label recognized that modern architecture actually did have a "style" and was not, as many had argued, simply a force of nature. The movement's major perpetrators tended to argue that their work was essentially "rational," that what they did was as scientific as designing a dynamo or a can opener. Le Corbusier, the most vigorous polemicist of the time, promoted the gruesome slogan "A house is a machine for living." Thanks to which analogy, machine imagery is one of the hallmarks of the style, especially anything with vaguely nautical overtones such as steel railings and shiny metal fittings. Also popular were glass-block-and-strip windows mounted flush with a facade. International Style buildings are almost invariably white and conceived in terms of planes—like houses of cards—rather than in terms of the solidity of neo-classical and Victorian architecture, against which many of these architects were reacting. (A sense of mass, it is often said, was replaced by one of volume.) Key monuments include Gropius' buildings for the Dessau Bauhaus (1926), Le Corbusier's Villa Savoie (1929), and Aalto's Paimio Sanitorium (1928). Fifty years later, the style would be much appropriated by restaurants: For a while there, it was next to impossible to dine out without staring at a wall of glass blocks from your Breuer chair.

The Bauhaus, Dessau, Germany; Walter Gropius, architect

The Yale Art and Architecture Building; Paul Rudolph, architect

Brutalism

The name, like so much in the modernist lexicon, comes from the French, in this case *béton brut*. Which is not, as you might suppose, an after-shave, but rather unfinished concrete, the kind that shows both the grain of the underlying wooden formwork and lots of rough edges. The French have a special genius for referring to the presumed ardors of the natural—"Eau Sauvage"—and nature has always emitted strong vibes, one way or the other, for modern architects. This is no doubt because the ideological basis for modern architecture (as for everything else worthwhile) comes from the Enlightenment and its problem child, Rationalism. On the one hand, it's resulted in a lot of buildings that look like grids; on the other, in a preoccupation with a kind of architectural state of nature, like that which preoccupied Rousseau. (Perhaps this is why renderings of modern buildings so often feature lots of trees.) Brutalism represents a reaction to the flimsy precision of the International Style, a reversion to roughness and mass. Characteristics include large expanses of concrete, dungeonlike interiors, bad finishes, and a quality of military nostalgia, a sort of spirit-of-the-bunker that might have gone down happily on the Siegfried Line. The style—popular in the Sixties and early Seventies—has pretty much taken a powder, but it's left behind the likes of Paul Rudolph's Art and Architecture Building at Yale University and Kallman and McKinnell's Boston City Hall.

Expressionism

A style whose day was, alas, brief. Concurrent with Expressionism's flowering in the other arts, architects (mainly German, mainly in the Twenties), managed to get a number of projects built in a style that will be familiar to you from *The Cabinet of Dr. Caligari* (see page 152). As you will recall, with Expressionism, things tend to get a little skewed, not to mention a little sinister, with materials often seeming to be on the point of melting. More than any other, this is the style that best embodies the kind of looney tunes sensibility, with its working out of the aberrations of the unconscious, that we all identify with the fun side of Twenties Berlin. The two greatest works in the genre are Erich Mendelsohn's Einstein Tower, an observatory in Potsdam that looks like a shoe, and Hans Poelzig's interior for the Grosses Schauspielhaus in Berlin, an auditorium that looks like a cave. The latter was commissioned by theatrical impresario Max Reinhardt, no slouch when it came to the visual. Expressionism is easily the funkiest of the modern styles.

The AT&T Building; Philip Johnson and John Burgee, architects

Postmodernism

A kind of portmanteau term (no relation to John Portman, the architect of all those ghastly hotels with the giant atriums), meant to describe a condition as much as a style, the condition of not being "modernist." As you have undoubtedly noticed, "modern architecture" in the 1980s came in for more than its share of lumps, with architects shamelessly scrambling to disavow what most of them only a few years before thought was the cat's pajamas. Postmodernism's most exemplary figure: Philip Johnson, the architect of the cocktail circuit and, until his death in 2005, the leading arbiter of architectural fashion. His premier contribution, as a postmodernist at least, was a New York skyscraper headquarters for American Telephone and Telegraph that looks a lot like a grandfather clock, or, according to some, a Chippendale highboy, allegedly the result of the postmodernist preoccupation with "history." Look for Corinthian columns in the foyer of such extravaganzas, as well as dirty pastel colors and ornament and detailing out the wazoo.

Just as postmodernism was beginning to seem really cloying, along came the deconstructivists, most of whom were into a deliberately chaotic, fractured, highly aggressive look: you know, skewed (not to mention windowless) walls, canti-levered beams and staggered ceilings, trapezoids where rectangles ought to be, slotted dining-room floors (one client actually got his foot stuck in his), a stone pillar in the bedroom, positioned so as to leave no room for a bed. Schizophrenic in those places where postmodernism had been merely hysterical, "deconstruc-tivism"—a play on Russian constructivism (see page 87) and the largely French intellectual movement known as deconstruction (see page 337)—was nihilistic but preening, an all-out attack on architectural embellishment and couch-potato comfort. Most often cited as practitioners: California's Frank Gehry, in his early days, and New York's Peter Eisenman.

The Chicago School

Not to be confused with the Chicago School of Criticism, which is known for its neo-Aristotelianism, or the Chicago School of Economics, which is known for its monetarism. The Chicago School of Architecture, which flourished around the turn of the century and comprised such immortals as William Le Baron Jenney, Dankmar Adler, Louis Sullivan, Daniel Burnham, and John W. Root, is widely touted as having been the source for modern architecture, American branch, and as having invented the skyscraper. Lecturers often show slides of the Monadnock Building (Burnham and Root, 1892) and the Seagram Building (Mies van der Rohe, 1958) side by side to demonstrate this lineage, citing such shared attributes as simplicity, regularity, and structural candor. This isn't really wrong, but it's not quite that simple, either. Most standard architectural historians take the technolog-ical determinist line with regard to the birth of the skyscraper. For them, the semi-nal event in the history of American architecture is the invention of cheap nails, which made possible the "balloon frame" (houses made of lightweight timber frameworks, nailed together and easy to erect), which in turn led—via the Bessemer steelmaking process and the Otis elevator—to the rigid steel frame, and thence to the profusion of tall buildings that sprang up in Chicago like mushrooms after a shower. This formulation may be too schematic, but there's no doubt that the Chicago architects made the first concerted and systematic effort to find new forms for the new type of building, often with lovely results.

FIVE MODERN ARCHITECTS

What would architecture be without architects? The five listed here, all dead, constitute the generally agreed-upon list of the modern immortals.

The Seagram Building;
Ludwig Mies van der Rohe, architect

Ludwig Mies van der Rohe (1886–1969)

Mies van der Rohe (always referred to simply as "Mies") is the one behind all those glass buildings, most famously the Seagram Building in New York. Although Mies is hardly to blame for it, one of the big problems with this kind of architecture is that it is fairly easy to copy, and that while one such building on a street may be stunning, fifty of them are Alphaville. The reason for the ease of imitation is that Mies was essentially a classical architect. That is, like the Greeks, he invented a vocabulary (cognoscenti use linguistics jargon as often as possible when talking about architecture) of forms and certain rules about how those forms could be combined, all of which he then proceeded to drive into the ground. Although his early work was influenced by Expressionism (as with the famous glass skyscraper project of 1921) and de Stijl (the brick houses of the Twenties), projects after the early Thirties were more and more marked by precision, simplicity, and rectilinearity. Prime among these is the campus for the Illinois Institute of Technology in Chicago, first laid out in 1939, on which Mies continued to work through the Fifties. To sound knowledgeable about Mies, you might admire the way in which he solved that perennial architectural problem, the corner.

Le Corbusier (1887–1965)

Le Corbusier (a.k.a. "Corb" or "Corbu," depending on where you went to school) is a self-appropriated pseudonym of obscure meaning, like "RuPaul" or "Bono." His real name was Charles Édouard Jeanneret. Like so many architects, Le Corbusier was something of a megalomaniac, who, perhaps because he was Swiss, thought that unhygienic old cities like Paris would be better off if they were bulldozed and replaced by dozens of sparkling high-rises. Fortunately, Parisians ignored this idea, although it did achieve enormous popularity in the United States, where it was called "urban renewal." On the other hand, Corb's buildings were superb. His early houses, including one for Gertrude Stein and her brother Leo at Garches, outside Paris, are legendary, supreme examples of the International Style, the most definitive of which is the Villa Savoie of 1929 (a big year indeed for modern architecture). Later in life, Corb discovered Cubism and concrete, and things began to change noticeably. Instead of thin planes and relatively simple geometries, Corb got into thick walls and sensuous, plastic shapes. Of this later work the best known is Notre Dame en Haut, a church whose form was inspired by the kind of headgear Sally Field wore as the Flying Nun. Toward the end of his life Corb did get to do an entire city: Chandigarh, in India.

Walter Gropius (1883–1969)

To be perfectly frank, Gropius was not really such a hot designer. He was, however, the presiding genius of the Bauhaus School, which, you scarcely need to be told, was the Shangri-la of modern architecture. Which makes Gropius, we guess, its high lama. The Bauhaus building—*bauen* (to build) plus *haus* (just what you'd imagine)—was designed by Gropius and is his most memorable work, the epitome of the International Style. During its brief life, before it was closed by Hitler (whose views on modern art and architecture we won't go into here), the Bauhaus was a virtual Who's Who of the modern movement, a home to everyone from Marcel Breuer to László Moholy-Nagy. Its curriculum, which was ordered along medieval master-apprentice lines, embraced the whole range of the practical arts, and its output was staggering in both quality and quantity. After it was shut down, Gropius (and most everyone else associated with it) came to the United States, bringing modern European architecture with them. This was either an intensely important or utterly dreadful development, depending on where you went to architecture school and when. Gropius was married to a woman named Alma, who was also married to Gustav Mahler and Franz Werfel, although not concurrently, and who is sometimes described as the first groupie.

Frank Lloyd Wright (1869–1959)

By his own admission, Wright was the greatest architect of all time. More than any other modernist, he went through several distinct stylistic phases. The conventional view is that the initial, so called Prairie style was his best. A college dropout, he worked for a time in the office of the Chicago architect Louis Sullivan before setting up on his own in Oak Park, a town he proceeded to carpet with his work. This early output—mainly houses but including such gems as the Unity Temple (1906) and the Larkin Building (1904)—was, despite European as

well as Japanese influences, at once very modern and very American, deriving its essence from Wright's near-mystical sense of the plains. Unique in proportion, detail, and decoration, these projects also "articulated" space in a new way. Rather than thinking of architecture as segmented, Wright perceived it as continuous and flowing, not as so many rooms added together but as a sculptable whole. Wright's later houses preserve this spatial sensibility but come in a welter of styles, ranging from zonked-out International to Mayan. The best-known house from Wright's middle period is Fallingwater (1936), built over a waterfall in Pennsylvania and designed, according to legend, in less than an hour. Many people, confused by the disparity between the prairie houses and something like the Guggenheim Museum or the Marin County Civic Center, find late Wright perplexing. Although Wright was, like Le Corbusier, a power freak, his version of utopia—which he called Broadacre City—was somewhat less threatening, resembling, as it does, the suburbs. Wright ran his office, which still exists, along feudal lines. His successor was married to Stalin's daughter, Svetlana.

Alvar Aalto (1896–1976)

Aalto, the hardest drinker among the twentieth-century masters, came from Finland, where dipsomania is the national pastime, and which has, unaccountably, produced more modern architects per capita than any other country. After the customary neoclassicist dalliance, Aalto took up the International Style and produced a number of masterpieces in a personalized version of same. The most important of these are the legendary Viipuri Library and the Paimio Sanitorium, both dating from the late Twenties. The Viipuri Library, now in the Russian Federation and undergoing restoration, had an auditorium with a beautifully undulating (and acoustically sound) wooden ceiling—the first instance of an Aalto trademark. No discussion of Aalto can omit mention of the tremendous responsiveness of his buildings to their particular (generally cold) environments, especially the way they introduce and modulate natural light. Of the five immortals, Aalto is the most unabashedly sensuous and tactile, full of swell textures and gorgeous forms. Aalto's best formal move was probably a fan shape, which allowed him to orient various rooms for best exposure to the sun over the course of the day; to illustrate this form in conversation, hold your hand parallel to the ground and stretch the fingers. As who wouldn't be, coming from Finland, Aalto was big on the use of wood both in his buildings and in his famous bentwood furniture. Unfortunately, most of Aalto's work—like the great Saynatsalo Town Hall (1952)—is located in places whose names are completely unpronounceable. This forces people to refer constantly to the several projects (e.g., the Imatra Church) that they *can* pronounce.

FIVE MODERN BUILDINGS

The Barcelona Pavilion

Built for an exposition in 1929, this is modern architecture's holy of holies, a status further enhanced by the fact that the pavilion was torn down shortly after it was built; such are the rules of expositions. What this means is that everything everyone knows about it must be received from photographs, the preferred medium of architectural communication. The Barcelona Pavilion—did we mention that it's by Mies?—is one of the most distinguished examples of a "free plan," that is, a plan not primarily based on the symmetrical imperative but rather on a sensibility derived from Suprematism and de Stijl (see page 90), yielding something rather like a collage. The result: spaces that flow and eddy, moving through large openings and expanses of glass into the out-of-doors and right on down the street. The Barcelona Pavilion is also remembered for its modern attitude toward materials. While retaining the International Style's predilection for crisp lines and planes, Mies enriches their formal potential by the use of a variety of posh materials, including chrome, green glass, polished green marble and onyx, and travertine. Many conclusions to be drawn here. First, the building affirms the displacement of craft (the hand) by precision (the machine); instead of carving the stone, Mies polished it. Second, Mies treats the surfaces of planes not as deep and solid (like a Gothic church) or as smooth and white (as in so much International Style shtik) but as highly reflective, like glass; in the Barcelona Pavilion, everything either reflects or gets reflected, then gets reflected again in two shallow pools, one inside and one out. Finally, this was the occasion for the design of the famous Barcelona chair, the most definitively upscale piece of furniture ever.

Top to bottom: The Barcelona Pavilion (1929); L'Unité d'Habitation (1952); The Robie House (1909)

*Top: Carson, Pirie, Scott (1904);
bottom: the Chrysler Building
(1930)*

L'Unité d'Habitation

Finished in 1952, this is the best of Corb and the worst of Corb, always referred to simply as "the Unité" despite the fact that there are actually three of them. (The original is at Marseilles, the other two at Nantes and Berlin.) So what is it? Well, you might say that it was an apartment house with social cachet, the result of an idea whose time had come. Also gone, some thirty years before. Back in the good old days of modernism, when architecture was seen as an instrument for progressive political transformation, architects talked about building "social condensers" and theorized vaguely about how people would learn to live in happy collective harmony if only they had the right kind of structures in which to do it. Corb, having glommed on to this idea, thought that if the whole countryside were dotted with "Unités" of his own design, everyone would get on fine. Fortunately, he was only able to build the three. By itself, the Marseilles Block (as some call it) is notable for a number of reasons, some social and others—the important ones—formal. The social program includes a shopping arcade on an upper floor, recreation and day care on the roof, and interior "streets" (big corridors, really) on every other floor: a variety of conveniences designed essentially to imprison. Formally, things are more positive and provide a golden opportunity for learning some key vocabulary words. Let's start with *pilotis*, the big legs on which the entire building is raised. Corb thought that these would free the landscape from the building (the former is supposed to flow uninterrupted underneath), but they had the reverse effect. The Unité is constructed in *béton brut* (we've had this one already), and its heavily sculpted facades incorporate *brisesoleils* (sun screens) and are heavily polychromed in primary colors. The roof vents, chimneys, elevator housings, and such are done in free-form shapes; together they make for a lovely silhouette.

The Robie House

The Robie House (1909) is the finest example of Wright's Prairie-style work. Prairie style was both a style and—as with so much great art—an anxiety. At the turn of the century the prairies still abutted Chicago, and Wright had them on the brain: their endless flatness, their windsweptness, and, dare we say, their romance. As a result, the longness and lowness of Prairie buildings (Wright was not the only architect so moved) is fairly easy to understand. Other elements, including decorative treatments and Wright's characteristic "flowing space," bespeak such influences as an early dose of Japanese architecture and a stint in Louis Sullivan's office. The Robie House itself is long, low, and brick. A tightly controlled but asymmetrical bi-level plan, a mature application of Wright's geometrical decoration, vertical windows arrayed in strips, and a low-hipped roof each does its bit. Next time you stroll past the Guggenheim with a friend, mention the Robie House and how incredible you find it that one architect could have done both.

Carson, Pirie, Scott

Designed by Louis Sullivan and built between 1899 and 1904, the Carson, Pirie, Scott department store (originally built as the Schlesinger and Meyer department store) is the hottest product of the Chicago School. Why? For starters, it has great structural clarity, which is to say, it is easy to "read" the underlying steel structure in the lines of the facades, which look like an arrangement of posts and beams filled in with glass. The proportions of the structural bays (the distance between columns, framed by floors above and below) are on the long side, a proportion that is considered particularly "Chicago." That old bugbear, the corner, is dealt with especially neatly by Sullivan, who, in effect, inscribes a cylinder there, accelerating the window proportions to help zing the viewer around the block. Less frequently noted is the incredible decoration that covers all surfaces (not counting the windows, dummy). Indeed, Sullivan was a great apostle of ornamentation, and the intricate system he finally arrived at was not so very different from Art Nouveau.

The Chrysler Building

The good news is that it's once again OK to like the Chrysler Building. For years seen as a detour on the way to boring modernism, we now acknowledge that the flowering of Art Deco (after the 1925 Exposition des Arts Décoratifs in Paris), which took place in the Twenties and Thirties, was one of the high points in modern design. In every sense, Deco's highest point is the Chrysler Building, designed by William Van Alen and, briefly, the tallest building in the world. It is still the most beautiful, most "classic" skyscraper ever built. The convention in talking about skyscrapers is to analogize them to classical columns, with their three-part division of base, shaft, and capital, or, if you prefer, beginning, middle, and end. The Chrysler is great because it succeeds at all levels. The lower portion contains a handsomely decorated lobby and dramatic entries, well related to the scale of the street. The shaft makes use of an iconography based, appropriately enough, on automotive themes (flying tires, a frieze of Plymouths), and the crown is that wonderful stainless steel top, the skyscraper's universal symbol.

FIVE MODERN MAXIMS

After all, what's a style without a slogan? Here are our favorites.

LESS IS MORE: Mies van der Rohe's coinage. Postmodernist wags had so much fun turning this on its head—"More is more," "Less is a bore," etc.—that you're advised to give it a rest for a decade or so.

ORNAMENT IS CRIME: Adolf Loos penned this goody (Anita wasn't the only aphorist in the family), an obvious reaction to fin de siècle excess. Given the recent upsurge of interest in ornament, be *sure* to keep your delivery ironic.

FORM FOLLOWS FUNCTION: The functionalist credo, generally attributed to Mies, but actually used by several eminences, including Louis Sullivan. The earliest use appears to be by Horatio Greenough, a mid-nineteenth-century Yankee sculptor remembered for his statue of George Washington in a peekaboo toga.

THE PLAN IS THE GENERATOR: Corb's version of the above. It means you should start (if you happen to be designing a building) from the floor plan, with all its implications of rational relationships, rather than impose some sort of "artistic" vision on a building a priori. Fortunately, Corb did not always practice what he preached.

ROAM HOME TO A DOME: From R. "Bucky" Buckminster Fuller (see page 42), that is, the apostle of geodesic domes, Dymaxion houses, positive effectiveness, and other benign nonsense. And meant to be sung to the tune of "Home on the Range." No doubt you'll be keeping your delivery ironic.

Snap Judgments

An intelligent, and quite cheeky, view of photography, by contributor **Owen Edwards**.

No one really knows that much about photography, and no one is even particularly sure what he likes. The history of the medium is so short—Nicéphore Niépce made the first photograph, a grainy little garden scene, in 1827 (though if you point out that Thomas Wedgwood might have been first, in 1802, many will be impressed)—that its salient points can be picked up in an afternoon. And the exact nature of photography is so much in dispute that you can call it an art, a fraud, or a virus without much danger of being provably wrong. Indisputably, however, there are categories, giving such comfort as categories do, and here's what you ought to know about each.

LANDSCAPE

Not long ago, everything you needed to say about landscape photography was Ansel Adams. The straight, somewhat unimaginative wisdom holds that Adams is the greatest landscape photographer ever. The revisionist stance is that Adams is passé by about a century, and that after Timothy O'Sullivan photographed the West following the Civil War, landscape was played out as a theme anyway. Neorevisionism, however, says it's OK to like Adams even if he *is* the Kate Smith of photography. Or you can end the discussion by saying that the only great landscape pictures nowadays are being made by NASA robots in the outer limits of the solar system.

A trendy group of landscapists now shows up at environmental disasters like Weegee homing in on a gangland hit in 1940s New York City. Poisoned horses and sheep, shot and skinned deer, and other gloomy slices of outdoor life are what the full moon rises on in the pictures of such as Richard Misrach and James Balog. It pays to know that nowadays, pretty pictures of awful scenery are a lot hipper than plain old pretty pictures.

FASHION

Though it was discovered only recently that fashion photographers might be artists, no one has ever mistaken them for plain working stiffs. The first fashion photographer of note was Baron de Meyer. His title was suspect, but useful nevertheless; he created the archetype of the social photographer, the inside man who not only knew about haute couture, but knew the women who could afford it. Then Edward Steichen came along and did a better de Meyer. (Steichen always did everything better; when in doubt, say Steichen.) Then a Hungarian photojournalist named Munkacsi appeared in the mid-Thirties and revolutionized fashion photography by making his models run along beaches and jump over puddles. Then Richard Avedon got out of the Coast Guard and did a better Munkacsi. And from then on, wannabes like Patrick Demarchelier, Herb Ritts, Bruce Weber, and Steven Meisel have been raking in mind-boggling fees trying, unsuccessfully, to do a better Avedon. Only Avedon could really manage that trick, however, reinventing himself right up until his death in 2004.

FINE ART

The answer to the tedious and irrepressible question "Is photography art?" is yes, but almost never when it thinks it is. Most of the avowed art photographers of the nineteenth century are considered quaint at best, grotesque at worst, while the pictures that have pried money out of the arts endowments look like what Fotomat used to promise not to charge you for. The great photographic art has been made by people doing something else: by Eugène Atget, trying to document Paris, or August Sander, trying to codify all the faces in prewar Germany, or Irving Penn (arguably America's greatest artist/photographer since Steichen) dutifully helping fill the pages of *Vogue*. It's perfectly safe, then, to dismiss any art photographer as hopelessly misguided. Except Man Ray, who was really a painter, and so can't be blamed for his failures. And László Moholy-Nagy, who discovered that the more things you did wrong, the better the photograph looked.

The great muddler of art photographers is also the medium's most revered saint, Alfred Stieglitz, who, early in this century, encouraged his fellow Photo Secessionists to blur, draw on, scratch, or otherwise manipulate their pictures to ensure that the hoi polloi would know they were artists. Stieglitz, by the way, was not Steichen, though even people with vast collections of lenses continue to think so. Steichen was a disciple of Stieglitz who fell out of favor when he began to make a bundle in advertising. (Stieglitz, being a saint, was not much fun.) In

Left: Edward Steichen,
The Flatiron Building
Below: Man Ray, Nusch Éluard

1961, Stieglitz discovered Paul Strand's unmanipulated masterpieces, decided that his followers were hopeless and misguided, and consigned them to oblivion. The resulting confusion has never quite cleared up.

The photographers most likely to be granted acceptance by the haute scribblers of the art world are those who have been careful to stay clear of the low-rent precincts of the world of photography. David Hockney, whose cubist collages of Polaroids command rapt respect, is one of these drop-ins. And William Wegman, a painter who makes unspeakably kitschy dogs-as-people pictures, is another. As is Cindy Sherman, high priestess of high concept who time-travels through female stereotypes with a few props—wigs, go-go boots, girdles—to create provocative reflections of the American psyche. My advice: When a photographer uses the word "artist," reach for your gun.

FINE ART, ABSTRACT DIVISION

Abstract photography is a disaster, invariably boring. Though photography is by nature an *abstract* of reality, it's always of something, so attempts to make it of nothing seem silly. The viewer wants to know what he's looking at, leans closer and closer, and ends up frustrated and peeved. The closest thing to true abstraction a photographer can manage is to take something and make it *look* like nothing. Most grants are awarded to photographers who are good at doing that.

FINE ART, STILL-LIFE DIVISION

The most overrated still-life photograph in the universe is Edward Weston's jumbo-sized pepper, made in the classic More-Than-Just-a-Vegetable style that has since accounted for more than half a century of abysmal amateur efforts. (Weston is probably the most overrated photographer, too, in large part due to the efforts of sons, lovers, and half the population of Carmel, California, to keep the legend alive.) The real contest for World's Greatest Still-Life Photographer is between Irving Penn, who studied drawing and illustration with Alexei Brodovitch in Philadelphia, and Hiro, who worked as a photographer for Brodovitch at *Harper's Bazaar*. (Remember Brodovitch—he was tough, selfish, often drunk, said, "If you look through the viewfinder and see something you've seen before, don't click the shutter," and was guru to two generations of great photographers.) Everybody knows about Penn; his prints are at least as good an investment as Microsoft stock. Few people know about Hiro except the knowing.

PHOTOJOURNALISM

This is the most problematic kind of photography for everybody, especially Susan Sontag, who couldn't bear the idea that the camera might tell an occasional fib.

It's what most people think of when they think of photography at all, and what most photographers start out wanting to be, and then spend a lifetime trying to retire from. The word—an awful-sounding hybrid (why not "journography"?)—was invented by Henri Cartier-Bresson so that he wouldn't be accused of making art while he made art, and it wrongly implies that one or more photographs can tell a story. Without words—usually a thousand or more—pictures are powerful but dumb.

Life magazine started the whole myth of photojournalism's storytelling power, but in truth *Life* was just a very good illustrated press, in which photographs were never allowed to wander unattended. The patron saint of photojournalists is Lewis Hine, who made pictures of child laborers and sweatshops at the turn of the century. Its greatest hero was W. Eugene Smith, who combined an honest concern for human suffering with a canny eye for dramatic composition and lighting, and a very cranky disposition. Now the reigning saint of the form is Sebastian Salgado, whose harrowing coverage of starving Ethiopians and miserable Third World workers manages, somehow, to be as glamorous as any high-fashion shot. When the question arises about whether this sort of agony 'n' ecstasy is ethically and morally proper, it's best to mention Picasso's *Guernica*, which ought to derail the conversation long enough for you to slip away.

PORTRAITURE

Cartier-Bresson (not to mention Coco Chanel) observed that after the age of forty, we have the faces we deserve. Portrait photographers tend to divide up between those who hide the evidence and those who uncover it. Bachrach and Karsh represent the first group, Avedon and Penn the second. Portraits of known people are more interesting than all the rest because we have a chance to decide whether what we see jibes with what we think we know about them—thus the outrage and/or delirium caused by Avedon's warts-and-all celebrities. The best of the nineteenth-century portraitists, and one of the best ever, was Nadar, a Parisian hobnobber whose pictures of that great self-imagist Sarah Bernhardt are unparalleled. Then again, since faces are the landscapes of lives, the best portrait ever made is probably mouldering in your family attic. Should an argument develop over who is the Greatest Portraitist of Photography, come down staunchly on the side of the aforementioned August Sander, a German who wandered the *Wälder* before World War II, chronicling his countrymen in a series of haunting stereotypes. Add Manhattan neurosis and the Age of Anxiety and you have Diane Arbus. Throw in mud-wrestling sitcom stars, body-painted movie stars, and the blithe belief that anything celebrities do, however silly, is worth recording for the ages, and you have Annie Leibovitz. Pile on hype and homosexuality and you have Robert Mapplethorpe.

DOCUMENTARY

In one way or another, all photographs are documentary, so all photographers are documentarists. Some, of course, are more so than others. A documentary photographer is a photojournalist whose deadline is a hundred years hence; posterity is the point. The first great large-scale documentary work was done by Matthew Brady and a group of photographers he hired to cover the Civil War (including Timothy O'Sullivan, who, as has been noted, later played the first, best notes in what has become the Ansel Adams songbook). The most famous and exhaustive documentary project was the misery-loves-company team put together by Roy Stryker to photograph sharecroppers, sharecroppers, more sharecroppers, and occasional other types during the Great Depression. This led to the discovery of the bribe in photography: If we take everybody's picture, maybe they'll go away and leave us alone.

Ironically, one of the great working-class heroes of documentary photojournalism was Walker Evans, a patrician sort who did much of his paying work for *Fortune* magazine. It seems highly likely that Evans viewed the whole idea of photography with some embarrassment, since many of his pictures show empty rooms, or people photographed from behind.

Much of the devotion and energy that used to fuel documentary photographers has been co-opted by television. Generations X, Y, and Z figure that it's way cooler to gather up old photographs, film them, add music and the voices of movie stars, and get famous. After all, Walker Evans never won an Emmy.

SURREALISM

In one way or another, all photographs are surreal, too, since that isn't actually Uncle Frank smirking on the beach, but just a little slip of paper coated with chemicals. But some photographers insist on being official surrealists. The harder they try to put things together in odd and unsettling ways, the more miserably they fail. Jerry Velsmann's cloud-covered ceilings are pretty obvious stuff. The problem is that life as we know it is already odd and unsettling. So for true surrealism, we are right back with documentary photography—especially when done by people who know where to look for the kind of juxtapositions the rest of us pretend we don't see.

Robert Frank is one of the great unofficial surrealists (his shot of a glowing jukebox certainly has the Magritte touch), as was Diane Arbus. Bill Brandt wasn't bad, though the credit is due mostly to the fact that he's a genius at the terrible print. The reigning king of the form these days is Joel-Peter Witkin, a masterful monster monger with a disturbing taste for amputees, dwarves, and severed heads. Somehow, Witkin presents your worst nightmares and makes you want to shell out big bucks to take one home. Surreal, isn't it?

WOMEN

The best of all women photographers is my aunt Isabel, who for several years was the only person on earth who could take my picture without causing me to vanish instantly. Other notable women are:

Lisette Modell, one of the world's smallest photographers, who had such a gravitational attraction to large people that her first pictures made in the resorts of southern France look like monuments come to life. As is the case with certain gifted photographers, Modell was as good as she would ever get on the first day of her career. She has been called the mentor of Diane Arbus, which she used to admit and deny at the same time, for reasons known only to her.

Imogen Cunningham, who lived so long that rumors circulated that she had been archivally processed. Like photographs, photographers almost inevitably benefit from great age (although they fade, their value inevitably rises). Cunningham was never better than just all right, but she had covered so much time and territory that eventually she became the art-photography world's unofficial mascot, a position she labored at by becoming adorably "feisty." As a result, feisty old Johnny Carson displayed her to the world on *The Tonight Show*, shocking the millions who thought women photographers looked like Faye Dunaway in *The Eyes of Laura Mars.*

Berenice Abbott, who made the best portrait ever of James Joyce, single-handedly saved the work of Atget from the trash bin, and who, whether she liked it or not, became an institution without ever being a great photographer.

Helen Levitt, almost unknown, shy, brilliant, virtually invisible in shabby coat and furtive mien, who crept around New York for forty years or more taking in street life. She's a genius in black-and-white or color, and when you state emphatically that Levitt is America's greatest woman photographer, you will have the rare pleasure of being both esoteric and right.

The natural inheritor of Levitt's mantle (*and* shabby coat) is Sylvia Plachy, a Hungarian immigrant with a wry, Frank-like eye but a far kinder heart. For years Plachy chronicled life at ground level, from sex workers in Times Square and tourists in Central Park to peddlers in Romania and refugees in war-torn Eastern Europe. Today, Plachy has moved uptown from the *Voice* to work for the *New York Times,* but she retains her edgy downtown sensibility, cranking out images that are sharp, surprising, and slightly off-kilter.

Finally, we'd better mention Nan Goldin, a photographer whose body of work is the antithesis of Plachy's (and who has famously shed *her* coat—as well as the rest of her clothing—for a series of nude, postcoital self-portraits). Goldin has internalized the personal-is-political mantra of Sixties feminism to spin intimate stories shot in tight, interior spaces. Drawn to the social underbelly, she explores it through pictures of herself and her close friends; her photo diary is both an intimate snapshot and the portrait of an era. One Goldin series documents the trajectory of her relationship with an abusive partner; another chronicles the demise of a friend from AIDS; still others capture the world of drugs and drag. The beloved poster child of the seedy counterculture, Goldin is not likely to age into an adorably feisty guest on the Jay Leno show.

CELEBRITY

Last and least among photographers are the paparazzi. But while it's perfectly all right to hold them in contempt, it's not OK to ignore them; they know where life is going, and for that matter *Life* (or what's left of it), *People*, and *Vanity Fair*. Andy Warhol predicted that someday everybody would be famous for fifteen minutes—the paparazzi work hard at reducing that to 1/125th of a second. Valedictorian of all celebrity photographers is Ron Galella, who has been sued by Jackie Onassis, punched by Marlon Brando, and deplored by even the most deplorable of his subjects. None of this has affected him adversely. Jackie and Brando are gone, and Ron, whose photos have recently been legitimized by an expensive art book, a major gallery show, a museum retrospective, and the sheer passage of time, now gets star treatment himself. Let's face it—celebrity snappers may be pond scum, but pond scum evolved into the likes of Albert Einstein and Greta Garbo, so there's still hope. On the other hand, in the age of Rupert Murdoch and reality TV, the ever-smarmier paparazzi would have to catch Al and Greta doing the nasty in the back of a Hummer to win a few minutes of audience attention. So much for evolution.

Economics

Contents

A good day on the stock market—a month before the Crash of '29

Now, What Exactly Is Economics, and What Do Economists Do, Again?

Economists are fond of saying, with Thomas Carlyle, that economics is "the dismal science." As with much that economists say, this statement is half true: It *is* dismal.

An equally helpful definition of economics was offered by American economist Jacob Viner, who said, "Economics is what economists do."

More to the point, perhaps, is the fact that economics concerns itself with the use of resources. It is about changes in production and distribution over time. It is about the efficiency of the systems that control production and distribution. It is, in a word, about wealth. This alone should be enough to engage our attention.

Over the past several decades, economics has experienced a substantial surge of interest and notoriety. Suddenly economists have found themselves not only studying wealth but also enjoying it. This is largely a result of their relationship with politicians. Where once rulers relied on oracles to predict the future, today they use economists. Virtually every elected official, every political candidate, has a favorite economist to forecast economic benefits pinned to that official's or candidate's views.

Besides, even if being in a position to feel on top of current events doesn't constitute a sufficient lure, people still want to be able to understand why their neighbors are all rushing out to buy mutual funds. Not that, as contributor **Alan Webber** is about to show, the economists are necessarily ready to tell them.

EcoSpeak

One reason economics is so hard to get a grip on is that economists speak in tongues whenever possible. They are, after all, being paid to come up with a lot of fancy guesswork, and they know how important it is to keep everyone else guessing about what they're guessing about since, in the end, your guess is as good as theirs. Anyway, here's what a few of their favorite terms really mean.

CETERIS PARIBUS: One of the things economists like to do is analyze a complicated situation involving a huge number of variables by changing one and holding the rest steady. This allows them to do two things: first, focus on the significance of that one particular element, and second, prove that a pet theory is correct. "Ceteris paribus" is the magic phrase they mutter while doing this. It means, literally, "Other things being equal."

COMMODITIES: Commodities generally fall into two categories: goods, which are tangible, and services, which are not. An easy way to remember this distinction: These days, goods are Chinese and services are American; they make textiles, we make lawyers.

CONSUMPTION AND PRODUCTION: Consumption is what happens when you actually use commodities; production is what happens when you make them.

EXTERNALITIES: Effects or consequences felt outside the closed world of production and consumption—in other words, things like pollution. Economists keep their own world tidy by labeling these messes "externalities," then banishing them.

FACTORS OF PRODUCTION: Ordinary people talk about resources, the things—like land, labor, or capital—used to make or provide other things. Economists talk about factors of production.

FREE-MARKET ECONOMY VS. PLANNED ECONOMY: In the former, decisions made by households and businesses, rather than by the government, determine how resources are used. Vice versa and you've got the latter. As long as you are living in the United States, it's probably a good idea to associate a free-market economy with the good guys, a planned economy with the bad guys. If you find yourself in Cuba or parts of Cambridge, Massachusetts, simply reverse the definition to get with the prevailing theology.

GROSS NATIONAL PRODUCT (GNP) VS. GROSS DOMESTIC PRODUCT (GDP): GNP is a dollar amount (in the United States, an enormous one) that represents the total value of everything produced in a national economy in a year. If the number goes up from year to year, the economy is growing; divide that number by the number of people living in the country and you get per capita income. An alternative measure, GDP, leaves out foreign investment and foreign trade and limits the measure of production to the flow of goods and services within the country itself. As a result, some economists believe it affords a more accurate basis for nation-to-nation comparisons. Either way, GNP or GDP, the basic idea is that more is better.

HUMAN CAPITAL: At first blush, "human" and "capital" may seem like strange bedfellows. But in the land of economics, human capital refers to the investments that businesses make in their workers, such as training and education, or, more broadly, to the assets of the firm represented by the workers and their skills.

INDIFFERENCE CURVE: This shows all the varying combined amounts of two commodities that a household would find equally satisfactory. For example, if you're used to having ten units of peanut butter and fifteen of jelly on your sandwich, and you lose five units of the peanut butter while gaining five of the jelly, and the new sandwich tastes just as good to you as the old one, you've located one point on an indifference curve.

INFLATION: One of the traditional villains of current events, inflation is most simply understood as a rise in the average level of all prices. Getting the definition down is one thing; getting the rate of inflation down once it has started to levitate is another.

LAISSEZ-FAIRE: It seems that whenever economists want to describe an imaginary world, they turn to a foreign language (see "ceteris paribus," above, or try to read the Annual Report of the Council of Economic Advisors to the President). Literally translated "let do," this phrase invokes the notion of an economy totally free of government intervention, one in which the forces of the marketplace are allowed to operate freely and where the choices driving supply and demand, consumption and production are arrived at naturally, or "purely." A kind of economic fantasyland.

LONG RUN VS. SHORT RUN: It's appalling, but economists take even perfectly obvious terms like "long run" and "short run" and try to invest them with scientific meaning. The short run refers to a period of time too short for economic inputs to change, and the long run refers to a period of time, as you may have guessed, long enough for all of the economic inputs to change. The terms are important when you get to thinking about how individuals or companies try to adapt to circumstances—and whether or not they can do it. For some economists, the long run, in particular, comes in handy when defending a pet theory. For example, during times of economic downturn and high unemployment, economists might argue against any form of government intervention, saying that in the long run the marketplace will adjust to correct the situation. The problem, of course, is that most people live in the short run, and that, as economist John Maynard Keynes once cautioned, "In the long run, we're all dead."

MACROECONOMICS VS. MICROECONOMICS: Further evidence of the tendency of economists to see things in pairs. Here, "macro" is the side of economics that looks at the big picture, at such things as total output, total employment, and so on. "Micro" looks at the small picture, the way specific resources are used by firms or households or the way income is distributed in response to particular price changes or government policies. One problem economists don't like to talk about is the difficulty they have in getting the two views to fit together well enough to have any practical application.

MARKET FAILURE: This is one of a number of terms that economists use to put down the real world. Here's the way it works: When things don't go the way economists want them to, based on the laissez-faire system (see above), the outcome is explained as the result of a "market failure." That way, it's not the economists' fault—they had it right, it's the market that got it wrong.

MIXED ECONOMY: Another term for economic reality, the "mixed economy" is the middle ground between the free market (the good guys) and the planned economy (the bad guys). When you look around a country like the United States and see the government manipulating the price and availability of money and energy, legislating a minimum wage, and so on, you have to conclude that ours is not really a free market. But neither is it a centrally planned economy. Grudgingly, economists have decided that what it is is a mixed economy, a kind of economic purgatory they will have to endure while they pray for ascension to the free market.

OPPORTUNITY COSTS: The idea behind the old line "I could've had a V8." In economics, there is a cost to using your resources (time, money) in one way rather than another (which represented another opportunity). Think of it this way: There is an opportunity cost associated with your studying economics instead of a really useful subject like podiatry.

PRODUCTIVITY: Another of the big words in the field, productivity, simply defined, is a measure of the relationship between the amount of the output and that of the input. For example, when you were in college, if it took you two days (input) to write your term paper (output) and it took your roommate one day to hire someone to write his term paper, your roomie's productivity was twice yours—and he probably got a better grade.

PROFIT: To get a firm grasp of profit and its counterpart, loss, you might consider the biblical quotation, "What does it profit a man if he gain the world but lose his soul?" For an economist, the correct way to answer this question would be to calculate the revenues received from gaining the world and subtract the costs incurred by losing one's soul. If the difference (known as "the bottom line") is a positive number, you have a profit.

SUPPLY AND DEMAND: Supply is the amount of anything that someone wants to sell at any particular price; demand is the amount that someone wants to buy at any particular price. Economists have a lot of fun making you guess what happens to the relationship between supply and demand when the amounts or the prices change. More on this game later.

VALUE ADDED: A real comer in the world of economics, the value added is a measure of the difference of the value of the inputs into an operation and the value of the product the operation yields. For example, when Superman takes a lump of coal and compresses it in his hands, applying superforce to turn the coal into a perfect diamond, the value added, represented by Superman's applied strength, is significant. The term explains how wealth is created; it's also what people use to justify all those hours they put in on the super pullover machine.

VALUE-ADDED TAX: Like the name says, a tax on the value added. At each stage of the value-added chain, the buyer pays, and the seller collects, a tax based on the value of the services added at that stage. The tax is rebated on exports and paid on imports. The VAT is a lot like a sales tax in that it's a tax on consumption (as opposed to income) and the consumer pays in the end, but it's less direct. All Western European countries have it, but in the United States the mere mention of a possible VAT, which does tend to hit the poor harder than the rich, is considered grounds for lynching the nearest politician.

EcoThink

Now that you can talk like an economist, the next step is to learn to think like one. The good news here: Economics is a closed system; internally it is perfectly logical, operating according to a consistent set of principles. Unfortunately, the same could be said of psychosis. What's more, once having entered the closed system of the economist, you, like the psychotic, may have a hard time getting out.

THE FOUR LAWS OF SUPPLY AND DEMAND: Economics as physics—something like the laws of thermodynamics brought to bear on the study of wealth. Basically, these four laws say that when one thing goes up, the other thing goes down, or also goes up, or vice versa, depending. When demand goes up, the price goes up; when demand goes down, the price goes down; when supply goes up, the price goes down; when supply goes down, the price goes up.

THE THEORY OF PERFECT COMPETITION: If the four laws of supply and demand are economics as physics, this is economics as theology. The theory holds that firms always seek the maximum profit; that there is total freedom for them both to enter into and to leave competition; that there is perfect information; and that no business is so large as to influence its competitors unduly. It is, according to economic dogma, a situation in which neither firms nor public officials determine how resources are allocated. Rather, the market itself operates like an "invisible hand" (see "Adam Smith," on the next page). And if you buy that one, there's this bridge we'd like to talk to you about.

THE PRINCIPLE OF VOLUNTARY EXCHANGE: Comes under the heading how-to-make-even-the-simplest-idea-sound-important; also known as people buying and selling to get what they want.

THE THEORY OF COMPARATIVE ADVANTAGE: The basis for much of our thinking about international trade. Most simply, it says that everyone's economic interests are served if each country specializes in those commodities that its endowments (natural resources, skilled labor, technology, and so on) allow it to produce most efficiently, then trades with other countries for *their* commodities. The classic example: Both England and Portugal benefit if England produces woolens and Portugal produces port and the two countries trade their products—rather than both countries trying to produce both products. Once you've arrived at an understanding of the theory of comparative advantage, the next thing to think about is how it is that Japan—without natural resources, native technology, or capital—ever became dominant in steel, cars, motorcycles, TVs, and Nintendo. The answer may tell us more about the theory of comparative advantage than it does about the Japanese.

THE THEORY OF RATIONAL EXPECTATIONS: Maintains that people learn from their mistakes. It is illustrated by the story of the economics professor who was walking across the campus with a first-year economics student. "Look," said the student, pointing at the ground, "a five-dollar bill." "It can't be," responds the professor. "If it were, somebody would have picked it up by now."

THE THEORY OF REVEALED PREFERENCE: Another of those laws that stipulate how people are *supposed* to behave. According to this one, people's choices are always consistent. In other words, once you have revealed your preference for a pepperoni pizza over a Big Mac, you'll always choose the pizza, provided it's available. Reduce it to this level, and it's easy to see the limits of the theory.

ECONOMIES OF SCALE: At the heart of manufacturing strategy since the days of Henry Ford. The principle is a simple one: With big factories using long production runs to make a single commodity, you can reduce manufacturing costs. In addition, the more you repeat the same operation, the cheaper it becomes. Following this principle, American factories have turned out some very cheap goods, indeed.

THE PHILLIPS CURVE: Had everything going for it. Based on data compiled in England between 1861 and 1957, this theory held that when inflation goes down, unemployment goes up, and vice versa. For politicians, it was an invaluable guide: If you had too much unemployment, you let inflation go up and—presto!—down went unemployment. If inflation was raging out of control, you put a few people out of work and down went inflation. All in all, a handy little tool. Then along came stagflation, which combined high unemployment with high inflation, and the Phillips curve turned into the Phillips screw.

EcoPeople

ADAM SMITH (1723–1790)

The first economist, this Adam Smith was an actual person, not some contemporary telejournalist's pseudonym. His historic book, *An Inquiry into the Nature and Causes of the Wealth of Nations* (1776), propounded the idea that competition acted as the "invisible hand," serving to regulate the marketplace. His theories, some of them derived from observations he made while visiting a pin factory, would prompt skeptics to ask, "How many economists can dance on the head of a pin?"

DAVID RICARDO (1772–1823)

With Malthus (see next page), a leader of the second generation of classical economists. Early on, Ricardo made a fortune in the stock market when he ought to have been going to school. He next gravitated to economics, where his lack of education, naturally, went undetected. In his most famous work, *The Principles of Political Economy and Taxation* (1817), he advanced two major theories: the modestly named Ricardo Effect, which holds that rising wages favor capital-intensive production over labor-intensive production, and the theory of comparative advantage (see "EcoThink," page 130).

THOMAS MALTHUS (1766–1834)

A clergyman who punctured the utopianism of his day by cheerfully predicting that population growth would always exceed food production, leading, inevitably, to famine, pestilence, and war. This "natural inequality of the two powers" formed, as he put it, "the great difficulty that to me appears insurmountable in the way to perfectability of society." Malthus' good news: Periodic catastrophes, human perversity, and general wretchedness, coupled with the possibility of self-imposed restraint in the sexual arena, would prevent us from breeding ourselves into extinction.

JOHN STUART MILL (1806–1873)

A child prodigy, Mill learned Greek when he was three, mastered Plato at seven, Latin and calculus by twelve; at thirteen he digested all that there was of political economy (what they called economics back then), of Smith, Malthus, and Ricardo. For the next twenty years he'd write; in 1848 (noteworthy also for the publication of the *Communist Manifesto* and a passel of revolutions, see page 596) he published his *Principles of Political Economy, with Some of Their Applications to Social Philosophy*. A couple of critics complained that the book was unoriginal—calling it "run-of-the-Mill"—and that Mill's mildly Socialist leanings (he argued for, among other things, trade unions and inheritance taxes) were antithetical to the Spirit of England. Many more, though, appreciated his making the distinction between the bind of production and the flux of distribution—how, while we can produce wealth only insofar as the soil is fertile and the coal doesn't run out, we can distribute it as we like, funneling it all toward the king or all toward the almshouse, taxing or hoarding or, for that matter, burning it. Sociopolitical options took a seat next to economics' abstract—and absolute—laws, and ethics eclipsed inevitability. Mill would be revered as a kind of saint (and *Principles* serve as the standard economics textbook) for another half century.

JOSEPH SCHUMPETER (1883–1950)

An Austrian who came to America in the early Thirties and whose best-known work was published a decade later, Schumpeter is remembered today as the man who argued that government should not try to break up monopolies, that, in fact, a monopoly was likely to call into existence the very forces of competition that would replace it. This dynamic, labeled the "process of creative destruction," is now much brandished by more conservative political and economic observers, who use it to explain to old industries why it's OK for them to go out of business. "Don't think of it as bankruptcy and massive unemployment," the rationale goes. "Think of it as 'creative destruction.' "

JOHN MAYNARD KEYNES (1883–1946)

The most influential economic thinker of modern times, known to his close friends and intimates as Lord Keynes (remember to pronounce that "kanes"). Pre-Keynesian economists believed that a truly competitive market would run itself and that, in a capitalist system, conditions such as unemployment would be temporary inconveniences at worst. Then along came the Great Depression. In 1936 Keynes published his major work, *The General Theory of Employment, Interest, and Money* (now known simply as *The General Theory*) in which he argued that economics had to deal not only with the marketplace but with *total* spending within an economy (macroeconomics starts here). He argued that government intervention was necessary to stimulate the economy during periods of recession, bringing it into proper, if artificial, equilibrium (the New Deal and deficit spending both start here). Keynes' system, brilliant for its time, has proved less valuable in dealing with modern inflation, and has been considered officially obsolete ever since Richard Nixon declared himself a Keynesian back in 1971. Later, however, Ronald Reagan's supply-side economists set Keynes up in order to knock him down again in an uprising known in economics circles as "The Keynes Mutiny."

JOHN KENNETH GALBRAITH (1908–)

One of the first (and certainly one of the tallest) New World economists to give a liberal twist to the field's dogma. In his *The New Industrial State* (1967), Galbraith, a Canadian, argued that the rise of the major corporation had short-circuited the old laws of the market. In his view, such corporations now dominated the economy, creating and controlling market demand rather than responding to it, determining even the processes of government, while using their economic clout in their own, rather than society's, interests. More traditional economic thinkers have agreed that Galbraith is a better writer than he is an economist.

Five Easy Theses

Even though economies are always in flux, economic theories aren't built to turn on a dime. As a result, it doesn't take long for even the most hallowed hypothesis to stand exposed as just another version of the emperor's new clothes. Here, for the record, a few items we've recently found balled up on the floor of the emperor's closet.

THE LAFFER CURVE: A relic of the Reagan years, this was Economist Arthur B. Laffer's much-applauded hypothesis, rumored to have been first sketched on the back of a cocktail napkin, stating that at some point tax rates can get so high—and the incentive to work so discouraging—that raising them further will reduce, rather than increase, revenues. The converse of this theory, popularly known as supply-side or trickle-down economics, maintains that a government, by cutting taxes, actually gets to collect more money; this version has been widely credited with creating the largest deficit in American history—before the current one, of course.

KONDRATIEFF LONG WAVE CYCLE: Obscure theory dating from the Twenties and periodically enjoying a certain gloomy vogue. Nikolai Kondratieff, head of the Soviet Economic Research Center, postulated that throughout history capitalism has moved in long waves, or trend cycles, which last for between fifty and sixty years and consist of two or three decades of prosperity followed by a more or less equivalent period of stagnation. Kondratieff described three such historical cycles, and when economists dusted off his graphs and brought them up to date in the 1960s and 1970s, they found his theories to be depressingly accurate. According to their predictions, we were all in for another twenty years with no pocket money. The Russians, by the way, weren't thrilled with Kondratieff's hypothesis, either, since it implied that the capitalist system, far from facing impending collapse, would forever keep bouncing back like a bad case of herpes. Sometime around 1930, Kondratieff was shipped off to Siberia and never heard from again.

ECONOMETRICS: Yesterday's high-level hustle. Econometrics used to mean studies that created models of the economy based on a combination of observation, statistics, and mathematical principles. In the Sixties, however, the term referred to a lucrative mini-industry whose models were formulated by computer and hired out to government and big business to help them predict future trends. Government, in fact, soon became the biggest investor in econometrics models, spending millions to equip various agencies to come up with their own, usually conflicting, forecasts—this, despite the fact that the resulting predictions tended, throughout the Seventies, to have about the same record for accuracy as astrology. Today, econometrics models are still expensive and still often wrong, but they're accepted procedure and nobody bothers making a fuss about them anymore.

MONETARISM: One of two warring schools of thought that feed advice to politicians on how to control inflation. Monetarists favor a laissez-faire approach to everything but the money supply itself; they have misgivings about social security, minimum wages, and foreign aid, along with virtually every other form of government intervention. They stress slow and stable growth in the money supply as the best way for a government to ensure lasting economic growth without inflation, and they insist that, as long as the amount of money in circulation is carefully controlled, wages and prices will gradually adjust and everything will work out in the long run (see page 128). Monetarism owes much of its appeal to one of its chief proponents, Nobel Prize–winning economist Milton Friedman, whose theories are generally acknowledged to have formed the backbone of Prime Minister Margaret Thatcher's economic policy in Britain (as well as Ronald Reagan's here). Liberal critics say Friedman owes his own appeal to the fact that he looks like everyone's favorite Jewish uncle.

NEO-KEYNESIANISM: Monetarism's opposite number, a loose grouping of economists who are less inclined to wait for the long run. The neo-Keynesians argue that there are too many institutional arrangements—things like unions and collective-bargaining agreements—for wages and prices to adjust automatically. They maintain that the best way for a government to promote growth without inflation is by using its spending power to influence demand. Who wins in the monetarist/neo-Keynesian debate seems less important than the fact that each side has found someone to argue with.

Action Economics

OR, PUTTING YOUR MONEY WHERE THEIR MOUTHS ARE

So much for theory. Although no self-respecting economist ever dispenses with it entirely, there *are* areas of economics in which interpreting—or inventing—economic gospel takes a backseat to delivering on economic promises. That is, to keeping things—money, interest and exchange rates, deficits—moving in what's currently being perceived to be the right direction. Here, contributor **Karen Pennar** explains what some of those promises (and some of those directions) are. Come to terms with them and you'll be ready to queue up for her tour of the markets, stock and otherwise, where action turns into hair-raising adventure.

THE FEDERAL RESERVE BOARD

Known in financial circles as the Fed (and not to be confused with the feds), this government body, our central bank, wields enormous control over the nation's purse strings. In fact, it's said that the Fed's chairman is the second most powerful man in Washington. He and his six colleagues, or governors of the Federal Reserve Board, direct the country's monetary policy. Simply put, they can alter the amount of money (see "Money Supply") and the cost of money (see "Interest Rates"), and thereby make or break the economy. When the Fed tightens, interest rates rise and the economy slows down. When the Fed eases, interest rates fall and the economy picks up. Or so it used to be. The balancing act is so difficult, and the Fed so mistrusted, that its actions often have a perverse effect. So much for simplicity.

Many swear that the Fed is the root of all economic evil. In his landmark work, *A Monetary History of the United States, 1867–1960* (coauthored by Anna J. Schwartz), Milton Friedman placed blame for the Great Depression squarely on the Fed (for tightening too much). He hasn't stopped berating it since, and he has plenty of company. Beating up on the Fed is a popular sport—unfair, perhaps, but understandable. A little history: The Fed, created in 1913 by an act of Congress, grew steadily in strength during the Depression years. By the 1950s, it had evolved into an independent force, free of the pressures of Congress and the president. Checks and balances for the economy, you might say.

This explains why many presidents have had a love-hate relationship with the Fed, praising it when interest rates are falling, then cursing it when they climb. Members of Congress, similarly, are often frustrated by the Fed's independence, and periodically threaten to limit its autonomy.

But the Fed tends to be blissfully immune to criticism. Board members pursue their own lofty economic objectives and routinely cast blame on Congress and the president for mismanaging the economy.

MONEY SUPPLY

This is what the Fed is supposed to control but has a hard time doing. For decades, the Fed, and the people who make a living analyzing what money is doing, monitored the money supply because of the effect it was believed to have on the national economy. The Fed measures the money supply in three ways, reflect- ing three different levels of liquidity—or spendability— different types of money have. By the Fed's definition, the narrowest measure, M1, is restricted to the most liquid kind of money—the money you've actually got in your wallet (including traveler's checks) and your checking ac- count. M2 includes M1 plus savings accounts, time de- posits of under $100,000, and balances in retail money market mutual funds. M3 includes M2 plus large- denomination ($100,000 or more) time deposits, balances in institutional money funds, repurchase liabilities, and Eurodollars held by U.S. residents at foreign branches of U.S. banks, plus all banks in the United Kingdom and  Canada. Last time we looked, the M1 was around $1.2 trillion; the M2, $6 tril- lion; and the M3, $8.8 trillion. The Fed, by daily manipulation, can alter these numbers. If the Fed releases less money into the economy, interest rates rise, cor- porate America borrows and produces less, workers are laid off, and everyone's spending is cut back. When the Fed pumps more money into the economy, the reverse happens. And if it moves too far in one direction or another, the Fed can create a depression (the result of too much tightening) or hyperinflation (the re- sult of too much easing).

In theory. The problem is that in practice, the Fed is far less able to control the economy than it was twenty years ago. There are billions of dollars sloshing around outside the banking system (some of which have even found their way to places like Russia and Argentina). What's more, today a lot of people are hold- ing money that used to be counted as checking or savings deposits in mutual funds. Oh yes, and let's not forget booming credit, which in effect creates a money supply of its own.

INTEREST RATES

Money, like everything else in the economy, has a price. Beginning in the late 1970s and lasting right through the 1980s, that price was high. Home mortgages carried double-digit rates, and borrowing on a credit card routinely cost about 19 percent. The Vietnam War, wage and price controls in the early 1970s, the quadrupling of oil prices, a flabby Fed, and a ballooning budget deficit had all done their part to push prices up—including the price of money.

Eventually, though, a tougher Fed and a sluggish economy brought down in- flation, which allowed interest rates to fall. By 1993, some rates were at their

lowest levels in thirty years. And to everyone's surprise, they were even lower ten years later. This is at least partly because of the huge U.S. trade deficit. Foreign central banks and investors now hold much of the United States' debt. Because their interest rates tend to be even lower than ours, they take the dollars we send them in exchange for record amounts of imported goods and send the dollars back to the United States, in effect recycling them, in order to take advantage of *our* interest rates.

DISINFLATION

It's an awkward word, for sure. Simply put, disinflation occurs when prices rise, but at a slower rate than they did before. So what was so significant about it? First off, it was a big and welcome change from the 1970s and early 1980s, when rising prices (and wages that didn't keep pace) eroded incomes, and consumers faced sticker shock every time they went shopping. Disinflation, and continuous low rates of inflation—say 2 percent to 3 percent a year—provide greater certainty and stability and allow economic activity to proceed at a steadier pace. (Though folks who expect to earn 10 percent on their certificates of deposit aren't necessarily happier.)

In the 1970s, galloping inflation was our biggest problem. In the 1980s, we were obsessed with the budget and trade deficits. The 1990s shaped up as the decade of disinflation and price increases have been very moderate ever since. First, both the Fed and the financial markets will work hard to push interest rates higher if prices start rising. That, in turn, will immediately dampen animal spirits and lower the inflation threat. Second, the U.S. recession of 2001 made it harder for manufacturers to raise prices, and the slow recovery has kept price increases tame. But the stiffest curb on inflation comes from the growth in world trade. Read on.

GLOBAL COMPETITION

The bulk of economic theory, and our understanding of how economies actually work, is based on the assumption that most nations are largely closed—that is, self-sufficient in the production of most goods and services, open to trade only at the margin. In the real world, however, trade across borders has been going on for centuries. And in recent decades, with the growing sophistication of technology, communications, and transport, it's become easier and cheaper for more people in more places to make and ship goods and provide services. The value of world trade, in real or after-inflation terms, has grown 6.5 percent a year since 1950. For every $100 billion more in goods that are traded around the world, growth is pushed about $10–20 billion higher than it otherwise would be, economists say.

Free trade, or relatively free trade, unencumbered by stiff tariffs or quotas, is responsible for this heady growth. That sounds positive and, for the world as a whole, it is. New workers and consumers join the global community as trade increases—witness the way millions of Chinese have gotten rich, thanks to China's adoption of decidedly uncommunist economic policies. Consumers in industrialized nations like the United States can obtain goods that are cheaper than those made at home, and that should improve living standards. But that benefit is not uppermost in the minds of workers in the United States, say, who lost their jobs because U.S. manufacturers decided to set up shop in Taiwan or Mexico and produce the same goods more cheaply there.

Today Americans are more and more aware of an alphabet soup of trade and economic relationships, from APEC and ASEAN to NAFTA and the WTO (see "Dead-Letter Department," page 407). All these groups spin an elaborate web of relationships on which future growth will be based, often within loose confederations of nations. Are these relationships progrowth? Definitely. But they also guarantee that economies are anything but closed. So long as trade continues to grow, wages and prices in relatively wealthy countries will be under downward pressure. And that means that global competition keeps the inflation threat low.

FLOATING CURRENCIES AND THE GOLD STANDARD

All that trade is being financed with U.S. dollars, Japanese yen, the E.U.'s euro, and a whole lot of other currencies. Every day the value of those currencies vis-à-vis each other shifts—or "floats"—according to supply and demand on foreign-exchange markets, and in recent years there've been some mighty big swings as economic policies change and speculators and investors make big bets.

Businessmen and tourists complain about the uncertainty that accompanies floating rates, but there's little alternative. Once upon a time, back in the 1960s (and for almost a century before), foreign-exchange rates were rigidly fixed—and only occasionally repegged—and major currencies such as the dollar were valued in terms of gold. (By this standard, gold was worth $35 an ounce, and dollars could be turned in for gold.) This setup supposedly lent stability to the world trading system and ensured that currencies possessed real, not inflated, value. But currency and investment flows across borders became so enormous in the late 1960s and early 1970s that the system (known as Bretton Woods, after the New Hampshire town where it was devised following World War II) unraveled. In 1971, Nixon took the United States off the gold standard.

Today there are still people who hanker for a gold standard. Gold, the argument goes, has intrinsic value, while paper does not. But advocates of a return to the gold standard are like octogenarians who reminisce about the good old days, forgetting about gas lamps and outhouses. The mechanistic inflexibility of the gold standard is what forced us to go off it. Floating rates allow these corrections to occur continually and with relative calm. The system may not be perfect, or even comprehensible, but it looks as though it's here to stay.

Adventure Economics

OR, PUTTING YOUR MONEY WHERE YOUR MOUTH IS

B ecause so many people share in the national pastime known as playing the market (which means, of course, the stock market, and used to refer specifically to the granddaddy of them all, the New York Stock Exchange, but now includes nine markets that are linked electronically), it's worth your while to know the rudiments. The way to do that is to follow the stock tables and read the daily market summaries. And if you're really ambitious, you can learn about a few other types of markets—like the bond and futures markets—and think of yourself as a financial polyglot.

THE STOCK MARKET

A *stock* represents a share, or fractional ownership, in a company, and a very fractional one indeed. Large companies have tens of millions of shares outstanding. Companies sell stocks (the first time they do it's called going public) because they need other people's money. With a strong base of stockholders' equity, as the pool of ownership is known, a company can buy machinery, fill orders, pay its executives handsomely (and its workers not so handsomely), and even borrow money.

Stock comes in two forms—common and preferred. The difference lies chiefly in dividend policy (see below) but is also important when a company liquidates. Then the preferred shareholder is, as the designation implies, in a better position than the common shareholder.

A *dividend* is the reward, or payoff, a company gives the stockholder for investing in it. It's actually a piece of the profits, but don't imagine for a minute that all the profits are distributed proportionally. No way: Profits must be plowed back into the company's operations (and, some might say, into executives' pockets). But something has to be given to the investor who helped make things happen, so dividends of anywhere from a few cents to a few dollars per share are handed over quarterly. The company sets the dividend rate, and every so often may decide to toss a few more coins the shareholders' way. But a company, if it is in poor financial shape, may also suspend paying dividends on common stock or cut a dividend. The company, however, must distribute dividends in full to preferred stockholders before it pays common stockholders, so it is the latter who gets their dividends axed first in a pinch.

A *capital gain* is the profit you make on the sale of your ownership in a company, provided the company has done well, its stock is in demand, and its stock price has risen: You hit big in the market.

A *loss* is a loss. Today—or the day you bought stock—was not your day.

The *stock market* is where winners and losers get together. Sometimes it seems like a party, other times like a wake. Big winners and losers determine the mood, because the real market makers are pension funds, banks, corporations, and other money managers, all known as institutional investors. The little guy is just that, and he tends to get swept up in or under the tidal waves institutional investors create. The cardinal rule of any market, the stock market included, is buy low, sell high, but if everyone did that successfully, there'd be no markets to speak of. For any person who buys low, there's somebody selling low, and for anyone selling high, there's someone willing to buy high. Why? Because of expectations and greed. A person selling low is trying to cut his losses and figures the worst is yet to come, so it's time to bail out. And a buyer shelling out big bucks is convinced that stock prices will go still higher, and he wants to cash in, even if belatedly.

The *herd instinct* accounts for the tidal waves and derives from the fact that people are always looking over their shoulder to see what the next guy is doing. More often than not, for no good reason, they figure he must be right and they must be wrong. Institutional investors can suffer this market paranoia in the worst way, so you see how a herd can form and really trample the market. Since institutions invest in many names, stock prices across the board tend to move in line with each other during big market swings. All sorts of things can affect the herd, from a change in tax legislation to a political assassination. But the herd can also behave in ways that have no obvious explanation, as it did when the bull market began in August 1982. And it can turn tail and run in the other direction, as it did when the market crashed in October 1987. It can also be spot-on correct, as it was throughout the 1990s.

If you watch stocks on a daily or even weekly basis, the numbers will tell the story of how the market is behaving.

The Dow Jones Industrial Average (DJIA), or simply "the Dow," the most widely used measure of market activity. It's an index of the price of 30 stocks (but a huge amount of money) which trade on the New York Stock Exchange, or NYSE, where the largest companies are listed. Dow Jones publishes the *Wall Street Journal* and *Barron's* and provides financial information.

NASDAQ stands for National Association of Securities Dealers' Automated Quotations system. The NASDAQ stock market is now the fastest-growing, most technologically advanced market, listing everything from hot new issues to established companies such as Apple Computer. Trading volume is second to the NYSE's.

AMEX stands for the American Stock Exchange, a distant third in trading volume.

Some other averages are far more comprehensive. Among those widely cited: the Standard & Poor's 500, which tracks large stocks, and the Russell 2000, which tracks small ones.

Then, too, remember that the stock market isn't the only market around. There's the *options market*, where people buy and sell the rights to buy and sell stocks, believe it or not. This way, for less money than it would take to actually buy stocks outright, people can play the market. Without ever owning a stock, they can win big or lose big on its movement. Playing the options market can be (if that's possible) even more of a crapshoot than playing the stock market.

Also dicey for some, though useful for others, is the *futures market*. This market was originally devised to help out farmers and manufacturers who used farm products. Contracts for future delivery (within a few months) of grains, pork bellies, and assorted other items could be bought and sold, providing a hedge against anticipated rising costs or falling revenues. But the market has burgeoned in recent years with the inclusion of a host of new contracts (from foreign exchange to stock indexes) and scores of new players. Today hardly anyone active in the futures market takes actual delivery on a contract. The fastest-growing component of the market is in financial futures—Treasury bills and the like—because fluctuating interest rates are still another cost businessmen want to hedge against and speculators bet against.

Once the staidest of them all, the *bond market* is not the safe haven many conservative investors think it is. Used to be, a company that wanted to fix its borrowing costs for ten or twenty years would borrow money from investors by issuing bonds. The U.S. Treasury did the same, as did the individual states and thousands of municipalities. The investor would buy the bond, receive a fixed amount of interest each year from the issuer, and get back his principal when the bond matured. Bonds were boring because usually, nothing changed. Prices were steady because interest rates were generally steady. If interest rates moved slightly higher, the resale price of the bond, or its price on the secondary market, moved down a notch. No big deal.

That's all changed. Low inflation has brought low interest rates and big profit-taking to the bond market since the early 1990s. But bond market investors, who only get paid the value of the dollars they lend, aren't trusting, and that makes the bond market anything but staid. Who knows where interest rates will be ten or twenty years from now? A sharp upturn in rates would send prices plummeting—producing big losses for investors holding long-term (twenty- to thirty-year) bonds. So this nightmarish guessing game has buyers and sellers tripping over each other to secure mere fractions of a percentage point in interest.

So much for the markets. If you feel like dipping your big toe in, be forewarned: The old adage that you should never invest more than you can afford to lose still holds true. In fact, it's truer than ever. Leave the fancy stuff and the big bets to the old hands. After all, they know more than you.

Or do they?

Economics Punch Lines

OR, PUTTING YOUR MOUTH WHERE YOUR MOUTH IS

In the past, all the good jokes were about doctors, lawyers, and politicians, but now that economists control the politicians and make more money than the doctors and lawyers, it's they who've become the butt. As it happens, the jokes themselves are far too long to recount here. Which means you'll have to be content with the punch lines:

Joke 1: "Do you have any idea how many economists you have to kill just to get a pound of brains?"

Joke 2: "Who do you think was responsible for creating all this chaos in the first place?"

Joke 3: "The economist says, 'First, assume the existence of a can opener.'"

Joke 4: "The good news is that the bus just went over the edge of the cliff. The bad news is that there were three empty seats on it."

FILM

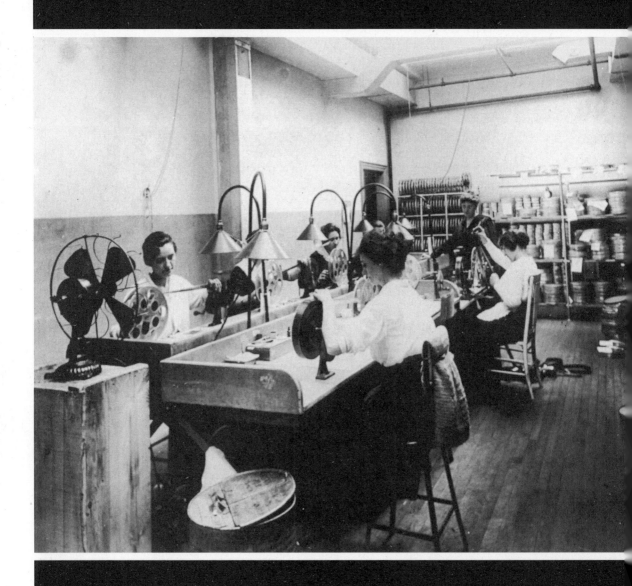

Contents

Careers in filmmaking: Worth the bus fare to Hollywood?

Remedial Watching
for Chucky *Fans*

I t's one thing when they try to get you on opera: You really *can* simply wave
your passport in their faces and announce that that isn't what we do here. It's
quite another when they hit you with movies, which are as American in spirit and
allure as you are—or aren't. *Birth of a Nation* got you down? Or *Potemkin*? Or
Citizen Kane? This'll help.

THE BIRTH OF A NATION
(American, 1915)

Director

D. W. (for David Wark) Griffith. The original and still, to some, the greatest.
Newcomers to Griffith (and, obviously, to film history, in which he is always a
long Chapter 3, right after "The Movies Are Born" and "The Movies Find a
Public") may, however, appreciate a couple of touchstones. The first: Thomas
Edison. Like him, Griffith was a practical genius, a boy-scientist type who
wanted to solve the problem, not promulgate the theory. The second: Charles
Dickens. Like *him*, Griffith was sentimental, melodramatic, and hopelessly Vic-
torian. A reactionary in terms of his subject matter (big moments in history,
American rural and domestic life, moral-religious allegories) and a philistine
when it came to "art," he nevertheless single-handedly propelled movies out of

the realm of stage-bound theatricality and into that of the cinematic. He also realized, a full decade before anybody else even got around to thinking about it, the possibilities of the new medium, and contributed its two most basic techniques: the cross-cut (in which we watch a little of one scene, then a little of another, then back to the first, etc., in a way that suggests simultaneous action) and the close-up (in which we get to feel we know, and are maybe not so very different from, the characters up there on the screen). *Birth of a Nation* and *Intolerance* (1916, an interweaving of stories of cruelty from four different civilizations, from Babylonian times to Griffith's own) are the "core" Griffith; cultists, by contrast, dote on *Broken Blossoms* (1919). Ironical note: Griffith lived too long, with industry honchos first stripping him of his creative freedom, then forcing him to edit the botched efforts of other directors, and finally refusing even to take his phone calls. He died, forgotten, of alcoholism, in a Hollywood hotel room.

Story

Nation—in the form of two families, the abolitionist Stonemans of Pennsylvania and the plantationist Camerons of North Carolina, who are, despite their differences, great friends—is torn apart by Civil War. Reconstruction proves even worse: Negroes are uppity; Flora Cameron (Mae Marsh)—a.k.a. the Little Sister—jumps off a cliff to avoid being raped by Gus, an emancipated house slave, and it takes the Ku Klux Klan, led by Ben Cameron—a.k.a. the Little Colonel—who, by the way, is in love with Elsie Stoneman (Lillian Gish), to set things right. Stay put for the climax: cross-cuts between two simultaneous Klan rescues, one of Elsie, whom a mulatto with a heavy black-supremacy rap wants to make "queen" of an all-black empire, the other of the entire Cameron family, with a Stoneman thrown in for good measure, from a cabin being besieged by Negroes and carpetbaggers.

What All the Fuss Was About at the Time

Nobody had ever seen anything remotely like this: a three-and-a-half-hour epic, with a coherent plot, persuasive performances, chase scenes, lots of camera movement, brimming over with emotion and what appeared to be ideas; plus, it had been budgeted at an unheard of $100,000 and cost an equally unheard of $2 a head to see. Without warning, movies emerged from the penny arcades into respectability. The era of the feature film was born and with it the pattern for the blockbuster, in which huge sums of money are invested in the hopes of even huger returns at the box office. Needless to say, not all the East Coast reviewers thought much of the movie's bathetic story, simple-minded thesis, and overwritten title cards (e.g., "Bitter memories will not allow the poor bruised heart of the

South to forget"). And the racism riled black and liberal viewers. There were riots in New York, Boston, and Chicago; city fathers demanded cuts; and Jane Addams and the president of Harvard, among others, wrote chiding letters. All the brouhaha did, though, was (1) incite Griffith, himself the son of a Kentucky colonel, to counterattack, first with pamphlets and then with *Intolerance*—in his opinion proof positive that *he*, at least, was free from prejudice; (2) suggest to anybody who'd managed to keep his cool just how inflammatory this new medium could be; and (3) fuel the movie's publicity and box-office operations. Not that *Birth* needed a shot in the arm; it was an immediate hit. As President Wilson said, "It is like writing history with lightning."

What All the Fuss Is About Today

Some people are still stuck on the racism, but most of us have moved on to Griffith as fashioner of the "grammar and rhetoric" of film, from his stockpiling of technical devices to his discovery that the emotional content of a scene, rather than its physical setup, determined where to place the camera and when to cut. Then there was his overall success with actors—how he got them to function as an ensemble as well as to underact (well, for the times it was underacting)—and his particular success with those contrasting types of womanhood, Lillian Gish (idealized femininity, purity, frailty) and Mae Marsh (the girl next door). *Birth* is also a valid historical document, not of Civil War days, but of the country fifty years later, still in reaction to that war. None of which makes for easy viewing: *Birth* (ditto *Intolerance*) has most modern audiences checking the minute hands of their wristwatches.

THE CABINET OF DR. CALIGARI
(German, 1919)

Director

Robert Wiene, but don't give him another thought: He was a one-shot and he got the job only because Fritz Lang was tied up making something called *The Spiders*. Instead, be mindful of the screenwriters, a Czech named Hans Janowitz, who'd happened to witness a sex murder in Hamburg's Reeperbahn, and an Austrian named Carl Mayer, who'd been examined once too often by army psychiatrists during World War I; the set designers, a four-man contingent headed by Hermann Warm, who used expressionist principles and techniques to create the

movie's warped, angular look, going so far as to paint in, rather than throw, those eerie lights and shadows; and even the producer, Erich Pommer, who financed the whole crazy package and hoped the public would bite.

Story

Check out the frame-tale setup: Patient in mental hospital tells elaborate and horrifying story of weird, heavily bespectacled carnival-circuit hypnotist (Werner Krauss), who controls lurching somnambulist, Cesare (Conrad Veidt), inducing him to commit series of murders. His story told, patient freaks out and is taken to office of mental hospital's benign director, who, in the course of examination, puts on pair of horn-rimmed spectacles and . . .

What All the Fuss Was About at the Time

German intellectuals liked the sick settings, the way a madman's fantasy life had been translated into visual terms; French intellectuals went one step further and coined the term *caligarisme*, which they used to describe cinema that was abstract, like a "painting in motion," rather than realistic narrative of natural events in natural settings—a useful enough idea in a postwar world that was striking almost everyone as sinister and unworkable. This sort of distortion was not unknown in the theater, of course. The amazing thing was that now a movie camera was eschewing reality, apparently no longer interested in recording the "look" of things, the very purpose it had been devised for. But apart from getting the intellectuals going and setting a certain standard for future "art" films, *Caligari* would not seriously influence the course of movies.

What All the Fuss Is About Today

For horror-movie aficionados, this is the granddaddy, happily fleshed out with mental illness (persecution, hallucination, breakdown) and the chilling ambiguities generated by the tale-within-a-tale format. More than mere horror, however, *Caligari* purveys the kind of weirdness that fuels cultism: Here's a way to get the jump on friends who are still gaga over Kafka or, what's worse, *Twin Peaks*. Then there's the movie's inherent appeal for painters and set designers: Unlike other classics of the cinema, this is one in which stagecraft and painted flats, rather than camera movement and dynamic editing, do the job—and get the credit. Finally, it's a traditional favorite of sociologists and portent readers: German film theorist Siegfried Kracauer, for instance, sees in it the beginnings of a "cortège of monsters and tyrants" that would eventually culminate in Hitler.

NANOOK OF THE NORTH
(American, 1922)

Director

Robert J. Flaherty. Boy with a camera (and a Jean-Jacques Rousseau streak), intent on revealing the essence and the quality of life as it was then being lived in such exotic outposts as the frozen Arctic (*Nanook*), the South Seas (*Moana*), the barren, storm-tossed islands off Ireland's west coast (*Men of Aran*), and the bayous of Louisiana (*The Louisiana Story*). The first—and most legendary—of the documentary filmmakers, he sidestepped studios and story lines for what he could observe out there on his own. Intense and gentle; paragon of integrity; like Renoir (whom he helped smuggle out of France and into America during the war), a "poet" among directors.

Story

Eskimo family—stalwart Nanook, jolly wife, Nyla, two small children, plus infant in pouch of Nyla's sealskin parka—survives elements and sculpts nature as best it can on the shores of Hudson Bay. Very cold, the shores of Hudson Bay. And crawling with seals. Sequences to note: Family emerges from kayak, one by one, like circus midgets from a tiny car; Nanook, at trading post, goes wild over phonograph and tries to eat phonograph record; Nanook, on big ice floe, stands alone at edge, spearing fish; Nanook builds igloo, from (just as you'd always suspected) blocks of compacted snow. But we bet you didn't know he was going to install a chunk of frozen river as a window.

What All the Fuss Was About at the Time

Unpredictably, a big commercial as well as critical hit. Of course, it helped that the picture opened in New York in the middle of one of the hottest Junes on record, but beyond that, viewers couldn't get over the way they were invited not only to travel to a distant clime, but to look into somebody else's mind and heart. Plus, everybody wanted to know how Flaherty had done it, had lived for months in subzero temperatures—a thousand miles from the nearest restaurant, photographic supply store, oral surgeon, whatever—and had gotten all these Eskimos not only to trust him, but to take direction (a matter that bothered some critics so much that they charged Flaherty with misusing "facts"). Then there was Nanook himself: the bright eyes, the continual smile, the weather-beaten face. Within a matter of months, Eskimo pies were being sold on both sides of the Atlantic, and words like "igloo," "kayak," and "anorak," formerly known only to anthropologists, were popping up in grade-school civics tests and sporting-goods store windows. Too bad Nanook couldn't have basked in his new fame: He died of starvation, out there on the ice, shortly after the film was released.

What All the Fuss Is About Today

Three things. First, the documentary tradition, of which Flaherty is held to be the father; how it was discovered that dramatic content could be derived from the depiction of fact, how documentary is both more "real" and more "respectable" than the fiction film. Second, Flaherty as counterpoint to Hollywood, as the great director who, unlike Griffith and Stroheim, wasn't crushed by it; and who, unlike Sternberg, didn't collaborate with it; but who simply abandoned it for places where he couldn't be reached by phone. Third, the final product, a triumph of structure, editing, and sympathy, even if he did force all those Eskimos to wear skins and furs that were more Eskimoish than anything they'd ever have picked out for themselves.

THE LAST LAUGH (German, 1924)

Director

F. W. (Friedrich Wilhelm) Murnau. Most revered director of Germany's Golden Age, which was conceived in the rubble of World War I, thrived through the heady days of the Weimar Republic, and withered away in the early Thirties, the result either of Hitler's crackdown on creative types or of Hollywood's buying them all up, or both. A pupil of Max Reinhardt, the Austrian theater impresario, Murnau jettisoned the expressionism and eerieness of *Caligari* days and began serving up bratwurst-and-boiled-potatoes realism. (Even his 1922 *Nosferatu*, based on Bram Stoker's *Dracula*, used everyday, business-as-usual, port-city-of-Bremen settings.) Hollywood got its hands on Murnau, too: He made *Sunrise*, about a young wife threatened by her unbalanced husband, for Fox in 1927, then collaborated with Flaherty on a quasi-documentary South Seas drama called *Tabu* (1931). Only forty-three, he died in a car crash a week before *Tabu*'s premiere, thereby affording film historians a favorite example of directorial careers nipped in the bud.

Story

Dignified old man (Emil Jannings) at top-drawer hotel is exalted by braided and epauletted uniform that is part and parcel of job. One morning arrives at work to find that new, young doorman is hailing cabs, lugging suitcases, etc., and that he has been demoted to washroom attendant and must wear simple white smock. More humiliation follows, especially at home, where old man, formerly treated like grand duke, is now treated like dirt. Not to worry: Tacked-on happy ending has him inheriting fortune of rich American hotel guest and dining sumptuously in hotel dining room.

What All the Fuss Was About at the Time

Hailed by American critics as "the best film in the world," *Laugh* was also a big popular success. Jannings' performance, if broad, was a great crowd-pleaser; besides, the world on screen looked real again, instead of like some crazy—and probably subversive—artist's nightmare. But the biggest impact was technical, and Hollywood felt it more deeply than that from any other foreign film: Suddenly, the movie camera was actually *moving*, up and down, forward and back, through the lobby of the hotel and out onto the street—even in simulation of the shakiness of a hangover, tracking and tilting and swinging and twirling. Freed from its fixed tripod (though not yet provided with cranes and dollies), it had become flexible and aggressive, had become—as the film historians like to observe—an actor.

What All the Fuss Is About Today

The situation's been in hand for a while now—unless you're stranded in a roomful of NYU film students, all of whom will be noting, in addition to the moving cameras and the realism, the fact that said realism is subjective (i.e., filtered through the consciousness of the central character) and that a great deal of attention is being paid to his emotional and psychological state. Even nonstudents, though, tend to marvel at how easy this movie is to watch, how modern in its narrative flow. Moreover, the story is told without so much as a title card, so efficient and eloquent are the visuals—until, that is, a series of cards announce (and apologize for) the tacked-on, trumped-up ending. Poignant oddity: the signs in the washroom, which are printed in Esperanto, a token of Murnau's conviction that cinema (at the time still silent) was destined to level the linguistic barriers between nations.

GREED (American, 1924)

Director

Erich von Stroheim. More precisely, either Erich Oswald Hans Carl Marie Stroheim von Nordenwald, son of a colonel on the Austrian general staff and himself a former officer in the Austro-Hungarian cavalry, or Erich Oswald Stroheim, son of a Prussian-Jewish hatter who'd emigrated to Vienna and himself a former frustrated foreman in his father's straw-hat factory—depending on whether you believe Stroheim's own publicity or its subsequent debunkers. Either way, the man who, as director and genius, suffered more than anybody else at the hands

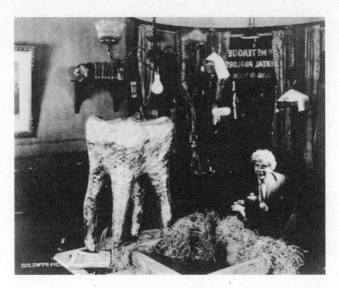

of Hollywood. A meticulous craftsman who exceeded budgets and audience attention spans as a matter of course, he met his nemesis in profit-minded Irving Thalberg. Of the eight and a half films he managed to turn out in over fifteen years of directing, all but the first two were mutilated by studio cutters, one was taken away from him in midproduction, and a couple weren't even released. Even so, he remains, after Griffith, the most influential director Hollywood turned out in the years before talkies. (The other bottom-line Stroheim: *Foolish Wives*, 1922, and *The Wedding March*, 1928.) Also an actor, both in the Teens (when he invariably portrayed nasty, stiff-backed Huns and was billed as "the man you love to hate") and, following the asphyxiation of his directing career, in such classics as Renoir's *Grand Illusion* (as the aristocratic Colonel von Rauffenstein) and Billy Wilder's *Sunset Boulevard* (as Norma Desmond's butler and playmate).

Story

From Frank Norris' turn-of-the-century naturalistic novel *McTeague*. San Francisco dentist (that's McTeague), practicing without a license, fixes tooth of, then courts and marries, sweet young thing (Zasu Pitts), who, at their engagement party, learns she's won $5,000 in lottery: the beginning of the end. A long and elaborate wedding banquet (a scene in which, among other things, a funeral cortège can be glimpsed through an open window) follows, along with boredom, estrangement, blackmail, penury, murder, and a Death Valley climax, in which ex-dentist and blackmailer fight and die like dogs. Interspersed with above: shot of long bony arms, belonging to no one in particular, clutching at pile of gold coins.

What All the Fuss Was About at the Time

The Stroheim method: How he'd shot the Death Valley scene *in* Death Valley (in 132° heat); how he'd made the cast and crew live in the San Francisco house they were using as a set; how he kept his actors working till four in the morning; how no detail, no bit of atmosphere, no bow in the direction of verisimiltude was, for this man, too much. (For other movies, he'd demand that a life-sized replica of Monte Carlo be built, that his movie archdukes wear only authentic medals and have crests on their—perforce—silk underwear.) The fact that he'd submitted a forty-two reel (i.e., ten-hour) movie, edited it to twenty-four reels under duress, then sat back and watched as the studio hacked it—and all its subplots, bit parts, symbolism, and narrative continuity—to ten reels and two and a half hours. Also, the subject matter (avarice and human degradation, dirty dishes and unmade beds, à la Zola), which had one popular critic branding the film "a vile epic of the sewer," another "the sour crème de la sour crème." The few colleagues who'd seen the original forty-two-reel version were dumbstruck, enthralled; anybody who saw the ten-reel one had a hard time knowing what was going on. A monumental commercial failure.

What All the Fuss Is About Today

The Stroheim legend—the man more than the movie. How he, a hatter's son, created himself: the aristocratic past, the monocle, the super-erect posture, the extra-long cigarettes. The fact that while the only version of the film we have is the two-and-a-half-hour one, the complete screenplay *does* exist, along with a few extra stills—a constant provocation to cinephiles, who keep hoping one of Stroheim's own original forty-two-reel prints, with coins, fillings, picture frames, and a canary, all allegedly hand-tinted in gold, will turn up. How we still don't know whether a ten-hour movie narrative is aesthetically, let alone commercially, possible. Then there's the object lesson for young directors: One is overweening at one's own expense. Finally, for the trivia buffs, the realization that Zasu Pitts hadn't always played ditzy manicurists.

THE GOLD RUSH (American, 1925)

Director

Charlie Chaplin. Tripped over his own mystique. The product of a Dickensian English boyhood (complete with drunken father, insane mother, orphanages, and floggings), Chaplin never stopped acting out his anxieties regarding food, security, social injustice, ostracism, bullies, and the human condition. Touring America in a music-hall act, he had been discovered by Mack Sennett, who employed him in a series of shorts as a puppet and pratfaller. Within a year, Chaplin had evolved the Tramp persona, with a cane, a hat, floppy shoes, and a pair of Fatty Arbuckle's trousers as props, and negotiated a contract to make his own pictures. Ahead lay, in addition to enormous popular success, the acclaim of the culturati; his conviction that he *was* the Little Man, the Tragic Clown; a loss of touch with his fans, who were being provided with fewer and fewer laughs and more and more sentiment; increasingly "heavy" films (*City Lights*, 1931; *Modern Times*, 1936; *Monsieur Verdoux*, 1947; *Limelight*, 1952) that garnered mixed reactions; several marriages, most notably his last one, to Eugene O'Neill's daughter Oona; deportation from the United States as a Communist sympathizer; a couple of less-than-successful English-made movies, à la *A Countess from Hong Kong* (1966); and official rehabilitation in the form of a special Oscar in 1972. He died in 1977.

Story

The Lone Prospector (Chaplin) joins mass trek to frozen Alaska gold fields; that's him looking out at you from the lower left-hand corner of the group picture. Arrives pursued by bear, and with frying pan spanking buttocks at every step. Is isolated in tiny cabin in blizzard with two larger and hungrier prospectors; eats own shoe. Meets dance-hall girl and falls in love, but is stood up on New Year's Eve, in course of which he dreams he spikes two hard rolls with forks and causes them to do variety of dances (famous sequence, this). Cabin almost falls over cliff. Strikes gold. Boards ship for San Francisco. Runs into dance-hall girl, who, it turns out, loves him back.

What All the Fuss Was About at the Time

To a degree, comedy in general. Chaplin was simply the favorite in a ragtag, anyone-can-play segment of the industry that boasted Langdon, Lloyd, Laurel and Hardy, and—the only one now regarded as being in Chaplin's league—Buster Keaton. Primed, the public applauded. To a degree, Chaplin in general, too. The first movie-spawned personality to be widely regarded as a genius, as well as the first international movie star, Chaplin fueled an icons-and-

memorabilia industry that compares favorably with those of Mickey Mouse and Harry Potter. The Little Man confronting power and wealth, less hostilely than ambivalently, appealed to the little man in everybody; the only difference was *they* couldn't use every last body part to convey the pathos, whimsy, and acuity of it all. As for *The Gold Rush* itself: Great moments (the bear, the shoe, those rolls, the precipitously placed cabin), with a nice thematic unity that critics had not yet started complaining was undermined by too episodic a structure.

What All the Fuss Is About Today

Most of it's in the backlash. Chaplin hasn't been artistically discredited, exactly, but he's been made to seem self-serving, even circumscribed. The big beneficiary is Keaton, whose *The General* has replaced Chaplin's *The Gold Rush* and *Modern Times* on all-time ten-best lists, as critics rushed to prefer the former's athletic naturalness and sense of film's "possibilities" to the latter's balletic self-consciousness and solipsism. Not that anybody's denying Chaplin's genius—only his modesty, sincerity, and devotion to the art form. Flashiest critical line for the undecided to take: that Chaplin, unlike Keaton, put the exterior world behind him—at the expense of his popularity—and lived out of "the interior, almost schizophrenic relationship between director and actor." (That's Andrew Sarris, by the way.) A saner tack: Be moved by the grace, the eloquence, the expressiveness of Chaplin's fingertips, and appreciate how he, like Griffith and Orson Welles, bridges the gap between movies as art and movies as entertainment.

POTEMKIN (Russian, 1925)
Director

Sergei Eisenstein, to movies what Freud is to psychology: the theoretician who's never been surpassed, the practitioner who's never been entirely superseded. Also, like Freud, the right man in the right place (in this case, Russia) at the right time (the fifteen turbulent years following the revolution, during which Soviet films were the most exciting in the world). You may feel he's manipulating you, and he is: Eisenstein subscribed to Lenin's belief that art could influence politics and that "the most important of all the arts, for us, is cinema"; saw that it could not only capture reality, but transmute it, less through the stories it told than through bold imagery, stylized compositions, and, most of all, rhythmic editing. Only twenty-six when he made *Potemkin* (Russians and purists pronounce that "po-*TYOM*-kin," by the way), Eisenstein would live both to employ his genius and to suffer for it. Under Stalin he was alternately purged and reinstated a couple of times a decade until his death in 1948; as personally devastating was his sojourn in Hollywood in the early Thirties, during which he made conversation with Charlie Chaplin and Mary Pickford, posed for press photos with Rin Tin Tin, collaborated unsuccessfully with Theodore Dreiser and Upton Sinclair, and watched his dream of filming an epic about Mexico from Toltec days to the present be sandbagged by the capitalists. Other seminal Eisenstein: *Strike* (1924), *Ten Days That Shook the World* (a.k.a. *October*; 1927), the two-part *Ivan the Terrible* (1942–1946).

Story

It's 1905. Sailors on the tsarist battleship *Potemkin*, anchored off the Black Sea port of Odessa, grow tired of, among other things, maggots in their meat. Group of them rebels and is ordered shot by firing squad made up of their mates. "Brothers! Who are you shooting at?" shouts rebels' ringleader, and rebellion becomes shipwide mutiny. As it happens, the citizens of Odessa—workers, mothers with baby carriages, bearded university professors, plus an amputee and an unforgettable old lady with pince-nez—see rightness in all this, and gaily assemble on the broad white steps in the middle of the town, where, within five minutes, they are gunned down and trampled on by a couple of hundred Cossack soldiers. But the spirit of revolution lives on. In the final segment, the *Potemkin* races toward an imperial squadron, prepared to do battle. Guns are drawn on it, but, in the nick of time, it runs up flags spelling out "Join us." The fleet does not fire. Everybody cheers.

What All the Fuss Was About at the Time

First off, that *Potemkin* didn't look like a movie, didn't look staged (as the high-artifice films that were coming out of Germany did) or even acted; in fact, it read as a newsreel. Second, that it was such powerful stuff: Nobody who's seen the Odessa Steps sequence will ever forget it (or admit that he has, anyway). Of course, that's not to say that he'll be aware of what went into it: on the one hand, of Eisenstein's commitment to "actuality," to using real people rather than actors (a furnace man as the ship's doctor, a gardener as the ship's priest, and sailors as the sailors) and shooting on location rather than in the studio; on the other, of his clever and intense use of montage, a kind of hyper-rhythmic editing in which Image A (shot of boots of soldiers marching relentlessly toward top of steps) is juxtaposed with Image B (shot of woman protesting soldiers' butchery) in such a way that the audience anticipates and becomes psychologically involved with a third, as yet unseen Image C, resulting from the "collision" of the first two. Thinkers pointed out that this was really just the application of the principles of dialectical materialism to art, but that wasn't what had Mary Pickford, Douglas Fairbanks, and Cecil B. De Mille making pilgrimages to Moscow, or young American intellectuals sitting night after night in Eighth Street movie houses. This movie seemed to be ushering in the twentieth century, taking up where Griffith had left off. With *Potemkin*, cinema had at last given up the theatrical, and the literary, and spoken in its own language. And, in just five reels and eighty-six minutes, it blew you away besides.

What All the Fuss Is About Today

The montage is still right in there: How, without it, is any true cinéaste going to go on to deal with, say, Godard? An even bigger come-on: the fact that this exciting, dynamic, idealistic, ideological, brave era of Soviet moviemaking didn't last; that Eisenstein and his colleagues would, within five years, be branded formalists and decadents by Stalin and company and that Soviet film would take a nosedive into banality. (Of course, the same thing was taking place in Germany under Hitler, but at least the Germans—producers, directors, actors, screenwriters, cameramen, and, for all we know, hair and makeup people—got to relocate to LA.) Finally, there's the sheer power of it all. Even if the story seems a little cartoonish, the idea of Eisenstein defining an art form, seizing the moment, defying hubris and Hollywood is *very* Promethean. For those who prefer the statistical angle: With Renoir's *La Règle du Jeu* and Welles' *Citizen Kane*, *Potemkin* is one of the three movies guaranteed to show up, decade after decade, on every international critic's all-time ten-best list.

THE PASSION OF JOAN OF ARC
(French, 1928)

Director

Carl-Theodor Dreyer, a Dane then working in Paris. And that's not all: The set designer was a German (Hermann Warm, from *Caligari* days), the cameraman a Pole, and the star, Maria Falconetti, an Italian, but the picture, from subject matter to aesthetics, is strictly French. Spoken of in the same hushed tones as Griffith, Eisenstein, and Renoir, but for most of us, even harder to get down with. Three possible ins: the supernatural angle (Dreyer's obsessed with witches and vampires, even if he does see them as all-too-human martyrs), the Bergman connection (having learned to tolerate one Scandinavian's bottomless guilt and pain, you shouldn't have too much trouble plugging into another's), and the old sympathy ploy (Dreyer, unappreciated in his own lifetime, could pursue his art only by dint of the money he made as manager of a Copenhagen movie theater, never got to make a movie about the life of Christ, never got to work in Hollywood like his mentor Griffith, etc., etc.). Other vintage Dreyer: *Vampyr* (1932), *Day of Wrath* (1943), and *Ordet* (1955).

Story

Based on actual trial records that, in 1928, had just come to light: A series of five grueling cross-examinations, culminating in the execution, at the stake, of Joan (Falconetti), but not before giant close-ups have told us everything we ever wanted to know about Joan and her accusers (among them Antonin Artaud, pre-

"Theater of Cruelty," as the only compassionate one). But plot isn't the point here. Go instead for the passion, in this case almost equal parts eroticism and religious persecution.

What All the Fuss Was About at the Time

The camerawork, especially as it fixed on faces (not to mention Joan's dirty fingernails) rather than action and events, faces that fill the screen and come complete with sweat, tears, wrinkles, warts, and spittle, and are thrown into even higher relief by the starkness of the sets and the dead whiteness of the sky. And, equally, Falconetti's performance as Joan: the way she managed to emanate sainthood, sorrow, and suffering, all without benefit of makeup—or, for that matter, much in the way of hair. (As one of Dreyer's assistants remarked later, "It was a film made on the knees.") An enormous success with the critics, who hailed it as the ultimate silent film, the distillation of a decade of creative filmmaking in Europe; the man from the *New York Times*, for instance, announced that it made "worthy pictures of the past look like tinsel shams." Banned in Britain, by the way, for its depiction of English soldiers stealing Joan's ring and sticking their arrows in her arm.

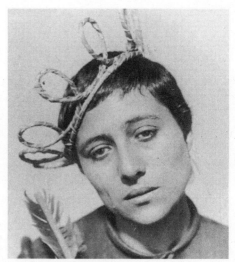

What All the Fuss Is About Today

Ignore the comparisons of *Passion* to various musical forms (most often an organ fugue); what you really have to grasp is the fact that this, of all the standard masterpieces of world film, is the one that separates the sheep from the goats, the aesthetes from the philistines, the devotees from the hangers-on. The former have largely shut up about Falconetti, who was so drained by this film she never made another. But they still can't get over those faces. Ditto the wild blend of fleshiness and spirituality. If you must find fault, cite the title cards—so disruptive, so unnecessary, and so emblematic of the silent film's increasing frustration at not being able to speak. By all means, point out that sound had already arrived in France as Dreyer began *Passion*, and that, had he succeeded in obtaining financing, the last great work of silent film might have been the first great masterpiece of the sound era. Then finish your espresso and go home.

L'AGE D'OR (French, 1930; English title, *THE GOLDEN AGE*)

Director

Luis Buñuel. The Spanish maverick who, yoking the outrageous with the matter-of-fact, the blasphemous with the banal, managed to parlay one of the least flashy—and, frankly, least cinematic—of directing styles into a career that, a half century later, was still going strong. In 1930, though, Buñuel was just getting started, having arrived in Paris five years earlier with his friend and fellow surrealist Salvador Dalí. The year before, the two had collaborated on *Un Chien Andalou*, the seventeen-minute manifesto-on-film, having nothing to do with either dogs or Andalusians, in which a girl's eye gets slashed with a razor, a man's hand is shown crawling with ants, and dead burros lie sprawled across two grand pianos. Now they undertook something more ambitious: an hour's worth of denunciation, obsession, and mania, financed by the famous French "angel," the Vicomte de Noailles. Dalí, who wasn't the easiest man in the world to work with (he'd try to convince you, for instance, that his waxed moustache served as an antenna for his muse, then turn around and expect you to buy a painting from him), had gotten that much worse since all the *Chien* notoriety, and lasted only a day on the *L'Age* set. Despite the credits (and with the exception of one gag, in which a man walks with a large stone on his head), the film is pure Buñuel.

Story

May as well begin with the documentary footage of the scorpions. Not that it prepares you for the bandits, or the Majorcans, or the fellow kicking a violin down the street. In a way, it *does* prepare you for the man and his mistress, though not necessarily for the mud they're rolling in. Things are a little more upbeat at the marquis' party (ignore the kitchen fire and the gamekeeper who shoots his little boy), especially once the man and mistress get out to the garden, where they try to have sex while seated in two wicker garden chairs. Try, that is, until he is summoned inside to take the minister's phone call and she busies herself with the toe of the statue. At some point somebody throws a Christmas tree, an archbishop, a plough, a stuffed giraffe, and several pillowfuls of feathers out a window. Then, before you know it, we're leaving a chateau in the company of four worn-out orgiasts; look for a cross, covered with snow and festooned with a woman's hair. The End—accompanied by a happy little Spanish march, the kind you might hear at a bullfight.

What All the Fuss Was About at the Time

Le bourgeois wasn't just *épaté*—he was livid. A funhouse mirror full of the pressures and postures of the day, *L'Age* pilloried Church, State, and Establishment, and monkeyed with morals, manners, and bodily functions. To get it past the censors, Buñuel had to position the film as "the dream of a madman"; now he billed it as "a desperate, passionate appeal to murder." Although it took a few weeks for the news to get around, eventually gangs of Fascists, Catholics, and anti-Semites broke into the theater, threw stink bombs and purple ink at the screen, and slashed the paintings by Dalí, Max Ernst, and Man Ray hanging in the lobby. Then the right-wing press got in on the action, along with the police chief. The film was banned, and Buñuel was branded a subversive. He went back to Spain and made a scathing documentary called *Land Without Bread*, likewise banned; he wouldn't direct another movie for fifteen years.

What All the Fuss Is About Today

Unlike *Chien*, which seems a little on the adolescent, look-Ma-no-hands side, *L'Age* comes across as fresh, stringent, biting, if anything enhanced by all that's gone on between then and now. It's your single best introduction to (1) avant-garde cinema (marked by its fondness for abstraction, its eschewal of narrative, and its overall flakiness), (2) surrealism (with all its jarring, illogical literalness, plus more Freudian bric-a-brac than you can shake a phallus at), and (3) Buñuel himself (whose later themes, targets, and preoccupations it sets in motion). The other avant-garde—and quasi-surrealist—film of the period: Jean Cocteau's *Blood of a Poet* (also 1930, also financed by the Vicomte de Noailles), a "poem on celluloid," according to Cocteau, featuring a mouth in a drawing that comes alive, a hermaphrodite with a *Danger de Mort* sign in its crotch, and a fatal snow-ball fight. After its rhapsodizing and self-congratulation, you'll appreciate Buñuel's outrage all the more.

STAGECOACH (American, 1939)

Director

John Ford. The grand old man of American movies. Gruff, big-hearted, meditative Irishman with a taste for folklore and nostalgia. In many ways a throwback to Griffith (sentimental, moralistic, committed to the probing of character and

motive), Ford remained, through the Forties and Fifties, the single most important director whom Hollywood didn't totally undo. Instead it gave him four Oscars (for *The Informer*, 1935; *The Grapes of Wrath*, 1940; *How Green Was My Valley*, 1941; and *The Quiet Man*, 1952), plus a couple more for his wartime documentaries. He also received, in 1973, the first of the American Film Institute's Life Achievement Awards, a fitting tribute to a man who, over the course of fifty years, made some 130 movies (including silents), the majority of which dealt with the American experience—the history, the dream, the legend—in one form or another, most notably the western. You can complain that Ford's maudlin and simplistic; you can regret that he ever took on such highfalutin, arty projects as *Informer* and *Grapes*; and you can explain how, unlike his confrère Howard Hawks (more on him in a minute), he needed a strong screenwriter at his side, but you can't not stand up when he enters the room.

Story

Grand Hotel with sagebrush and on wheels. Stagecoach in question is bound for Cheyenne; on board are a former Confederate officer turned cardsharp (John Carradine), an alcoholic doctor (Thomas Mitchell, who'd played Scarlet O'Hara's father that same year), a prostitute (Claire Trevor) who's just been run out of town, a timid whiskey salesman, an escaped convict, a bank embezzler, and, of course, the pregnant wife of a cavalry lieutenant, who refuses to speak to the prostitute. Andy "Jingles" Devine is the driver. Along the way they're joined by the Ringo Kid (John Wayne), who's lost his horse; both the prostitute and the doctor undergo radical transformations (he becomes Marcus Welby); the army wife gives birth; the Apaches attack; the cavalry comes to the rescue; and, finally, in Cheyenne, the Ringo Kid settles an old score with the Plummer boys, then rides off with the prostitute to start a new life.

What All the Fuss Was About at the Time

The western, already an established Hollywood genre, gained new respectability. It also gained a form, a flexibility, and an overall relevance: Now "prestige" directors could make westerns without being accused of slumming. John Wayne, previously no great shakes, became a star—as did Monument Valley, the tract on the Utah-Arizona border with all those buttes, mesas, and sandstone spires; both would figure in many John Ford westerns to come, notably the so called cavalry trilogy (*Fort Apache*, *She Wore a Yellow Ribbon*, and *Rio Grande*). Literary types got to note the resemblance to Guy de Maupassant's short story "Boule de Suif," about a prostitute traveling in a carriage with a bunch of bourgeois during the Franco-Prussian War, while everybody else in the theater watched for the Indians to mass on the horizon.

What All the Fuss Is About Today

To be honest, there isn't much. *Stagecoach* was remade in the Sixties, with Ann-Margret in the Claire Trevor role, but the fact that we're even telling you that shows you how little news there is here. However, *Stagecoach* is still the best choice for those who want in on the Ford mystique, an important first stop on anybody's road toward the bitter, dark (and cultish) *The Searchers*. Do be careful with the important Ford/Hawks polarity. Born in 1895 and 1896, respectively, they both made westerns (Hawks was even smart enough to hire Ford's boy, John Wayne) and they both hung around forever, with Peter Bogdanovich hounding them for interviews and dinner invitations every step of the way. But Hawks was never the Establishment favorite Ford was (no Academy Awards, for instance, unless you want to count a "special" one), perhaps because he eschewed art for action, sentimentality for cynicism, the safe idea of woman as Maureen O'Hara for the sexy idea of woman as Lauren Bacall. With no folklore and great humor (Ford had none), Hawks made at least one film in every important genre: the gangster picture (*Scarface*), the screwball comedy (*Bringing Up Baby*), the film noir (*The Big Sleep*), the musical (*Gentlemen Prefer Blondes*), and yes, the western (*Rio Bravo*). He wasn't an innovator, as Ford could be when he chose, but he was the most artless of the great Hollywood directors—so craftsmanlike, so in control as to be "invisible." And it was Hawks, not Ford, who stopped those *Cahiers du Cinéma* French boys cold when they first discovered Hollywood.

LA RÈGLE DU JEU (French, 1939; English title, *THE RULES OF THE GAME*)

Director

Jean Renoir. The grand old man of world cinema, impossible to dislike and even harder to disparage. Had his ups (sunny, unfettered childhood overseen by his father, Pierre Auguste, the Impressionist painter; unbroken lifetime string of supportive women and creative collaborators, what he called his *équipe*; at least one film that was both a popular and critical smash, namely the 1937 *La Grande Illusion*, about national loyalties and class affinities in a World War I German prisoner-of-war camp). And his downs (majority of his films misunderstood and cold-shouldered at the time they were released; *Règle*, his masterpiece, first butchered, then withdrawn, finally bombed to smithereens; personal inability to cope with Hollywood during his exile there in the Forties). Words to brace yourself for in any discussion of Renoir: humanism, realism (and/or naturalism), lyricism; luminosity, spontaneity, generosity; nature, artifice, civilization. What they're really trying to say: that Renoir's heart was in the right place, that he took the long view, that he cared about people (especially his actors, for the sake of whom he was willing to sacrifice plot, dialogue, or technique), that he had an artist's soul as well as eye and winked at his audience with both, that he understood how—as one of the characters in *Règle* puts it—"The terrible thing is that everyone has his own reasons." Basic Renoir, in addition to *Règle* and *Illusion*,

the two big guns: *Boudu Saved from Drowning* (1932; the inspiration for *Down and Out in Beverly Hills*), *A Day in the Country* (1936), *The Southerner* (1945; about a family of sharecroppers, the best from his Hollywood period), *The River* (1951; shot in India), *The Golden Coach* (1952; in which Anna Magnani plays an actress on tour in eighteenth-century Peru).

Story

Rich marquis throws elaborate country house party for high-toned (if, *entre nous*, somewhat vulgar) friends; sex, games, and the chase on everybody's mind, notably those of marquis, marquis' wife, her aviator lover, marquis' mistress, estate gamekeeper, his wife the lady's maid, and poacher new to the neighborhood. (Also at the party: Octave, the friend of the family, played by Renoir himself.) In the course of the week or two that everyone's together, there's a hunt (watch for the beaters flushing the rabbits and pheasants), elaborate theatrics and a fancy-dress ball, the shooting of the aviator by the gamekeeper, and a tour of the marquis' collection of wind-up toys.

What All the Fuss Was About at the Time

To begin with, that Renoir had gotten carried away. Because of bad weather and casting problems, *Règle* wound up costing twice what it was supposed to; plus it ran 113 minutes and the front office insisted it be shaved down. Also, what with Europe in a tizzy and war about to break out, a lot of people weren't much in the mood for what Renoir called "an exact depiction of the bourgeois of our time"; for the ultranationalists and anti-Semites among them, the presence in the cast of a Jew (the marquis) and an Austrian (the marquis' wife) was the last straw. Then there were those who merely found the movie immoral, decadent, or incomprehensible. More footage was cut. Even so, *Règle* was banned as demoralizing; when the Nazis arrived on the scene, it was banned all over again. To add insult to injury, in 1942 the Allies inadvertently destroyed the film's original negative. (English-speaking audiences wouldn't get to see the complete, painstakingly reconstructed version until the late 1950s.) In the meantime Renoir had fled to America; by the time he returned to France in the early 1950s his spirit was broken.

What All the Fuss Is About Today

Half the crowd raves about how dazzling, complex, brilliantly structured and ironic it is; the other half about its richness, sensuality, egalitarianism, and drollness. Then they get down to specifics: the multiple viewpoint, how *Règle* doesn't root for one side or the other in the class war, how it was the first psychologically sophisticated film in which the notion of "good" people and "bad" people was completely eliminated. Alternatively, Renoir's use of the deep focus, in which the camera pulls back to show us a landscape as clear and sharp as characters busily ensnaring each other in the foreground—a perfect way to probe human relationships, establish man's interaction with the world, and engage the viewer by bringing him into the field of action. Or maybe you prefer to think of Renoir as the spiritual leader of the French cinema, whose artistry and humanity served, in the Thirties, as the only alternative to Hollywood brashness and glamour. If you aren't swept away by any of the above, at least be mindful of Renoir's enormous influence on the next generation of filmmakers, from Truffaut and the New Wave in France, to the neo-realists (De Sica, Rossellini, et al.) in Italy, to Satyajit Ray, who never stopped talking about how he met Renoir when the latter was filming *The River* on the banks of the Ganges. Finally, there's critic Pauline Kael, who pointed out how *Règle* foreshadows all those jaundiced house-party movies of the 1960s—*L'Avventura*, *La Dolce Vita*, *Last Year at Marienbad*—in which the big house symbolizes the remains of European civilization.

CITIZEN KANE (American, 1940)

Director

Orson Welles. The wunderkind: *Kane*, which he produced, directed, wrote (sort of), and starred in, all at the age of twenty-five, remains the most impressive directorial—and entrepreneurial—debut in movie history. Keep in mind that Welles already had an out-sized reputation when he got to Hollywood, as an actor and director for the stage (he had founded the Mercury Theater in 1937) and radio (he was the force behind the weekly *Mercury Theater of the Air*); it was this reputation that accounted for the degree of artistic and financial control he was given on *Kane*, and the degree of suspicion and dislike Hollywood instinctively felt for him. After *Kane*, which turned out to be a commercial failure and a public-relations fiasco, it was all downhill. His next (and next best) film, *The Magnificent Ambersons* (1942), was reedited in his absence, and everything from then on suffered from either funding or quality-control problems. Still, nobody's had more influence on young filmmakers over the last fifty years. Many of them see Welles as a titan, committed to art and personal vision, eager to experiment with storytelling and cinematography, a man brought down by nothing less than hubris. Others see him as a big chubby boy given to overstatement, unnecessary camera move-

ment, and half-baked profundity, a man done in by simple egomania. Our favorite summation of Welles: that of Herman J. Mankiewicz, coauthor of the *Kane* screenplay, who, observing the big man on the set one day, was heard to mutter, "There, but for the grace of God, goes God." Other Welles you might consider turning out for: *The Lady from Shanghai* (1948), *Macbeth* (1948), *Touch of Evil* (1958), *Mr. Arkadin* (1962), *The Trial* (1963), *Chimes at Midnight* (1966, with Welles as Falstaff).

Story

Never a dull moment. Media baron and thwarted politician Charles Foster Kane (played by Welles and based largely on William Randolph Hearst) dies, in bedroom of fabulous castle home, Xanadu (cf. San Simeon), with "Rosebud" his last spoken word. Cut to *March of Time*–style newsreel acquainting us with the outline of his overscale, somewhat unsavory, and absolutely enigmatic life. Cut to newspaper office, whence young reporter is dispatched to discover essence of same, especially as it might be summed up by word "Rosebud." He visits library established by Thatcher, Kane's childhood guardian (George Coulouris), where he reads of Kane's youth and, of course, this being the twentieth century, of Kane's mother (Agnes Moorehead); then interviews, in succession, Kane's business manager (Everett Sloane), Kane's best friend (Joseph Cotten), Kane's mistress (Dorothy Comingore), and Kane's majordomo at Xanadu. Loads of flashbacks, in which we observe Kane run newspaper, stir up war with Cuba, marry niece of president (Ruth Warrick), meet toothachy mistress and attempt to turn her into diva, run for office. But reporter never finds out what "Rosebud" means. We do, though: After everybody's gone home, camera registers it as name of sled, now being consigned by workmen to Xanadu's furnace, that Kane hit Thatcher in stomach with when, so many years ago, latter tried to separate him from mother.

What All the Fuss Was About at the Time

Prime example of a film undone by advance publicity, most notably attempts by Hearst to suppress, buy up, calumniate, etc., *Kane*. He succeeded in making distribution a nightmare for parent studio RKO and in infuriating, boring, and perplexing enough people so that, when the film finally came out, it died on the vine. (Hollywood, ever vulnerable in the manners-and-morals department, and fearing another Fatty Arbuckle–type scandal, got so roiled it booed *Kane* at the Academy Awards every time one of its nine nominations came up; that year John Ford's *How Green Was My Valley* was the big winner.) Then there was Welles the man, the sacred monster, the virtuoso, who in *Kane* did with the moving picture almost everything that could be done with it, yanking his audiences forward and backward in time, montaging sound as well as image, plunging his camera through, say, the skylight of a New Jersey cabaret rather than using the front door—and then, on top of the pyrotechnics, starred in the thing himself. Scandal and bravura—but *Kane* remained out of circulation from its initial release till its late-1950s art-house revival.

What All the Fuss Is About Today

Welles and *Kane* zoom to very top of 1972 *Sight & Sound* international critics poll! The most written about, most controversial movie ever! America on map as producer of sound films to rival Europe's! The one American talking picture that "seems as fresh today as the day it opened"! (That last is Pauline Kael, whose *The Citizen Kane Book* is required reading for zealots.) On the other hand, you can, as far as fashioning a personal reaction to *Kane*, do better. Revel in the film's unabashed theatricality, its sleight of hand, its highly visible "insides." Note the polished camera work of Gregg Toland, the Bernard Herrmann score. Suggest that *Kane* hints at the insanity implicit in American pop culture—and American life—as broadly as a Busby Berkeley musical number. (Or Jeffrey Dahmer.) Get behind Kael's assertion that screenwriter Mankiewicz is the real genius behind *Kane*; then cite Peter Bogdanovich's refutation of same. And rather than alluding to Rosebud (a gimmick in the film, a cliché in film talk), take as your favorite scene the one in which old Bernstein, Kane's business manager, reminisces about seeing the girl in the white dress on the Jersey ferry: "She didn't see me at all," he says, "but I'll bet a month hasn't gone by since, that I haven't thought of that girl."

For Extra Credit

THE THIRTEEN NEXT-BIGGEST-DEAL MOVIES THEY MADE BEFORE YOU—OR STEVEN SPIELBERG—WERE BORN

1. *The General* (Buster Keaton, 1926). Now widely held to be the best of all Twenties comedies, bar none. (In case you hadn't noticed, Keaton's no longer playing Garth to Chaplin's Wayne.) The reasons: action that's all of a piece, rather than episodic and "taped together" (Southern engineer gets back the supply train Yankee soldiers have hijacked, as well as his girlfriend, who was accidentally aboard), plus technique that integrates character and environment, incident and existence, instead of just capturing a few brilliant pantomimes on celluloid. Unlike Chaplin, Keaton doesn't mime, emote, or ingratiate—he merely stares, a man up against a whole army (not just the town bully), with a face as quintessentially American as Abe Lincoln's (cf. Chaplin's Old World one) and a girl who's more pain in the ass than Holy Grail.

2. *Mother* (Vsevolod Pudovkin, 1926). Soviet movies aren't just Eisenstein. In fact at the time, many critics preferred the work of his contemporary Pudovkin, who was lyric and emotional where Eisenstein was epic and intellectual, and who, as Dwight Macdonald remarked, used his shots as a novelist uses words rather than, à la Eisenstein, as a musician uses notes. Case in point: *Mother*, Pudovkin's masterpiece, the tale of a woman who, tricked by the police into betraying her own son (who's in league with a bunch of striking workers), learns that radicalism is the only way to fly; it's all from a Maxim Gorky story you may know in its subsequent *Mother Courage* incarnation. To be noted: The professional actors (cf. Eisenstein's insistence upon using nonpro-

fessionals); the fact that the movie's hero while symbolic, is nevertheless an individual (cf. Eisenstein's masses); the way in which montage here is a function of "linkage," of shots being used like so many building blocks (as opposed to Eisenstein's dialectical "collision" of images).

3. *Metropolis* (Fritz Lang, 1926). As *Caligari* begot the horror film, *Metropolis*—futuristic and allegorical—generated the sci-fi one. Here we're in a city (said to have been inspired by Lang's first shipboard view of New York) built on two levels, one for the rich, with skyscrapers and hanging gardens and air taxis, the other—subterranean and prisonlike—for the workers who keep the aboveground society going. The story, which is perfectly preposterous, concerns a banker's son who decides to go live with the workers, whereupon he falls in love with a girl name Maria. Do note, however, the sets (not that it's easy to miss them) and the way in which the cast of hundreds is made to function more as scenery than as crowd. As for Lang: He's a tough nut, and a bitter one (half-Jewish, he'd fled Germany even though Hitler wanted him to stay and make pro-Nazi movies), with a penchant for criminality and angst, the guilty innocent and the femme fatale.

Life underground in Metropolis

4. *Napoléon* (Abel Gance, 1927; full title, *Napoléon vu par Abel Gance*). The highlight of the 1927 movie season, when the original seven-hour version premiered at the Paris Opéra. Also, the highlight of the 1981 New York movie season, when a painstakingly reconstituted four-hour version (by movie scholar Kevin Brownlow, egged on by Francis Ford Coppola) was shown at Radio City Music Hall. You're up against two things here. The first is scale: from the 6,000 extras and 150 sets to the nicely matched ambitions of subject Napoleon and director Gance, plus the sheer enveloping scope of the tripartite, fifty-foot-by-twelve-and-a-half-foot screen. The second is technology. Gance's Polyvision, as wraparound as Cinerama, in fact predates it by thirty years. What's more, scholars see *Napoléon* as a clearinghouse for silent-screen techniques (Gance wasn't known as the French Griffith for nothing) and tend to be especially overwhelmed by his moving cameras, sometimes handheld, sometimes suspended by wires, sometimes strapped to horses, pendulums, or, we're told, dancers' bellies.

5. *Pandora's Box* (G. W. Pabst, 1929). By the other Golden Age German director who, along with Murnau and Lang, you maybe should have heard of. Not Pabst's most famous movie (that would be *Joyless Street* or his bastardization of Brecht's *The Threepenny Opera* or maybe *Kameradschaft*, about German miners who rescue French ones), but probably your best investment. For one thing, it'll prepare you for the big-deal Alban Berg opera *Lulu*, all about sex and parasitism. For another, it'll afford you the chance to watch American actress Louise Brooks do her thing as Lulu. The movie goes on forever before Lulu, having devoured her fifth or sixth mate, praying-mantis-style, and now down and out in London, meets her match in Jack the Ripper; but there are enough high-perversity moments along the way to keep most of us latter-day sexual sophisticates satisfied.

6. *The Blue Angel* (Josef von Sternberg, 1930). Perverse, psychoerotic saga of how cabaret queen Lola Frohlich (Marlene Dietrich), who sings "Falling in Love Again" several times a night and spits into her mascara, transforms poor, respectable Professor Rath (Emil Jannings) into a whimpering clown given to doing his chicken imitation in front of an audience of vindictive former pupils. May give you another interesting insight or two into the frenzy and murkiness of Twenties Germany; will certainly acquaint you with the von Sternberg mystique— the visual bravura; the aspirations toward high art and European culture; the all-in-the-same-breath preoccupation with glitter and gutter; and, of course, with Dietrich, whom von Sternberg subsequently brought to Hollywood and directed in a string of cult classics full of veils, nets, fog, and smoke. After their collaboration petered out in the mid-Thirties, von Sternberg ceased to count for much, but the personal legend, the mastery of cinematic illusion and sexual delusion, the commitment to languor and decadence at a time when other directors

*Showgirl (Marlene
Dietrich) ensnares
educator (Emil
Jannings) in*
The Blue Angel

were trying to say something meaningful about society, vouchsafe him classic status.

7. *Earth* (Aleksandr Dovzhenko, 1930). For those desiring a glimpse of the Russian countryside beyond what they got in *Dr. Zhivago.* Dovzhenko, the third genius of Soviet silent film, stands apart from his illustrious colleagues: The son of an illiterate Ukranian peasant, he taught himself filmmaking, didn't choose to theorize, and had a predilection for the folkways, nicely blended with poetry and satire. His movie world has less to do with montage than with horses that talk (in title cards, of course), paintings of military heroes that roll their eyes, and animals who, as one critic notes, sniff the air and smell the revolutionary spirit. In *Earth*, his masterpiece, one's confronted by nature, life, death, childbirth, and a farm in the process of being collectivized. Unfortunately, the shot in which a group of peasants urinate into a tractor's radiator to keep it from boiling over has been removed from the foreign-release prints.

8. *Le Million* (René Clair, 1931). Breezy, flirtatious tale of Parisian artist Lothario who leaves winning lottery ticket in pocket of sports jacket, subsequently lent by softhearted girlfriend to passing thief, who happens to run secondhand clothing store on the side, where jacket is purchased by touring Metropolitan Opera tenor. Somehow, everybody (and all his friends) winds up on stage at the opera that night, then goes back to the hero's garret for an *8½*-style snake dance. Stylized (somewhere between ballet and puppet theater) and a musical (perhaps the first in which the music really carries the story forward), *Million* is immensely likable; it's also the prototype for the Marx Brothers' *A Night at the Opera*. Watch what you say about Clair, though. A founding father of the talking picture and considered a paragon of levity and wit as recently as thirty years ago, he's now written off by many as a fluffhead who relied too much on special effects.

9. *Trouble in Paradise* (Ernst Lubitsch, 1932). The plot doesn't recount well (in a sentence, male-female pair of jewel thieves, impersonating aristocrats, set up French perfume heiress) and the stars are disappointingly second-order (Herbert Marshall, Miriam Hopkins, Kay Francis). But you'll find out, in no time flat, what those "Lubitsch touches" are: the "dry sparkle" of language and sexuality; the "artless"

Jewel thieves (Herbert Marshall and Miriam Hopkins, right) ensnare perfume heiress (Kay Francis) in Trouble in Paradise

wit, visual and otherwise; the "moderne" period sense; the ellipsis, the polish, the perfectionism; the total grasp of Americans' preoccupation with sex and money; the caress. Lubitsch (according to Andrew Sarris, "the least Germanic of German directors as Lang was the most Germanic") was also the only silent-era director Hollywood imported from Europe whom it didn't wind up disappointing, defeating, or, as in the case of Murnau, sending home for burial. Gliding easily from silents to talkies, he pioneered the cinematic, as opposed to the theatrical, musical, adapted himself to Hollywood business ways, coaxed intelligent performances out of empty Hollywood heads, and kept the champagne flowing.

10. *Zéro de Conduite* and *L'Atalante* (Jean Vigo, 1933 and 1934). Counts as one selection: The revival houses always show them together (*Zéro* is only forty-five minutes long); besides, having seen the two of them, you'll have seen Vigo, who died when he was only twenty-nine. One of those poetic rebel types, constantly being compared with Rimbaud and James Dean, he defies categorization and gives the avant-gardiste goose pimples; after Renoir, he's the single biggest deal in the first golden age of French filmmaking. *Zéro*, a study of revolt and freedom in a boys' boarding school, is alternately real and surreal, and so virulently antiestablishment that it was banned, from the critics' screenings in 1933 (during which fistfights broke out) until after the Liberation. Today's critics like to note the debts owed to it by such subsequent boys' school pictures as Truffaut's *The Four Hundred Blows* and Lindsay Anderson's *If. . . . L'Atalante*, about a couple of newlyweds attempting to adjust to life together on his river barge, is a less experimental, more commercial affair, adapted from somebody else's screenplay and tarted up with a *Man and a Woman*–type theme song, but it's still pure Vigo: imaginative, iconoclastic, clearheaded.

11. *Triumph of the Will* (Leni Riefenstahl, 1936). The official film record, ordered by Hitler himself, of the sixth Nazi Party Congress, held in Nuremberg in 1934. The prologue has the Führer en route, flying in his airplane over the waiting city, then descending Messiah-like out of the clouds and subsequently marching blithely by tens of thousands of Nazi soldiers, who might as well be soldier ants. Torchlight parades; Brown Shirts and Black Shirts, listening transfixed one minute, *Sieg Heil!*-ing the next; naked-from-the-waist-up Hitler Jugend; speeches; some drilling of the troops; even dinnertime. Of course we'll never know for sure whether Hitler really had a crush on the red-haired dancer-skier-actress to whom he encharged the making of movies on his political conventions and on the 1936 Olympics, but she stands enshrined as one of the few truly creative types (and virtually the *only* truly creative woman type, everyone but Susan Sontag seems agreed) to work in the medium.

12. *Henry V* (Laurence Olivier, 1944). The first of the trio of Shakespeare films he directed and starred in (the others are *Hamlet*, 1948, and *Richard III*, 1956); the first time Shakespeare was ever made into a good movie; and the first sign from England—apart from Hitchcock and the documentarists—that that country could bring anything at all to the art of the sound film. What's in it for you? Well, there's the sheer gloss on the enterprise, from its unprecedented $2 million budget through the Olivier screen presence (in this case, under a haircut that Grace Jones would be proud to have come up with). There's the enchantment of the movie's structure, which features a camera traveling over a model of early-seventeenth-century London, on into the hexagonal Globe Theatre, where, get this, the premiere performance of *The Chronicle Historie of Henry the Fifth* is just getting under way. Finally, there's the play itself: You get a free crack at *Henry V* (see page 204) and its "Once more unto the breach, dear friends" and "We few, we happy few, we band of brothers" speeches. On the other hand, you're not going to recognize anybody in the cast besides Olivier (no Gielgud, no Richardson, etc.). And you aren't fighting the Battle of Britain, as audiences felt *they* were when the movie first came out; if a lump in the throat or a surge of feeling is what you're after, you stand a better chance of acquiring it at the Kenneth Branagh version—or at *Braveheart*.

13. *Les Enfants du Paradis* (Marcel Carné, 1945; English title, *Children of Paradise*). A lot of movie: sumptuous sets re-creating the Paris of Balzac; six central characters (most notably the mime Baptiste, played by Jean-Louis Barrault; the ham actor Lemaître, played by Pierre Brasseur; and the courtesan Garance, whom they both love, played by the legendary Arletty); two distinct acts; a whole set of art-is-life, life-is-art, play-within-a-play-within-a-movie undercurrents; and a running time of three hours and fifteen minutes. Either you love the "literary," deliberately old-fashioned style of this superromantic, super-fatalistic spectacle or you side with Truffaut and the New Wave (see next page) and wonder how a director, still in his early thirties, for crying out loud, could make such a reactionary, pretentious piece of crap. Whichever, *Enfants* is an eyeful, concocted by Carné and the poet/screenwriter Jacques Prévert, one of the most celebrated pairs of screen collaborators ever.

French, Likewise Hollywoodese, for the Movie-Goer

Don't know the grip from the gaffer—or from the dolly? How about the gaffer from the auteur? And what's a McGuffin for, anyway? Read on.

First, the French. The two most important terms are *montage* and *mise en scène*, and, for cinema buffs, they're opposed. *Mise en scène* (literally, "put into the scene") refers to everything that takes place on the set: direction of actors, placement of cameras, deployment of props, choice of lenses, and so on. *Montage* can mean simply "editing," or it can mean the kind of creative editing that, à la Eisenstein, juxtaposes specific shots so as to create whole new meanings. For what it's worth, film-theory fans point out that realists prefer *mise en scène*, expressionists *montage*.

Next, three terms rooted in the Fifties and Sixties. The (1) *Cahiers du Cinéma* reference you occasionally trip over is to a film magazine (literally, "Notebooks of the Cinema") founded by, among others, the French theorist André Bazin, and contributed to by, among others, such (2) *Nouvelle Vague* (or "New Wave") directors as François Truffaut, Jean-Luc Godard, Eric Rohmer, and Claude Chabrol, all of whom were determined to do in, once and for all, the talky, theatrical, studio-crafted movies of France's postwar years. For inspiration, they went back a generation to the more spontaneous, more heartfelt Thirties of Renoir, Clair, and Vigo, who, in their opinion, constituted the "authentic" French tradition. They also cast their gaze on Hollywood, on Hitchcock and Hawks and a clutch of other, less prominent directors. Soon they, like their mentors, would be seen as the prime forces, the (3) *auteurs* (literally, "authors") behind their movies, mediating style, theme, and technique through a single consistent vision. Truffaut first used the term in 1958; Andrew Sarris, film critic for *The Village Voice*, is most responsible for promoting the *auteur* theory in this country.

Two more French terms, by the end of which we'll find ourselves at the corner of Hollywood and Vine. The first is *cinéma vérité* (the second word means "truth"), which can be used loosely to describe almost any kind of documentary technique (including the application of such techniques to fictional subjects), or strictly to describe movies that—starting in the Sixties—were made with lightweight (and hence very mobile) equipment, two-person camera-and-sound crews, and extensive on-camera interviewing.

The other French term: *film noir* (the second word means "black"), a term coined by French critics to describe the kind of Hollywood gangster picture in which the crooks aren't so much bad as sick, and the passions run dark and

François Truffaut, body-surfing on the Nouvelle Vague

brooding. John Garfield was the *film noir* protagonist par excellence, Gloria Grahame or Shelley Winters its abused and no-better-than-she-should-be female lead.

John Garfield, film noir protagonist par excellence

Shelley Winters, as the woman men loved to abuse

Another genre term—strictly American—worth noting: "screwball comedy," which reached its height in the Thirties, in such films as *Bringing Up Baby* (1938, directed by Howard Hawks, with Katharine Hepburn and Cary Grant), and which focused on sexual relationships, madcap action, and verbal one-upmanship, usually among the upper class, and which is to be opposed to the *slapstick comedy* of the silent era. The one other genre-related term not immediately obvious: Alfred Hitchcock's *McGuffin*, the plot element or device that, according to him, drives the plot and fuels the audience's interest, but that can be ignored once it's served its purpose (for instance, the whole Janet Leigh, love-and-money business at the beginning of *Psycho*).

Then there's the technical, get-to-know-your-cameraman vocabulary. Here, it's a seminal—and tricky—distinction between the *zoom* and the *track* that's most worth paying attention to. Both describe ways of following a moving subject with a camera, the zoom with a lens that automatically refocuses to allow for a variable distance between camera and subject (and subject and background), the track with a moving camera, usually mounted on rails, that maintains a single focus on—and consequently a constant distance from—its subject. Tracking is as a result a steady process; zooming a fast, somewhat arhythmic one in which distant objects can be magnified, or close ones moved rapidly away from.

A *pan* is what a stationary camera does when it wants to survey its vicinity, simply moving on its axis from left to right, or right to left. Other stationary shots include the *tilt* (the camera moves up or down) and the *roll* (the camera lies on its side and maybe turns over). Pans are common, tilts less so (just as one looks up less often than one looks to the side), rolls least common of all, in general relegated to "trick" shots, up to and including the one in which Fred Astaire, in *Royal Wedding*, seems to be dancing on the ceiling.

Also an issue: Getting from one scene to another. Here the choices include the *fade-out* (the image gradually goes to black) followed by the *fade-in*; a *dissolve* superimposes one image on another, so that the screen is never entirely image-free. With a *wipe*, more common in Thirties movies than in contemporary ones, an image appears to wipe off a preceding one. Of course, transition can also be effected by out-and-out cutting. A *jump cut* within a scene gets us from point A (hero enters room) to point B (hero flops down on bed at far side of room) without forcing us to watch him walk by his desk, his bureau, and his bulletin board with the pennants pinned to it. *Cross-cutting* establishes a feeling of parallel action by cutting repeatedly from one scene (and mood, and set of characters) to another.

About the equipment: The *boom* is a traveling arm used to hold the microphone above the actors (and, with any luck, out of the frame), the *dolly* a set of wheels on which the camera is mounted so as to be able to "track."

And the personnel. The *gaffer*, from a nineteenth-century nautical term, is the chief electrician responsible for the placing of light. The *grip* casts the shadows, working with "flags, nets, and silks," as a grip of our acquaintance put it, somewhat archaically, we thought. (The *gofer* makes Danish and Xerox runs.) As for that most mysterious of all cinema terms, *best boy*, we're sorry to report that he plays neither page to the director's knight nor paramour to the leading lady. All he does is assist the gaffer or the grip, a reminder of just how workaday studio, as opposed to *Cahiers*, life can be.

LITERATURE

Contents

Enemies of the Book, *drawing by Gustave Doré*

A Whirlwind Tour of BritishPoetry

IF IT'S TUESDAY, THIS MUST BE BROWNING

Don't even think of unpacking. Just wash out yesterday's socks, then prepare to get a grip on six hundred years of poetry in motion.

GEOFFREY CHAUCER

> Bifel that in that seson on a day,
> In Southwerk at the Tabard as I lay,
> Redy to wenden on my pilgrimage
> To Canterbury with ful devout corage,
> At night was come into that hostelrye
> Wel nine and twenty in a compaignye
> Of sondry folk, by aventure yfalle
> In felaweshipe, and pilgrimes were they alle
> That toward Canterbury wolden ride.
> The chambres and the stables weren wide,
> And wel we weren esed at the beste.
> And shortly, whan the sonne was to reste,
> So hadde I spoken with hem everichoon
> That I was of hir felaweshipe anoon,
> And made forward erly for to rise,
> To take oure way ther as I you devise.

from "The General Prologue,"
The Canterbury Tales (1386–1400)

The first wave of English poetry (give or take *Beowulf*), the tales-within-a-tale being shared by twenty-nine pilgrims en route to the shrine of Saint Thomas à Becket in Canterbury provide a bard's-eye view of social classes, economic brackets, and personality disorders in medieval England. Note that the Tabard, where the pilgrims spend their first night out, is one of the famous inns of literature. And that the pilgrims, from the Knight to the Wife of Bath to the Miller, will come to seem as recognizable a bunch of human types as, say, the ensemble in

Robert Altman's *Nashville*. Note, too, that three hundred years after the Norman Conquest, French words are almost as integral to Middle English (that's what Chaucer's writing in) as Anglo-Saxon ones. Speaking of which, if you're going to tackle the *Tales* at all, you might as well go for the authentic Middle English version rather than a lame modernization (although you'll certainly need all the footnotes you can find). And try reading the "Prologue" aloud; once you get the hang of it, Chaucer's English is surprisingly melodious, even if it does sound a little like Norwegian.

EDMUND SPENSER

He there does now enjoy eternall rest
And happie ease, which thou doest want and crave,
And further from it daily wanderest.
What if some little paine the passage have
That makes fraile flesh to feare the bitter wave?
Is not short paine well borne, that brings long ease,
And layes the soule to sleepe in quiet grave?
Sleepe after toyle, port after stormie seas,
Ease after warre, death after life does greatly please.

from *The Faerie Queene* (1590–1596)
Book I, Canto 9

With characters like King Arthur, Queen Elizabeth, Venus, the Angel Gabriel, Adam and Eve, and Despair (that's him above, trying to convince the Red Crosse Knight to commit suicide), *The Faerie Queene* isn't just England's first epic, it's also its first theme park. Though Spenser meant to write twelve books, each celebrating a different knightly virtue, he managed to finish only the first six—to almost nobody's chagrin. Wildly uneven, *The Faerie Queene* can go on for pages without producing a single line, image, or insight you care about, then dazzle you by summing up (and sometimes even solving) the sort of personal problem you've spent the last five sessions trying to thrash out with your shrink. The two main themes (both fleshed out allegorically, with characters and scenery embodying historical events and ideas): medieval chivalry (already, in Spenser's day, pretty much a memory) and Protestant Christianity (still, in Spenser's day, requiring some getting used to). But don't worry too much about who's supposed to be Mary Tudor and who's supposed to be Francis Drake. Better to keep moving, just the way you would at Six Flags.

JOHN DONNE

Our two souls therefore, which are one,
    Though I must go, endure not yet
A breach, but an expansion,
    Like gold to airy thinness beat.

If they be two, they are two so
    As stiff twin compasses are two;
Thy soul, the fixed foot, makes no show
    To move, but doth, if th' other do.

And though it in the center sit,
    Yet when the other far doth roam,
It leans and harkens after it,
    And grows erect, as that comes home.

from "A Valediction: Forbidding Mourning" (1633)

The first and best of the Metaphysical poets, Donne broke away from the conventions of the Elizabethan sonnet and the courtly love poem to invent a poetry characterized by a dense, almost incomprehensibly learned style, extremely complicated imagery, a zillion offbeat references to the arts, sciences, crafts, and daily life of the times, and a fractured meter and syntax that were meant at times to sound conversational, at other times simply to knock your socks off. His poetry tends to be ironic and erotic or heartfelt and impassioned, depending on which of his two favorite obsessions—love or death—he is focusing on at the time (love, naturally enough, in the early poems; death later on). In both he is wise and intellectually astute, and in the love poems—more precisely, the dissection-of-the-psychology-of-love poems—he's not only sharp and smart, he's also more modern than you are. Metaphysical poetry enjoyed a brief vogue in the early seventeenth century, but Donne didn't really come into his own until the twentieth.

JOHN MILTON

High on a throne of royal state, which far
Outshone the wealth of Ormus and of Ind,
Or where the gorgeous East with richest hand
Showers on her kings barbaric pearl and gold,
Satan exalted sat, by merit raised
To that bad eminence; and, from despair
Thus high uplifted beyond hope, aspires
Beyond thus high, insatiate to pursue

Vain war with Heaven; and, by success untaught,
His proud imaginations thus displayed:—
"Powers and Dominions, Deities of Heaven!
For, since no deep within her gulf can hold
Immortal vigour, though oppressed and fallen,
I give not Heaven for lost: from this descent
Celestial Virtues rising will appear
More glorious and more dread than from no fall,
And trust themselves to fear no second fate!—"

from *Paradise Lost* (1658–1665), Book II

Milton claimed to have written it to "justify the ways of God to man," but you'd be smart to interpret it as his attempt to one-up Homer, Virgil, and Dante; an outcry by a no-nonsense Puritan against the high-flown Church of England; and an exercise in style-as-substance, with loftiness the upshot in both departments. The most celebrated English poet after Shakespeare, Milton erected a major edifice, gilded and soaring, where Spenser had gone for sheer acreage. Keep three things in mind as you read: (1) It's still the Renaissance, at least up north, that time during which man was trying to get a bead on who he (or she) was even as he (or she) sought to outperform the Greeks and Romans at their own games; (2) it's not the theology that matters most here, it's the scheme, sweep, effect; and (3) you aren't the only one who thinks Milton's Satan is infinitely more interesting than Milton's God. Not enough hours in the day? Forget *Paradise Lost* and read "Lycidas," Milton's bite-sized elegy on the death of a sailor friend—sweet and intimate, yet abristle with the kind of poetic conviction you came to him for in the first place.

ALEXANDER POPE

Know then thyself, presume not God to scan;
The proper study of mankind is man.
Placed on this isthmus of a middle state,
A being darkly wise, and rudely great;
With too much knowledge for the sceptic side,
With too much weakness for the stoic's pride,
He hangs between; in doubt to act, or rest;
In doubt to deem himself a god, or beast;
In doubt his mind or body to prefer;
Born but to die, and reasoning but to err;
Alike in ignorance, his reason such,
Whether he thinks too little, or too much;
Chaos of thought and passion, all confused;
Still by himself abused, or disabused;
Created half to rise, and half to fall;
Great lord of all things, yet a prey to all;

> Sole judge of truth, in endless error hurled:
> The glory, jest, and riddle of the world!

from *An Essay on Man* (1733–1734),
Epistle II

Poor Pope: He was a hunchback, he was barely five feet tall, and he was a Catholic, on account of the last of which he stands outside the Grand (read Protestant) Tradition of English poetry. His revenge: being more epigrammatic than anybody ever (with the possible exception of Oscar Wilde) and so quotable you don't even know you're quoting him—e.g., "A little learning is a dangerous thing," "Damn with faint praise," "Fools rush in where angels fear to tread," and on through column after column of Bartlett's. Historical note: This is the Augustan Age (also starring Swift, Addison, and Steele; so called because London had come to fancy itself the equal of Augustus' Rome), a conservative, well-ordered era when rhyming couplets, fine manners, powdered wigs, and elaborate gardens were all you needed to get a reputation as a tastemaker. Not that Pope was himself one of the smugs. For sheer venom, spleen, and bile, his satires still haven't been beat.

WILLIAM WORDSWORTH

> Our birth is but a sleep and a forgetting:
> The Soul that rises with us, our life's Star,
>   Hath had elsewhere its setting,
>   And cometh from afar:
>   Not in entire forgetfulness,
>   And not in utter nakedness,
> But trailing clouds of glory do we come
>   From God, who is our home:
> Heaven lies about us in our infancy!
> Shades of the prison-house begin to close
>   Upon the growing Boy
>   But he
> Beholds the light, and whence it flows,
>   He sees it in his joy;
> The Youth, who daily farther from the east
>   Must travel, still is Nature's Priest,
>   And by the vision splendid
>   Is on his way attended;
> At length the Man perceives it die away,
> And fade into the light of common day.

from "Ode: Intimations of Immortality" (1807)

A revolutionary in a revolutionary age and the first of the Romantics (Coleridge, Byron, Keats, and Shelley were the others, Blake a precursor), Wordsworth hated Pope, arguing that memory counted for more than wit, imagination for more than reason, and nature for more than gazebos and topiary hedges. Visual, subjective, and basically all het up, he introduced a style he thought of as conversational (though you won't), favored an everyday, even tabloid sort of subject matter (look for lyrics written to "The Idiot Boy," "The Mad Mother," and "The Female Vagrant"), and redefined poetry famously as "emotion recollected in tranquillity." Two big don'ts: Don't think you have to read *The Prelude*, his longest, most ambitious, and most lethal poem. And don't adopt him wholesale as your mentor: Wordsworth the revolutionary is notorious for having turned into Wordsworth the reactionary, a nasty old man given to campaigning against the abolition of slavery, the reform of Parliament, and the prevention of cruelty to animals.

ROBERT BROWNING

> I, painting from myself and to myself,
> Know what I do, am unmoved by men's blame
> Or their praise, either. Somebody remarks
> Morello's outline there is wrongly traced,
> His hue mistaken; what of that? or else,
> Rightly traced and well ordered; what of that?
> Speak as they please, what does the mountain care?
> Ah, but a man's reach should exceed his grasp,
> Or what's a heaven for? All is silver-gray
> Placid and perfect with my art: the worse!
> I know both what I want and what might gain,
> And yet how profitless to know, to sigh
> "Had I been two, another and myself,
> Our head would have o'erlooked the world!"
>   No doubt.

from "Andrea del Sarto" (1855)

His contemporary, Tennyson, got most of the attention at the time, but lately it's Browning who's become the hero, for blazing the trail of modernism in poetry with his jagged-edged dramatic monologues (in which the speaker reveals things about himself he has no idea he's revealing) and his jazzy beat. Jettisoning the confessional style of the Romantics in favor of first-person narrative, Browning, though pre-Freud, manages to come across with a fair amount of sexual heat and even more psychoanalyzable content. On the negative side: He tries too hard ever to seem cool or commanding; he can drift off into stupid, just-what-you'd-expect-from-a-Victorian moralizing; and sometimes he sounds as if he thinks he's writing for children. Personal note: Before he got famous, he was, for most people, Mr. Elizabeth Barrett.

WILLIAM BUTLER YEATS

That is no country for old men. The young
In one another's arms, birds in the trees
—Those dying generations—at their song,
The salmon-falls, the mackerel-crowded seas,
Fish, flesh, or fowl, commend all summer long
Whatever is begotten, born, and dies.
Caught in that sensual music all neglect
Monuments of unageing intellect.

An aged man is but a paltry thing,
A tattered coat upon a stick, unless
Soul clap its hands and sing, and louder sing
For every tatter in its moral dress,
Nor is there singing school but studying
Monuments of its own magnificence;
And therefore I have sailed the seas and come
To the holy city of Byzantium.

from "Sailing to Byzantium" (1927)

Yeats (pronounce that "yates," please) is generally ranked as one of the greatest—oh, let's just go ahead and say *the* greatest—of twentieth-century poets. Partly mystical, partly earthy, and partly just plain Irish, he saw himself and his generation as the Last of the Romantics, and resisted all further categorization. His poetry varies from period to period, as does what can be deduced of his philosophy, but it tends to be made up of anecdotal material—some of it autobiography, some of it folklore, some of it occult theory, some of it current events—overlaid by symbolism and sensuality, all honed for maximum precision. Although he got bad press for becoming a Fascist later in life, he did not, like Wordsworth, turn into a bore, and his "mature" period is considered his best. In fact, he's the poet laureate of old age, a subject with which he became obsessed, and several of his better-known poems, like the one above, provide models for growing old.

HOW TO TELL KEATS FROM SHELLEY

John Keats

Percy Bysshe Shelley

Keats is the one you'd play squash with. He wasn't happy exactly, but he was better adjusted and less the outcast than Shelley, and it shows. (As a kid, Keats had been noisy and high-spirited, a bit of a hellion; Shelley was always coming home from the playground in tears.) Keats wrote letters that his friends couldn't wait to get, and that literary critics and biographers delightedly pore over alongside his poetry; Shelley wrote letters in which he talked about himself a little too much, and it's his essays—philosophical, high-flown, full of abstractions—that the scholars note. Of all the Romantic poets, Keats has worn the best, his stock never varying by more than a point or two; Shelley's has wavered significantly, ever since T. S. Eliot branded his poetry "an affair of adolescence" and Lionel Trilling said he "should not be read, but inhaled through a gas pipe." Be that as it may, it's Shelley, high-principled and farsighted, you'd want by your side at the barricades.

As for the poetry, Keats' is sensuous, concrete, and concentrated, with art-for-art's-sake overtones. (It was he, after all, who wrote, " 'Beauty is truth, truth beauty,'—that is all / Ye know on earth, and all ye need to know," though there's some question as to whether he was being sarcastic.) Keats was a craftsman, with no theory to speak of; it's commonplace to compare him, in the richness and confidence of his language, to Shakespeare, as in these lines, from "Ode to a Nightingale":

> Thou wast not born for death, immortal Bird!
>   No hungry generations tread thee down;
> The voice I hear this passing night was heard
>   In ancient days by emperor and clown:
> Perhaps the selfsame song that found a path
>   Through the sad heart of Ruth, when, sick for home,
>   She stood in tears among the alien corn; . . .

HOW TO TELL KEATS FROM SHELLEY

Shelley's poetry is less solid, more shifting and translucent, more volatile. Unlike Keats, who was at home in the world of things and who was capable of both greed and earthiness, Shelley was able to say of himself, "You know, I always seek in what I see the manifestation of some thing beyond the present and tangible object." (He was also able to address an unsuspecting skylark, "Hail to thee, blithe Spirit!") A radical, full of black despair, Shelley, like Wordsworth, was deemed "a voice of the age." This is how that voice sounds, in the early "Hymn to Intellectual Beauty":

> I vowed that I would dedicate my powers
> > To thee and thine—have I not kept the vow?
> > With beating heart and streaming eyes, even now
> I call the phantoms of a thousand hours
> Each from his voiceless grave: they have in visioned bowers
> > Of studious zeal or love's delight
> > Outwatched with me the envious night—
> They know that never joy illumed my brow
> > Unlinked with hope that thou wouldst free
> > This world from its dark slavery, . . .

Shelley had the more interesting—and marginally longer—life. Born an aristocrat (whereas Keats' father owned a livery stable), he came to be regarded as an atheist, a revolutionary, and an immoralist; he was, in addition, married to Mary Wollstonecraft Godwin, daughter of the radical social philosopher William Godwin and author of *Frankenstein*, with whose half-sister Byron would later have a much-remarked-on affair. Keats didn't hang out with Shelley and Byron, was preoccupied with the financial and medical problems of his brothers, and had a traumatic relationship with a girl named Fanny Brawne. Both Keats and Shelley died miserably, Keats in Rome in 1821 from tuberculosis, Shelley off the Italian coast in 1822 when his boat was swamped in a squall. Keats was twenty-six, Shelley thirty.

Triple Play

You say the dishes are done, the kids are in bed, and the DVD player is broken? Good: This is your opportunity to take a few minutes and bone up on literary devices. And we don't mean foreshadowing and onomatopoeia. *They're* for high-school sophomores. If you want to sound like an adult, it's wit, irony, and ambiguity you've got to be able to field—and every so often manifest. But what, exactly, are they? We don't blame you for not being sure; each is booby-trapped in some way. The first has a complicated history, the second comes in too many shapes and sizes, and the third leaves you wondering whether it's good or bad. To, er, wit:

WIT

At its best, it's—as you've doubtless heard—like a rapier: fast, clean, intensely civilized. And it's immediately recognizable: Oscar Wilde, Dorothy Parker, and Tom Stoppard are witty; Groucho Marx is funny, even trenchant, but too interested in being *unciv-ilized* to be witty; nor is David Letterman (too scattershot, too sloppy). Not that wit is necessarily grand or preening: *The Simpsons* provides a pretty fair version of it.

But that's lately. In past centuries, the word was both more incendiary and more central, and how you used it revealed which side of the politico-literary fence you were on. From its original Anglo-Saxon sense of "mind, reason, intelligence," it had come by Elizabethan times to be used

Oscar Wilde

of anything clever or ingenious, especially if it was also a little bizarre, paradoxical, or farfetched. The Metaphysical poetry of John Donne (see page 190) in which, as Dr. Johnson noted, "The most heterogeneous ideas are yoked by violence together," was the height of wit in this sense—which was soon being equated with the spirit of poetry itself. So far, so good.

Enter the Augustans of the eighteenth century, who, enamored of the classical proportions and strictures of ancient Rome, had other plans for the word, insisting that, properly used, *wit* tended not toward bizarrerie but, rather, eloquence and precision. Alexander Pope (see page 191) used the word at least forty-six times in his *Essay on Criticism*, most memorably in the lines "True wit is nature to advantage dressed, / What oft was thought, but ne'er so well expressed"; John Dryden said, among other things, that wit, "like a nimble spaniel, beats o'er and ranges thro' the field of memory, till it springs the quarry it hunted after." Their point: that everybody should stop associating wit with the Metaphysicals (whom the Augustans loathed, and who wouldn't be reconstructed until T. S. Eliot spoke up for them a couple of centuries later) and start associating it with *them*.

The nineteenth century didn't care much for the word "wit" (preferring, among others, imagination) and allowed it to languish, to the point that it was soon synonymous with mere levity; Matthew Arnold, for instance, struck Chaucer—not to mention Pope—from the list of great poets because he was "witty": He lacked high seriousness. Now the word, like the Metaphysicals—not to mention Pope—has achieved respectability once more: It's not that high seriousness is out (like heavy meals), just that getting it said fast, and maybe even piquantly, is, like the perfect sorbet or the perfect chèvre salad, very much in.

IRONY

Socrates

Unlike *wit*, its meaning, or rather bundle of meanings, has held fairly steady over time: Always it's implied that there are two sets of listeners keyed in to the same statement, story, or piece of information, and that one of them gets it—sees it for what it is, in all its poignancy or complexity or awfulness—and the other one doesn't. If you're in the former set, congratulations: The ability to recognize irony, especially in writing (where there are no facial expressions or vocal inflections to help it, and you, along), has for centuries been regarded as one of the surest tests of intelligence and sophistication.

The word derives from *eiron*, one of the basic character types in Greek drama, the trickster who pretends he's ignorant, thereby provoking somebody else to reveal his most ludicrous side. Not that this technique was confined to the stage:

Socrates, for instance, acted the part of the *eiron* when he asked those apparently pointless, naïve questions of his students, only to demolish the kids in the end. Thus was born *Socratic irony*, where those who are in on the game smile knowingly as their master's feigned ignorance routs dogma, superstition, and/or popular wisdom.

More common is *dramatic irony*, also called *tragic irony*, where the audience knows something—or many things—the characters on stage don't, and consequently can read doom into all the innocent, trivial remarks they make. You know: Oedipus vows revenge on the murderer of his father, and all of us (whether because we're already familiar with the tale, as even children were in ancient Greece, or whether because the omniscient chorus spilled the beans while Oedipus was out of earshot) gasp.

Verbal irony, by contrast, is no more complicated than calling a three-hundred-pound linebacker Tiny, or saying "Brutus is an honorable man" when what you really mean is that he's a junkyard dog. It is, though, more complicated than sarcasm, which is almost always heavy-handed and caustic (and spoken), and it can sometimes leave you wondering what, exactly, the intended meaning is. It can also be extremely moving, as when Mercutio says, of his death wound in *Romeo and Juliet*, "No, 'tis not so deep as a well, nor so wide as a church door; but 'tis enough, 'twill serve."

For the graduate student: You'll also want to take note of *cosmic irony*, where God mocks, thwarts, or sports with us mere-mortal types; the classic example here is the last sentence of Thomas Hardy's *Tess of the D'Urbervilles*: "The President of the Immortals, in Aeschylean phrase, had ended his sport with Tess." And of *romantic irony*, especially prominent—as the name suggests—in the early nineteenth century, in which the author reveals that his characters are just fictions, after all, being created and manipulated by him, as in Byron's long satiric poem "Don Juan" (pronounced, just this once, "JOO-en").

And everybody: Given that you've bothered to read (and we to write) all of the above, promise you'll stop saying, "It's ironic," when all you mean, really, is that it's a little odd.

AMBIGUITY

You're right to be suspicious of it in a contract, even in a conversation. But ambiguity—from the Latin *ambi-*, "both," plus *agere*, "drive"—is, it turns out, not such a bad thing in literature, especially poetry, where nobody has to choose between meanings the way he might have to in a courtroom or on a street corner. Classic example: in Shakespeare, Hotspur's drumming up antagonism to Henry IV by saying, "We must have bloody noses and crack'd crowns / And pass them current too"—where the crowns in question are first of all coins, second heads,

William Empson

and third what kings wear, and where a single word thus manages to hint at the action, and the most important theme, of the play.

The final authority on ambiguity, by the way, is William Empson, the British literary critic who wrote, in 1930, *Seven Types of Ambiguity*, still beloved of English professors and comp-lit grad students, where he defined "ambiguity" as "any verbal nuance, however slight, which gives room for alternative reactions to the same piece of language." The seven types, for the record, range from seemingly unconnected meanings contained in a single word, to alternative meanings that together clarify an author's state of mind, to a statement that's so obviously loopy that the reader has no choice but to invent his own meaning.

Empson goes on and on about all this, but all you have to worry about remembering is that, even in poetry, ambiguity can be a good thing (involving, in Empson's words, "intricacy, delicacy, or compression of thought") or a bad one (reflective of "weakness or thinness of thought"). That, and not using "ambiguous" when what you really mean is "ambivalent"—when you mean somebody is *feeling* conflicted about something, is of two minds about it: Language exhibits ambiguity; people feel ambivalence.

Bellying Up to the Bard

It's not just that we don't know much about Shakespeare the man; it's not just that what he wrote presents so many obstacles (the overwhelming textual complexities, the outmoded theatrical conventions, the fact that the heroes have all been played by Richard Burton); it's that there's so much riding on having a meaningful relationship with him. Sorry, we can't do much more than make the introductions; what the two of you do in the clinches is your problem.

In the meantime, whether things ultimately work out for you or not, you still ought to know what the plays are all about. Like everyone else, we've divided them up into four categories. Also, we've asked **Henry Popkin**, a Shakespeare-scholar neighbor of ours, for some deep background on one play from each category, plus a once-over of the rest. Still don't know what to make of the whole business? Take a look at what some other literary titans have had to say about Shakespeare over the years.

As to who it is, precisely, that you're spending time with here, well, that's been the source of endless gossip. Skeptics have ascribed authorship of Shakespeare's plays to everyone from Francis Bacon and the seventeenth Earl of Oxford to an Arab sheik named Zubair.

THE HISTORIES

Shakespeare's history plays—there are ten of them—tell the story of England from the end of the fourteenth century to the reign of Henry VIII, father of Elizabeth, the woman who gave us the adjective "Elizabethan." (One, about Bad King John, is set roughly two centuries earlier than the rest.) It's hard to find a contemporary analogue to what Shakespeare was doing in his histories, obsessed as they are with civil strife and rebellion, with "order and degree." The historical novel comes to mind, of course. But in terms of the popularity these plays enjoyed, the way they came out in installments, and the extent to which they focused on certain rich, ingrown, and acrimonious families, it's probably *The Sopranos* we really should be talking about.

Close-up: *Henry IV, Part I*

> Can honour set to a leg? No: Or an arm? No: Or take away the grief of a wound? No. Honour hath no skill in surgery then? No. What is honour? A word. What is in that word honour? Air. A trim reckoning! Who hath it? He that died o' Wednesday. Doth he feel it? No. Doth he hear it? No. 'Tis insensible then? Yea, to the dead. But will [it] not live with the living? No. Why? Detraction will not suffer it. Therefore, I'll none of it. Honour is a mere scutcheon—and so ends my catechism.
>
> Act 5, scene 1

A Scene from Henry IV, Part I

A play that got away from its author. While surely intended to focus on Hal, the future Henry V, as the embodiment of the perfect prince, a model of courage, common sense, and fidelity to his father, King Henry IV, it winds up lingering most fondly over—and etching most sharply—the volatile young rebel Hotspur and the Rabelaisian old reprobate Falstaff. Granted, the former, full of foolhardiness and childish resentments, and the latter, with his steadfast refusal to take anything to heart beyond simple self-preservation, could not have governed England (at least not an England we could bear living in), but we'd rather share a pot of ale (or a container of yogurt) with either than with Shakespeare's cold-blooded paragon.

The first half of the play enforces the contrasts by cutting back and forth between the conspiracy that Hotspur, his father, and his uncle—the redoubtable Percy family, who had helped Henry IV depose Richard II and now think themselves unfairly ignored—lead against the King, and the highway robbery being planned by Falstaff. Hal eventually scotches both schemes, thwarting Falstaff's plan to rob the King's treasury at Gadshill and Hotspur's plan to rob him of his realm at Shrewsbury. The dual successes may make a man of Hal, but they don't make him any more endearing.

The genius of the play lies in its integration of something like realistic comedy into a chronicle-play format and in its depiction of Falstaff—equal parts wit and fool, philosopher and con man, hypocrite and debunker. In fact, Falstaff was such a favorite of Elizabethan audiences that he was brought back in both *Henry IV, Part II* and *The Merry Wives of Windsor* (and his death reported at the beginning of *Henry V*). Critics disagree on whether Falstaff is a coward or not, and on whether he really expects his lies to be believed, but the majority of them maintain not only that he is the most superbly rendered comic figure in all of Shakespeare, but that, in six centuries of English literature, only Chaucer's Wife of Bath gets off anywhere near the same number of good lines.

The Other Histories

Henry VI, Parts I, II, and III—Early Shakespeare, set against a background of England's sixty-three-year Wars of the Roses, between the House of Lancaster and that of York, and guaranteed to induce such objections on the part of the uninitiated as: What's the plot? Who's the hero? Isn't there too much going on? And how can you do that to Joan of Arc? The three-part sequence examines the problems created by a king who is weak and who has only a dubious title to his throne. Shakespeare would deal more neatly with the same issues a few years later, with *Richard II*, his study in weak character, and *Henry IV*, his study in dubious title.

Richard III—You may want to think of it as *Henry VI, Part IV*. No shades of gray here: Richard is totally evil. He's also totally entertaining, and ascends to the throne by slaughtering a clutch of its legitimate heirs. Eventually he's over-

---

I remember, the Players have often mentioned it as an honour to *Shakespeare*, that in his writing, (whatsoever he penned) he never blotted out a line. My answer hath been, would he had blotted a thousand.

Ben Jonson

thrown—by a prince not in the least evil and much less entertaining, but whose dynastic claims are impeccable, whose marriage ends the Wars of the Roses, and whose granddaughter will turn out to be Elizabeth I. The best scenes: Richard's wooing of the Lady Anne and the downfall of the Duke of Buckingham, his early supporter. The most famous lines: "A horse! a horse! My kingdom for a horse!" and "Now is the winter of our discontent / Made glorious summer by the sun of York."

King John—He of the Magna Carta, which means another history with, instead of a royal hero, a royal villain. But not without a hero altogether: That's the Bastard Faulconbridge, son of Richard the Lion-Hearted. More rhetoric here than poetry, it's often said, specifically much noodling about such contemporary political issues as the rights and duties of kings, the wisdom of inheritance by primogeniture, and the relation of secular rulers to spiritual ones.

Richard II—Richard loves to play at being king and gets off some rather good poetry on the subject, but he is the victim of indecision, effeminacy, and bad advisors, and he is eventually overthrown by the hard, efficient Bolingbroke, who'll take the throne as Henry IV. The first really developed "tragedy of character" in the English drama—and the first of the four parts of Shakespeare's second, or mature, history cycle, to be followed by the two halves of *Henry IV* and *Henry V*. Most famous speech, hands down: "This happy breed of men, this little world, / This precious stone set in the silver sea." Runnerup: "For God's sake, let us sit upon the ground, / And tell sad stories of the death of kings."

Henry IV, Part II—In which Prince Hal is required to reject the irrepressible Falstaff for the sake of higher duty: "Reply not to me with a fool-born jest: / Presume not that I am the thing I was." Comedy looms larger here than history, though, and Falstaff (especially with Hotspur gone) larger than any other three characters put together. Perhaps to make Hal look better, the play also gives us a really shameless opportunist in the person of his brother John.

Henry V—Prince Hal, now a hero-king, conquers France. His old drinking buddies get the worst of it again, being unfavorably contrasted with a cross-section

Shakespear, (whom you and ev'ry Play-house bill
Style the divine, the matchless, what you will)
For gain, not glory, wing'd his roving flight,
And grew immortal in his own despight.
                                      Alexander Pope

of doughty British soldiers (reminiscent of the bomber-crew movies of World War II, with Wales and Scotland corresponding roughly to Brooklyn and Chicago). The two most famous lines: "Once more unto the breach, dear friends, once more," and "We few, we happy few, we band of brothers."

Henry VIII—This play, Shakespeare's last, has had its problems: Shakespeare didn't write it alone, the portrait of the King is blurry, and the Globe Theatre burned down when wadding from onstage cannon charges ignited during its production. Still, the characters of Catherine of Aragon and Cardinal Wolsey have managed to catch the occasional fancy of actors and/or audience.

THE COMEDIES

It helps to keep in mind that, during the Renaissance, a play did not have to be a barrel of laughs to be called a comedy; any drama with a happy ending and a generally optimistic point of view fulfilled the requirements. If the plot also revolved around a temporarily troubled love affair, you had romantic comedy, the genre that, from about 1595 to 1600, was Shakespeare's forte and that hit its peak with his three so called joyous comedies, *Much Ado About Nothing*, *As You Like It*, and *Twelfth Night*, all of which satisfied their audiences' desire for escapist entertainment. After 1600, with a more somber mood reigning in England and theater audiences becoming both more sophisticated and more cynical, the tone of the plays changed; the three "problem" comedies, *Troilus and Cressida*, *All's Well That Ends Well*, and especially *Measure for Measure*, hardly seem like comedies at all, except for those inevitable—and barely believable—happy endings.

Close-up: *Twelfth Night*

> What is love? 'tis not hereafter;
> Present mirth hath present laughter;
>   What's to come is still unsure:
> In delay there lies no plenty;
> Then come and kiss me, sweet and twenty,
>   Youth's a stuff will not endure.
>
>   Act 2, scene 3

Illyria is a center of self-indulgence, a morass of misplaced love and the rejection of life—or the overeager embracing of it, sometimes by the same person. Its duke, Orsino, wastes most of his energy being lovesick over Olivia, who has spurned him. She, having renounced life to mourn her dead brother, switches

Twelfth Night

over to another losing proposition, a fixation on Cesario, who is really Viola in drag. Malvolio, obsessed by self-love, is soon convinced that Olivia is as crazy about him as he is about himself.

That most of the major characters spend most of the play mooning about or making fools of themselves is not surprising, given that *Twelfth Night* is the closest thing Shakespeare ever wrote to a *musical* comedy—someone is forever breaking into a pavane or one of those apparently tuneless Elizabethan ditties (like the one above), and nearly everyone in the play seems to be taking a holiday, like they did in old Fred Astaire–Ginger Rogers movies. In fact, *Twelfth Night* was named for a holiday, the twelfth night of Christmas.

Viola, of course, is taking a holiday from her true identity by dressing up as a man. But although Malvolio and Sebastian also disguise themselves, very little of this play's comic effect depends on mistaken identity. Instead, its humor comes from the human failings of its characters. It is the characters—even the minor ones—that really make *Twelfth Night*: The sensible Viola is probably Shakespeare's most lovable heroine, and the conceited, priggish Malvolio is the character everyone remembers best, partly because narcissists were rare in Elizabethan drama and partly because the rather cruel way he's treated by the other characters was immensely satisfying to Elizabethan audiences and wrings sympathy from modern ones.

Shakespeare approximates the remote, and familiarises the wonderful; the event which he represents will not happen, but if it were possible, its effects would probably be such as he has assigned; and it may be said, that he has not only shown human nature as it acts in real exigencies, but as it would be found in trials, to which it cannot be exposed.

Samuel Johnson

The Other Comedies

The Comedy of Errors—This very early, uncharacteristically farcical comedy, drawn from two Roman plays by Plautus, gets most of its laughs from mistaken identity, with a sprinkling of marriage jokes thrown in. What's surprising is that, as pure sitcom, it still works on the modern stage.

The Two Gentlemen of Verona—An interesting forerunner of the kind of romantic comedy that Shakespeare was to make one of his distinctive genres, exhibiting all the imaginable extremes of fidelity, gallantry, and melancholy, as if the dramatist was staking out the boundaries within which his subsequent comedies would be enacted. In Valentine and Proteus, the "two gentlemen" whose friendship turns to rivalry, and Silvia and Julia, their lady friends, he also begins to formulate his method of using contrast to establish character.

Love's Labours Lost—Lots of learned wit, not all of it easily decipherable by contemporary audiences, in this story of a king and three courtiers who undertake a rest-and-study cure but quickly change their plans when a princess and her three ladies-in-waiting turn up. Shakespeare's attention keeps shifting—probably a sign that the play kept being rewritten.

The Taming of the Shrew—Let's not kid ourselves. This *is* a male-chauvinist play: Petruchio does eventually subjugate the self-willed Katharina. The best that can be said for her, finally, is that she learns to exchange clever remarks with him, but she must submit totally on every issue that counts. Shakespeare's treatment of his heroine, however, merely reflects the standard Elizabethan view of a woman's place, according to which Petruchio really does Kate a favor by forcing her to accept her proper role. By the way, in those days, *shrew* was pronounced "shrow," which explains why many of the play's rhymes seem a bit off.

A Midsummer Night's Dream—Shakespeare's first comic masterpiece is a compliment to love, but a backhanded one, given the quarrelsome marriage of Oberon and Titania, the marriage by conquest of Theseus and Hippolyta, the lampooning of tales of true love in the play within a play, and the mismatched infatuations in the forest. All of which makes it hard to tell the difference between love and lunacy. In Puck, the beneficent goblin, and Bottom, the weaver, who winds up with an ass's head, Shakespeare created two of his most memorable minor characters.

*L*ike a miraculous celestial Light-ship, woven all of sheet-lightning and sunbeams.
Thomas Carlyle

The Merchant of Venice—In this double plot, the courtship of Portia pits the true values of Belmont, her home, against the false values of Venice, which thinks life is all about gold, silver, and justice (as opposed to mercy). Although the play is classed as a romantic comedy, the emphasis is more on friendship than on love, and the question of anti-Semitism inherent in Shakespeare's portrayal of Shylock always gets more attention than either.

Much Ado About Nothing—The witty exchanges of the unwilling lovers Benedict and Beatrice make for much of this comedy's charm. On the other hand, Claudio's bitter denunciations of Hero, the woman he so recently adored, tend to distress modern audiences with their cruelty. As the title suggests, confusions and misunderstandings abound, compounded by the two monumentally incompetent constables, Dogberry and Verges.

As You Like It—We're in the idyllic Forest of Arden, to which all the good characters have fled from the corrupt court. Our backpackers include: the young nobleman Orlando, who falls in love with Rosalind, daughter of the banished duke (and the first of Shakespeare's self-reliant, no-nonsense heroines), Rosalind's cousin Celia, Jaques (always referred to as "the melancholy Jaques"), and the fool Touchstone. The exiles praise the free life of the forest, but, except for Jaques, they all jump at the chance of going back to civilization.

The Merry Wives of Windsor—Said to have been written in response to Queen Elizabeth's request to see Falstaff in love. If so, the monarch got short weight. This is Falstaff bereft of his wit, and he's not in love, or even in lust, just prodded by vanity and greed. Amiable enough on the whole, however, and the only play in which Shakespeare presents (and defends) the life of his own middle class.

Troilus and Cressida—A romance with an unfaithful woman (Cressida) conducted in the middle of a war (Trojan) over another unfaithful woman (Helen).

Shakespeare's name, you may depend on it, stands absurdly too high and will go down. He had no invention as to stories, none whatever. He took all his plots from old novels, and threw their stories into a dramatic shape, at as little expense of thought as you or I could turn his plays back again into prose tales. That he threw over whatever he did write some flashes of genius, nobody can deny: but this was all. Suppose anyone to have had the dramatic handling for the first time of such ready-made stories as Lear, Macbeth, &c. and he would be a sad fellow indeed, if he did not make something very grand of them.

George Gordon, Lord Byron

War and love are shown to be equally vicious and destructive. Or, as Thersites says, "Lechery, lechery; still wars and lechery; nothing else holds fashion." This play squeaks through as comedy on a technicality: The two principals are still alive at the end.

All's Well That Ends Well—Classed, along with *T & C* and *Measure*, as one of the "dark" or "problem" comedies, said to mirror the increasingly pessimistic side of Shakespeare and/or Elizabethan England. This one is the lightest of the three and Helena one of the most endearing of Shakespeare's heroines. Having cured her king of an ailment that baffled the court physicians, she sets out resolutely to track down (and bag) her man, a self-centered nullity under the influence of his friend, the boastful and opportunistic Parolles. That she wants him at all is problematic, but then, Shakespeare never said love had to be reasonable.

Measure for Measure—Scholars like to roll out religious allegory to explain this play, but even with the special pleading it can seem bitter and cynical. The Duke appoints his deputy, Angelo, to clean up the mess he has made in Vienna. Why can't he do it himself? Doesn't he see through Angelo's hypocrisy? If so, he is at fault for putting Vienna at the deputy's mercy. If not, he is incompetent. Isabella's refusal to lay down her virginity to save her brother is understandable, but must she then tell him about it? Isn't the Duke's revenge for Lucio's verbal insults a bit excessive? And what real satisfaction can anybody take in a finale in which sordidness is converted to happiness by fiat? Are you starting to see the problem? Do you care?

I keep saying Shakespeare, Shakespeare, you are as obscure as life is.
Matthew Arnold

What is he? You might almost answer, He is the earth . . . the globe . . . existence. . . . In Shakespeare the birds sing, the rushes are clothed with green, hearts love, souls suffer, the cloud wanders, it is hot, it is cold, night falls, time passes, forests and multitudes speak, the vast eternal dream hovers over all. Sap and blood, all forms of the multiple reality, actions and ideas, man and humanity, the living and the life, solitudes, cities, religions, diamonds and pearls, dunghills and charnel houses, the ebb and flow of beings, the steps of comers and goers, all, all are on Shakespeare and in Shakespeare; and, this genius being the earth, the dead emerge from it.
Victor Hugo

THE TRAGEDIES

Amazingly, nineteenth-century audiences preferred the comedies; it's only since the twentieth century that they have been impressed by Shakespeare's tragedies—at least, with those four tragedies generally acknowledged as his greatest: *Hamlet*, *Othello*, *Macbeth*, and *King Lear*. All of these were written between 1601 and 1606, after Shakespeare began leaning toward heavily symbolic, multilayered plots that clearly juxtaposed good and evil. Combine these elements with the kind of psychological complexity that only a terribly unhappy character can put across, and you can see why the tragedies jibe so nicely with the modern sensibility.

Close-up: *King Lear*

> Blow, winds, and crack your cheeks! Rage! Blow!
> You cataracts and hurricanoes, spout
> Till you have drench'd our steeples, drown'd the cocks!
> You sulphurous and thought-executing fires,
> Vaunt-couriers to oak-cleaving thunderbolts,
> Singe my white head! And thou, all-shaking thunder,
> Smite flat the thick rotundity o' the world!
> Crack nature's molds, all germens spill at once,
> That make ingrateful man!
>
> Act 3, scene 2

"If you have tears, prepare to shed them now." Though this line comes from *Julius Caesar*, it applies best to *King Lear*, which, increasingly, scholars and critics have come to regard as the most bitter, bleak, and pessimistic—as well as the greatest—of Shakespeare's tragedies.

King Lear, Act I, Scene 1, *painted by Edwin Austin Abbey*

The play's opening events hardly prepare us for the bombshells that follow. Retiring from power and dividing his kingdom, Lear relies, outrageously, on a single test—his daughters' public declarations of love. Offended by this silliness, Cordelia, his favorite and the only one of his three daughters who is genuinely devoted to him, brusquely rejects his demand. That's all it takes to propel Lear—and us—inexorably through five acts of unspeakable anguish, culminating in the deaths of both Lear and Cordelia. And why? Not just because Lear has a dumb view of human relations. The fact is that this is a terrible world, filled with evil and unimaginable cruelty. What comfort there is doesn't derive from anything as trivial (and as unattainable) as a happy ending, but from the warmth and joy Lear and Cordelia feel when they are temporarily reunited. Lear has learned a lot, but the tuition was a killer.

There is nothing halfhearted about the play's tragic effects; no one gets hurt just a little. Lear, having abdicated, doesn't shuffle off to a tower room to do jigsaw puzzles; he is driven out, crazed, to seek shelter on the heath in a raging storm. Cordelia is hanged in prison. Gloucester's punishment for being misled about his legitimate son, Edgar, and for being faithful to his king is to be blinded—on stage.

King Lear is full of the kind of significant parallels Shakespeare liked to use to reinforce his effects. Gloucester is a second tragic father, also brought to grief for failing to distinguish between his good and bad children. Lear, judging his daughters' devotion to him by the number of knights they will allow him, is repeating his original mistake of trying to measure love. Meanwhile, a virtual symphony of madness is being played out in the delirium of Lear, the feigned lunacy of Edgar, and the addled wisdom of the Fool, who pretty much sums up the moral of the play when he tells Lear, "Thou shouldst not have been old till thou hadst been wise."

The Other Tragedies

Titus Andronicus—Lots of blood and gore, with about as much substance as a Charles Bronson movie and a similar cumulative effect—that is, if you can imagine Bronson as a victorious Roman general who sets out to avenge the rape and mutilation of his daughter, Lavinia. Not a play to win raves from the critics, who like to think of it either as the work of a young Shakespeare out to have a hit at any cost, or as not the work of Shakespeare at all.

Romeo and Juliet—The world's most famous star-crossed lovers play out the world's worst run of luck. Although it contains some beautiful poetry and a couple of brilliantly developed minor characters (Mercutio and the Nurse), and despite the moralizing of twentieth-century remakes like *West Side Story*, this one is really just what it appears to be—a classic tearjerker.

Julius Caesar—Ruined for most of us by being taught in high school, when we were too young to care about anyone as noble and good as Brutus, whose tragedy this really is. (We were just confused and irritated when the title character got killed off in the middle of the action.) True, the plot is more straightforward than most of Shakespeare's, but the play's austerity isn't for sixteen-year-olds.

Hamlet—The Master's shot at one of the big box-office genres of his day—the revenge tragedy, in which, nine times out of ten, a treacherous murder is avenged by a tireless pursuer, with plenty of carnage along the way. Shakespeare's addition of a psychological and philosophical dimension, and his creation of a hero who thinks so much that he can't get the job done, have, however, sufficed to discourage Jean-Claude Van Damme (though not, it's true, Mel Gibson) from attempting a movie version.

Othello—All about the deceptiveness of appearances. Othello's black exterior is no guide to his noble character. "Honest Iago" is untrustworthy. Desdemona, who is innocence itself, gets smeared. And Cassio, who has been fooling around with a courtesan, is really a fine fellow after all.

Macbeth—Don't fall for the victim-of-circumstances line. Not only does Macbeth murder his king and slaughter a whole family of innocents, but the business about his wrestling with his conscience has been greatly exaggerated. He worries only about the practical consequences, not the ethical implications, of his evil deeds. When his wife judges him to be "too full o' th' milk of human kindness," she doesn't mean what we mean by "kindness," and besides, she's hardly an authority on the subject.

Antony and Cleopatra—Overly complex, perhaps, but then Shakespeare had a lot to deal with here: the decline and fall of Antony, who, although he's the victim of his own unbridled passion, can't be made to seem a total fool; the development of Cleopatra from a selfish little twit into someone whose death by asp moves us; and the depiction of Rome and Egypt as two different and opposing worlds, without the benefit of split-screen technology.

Timon of Athens—A kind of morality play about worldly vanity. Timon, a nobleman, goes broke entertaining his friends, who then refuse to have anything to do with him. He becomes a hermit and a cynic, whom, for all practical purposes, we can forget about. An acknowledged mess, *Timon* was probably tinkered with beyond recognition.

Coriolanus—At last, a tragedy in which *both* sides repel us—the aristocratic Coriolanus with his noblesse oblige and his contempt for the masses, and the scheming tribunes who play on those masses' foolishness, fickleness, and gullibility. Because of its ambiguity, the play has been easy to use propagandistically; it was staged as a pro-Fascist parable in France between the wars, and later rewritten from a Marxist perspective by Bertolt Brecht.

THE ROMANCES

"Romances" is what scholars call the four comedies that Shakespeare wrote after his prosperous company took over the Blackfriars Theatre in 1608 and began requiring texts different from those he had been supplying earlier. More wistful, more melancholy, and more atmospheric than anything that had preceded them, the Blackfriars plays were staged at night in a closed, artificially lit environment, and cost considerably more money. Their wealthier, better-educated audience expected emotional, heart-wrenching poetry, extravagant incident, extended suffering, and perilous escapes—then a happy ending.

Close-up: *The Tempest*

Scene from The Tempest, *rendered by Henry Fuseli*

> . . . These our actors,
> As I foretold you, were all spirits and
> Are melted into air, into thin air;
> And, like the baseless fabric of this vision,
> The cloud-capped towers, the gorgeous palaces,
> The solemn temples, the great globe itself,
> Yea, all which it inherit, shall dissolve,
> And, like this insubstantial pageant faded,
> Leave not a rack behind. We are such stuff
> As dreams are made on, and our little life
> Is rounded with a sleep. Sir, I am vexed.
> Bear with my weakness; my old brain is troubled.
> Be not disturbed with my infirmity.
> If you be pleased, retire into my cell
> And there repose. . . .

Act 4, scene 1

The Tempest is the last play wholly written by Shakespeare. As a result, generations of readers have viewed it as the culmination of his vision, identifying Prospero, the magician and duke-in-exile, who now presides over a desert island, with the playwright, and the play itself with Shakespeare's farewell to his art and subsequent retirement to Stratford. This may or may not have been conscious on Shakespeare's part, but certainly *The Tempest* represents a heartfelt return to naïveté after the complexity and weight of the great tragedies.

Here's the plot: Prospero seizes an opportunity to get back at his usurping brother and restore himself as Duke of Milan. He creates a storm and shipwreck, netting not only the brother, but also a fit suitor for his daughter, Miranda; the suitor's father, the King of Naples; the suitor's father's brother, likewise treacherous; and all their retainers. Conspiracies ensue, some "upstairs," some "downstairs," but Prospero's magic is sufficient to vanquish all comers. Ultimately *The Tempest*, like all the romances, is a play of reconciliation, and Prospero turns benign and forgiving. He arranges a marriage that unites two previously hostile families—and presents a masque that elegantly celebrates that marriage. (Appropriately, the play helped to celebrate the betrothal of King James' daughter, Elizabeth.)

When Shakespeare wrote *The Tempest*, he had been reading travelers' tales and was mindful of a recent shipwreck that had taken place off Bermuda. He must also have been thinking about the practical effects of such travelers' activities; accordingly, *The Tempest* is in some respects a parable of colonialism. In the two creatures who had greeted Prospero after his own shipwreck years earlier (and who then became his servants), we have the perfect image of the good and the bad native: Ariel cooperates and serves his master by helping to oppress the rest of the population, while the bestial Caliban (a near anagram for "cannibal") instigates the archetypal colonialist nightmare by trying to rape Miranda. All of which raises larger issues, i.e.: Is nature superior to civilization and, by extension, to art? And in which state—nature or civilization—is man nobler?

---

*T*he fact is, we are growing out of Shakespeare. Byron declined to put up with his reputation at the beginning of the nineteenth century; and now, at the beginning of the twentieth, he is nothing but a household pet. His characters still live; his word pictures of woodland and wayside still give us a Bank-holiday breath of country air; his verse still charms us; his sublimities still stir us; the commonplaces and trumperies of the wisdom which age and experience bring to all the rest of us are still expressed by him better than by anybody else; but we have nothing to hope from him, and nothing to learn from him—not even how to write plays, though he does that so much better than most modern dramatists.

George Bernard Shaw

The Other Romances

Pericles—Apparently an old play partially rewritten by Shakespeare, and the first of the romances, complete with wonderful adventures in strange places, long separations, deaths not real but feared, etc., etc. Consider Marina, unpredictably saved from a murderer by pirates, sold by her rescuers to a brothel, and so resolute in her purity that she's able to convert the brothel's patrons. Realism it's not, but it has a certain archaic charm.

Cymbeline—An odd concoction, mingling Celtic Britain and ancient Rome, with a plot that is no more than a machine for producing sensations, overflowing with abductions, disguises, magic potions, and mistaken identities. The central story pits Princess Imogen, daughter of King Cymbeline of Britain, against the new queen, her stepmother, who's determined that Imogen marry her cloddish son Cloten. Still to come: Imogen's "seduction" by Iachimo, a kind of cut-rate Iago; her encounter with her two long-lost brothers; her mistaking Cloten's headless body for that of her true husband, Posthumus; and the dream sequence, featuring a personal appearance by Jupiter.

A Winter's Tale—The fact that a character exits "pursued by a bear" is no more outrageous than King Leontes' sudden, entirely unmotivated jealousy of his wife, Hermione, or her decision to teach him a lesson by turning into a statue for sixteen years. Then there's the matter of Bohemia, notoriously landlocked, having been issued a seacoast. In other words, the events of the play are patently fantastical, contributing to an atmosphere that is part fairy tale and part allegory, in which we travel from court to countryside, from winter to summer, and from death to life.

I do not believe that any writer has ever exposed this *bovaryisme*, the human will to see things as they are not, more clearly than Shakespeare.

T. S. Eliot

---

*W*hen I read Shakespeare I am struck with wonder
That such trivial people should muse and thunder
In such lovely language.

D. H. Lawrence

FIVE DEFINITIONS (OUT OF FIVE THOUSAND OR SO) THAT MIGHT MAKE THE GOING A LITTLE EASIER

DIE—Can mean "to come in lovemaking: to have an orgasm." This is what Benedick means in *Much Ado About Nothing* when he says, "I will live in thy heart, die in thy lap, and be buried in thy eyes." Heady knowledge, but use it sparingly: "Die" usually means "to die."

FOOL—Often a term of endearment, as it is at the end of *King Lear* when Lear says, "My poor fool is dead." He means Cordelia, not the Fool, whose absence from the latter part of the play nobody ever bothers to explain.

HORNS—The adornment and symbol of the cheated-on husband, the cuckold. Alluded to when Othello says, "I have a pain upon my forehead here." More often, the basis of the favorite family of jokes among the Elizabethans, who seemed to think any reference to horns was in and of itself uproarious.

HUMOUR—Mood, idiosyncrasy, temperament. Bottom in *A Midsummer Night's Dream* means the first when he says, "Yet my chief humour is for a tyrant." (He likes to play tyrants.) Never as in our "sense of humor." But in making "humour" such a prominent word in *The Merry Wives of Windsor*, Shakespeare was probably giving a nod to Ben Jonson, who in such plays as *Every Man in His Humour*, popularized a more formal concept of the "four humours": When phlegm, or blood, or yellow bile, or black bile is dominant in somebody, he is rendered phlegmatic, or sanguine, or choleric, or melancholic, rather than "good-humoured," i.e., emotionally balanced.

QUICK—In addition to the meaning we're most familiar with ("acting speedily"), can mean "vital, vigorous, full of energy"; "sharp, piercing"; or—here's the important one—"living, endowed with life," and, by extension, "pregnant." Hence a phrase like "the quick and the dead" and a line like, in *Love's Labour's Lost*, "The poor wench is cast away; she's quick; the child brags in her belly already."

That would be George Bernard Shaw, who lived about three hundred years after Shakespeare and who beats out Christopher Marlowe, Ben Jonson, William Congreve, Richard Brinsley Sheridan, and Oscar Wilde for the slot. True, he's not really English, but Anglo-Irish. And, unlike Shakespeare, he's not just a dramatist (or, more precisely, a dramatist with a taste for sonnet sequences). He's an insatiable critic, a prolific letter writer, and an indefatigable social reformer. A know-it-all with a sense of humor, Shaw took it upon himself to lecture (and upbraid) his era on his era, and went on doing so from the late nineteenth century to his death in 1950.

The plays are of varying degrees of heaviness, acerbity, and outrage, with varying ratios of polemic to farce. Even a relatively benign one like *Pygmalion* (the basis for *My Fair Lady*) manages to send up the class structure, relations between the sexes, and the idea of education. In the early *Widowers' Houses* and *Mrs. Warren's Profession*, Shaw skewers slum landlordism and prostitution, respectively; in *Major Barbara*, soup-kitchen evangelism; in *Heartbreak House*, the human species and civilization in general. Shaw's masterpiece (or, as his critics would have it, his attempt at a great play): *Saint Joan*, in which the famous martyr is revealed as a model of clear-eyed common sense.

In all the plays, Shaw's intention is to shake his audience's complacency, challenge its hypocrisy, and demonstrate how anybody who isn't part of the solution is de facto part of the problem. And neither the problem nor the solution is, in Shaw's hands, what you may have begun by thinking it was. Thus, he writes in a preface, *Mrs. Warren's Profession* was written "to draw attention to the truth that prostitution is caused, not by female depravity or male licentiousness, but simply by underpaying, undervaluing, and overworking women so shamefully that the poorest of them are forced to resort to prostitution to keep body and soul together."

Three cautions when approaching Shaw: Wit is one of his hallmarks, but it's in the service of intellect rather than simple entertainment; don't expect a cascade of Oscar Wilde–style epigrams and absurdities from him. Then: It's easier to read Shaw than to see it performed; in fact, with their explicit and endless stage descriptions, his plays can verge on novels, and a lot of the arguments repay (and require) study. Finally: Remember the adjective form of Shaw's name— "Shavian," with a long *a*.

Let's Pause for a Moment and Consider Boswell's Life of Johnson

He received me very courteously; but it must be confessed that his apartment, and furniture, and morning dress, were sufficiently uncouth. His brown suit of clothes looked very rusty; he had on a little old shrivelled unpowdered wig, which was too small for his head; his shirtneck and knees of his breeches were loose; his black worsted stockings ill drawn up; and he had a pair of unbuckled shoes by way of slippers. But all these slovenly particulars were forgotten the moment that he began to talk.

Published in 1791, James Boswell's *The Life of Samuel Johnson, LL.D.* is still the greatest biography in the English language and a gold mine of conspicuous erudition. In fact, in the days, not so very long ago, when people aspired to intellectual superiority the way they currently yearn for vast real estate holdings, the ability to quote Boswell quoting Johnson constituted the basic literacy test in some (admittedly preposterous) social circles.

Don't look for a story line; just think of the book as a talk show with a particularly entertaining guest and an interviewer who knows enough to shut up and listen. And don't let the scholarly reputation scare you off; Johnson the eighteenth-century savant seemed awesome even to his contemporaries, but making him accessible was Boswell's mission in life.

Essentially a quick succession of close-ups of Johnson holding forth, the biography is three-dimensional and so fast-paced that you may feel like you're being whisked from one dinner party to another without ever having time for a cigar. Before the evening's over, however, Johnson will have come alive, and, although none of his aphorisms will help you get rid of cellulite or make a killing in corn futures, you'll probably find both his unshakable moral certitude and his way with words fortifying.

Keep in mind that Johnson was not only a great conversationalist but the author of the *Dictionary of the English Language*—which he wrote, by himself, over the course of eight years, after reading every notable piece of English literature from Shakespeare's time to his own day and jotting down all the words he thought needed explaining—and a famous "Preface to Shakespeare," among a great many other works. Also that Boswell was no ordinary biographer but a man obsessed with his subject, a writer whose prodigious memory, application, and style revolutionized the genre.

Finally, you might want to memorize a few bits of Johnsonese yourself, just in case intellectual snobbism comes into vogue again during your lifetime. Here are some good ones to toss off in the drawing room, bearing in mind, of course that your timing, as well as your delivery, must be impeccable:

If he does really think that there is no distinction between vice and virtue, why, sir, when he leaves our houses let us count our spoons.

Sir, a woman preaching is like a dog's walking on his hind legs. It is not done well; but you are surprised to find it done at all.

A man of genius has seldom been ruined but by himself.

That fellow seems to me to possess but one idea, and that is a wrong one.

No man but a blockhead ever wrote except for money.

A cow is a very good animal in the field; but we turn her out of a garden.

Patriotism is the last refuge of a scoundrel.

Were it not for imagination, sir, a man would be as happy in the arms of a chambermaid as a duchess.

Worth seeing? Yes, but not worth going to see.

He is not only dull himself, but the cause of dullness in others.

I have found you an argument; I am not obliged to find you an understanding.

It is better to live rich, than to die rich.

A Bedside Companion to the Nineteenth-Century English Novel

In general, English novels of the nineteenth century are a lot easier to read than, say, Faulkner; they don't ask much more of you than sheer stick-to-it-iveness. But there *is* the problem of understanding what all those characters are traipsing across, riding in, and being offered a glass of. Not to mention the varieties of clergy and degrees of aristocracy they always seem to be bumping into. And then there's the money. Herewith, a partial exegesis of seven difficult areas in Austen, Dickens, Thackeray, Eliot, Meredith, Trollope, Hardy, and yes, the Brontës.

THE TOPOGRAPHY: PICKING YOUR WAY THROUGH THE COUNTRYSIDE

In general, it's gentle. And it's Anglo-Saxon: No buttes, mesas, or steppes need apply.

The Cornfield *by John Constable*

At the Seashore

STRAND—Land bordering a river, lake, or sea; a beach. But especially the area between tidemarks (which means the body of water is more often than not the ocean). In London, the street called the Strand occupies the former shore of the Thames.

SHINGLE—A stretch of beach covered with loose, smooth pebbles and little or no sand. Also, the pebbles themselves.

BIGHT—A bend or indentation in a shoreline (sometimes used of a bend in a river, as well). Therefore, a wide bay formed by such a bend. From an Old English word that meant "bend" or "angle," including those of the body, like the inside of the elbow and the armpit.

In the Woods

GLADE—A clearing in a forest where the sunlight shines down between tall trees. Has a strong positive charge: A glade is a pleasant place to be. ("Glade" is related to "glad," and originally meant "bright.")

COPSE—A thicket of small trees or shrubs. It derives from the French *couper*, "to cut." Emotionally neutral: One might use it as a trysting-place or as a source of kindling wood. Also called "coppice."

GROVE—This one's second nature, but don't lose sight of its salient feature: no undergrowth.

On the Moor

MOOR—A broad tract of open land, usually high but poorly drained, with patches of heath (see below). An expansive, potentially threatening place: Lots happens, emotions run high, limits are hard to set, and Heathcliff goes at it with Cathy.

HEATH—In common parlance, synonymous with "moor," but refers more specifically to that part of a moor that is not quite so soggy and, not totally surprisingly, covered with heather.

FEN—Flat, swampy land; a bog. But especially the kind of swampy land where peat forms, hence a frequent component of moors. The Fens are certain low-lying districts in central England, not far from Cambridge.

In the Meadow

SWARD—Basically, any land covered with grassy turf, whether man-made (a lawn) or natural (a meadow); a wide expanse of green. Usually in heavily forested, densely populated, or somewhat arid areas, swards stand out by contrast. Also spelled "swarth."

LEA—A grassland or meadow, especially one that's gone untilled for a while, as in Gray's "The lowing herd winds slowly o'er the lea." Also spelled "ley" (both forms are pronounced either "lee" or "lay"), it's more aggressively poetical than most of these terms.

SWALE—The thing is, it's cool. Either it's cool because it's shady, or it's cool because it's moist, if not out-and-out marshy. Or both. (They don't always say which.) Also spelled "swail."

In the Valley

VALE—A broad, low-sided valley, generally with a good-sized stream running through it. (By extension, it's the world as a scene of sorrows, with that stream turned into tears.)

DALE—Same as vale, though both more intimate (it's not always broad) and more upbeat (as in the expression "up hill and down dale"). A related word is "dell," guaranteed to be both secluded and woodsy.

GLEN—From a Gaelic word meaning "mountain valley." Now any steep, narrow valley, generally remote and unfrequented—unless by elves.

In the Hills

DOWNS—A plural form (or, less frequently, "down," the singular). An expanse of hilly, grassy upland, good for grazing. Also, the short-wooled sheep developed there. After the Downs, two parallel hill ranges in southern England.

WELD—The same open, rolling country, but with lots of woods. After the Weald, a once-forested area of Kent, Surrey, and Sussex, in southern England. Say "weeld." (From the same root: "wold," an elevated tract of open country or moorland, not necessarily wooded, as in the Cotswolds.)

TOR—England's short on mountains, and this is about as rugged as the landscape gets: a rocky peak, craggy hill, or—at its least dramatic—a pile of rocks on top of a hill.

TARN—A small mountain lake without significant tributaries. Wordsworth and D. H. Lawrence liked to pause by same.

By the Lake

MERE—Not just the lakes of the Lake District (e.g., Windermere, Grasmere, Buttermere). Can be as small as a pond, and is sometimes used of a marsh. Water's what's important: The word is related to the Latin word for "sea."

RILL—A small brook or stream, a rivulet. No big deal, but your mere's probably fed by a few.

WEIR—A fence, enclosure of stakes, wattle, or what-have-you placed in a stream to trap fish. On a larger scale, a dam placed across a river or canal to raise or divert the water or to regulate its flow.

On the Farm

CROFT—A small enclosed field or pasture near a house. Sometimes the whole farm, if it's small and down on its luck (a tenant farm, for instance).

STILE—A set of steps or rungs up one side of a fence or hedge and down the other, of a sort that a person can negotiate easily but a cow can't.

THORP—Where they'll try to take you on Saturday night: the nearest small town or village. They may instead call it a "ham" or a "wick." Look for all three words, now archaic, as elements in English place names.

At the Manor

CHASE—A privately owned, unenclosed game preserve. It's here that one rides to hounds. And that Lady Chatterley dallies with the gamekeeper.

HEDGEROW—A closely planted row of bushes, shrubs, or trees meant to function as a fence or boundary, or as a deliberate interruption of the view. One might make use of a stile to get over a low-slung hedgerow—though ideally not while a guest at a great estate. Save that kind of behavior for your weekend at the croft.

SHIRE—Another word for each of the counties into which England is divided. But the Shires is specifically the fox-hunting district of central England, consisting mainly of Leicestershire and Northamptonshire. Bear in mind, too, that "country life" counted (and counts) for a great deal in England: If one couldn't dazzle London, one might still dazzle one's shire.

In the Garden

BOWER—A shaded, leafy recess, an arbor, into which one withdraws to read or think, and which may be either natural or man-made. (Also, in poetry, a rustic cottage or similar country retreat, or simply a private chamber, even a boudoir.) Spenser's Bower of Bliss is the legendary one, but it's the rare country house that doesn't provide something that passes for a bower.

GAZEBO—A pavilion in the middle of a garden, usually trellised, latticed, cupolaed, and gingerbreaded within an inch of its life. The idea is to stand in it and look all around you: The word is a fanciful takeoff on the Latin future-tense construction and means roughly, "I shall gaze."

HAHA—A staple in Jane Austen novels. It can be a moat, or just a fence, stone wall, or hedge sunk into the ground; either way, it encloses a garden or park without impairing the view. So called after the presumed exclamation of somebody encountering a particular haha for the first time.

THE CLASS STRUCTURE: THE DUKE AT THE TOP OF THE STAIRS

Frankly, it's a relentless business. Also, complicated and patently unfair. And that's today. In the nineteenth century, things were considerably worse; just ask Becky Sharp, Elizabeth Bennet, or Pip. But before you do, glance over this table, which, begging your pardon, sir or ma'am, begins just where you'd expect it to: at the very top.

The Royals

A class—and a law—unto themselves. Even now there are those who consider everyone not born into it (and that includes dukes, duchesses, and the Queen Mother) little better than commoners.

KINGS AND QUEENS: Inaccessible, perhaps, but easy to pick out in a crowd, especially in the nineteenth century, during which there were only four of them. Victoria (reigned 1837–1901) needs no introduction here. Before her came a couple of Georges (between them, they reigned 1760–1830) and one William (IV, 1830–1837). N.B.: The younger George (who would become George IV) ruled 1811–1820 for his father (III), who was declared hopelessly insane (al-

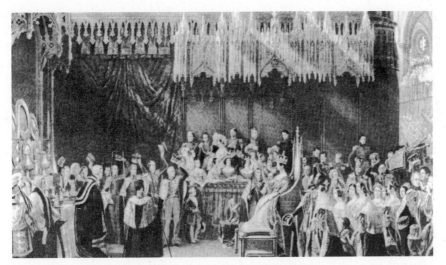

The Coronation of Queen Victoria *by Sir George Hayter*

though he did eventually recover). This period—the Regency—was one of social complacency, moral laxity, and ostentatious display; provided abundant opportunities for clotheshorses and adventurers; and, in a way, provoked Victorianism.

Upon meeting the king or queen: Bow or curtsy—depending on your gender, not theirs—and say "your majesty." Thereafter, say "sir" or "ma'am."

PRINCES AND PRINCESSES: Although in fairly wide use on the Continent (French princes, for instance, are usually *not* royal and rank below dukes), in England the titles are reserved for the children of the sovereign and—feminists take note—those of his grandchildren who are descended through his sons; a ruling queen typically makes her husband a prince, too. (The grandchild provision explains today's Princess Alexandra, a granddaughter of George V through her father, the Duke of Kent; the husband one explains Prince Philip.) In the nineteenth century two princes figured prominently: George, the prince regent, and Albert, Victoria's husband, the prince consort. Prince of Wales is, as you've heard, the title traditionally conferred on the sovereign's oldest son.

Upon meeting a prince or princess: Bow or curtsy and say "your royal highness," subsequently "sir" or "ma'am."

The Nobles

Or, as the English like to say, the peers of the realm, each of whom passes on his title—or as often, package of titles—to his oldest son. Originally the whole business had to do with ownership of land, discharge of feudal obligations, and the wielding of actual power rather than with mere wealth and privilege. For the last few centuries, though, it's meant only that such hereditary peers (who come in five strengths), together with a few "life" peers (who come in only one and whose titles are not bequeathable) and Church of England bigwigs, sit together in the House of Lords and continue, with their wives and children, to provide England with her lords and ladies—and her much-debated class system. (The mnemonic you'll need to remember the five-tiered structure is "Do men ever visit Boston?") N.B.: A duchess, marchioness, etc., is most often the wife of a duke, marquess, etc.; however, if a woman is the oldest daughter of a duke (etc.) in a family with no male heirs, she becomes a duchess (etc.) "in her own right."

DUKES AND DUCHESSES: A very big deal, head and shoulders above the other degrees of the peerage. Historically, throughout Europe dukes controlled vast areas—like Bavaria and Normandy—and pretty much called their own shots. This was never the case in England, where the first duke wasn't created until 1338, but even so, they're a rare and much-deferred-to breed, a couple of dozen in number. There are a few "royal dukes," too, relatives of the sovereign like the late Duke of Windsor or the present Dukes of Gloucester, Kent, and York, who seem to like having a title beyond the "prince" that's theirs by birth. The title has also served as a reward for military heroes, like the Dukes of Marlborough and Wellington.

Upon meeting a duke, say "your grace." His wife, the duchess, is "your grace," too.

MARQUESSES AND MARCHIONESSES: First of all it's "MAR-kwiss" (even when spelled "marquis," in the French manner) and "MAR-shuness," and it comes from "march," an old word for a border territory. The title wasn't well received at first (the first and second honorees complained that "Marquess is a strange name in this kingdom"), but eventually, with Tudor persistence, it gained acceptance. Formerly a reward for viceroys of India upon their return home, and, in 1917, a compensation to relatives of George V when he made them give up their obviously inappropriate German titles, there are almost as few marquesses around as there are dukes.

Upon meeting a marquess—or anybody from the four lower grades of the peerage— say "my lord." Call his wife "madam."

EARLS AND COUNTESSES: William the Conqueror tried, back in the eleventh century, to substitute the Continental title "count," but nobody bit: They were all too fond of the distinction between *eorl*, an Old English word meaning "man of position," and *ceorl*, an Old English word meaning "churl"; besides, "earl" was the only hereditary title around at the time, and it damn well *should* have a native flavor. (Women, on the other hand, seem to have had less resistance to the chic French import—hence "countess.") Today there are a couple of hundred earldoms; particularly effective prime ministers, like Disraeli, the Earl of Beaconsfield, and Anthony Eden, the Earl of Avon, are rewarded with them when they retire.

VISCOUNTS AND VISCOUNTESSES: That's "VYE-count" and "VYE-countess," and the title originally designated the fellow who stood in for the count or, more precisely, given that this is England, the earl. (The "vis-" is like the "vice" in "vice president.") The most recently instituted of the five grades (1440), it's the accepted way to say thank you to a good speaker of the House of Commons.

BARONS AND BARONESSES: Low men on the peerage totem pole, taking in, originally, those Englishmen whose ancestors had fought during the Middle Ages in Wales, Scotland, and France, and more recently a number of industrialists and trade-union leaders (who are generally given the title only for life). As demonstration of their lack of precedence, barons are never referred to by their title, merely as Lord So-and-so. (For the record, the sequence goes: the Duke of U, the Marquess of V, the Earl of W, the Viscount X, and Lord Y.) Lord Y's wife is, similarly, Lady Y, never the baroness. Sometimes a given name sneaks in, as with Alfred, Lord Tennyson.

AS FOR THE KIDS: In general, only the oldest son comes out on top—though not until the old man kicks off. In the meantime, if that old man is a duke, marquess, or earl, the son is awarded a "courtesy" title, one of his father's lesser ones, to use: e.g., the son of a still-living Duke of Wellington would be titled the Marquess Duoro until the major title comes free; eldest sons of viscounts and barons just have to wait. They, and everyone else in the second generation, make do—most of them for life—with what's called a courtesy style. If you're lucky (Daddy's a duke or marquess), you're "Lord" or "Lady": Lord John Brown, Lady Mary Brown (daughters of earls are "Lady," too). If you're not so lucky, you get a simple "The Hon." (read: "The Honourable") to put before your name: The Hon. John Doe, The Hon. Jane Doe. As for the grandchildren: They're on their own unless they belong to the oldest son.

The Lesser Nobles

Or, depending on your point of view, the titled commoners. They come in two sizes: the baronet and the knight. Don't look for either in the House of Lords.

BARONETS: Literally, "little barons." In 1611, King James I, needing capital, instigated "a new dignitie between Barons and Knights," open to anyone whose paternal grandfather had borne arms, who possessed an annual income of at least a thousand pounds, and who was willing to make a £1,095 down payment. While these Johnny-come-latelies were not, under any circumstances, to think of themselves as noble, they were encouraged to adopt the style Sir John Lately, Bt., and they could pass their title on to their—that's right—oldest son. *Vanity Fair's* Sir Pitt Crawley—dirty, cynical, coarse—is one side of the baronet story.
  Say: "Sir John." His wife is "Lady Lately."

KNIGHTS: The knight was the most significant figure in the feudal system, a mounted horseman who fought for his liege lord and defended the honor of his lady. For a while now, it's been the most frequently conferred "dignity" in England by far; allows the male recipient a "Sir" (his wife is "Lady") and the female recipient a "Dame" (her husband gets nothing); but wouldn't you know, it's guaranteed for one lifetime and one lifetime only.
  Say: As with a baronet. Plus, "Dame Agatha."

The Gentry

They can be of birth as high and breeding as fine as the nobility; in fact, many of them are the descendants of that nobility's younger sons and daughters. But there's no getting around the fact that, as intimidating as their manners and as awesome as their fortunes may be, they are sadly lacking in one thing: titles. As the people at *Burke's* point out, they're the only untitled aristocracy in the world.

ESQUIRES: In the Middle Ages, the esquire (or squire) attended the knight and carried his gear. Once the Middle Ages were over, though, somebody decided that the category might be usefully applied to—and we quote—"the sons of peers, the sons of baronets, the sons of knights, the eldest sons of the younger sons of peers, and their eldest sons in perpetuity, the eldest son of the eldest son of a knight, and his eldest son in perpetuity, the king of arms, the herald of arms, officers of the Army or Navy of the rank of captain and upward, sheriffs of counties for life, J.P.'s of counties whilst in commission, serjeants-at-arms, Queen's counsel . . ." and, well, you get the picture: It's a catchall, really, albeit one with connotations of both rank and real estate, and a way of appeasing any number of people who would otherwise risk seeming, in the eyes of the world, no better than their neighbors. It didn't really work out, though. While the Victorians jealously reserved "esquire" for the landed gentry, and withheld it from commercial and industrial types with too much and too new money, by the start of this century, the word had lost—through careless usage—almost all its distinction. Today the entire male population of Britain and Ireland is regularly so addressed (an "Esq." after their name taking the place of a "Mr." before it) by mail-order houses and book clubs.

A note on squires: Not so much an honor or even a slot in the hierarchy as a way of life. They were the big country landowners who exercised authority and financial leverage over their districts or villages, like Squire Western in *Tom Jones*. A paternal lot, who spoke in broad provincial dialect, rode to hounds, and weren't necessarily esquires (although they were certainly gentlemen; see below), the squirearchy was extinguished in England by the increasing taxes and creeping urbanism of the nineteenth century.

GENTLEMEN: Historically, of "gentle" birth, entitled to bear arms, owning at least three hundred acres of land, but lacking the larger distinction of being an esquire, let alone a knight or better. For more than a century now the word has had almost no agreed-upon meaning at all (as that old curmudgeon H. W. Fowler lamented, "We are all of us esquires now, and we are none of us gentlemen"), but in Jane Austen's day it was still something to keep in mind: Mr. Collins was considered an appropriate suitor for Elizabeth Bennet precisely because he was a gentleman, even though he was also a fool, a clergyman, and her cousin. (And Charlotte Lucas, a knight's daughter, no less, was happy to land him.)

And So On

Ugh: mostly peasants, servants, grooms, tradesmen, and the like. Obviously, you won't be paying *them* your respects. It's enough that you're civil (but firm) with them and occasionally throw a little business their way. Nevertheless, there are a handful of folks whom, while they aren't gentry, mind you, one just might consider having a dance or two with on a slow Saturday night. They are the . . .

YEOMEN: And here we pass from what is basically the upper middle class to what is, at most, the middle middle one—small, independent farmers who, like the squirearchy, would be forced out of existence by the pressurized ways of nineteenth-century life, but who up until their demise as a class had a reputation for being sturdy and hardworking, sometimes even educated, and possessed the kind of integrity that England is always tapping you on the shoulder to tell you it has. Respectable, landowning, and they could vote, but Emma Woodhouse (see page 245) wouldn't let poor Harriet Smith marry one.

THE CLERGY: KEEPING THEM—YOU SHOULD PARDON THE EXPRESSION—STRAIGHT

One of the quainter, and more confusing, fixtures in your nineteenth-century novel is the local clergyman. On the one hand, it was apparently hard to arrange an evening of whist without deferring to the rector; on the other hand, his wife always seemed to show up wearing someone's cast-off frock. Or was that the vicar's wife? And why, pray tell, wasn't the curate invited?

RECTOR: The head clergyman of a country parish, who had rights to the parish lands and owned its tithes. He held his post for life and could pass it on to his sons. In the eighteenth century, most rectors were the children of farmers and tradesmen, with no social status to speak of, but by the beginning of the nineteenth century, enough of them had made a killing in local agriculture to turn the clergy into a fit calling for the younger sons of gentry. As a result, the nineteenth-century rector was usually an educated gentleman, who in theory at least, was the social equal of the local squire, with whom he was expected to play cards and go grouse hunting. He functioned as if he were a landowner and often devoted most of his time to raising crops profitably while his underpaid assistants ran the church. In reality, however, most rectors had neither the independent income, nor the knack for turning a profit from parish lands, necessary to keep up a gentleman's lifestyle. They were often dependent on upper-class patrons who treated them like poor relations. The classic example of this type of rector is, once again, the insufferable Mr. Collins, who spends his life fawning upon his patroness, the Lady Catherine de Bourgh.

VICAR: A sort of freelance parson who stands in for a dead or absent rector or who heads a parish in which the tithes belong to someone else (e.g., the local squire). The vicar lived in a vicarage instead of a rectory, collected an allowance or salary in lieu of tithes, had no control over the land, and was only a transient (which is to say, he hadn't been established in the neighborhood for generations). In terms of education and breeding, however, he was the equal of a rector and, if he had a big enough independent income, could one-up him. After tithes were abolished in England in 1936, the terms "rector" and "vicar" became synonymous.

PARSON: A very general term (thought to derive from the French *personne*, which, reassuringly, means "person") for the head of a parish—i.e., a rector or a vicar—or for any Protestant minister below the rank of bishop who has enough authority to conduct religious services.

CURATE: Assistant to the rector or vicar, who usually did most of the tedious church work of the parish. Members of the "inferior clergy," curates were known for being poor, insecure, and a little uncouth; in your novel, the curate will probably have a large brood of ragged children for whom the gentle heroine is constantly making up baskets of provisions. Don't confuse the English curate with the French *curé*, or "parish priest." (And *le vicaire* is conversely, *le curé*'s assistant.)

BEADLE: A minor parish officer who along with various nonecclesiastical tasks, ushers people in and out of Sunday services, delivers messages for the parson, and generally keeps the parishioners, especially the small boy parishioners, in line. In short, a sort of church constable.

SEXTON: A kind of dignified janitor, who takes care of church property, rings the church bells, and digs the graves.

THE DRINKS: WHAT TO SERVE WITH THE OYSTERS, THE SOUP, THE FISH, THE SAVOURY, THE GAME, THE TRIFLE, AND THE CIGAR

First, you need to know that upstairs, the lords and ladies drank wine, bottles and bottles of it. Oh, a gentleman in need of fortification might have the occasional brandy or, if the day was hot and he was in a democratic mood, a beer, but wine was, for centuries, the traditional beverage of the upper classes. In the nineteenth century, when French wines became available again for the first time in a hundred years and vintage wines were all the rage, any gentleman worthy of the name was expected to keep a well-stocked cellar, to provide six or seven varieties with dinner, and to deal with them as a connoisseur. As Routledge's *Etiquette for Gentlemen* put it back in 1865, "How to eat soup, and what to do with a cherry-stone are weighty considerations when taken as an index of social status; and it is not too much to say, that a man who elected to take claret with fish, or ate peas with his knife, would justly risk the punishment of being banished from good society." We agree, in principle . . . but what's claret?

CLARET: The British term for any red Bordeaux wine (luckily, they call their Burgundy Burgundy). Claret has a special niche in the English heart because back in the Middle Ages, when Eleanor of Aquitaine married Henry Plantagenet (see page 589), Bordeaux and its vineyards became British possessions. Ever since, claret has been the preferred table wine in upper-class British households. Even during the Francophobic eighteenth century, when the English monarchy tried to replace the French wine trade with that of the Portuguese, the French managed to smuggle claret into England by shipping it via Portugal. Still, claret didn't really come into its own in England until the nineteenth century and the onset of the vintage-wine obsession. Claret was served with several different courses at Victorian dinners, and it was standard practice to have a few bottles on hand for high tea. Toward the end of the century, when society began to regard the seven-wine dinner as a bit excessive, claret, along with champagne, became the all-around dinner wine, and some young lords even began to substitute it for port as an after-dinner. drink.

PORT: The drink of choice of the upper class; a sweet, red, fortified wine originally from Oporto, in Portugal. Although early port was simply mediocre Portuguese table wine, Portugal (as Britain's oldest continuous ally) always got such favorable trade agreements, and shipped so much wine to England, that eventually the English got used to the stuff. The *cult* of port, however, didn't start until the nineteenth century, by which time the Portuguese had learned two important things: One, if they put the wine in a flat-sided bottle and left it lying around for a long time, it tasted better; and two, adding a little brandy not only helped it "travel," but also provoked an altogether more enthusiastic response from the consumer. Before long, the British nobility was passing the port, tenderly decanted, with the venison, the game, the cheese, and again with dessert; and gentlemen looked forward to tossing off another glass or two (which in the parlance of the day meant at least a bottle apiece) after the ladies had retired to the drawing room. This, by the way, was vintage port that had been aged at least twenty years, the absolute minimum before the wine was considered fit to drink. It was traditional for the well-heeled Victorian father to lay down a pipe of port (about 140 U.S. gallons' worth) at the birth of his son or godson, to be opened after the boy's twenty-first birthday. The equivalent gesture today, in terms of generosity, might be to present the boy with a kilo of cocaine.

HOCK: Although "hock" originally referred to wine from the area around Hochheim, Germany, it became a general British term for any white Rhine wine. In Victorian times, hock's place was on the dinner table, in its traditional green glass, next to the claret with the roast meat course and the dessert.

SACK: At various points in British history, sack referred to a dry white wine from Spain or the Canary islands, or to a heavy, sweetened, amber-colored wine from any of several Mediterranean wine-producing regions. Very popular in Shakespeare's day, it eventually gave way to sherry-sack, or sherry.

SHERRY: The world's most popular fortified wine. Sherry comes from Spain, although the British are, in a way, its adoptive parents. Real sherry, according to them, comes from Andalusia, Spain (the name "sherry" is an anglicization of Jerez, the capital of the sherry region), the way real champagne comes from the Champagne region of France. The British have always preferred the *finos*, the light, dry sherries, which make the best aperitif. Americans, by contrast, are mainly familiar with the *olorosos*, the second, and inferior, type of sherry, which is sweet, heavy, earthy, and the basis for brands like Harvey's Bristol Cream. There's no such thing as a vintage sherry, but *finos* can be very elegant; the Victorians used to like them with the fish and soup at the beginning of a meal, and again at the end, with dessert. They believed sherry should be properly decanted and served in ordinary wine glasses, never in those thimble-sized "sherry glasses" common today. Amontillado, which you probably remember from Edgar Allan Poe's horror story, is a medium-dry sherry, halfway between a *fino* and an *oloroso*.

MADEIRA: A heavily fortified white wine from the Portuguese island of Madeira. This was one of the first fortified wines to make it big in England, having arrived in the seventeenth century along with the Portuguese bride of Charles II, Catherine of Braganza. (Actually, Catherine brought the whole island as part of her dowry, but Charles, who was having a cash-flow problem at the time, settled for money instead.) Catherine loved to sip Madeira in the morning as she munched a slice of Madeira cake; before long all the fashionable ladies of the kingdom got into the habit of tossing off a little glass to get the day started, a practice that lasted well into the Victorian era. As a result, Madeira, besides being a standard dessert wine, had a reputation as a ladies' drink. For the record, Madeira comes both dry and sweet; malmsey, in a butt of which George, Duke of Clarence, was allegedly drowned by order of his brother, later Richard III, was one of the sweet varieties.

SAUTERNE: The greatest of the white Bordeaux wines, grown in the S region of the province of Bordeaux. It is a sweet, intense, fruity wine s and now, with dessert.

TOKAY: Another sweet dessert wine; as you can see, the end of a ner was a little like the climax of a fireworks display, with five o presented simultaneously, along with the cakes. This one is comes from the town of Tokay, or Tokaj, in Hungary.

NEGUS: Back in Samuel Pepys' time, this was a simple mixture o sugar named for one Colonel Negus, whose accomplishments are at vague. Johnson and Boswell (see page 218) drank about a bottle of neg ece every night. Later, because port was the wine most commonly used to make the concoction, "negus" came to mean mulled port.

MEAD: A sweet, fermented honey or honey-flavored wine the Babylonians were drinking back in 2000 B.C. (For your trivia collection: They declared mead the official wedding drink, stipulating that the bride's parents be required to keep the groom well supplied with "the wine of the bee" for the month following the marriage; that month became known as *honeymonth*, hence our *honeymoon*.) It was a great favorite of the ancient Britons, who believed in its powers as an intoxicant, a medicine, and an aphrodisiac. For centuries, making mead was a sort of cottage industry in English monasteries. It began to die out, partly because Henry VIII suppressed the monasteries and partly because the English honeybee went into a slump. Samuel Pepys caught Charles II drinking metheglin, a kind of spiced mead, as late as the seventeenth century, but the wine became virtually extinct after that. Two reasons to know what it is: You're sure to run across the term somewhere in English Lit., and recently, in a fever of nostalgia, mead-making became a British cottage industry all over again.

So much for the goings on upstairs. Downstairs and out on the farms, respectable working folk were consuming vast quantities of beer (in 1876 alone, they downed thirty-four gallons for every man, woman, and child in the country). Beer drinking was not only respectable, it smacked of patriotism; nearly everyone brewed his own at home (or rather, *her* own—brewing was considered woman's work) from local English barley. What's more, it was a lot safer than drinking from the typhoid-ridden public water systems, which is why ten-year-old boys at Eton and Harrow drank beer for breakfast as a matter of course. Naturally, with a lifetime of beer drinking—and custom-beer drinking at that—behind one, some very specific tastes arose, such as:

BITTER: A traditionally English and still very popular type of draught, or keg, beer (although now you can find it in little bottles) that is light, dry, strong, and relatively high in both hops and alcohol content (compared, that is, with the lager-type beers favored in the United States; bitter is neither the strongest nor the bitterest beer in England). Always ordered as "a pint of bitter," which will get you a tankard, and never to be confused with bitters, the root extract used to spike a cocktail.

PORTER: A dark brown, heavily hopped brew with a 6 to 7 percent alcohol content (most U.S. beers average 3 to 6 percent) and a taste of roasted malt. Porter, which was originally called "porter's beer" or "porter's ale," probably because it started out as a drink for porters and other common laborers, was an exception to the nineteenth-century trend toward lighter, less alcoholic beers, and it became one of the great pop hits of its time. Rumored to be more healthful than beer, it was a big favorite with actresses and singers, who swore by its salutary effects on their voices, and one election campaign revolved around the slogan "Peace, Plenty, and Porter." It turned out to be just a flash in the pan, though; today porter is virtually extinct.

STOUT: An even stronger, more heavily hopped version of porter. This one managed to hang on, thanks to the Guinness family, with whom the word "stout" is now more or less synonymous.

As for the class distinctions of beer (which, by the way, is the same thing as ale in Britain), they're a little trickier than those of wine. Although, on the whole, beer was a working-class drink, it did have its fans among the upper echelons, including the residents of certain colleges at Oxford and Cambridge—most of which had their own breweries—who became famous for producing a very dark, semilethal collector's item called "Audit Ale." Moreover, the rise of the big English breweries around the beginning of the nineteenth century changed the whole picture. Great fortunes were made, and with them great families, whose members suddenly bore titles and sat in the House of Lords. Under the circumstances, beer drinking pretty much had to become socially acceptable. Today, among beers, anything goes, with the possible exception of a sweetish variety called "mild," which still has a faintly low-class image.

Meanwhile, sailors and other rough trade, when they weren't drinking beer, were downing:

GROG: Any liquor, but especially rum, that's been diluted with water. Grog was named after Admiral Edward Vernon (whom the sailors called "Old Grog" because he always wore a grogram coat), who gave the order that the daily rations of rum aboard Her Majesty's ships be diluted. Pretty soon, taverns catering to sailors had taken up the practice, and grog became what one settled for when one couldn't afford a stiffer dose.

And at the bottom of the barrel, so to speak, the wretched rabble were killing themselves with bad English GIN. Gin had been promoted back at the start of the eighteenth century by William of Orange, who considered it the perfect drink for the workingman, forgetting, for the moment, that the only decent gin was still being produced in Holland and was much too expensive for poor people. So the lower orders bought what they could afford, lured by the promise of getting "drunk for a penny, dead-drunk for two-pence, and straw for nothing" (meaning that the pub owner would drag them to the cellar to let them sleep it off), and for the rest of the century, gin drinking leveled the poor like a plague. By the mid-nineteenth century, the gin epidemic had begun to taper off, except for the curious defection of many respectable working-class women from beer to gin, after which gin was nicknamed "Mother's Ruin."

THE CARRIAGES: WHEELS OF FORTUNE

In the nineteenth century, one's carriage, or carriages, had as many social connotations as one's car, or cars, do in Los Angeles today. (Of course, back then, one had to be at least moderately upper crust to own a carriage at all.) Yet most of us, faced with the mention of a cabriolet, are at as much of a loss as Jane Eyre would have been at the mention of a Volvo station wagon. The following guide may be of some help; keep in mind, however, that *all* carriages were custom-made, and hybrids abounded.

PHAETON: Any of a bewilderingly large family of four-wheeled open carriages that marked the carriage's turning point from means-of-transportation to status symbol. The earliest models, the eccentric and risky Highflyers, inspired the prince regent—and everyone else—to

Phaeton

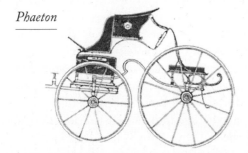

take up driving as a sport. Later, when the regent, now George IV, became too fat to climb into the original version, a low phaeton (pronounced "FAY-ut-en") was devised. Drawn by docile ponies, the low phaeton became the only acceptable vehicle for a lady to drive.

CURRICLE: A racy little Italian import, also fashionable during the Regency, when young gentlemen prided themselves on being accomplished "whips." Two-wheeled, and drawn by a pair of horses instead of just one, curricles were built for speed. They were used for both town and country driving and became very popular in the trendy aristocrat's version of drag racing.

CABRIOLET: The sports car of its time; superseded the curricle as the carriage for the fashionable man-about-town. Considered the perfect bachelor's carriage, it held two passengers comfortably, sheltered by a hood with a curtain that could be drawn for privacy. Relatively economical since it was pulled by only one horse, the cabriolet nevertheless allowed for a certain amount of ostentation: One could—and did—equip one's carriage with the largest, finest horse one could find, accessorized, in

Cabriolet

case anyone missed the point, by the tiniest available groom.

BROUGHAM: The discreet, black, coachman-driven affair used by nervous peers in old Jack-the-Ripper movies. Simple, practical, and dignified, the brougham (pronounced "broom" or "BROO-em") was named after its originator, Lord Brougham, the lord chancellor of England. It was the one major innovation in

Brougham

Landau

coach-making under Queen Victoria, reflecting the shift to a more sober, moralistic mood, and it remained England's most popular closed carriage throughout the Victorian era.

VICTORIA: A French import, known on the other side of the Channel as a "milord." This was another very popular, coachman-driven town carriage but, being open, or at most equipped with a folding hood, it was used mainly in summer. A great favorite with Victorian ladies, it was light, low, elegant, roomy, and easy to climb into, and it

Victoria

came with sweeping mudguards to protect voluminous skirts.

LANDAU: The nineteenth-century equivalent of a limo, the landau (pronounced "LAN-dow") was second in formality to the closed town coach (the nineteenth-century equivalent of a stretch limo). A large four-horse carriage used for long-distance travel and formal-dress occasions, it held four passengers seated opposite each other

(which led to its sometimes being called a "sociable-landau") and had a jointed hood that could be raised or lowered, as with a hard-topped convertible. At its most elaborate, the landau was led by two postillions and accompanied by two liveried outriders; all six horses were perfectly matched, of course.

BAROUCHE: Like a landau in structure and status but, because its folding hood covered only one of its seats, used almost exclusively as a summer carriage. The fact that owners usually liked to drive their barouches themselves also made them a little less formal than landaus. But the barouche is the one you'll find most often referred to in novels, marking ceremonial occasions, family outings, and sporting events. The snobbish Mrs. Elton, in Jane Austen's *Emma*, never misses a chance to tell everybody that her brother owns one, and Mr. Pickwick first meets amiable old Mr. Wardle while the latter is climbing out of his for a family picnic.

Barouche

GIG: The Volkswagen of the Victorian era; a light, open, one-horse carriage that carried one or two passengers perched directly above the two wheels. Not particularly elegant but compact,

Gig

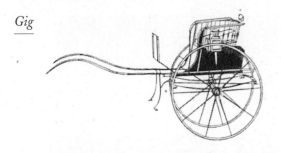

economical, and maneuverable, gigs became increasingly popular as the century wore on. The country doctor, for one, nearly always drove up in his gig. Not acceptable for town use.

DOGCART: As popular as a suburban station wagon, and used in much the same way. Originally built to hold a sportsman's dogs in a ventilated storage boot beneath the seat, the dogcart had a fold-up footboard that could double as a seat, thereby accommodating four passengers back to back. Since practicality, not fashion, was what counted in country vehicles, most landowners kept at least one dogcart on the estate.

WAGONETTE: A big, plain, open wagon of a thing, with bench seats inside, made specifically for family excursions in the country. Although not elegant, wagonettes were very much in vogue for a while; Queen Victoria and the earl of

Chesterfield didn't mind owning them, and King Louis Philippe once sent Victoria the French version, called a *char-à-bancs*, as a gift.

POST CHAISE: The gentlemanly alternative to sharing legroom in a large mail or passenger coach. One hired the post chaise in stages, from inn to inn. They were always painted yellow and were traditionally driven by an elderly postillion dressed in a yellow jacket and a beaver hat. Although this was considered the first-class way to travel long distances, anyone looking for the equivalent of flying the Concorde had to own the private version of the post chaise, called a traveling chariot, emblazoned with the family crest.

HANSOM CAB: The "Gondola of London"; the vehicle hired taxi-style by Sherlock Holmes and any other gentleman who couldn't afford, or didn't want, to keep a private carriage. For a long

Hansom cab

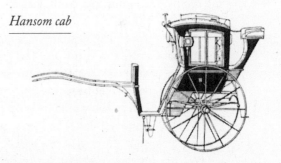

time, hansoms were considered quite dashing; no respectable lady would be caught dead riding alone in one, or with any man other than her husband.

THE MONEY: A GUIDE FOR PICKPOCKETS, WASTRELS, AND FORTUNE HUNTERS

As some of you no doubt remember, David Copperfield was born with a caul, that is, with a portion of fetal membrane encasing his infant head, believed in those days to be a sign of good luck and a safeguard against drowning. David's mother having just been widowed (and financially reduced), the caul "was advertised for sale, in the newspapers, at the low price of fifteen guineas." A solitary bidder "offered two pounds in cash, and the balance in sherry," and subsequently the caul "was put up in a raffle . . . to fifty members at half-a-crown a head, the winner to spend five shillings." It was won by "an old lady with a handbasket, who, very reluctantly, produced from it the stipulated five shillings, all in halfpence, and twopence halfpenny short."

Now, how much money did the raffle realize—more than the desired fifteen guineas or less? And how much did the old lady pay? And what's a guinea anyway? We're glad you asked. Herewith, a guide to the intricacies of the English monetary system, back when England was calling the shots.

POUND: Or, more formally, the pound sterling, for over nine hundred years a symbol and index of Britain's power, wealth, and determination to get her way in the world. Originally equivalent to a pound-weight of silver pennies, called sterlings (or "little stars," after the mark each was stamped with), later simply the basic unit of English currency—currency that was not foreign, not colonial, not debased, but "sterling," or lawful. It came in the form of a pound note (paper) or a sovereign (gold coin). The slang term is "quid," always in the singular, and the sign, equivalent to our $, is a crossed L, £, from the first letter of *librum*, the Latin word for pound. Divided, prior to 1971's shift to decimals, into shillings and pence.

SHILLING: Twenty of them used to make up a pound, before they were discontinued in 1971. In its mood, not unlike our quarter: Lots of routine daily business was done in them; books, lunches, shoeshines, magazines, and gloves bought. Abbreviated *s.*, as in 12*s.*, or symbolized by a slash, as in 12/-, "twelve shillings even." The slang term is "bob."

PENNY: In the plural, "pence," twelve of which used to make up a shilling (and 240 a pound). Now the pound comprises one hundred *new* pence (or one hundred p, pronounced "pee"). Used to be available in several denominations, among them the ha'penny (or halfpenny), tuppence (or twopence), thrippence (or threepence), fourpence (also called a groat), and sixpence (also called a tanner, also a teston). Abbreviated *d.*, from the Latin *denarius*, an old Roman coin. Thus £8 3*s.* 8*d.*— or, alternatively, £8/3/8—is eight pounds, three shillings, and eight pence.

There you have the basic units, simple enough provided you can remember there are twenty shillings in a pound and twelve pence in a shilling and not the other way around. But, as you know, the English don't like things to be *too* simple. So we have:

GUINEA: A little bigger than a pound—one shilling bigger, to be precise. At first a coin, made from gold from Guinea, with a little elephant stamped on it and meant to be employed specifically in the Africa trade. Since 1813, simply a unit—£1 1*s.*—traditionally used to state such quantities as professional fees, subscription amounts, and the value of pictures, horses, and estates. A "prestige" way of stating the cost of something, as well as a way of understating, psychologically—à la $9.98—that cost.

FLORIN: A silver coin, with a flower on it, worth two shillings.

CROWN: Likewise silver, with a you-know-what stamped on it. Worth five shillings. (A half crown is, obviously, $2\frac{1}{2}$ shillings.)

FARTHING: A quarter of a penny.

MITE: Still less worth having: an eighth of a penny.

So Mrs. Copperfield advertised the caul for £15 15*s.* She received a £2-plus-sherry offer (not alluring, given that her own sherry was already on the market). At the raffle, fifty people paid $2\frac{1}{2}$ shillings (or a half crown) each, £6 5*s.* altogether. The old lady came up with an additional 5*s.*, less $2\frac{1}{2}d.$ Total: £6 9*s.* $9\frac{1}{2}d.$, or considerably less than half the amount that had at first been asked. On the other hand, those were the days when a pound sterling really was a pound sterling.

Talking about what money will buy is tricky enough in one's own country on the day one is actually considering spending some of it. Arriving at exact equivalences over the decades and across national boundaries is almost impossible. Still, certain generalizations can be made. Among them:

1. Inflation is not the inexorable force recent history—and especially recent British history—would lead us to believe it is. Since 1661, prices in Britain have alternately risen and fallen, fallen and risen, and only in the last generation gone haywire. While there was considerable inflation during the early part of the nineteenth century (what with the Napoleonic Wars), by the 1820s, things had pretty much leveled off. In fact, in 1911, on the eve of World War I, a pound would buy more than it did on the eve of the Great Plague of 1665.

2. International events gravely affect how many francs or dollars or quetzals the pound—or any other unit of currency—is worth. Around the time of the American Revolution, a pound brought between $4.50 and $5.00; that figure shot up to $12.00 during the American Civil War, returning to "normal" during 1880, not falling to a new "normal" level of about $2.50 until after World War II. Today it's worth well under $2.00.

3. Not only does the perceived "formal" value of the pound fluctuate, so does the living standard of the society it serves, not to mention the degree to which transfer of cash, as opposed to, say, barter, or the providing of room and board by an employer, accounts for how that society spends its money. Thus, as the nineteenth century drew to a close, though few people were making more than a couple of pounds a week, just one pound would buy six bottles of whiskey or thirty gallons of fresh milk or the rent of a shop or house for nearly a month or fifteen pairs of serviceable ladies' shoes.

4. Not only do the perceived formal value of the pound and the living standard of the society fluctuate, so do buying habits, human needs, and customs of the country. For instance, money seems to go further in an agricultural society than in an industrial one, and in a part of the country—or of the century—that boasts a lot of gardens and pastures, where the price of tomatoes, milk, and brussels sprouts seldom packs much of a wallop, than it does in town. Then, too, if there are no music halls or gin mills within a twenty-mile radius of your house, you don't allow for many evenings out in your entertainment budget.

All that said, let's look a little more closely at Dorothea Brooke, the heroine of George Eliot's Middlemarch (see page 245), who, in 1832, the year the First Reform Bill was passed by Parliament, can be overheard describing herself to a distraught Lydgate (who's just lost four or five pounds at the billiard table) as having "seven hundred a-year of my own fortune, and nineteen hundred a-year that Mr. Casaubon left me, and between three and four thousand of ready money in the bank." Keeping in mind that a few years before, it has been estimated by a journal of the day, a family could live on a minimum income of one guinea a week, provided they didn't drink or "seek entertainment," you can see that this makes Dorothea—while no Barbara Hutton—a very wealthy woman. Moreover, not only was an 1832 pound worth at least fifteen of today's pounds, it went further, and living standards were lower, especially in Dorothea and Lydgate's small, not-yet-industrialized, north-of-England town. Given all of this, our Miss Brooke had an annual income that was the equivalent of at least $75,000 a year, with another $115,000 in her savings account, which, since she owned her own home and didn't care about jewels or parties, was more than enough to endow hospitals, found a village, and bail Lydgate out. As to where her income came from—that is, what it meant to have "seven hundred a-year" in the first place—you should know that rents on the land he owned were the major source of every aristocrat's income (as they still are for, say, Prince Charles). Of course, there were such things as a commercial class (relegated to London and other big cities), as profit, interest, and investment, but most country folk didn't get embroiled to any great extent. Better to "live on" one's own estate, in both senses of the phrase.

THE NAMES: ENGLISH AS A SECOND LANGUAGE

So we say Lord Tomato and they say Lord Tomahto; what's the big deal? We all speak the same language, right? Wrong. It turns out that *they* speak English and we just translate, more or less successfully, as you'll see from the following list of well-known names.

1. Bolingbroke (as in Henry IV's surname): BOLL-in-brook
2. Pepys (as in Samuel, the diarist): PEEPS
3. Cowper (as in William, the poet): COOP-er
4. Crichton (as in James, the Scottish Renaissance man known as "the Admirable Crichton," as well as all British families named Chrichton or Chreighton, and even the American novelist, Michael): CRY-ten
5. Cockburn (as in Alicia, the eighteenth-century wit; Sir Alexander, the nineteenth-century lord chief justice of England; plain old Alexander, the expatriate journalist; plus Cockburn Harbour and Cockburn Sound): CO-burn

Two Scottish cities:
6. Edinburgh: ED-in-burra
7. Glasgow: GLAZ-ko or GLAZ-go

Two place names that are easier to pronounce correctly if you don't smoke:
8. Marlborough: MARL-burra or MAR-burra
9. Pall Mall: PELL-MELL

One whose correct pronunciation may sound like an affectation, but isn't:
> 10: Queensberry (as in the marquess of): QUEENS-bry (and that's MAR-kwis)

One case of the language doing a double take:
> 11. Magdalen and Magdalene (the college at Oxford and the college at Cambridge): pronounced like "maudlin," which derives from the name Magdalen

And a few that follow rules:
> 12. The county names ending in *cester*—drop the *c* and the letter preceding it: Gloucester, Worcester, Leicester: GLOSS-ter, WOOS-ter, LESS-ter, also, their alternative names: Gloucestershire, Worcestershire, Leicestershire: GLOSS-te-sher, WOOS-te-sher, LESS-te-sher
> 13. The *wich*es—drop the *w*: Norwich, Woolwich, and the tip-off, Greenwich: NOR-ich, WOOL-ich, GREN-ich
> 14. The *wick*s—ditto: Northwick, Southwick, Warwick, Smithwick: NORTH-ick, SOUTH-ick, WAR-ick, SMITH-ick
> 15. A London *wark* that can get you coming and going: Southwark: SUTH-erk
> 16. The *er*s—say "ar" (but stay on your toes; the rule doesn't always apply): Berkeley (as in George, the Irish philosopher; Sir William, the colonial governor of Virginia; also, the former earldom and the square), Berkshire (the county), Derby (the borough, the earldom, and the English horse race): BARK-lee, BARK-sher, DAR-by. And a tricky one: Hertford: HAR-ferd

Finally, a couple of instances in which they insist on speaking English when they should be speaking French:
> 17. Beauchamp (as in Guy de, Richard de, Thomas de; London's Beauchamp Place, and Beauchamp Tower in the Tower of London): BEECH-em
> 18. Beaulieu (the town and the abbey): BYOO-lee

And, the ultimate in inscrutable British English:
> 19. Cholmondeley (a common last name): CHUM-lee

Guess Who's Coming to Dinner?

TWELVE FICTIONAL CHARACTERS WITH WHOM YOU SHOULD HAVE AT LEAST A NODDING ACQUAINTANCE

Literature does have its practical applications. For instance, suppose you're at a dinner party and you overhear your hostess describing you to the person on your left as "a real Baron de Charlus." What do you say to your new acquaintance? And how should you feel about your hostess? Or yourself? See below.

Baron de Charlus (from Proust's *Rememberance of Things Past*): A closet case. An aristocrat who travels in the best society, the Baron cultivates his image as a woman chaser while dating an eclectic assortment of boys on the sly. French aristocrats do this all the time, of course, but the Baron suffers from such a virulent strain of depravity that it not only leads him into scandal, it makes him prematurely senile.

Cousin Bette (from Balzac's *Cousin Bette*): An aging spinster consumed by hatred. An ugly duckling who, for various reasons, never metamorphosed into a swan, Bette is dependent on her relatives and is, therefore, forced to hide her envy and bitterness behind a facade of goodwill. She's nobody's fool, however; secretly, she's dedicated her life to ruining other people's.

Father Zossima (from Dostoevsky's *The Brothers Karamazov*): A famous church elder, holy and ascetic, who teaches a doctrine of love and forbearance. When he dies, a miracle is expected, but instead, his body begins to decompose almost immediately. Cynics point to this as a sign that his teachings were false. Ask yourself (*a*) if your hostess is a cynic, and (*b*) if you've had a checkup recently.

Isabel Archer (from James' *The Portrait of a Lady*): An intelligent, vivacious, high-minded American girl who's off to Europe in search of her Destiny. Which is to say she's headed for trouble. Isabel has her faults: She's naïve and a little presumptuous, she gets huffy when criticized, and she could do with a lesson or two in picking her friends. Still, you can't blame her for wanting to get out of Albany.

Julien Sorel (from Stendhal's *The Red and the Black*): A brilliant, hypocritical young parvenu. A misfit determined to make it in a society he despises, Sorel uses his love affairs to get ahead and almost manages to become a successful cad. He is both too smart and too sentimental for his own good, however; ultimately, he self-destructs.

Dorothea Brooke (from Eliot's *Middlemarch*): A young woman of great intelligence and integrity who longs to devote herself to a worthy cause. Her idealism gets her into a disastrous marriage with Mr. Casaubon, an arid scholar who can't see the forest for the trees. Dorothea's a sweet kid, but she really ought to lighten up a bit.

Alexey Vronsky (from Tolstoy's *Anna Karenina*): The dashing young officer for whom Anna Karenina abandons her husband, child, and respectable society life. Vronsky isn't really a bad sort; he just isn't neurotic enough to cope with a tragic love affair. He really does seem to take it hard when Anna throws herself under the train that's taking him away to war. Heck, all the poor guy wanted was a little space.

Emma Woodhouse (from Jane Austen's *Emma*): "Handsome, clever, and rich, with a comfortable home and a happy disposition," Emma has "lived nearly twenty-one years in the world with very little to distress or vex her." Too bad she's a terrible snob, an incurable gossip, a cold fish, and utterly blind both to her own faults and to the mess she makes trying to run everyone else's life.

Stephen Dedalus (from Joyce's *A Portrait of the Artist as a Young Man* and *Ulysses*): Well, you can take this one of two ways, as the critics have. On the one hand, Stephen may be a pretentious aesthete, an egomaniacal little prig who only *thinks* he's an artist. On the other hand, he may have talent. At any rate, he's not a bore; he has depth, intelligence, an abundance of Catholic guilt, a driving need to find a father figure, and a striking resemblance to James Joyce.

Eustacia Vye (from Hardy's *The Return of the Native*): Caution: Contents Under Pressure. Eustacia is stuck out on the heath with nothing to do and no one to talk to until Clym Yeobright comes home from Paris. Seeing him as her ticket to glamour and adventure, she marries him. Unfortunately, all he wants to do is teach school and spend quiet evenings in front of the fire. After a period of making herself and everyone else miserable, Eustacia drowns herself in a bog.

Marlow (from Conrad's *Lord Jim*, *Heart of Darkness*, and other tales): The narrator of long stories, usually told late at night over booze and cigars, in which one or another of Conrad's outcasts works his way through some agonizing and frequently fatal moral dilemma. Although Marlow claims to be baffled by whatever it is that "causes me to run up against men with soft spots, with hard spots, with hidden plague spots, by Jove! and loosens their tongues at the sight of me for their infernal confidences," he is really a sleuth of the soul, as perpetually on the lookout for a knotty problem as Ted Koppel.

Mrs. Ramsay (from Woolf's *To the Lighthouse*): Somebody's ideal of womanhood. Loving, tender, sensitive, instinctual, compassionate, and efficient, she copes gracefully with eight children, a demanding husband, a steady stream of house-guests, and the village poor—all on a tight budget—and still manages to age so beautifully that everyone who meets her wants to paint her portrait or carry her bundles. If you're anything like her, give us a call.

Three Important-Sounding Fallacies (and Two Important-Sounding Other Things) You May or May Not Want to Watch Out For

PATHETIC FALLACY

A phrase coined by the British critic and essayist John Ruskin to call attention to the tendency on the part of second-rate poets to attribute to nature the emotions and motivations of human beings. Ruskin cites a passage from a poem of the day, "They rowed her in across the rolling foam— / The cruel, crawling foam," then comments dryly, "The foam is not cruel, neither does it crawl. The state of mind which attributes to it these characters of a living creature is one in which the reason is unhinged by grief." However, while this practice might have struck Ruskin as morbid, "pathetic fallacy" is now a fairly neutral term used to designate any nature-as-human image, whether convincing (as in the hands of Shakespeare or Keats) or absurd (as above). Look for a lot of pathetic fallacy in the Romantic poets (where mountains mourn and fields smile) and in the novels of Thomas Hardy.

INTENTIONAL FALLACY

Or don't believe everything the author tells you—especially if he's trying to explain why he's written the book or play or poem at hand. For instance, Milton, up front in *Paradise Lost*, tells us he wants to "justify the ways of God to men." Don't (according to critics William K. Wimsatt Jr., and Monroe Beardsley, who came up with the term "intentional fallacy") count on it. And even if it's true, if that's precisely why Milton thinks he wrote his epic, so what? Who *cares* why he thought he wrote it? The Big Critical Issue here: Which counts more, the Author or the Work? Intentional fallacy was a favorite thing of the New Critics of the Forties and Fifties, who, having been force-fed historical and biographical background material when they were kids, now insisted on "close readings of the text." In other words, forget the Author, forget his Period; it's you and the night and the music. And the Critic, of course.

AFFECTIVE FALLACY

The flip side of the intentional fallacy, and likewise introduced by Wimsatt and Beardsley, who now warned against the "confusion between the poem and its *result* [what it *is* and what it *does*]"—i.e., it doesn't matter whether the night and the music (and the Critic) make you feel amorous, or melancholy, or afraid of the dark. Your emotional response to the poem or story or whatever doesn't matter any more than how the poet or novelist or whoever felt as he wrote it. How you react isn't the point; the poem (etc.) is the poem. Is the poem. Note that (1) the affective fallacy is what some critics think happens when somebody puts a lot of emphasis, as Aristotle did, on a goal like catharsis (see page 263), and (2) both the intentional and affective fallacies are battle cries, not neutral terms like "pathetic fallacy," and not open-and-shut cases.

OBJECTIVE CORRELATIVE

T. S. Eliot's idea. It means that a good poet, playwright, or novelist doesn't write, "Hmm, how sad, even pathetic, that girl looks, the one over there by that rock, who lives, I think, by the River Dove"; he says instead, at least if he's Wordsworth, "A violet by a mossy stone." Eliot maintained that the objective correlative—the concrete and specific image—is "the only way of expressing emotion in the form of art," and he defines it as "a set of objects, a situation, a chain of events which shall be the formula of that *particular* emotion, such that when the external facts, which must terminate in sensory experience, are given, the emotion is immediately evoked." Whatever; she still looks sad to us.

NEGATIVE CAPABILITY

Hard to get a clear definition here, even though everybody from F. Scott Fitzgerald to service-magazine journalists behaves as if he knows exactly how and when to deploy it. The phrase is Keats', and he kept using it in letters to friends in slightly different, and slightly vague, senses. Somebody must have called him on it (not that it did much good), because, in 1817, Keats glosses "negative capabil-ity" in yet another letter: "that is, when a man is capable of being in uncertain-ties, Mysteries, doubts, without any irritable reaching after fact & reason." Lionel Trilling (see page 34) interpreted this to mean "a way of dealing with life," "to make up one's mind about nothing—to let the mind be a thoroughfare for all thoughts," to trust the subconscious and not "try too hard in coming at a truth." F. Scott's reading of it (in *The Crack-Up*) was a little different: "The test of a first-rate intelligence is the ability to hold two opposed ideas in the mind at the same time, and still retain the ability to function. One should, for example, be able to see that things are hopeless and yet be determined to make them otherwise." Other people seem to think negative capability is related to empathy. Or in-tegrity. Or objectivity. Anyway, according to Keats, Shakespeare had a lot of it. Who knows? So might you.

Three Twentieth-Century Novels to Reckon With

Sure they're long, and none of them's exactly a cliff-hanger. But that doesn't mean you have to spend the rest of your life tiptoeing around these monuments of high modernism, one Irish, one French, one German.

ULYSSES (1922)
JAMES JOYCE

What did his limbs, when gradually extended, encounter?

New clean bedlinen, additional odours, the presence of a human form, female, hers, the imprint of a human form, male, not his, some crumbs, some flakes of potted meat, recooked, which he removed.

If he had smiled why would he have smiled?

To reflect that each one who enters imagines himself to be the first to enter whereas he is always the last term of a preceding series even if the first term of a succeeding one, each imagining himself to be first, last, only and alone, whereas he is neither first nor last nor only nor alone in a series originating in and repeated to infinity.

The novel as cab ride: potholes, gridlock, minority-group parades, plus the springs are shot and the driver's smoking a cigar. The trick is to sit back, ignore the meter, and try not to anticipate the destination. Go easy on yourself: Linearity—getting from A to B—was never much on Joyce's mind, and it doesn't have to be much on yours either. More than any other, this is a book not to stand on ceremony with.

But it is a book to be careful around. An eyes-in-the-gutter, *Life*-goes-to-a-bad-dream mutant of a novel, it's still every bit as off-putting as you found it the first time around. (The passage on the previous page, from the "Ithaca" chapter, in which Leopold Bloom—an advertising-space salesman in 1904 Dublin, exhausted husband to Molly, would-be father to Stephen Dedalus, and twentieth-century analogue to Ulysses, a.k.a. Odysseus [see page 255], the most down-to-earth yet cunning of the Greek heroes—comes home and goes to bed, is as easy as the going gets.) The basic problem with *Ulysses* is, of course, that there's too much in it: The *Odyssey*-mimicking structure, the linking of each of the eighteen episodes with a different academic discipline *and* a different bodily organ, the symbols and allusions, the puns and parodies, the cast of dozens (each of them Irish and voluble), the determination to do it all, both expressionistically and documentarily, and in eighteen hours and forty-five minutes of novel time, no less. Then there's Joyce himself, who, while he may be, as Eliot pronounced, "the greatest master of language in English since Milton," is also a show-off of the worst, third-grader-with-a-father-who-writes-for-television sort.

Two tips: Don't be afraid to browse. Find an episode you like. *Then* graze: Let Joyce's precise, unflagging, comic, and consolational portrayal of life take hold. And don't be proud: A guide, like Stuart Gilbert's *James Joyce's "Ulysses"* or Harry Blamires' *The Bloomsday Book*, both of which provide page-by-page assistance, will help you over the rough patches.

REMEMBRANCE OF THINGS PAST
(1913–1927)
MARCEL PROUST

[S]ince the accident to her jaw, [Mme. Verdurin] had abandoned the effort involved in real hilarity, and had substituted a kind of symbolical dumb-show which signified, without endangering or even fatiguing her in any way, that she was "laughing until she cried." At the least witticism aimed by any of the circle against a "bore," or against a former member of the circle who was now relegated to the limbo of "bores"—and to the utter despair of M. Verdurin, who had always made out that he was just as easily amused as his wife, but who, since his laughter was the "real thing," was out of breath in a moment, and so was overtaken and vanquished by her device of a feigned but continuous hilarity—she would utter a shrill cry, shut tight her little bird-like eyes, which were beginning to be clouded over by a cataract, and quickly, as though she only just had time to avoid some indecent sight or to parry a mortal blow, burying her face in her hands, which completely engulfed it, and prevented her from seeing anything at all, she would appear to be struggling to suppress, to eradicate a laugh which, were she to give way to it, must inevitably leave her inanimate. So, stupefied with the gaiety of the "faithful," drunken with comradeship, scandal, and asseveration, Mme. Verdurin, perched on her high seat like a cage-bird whose biscuit has been steeped in mulled wine, would sit aloft and sob with fellow-feeling.

The novel as flotation tank. Except that it feels more like you're suspended in mayonnaise than floating on water, and, far from sensory deprivation, it's sensory inundation that the experience winds up being all about. Your host(s): Marcel, a fictitious first-person narrator as well as the author whose name appears on the cover. The length of your session: three thousand pages, distributed over seven dense volumes, five resonant locales, half a dozen impressive drawing rooms, and between seven and ten major love affairs (depending on whether you count Marcel's infatuation with his mother and his grandmother as one or two, and his passionate discovery of his literary calling, on page two thousand nine hundred and something, at all).

Begin (and, if you must, end) with *Swann's Way*, the first volume in the heptology; for conversational purposes, at least, you'll have read Proust. You won't meet many people who've made it through the whole thing; besides, the narrative eventually comes full circle, and virtually all its important themes and characters are presented here. Shifting back and forth in time and space, the narrator first recalls his childhood in the relatively innocent town of Combray, then goes on to tell of the doomed obsession of Robert Swann, an elegant dilettante, with an unworthy tart named Odette de Crécy. (Later, all the characters will exchange roles and masks until they're unidentifiable, and everyone you've met along the way will either die or turn out to be gay.) This segment will also give you a perfectly adequate take on Proust's prose style; in fact, by the time you come stumbling back into the sunlight, you'll feel positively intimate with the interminable, serpentine sentences; the constant, unstoppable metaphors, analyses, and digressions; and the schizophrenic shifts from gloomy reverie to bitchy social comedy—all in a way that you'll find hard to explain to your roommate.

Chic and snobbish, Proust is nevertheless out to alter consciousness, to make the impossible connections, to demonstrate the relationships, real or illusory, between transcendence and trendiness, art and love, the self and the other, people and birds: His theories of relativity give Einstein's a run for their money.

THE MAGIC MOUNTAIN (1924)
THOMAS MANN

They even took Karen, one afternoon, to the Bioscope Theatre in the Platz—she loved it all so very much. The bad air they sat in was offensive to the three, used as they were to breathing the purest; it oppressed their breathing and made their heads feel heavy and dull. Life flitted across the screen before their smarting eyes: life chopped into small sections, fleeting, accelerated; a restless, jerky fluctuation of appearing and disappearing, performed to a thin accompaniment of music, which set its actual *tempo* to the phantasmagoria of the past, and with the narrowest of means at its command, yet managed to evoke a whole gamut of pomp and solemnity, passion, abandon, and gurgling sensuality. It was a thrilling drama of love and death they saw silently reeled off; the scenes, laid at the court of an oriental despot, galloped past, full of gorgeousness and naked bodies, thirst of power and raving religious self-abnegation; full of cruelty, appetite, and deathly lust, and slowing down to give a full view of the muscular development of the executioner's arms. Constructed, in short, to cater to the innermost desires of an onlooking international civilization.

The novel as triathlon, with politics, philosophy, and science where the bike, the water, and the foam-rubber inner sole should be. Not hard to read, exactly: Unlike Joyce and Proust, Mann—ever the burgher, never the bohemian—gives you a crystal-clear picture of the action; while things get strange, they're never impenetrable. But you do need a whole lot of endurance to get through the lectures on duty and rationalism and Marxism and Eros and vitalism, each delivered by a different Old World spokesperson with an ax to grind.

Itself exhausted, yet moving relentlessly from minute to minute, week to week, and finally year to year, *The Magic Mountain* keeps its hero, the "unremarkable" Hans Castorp, virtually immobile in a sanitarium for the tubercular, located high in the Alps in the days "before the Great War." The sanitarium, of course, is Europe, and Castorp's fellow inmates are Europe's dispossessed: progressive radicals, reactionary Jesuits, cat-eyed Russians. Everyone's a patient. And a captive. Ditto the reader. And the amazing thing about the book is that, as a Munich woman wrote to Mann, "I was not bored by your novel, and with every page I read I was astonished that I was not bored."

If you don't get bored, it'll be despite Mann's craftsmanship (labored, ham-fisted) and storytelling technique (old-fashioned, digressive), and because of his subject, which couldn't be more to the point: art, alienation, and apocalypse. Mann, an architect (to Proust's painter, Joyce's sculptor), has taken a condemned site—all that rotting yet reassuring pre–World War I culture—and built a skyscraper on it. And everybody from J. Alfred Prufrock to Woody Allen has had lunch in its ground-floor restaurant.

Gifts from the Greeks

A FEW ENRICHING IDEAS FROM THE CLASSIC CLASSICAL CIVILIZATION

HOMERWORK

True, the scholars can't be sure that he was really blind, that he was really a wandering minstrel, that he really wrote both (or either) the *Iliad* and the *Odyssey*, or that he even really existed. For the record, most of the scholars now seem to believe that there were two poets at work here, the *Odyssey* poet having been preceded (and influenced) by the *Iliad* poet, and some of them seem to think that *homer* was an archaic Greek verb meaning "to set to verse." Whatever; given how old you—not to mention the poems—are, it's probably easier just to go on filing them under the name Homer and hoping for the best.

What we do know: that both poems are epics, telling memorable, larger-than-life stories in memorable, larger-than-life language; that both concern the Trojan War (but, even taken together, tell only a small part of the story of that war); that they were almost certainly composed sometime in the eighth century B.C., nearly four hundred years after the events they describe; and that they were meant to be recited, not read.

We also know that Western literature begins here. Not only have the *Iliad* and the *Odyssey*, like the Old Testament, never been dropped from the syllabus, they're the cornerstone for the whole epic tradition: Virgil's *Aeneid*, Dante's *Divine Comedy*, Milton's *Paradise Lost*, down through—with the emphasis on the "down"—Joyce's *Ulysses* (see page 250). None of which makes for the world's easiest read; those embarking on same are advised to bear in mind that (1) people in the eighth century B.C. thought of people in the twelfth century B.C. as being bigger, stronger, and better acquainted with the gods than they themselves were (result: a degree of overstatement, and of man/god interaction, that's less just for effect than it is from the heart), and (2) all those "wine-dark sea"s, "rosy-fingered dawn"s, and "Poseidon, shaker of earth"s, while they might have you nodding off, helped both the poet remember his lines and the audience get into the mood (after all, you didn't object when Billy Joel sang "uptown girl" a dozen times in the same song).

Attention, please: While you don't really have to read both (or either) the *Iliad* and the *Odyssey*, you'd be advised to at least have an opinion as to which you like better; some people will even treat your preference as a short-form personality inventory. Which is precisely why we've prepared the following chart, *Iliad* on the left, *Odyssey* on the right:

Iliad	*Odyssey*

	Iliad	*Odyssey*
Setup	Prepare to stay put: a bleak, embattled beach outside the gates of Troy (a.k.a. Ilium—hence the title—in present-day Turkey), in the last months of the ten-year siege the Greeks have undertaken to avenge the wifenapping of luscious Helen from Spartan king Menelaus by Trojan prince Paris	Don your life jacket: thousands of nautical miles and dozens of ports of call, over the course of ten years and much of the eastern Mediterranean, as Odysseus—one of the heroes of the siege of Troy—tries to get home to Ithaca
Main Characters	The Greek Achilles (your basic tragic hero, noble in all things and dashing to the max, but too proud and vengeful for his own good) and the Trojan Hector (a hero himself, stuck fighting a war neither of his own making nor worthy of him)	Odysseus (alias Ulysses, prudent, resourceful, and a born survivor), his son Telemachus (left at home for twenty years, trying to keep things together while wondering where his father—and his sense of self—is), his wife Penelope (long-suffering, likewise resourceful, fending off a clutch of suitors by weaving and unweaving her prenuptial tapestry)
Supporting Cast	On the Greek side: Agamemnon (the king and general, brave but flusterable), Ajax (the consummate soldier, strong, daring, not too swift), Odysseus (see opposite), Patroclus (sweet and gentle, Achilles' longtime companion); on the Trojan side: Priam (king of Troy, father of both Hector and Paris); hovering over all: most of the gods and goddesses, rooting for one team or the other	The fantastical creatures (the women are especially memorable) Odysseus encounters along the way, like Calypso, Circe, the Sirens, the Cyclopes, Scylla and Charybdis, etc., etc.; the kings Telemachus preps under, Nestor (wise and seasoned) and Menelaus (courtly and considerate); Penelope's suitors, as a group; the goddess Athena, presiding over the whole and protecting Odysseus and company

	Iliad	*Odyssey*
Plot Summary	Agamemnon and Achilles quarrel over distribution of booty; Achilles goes off to sulk in tent; war goes on without him; Patroclus, wearing Achilles' armor, is slain by Hector; Achilles, in rage and despair, slays Hector; Achilles and Priam weep together at Hector's funeral	Double (but simple) plot: Odysseus tries—and tries and tries—to get home as Telemachus defies suitors and finally sets out in quest of him; two (characters and plots) are finally united on Ithaca; father and son slay suitors
Genre	Tragedy (said to be ancestor of the drama)	Comedy (said to be ancestor of the novel)
Themes	Manliness, force, duty, *arete* (see page 264); war (obviously), including fighting, killing, plundering; the male impulse	Sensitivity, longing, home and family; the quest for identity and intimacy; the roles of wit and luck, treachery and loyalty; the female principle
Structure	An examination, lasting 16,000 lines, of a single, well-defined incident in the Trojan War (and including neither the war's beginning nor its end); focused, unified, selective	The double plot, natch, plus 12,000 lines of stories from everybody you meet along the way; more story lines than a year's worth of *All My Children*; complex, inclusive, digressive
Tone	Sublime, intense	Sophisticated, wry
Rating	Preferred throughout antiquity; the aristocratic choice (everybody in it is an aristocrat or a god, and everybody who listened to it was probably one, too)	Favorite of contemporary readers (as borne out by trade-paperback sales figures); the popular choice (a vote for people in all shapes and sizes, including women, and with all manner of tales to tell)

But don't cast your ballot now; better to read a passage or two in each, decide which speaks to what's going down at the moment for you. (Try Priam's speech to Hector, *Iliad*, Book XXII, lines 25–76; with the *Odyssey* you're better off skimming till you find something you like.) Then take sides. And one more thing: Hit a dull or a bumpy spot—in the *Iliad*, the *Odyssey*, or anyplace else where for the most part you've been getting a smooth ride—and you can invoke the favorite formula of academics and book reviewers everywhere, coined by the Roman poet Horace in the first century B.C.: "Even Homer nods."

HERO WORSHIP

Of the four great Greek heroes in the days before the Trojan War—before, that is, Agamemnon and Achilles and the *Iliad*—one poses no problem. That's Hercules. The other three are at least as worthy but, scanted by Hollywood, they're short on fan clubs. Here, then, is the rundown on Perseus, Theseus, and Prometheus.

Perseus first, whose father was Zeus—making him a demigod as well as a mere hero—and the one who slew Medusa, she of the snakes-for-hair and the petrifying (literally) countenance; he also rescued Andromeda from the sea monster. With Perseus, we're in what reads like a fairy tale (complete with winged sandals, magic sack, a cap that makes its wearer invisible, and so on). We're also in what could pass for a matriarchy: From his boyhood on, women loom large in Perseus' story, beginning with his mother, Danaë (whom Zeus had gotten pregnant by covering her in a, you should pardon the expression, golden shower), continuing through the three Gray Women (whom Perseus tricked into revealing vital information by stealing the single eye they shared), the three Gorgons (of whom Medusa was one), and Andromeda (who wouldn't have been sea-monster bait if *her* mother, Cassiopeia, hadn't bragged in front of a god about her own beauty). Scholars compare Perseus to Saint George, who likewise slew a dragon and rescued a princess.

Theseus is in every way more difficult; the great Athenian hero, celebrated not only in myth but in three plays by Euripides and one by Sophocles, he has a legend that doesn't quit. Or, as the Athenians themselves used to say, awestruck by the sheer number of his exploits and enterprises, "Nothing without Theseus." Unlike Perseus, Theseus was pure mortal; his father was King Aegeus of Athens, after whom the Aegean Sea would be named. His best-known early adventure was slaying the Minotaur (the half-bull, half-man monster who lived in the labyrinth on Crete) with the help of the princess Ariadne and her ball of thread; his best-known late one had him dealing with his wife Phaedra's infatuation with his son by a previous marriage, Hippolytus. In between there range an ongoing friendship with Hercules, an encounter with Medea, a war with the Amazons, the slaying of Procrustes (with the one-size-fits-all guest-room bed), the forgiving of Oedipus, and much, much more. Quasi-legendary, quasi-historical, Theseus is also an intellect, a man of conscience and compassion, and a father to his people—more King Arthur than just another knight.

The most difficult (and the most senior) of all is Prometheus. Son of one of the Titans, the first wave of rulers in prehistoric Greece, predating Zeus, Hera, Poseidon, and the rest of the Olympians, not to mention the mortals, by at least a generation, Prometheus (literally, "foresight") helped Zeus overthrow their shared ancestors. In gratitude, the new gods delegated Prometheus to create man out of clay. Not knowing when to stop, Prometheus then stole fire from the sun, with the help of which he was able to breathe wisdom (plus a little of what we now call style) into his new creation. Not surprisingly, Zeus saw the fire business as a combination of disloyalty and audacity. Prometheus was chained to a rock, where an eagle pecked daily at his liver, until Hercules finally set him free.

Several things here: First, note that Prometheus pursues and receives fire (a.k.a. inspiration), and is hence a poet; that he has flown in the face of the tyranny of established power, and is hence a rebel; and that his predicament prefigures the Crucifixion, and he is hence a martyr and proto-Christ-figure. Various ages have made various big deals of all this, most notably Aeschylus in the trilogy *Prometheus Bound*, *Prometheus Unbound*, and *Prometheus the Fire Bringer*; and, in the Romantic Age, Goethe, who saw Prometheus as a symbol of man's creativeness and independence of spirit, and Shelley, who wrote *Prometheus Unbound*, part psychodrama, part political allegory, and all antiestablishment hullabaloo. (In it, Prometheus, like Lucifer in *Paradise Lost*, is a rebel with a cause, and Jupiter/Zeus, like Milton's God, is literal-minded and overbearing.) So what are you to make of your cousin's new fiancé when she describes him as "Promethean"? Well, either he's artistic or he's martyred or he's mad as hell; on the other hand, knowing your cousin, he may just wear nail polish.

A word about Hercules: Sure, he's strong. Also simple, blundering, brash, and big. But he's not *just* about strangling snakes, killing lions, diverting rivers through stables, and spelling Atlas for a while. He also has a great midcareer mad scene, is known to dress up in drag, and eventually commits suicide.

TWO GUYS FROM DELPHI

Of the myriad gods and goddesses who habitually messed with the Greeks' heads, only two are still worth getting steamed up about. Apollo, tagged "the most Greek of all the gods," was the god of light, inventor of medicine, master musician, number-one archer, ideal of manly beauty, and symbol of all that was cool, civilized, and rational in Greek life. Like the young JFK, he had a flashy pedigree (son of Zeus and Leto; twin brother of Artemis), wielded enormous political power, had numerous love affairs, and was widely admired for his ability to dispense impartial justice and play a mean game of touch football (or its ancient Greek equivalent) with equal panache. He was definitely a representative of the Establishment, but then, being the law-and-order candidate was no social handicap during the Golden Age, and Delphi, the seat of his oracle, was both a religious shrine and the political power center of Greece.

Dionysus, by contrast, was an arriviste among Greek gods. Although he was fathered by Zeus, his mother, Semele, was a mortal, and no one was ever really sure where he'd spent his presumably wild youth before he arrived on the Greek mainland and started raising hell. While Apollo passed his time inculcating high moral principle and urging moderation in all things, Dionysus and his followers roamed the hills celebrating sex, drugs, and rock 'n' roll. (Actually, as far as we know, the Greeks weren't into hash, coke, or acid at the time, but Dionysus was the god of wine, a substance that, being new to the populace, amounted to the same thing.) Before long, Dionysus had amassed enormous popular appeal and a huge following of bored Greek housewives who were delighted at the chance to slip away from their looms for a night of dancing, shrieking, and ripping small animals to shreds with their teeth. The point, for these Dionysian groupies, was *enthousiasmos*, a state of transcendent ecstasy in which possession was nine-tenths of the fun. Interestingly, the conservative male power structure (we know, we know) was prepared to tolerate these periodic lapses from wifely virtue; instead of banning the Dionysian revels, it simply co-opted them. Dionysus was given his own place of honor at Delphi, time-sharing with Apollo on an alternating six-month basis, and the celebrations became official state occasions. Since Dionysus doubled as the god of drama, these rites turned into theatrical events at which plays were presented as offerings to the god—and there you have the beginnings of theater as we know it.

It may have seemed an unlikely partnership even at the time, but the Apollo/Dionysus alliance worked tolerably well for the Greeks. Having made Dionysus an official element of state religion, they were in a position to regulate his behavior, making him less threatening and more socially acceptable as Greek life became more conservative and rationalistic.

In a way, the rivalry between the two gods didn't really start until the nineteenth century, when Nietzsche, in his *Birth of Tragedy*, contrasted what he saw as the primitive, creative, emotional "Dionysian" state of being, where life is dominated by music, dance, and lyricism, with the formal, analytical, coldly rational, and ultimately static "Apollonian" state, in which art and originality are squelched. Later, Spengler picked up on this notion in *The Decline of the West*, where he theorized that the uninhibited Dionysian element was the mark of a culture on the rise, the overcivilized Apollonian one the beginning of the end. In the Sixties and early Seventies, these characterizations fueled a lot of radical theater and caused a great many people to take off their clothes in public; eventually, however, the Dionysian element began to lose its rough edges once again, and everybody put his or her clothes back on and went to work on Wall Street.

YOU SAY YOUR FATHER SACRIFICED YOUR SISTER,
YOUR MOTHER AMBUSHED YOUR FATHER,
YOU SLAUGHTERED YOUR MOTHER,
AND NOW YOU'VE GONE BLIND AND ARE
BEING CHASED AROUND THE COUNTRYSIDE BY THREE
BLOOD-SOAKED WOMEN WITH SNAKES FOR HAIR?
IS THAT WHAT'S BOTHERING YOU, BUNKY?

Not every civilization has the taste for tragedy that the ancient Greeks had. Not only did they invent the genre, but many critics insist that, in all of Western literature, there have been only four truly great tragic poets, three of whom wrote within fifty years of one another in Periclean Athens, a city whose population, not counting slaves (who didn't have much time to write poetry), was roughly equal to that of present-day Dogpatch. Although this traffic jam of talent has never been adequately explained, it probably stemmed from the Greeks' need to blow off steam (see "Catharsis," page 263) after trying to behave rationally all day instead of sacrificing virgins and praying to rocks the way their ancestors had. In fact, it was part of the function of tragedy to help the man in the street make sense of a lot of decidedly *irrational* gods and goddesses—who were holdovers, for the most part, from more primitive times—while purporting to pay homage to them.

In the absence of public television, it was also up to the tragic poets to combine enlightenment with entertainment. Aeschylus and Sophocles pulled this off with great success; Euripides, on the other hand, was a box-office flop. Nevertheless, given the right translation, all three still have the power, not necessarily to make you cry (if that's all you're after, you can make do with *Terms of Endearment*), but to inspire the "pity and awe" that Aristotle considered hallmarks of any tragedy worth the price of admission. Reading the three in sequence will also give you a bird's-eye view of mankind jockeying for its current position at the center of the universe.

Aeschylus (525–456 B.C.): The granddaddy of Greek tragedy, Aeschylus (ES-ku-lus) was the first playwright to get some real action going by putting two actors on stage at the same time, instead of making audiences listen to one man rapping interminably with a chorus (and, of course, the Greek chorus didn't do high kicks; it just talked). In fact, action was Aeschylus' strong suit. He was a master of the bold stroke—the stirring speech, the grand gesture, the relentless buildup of tension followed by the inevitable thwack of the ax. If he is a little heavy on febrile metaphor ("Behold the orphaned children of the eagle father, now that he has died in the binding coils of the deadly viper, and the young he left behind are worn with hunger of starvation, not full grown to bring their shelter slain food, as their father did") and a little light on verisimilitude (Electra recognizes her long-lost brother, Orestes, by the fact that their footprints match), he is still the tragic poet best equipped to make the hairs stand up on the back of your neck. Armed with the charge-forth morality of the war hero (which, in fact, he was, having participated in the Athenian victory over Persia; see page 606), he never wastes time questioning the motivation of the gods, who seem to get their kicks from making mankind cry uncle, or of his characters, none of whom is notable for thinking things through when there's a suicidal act of courage to commit before breakfast. Nietzsche, one of history's three or four most prominent definers of tragedy, saw Aeschylus' plays as the pinnacle of the form, an expression of the "reaffirmation of the will to live in the face of death." Certainly, his plays are page-turners, and the vision of Clytemnestra boasting that not only has she just slaughtered her husband, the king, but that if she were the teensiest bit less circumspect, she'd drink a toast with his blood, does provide a refreshing alternative to all those *Married . . . with Children* reruns.

Sophocles (c. 496–c. 406 B.C.): The biggest box-office success of the three trage-dians, Sophocles was also the most innovative (he put yet a third actor on stage, thereby thickening the plot considerably; wrote the first self-contained tragedies—as opposed to the trilogies, the Greek version of the miniseries, that audiences were accustomed to; and even came up with the idea of using painted sets), as well as the most craftsmanlike. Although he, too, based his plays on tra-ditional myths, he wasn't opposed to tinkering with the conventions a bit in order to make the stories more believable: There are no matching footprints in *his* ver-sion of the Electra-Orestes reunion; Orestes simply tells Electra who he is. Sophocles is also considered by far the best poet of the lot, an artist who was more interested in perfecting the form than in proving a point. Not that he didn't have a point to prove; as the undisputed champion of the status quo, he virtually defined the poetic tradition of Apollonian classicism (see "Two Guys from Delphi," page 258). When his heroes come to grief, it's because they've failed—albeit through no fault of their own—to follow one of Apollo's two fa-vorite maxims: "Know thyself" and "Nothing to excess." Still, by ascribing his protagonists' inevitable downfall to some fatal flaw of character (see "Hamartia," on the next page) rather than to a fit of pique on the part of some Idi Amin–like deity, Sophocles scored a subtle point for man as more than a spear-carrier in the shaping of his own destiny. Whether Greek audiences grooved on this new power position or just appreciated solid workmanship, they awarded Sophocles a score of first prizes—and never anything less than a second—at the annual Dionysian festival at which all Greek tragedies made their debut. Aristotle pro-claimed Sophocles' *Oedipus Rex* the most perfect of all tragedies; modern critics call his work Greek drama at its most rational, most balanced, and, as some like to point out, most middle-aged.

Euripides (480 or 485–406 B.C.): Last born of the trio, Euripides had the misfor-tune to come of age as the sun began to set on Athenian democracy. While the older generation was still holding pep rallies for the glory that was supposed to be Greece, he started taking potshots at the gods, the established order, and the growing Athenian penchant for power-tripping. Partly because of his vehement antiauthoritarianism, and partly because of his willingness to get so upset over individual human suffering, Euripides is considered the most modern of the tragedians. Psychologically, he was certainly ahead of his time. His characters seem more neurotic than heroic; they're continuously aware of the fact that they're in pain and they never let us forget it, either. Unfortunately, this didn't play as well in the fifth century B.C. as it does nowadays. Euripides ended up a bitter recluse, having won only five first prizes at the Dionysian festivals. In fairness to his audiences, it must be said that he really wasn't the playwright his predecessors were; his plots tend to drift, his pace to drag, and his protagonists to exit the stage more often than not via a *deus ex machina*, literally carried off to meet their destinies by gods and goddesses who suddenly flew in on invisible wires. A couple of millennia later, however, Euripides was to become the ancient-Greek-poet-of-choice for a whole roster of Sixties protest groups, who used his *Trojan Women* to underscore the horror of napalming babies in Vietnam, and his *Medea* to explain why they were burning their bras.

SPEAK ANCIENT GREEK LIKE A NATIVE: TAKE THIS SIMPLE QUIZ

How Is Greek Tragedy Different from the Six O'Clock News?

In Greek tragedy, whenever a construction crane crushes a hapless shopper or a successful politician butchers his next of kin, you'll generally find, in lieu of a camera crew, the following elements:

HAMARTIA: Usually translated as "fatal flaw" (or "error" or "shortcoming"), it's what, according to Aristotle, it takes to be a tragic hero. Sometimes hamartia can verge on vice; sometimes it can seem a misstep no more shameful than choosing the wrong door on a game show. In either case, it functions like a renegade gene, biding its time until the moment is right to bring some otherwise healthy individual to his or her knees. Hamartia is a necessary component of tragedy because, Aristotle reasoned, there is no point in witnessing the destruction of a man who is thoroughly virtuous, on the one hand, or thoroughly corrupt, on the other.

HUBRIS: Everybody's favorite example of hamartia. It adds up to arrogance or pride, although it can start out as an essentially harmless character trait taken to extremes, or, according to some critics, as merely a hero's attempt to express too much in the way of human vitality and choice, thereby violating the social—or the cosmic—order.

NEMESIS: What's going to get a hero whose hubris starts showing. Originally, Nemesis was a quasi-goddess who epitomized righteous anger at a breach of the rules and who liked to mete out punishments. Subsequently, a hero's highly specific, individual, and thoroughly inevitable undoing.

CATHARSIS: The experience of purgation, or purification, of the emotions that Aristotle claimed tragedy could be counted on to produce, thereby rendering it socially useful. Ideally, catharsis is something that both hero and audience will undergo simultaneously, although it's going to hurt the hero a lot more. Of course, we've lost the volume in which Aristotle explained what catharsis was, exactly, but don't let that stand in the way of your having a good cry.

How Is an Ancient Greek Like a Modern Californian?

Both base their way of living on the concept of *arete*, or inborn capacities, the development of which is, for each, the highest purpose of the individual. (The classic example of *arete* is the acorn that, right from the start, has the potential to become a mighty oak.) The Greeks assumed, however, that *arete* had as many social as personal reverberations and that, given all the freedom in the world to develop one's potential, one would naturally develop it in a way that was best for everyone. Self-actualizing as it may be, leaving one's spouse and children to marry one's eighteen-year-old freshman composition student probably wouldn't have counted as full-fledged *arete* for the Greeks.

What's Love Got to Do, Got to Do with It?

The Greeks wrote the book on forms of affection, and Western civilization hasn't done much but muddy the waters ever since. Our umbrella-term "love" didn't exist back in fifth-century Athens; instead there were seen to be three very distinct and powerful love-related forces at work in the world: *eros* (what we would call "sexual love," only more complex), *philia* (what we would call "friendship," but ditto), and *agape* (what we would call "love of God" or "love of God's creatures" if we ever gave it a second thought). Having organized the whole business from the ground up, the Greeks were able to appreciate its subtleties: *Eros*, for instance, while it is the basis for our word "erotic," didn't just refer to the feelings evoked by pornographic vases, or even to the heat generated between men and women (for that matter, the Greeks gave more credence to the heat generated between men and men), but to all sorts of passions, including spiritual ones, that were based on a yearning for union or self-fulfillment; it also recognized the fact that fulfillment inevitably neutralized desire. The social implications of *philia* can't even be translated into English, and under the joint heading *eros/philia* the Greeks had room for a whole roster of good feelings, ranging from kindness toward creatures of the same race (*physike*) to benevolence toward guests (*xenike*). On the other side of the cosmic coin was *agape* (say it like "canapé," sort of), which implied the giving of affection without expecting anything back, and which was soon twisted beyond recognition by overenthusiastic Christian theologians. None of this is to say that the Greeks' clearheaded perspective was responsible for their minuscule divorce rate, only that the Greeks spent a lot of time thinking about the meaning of love, whereas the rest of us have opted just to dance to it.

CHAPTER

MUSIC

W. S. PRESTON.

Contents

Imperial Ladies' Orchestra, Hoag Lake Theater, Woonsocket, Rhode Island; Miss Lizzie A. Otto, directress

Classical Music for the Disconcerted

PLAY IT AGAIN, SAM—AND THIS TIME WE'LL TRY TO LISTEN

Ten paradigmatic works, offered as a map for the ear by contributor **Jon Pareles**.*

JOSQUIN DESPREZ: *LA DÉPLORATION SUR LA MORT D'OCKEGHEM*

IOSQVINVS PRATENSIS.

For most regular concertgoers, music before Bach is a mystery. Even a lot of early-music fans think of it simply as intensely dulcet, fa-la-la-filled madrigals and jaunty dances played on nasal instruments. But that's not all there is to it. This is, after all, music that has survived almost five centuries; one way to enjoy it is to savor its alienness. Its structures can seem whimsical or perverse, as with "cantus firmus" pieces whose important melody is the slowest-moving part, in the bass. And early harmonies sound a little off today, both because the tuning of instruments has changed and because the fifteenth-century ear had its own notions of dissonance and consonance. So, early music moves in mysterious ways—often, it just seems to mosey along, coming to a rest here and there, then moseying on again via the occasional utterly peculiar turn. *La déploration sur la mort d'Ockeghem*, by the Fleming Josquin Desprez, is the sound of the Middle Ages becoming the Renaissance. Johannes Ockeghem, who died in 1495, was the last great medieval composer, writing seamless, otherworldly pieces, all of whose parts moved independently. Josquin's requiem piece for him, with "Requiem aeternam" as its cantus firmus, begins as an homage to Ockeghem, then changes to the more modern style: clearer phrases, voices sometimes echoing each other, something akin to modern chords. In half a century, there would indeed be madrigals; a century after that, Bach would be born.

*Jon Pareles is a music critic for the *New York Times*.

JOHANN SEBASTIAN BACH: MASS IN B MINOR, BWV 232

Bach was the greatest Baroque composer because he was also the last Renaissance composer; that is, he wrote brilliantly in both the newfangled *concertante* style—with a clear separation of melody and accompaniment, in forms built from contrasting sections—and the older, free-flowing counterpoint. Written between 1733 and 1748 (Bach died in 1750), the Mass is a virtual Bach encyclopedia, with each chunk of text set as the composer saw fit. It has solo arias; sections in which voices and instruments intertwine; massive concertante choruses in which solo and instrumental groups trade off with full chorus and the Baroque orchestra of strings, organ, recorders, oboes, bassoons, trumpets, and drums; and sublime, complex fugues, pieces in strict counterpoint derived from the staggered entrances of the theme, or "subject." Some arias, such as the "Agnus dei" for alto and the "Domine Deus" for soprano, tenor, and recorder, are so devout it's hard to remember that Bach was only a Lutheran.

WOLFGANG AMADEUS MOZART: SYMPHONY NO. 41 IN C MAJOR ("JUPITER"), K. 551

In *Lucky Jim*, Kingsley Amis called Mozart's music a "skein of untiring facetiousness." Maybe. But not the "Jupiter." True, its themes are typically Mozartian question/answer pairs, ever so neatly balanced. And, as with most classical symphonies, each movement proceeds duly away from, then back to, its starting point. (In sonata form, used in first movements of symphonies and sonatas, themes are introduced, taken for a ride, then returned home safe and sound.) But in Mozart's music, the process is displayed with diagrammatic clarity and absolute poise. Even when the writing seems effortless, it moves forward; its symmetries pull it ahead gracefully yet inevitably, disturbing their own balance, only to set it straight again. The three final symphonies Mozart wrote in sum-

mer 1788 (the "Jupiter" is the last one) are the peak of classical form, congenial and precise. At his best, Mozart wasn't facetious—he was Olympian.

LUDWIG VAN BEETHOVEN: PIANO SONATA NO. 29 IN B FLAT MAJOR, OPUS 106 ("HAMMERKLAVIER" SONATA)

When the movies show Beethoven in creative agony, the soundtrack ought to be the "Hammerklavier," which took him two years to write (1817–1818) and blew the roof off the sonata while honoring its form (see Mozart). The "Hammerklavier" is an obsessive work, longer and probably more difficult than any previous piano sonata, yet so concentrated that almost every detail, large and small, derives from a single idea: in musical terms, a chain of descending thirds. Like the iodine crystal that seeds a cloud, that idea generates not only all of the sonata's themes, but its harmonic plan and even the relation between movements. Beethoven's relentless logic leads him far afield (the Adagio has moments that sound like Chopin) but he never, ever rambles. Despite its length, the "Hammerklavier" is no-frills writing with a vengeance.

FRÉDÉRIC CHOPIN: TWENTY-FOUR PRELUDES, OPUS 28

In some of the greatest salons of all time, Chopin was *the* salon pianist. He was much loved for his pianistic technique, and for the sense of melancholia in even his most triumphant pieces. He was also a harmonics pioneer, charting extraordinary new chords. Like most of his contemporaries, Chopin was better at writing tunes than at sustaining large-scale structures; unlike them, he had the sense to concentrate on miniatures (the preludes, waltzes, mazurkas) and on extended miniatures (ballades, nocturnes, polonaises). In 1839 he completed the twenty-four preludes—one in each major and minor key, just like Bach's *The Well-Tempered Clavier*; none is longer than five minutes, most under two. Each is a gem: the C Minor, whose chord sequence was stolen for the *Fame* theme song; the E Minor, with its sustained melody floating above an astounding sequence of chords; the lithely filigreed E Flat Major; the vociferous, breakneck, where-the-hell-are-we-going G Minor. Chopin doesn't make more of his ideas than he ought to; if thirty-three seconds is enough, that's where the prelude ends. A few composers could take the hint.

PETER ILYICH TCHAIKOVSKY: CONCERTO IN D FOR VIOLIN AND ORCHESTRA, OPUS 35

Think of Romantic man, alone and heroic, bending a universe to his will—what better analogue than the concerto? The soloist faces the orchestra and battles it with his virtuosity until, finally, they join in triumphant partnership. From Mozart's time, the concerto had been a star vehicle, but the classical-era composers at least remembered that the orchestra existed. By the time Tchaikovsky wrote his Violin Concerto in 1878, the orchestra is lucky to get a few rumbles and forebodings in edgewise before the soloist enters with his first sweet, soulful melody. That tune comes back as a rabble-rousing march, complete with trumpets, but not before a tear-jerking second theme and considerable violinistic showing-off. The showing-off is the point, of course. After a short, tearful Andante, the concerto's finale is a violin decathlon. Upon hearing the premiere, Vienna's top critic wrote: "The violin is no longer played but rent asunder, beaten black and blue." What fun.

ARNOLD SCHOENBERG: *PIERROT LUNAIRE*, OPUS 21

Schoenberg blueprinted quite a bit of twentieth-century chamber music with his 1912 song cycle, *Pierrot Lunaire*. Loony (or, if you prefer, moon-drunk) Pierrot the harlequin drifts through Albert Giraud's twenty-one poems to the sinuous dissonances of a "broken consort," instruments from different families: piano, flute, clarinet, violin, and cello. The poems are declaimed in *Sprechstimme*, literally "speak-sing," which Schoenberg devised as a combination of song's melodic contours and speech's indeterminacy. After *Pierrot*, Schoenberg (along with Anton von Webern) went on to further compress and systematize atonal pointillism in the serial or twelve-tone style (see page 281), all the rage in the latter part of the twentieth century. Meanwhile, the instrumentation, *Sprechstimme*, text-centered form, tiny musical gestures, and atonality all gave other composers ideas. So did Pierrot's light-headedness.

IGOR STRAVINSKY:
LE SACRE DU PRINTEMPS (THE RITE OF SPRING)

The Rite of Spring is Tarzan among the classics: pagan, ill-mannered, passionate, suffused with jungle rhythms. No wonder there was a riot at the 1913 premiere, where it backed a Diaghilev ballet that Stravinsky never much liked. What the vociferous audience missed, however, was the music's astonishing intricacy and delicacy. Between its percussive, brassy climaxes—the rite ends with a young girl dancing herself to death—*Le Sacre* is deeply melodic without an atom of sentiment (the bassoon call that opens the piece may haunt you forever). Stravinsky studied orchestration with Rimsky-Korsakov (of *Scheherezade* fame) but turned all the old tricks inside out, using woodwinds in particular to achieve an eerie, pungent sound. Half a century later, *Le Sacre* is still galvanizing for audiences and hellishly difficult for orchestras and conductors. It has, moreover, left its mark. Leonard Bernstein brought its choppy rhythms to Broadway in *West Side Story*, and its obsessively repeated motifs, energizing harmonies that barely move, predicted late-twentieth-century minimalism.

BÉLA BARTÓK: THE SIX STRING QUARTETS

String quartets, historically, are a composer's most rigorous private utterances; with just two violins, viola, and cello there's no room for anything but purest form expressed in intimate counterpoint. The six string quartets Bartók wrote between 1908 and 1939 are, with Beethoven's final six, the form at its most intense. Bartók's sum up his growth from an impressionable pan-European eclectic to a visionary native (in this case Hungarian) voice. In the first three, Bartók puts the squeeze on received lyricism: He reduces themes to angular motifs, develops those motifs with merciless concision, replaces comfortable Europeanisms with dissonances and rhythms out of Hungarian folk tradition. The third quartet, his shortest, is so distilled and dramatic it feels like a single indrawn breath. For the final three, Bartók loosens up a bit, singing in the atonal phrases of his own new language. Along the way, he uses every bit of the string quartet's sonic vocabulary, including sliding notes and glassy harmonics and grainy *col legno* (playing with the wood of the bow), yet never sounds as if he's showboating because every effect is at the service of the whole.

TERRY RILEY: IN C

It's only a page or two of music, a collection of fifty-three motifs in the key of C. Any number of musicians, the more the better, can play it without a conductor. While somebody plunks out steady Cs on a keyboard, the other musicians play a motif, repeat it for some time, then move on to the next one. They all listen to each other so that no one gets too far ahead or behind. And the nigh-miraculous result is a monumental work: a rich, pulsing C chord encompassing ceaseless activity, change within stasis. Written in 1964, *In C* was Riley's seminal work of minimalism, or trance music, or process music, or going-nowhere music, or cooperative music, or whatever you want to call it. Because it was so warmly consonant, minimalism attracted a new audience to contemporary music; because it ignored most classical ideas of form and drama, it had the old guard outraged.

The Parts of an Orchestra, Dear, Once and for All

Actually, you have a right to be confused; orchestra structures come and go—as they've been doing for about three centuries—and a conductor will add or subtract instruments at the drop of a baton, depending on the demands of the piece to be performed. In general, however, when people today say "symphony orchestra," they mean pretty much what they meant in the nineteenth century, and what you see below. Of the four sections of instruments, the string section is the largest, most important, and usually the most continuously played. Woodwinds are second in the pecking order; they add color and sometimes carry the melody. The brass, which acts as the muscle, or amplifier, in those swelling, passionate passages, is generally used sparingly. And, of course, the percussion section provides the beat. If you still don't know a cornet from a clarinet, study this page, then clip and pin it to your sleeve.

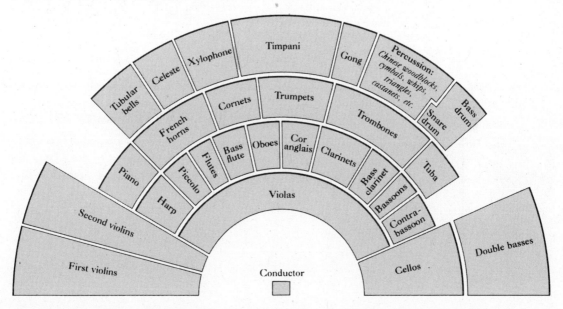

STRINGS: First and second violins (they're all the same instruments, they just play different parts), violas, violoncellos (or simply cellos), double basses, and, sometimes, a harp.
WOODWINDS: Piccolo, flutes, clarinets, oboes, cor anglais, bassoons.
BRASS: French horns, cornets, trumpets, trombones, tuba.
PERCUSSION: Timpani, bass drum, snare drum, cymbals, triangles, assorted instruments such as woodblocks, castanets, celeste, gongs, glockenspiel, xylophone, etc.

Practical Italian for the Concertgoer

First, there are the words indicating the speed and volume at which a composition is to be played; we've ranged them from the least to the most.

SPEED		VOLUME (with abbreviations)	
grave (= solemn) largo (= wide, broad)	very slow	pianissimo (pp)	very soft
adagio (= at ease)	quite slow	piano (p)	soft
lento	slow	mezzo piano (mp)	sort of soft
andante (= walking)	steady, flowing	mezzo forte (mf)	sort of loud
andantino	either somewhat faster or somewhat slower than andante, depending on your conductor's reading of that diminutizing suffix	forte (f)	loud
		fortissimo (ff)	very loud
moderato	moderate		

Note: More *p*'s or *f*'s can be added as desired by the composer; there are even *pppppp* passages in Tchaikovsky's "Pathétique."

allegretto	moderately fast		
allegro (= cheerful)	fast		
vivace	lively		
presto	fast		
prestissimo	very, very fast		

CHANGE IN SPEED		CHANGE IN VOLUME	
accelerando	getting faster	crescendo	getting louder
ritardando rallentando	getting slower	decrescendo diminuendo	getting softer

You've noted that the Italians like to qualify things. Sometimes they do this with suffixes (that *-issimo*, for instance, means "very," *-ino* and *-etto* both mean "a little"). Sometimes they use whole words, as with:

molto	much
meno	less
mezzo	half
poco	a little
non troppo	not too much

But that's just the basic, strike-up-the-band stuff. Other, less blatantly quantitative terms, in simple alphabetical order, include:

A CAPPELLA (literally, "as in church"): Used of vocal music without instrumental accompaniment, even though instrumental accompaniment has been common in churches since the Middle Ages.

ARPEGGIO (literally, "as played on a harp"): A broken chord in which the notes are played in succession so as to recall—on a piano, violin, whatever—a harpist "sweeping" the strings.

CADENZA (literally, "cadence"): A passage in a concerto (and a display of virtuosity, florid, brilliant, or both) in which the solo instrument plays without the orchestra. It was up to the performer to decide to execute a cadenza until the time of Mozart; now always indicated by the composer.

CANTABILE (literally, "singable"): In a flowing style.

CODA (literally, "tail"): A concluding, rounding-off section to a piece of music, or a portion of it.

DA CAPO (literally, "from the head"): An indication that a previously played section of music is to be repeated.

GLISSANDO (from an Italian version of the French *glisser*, to slide): Sliding from note to note, as by running one's fingers over the keys of the piano, strings of the harp, etc.

LEGATO (literally, "bound together"): Describes a smooth performance without accentuated notes (cf. "staccato," on the next page).

OBBLIGATO (literally, "obligatory"): Denotes some indispensable part: an elaborate embellishment of a main melodic line, an instrument that's critical (but subordinate) to a vocal performance. Careful: Some people use the term to signal precisely that element which *can* be dispensed with; the point is, according to them, if it's a key support, it can't also be the heart of the matter.

PIZZICATO (literally, "pinched"): Directs that, with stringed instruments, the strings are to be plucked with the fingers, not bowed.

RUBATO (literally, "robbed"): Indicates that a player should "play around" with a given tempo, marginally accelerating or relaxing it, for effect; sometimes on a piano keyboard one hand might play "normally," the other go with the *rubato*. Also known as swaying the rhythm.

SCHERZO (literally, "joke"): A sped-up form of the minuet, much beloved of Haydn and Beethoven. Common today as a component of sonatas, symphonies, etc.

SFORZANDO (literally, "forced"): Designates a note to be played with special emphasis.

STACCATO (literally, "detached"): Opposite of "legato" (on previous page), with notes to be played in a sharp, highly differentiated manner.

TESSITURA (literally, "texture"): Refers to the basic range of a part, vocal or musical, excluding any very high or low notes.

TOCCATA (literally, "touched"): A piece that shows off the "touch"; originally often used of a trumpet fanfare, now more often of a free-form keyboard piece.

TREMOLO (literally, "tremulous"): A "trembling" effect, either from the rapid repetition of a single note (by, say, fast backward-and-forward bowing) or from the rapid alternation of two notes more than a whole tone apart.

VIBRATO (literally, "shake"): A rapid, slight wavering of pitch.

Five Composers Whose Names Begin with the Letter P

WE'D HAVE THROWN IN PAGANINI, BUT WE KNOW HOW BUSY YOU ARE

GIOVANNI PIERLUIGI DA PALESTRINA (1525–1594): No pioneer. A native Roman who composed almost entirely for the Church, Palestrina wrote masses, motets, and hymns in the same polyphonic texture—where separate strands of melody, each provided by an independent voice, count for more than the harmony they go to make up—that characterizes all music composed before 1600. But if he only marks the end of the medieval era, with all its ritual and mysticism, rather than the dawn of a new one, Palestrina's still one of the most important figures before Bach and Handel. Think of him as the Homer of music.

FRANCIS POULENC (1899–1963): Wrote avant-garde music with the working man in mind. Poulenc belonged to the group of irreverent young composers called the Six, a fixture of between-the-wars Paris (Erik Satie, who'd made a career of irreverence, was the group's sponsor; it also included Darius Milhaud and Arthur Honegger). Against authority (in this case, traditional French good taste), fond of jazz and the music hall, susceptible to the Dadaist and Surrealist movements in art, these guys would all be hanging out in yet-to-be-gentrified pockets of Brooklyn today. Of the Six, Poulenc was the most gamin, mischievous and flippant, squarely on the side of everyday music for everyday people. Who'd have predicted that, by the late Fifties, he'd be writing opera and religious music?

SERGEI PROKOFIEV (1891–1953): One of three Russian composers of this century you can't not know something about. Despite some youthful iconoclasm (and an ongoing astringency), Prokofiev is about as accessible as good twentieth-century music gets: melodious but not bland, rhythmic but not blatant. He may also be the first classical composer you ever heard, if your first-grade teacher played you *Peter and the Wolf* the way ours did. The other two de rigueur Russians: Igor Stravinsky (see also page 273, with as many moods, phases, and ego needs as Picasso), and Dmitri Shostakovich (the heir to Tchaikovsky, but also the number one product—and victim—of Soviet musical training and strictures).

GIACOMO PUCCINI (1858–1924): If Italy were on fire and only a single Italian opera could be saved, it wouldn't be one of Puccini's. Though there's no arguing with *La Bohème*, *Tosca*, and *Madame Butterfly* at the box office, they can, next to the best of Verdi, strike bona-fide opera lovers as a little, well, vulgar. A showman and crowd-pleaser (not to mention a pirate who wasn't above stealing an idea or two from a colleague), Puccini has had his greatest influence on the development of the popular musical theater.

HENRY PURCELL (1659–1695): First, the good news. Purcell is virtually the only pre-twentieth-century English composer you have to know anything about at all. Now, the bad news. You *do* have to remember that it's pronounced "PURS-el," with the accent up front. For his short life, Purcell was the great Baroque master, not only of English music, but of European music in general; technically brilliant, exceptionally versatile, he was the first winner of the coveted Wünderkind Award that would later go to Mozart. Purcell's gifts included an ability to adapt musical composition to the peculiar inflections of spoken English; it's rumored that, had he lived a little longer, he'd have made something of English opera.

The Day the Music Died

ATONALITY, TWELVE-TONE THEORY, AND SUCH

Depending on whether you're one of the cognoscenti or just an average listener, atonality is either the biggest breakthrough of the twentieth century or what's wrong with modern music. Before you can understand what atonality *is*, however, you have to know a little about what it isn't—namely, tonality. Think, for a moment, of how nicely "do re mi fa sol la ti do" fit together—that's tonality for you. It has to do with the idea that, of the twelve tones in a chromatic scale (all the notes from, say, one C to another on the piano keyboard), only seven have a natural affinity for, hence are capable of sustaining meaningful relationships with, each other. These tones interact as family members, experiencing their little tensions (dissonances) from time to time, but managing to work things out between themselves (consonances), and always, ultimately, gravitating toward one restful "home" note (the tonic), which determines their key. Such groupings—orderly, reassuring, full of familiar emotional associations—are the basis of tonality and of virtually all Western music from Bach to Brahms.

In the early 1900s, however, the Viennese composer Arnold Schoenberg, heavily influenced by Wagner (who had played around with dissonance in *Tristan und Isolde*), by twentieth-century malaise, by German Expressionism, by the radical thinking then rampant in Vienna, and by his own Teutonic angst, began to chafe under the old tonal tradition—and under the idea that music was supposed to make people feel better. In 1921 he did the first really new thing in three hundred years of musical history: He threw out tonality altogether and composed an opus in which he gave equal importance to all twelve tones of the chromatic scale. In order to keep his early compositions from slipping naturally into tonality, Schoenberg filled them with dissonance, in much the same way German Expressionist painters filled their paintings with the grotesque: Dissonance broke up the notes, kept them from forming cliques, as it were, and evoked a kind of unrelieved tension—near hysteria, in fact—which seemed right for the times.

There was still the problem of how to hold a piece together without tonality, however. Schoenberg eventually solved it by inventing the twelve-tone row, which became the basis for twelve-tone, or dodecaphonic, music, as well as for later serial music. Composing with twelve tones is a little like playing a very complicated board game, minus the entertainment value. First, the composer decides on a row—a particular order for the twelve pitches. The row then becomes the basic material of the piece, with variations unfolding according to a very specific set of rules. It can, for instance, be played forward, backward, upside-down, or upside-down and backward, so long as the whole row is played through before any of the tones is sounded again. (Are you beginning to see why twelve-tone music has failed to capture the popular imagination?) In short, the twelve-tone form was a necessarily arbitrary, highly intellectual way of exerting control over the chaotic elements of atonal compositions, of imposing the strictly rational over the basically irrational.

Later, the idea of the tone row as the organizing principle of a piece led composers to attempt to exercise the same kind of control over all the elements of a piece: pitch, rhythm, timbre, dynamics, you name it. This all comes under the heading "serial music," which can include, but isn't limited to, twelve-tone and atonal forms. Absolute control! To the public, this was simply not an idea whose time had come; to many critics, it was an idea whose time had come and gone. In fact, the whole business of atonal and serial music shouldn't worry you too much; only composers really understand it and they rarely talk to anyone but each other anyway. Just keep in mind that atonality aims at a whole new concept of what music, and listening to music, is all about, and be aware that, silly as serial music can get at times, virtually every modern composer has flirted with its various forms at some point in his or her career—as contributor **Ronald Varney** documents here.

TUNEBUSTERS

In 1899, after trying in his early compositions to out-Wagner Wagner, the twenty-one-year-old Arnold Schoenberg composed a string sextet entitled *Transfigured Night*. It was a milestone in the history of music, perhaps the first really atonal work.

In 1904 Alban Berg and Anton von Webern, also Austrians, apprenticed themselves to Schoenberg in Vienna and became the two chief disciples of his radical musical teachings. While Berg, handsome and aristocratic, always displayed somewhat romantic tendencies in his composing, Webern, squinty-eyed and professorial, would become more daring and radical than the master himself. In 1910, with these two firmly under his wing, Schoenberg crowed, "In ten years, every talented composer will be writing this way, regardless of whether he has learned it directly from me or only from my work."

In 1912 Schoenberg composed *Pierrot Lunaire* (see also page 272), a fully atonal, slightly bizarre song cycle which is considered his masterpiece. About it, Leonard Bernstein wrote: "This is a piece which never fails to move and impress me, but always leaves me feeling a little bit sick. This is only just, since sickness is what it's about—moon-sickness. Somewhere in the middle of this piece you have a great desire to run and open a window, breathe in a lungful of healthy, clean air."

Berg, though not prolific, wrote three works that have become recognized as major additions to the classical repertoire: his *Violin Concerto* and two operas, *Wozzeck* and *Lulu*.

The enigmatic Webern concentrated on chamber music, emphasizing silence as much as sound in almost painfully short works that reduce music to its barest elements. His *Six Bagatelles* for string quartet is only three and a half minutes long. Other works, like his *Variations* for orchestra or *Symphony for Chamber Orchestra*, seem to last a lifetime. "The pulverization of sound into a kind of luminous dust" is the way Virgil Thomson described one of Webern's pieces.

It is ironic that, of atonality's Big Three, Schoenberg probably enjoyed the least success. During the 1930s he fled Germany and wound up in Los Angeles, where he taught at UCLA and continued to compose. He died in 1951, embittered by his lack of recognition. And when atonal music and the twelve-tone theory swept Europe and the United States during the Fifties and Sixties, it was Webern, not Schoenberg, who was hailed as the high priest of atonality. Webern's works were so influential, in fact, that they prompted a binge of international experimentation. Some examples:

Iannis Xenakis: One of the most often booed of modern composers. Has written music based on far-out theories from math and engineering.

Pierre Boulez: Noted for his contempt for every composer in history (except himself, the Big Three, and maybe a few of his own followers). Has generally sought in his music a sound expressing, as he puts it, a "collective hysteria and spells, violently of the present time."

John Cage: Achieved renown for cramming all kinds of junk, from bits of wood to weather-stripping, into his "prepared pianos" and then having the pianist strike the keys at random. Tireless in his efforts to do away with the role of the composer. Known for two particularly eccentric works: *Imaginary Landscape No. 4*, in which twelve radios are "played" by twenty-four performers; and the most famous silent piece of history, *4'33"*, in which a pianist sits silently at the keyboard for four minutes and thirty-three seconds, creating a sort of musical vacuum in the concert hall. Also fun: his *0'0"*, to be played "in any way to anyone."

Karlheinz Stockhausen: A specialist in electronic music. Like Cage, explores the outer frontiers of musical pointlessness. In the epic cycle *Gold Dust*, asked the performers first to starve themselves for four days while living in complete isolation. Then, in his own words, to "late at night, without conversation beforehand, play single sounds, without thinking which you are playing, close your eyes, just listen."

The atonality craze that began after Webern's death in 1945 was, by the mid-1970s, already winding down. The music had become incredibly complicated; audiences felt increasingly bored and alienated by it; and the composers found themselves with nothing more to say on the subject. The next generation of avant-garde composers, such as Philip Glass (see page 291) and Steve Reich, while still in the atonal tradition, took to writing music that was less grating and more hypnotic.

Still, two things must be said for atonality: It broke classical music wide open, and it left audiences reeling. Neither has fully recovered.

Beyond BAY-toe-v'n
and MOAT-sart

It's not that music is strewn with unpronounceable names; in fact, if you can fake your way in French, remember a handful of basic German pronunciations (like the two in the title), and treat all Italian proper names as if they were varieties of pasta, you'll do fine. There are, however, a few classic pitfalls.

1. The sole Brazilian composer to achieve international status: Heitor Villa-Lobos (AY-tor VEE-la LOW-bush).
2. The German expatriate composer, now best known for his theater work: Kurt Weill (VILE).
3. The two Czechs, one best known for his symphonies, the other (see page 290) for his operas, Antonin Dvorák and Leoš Janácek (AN-toe-neen DVOR-zhock and LEH-osh YAN-a-check).
4. The highly polished turn-of-the-century French composer: Camille Saint-Saëns (ka-ME-YA sanh-sawnhs; lots of nasality, please, and only one vowel sound in "Saëns").
5. The only really important pre-twentieth-century English composer: Henry Purcell (PURS-el).
6. The Hungarian-born conductor: Sir Georg Solti (SHOAL-tee); pronounce the Georg part "George."
7. The New Zealand–born soprano: Kiri Te Kanawa (KIR-ee Tuh-KON-a-wa). And then there's the one about how Barbara Walters calls her "Kiwi."
8. Those two composing, conducting, former enfants terribles of contemporary music, one French, the other American: Pierre Boulez (see page 283) and Leonard Bernstein (it's boo-LEZ and BERN-stine (stein, as in Steinway).
9. Finally, the iconic German composer: Richard Wagner (RICK-art VOG-ner). Germanicize the first name too.

Opera for Philistines

350 YEARS OF OPERA AT A GLANCE

THE ITALIANS

Invented opera, the Mediterranean equivalent of baseball, c. 1570. Encouraged enthusiastic audience participation. Had knack for creating catchy tunes. Ruled the roost until the twentieth century.

THE COMPOSERS

THE OPERAS

Claudio Monteverdi (1567–1643)
Opera's first musical genius; turned early academic theory into stage success by hitting his audiences where they lived. Speak his name with respect.

Heavy on recitative and short on show-stoppers, but the passion and musicianship still come across; highly respected museum pieces. The masterpieces, *Orfeo* and *L'Incoronazione di Poppaea*, continue to draw crowds, especially in Europe, where Baroque opera (of which Monteverdi's work is a prime example) has periodic revivals.

Alessandro Scarlatti (1660–1725)
One of the fathers of classical opera; a scholar's composer. Historical landmark only.

Of the 115 he wrote, about 70 are extant and you've never heard of any of them. Big deal in their day, however. Established opera as a going concern. Laid structural foundation for *opera seria*—serious opera, Italian style, of the seventeenth and eighteenth centuries, with heroic characters, tragic predicaments, usually mythical settings, strictly delineated arias and recitatives.

Gioacchino Antonio Rossini (1792–1868), Vincenzo Bellini (1801–1835), Gaetano Donizetti (1797–1848)
Hottest composers of their time; big box-office draws.

Rossini's *The Barber of Seville* was the pinnacle of *opera buffa* (comic opera about common people and everyday life, usually revolving around boisterous romantic intrigues; a reaction against the stuffy formality of *opera seria*). Bellini and Donizetti, on the other hand, were rivals in the *bel canto* category (see page 295). Major entries: the former's *Norma*, the latter's *Lucia di Lammermoor*. Donizetti's operas were sloppier but contained more memorable tunes and the most sentimental atmospheres. Bellini's works were more meticulous but thin on story line and orchestrally clumsy; he might have won in the end, but he died young.

Giuseppe Verdi (1813–1901)

Mr. Opera; the greatest Italian composer in a predominantly Italian art form. Like Shakespeare, had innate sense of theater: instinct for constructing plot, creating character, moving action along, suffusing the whole with universal themes; wrote unforgettable melodies. Of humble origins; a patriot. Changed the nature of traditional Italian opera simply by outgrowing it.

For the most part, melodramas that transcend their genre. Any Verdi opera is considered a class act, but the three of his "middle period," *Rigoletto*, *Il Trovatore*, *La Traviata*, are the most popular; *Aïda* is the grandest; *Otello* and *Falstaff*, his one comedy, are the prestige choices, both "mature Verdi."

Giacomo Puccini (1858–1924)

Most bankable composer ever. The Steven Spielberg of opera. (See also page 279.)

Superficial, sentimental, border on the vulgar and, in some cases (notably *Turandot*), the perverse. But *Tosca*, *La Bohème*, and *Madame Butterfly* are supremely accessible, undeniably heartrending, and laden with catchy tunes. Watch for the earmarks of *verismo*, the trendy gutter realism of the period.

THE GERMANS

Heavily into symbolism, weighty themes, philosophical and sometimes erotic undertones, and, after Wagner, orchestration. Top of the charts in the twentieth century.

THE COMPOSERS

THE OPERAS

Christoph Willibald von Gluck (1714–1787)

Opera's first great reformer; attempted to streamline the form, do away with the florid excesses of *opera seria*, create a balance of power between drama and music. Of great historical, but little practical, importance, because no one followed his lead.

Formal, well balanced, critically respected, and largely forgotten because they lack immediate musical appeal. You're not likely to see *Orfeo ed Euridice* or *Iphigénie en Tauride*, at least where opera houses depend on audiences to pay their expenses.

Wolfgang Amadeus Mozart (1756–1791)

No great innovator, but had that magic touch; personalized and humanized opera and succeeded in balancing all of its pain-in-the-neck elements. A master musician, a sophisticate, a "natural." With Verdi and Wagner, forms the triumvirate of opera "greats."

Remember Mozart's three great "Italian" operas: *Le Nozze di Figaro*, a comedy with political overtones; *Così fan tutte*, a sexual farce, sort of, that scandalized all but late-twentieth-century audiences; and *Don Giovanni*, the greatest example of Mozart's unconventional mix of tragedy and comedy. The two "German" operas to know about are *Die Entführung aus dem Serail (The Abduction from the Seraglio)* and *Die Zauberflöte* (*The Magic Flute*, which some critics consider the most perfect opera ever written). Both are advances on the traditional German "singspiel," a loose construction of popular and folk tunes, and together laid the foundations for indigenous German opera.

Ludwig van Beethoven (1770–1827)

The Romantic genius; wrote only one opera, but it's a doozy.

Fidelio took nine years to write, blazed no new trails, and has some serious problems in the structure department; still, it's Beethoven, it's big-time, and to its admirers, it's the greatest opera ever written. It is also, in its moralistic themes, the polar opposite of the frivolous immorality Herr B. deplored in Mozart.

Richard Wagner (1813–1883)

Opera's towering intellect, its second Great Reformer (this one had influence in spades), and the pinnacle of German Romanticism. A megalomaniac and a visionary.

Wagnerian "music drama" (his term) aimed at a union of all theatrical arts: poetry, drama, music, and stagecraft. Major innovations: symphony-scale operatic orchestration (and singers powerful enough to be heard over it); the dripping-with-significance leitmotif (an orchestral theme recurring throughout a work and representing a particular character or idea). All Wagner operas are narcotic, hypnotic, and very, very long. *Tannhäuser* is considered the most accessible, *Parsifal* the least. In between, remember *Tristan und Isolde*; the four-opera *Ring* cycle; and the lone comedy, *Die Meistersinger von Nürnberg*. All are full of psychosexual undertones and all are holy, holy, holy.

Richard Strauss (1864–1949)

Most popular composer of the turn of the century. Not to be confused with Johann Strauss, "The Waltz King," although Richard capitalized on the association by sprinkling his operas with waltz tunes.

Lovely, easy-to-swallow operas that made lots of money. *Salomé* is best remembered as a succès de scandale, *Der Rosenkavalier* for its pretty waltzes.

Alban Berg (1885–1935)

Probably the most important modern opera composer; an experimentalist working with atonality and post-Freudian themes (see also page 282).

His two operas, *Wozzeck* (pronounced VOY-check) and the unfinished (but recently reconstructed) *Lulu* are both highly cerebral, avant-garde works with complex musical structures unlike anything you ever thought of as opera. Don't bother looking for melodies (there aren't any), but the plots are full of sinister sexuality and twentieth-century angst.

THE FRENCH

In it for the spectacle: the storyline, the costumes, the courtly dances, the divine special effects, and *le pauvre* who gets boiled in oil in the second act.

THE COMPOSERS

THE OPERAS

Giacomo Meyerbeer (1791–1864)

A German who went to Paris and wrote the most successful French operas of his time. The master of grand opera. His works are now rarely performed.

Les Huguenots, the best-known and longest lived, is grand opera par excellence. The dominant style in nineteenth-century France, grand opera was long, epic, historical, and loaded with spectacle, always including a ballet or two and usually at least one massacre. Never the most subtle or best-knit of plots, but large, expensive, and exciting.

Louis-Hector Berlioz (1803–1869)

Either France's greatest opera composer or a genius *manqué*, depending on taste. Much maligned in his own day ("The French wanted talent, not genius," says a critic). Brilliant anti-Wagnerian opera theorist; unconventional, unclassifiable. Remains a controversial figure.

No two alike, though all aimed at drama *through* music (as opposed to the Wagnerian ideal of drama *and* music); *Benvenuto Cellini*, an early, resounding failure, cut short his operatic career; *Les Troyens (The Trojans)*, his "gigantic masterpiece," brought vindication in the twentieth century.

Charles François Gounod (1818–1893); Georges Bizet (1838–1875)
Each wrote one masterpiece.

Gounod's *Faust*, once ubiquitous, has dropped down the charts recently, but is still one of the few French operas performed all over the world. Bizet's *Carmen* is the most famous example of *opéra comique* (the French alternative to grand opera; not necessarily humorous, although usually equipped with a happy ending; the term applied to any opera that included spoken dialogue) and, although often badly produced, one of the most popular operas ever.

THE ENGLISH

Always a bridesmaid, never a bride.

THE COMPOSERS

Henry Purcell (1659–1695)
England's Great White Hope. Alas, he died young. (See page 280.)

George Frideric Handel (1685–1759)
German-born, naturalized Englishman who lived in London and wrote mainstream Italian operas. Because he and they were so successful, gave English colleagues a permanent inferiority complex.

Benjamin Britten (1913–1976)
England's postwar contender; not in the Hall of Fame just yet, but the best they've got and the only modern English composer whose name you're likely to hear. Known for eclecticism, passionate music, a feeling for the human predicament.

THE OPERAS

Dido and Aeneas, the only English opera to rank as a world masterpiece.

Quintessential *opera seria*; of Handel's many operas, a few are still performed, e.g. *Orlando*, *Giulio Cesare*, *Rinaldo*. Beautiful music, lame dramas, highly formalized structures; once considered white elephants, now have a limited but enthusiastic following.

Peter Grimes and *Billy Budd* are his two well-known, full-scale operas; lack of English opera tradition and consequent lack of funding resulted in chamber (small) operas such as *The Turn of the Screw*, *Let's Make an Opera*, *The Beggar's Opera* (a remake), etc.

THE RUSSIANS

Had a penchant for collective singing, heroic themes, folk idioms; can get as gloomy as a rainy day in Vladivostok.

THE COMPOSERS

THE OPERAS

Modest Petrovich Moussorgsky (1839–1881)
Mother Russia's number-one operatic son.

His one complete opera, *Boris Godunov*, based on a play by Pushkin, is considered uniquely Russian in the way Dostoevsky is considered uniquely Russian; original, both musically and dramatically, impassioned, nationalistic, imbued with intense feeling for the "Russian people." Also, a little grim.

Peter Ilyich Tchaikovsky (1840–1893)
Educated in the West; the first to pour Russian themes and melancholia into Western classical molds.

His masterpiece, *Eugene Onegin*, has moments of greatness but is criticized for being "too pretty."

THE CZECHS

Passionate, colorful, high on folklore.

THE COMPOSERS

THE OPERAS

Bedrich Smetana (1824–1884)
Czech patriot; one of the leaders of the movement toward nationalistic opera; a major force behind development of a Czech style.

The Bartered Bride, a colorful peasant comedy, is the only one of his works well-known outside the homeland. His other operas tend more toward the heroic than the folksy, their patriotism troweled on.

Leoš Janácek (1854–1928)
Former cult figure, increasingly recognized as a master composer.

Lyrical, theatrical, and thoroughly accessible, his operas have run into trouble because translating opera from the Czech is no mean feat. The composer's humanism, love of nature, and obsession with folk idioms and speech rhythms are evident in his three best-known works, the tragic *Jenufa*, the fantastical *Makropoulos Affair*, and the pantheistic *Cunning Little Vixen*, with its cast composed entirely of animals.

THE AMERICANS

Have suffered from Old World/New World schizophrenia; worked it out in a diversity of styles and genres. Keep trying.

THE COMPOSERS

THE OPERAS

Douglas Moore (1893–1969)
Minor explorer of American regionalism and roots.

The Devil and Daniel Webster, from Benét's literary tall tale, and the folkloric *Ballad of Baby Doe*, popular with touring companies and university music clubs.

Virgil Thomson (1896–1989)
Sophisticated music critic and composer who made brief forays into opera.

Four Saints in Three Acts and *The Mother of Us All*, two charming, cerebral, short operas, notable for the cachet of Gertrude Stein's collaboration.

Gian Carlo Menotti (1911–)
Well-known Italian-American lightweight; forthright defender of opera as mass entertainment and promoter of television as operatic medium.

A long string of hits, of which the most famous are *The Medium*, a melodramatic supernatural thriller; *The Consul* and *The Saint of Bleecker Street*, serious operas about, respectively, political refugees and religious skepticism; and *Amahl and the Night Visitors*, the first opera to be written for television, perfect Christmas family fare.

Philip Glass (1937–)
Postmodernist with a predilection for hypnotic repetition, electronic technology, and mixed-media effects.

Einstein on the Beach and *Satyagraha*, the former a marathon collaboration with then-wunderkind Robert Wilson, having something to do with relativity theory; the latter all about (sort of) Gandhi and passive resistance.

Eleven Arias to Sing in the Shower

BRING YOUR OWN SOAP

Tosca (Puccini), act 2, "Vissi d'arte": Famous singer (that's Tosca) and her painter boyfriend fall into the clutches of evil police chief. He threatens to liquidate boyfriend unless she submits to his advances. She protests: "Vissi d'arte, vissi d'amore, non feci mai / Male ad anima viva!" ("I have lived for love and my art / Never harming a living soul!")

Rigoletto (Verdi), act 3, "La donna è mobile": Dad, a court jester (Rigoletto), tries to shield daughter from worldly corruption. Things start to slide when an old count puts a curse on him. After Dad's boss, the lascivious Duke, seduces his daughter, Rigoletto forces her to eavesdrop with him while the Duke reveals his true misogynist colors: "La donna è mobile / Qual piuma al vento / Muta d'accento / E di pensiero." ("Woman is fickle / Like a feather in the wind / She changes her tone / And her thoughts.") Aria recurs later, revealing to Rigoletto that it is murdered daughter, not murdered Duke, he carries in the sack on his back.

Lucia di Lammermoor (Donizetti), act 3, "Spargi d'amaro pianto" (just refer to Lucia's "Mad Scene"): Girl's brother tries to pressure her into marriage to bolster fading family fortunes. Forges letter announcing her true love's engagement to another woman. Plan backfires; on her wedding day, she goes bananas, stabs her tutor, and wanders babbling among the wedding guests. "Spargi d'amaro pianto / Il mio terrestre velo. Mentre lassù nel Cielo lo pregherò per te." ("Ah, shed your bitter tears / over my earthly remains. But meanwhile in Heaven above I will be praying for you.")

La Traviata (Verdi), act 1, "Sempre libera": Young man loves dying courtesan; Dumas' "La Dame aux Camélias" retold. Violetta contemplates possibility of returning Alfredo's love and leading a pure and simple life. Then she has second thoughts: "Sempre libera degg'io / Follegiare di gioia in gioia . . ." ("Ever light, ever free, / Flitting on from joy to joy . . .")

Die Walküre (Wagner), act 1, "Winterstürme" ("The Spring Song"): Hapless brother and sister, fall guys for the gods, are reunited after years of misery and loneliness. They fall in love. Things seem to be picking up. Little do they know . . . "Winterstürme wichen / Dem Winnemond, / In milden Lichte / Leuchtet der Lenz." ("Winter storms have waned in / the joyful May. / The spring is shining, / mild is his light.")

Don Giovanni (Mozart), act 1, "Madamina" (also known as "Leporello's Catalogue Aria"): Life in the fast lane with the notorious ladies' man (we're talking about Don Juan here, in case you don't speak Italian). After one particularly close shave, the Don leaves his servant, Leporello, to entertain a vengeful victim. Leporello tries to make conversation: "Madamina, il catalogo è questo, / Delle belle che amo il padron mio." ("Little lady, this is the catalogue / Of the Ladies my master has loved.") Best known for its refrain: "Ma, in Ispagna, son già mille e tre!" ("But in Spain, one thousand and three!")

Norma (Bellini), act 1, "Casta Diva": Love among the Druids. High priestess (Norma) has swapped sacred chastity for the affections of a Roman proconsul. Now she's left to contend with a guilty conscience, two illegitimate kids, and a crowd of restless locals itching for a rumble with the Romans. Craving peace (for the moment—she'll feel less pacific when she hears that the proconsul plans to leave her for a younger priestess), Norma invokes the Moon: "Casta Diva, casta Diva, che in argenti / Queste sacre, queste sacre antiche piante / A noi volgi il bel sembiante." ("Chaste Goddess, chaste Goddess, who makes silver / These ancient, sacred trees / Turn toward us thy lovely face.")

Fidelio (Beethoven), act 1, "Abscheulicher": Wicked governor imprisons political opponent. Opponent's wife, in drag, gets job as jailkeeper's assistant. Overhears governor's plot to assassinate husband. Is understandably upset: "Abscheulicher! Wo eilst du hin? Was hast du vor? / Was hast du vor im wilden Grimme?" ("Monster! Whither is thy haste? / What designs breed thy rage?")

La Bohème (Puccini), act 1, "Che gelida manina": Four carefree young artistes share substandard garret. The sensitive poetic one meets consumptive little embroideress from garret next door. Notices, as they proceed to fall in love, that she seems a bit under the weather: "Che gelida manina / Se la lasci riscaldar." ("Your tiny hand is frozen. Let me warm it into life.")

Le Nozze di Figaro (Mozart), act 1, "Non so più cosa son": Sexual intrigue, sexual revenge, marital infidelity, the breakdown of the class system—an Italian *Upstairs, Downstairs*. Here, the young page Cherubino describes what it feels like to discover his hormones: "Non so più cosa son, cosa faccio, / Or di fuoco, ora son di ghiaccio . . ." ("I can't give you a good explanation / For this new and confusing sensation . . .")

Carmen (Bizet), act 2, "La fleur que tu m'avais jetée" (known as Don Jose's "Flower Song"): Gypsy femme fatale (Carmen) seduces honorable young officer of the guard, leading him to betray his sweetheart and his post to join a band of smugglers. After doing time for helping Carmen escape from police, the hapless Don José, destined to be ditched for a toreador, pledges his love: "La fleur que tu m'avais jetée / Dans ma prison m'était restée. / Flétrie et sèche, cette fleur / Gardait toujours sa douce odeur . . ." ("The flower you threw me / Stayed with me in prison. / Faded and dry, this flower / Has kept its sweet scent.")

Practical Italian for the Operagoer

DIVA: Literally, "goddess": a great lady of the opera, a legend. The highest accolade given to a female singer, usually by adoring fans or an ecstatic press. Ranks above the more restrained "prima donna," which, properly speaking, simply refers to the leading lady of an opera company.

RECITATIVO (Actually, you're better off using the English "recitative," unless you happen to be in Milan.): Refers to the speechlike vocal sections used to advance the action in an opera, as opposed to the more lyrical, anchoring arias, duets, etc. In most pre-Wagnerian opera, the recitativo was kept rigidly separated from the moments of pure "song," and, if allowed to go on too long, had a tendency to make audiences drowsy. Later composers began to blur the boundaries between the two.

LIBRETTO: The text, or lyrics, of an opera; also a "little book" (the literal meaning of the word) containing the lyrics, a synopsis of the plot, and often, an accompanying translation. In the early days of opera, librettos (in Italian, *libretti*) were reduced to pocket size so that they could be carried to the theater to help spectators follow the words of an opera during a performance. This custom was made possible by the fact that, at the time, house lights were habitually kept on throughout the performance; if further illumination was needed, audiences were sold little candles that attached to the tops of the librettos.

BEL CANTO: Means, literally, "beautiful singing" and refers, historically, to the type of singer-dominated opera prevalent in Italy throughout the seventeenth and eighteenth centuries. In bel canto opera, pure vocal technique was emphasized, usually at the expense of drama and orchestration. With the advent of nineteenth century Romantic opera (and, in particular, Verdi's sweeping melodramas) the genre fell out of favor and was rarely heard until Maria Callas helped to revive it in the 1950s. Bellini's *Norma* and Donizetti's *Lucia di Lammermoor* are considered pinnacles of the bel canto style.

COLORATURA: A fake Italian word (possibly derived from the German *koloratur*) indicating elaborate ornamentation of the melodic line; a kind of vocal acrobatics consisting of runs, trills, and added flourishes, and demanding exceptional speed and agility on the part of the singer. A coloratura soprano is one who specializes in this type of singing. Joan Sutherland is the best-known contemporary example and is, some say, one of the greatest coloratura singers of all time.

Opera Houses

THE HEAVY HALF-DOZEN

TEATRO ALLA SCALA (MILAN)

Built in 1776 and named for a duchess, not a ladder, La Scala is still Italy's premier opera house, despite Mussolini's efforts to transfer the operatic action to Rome. Like most major European houses, La Scala was bombed during World War II; the theater was rebuilt along the old Baroque lines—horseshoe-shaped auditorium, elaborate decor, seats stacked vertically to the ceiling—and reopened in 1946. The house gained points through its close association with Verdi in the nineteenth century, but nearly everyone agrees that its "Golden Age" came during the on-and-off directorship of Toscanini, between 1898 and 1929; it had another flowering during the 1950s, when Maria Callas reigned as "La Regina della Scala" and both Visconti and Zeffirelli worked on productions.

Like Italy herself, La Scala traditionally operates in perpetual crisis mode, dominated by local politics, saddled with hordes of state employees who can't be laid off, and dependent on government subsidies that have been shrinking steadily for years. Whoever is mayor of Milan automatically becomes president of the opera's governing board, and the theater's administrators are appointed by the city council. As a result, critics complain, aesthetic decisions have too often been made along party lines. Still, La Scala is La Scala, as legendary for the passion of its *loggionisti*—holders of cheap upper-circle tickets—as for its high production standards, and forever synonymous with the glory days of Italian opera.

When the theater reopened in 2004, after a three-year renovation, its front-of-the-house silks and velvets had been faithfully restored and its backstage machinery thoroughly modernized. It now ranks with the Opéra Bastille and the refurbished Covent Garden as a state-of-the-art opera factory capable of staging three full-scale operas a day, provided it can find the money to pay for them. With an expanded season, we can hope to see more of La Scala's famous opening night ritual, in which Milanese big shots and their bejeweled, fur-dripping consorts settle into their box seats as ostentatiously as possible while unemployed auto workers and animal-rights activists wave banners and hurl insults in the streets outside the theater.

ROYAL OPERA HOUSE, COVENT GARDEN (LONDON)

Now the dowager queen of British opera (albeit a dowager queen who recently underwent an extreme makeover), Covent Garden didn't really come into its own until after World War II. Although it was traditionally known for its star-studded seasons and blue-blooded audiences, its performances were generally dismissed as more social than serious, its productions as more opulent than tasteful. During the war, the theater was converted to a dance hall, thanks to a lack of public support that still makes English opera buffs wince in humiliation. After opera was reinstated in 1946, the resident company had to contend with a virulent inferiority complex due, in part, to the stream of foreign guest artists by which it was continually being upstaged, and in part to the way everyone kept pointing to the humble Sadler's Wells company as the place where British opera history was *really* being made. During the 1950s, however, singing standards at Covent Garden were upgraded and production standards became, at the very least, dependable.

The present theater opened in 1858. It's the third incarnation to exist on the site, two earlier versions having both been destroyed by fire. Covent Garden, by the way, was originally a convent garden (hence the name) and was, until 1974, the central fruit and vegetable market of London.

Never quite as secure as the Royal Ballet, with which it shares headquarters, the Royal Opera was, by the latter half of the twentieth century, so plagued by management and financial crises that it was almost as well known for its frequent neardeath experiences as for its productions. In 1996, thanks to funds allocated, somewhat grudgingly, from a national lottery, the theater closed for renovations, promising to reinvent itself as a "people's opera." When it reopened at the end of 1999, however, spectacularly over budget and not quite ready for prime time, neither the price of a ticket nor the flow of Perrier Jouët in the dazzlingly refurbished Floral Hall was calculated to make the masses feel welcome. New management has since succeeded in stabilizing Covent Garden's finances and offering more affordable programs, but the Royal Opera House is still up against a lingering reputation as a clubby affair that caters mainly to stuffed shirts and society matrons.

STAATSOPER (VIENNA)

One of the most venerable opera houses and, according to some, the most important, the Staatsoper (or State Opera) has three distinct advantages over its rivals: (1) its location in what has been, since the seventeenth century, the music capital of the world; (2) its resident orchestra, the Vienna Philharmonic, which has been called "the world's supreme musical instrument"; and (3) a combination of generous government subsidies and high ticket prices, which allow it to hold a superlong annual season and to present more operas during that time than any other house (in some years nearly twice as many as the Met). On the other hand, the Staatsoper, and the Viennese in general, are notoriously conservative; although they insist on high standards, they won't brook innovation. Consequently, history is preserved here, not made, and the Staatsoper's reputation, for better or worse, is based on rigidly traditional productions of the classics, especially works by the perennial Viennese favorites: Wagner, Mozart, and Richard Strauss.

The original theater, built in 1869 to house the already successful Vienna Court Opera, was partially destroyed during World War II; although the rebuilt version, which opened in 1955, still boasts an ornate facade and a lobby and grand staircase not unlike those of the Palais Garnier, the auditorium is pencil-plain modern and not particularly attractive.

FESTSPIELHAUS (BAYREUTH, GERMANY)

Technically, Bayreuth, as it is universally known, is a festival, not a house, but it *is* one of the great operatic centers of the world, so let's not split hairs. Remember

that it's pronounced "BY-royt," unlike the capital of Lebanon, and that the name is virtually synonymous with that of Richard Wagner, who envisioned it as the ideal theater, supervised its design and construction, and ran it until his death. (His body, along with that of his father-in-law, Franz Liszt, is buried on its grounds.) After he died, Bayreuth was run by successive generations of Wagners and, since its opening in 1876, has been devoted exclusively to the production of

Wagnerian opera. Design-wise, the theater was revolutionary for its time. It was, in a sense, the first democratic opera house, eschewing the old Baroque box-and-tier system in favor of a fan-shaped auditorium with continuous rows of seating that provided uniformly good sightlines and spectacular acoustics. Under the direction of Wagner's grandson Wieland, Bayreuth exchanged opera's traditional naturalistic, painted backdrops for minimal sets and sophisticated lighting, calculated to evoke atmosphere and universal themes rather than specific locales. After Wieland's death in 1966, his brother Wolfgang took over and, by bringing in directors from outside the family, managed, more or less, to maintain Wieland's high level of technical innovation, which set the standards for modernist theater production throughout the world. Over the years, Wolfgang, now in his mid-eighties, also managed to alienate nearly every other surviving Wagner, setting the stage for a nasty battle over succession. Or so festival-lovers have long feared. As it happens, Wolfgang has a promising young opera-director daughter and, it appears, a plan. In the meantime, Bayreuth continues, season after season, to be swamped with half a million applicants for a tenth as many seats.

L'OPÉRA NATIONAL (PARIS)

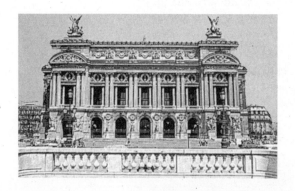 

Probably the most sumptuous opera house in the world, the Palais Garnier was, at its 1875 opening, certainly the biggest. Designed as a monument to Second Empire architecture by Charles Garnier, the house peaked between 1885 and 1906, then promptly went into a seventy-year decline. Its enormous stage and machine-laden backstage area, tailor-made for the spectacular processions, elaborate special effects, and ornate ballets the French had loved so much during the heyday of grand opera (when Verdi, working in Paris, contemptuously referred to the theater as "la grande boutique"), now played host to an endless string of shoddy productions complemented by second-rate singing. By the mid-twentieth century, l'Opéra had become just another elaborate piece of bric-a-brac in the Parisian landscape, as essential to the production of opera as the Eiffel Tower to the sending of telegrams.

During the 1970s and early 1980s, however, l'Opéra's honor was restored; not only did the house make a comeback, it made a name for itself as a showcase for experimental operas and for innovative, often controversial restagings of the classics. In 1989, the Paris Opéra relocated to the ultra—not to say brutally—modern new hall at La Bastille. Despite an abundance of bad press during its first few years, the mammoth Bastille, with its industrial-strength production facilities, programs to suit every taste, and inhouse Métro exit, soon succeeded in establishing itself as the "people's opera," attracting both younger, hipper patrons and tourists from the provinces. Now the Paris Opéra encompasses both the Opéra Bastille and the Palais Garnier (also home to the Paris Opéra Ballet), and, for at least a decade, has had no trouble packing both houses. Stay tuned, however; in the hands of its new, radical-modernist director, that could change.

METROPOLITAN OPERA HOUSE
(NEW YORK)

The original opened on Broadway in 1883 when a group of wealthy businessmen, irritated because they couldn't get boxes at the Academy of Music, decided to start their own theater. Despite its early policy of producing all operas in German, the Met had, by the turn of the century, shown a knack for attracting the biggest operatic guns of Europe (Caruso, Mahler, and Toscanini, among others) and the richest patrons of its hometown (the Vanderbilt clan alone took up five private boxes). In 1966, the company moved to contemporary glass-and-marble headquarters at Lincoln Center for the Performing Arts. The new theater drew raves for its acoustics, its huge warren of backstage rehearsal and administrative rooms, and its state-of-the-art technical facilities (the *New Yorker* music critic called it "the most efficient factory for the production of opera ever devised"); some pans for its less-than-perfect sightlines; and a mixed bag of gasps and snickers for the two huge Chagall murals adorning the Great Hall. Today the Met is one of the two or three wealthiest and most prestigious opera houses in the world, although, dependent as it is on private sponsors with pronounced likes and dislikes, it is hardly the most adventurous. Next door, at the decidedly less glamorous New York State Theater, the plucky New York City Opera has long played Betty to the Met's Veronica. Word is, however, that it will soon be moving to new digs.

A Night at the Opera

MANNERS AND MORALS FOR THE MTV GENERATIONS

Granted, you'd feel more comfortable if you'd absorbed opera etiquette as a tot, sitting between Mummy and Daddy at La Scala or Covent Garden. Just remember that the prospect of going to the opera is a lot more intimidating than the actual experience, and that, in America at any rate, at least half the audience will be made up of late bloomers like yourself. It does help, however, to know the rules of the game:

1. *Memorize the plot before you go.* This will only take a minute, given the complexity of most opera plots (but watch out for *Rigoletto*), and nearly everyone's written a book summarizing them. Opera, as you'll recall, is supposed to be the perfect combination of music *and* drama (nowadays, throw in film, sculpture, fashion, and occasionally sword swallowing, but that's for a later book), and you'll find it enormously helpful, as the curtain goes down on *Aïda*, for instance, to know why that nice young man and his girlfriend are still hanging out in the basement.

2. *Bring a libretto.* If you can't borrow it from the local library, you can usually buy one at the box office on the night of the performance. Cram during intermission. No one will expect you to understand even a third of what's being sung on stage, but after all, the librettist didn't deliberately write the lyrics in a language you wouldn't understand; he meant them to enhance the appeal of the songs, and, as the best of Broadway musicals, they often do. If you're going to a major opera house in a big city, however, forget all of this; there will probably be subtitles flashed on a screen above the stage (or on the back of the seat in front of you, if you're at the Met).

3. *Don't clap until the people around you do.* The moments of silence in an opera don't always signal breaktime; very often, the singer pauses for effect, or to indicate that something dramatic is about to happen, or to heighten the intensity of an orchestral interlude, which, by the way, is to be paid attention to. Opera orchestras, unlike Paul Shaffer and his boys, don't expect to have to play through applause.

4. *Go ahead and voice your enthusiasm,* if the spirit moves you, at the end of a well-executed aria. Strictly speaking, you're supposed to shout "Bravo!" if the singer is a man, "Brava!" if it's a woman, but American audiences tend to take a unisex approach, shouting "Bravo!" to everyone indiscriminately, and the singers don't seem to mind. (Just, please, refrain from yelling "Bravissimo!" which is simply pretentious. Some of the people around you may be doing it, but you don't want to know them.)

5. *Don't spend a lot of time worrying about what to wear,* unless you're going to La Scala or have an invitation to share a box at the gala with the Duke and Duchess of Bedford. Jeans, of course, are inadvisable (although not unheard of). And while we agree that arriving in diamonds and satin with a liveried footman to help one out of one's carriage can make the whole opera-going experience more meaningful, outside Milan, and especially in America, most people opt for comfort and just try to have clean hair.

6. *Don't choose Wagner your first time out.* Later, maybe, you'll come to relish sitting in the dark for four hours contemplating the erotic implications of death and listening to music that (to the untrained ear) all sounds alike. Right now, it's OK to go for one of the crowd-pleasers, maybe something by Puccini or Verdi (although, if we had to choose between them, we'd recommend the Verdi; they'll both make you cry, but even a novice will sense the presence of Quality). Some other obvious possibilities:

Carmen, the world's most popular opera, and one of the most accessible; this is a real *musical*, complete with Spanish dances and lots of gypsy flavor. It does, however, bring with it the risk of shoddy production values and overweight leading ladies.

The Magic Flute, a spectacular fairy tale, written to please ordinary people, not just opera buffs. The plot's so harebrained that you won't lose anything by not understanding German, and as pure entertainment it, like any Mozart, rates two thumbs up.

Norma, one of the greatest "singer's operas." It's harder to recommend this one; the plot's clumsy, you may not go for the bel canto style, and who knows—you could find it offensive to Druids. Given the right cast, however, the music will take your breath away.

PHILOSOPHY

Contents

Socrates, about to swig the hemlock, in Jacques-Louis David's 1787 you-are-there evocation of his death

Philosophy Made Simplistic

Philosophy is the study of everything that counts, just as those ancient Greeks, who were as interested in the structure of matter and the existence of God as they were in the nature of good, always said it was. Today, though, what with the pressures of specialization (not to mention the glut of Ph.D.'s), the physicists have walked off with matter and the theologians with God, leaving the philosophers either to go on pondering "What is good?" or to become computer programmers. Don't tell *them* that, though; they still think they have the last word on anything that falls within one or more of the following five areas of classical philosophical investigation:

1. *Logic:* What's valid, what's invalid; what can profitably be argued and proven, what can't; how to test a categorical syllogism; how not to keep making silly mistakes all the time. Or, as Tweedledee says in *Through the Looking Glass*, "Contrariwise, if it was so it might be; and if it were so, it would be; but as it isn't, it ain't. That's logic."

2. *Ethics:* Which actions are right and which ends are good. Moreover, does the rightness of actions derive from the goodness of their consequences? And while you're on the subject, is the virtuousness of a motive to be inferred from the rightness of the actions that it tends to prompt? Also, is it less bad to shoplift from Kmart than from the corner hardware store even though the salesperson at Kmart explained the fine points of home rewiring to you and the guy who runs the hardware store doesn't know a switch from a socket? And other more or less practical aspects of human conduct.

3. *Aesthetics:* Beauty and art and taste, standards and judgments and criticism, Aristotle and Oscar Wilde and Sharon Stone. Why do we like what we like? Does art per se exist, or is it just patches of color and hummable tunes and words in a row? Is the point of a work of art that it be representative of something, or that it express its creator's identity, or that it engage its audience? And is there a relationship between what's beautiful and what's good?

4. *Epistemology:* Do we *really* know anything and, if so, what? And how do we know it? And how do we know that we know it? And how do we know that we know that we know it? etc. Note: Ever since Wittgenstein (see page 329), formal philosophical inquiry has been centered less on classical epistemology and more on language, less on the question "How do you know?" and more on the question "What do you mean?"

5. *Metaphysics:* The big one: The search for (and ransacking of) ultimate categories, with its goal an understanding of the all-inclusive scheme of things otherwise known as the world and of the part man plays within it. Past discoveries have included existence, essence, time,

space, God, self, and cause. Stay tuned. But don't hold your breath: A lot of philosophers now characterize metaphysics as "overpoetic" and "prescientific."

Got Another Minute or Two?

Philosophy is, as befits the so called queen of sciences, rife with -ologies and -isms. Of these, let's take a closer look at three of the former (and you've already had epistemology, don't forget) and two of the latter.

Ontology is literally the study of being (the cancer speciality is oncology), and is sometimes used interchangeably with metaphysics. Depending on whom you listen to, it's either the most generic and abstract of all intellectual inquiries or it's a compilation of pseudo-problems only a fool would tackle. If you must field (or wield) the word, keep in mind that it implies getting to the heart of the matter, to the very essence of something. So, an ontology of the cinema would proceed by taking the thing called "moving pictures" and contrasting it with still photographs and with paintings, with television, with the landscape viewed through the windshield of a moving car. It would talk about other activities revolving around lenses and editing, and other art forms, most notably the theater, undertaken collectively and enjoyed communally. (What it wouldn't deal with: Eisenstein, Hollywood in the Thirties, David Lynch's career, censorship, the "zoom," what makes a movie fun to watch, or the insipidity of Oscars night.) Careful: "Ontology" is a word strictly for intellectual big spenders.

Two -ologies have to do with final affairs. One, *eschatology* (not to be confused with *sca*tology, a preoccupation with excrement or talking dirty), describes any doctrine or system focused on such end-of-the-line matters as death, the afterlife, immortality, and redemption. William Buckley, for example, has even described Communism as an eschatological system because it deals in a "millennial vision" of peace and equality, en route to which the present is just a way station, life less a process than a partial product.

The other, *teleology*, is applied to a belief in, or study of, an overall purpose, design, or end (*telos*, in the Greek), usually in nature. Teleologists like to invoke results as reasons: Of course the giraffe has a long neck, argued the pre-Darwinian biologist and teleologist, Lamarck (see page 565); he needs it to reach the tender leaves he feeds on. Teleology tends to thrive in systems structured around the existence of an active God, intent on revelation (see page 340). And to be treated as anathema by scientists.

Still with Us?

Great! Of the -isms, by far the most important are the diametrically opposed idealism and materialism, neither of which has its everyday meaning here.

Idealism stipulates that the nature of reality is completely bound up with mind and consciousness and thought, that your leg and your bandanna and your patriotism and Bruce Springsteen and his leg and his bandanna and his patriotism cannot be dealt with—perceived or proven to exist—except through the activity of your (or somebody's) knowing mind.

Materialism maintains that all entities—including everybody and everybody's leg and everybody's bandanna and everybody's patriotism *and* everybody's mind—can be explained only in terms of matter and energy, atoms and electrons. Thus had Madonna sung about being a material*ist* girl, she'd have been casting her vote not for net gloves and dangly earrings but for molecules over perceptions. Which, come to think of it, was more or less what she was doing anyway.

Rating the Thinkers

A CONSUMER'S GUIDE TO TWENTY PHILOSOPHERS

PLATO (c. 427–c. 347 B.C.)

Best-Known Works: The *Dialogues*, especially the *Apology, Crito,* and *Phaedo* (a trilogy about the imprisonment and death of Socrates); the *Symposium* (on the nature of love); and the *Republic* (on the principles of government).

Readability: Too bad you were asked to read the *Republic* at an age when you couldn't wait to get back to *Lord of the Rings.* As philosophers go, Plato is a live wire; the *Dialogues* read like screenplays, complete with sets, props, characters, and, of course, dialogue. True, that ancient Greek frame of reference takes some getting used to but, as with any vintage movie, switching into another mindset is half the fun.

Qualities of Mind: Abstract, absolutist, imaginative, moralistic, ironic; intellectually better equipped to walk on water than build bridges.

Catchphrases: The allegory of the cave (see page 331), philosopher-kings, the life that is unexamined is not worth living.

Influence: Metaphysics on a grand scale, from the world's greatest rationalist. Postulated the existence of a supreme order of archetypal, universal ideas, or pure Forms, of which all our existing forms and ideas are only cheap, transitory reflections; these paradigmatic Forms are independent of, and inaccessible to, sensory experience, and are graspable only through the power of the mind. Plato's confidence in the possibility of reasoning or conceptualizing one's way to Truth, together with his mistrust of knowledge obtained through the senses, pretty much defines philosophical rationalism, then and now. He is also our only source—albeit an unreliable one—for the teachings of Socrates.

Personal Gossip: A rich young aristocrat who could afford to spend his time contemplating pure ideas. His real name was Aristocles; Plato was a nickname meaning "broad," which may have referred to his forehead, his waistline, or the scope of his ideas. And yes, he was probably gay.

Current Standing: Some contemporary philosophers would agree with Alfred North Whitehead's remark that "philosophy is only a series of footnotes to Plato." (But then, no one can appreciate a philosopher-mathematician like another philosopher-mathematician.) Neither empiricists nor fitness buffs much go for his denigration of sensory experience, however, and, for much of the twentieth century, Aristotle, a nuts-and-bolts type, seemed more acceptable to the modern mind.

ARISTOTLE (384–322 B.C.)

Best-Known Works: Organon, Physics, Politics, Rhetoric, Poetics, Nichomachean Ethics.

Readability: If you enjoy reading leases, you'll love Aristotle; every thought is examined in detail and every detail meticulously numbered. To be fair, you should remember that his only extant works are treatises that were probably intended as lecture notes; his early popular works have been lost.

Qualities of Mind: Lucid, learned, practical, didactic, analytical, versatile. Dante called him "the master of those who know."

Catchphrases: The Golden Mean, the Unmoved Mover (see page 340), the Dramatic Unities (of action, time, and place), entelechy (in dictionary terms, "the condition of a thing whose essence is fully realized," or, to paraphrase the Army, "Being all that you can be"), catharsis (see page 263).

Influence: The roots of modern science and, probably, Western civilization. Discarded Plato's abstractions in favor of observation and analysis of the physical world. Systematically studied and categorized virtually everything: astronomy, physics, anatomy, physiology, psychology, natural history, political science, rhetoric, art, theology, whatever. Planted the ideas of the pursuit of happiness (a thoroughly modern, success-oriented morality, which tacitly relegates virtue to the level of a means to an end) and the Golden Mean (or "moderation in all things," a doctrine that, as Bertrand Russell pointed out, appeals mainly to the respectable middle-aged). Established the West's first, and until recently only, systematic study of logic. Still associated with modern concepts of scientific analysis, although many of his conclusions put scientists on the wrong track for a couple thousand years.

Personal Gossip: Student of Plato (remember the order: Socrates taught Plato, Plato taught Aristotle); teacher of Alexander the Great, who apparently didn't pay much attention to him.

Current Standing: Plato's opposite number and of the two, the top dog in a science-minded age.

SAINT AUGUSTINE (A.D. 354–430)

Best-Known Works: Confessions, The City of God.

Readability: Not difficult, exactly, but after reading seven pages on the wickedness of stealing a pear, or two chapters on the putative differences between good demons and bad demons, you may decide you'd rather spend your time discussing, say, fluoridation of the water supply with someone closer to your own age.

Qualities of Mind: Scholarly, fevered, guilt-ridden, dogmatic, idealistic.

Catchphrases: City of God, city of man.

Influence: Cornerstone of the Christian Church; attempted a rational defense of Christianity in light of the fall of the Roman Empire and tried to fit all of history into a Christian framework. Sometimes called the founder of theology. Gave us ideas of separation of Church and State and of history as progression toward a goal (see page 577). Biggest influence on Christian thinking, and especially on Roman Catholicism, after St. Paul. Wrote the first self-analytical autobiography, precursor of the genre as well as of the modern introspective novel.

Personal Gossip: Had a long-term mistress and an illegitimate child before his mother, St. Monica, finally talked him into becoming a Christian.

Current Standing: Out of date, but he had soul. Admired by Platonists (since he was an outspoken Plato fan himself) and by contemporary Protestant theologians in search of "the essence" of Christianity.

SAINT THOMAS AQUINAS (1225–1274)

Best-Known Works: Summa Theologica, Summa Contra Gentiles.

Readability: Elaborate and extremely formal; do not drive or operate heavy machinery while reading.

Qualities of Mind: Learned, dogged, systematic, analytical; they didn't call him "The Prince of Scholastics" for nothing.

Catchphrase: His epithet, "The Angelic Doctor."

Influence: Constructed the second great synthesis of Christian thinking, which superseded Augustine's as of the thirteenth century. Championed Aristotle, as opposed to Plato, and based his theology more on concrete analysis of this world than on irrational faith in the next. Reinterpreted Aristotle's ideas in Christian terms. Effected the classic integration of reason and revelation, proved conclusively the existence of God, and split hairs more brilliantly and systematically than nearly all his Scholastic colleagues. Provided the Catholic Church with much of its official dogma, then and now.

Personal Gossip: When he was a teenager, his mother had him locked up for two years to prevent him from becoming a Dominican monk. He escaped and joined the order anyway. He later became very famous and very fat.

Current Standing: A lesson in the rewards of thoroughness; beyond that, unless you're a Catholic priest, take him with a grain of salt.

NICCOLÒ MACHIAVELLI (1469–1527)

Best-Known Works: The Prince, Discourses.

Readability: A piece of cake; Machiavelli was forced to earn his living as a writer, so he understood the importance of keeping his audience awake.

Qualities of Mind: Shrewd, pragmatic, insightful, cynical.

Catchphrase: The chief foundations of all states are good laws and good arms.

Influence: Revolutionized political philosophy and shocked idealists by adopting a purely secular, scientific perspective toward statecraft; left out questions of morality altogether in order to focus, reporterlike, on what was, not what should have been. Wrote the classic how-to book for aspirants to power (*The Prince*). Based principles of government on the assumptions that man is fundamentally bad and that the end justifies the means. Was the rare philosopher whose name became a household word, in his case, synonymous with deception, unscrupulousness, and cunning.

Personal Gossip: A politician himself (as well as author and historian), Machiavelli wrote *The Prince* in an unsuccessful attempt to curry favor with the reigning Medici, who didn't like him and who probably never read it. (Among those who *did* read it: Mussolini, Hitler, Lenin, and Stalin.) For a more balanced and more honest picture of his ideas, read the *Discourses.*

Current Standing: His political views are more acceptable in our era than in any since his own; nowadays anyone who disagrees with him is assumed to be hypocritical or naïve. Considered a first-rate social scientist, but as a pure thinker, superficial, inconsistent, and generally shaky.

RENÉ DESCARTES (1596–1650)

Best-Known Works: Discourse on Method, Meditations on First Philosophy.

Readability: Rolls right along; philosophy with a sense of style for a change. Descartes writes like an intelligent adult addressing other intelligent adults. His prose, some say, is to the French language what the King James Bible is to English.

Qualities of Mind: Sophisticated, independent, lucid, methodical, individualistic.

Catchphrase: Cogito ergo sum.

Influence: Marks the point at which the world decided to go modern. Was determined to make a clean sweep of all the comfortable old assumptions, to take nobody's word for anything, to doubt everything in order to find something he could be sure of. Came up with the famous bottom line, "I think, therefore I am." Built a philosophical system based on deductive reasoning (see page 333) and a priori truths (see page 334), the basis for seventeenth-century Rationalism. Believed in innate ideas, ones that do not come to us through experience. As a mathematician, came up with the idea for analytic geometry and the mind-set behind the scientific method. Insisted on the complete separation of mind and matter (which would later split philosophy—not to mention personality—into warring camps) and on the purely mechanistic nature of the physical world.

Personal Gossip: Who can gossip about a mathematician? This was the kind of guy who would move rather than allow his friends to drop by and interrupt his train of thought.

Current Standing: Seminal figure of modern philosophy; usually off-base (who says "I am" just because "I think," and how do I *know* I think, anyway?) but always inspiring.

JOHN LOCKE (1632–1704)

Best-Known Works: An Essay Concerning Human Understanding, Second Treatise on Government.

Readability: Boring but bearable; like reading the Declaration of Independence, which, in fact, borrowed from his phraseology as well as from his ideas.

Qualities of Mind: Modest, sensible, utilitarian, tolerant.

Catchphrases: The mind as *tabula rasa* (blank page), the system of checks and balances, the labor theory of value, laissez-faire, the rights of man, "Knowledge is the perception of the agreement or disagreement of two ideas."

Influence: As a political philosopher, was the theoretical architect of what we call democracy; gave us basic liberal ideals (the primacy of the pursuit of happiness, the belief in the natural rights of man) and specific principles of government (majority rule, checks and balances). As a pure philosopher, was the first to make a really big deal out of epistemology, of *how* we know things. Pioneered modern empiricism, a vehement rebuttal of the Rationalist school of philosophy that ruled the day (see previous page), declaring that the mind at birth is *tabula rasa*, that there are no such things as innate ideas, that all ideas come to us through our senses from the material world—a science-oriented way of thinking that opted for limited, but immediately usable, knowledge of everyday reality.

Personal Gossip: A physician who came to prominence, politically and philosoph-ically, when he chose the winning side (William of Orange, see page 590) in the Glorious Revolution of 1688.

Current Standing: No towering intellect, just an eminently reasonable man with a head full of ideas whose time had come. A propounder of popular, rather than profound, political theories, the validity of which depend largely on how one feels about liberal democracy.

BARUCH SPINOZA (1632–1677)

Best-Known Work: Ethics.

Readability: Just conquered the Matterhorn? Looking for a challenge? Welcome to *Ethics*, a deadly morass of Euclidean definitions, axioms, theorems, and demonstrations of the impossible. Too bad; Spinoza could be a rather eloquent writer. We're told that if you can get through the whole thing—twice—it starts to grow on you.

Qualities of Mind: Analytical, realistic, idealistic, mystical, rational, patient, rig-orous, determined.

Catchphrases: Sub specie aeternitatis (in the light of eternity); all determination is negation.

Influence: The world's most sensible mystic. Constructed the first thoroughly logical, consistent metaphysical system and made the first attempt at an objec-tive, scientific study of human behavior. Carried all arguments to their logical conclusions, even when those conclusions meant trouble. A pantheist and a pure determinist, who believed, as all good mystics do, in the oneness of the universe, in the supremacy of immutable natural law, in the necessity of learning to go with the flow. Had no followers, but his freethinking religious views helped pave the way for the Enlightenment.

Personal Gossip: Excommunicated (and formally cursed with all the curses of Deuteronomy) by the Jewish community in Holland for refusing to keep his heretical thoughts to himself. Socially ostracized, he earned his living as a lens grinder, wrote philosophy on the side, and is best remembered for behaving, all the way to his deathbed, like a saint.

Current Standing: Nobody doesn't like Spinoza; he was smart, hardworking, and holy, one of the few intellectuals on record to have actually lived by his beliefs. Bertrand Russell called him "the most lovable of philosophers." On the other hand, the idea of bowing quietly to Natural Law has never been big box office in the West.

GOTTFRIED WILHELM VON LEIBNIZ
(1646–1716)

Best-Known Works: Monadology, Principles of Nature and of Grace, Theodicy.

Readability: Uninviting: dry, precise, businesslike; moves fast and seems likely to snap at you if you can't keep up.

Qualities of Mind: Rigorous, dynamic, logical, systematic, concise, humorless.

Catchphrases: Windowless monads, preestablished harmony; also Voltaire's parodistic phrase "This is the best of all possible worlds."

Influence: One of the great "Continental Rationalists," mainstream thinkers of the seventeenth century. Invented infinitesimal calculus, founded the first system of symbolic logic, furthered the development of exact logical analysis. A metaphysician in the tradition of Descartes, he created the famous analogy of the Cartesian Clocks, which postulates that mind and body do not interact, but only seem to, because they are synchronized by God. Publicly espoused a philosophy that was pious, logical, and somewhat simpleminded, for which he was caricatured as Dr. Pangloss in Voltaire's *Candide*. Secretly spent his life trying to perfect a brilliant, complex mathematical system that aimed at replacing thought with calculation.

Personal Gossip: An ambitious hypocrite who kept his best work secret and published whatever would make him popular with his employers. Admired and was influenced by Spinoza, whom he denounced as soon as it seemed expedient.

Current Standing: Considered by many to be one of the greatest logicians of all time. Although nearly all of his conclusions are either totally implausible or hopelessly obsolete, his methods for arriving at them are models of clearheadedness.

DAVID HUME (1711–1776)

Best-Known Works: A Treatise of Human Nature, An Enquiry Concerning Human Understanding (a simplified version of the first book of the *Treatise*).

Readability: Lucid, compact, direct; refreshing, though not, as Hume had hoped, riveting.

Qualities of Mind: Rigorous, no-nonsense, consistent, honest.

Catchphrases: The science of man. Also, Kant's famous remark that reading Hume "awakened me from my dogmatic slumbers."

Influence: The Scottish skeptic who took Locke's empirical arguments to their logical conclusion (which Locke had neglected to do) and wound up doubting our ability to know anything at all. That the sun will rise tomorrow morning, according to Hume, is not something we *know*, but something we *believe*, simply because it has risen every other morning. Effectively deflated metaphysical pretensions, made philosophers very nervous about their assumptions, and made it clear that the Age of Reason had arrived at a dead end.

Personal Gossip: A cheerful, easygoing sort, despite his skepticism; one of the few men capable of maintaining a friendship with Rousseau (although Rousseau did turn on him in the end). Always wanted to be a famous writer.

Current Standing: A watershed and a warning signal; has forced all subsequent philosophers to look before they leap. No self-respecting philosopher can wholly accept his conclusions (i.e., that we can't know anything), but none has entirely succeeded in refuting his arguments, either.

IMMANUEL KANT (1724–1804)

Best-Known Works: Critique of Pure Reason, Critique of Practical Reason, Critique of Judgment.

Readability: Confirms your worst fears. Kant wrote exclusively for his learned colleagues and succeeded in making even *their* eyes glaze over. Will Durant compared him to Jehovah, saying, "He speaks through clouds, but without the illumination of the lightning flash."

Qualities of Mind: Scholarly, complex, profound, moralistic, systematic, earnest.

Catchphrases: The categorical imperative, transcendental logic, "thing-in-itself" (*Ding-an-sich*).

Influence: Put Germany on the map as an intellectual power (and lent it the pedantic tone for which it soon became notorious); made sweeping revisions in nearly all branches of philosophy, thereby inspiring other philosophers to stop bickering among themselves and get serious about thinking again. Effected what he called a "second Copernican revolution": The origin of the world as we know it, he insisted, is the human mind itself, which, far from being *tabula rasa*, has an inherent structure through which we filter all experience and which imposes its own order on the world of phenomena (though not on the real/ideal world of "things-in-themselves," which is unknowable). Likewise, humans have an innate awareness of moral law, in the form of the categorical (i.e., unconditional) imperative (i.e., command), a sort of bottom-line ethical "ought." In attempting to make the world safe for both God and science, Kant managed to restore some dignity to the idea of the human mind; also to destroy the credibility of traditional metaphysics (since we can't "know" any external reality that isn't colored by our own "knowing"), to make modern philosophy more subjective than objective (and to prefigure such radically man-centered movements as existentialism), and to widen the rift between philosophy and the physical sciences.

Personal Gossip: The archetypal academic philosopher; a retiring, studious little man who didn't travel, never married, and lived a life of such extreme regularity that, according to legend, the citizens of his hometown used to set their clocks by his daily walks.

Current Standing: One of philosophy's all-stars, with Plato, Aristotle, and, if the judges are in a generous mood, Hegel. Often called "the founder of modern philosophy," which is not to say that anyone totally accepts—or ever accepted—his theories, but that every subsequent philosopher has teethed on them. Also, that his complex theories foreshadowed such hip twentieth-century systems as structuralism (see page 334).

GEORG FRIEDRICH WILHELM HEGEL
(1770–1831)

Best-Known Works: Phenomenology of Spirit, The Philosophy of Right, Lectures on the Philosophy of History (compiled and published posthumously).

Readability: The nadir of German prose; pompous, pedantic, obscurantist; every statement is qualified, as is every qualifying statement, and Hegel doesn't stop short of inventing his own words. Not only do you not have to read him, you should feel free to snigger when anyone suggests it.

Qualities of Mind: Abstruse, academic, methodical, with mystical leanings.

Catchphrases: The dialectic (thesis vs. antithesis leads to synthesis), Absolute Spirit.

Influence: Took Kant's mind-ordered world from the human level to the cosmic one, creating a totally awesome system into which all past, present, and future experience *and* thought fit together rationally in an encompassing dialectic that is constantly evolving toward supreme self-consciousness, or Absolute Spirit. At which point we'll know everything and see God. Plenty of energy and ambition here, not to mention enormous clout: By the end of the nineteenth century, most academic philosophers of any stature were Hegelians, which is to say they embraced, theoretically, the notion of Change, accepted Strife as essential to Progress, saw things as Parts of a Whole and themselves as characters in the Unfolding of History, argued dialectically, and tended to think in capital letters. They probably would have continued to run amok with the notion of Absolute Spirit if Marx and Engels hadn't come along and sold the world on Absolute Economics instead.

Personal Gossip: None, really, except that for a man whose philosophy could so easily be read as revolutionary at the outset, Hegel had become notoriously conservative by middle age. A classic example of what money, fame, and a few favors from the King of Prussia can do.

Current Standing: There *had* to be a backlash; by the early twentieth century Hegel's complexity and that crazily incomprehensible prose had made him a laughingstock among many philosophers. Nowadays, he's been more or less restored to a top-shelf position in the Philosophers' Hall of Fame, although his thinking is still mistrusted as leading to a glorification of the state over the individual and an end-justifies-the-means immorality.

ARTHUR SCHOPENHAUER (1788–1860)

Best-Known Works: The World as Will and Idea, Essays.

Readability: No problem: surefooted, vigorous prose, with plenty of examples, analogies, and, at moments, wit; often quotable.

Qualities of Mind: Cultured, pessimistic, arrogant, embittered, individualistic.

Catchphrase: The world is my idea.

Influence: The first to come right out and insist that there was something more important than knowledge or intellect: namely, will, and specifically, the will to live (Nietzsche and Freud were both to be influenced by this concept). Believing that will was inherently evil, he argued that the best one could strive for was renunciation of desire, a temporary absence of pain through the contemplation of high art (which made him very popular among artists), and, with any luck, the eventual extinction of the species. His rejection of the action-minded, essentially bourgeois confidence of the nineteenth century presaged the individualistic despair of the twentieth.

Personal Gossip: Spent twenty-five years without speaking to his mother, a literary lady who'd disliked him (although she continued to foot the bills) ever since she heard that two geniuses could not exist in the same family. Had a reputation for meanness and spent most of his life alone, save for the company of his dog (the authorities disagree here; it may have been a cat), whom he named Atma, or "World-Soul."

Current Standing: His system is generally regarded as a mishmash of oversimplifications and inconsistencies, peppered with a few brilliant insights; still, thanks to those insights and his skill in presenting them, he's been designated a historical landmark and, as one of the few pessimists in the history of philosophy, is considered something of a curiosity.

SØREN KIERKEGAARD (1813–1855)

Best-Known Works: Either/Or (more dramatic than theoretical), *Fear and Trembling, Sickness unto Death.*

Readability: A bit gristly (*you* try chewing on reflections like "Dread is a sympathetic antipathy and antipathetic sympathy"), but it has its moments.

Qualities of Mind: Melancholy, unorthodox, God-oriented, imaginative.

Catchphrase: The leap into absurdity.

Influence: No one paid much attention at the time; the idea that there were *no* reliable guidelines for human action, that one could only hope for enlightenment by committing oneself to a God who might very well never give one the time of day, just seemed like one man's personal problem. But once twentieth-century alienation had set in and people had begun wondering why they should get out of bed in the morning, Kierkegaard, with his Scandinavian gloom, started to make sense. In the hands of Sartre and Camus, his belief in God was replaced by a belief in the Void, the whole philosophy was given a leftist twist, and before you knew it, everyone in Paris was carrying on like a character out of *Last Year at Marienbad.*

Personal Gossip: Poor Søren; but what could you expect with that "Fall of the House of Usher" childhood and those spindly legs? Even so, people shouldn't have made fun of him the way they did, especially about his painful broken engagement. (On the other hand, he did ditch *her.*)

Current Standing: Acknowledged as the "founder" of existentialism (although existentialism is less a philosophical system than a bad mood), and a brilliant thinker whose neurosis was prophetic.

WILLIAM JAMES (1842–1910)

Best-Known Works: Principles of Psychology, The Will to Believe and Other Essays, The Varieties of Religious Experience, Pragmatism.

Readability: Chatty, colloquial, and direct; like an entertaining dinner guest.

Qualities of Mind: Cultured, commonsensical, optimistic, moralistic (New England Puritan style).

Catchphrases: The will to believe, the cash-value of ideas (also, in a more literary vein, stream of consciousness, the bitch-goddess success).

Influence: Almost put America on the map as an intellectual presence. Pioneer of pragmatism, our first indigenous school of thought. Attempted to make philosophy relevant by abandoning the search for absolutes in favor of a will-it-cut-down-trees approach to ideas. Theorized that reality is whatever we make it, that truth is tantamount to effectiveness, ditto goodness (thus, if believing in God makes you a better person, then God exists), and that philosophy should stick to answering questions that have a "cash-value," i.e., that will make a significant difference in people's lives. Set the tone for much subsequent twentieth-century philosophy.

Personal Gossip: Older brother of Henry James. Was a famous psychologist before switching to philosophy. Center of a clique of brilliant Harvard intellectuals. Attempted suicide in adolescence (more proof that bad things happen to good people).

Current Standing: One for our side—an American philosopher who won't embarrass you at black-tie dinners. Whatever his limitations as a systematic thinker, he made up for them by being well-rounded.

FRIEDRICH NIETZSCHE (1844–1900)

Best-Known Works: Thus Spake Zarathustra, The Will to Power (beware posthumous additions by his sister), *Twilight of the Idols, Ecce Homo* (his autobiography).

Readability: Looks easy enough; used ordinary language, specialized in short spurts and aphorisms, pulled no punches (sums up Socrates, for instance, as "the patron saint of moral twaddle"), but style is overheated and dense; reads a little like Norman Mailer in his apocalyptic mode.

Qualities of Mind: Impetuous, irreverent, individualistic, elitist, unstable.

Catchphrases: The will to power, transvaluation of values, *Übermensch*, God is dead.

Influence: One of the most flamboyant and controversial philosophers ever, vehemently opposed to virtually all established culture and morality. A prophet who announced the demise of God (and, more importantly, of all absolutes), prophesied the world wars (or something very like them), warned of democracy's tendency to promote conformity and suppress excellence; also, favored selective breeding. A cultural historian whose perceptions about unconscious human drives paved the way for Freud's. Insisted that the dominant force of history is the "will to power," and advocated a "transvaluation of values" in which the traditional "feminine" virtues espoused by Christianity (submission, compassion, being nice to other people) would be joined with "masculine" virtues (courage, strength, toughness) in a morality that aimed at greatness rather than goodness. Hoped for the ascendancy of the *Übermensch*, or superman, in whom Dionysian instinct and dynamism would be perfectly integrated with Apollonian reason and ethics (see page 258). Has been variously interpreted—and misinterpreted—as a spokesman for Fascist, Nazi, anti-Nazi, Romantic, anti-Romantic, and existentialist doctrines.

Personal Gossip: A frail, sickly boy raised in a household of pious women. Became a classics scholar. First an ardent admirer, then bitter enemy of Wagner. Went hopelessly insane at age forty-four. His sister, who had problems of her own, later distorted some of his writings, making him sound more racist than he really was.

Current Standing: It's no longer fashionable to call him the Antichrist, to blame him for World War II, or even to dismiss him as a brilliant but sophomoric "literary philosopher." These days, he's admired as a visionary theorist of language and knowledge. On the whole, however, philosophers are still busy trying to figure out exactly what he was driving at.

HENRI BERGSON (1859–1941)

Best-Known Works: Time and Free Will, *Creative Evolution,* Matter and Memory (see also *On Laughter,* a minor but famous work).

Readability: Smooth and seductive; Bergson was a master of visual imagery who didn't believe in arguing a point when he could paint a watercolor of it instead. You'll probably be wafted along in happy agreement with him, but good luck afterward trying to explain what you've read.

Qualities of Mind: Suave, sophisticated, mystical, optimistic, artistic.

Catchphrase: Élan vital.

Influence: The chic philosopher of Europe between the wars. Combated the depressingly mechanistic, deterministic, shut-up-and-reproduce outlook of Darwinism with his mystical "vitalism." Viewed human history as a contest between the inertia of matter (associated with reason, conservatism, laws, and social pressure) and the creative energy—or *élan vital*—of living things (associated with intuition, art, charisma, and the mysteries of life). Everyone was delighted to have some version of free will restored and to be given such a clear-cut distinction between people and rocks. His theories had a great impact on artists, political activists, and socialites: Shaw appropriated his concept of *élan vital* and Proust used his mystical concept of time and memory as the basis for *Remembrance of Things Past.* The party ended with the outbreak of World War II, however, when everybody began to prize sanity over spontaneity again.

Personal Gossip: Proust was best·man at his wedding.

Current Standing: Developed appealing theories that, though not without merit, are taken with a grain of salt. Reason is still at a premium, after all. Moreover, it's understandably difficult for any philosophy department to embrace a mystic, particularly one who, instead of producing a coherent system of thought, chooses to describe life as a "shell bursting into fragments which are again shells."

ALFRED NORTH WHITEHEAD (1861–1947)

Best-Known Works: Principia Mathematica (with Bertrand Russell), *Science and the Modern World, Adventures of Ideas.*

Readability: Perfectly accessible, provided you stick to the latter two, which were written for the layman.

Qualities of Mind: Idealistic, mystical, religious, balanced, thorough, disciplined.

Catchphrases: The philosophy of organism, occasions, and becomings.

Influence: A mathematician turned metaphysician; his work with Russell produced the first new system of logic since Aristotle, the *Principia*, which whether or not one cares about that sort of thing, is considered one of the great intellectual monuments of all time. On his own, worked out the most comprehensive metaphysical system of this century ("the philosophy of organism"), a synthesis of idealism, empiricism, mysticism, mathematics, God, Darwin, and Bergson, to name just a few. Aimed at a general theory that would, in the best metaphysical tradition, explain absolutely everything, and one that would make it OK for God to exist in the modern world. His philosophy, which revolved around theories of change and actualization of potentiality, is now called "process theology."

Personal Gossip: Reputed to have been a kind man whose wife was a great help to him, although they were always worrying about money.

Current Standing: Universally admired for the pure scope of his understanding, his balanced intelligence, his ability to incorporate dualities into vast schemas without getting silly, and his unwavering faith in the possibility of total understanding. But since no subsequent philosopher has shared that faith, and so few of them believe in God, his metaphysics is already obsolete.

LUDWIG WITTGENSTEIN (1889–1951)

Best-Known Works: Tractatus Logico-philosophicus, Philosophical Investigations.

Readability: Bedside reading for Bauhaus fans; oddly and intriguingly structured, especially the *Tractatus*, which was intended as a model of clarity and has the added advantage of being only seventy-five pages long. Not the kind of book you can't put down, but if you're in the right mood, it reads a little like poetry.

Qualities of Mind: Intense, penetrating, exacting, original, analytical.

Catchphrases: Language games; whereof one cannot speak, thereon one must remain silent; don't ask for the meaning, ask for the use.

Influence: Seminal—and central—figure in linguistic analysis, one of the dominant trends of modern philosophy (and Cambridge's answer to sloppy French existentialism). Was convinced that language creates a picture of the real world and that most philosophical problems are merely the result of philosophers' misuse of language; experience only *seems* complicated because of our confused descriptions of it, which represent knots in our understanding. Untangle the knots and, according to the theory, philosophical questions will simply dissolve. Was notable for having formulated two separate philosophical systems, the second of which (called ordinary-language philosophy) refuted the first (logical atomism, or picture theory). Was a major influence on yet another group of moderns, the logical positivists.

Personal Gossip: A rich kid who gave away his inheritance because, he said, he didn't want his friends to like him for his money. Quit philosophy after finishing his first book, spent a few years teaching grade school in the Alps and contemplating suicide. Built a mansion for his sister that is considered outstanding architecture. Could whistle difficult passages of music from memory. Took up philosophy again and became a cult hero at Cambridge.

Current Standing: Early Wittgenstein gets raves for sheer brilliance, even though no one is into logical atomism anymore; his later work gets mixed reviews, but the subject is still hot stuff in England and America. On the whole, a prestige philosopher.

JOHN DEWEY (1859–1952)

Best-Known Works: Democracy and Education, Reconstruction in Philosophy, The School and Society.

Readability: No laughs, no tears, just earnest American textbook prose.

Qualities of Mind: Robust, practical, down-to-earth, zealous, democratic.

Catchphrases: Progressive education, learning by doing.

Influence: An intellectual activist, a thinker for the heartland, and one of the dominant American philosophers of the century. Conceived of philosophy as an instrument for guiding human action, and turned James' theoretical pragmatism into an applied science, using pragmatic principles to help resolve contemporary social issues. Developed a biology-based theory of knowledge, emphasizing the problem-solving nature of human thought processes and the importance of experimentation in learning. Famous for using these theories to reform the American educational system, rejecting learning by rote in favor of learning by doing. A champion of collective social power.

Personal Gossip: None.

Current Standing: The thoroughly relevant philosopher. Hard to criticize him on the basis of his ideas because these were never supposed to be eternal verities; even harder to argue with his success in implementing them. Pragmatism itself is still open to debate; Bertrand Russell accused Pragmatists of "cosmic impiety" in making truth out to be nothing more than a tool for human use, and warned that Dewey's "intoxication" with social power was the greatest danger confronting modern man. All we know is, Johnny *still* can't read.

Toys in the Attic

FIVE FAMOUS PHILOSOPHICAL MIND GAMES

ZENO'S ARROW: One of the best-known of the paradoxes with which a whole contingent of early Greek logicians liked to amuse themselves; this one illustrated the impossibility of motion or change. The flight of an arrow, said Zeno, is an apparent example of motion. But at any given moment of its flight, the arrow is either where it is or where it is not. If it moves where it is, it must be standing still, and if it moves where it is not, then it can't be there; thus it can't move. This sort of thing drove Zeno's friends crazy, of course, but it also provoked a crisis among metaphysicians, who were, for a long time, concerned with reconciling the basic features of permanence and change. It also gave rise to a vast literature that set about trying to prove, disprove, or avoid Zeno's conclusions. In fact, you could probably still get a lively dinner-table conversation going on the subject today, given the right crowd and plenty to drink.

PLATO'S CAVE: The famous allegory with which Plato, using Socrates as his mouthpiece, tries to explain the nature of human knowledge. Picture, says Socrates, a bunch of people who've spent their whole lives chained up in an underground den, unable to turn around. Behind them a fire is blazing, but all they can see are their own shadows on the wall of the cave in front of them. Never having seen anything else, they naturally mistake these shadows for reality. In the same way, the rest of us mistake the world as we know it for the real world, whereas the objects, and even the qualities, of this world are only shadows of the pure forms that exist in the realm of ideas. Now, what does this mean for you? It means, for example, that somewhere above us in that realm of forms and ideas, there is one, and only one, perfect automobile, of which the lemon you've been driving is merely a crude imitation (you probably suspected something of the sort already). By training your mind to contemplate the idea of the perfect driving machine rather than the expensive heap of scrap metal in your driveway, you can eventually struggle up out of the cave into the sunlight where you'll see the car with utter clarity. True, you will then be confined to driving the idea of the car on the idea of a highway, but Plato never claimed that being a philosopher was easy, and at least you can be pretty certain you'll never encounter much traffic in the realm of ideas.

BURIDAN'S ASS: A famous stumbling block to the concept of free will. An ass, placed equidistant from two identical bundles of hay, has no basis for choosing one over the other and ends up starving to death. Although it was first suggested by Aristotle in connection with astronomy, the image is traditionally attributed to the medieval French philosopher Jacques Buridan, who claimed that a man must choose that which his reason tells him is the greater good, but that he may delay making a decision until his reason has had sufficient time to gather all the information it needs. Actually, it's a starving dog that Buridan refers to; the ass was his critics' idea.

OCCAM'S RAZOR: "Entities ought not to be multiplied, except from necessity." The maxim for which William of Occam, the Franciscan scholar, is best remembered. Actually, Occam never really said this, but he did say, "It is vain to do with more what can be done with fewer," which adds up to the same thing; moreover, he did uphold the principle of eliminating all unnecessary facts or hypothetical entities in analyzing a subject, and he *did* dissect every question as if with a razor.

PASCAL'S WAGER: The pragmatic approach to God, and the seventeenth-century French religious thinker Blaise Pascal's attempt to save the skeptical soul through commonsense reasoning. Basically, his argument goes: OK, so you'll never know for sure whether or not God exists, it's all a cosmic game of heads or tails. But you have everything to gain and nothing to lose by betting on His existence. Remember, you're only staking one finite, so-so little life—no, not even that, only the way you *live* that life—against a chance to win an infinity of an infinitely happy life. If you win (if God exists), you've won everything; if you lose (if God doesn't exist), you haven't really lost a thing. And don't say you'd rather not play, because you have no choice; you're already in the game.

Dueling Dualities

TWO PAIRS OF CONCEPTS DEAR TO THE HEARTS OF PHILOSOPHERS, LOGICIANS, LITERARY POSEURS, AND INTELLECTUAL BULLIES EVERYWHERE

DEDUCTION VS. INDUCTION: Begin by forgetting what Sherlock Holmes used to do; to a philosopher, deduction is much more serious and far-reaching than being able to guess Watson was at his club all day because it's been raining and his clothes aren't wet. So what is it? It's a formal argument that assumes one or more principles as self-evident, then, following rigid rules and forms and proceeding from the general to the specific, infers one or more conclusions from those principles. The example you've heard before: "All men are mortal. Socrates is a man. Therefore, Socrates is mortal." Pay attention to that form. It's called a syllogism, and it's deduction at its most classic—though you can substitute Michael J. Fox for Socrates if you want.

Induction, by contrast, is empirical, factual, ordinary-feeling; it makes use of experiment and/or experience—the scientific method, if you will—to arrive at an inference and proceeds from the specific to the general. When you make an induction, you begin by recording instances, monitoring behavior, counting noses. If you go out to dinner at a Mexican restaurant a dozen times and each time you wake up at 3 A.M. with horrible indigestion, you may well induce that your digestive tract can't take Mexican food, at least not late at night. Of course, you could be wrong; maybe you'd have gotten sick those nights anyway, or maybe it's the particular Mexican restaurant, not Mexican food in general. Or maybe your roommate is poisoning you and trying to make it look like Mexican food. Don't worry, though: Unlike deduction, which, assuming its premises are sound, is certain, absolute, and airtight, induction is about mere probabilities; its success depends on how accurately you observe and over how many cases.

Historical note: For at least two hundred years philosophers have been looking for a logical proof for why induction works as well as it does or, failing that, even just an orderly way to think about it. No soap. About the closest anybody's come to actually legitimatizing it as a philosophical entity, as opposed to a useful day-to-day skill, is John Stuart Mill, who cited "the uniformity of nature" as one reason why induction has such a good track record. Of course, that nature is uniform is itself an induction, but Mill was willing to give himself that much of a break.

Sometimes the line between deduction and induction is clear-cut: For instance, noting (with many a famous philosopher) that the sun always rises, you may have deduced it from the laws of planetary motion, or you may have induced it from the last three thousand or so dawns. Sometimes you think you spot incest—after all, whoever first said that all men are mortal must surely have felt the need to do a little field work first, thereby inducing deduction's single most famous premise. But the flavors of the two will always be distinctive: Deduction is, in the end, all about the axiom ("A triangle has 180°"), while induction has the ring of the maxim ("Faint heart ne'er won fair lady").

A PRIORI VS. A POSTERIORI: In a way, we're back with deduction and induction. That is, a priori knowledge is based on assumption-as-bottom-line, on belief that doesn't depend on experience for validation, on "general principles" of the two-plus-two-equals-four, no-plant-can-get-up-and-walk variety. And, like deduction, it's absolute. A posteriori knowledge derives from observation, of the this-box-is-red, everybody's-sentimental-on-Valentine's-Day variety. You get to it after (*post-*) looking around for yourself. (Your professor probably added that a priori reasoning proceeds from cause to effect, a posteriori reasoning from effect to cause, but that seems like a harder way to think about the whole business.) A good example here, and we owe it to English grammarian, lexicographer, and all-round curmudgeon H. W. Fowler: Browning's famous line "God's in his heaven—all's right with the world" would be interpreted by an a priorist to mean "Given we know there's a God, the state of the world must be OK," by an a posteriorist to mean "The world's so obviously OK, there's got to be a God." Caution: A priori thinking can have negative connotations in some circles, implying arbitrary judgments based on preconceived notions.

What Was Structuralism?

AND WHY ARE WE (with a little help from contributor Stephen Nunns) TELLING YOU ABOUT IT NOW THAT IT'S OVER?

Structuralism was a French intellectual movement that peaked in the Sixties. Because it was French, as opposed to, say, German, it had automatic chic and cachet. And because it was French, as opposed to, say, English, it was a problem for the Anglo-Saxon mind right from the start.

Even less focused, less definable, and less happy-go-lucky than existentialism (its immediate predecessor on university daises and at Left Bank café tables), structuralism wasn't a philosophy exactly, but a *method*, a way of analyzing and, with any luck, understanding things. Many, many things. Everything, in fact. As such, it cut across academic disciplines and art forms, from linguistics and anthropology (its two major incubators), to literary criticism, film, history, and sociology, to psychology and politics.

Structuralists believed, fervently and at great length, that (1) the component parts of any system have meaning only in terms of their relations to one another; that (2) those relations tend to be binarily organized, i.e., to involve a pair (or many pairs) of terms, each half of which is parallel, or opposed, or inverted, or equivalent, or duplicative, or whatever, with regard to the other; and that (3) all cultural phenomena, from linguistic structures to kinship practices, table manners to skirt lengths, wrestling to insanity, and so on, long into the Paris night, are governed by the same principles, and hence related to each other. They, as well as all patterns of human behavior, are codes in which the inherent structuring tendencies of the human mind are reflected. And they directly reflect the ways in which the mind sorts, clusters, and mediates every image, every stimulus, every bit of information it stumbles across. Structuralists claim that if you pay close enough attention to these phenomena, ask the right questions, and construct the appropriate "model," eventually you couldn't help getting to the bottom of things.

Structuralism had its beginnings in linguistics, in the work of the Swiss (but French Swiss, if you get our drift) linguist Ferdinand de Saussure, who observed, among other things, that the "signifier" c-a-t was an arbitrary way of calling attention to the "signified" concept of cat and an even more arbitrary way of designating Muffin over there, the "referent." And that all that kept c-a-t from being c-o-t or b-a-t was a single sound, more specifically, a single sound difference, enough of which differences together went to allow us to encode meaning in language—arbitrarily, granted, but with a high degree of success. Also, to decode meaning. And what's more, Saussure hinted knowingly, it's not just language. We "understand" Coke in terms of its not being Pepsi, a mimosa in terms of its not being a Bloody Mary, Top-Siders in terms of their not being motorcycle boots.

Saussure, who died in 1913, had been very provocative. But outside the linguistics community, which he'd provided with a whole new lease on life, it took decades for the news to trickle down to intellectuals-at-large. Enter Claude Lévi-Strauss, the anthropologist (and the high priest of structuralism), the publication of whose *Elementary Structures of Kinship* in 1949 launched the structural phase of anthropology. For the next thirty years, Lévi-Strauss chiseled away at

Claude Lévi-Strauss

primitive cultures and mythologies (as he called them) as if no white man had ever seen a clay pot or a loincloth or an incest taboo before.

Picture him, for instance, in residence among the Bororo Indians of central Brazil, dealing with their every routine, from cooking to marital fidelity, as if each were a language, a system of communication, structured by unconscious but absolutely binding and consistent laws, laws that were binary in nature (as suggested by two of Lévi-Strauss' better-known titles, *The Raw and the Cooked* and *From Honey to Ashes*).

Of course, the Bororo Indians could themselves have applied the structuralist method to an analysis of Parisian department-store layouts or social-kissing practices had they cared to make the trip. The method is, you understand, up for grabs, employable by anybody who's familiar with it precisely because it is rooted in the structures of the mind. Or, as Lévi-Strauss himself put it, "We do not claim to show how men think in myths, but how myths think themselves in men, and without their knowledge. . . . Myths think themselves among themselves." In fact, Lévi-Strauss had already sorted through a lot of those myths, eventually decreeing the existence of units called mythemes, the equivalent in culture of phonemes, the lowest-common-denominator elements of speech.

Structuralism was an attempt to apply science to areas where it had never been applied before, to banish the old belles-lettres approach to literary criticism, the old pencil-and-notebook approach to anthropology, the old roots-and-prefixes approach to linguistics. But it also had certain Marxist overtones (and what French intellectual movement does not?): By questioning the codes—of behavior, of meaning, of authority—it implicitly questioned who had power and why we went along with his having it. Its real beauty, though, lay in its ordering principles. Lévi-Strauss would hear everybody's folktales and kinship-system stories, thousands and thousands of variations of a theme, and, working structurally, reduce them to a few potent—and lucid—"systems of difference."

Roland Barthes, the bottle imp of Paris intellectual life from the Fifties until his death in 1980, could watch a wrestling match or a Molière play, read a fashion magazine or a novella by Balzac, spend an hour at a striptease parlor or several months in Japan, and break the experience down into its component, binarily opposed parts—many of which would then be interchangeable from spectacle to spectacle, experience to experience. Other structuralists worth knowing about: Michel Foucault, the French historian (see page 587), decoder of insanity, imprisonment, sexuality, and other "marginal" social institutions; Jacques Lacan, the French psychoanalyst (see page 446), who maintained that the unconscious is structured the same way a language is; and Umberto Eco, the Italian scholar and cultural commentator, a specialist in semiotics, or communication through signs, a variant of structuralism that emphasized subject matter over methodology. (Sometimes called structuralists, but not exactly in this way: Noam Chomsky, the American linguist, and Jean Piaget, the French child psychologist.)

So, why have we chosen to tell you about structuralism, given that it's pretty much yesterday's papers? Two reasons. First, it's the immediate ancestor of—and force behind—*post*structuralism, which is, in turn, the kissing cousin of deconstruction and postmodernism (the literary variety, *not* the architectural one; see page 106). All three were incredibly hot French theories that had a huge impact not only on philoso-

Roland Barthes

phy, but on art theory, cinema studies, cultural studies, queer studies, and a host of other "studies" at the end of the twentieth century.

The deconstructionists were led by the philosopher Jacques Derrida, who in 1966 started one of the greatest academic food fights of all time when he took on the structuralists at a conference at Johns Hopkins University. Derrida lobbed his sloppy joe: Lévi-Strauss and his gang were wrong about their binaries leading to reality. There was no such thing as "objective reality." Indeed, according to Derrida, "Il n'y a pas de hors-texte" ("There is nothing outside of the text"). Signifiers just keep stacking up on top of more signifiers, until there's an endless chain of words. And we, of course, are stuck in the middle of all those signifiers ourselves. That means that our "selves" are really nothing more than by-products of language.

Derrida was joined by (before their deaths) the "late" Barthes, "late" Foucault, and "late" Lacan, though it's worth noting that these guys shot a few peas across the cafeteria at each other as well. *Et voilà*—out of the free-for-all, postmodernism was born.

This "method"—again, it can't *really* be called a philosophy, since it denounces grand theories—was all the rage in American academic circles during the Eighties and Nineties. (The French, interestingly enough, had had enough of this stuff by the early Seventies, which explains why most of these fellows ended up in American universities.) The deconstructionists' intent was, in the words of one convert, to "disturb" the work "along its own fault lines." In a similar vein, postmodernists questioned all such supposedly self-evident structures as superior/

inferior, in/out, original/belated, and man/woman, and accused all systems—power structures no less than paragraph structures—of being propped up from the inside and, get this, of unwittingly betraying, under cross-examination, exactly how, and how much, they are propped up.

Though the influence of thinkers like Derrida and Foucault is still evident—particularly in the ivory towers—it has fallen out of favor recently. Part of this has to do with the impenetrability of the jargon, which often made it difficult to tell whether the theorists were on to something new and genuinely complex, or just covering their tracks. Check out, for example, Derrida in the early Nineties: "Needless to say, one more time, deconstruction, if there is such a thing, takes place as the experience of the impossible."

At a certain point it also seemed as though deconstruction could never be much more than a literary parlor trick. OK, maybe signifiers *are* arbitrary, and the meaning of a text *can* be pulled apart to the point of incoherence. But generally speaking, that happens only in graduate English departments. In the rest of the world, things *do* hang together pretty well—and that includes texts, too. (With occasional exceptions, like deciphering directional text for assembling children's toys late on Christmas Eve—a postmodern post-eggnog moment.)

The big issue with postmodernism, though, was its relativity. While a lot of us could get behind the thinkers' attacks on the nasty consequences of modernity (which was, after all, the target of their critiques), other conclusions—that we can't confidently declare one idea or way of life better than another (which was postmodernist extraordinaire Jean-François Lyotard's point), that there is no such thing as universal "truth" or even right or wrong, that it all comes down to language (Derrida's point) or various forms of power and discourse (Foucault's point)—made a lot of people uncomfortable. (It didn't help matters when it turned out that Derrida's friend, fellow Yale professor, and deconstructionist Paul de Man had written anti-Semitic articles for a Nazi newspaper in Belgium during World War II, or when vague rumors surfaced that Foucault had engaged in unsafe sex in San Francisco bathhouses after he had been diagnosed as HIV-positive.) When the terrorist attacks of 9/11 took place, critics of postmodernism and deconstruction—and there have always been plenty—took the opportunity to say, "I told you so! There *is* evil in the world!" and claimed that the "age of relativism" was over.

Of course, nothing's quite that simple. The spread of the Internet and the "virtual" world—not to mention the proliferation of reality TV—has blurred the lines between the real and the unreal (or, as one of the last recalcitrant postmodernists, Jean Baudrillard, likes to put it, "the simulacrum"), making a lot of postmodern ideas seem just a little less loopy.

And that brings us to the second reason we've decided to talk about structuralism as well as postmodernism and deconstruction: Questioning authority—wondering not only who's in charge but also why we're behaving as if he or she were *really* in charge—has never been a bad idea, though lately it seems to have become riskier. While French theories like structuralism and poststructuralism are less fashionable in the United States these days (not unlike the French themselves—think "patriot fries"), it's worth noting that no other new, noteworthy ways of thinking have really risen to take their place. When they do, we'll get back to you.

Three Well-Worn Arguments for the Existence of God

These old chestnuts mark the point at which philosophy—which supposedly bases its arguments on reason—and theology—which gets to call in revelation and faith—overlap. The result, as you'll see, sounds an awful lot like wishful thinking.

THE COSMOLOGICAL ARGUMENT: This one dates all the way back to Aristotle's theory of motion and encompasses Thomas Aquinas' version, known as the argument from contingency and necessity. We know from experience that everything in the world moves and changes, said Aristotle (or simply *exists*, said Aquinas), and everything that moves, or exists, has a mover, i.e., a cause, something that precedes it and makes it happen. Now, we can trace lots of things in the world back to their immediate causes, but there is always another cause behind them and another behind *them*. Obviously, said Aristotle & Co., we can't keep tracing effects back to causes indefinitely; the buck has to stop somewhere, there has to be one cause that isn't, itself, caused by something else, or one entity that existed before all the others could come into existence. This first cause, the Unmoved Mover, is God. The cosmological argument, widely accepted for centuries, started running into snags when Hume decided that the whole principle of cause-and-effect was a mirage. Later, Kant made matters worse by pointing out that while there may be cause-and-effect in *this* world, we don't get to assume that the same holds true out there in the Great Unknown. Today, critics counter the cosmological argument by pointing out that there's no reason to assume we *can't* have an infinite series of causes, since we can construct all sorts of infinite series in mathematics. Also that the argument never satisfactorily dealt with the question any four-year-old knows enough to ask, namely, Who made God?

THE ONTOLOGICAL ARGUMENT: This is an example of the old philosopher's dream of explaining the nature of the universe through sheer deduction (see page 333); also, of how slippery a priori reasoning (see page 334) can get. The argument, which probably originated with St. Anselm back in the Middle Ages and which hit its peak with Descartes, Spinoza, and Leibniz, the Continental Rationalists of the seventeenth century, runs as follows: We can conceive of perfection (if we couldn't, we wouldn't be so quick to recognize imperfection) and we can conceive of a Perfect Being. God is what we call that Being which embodies all imaginable attributes of perfection, the Being than which no greater Being can be conceived. Well, if you're going to imagine a Perfect Being, it stands to reason that He exists, since a Perfect Being that didn't exist wouldn't be as perfect as a Perfect Being that did, and isn't, therefore, the most Perfect Being you can imagine. (Is He?) Hence, by definition, God exists. (Doesn't He?) If you're still reading at this point, you may already have noticed that the ontological argument can be criticized for begging the question; that is, it assumes, at the outset, the very thing it purports to prove. Still, when you think about it, the argument is not nearly as simpleminded as it appears. Just where *did* you get your idea of a Perfect Being if you're so sure no such thing exists?

THE TELEOLOGICAL ARGUMENT, OR THE ARGUMENT FROM DESIGN: You've probably heard this one before. The gist of it is that simply by looking around you can see that the world is a strange and wondrous place, something like an enormous machine with millions of perfectly made and perfectly interlocking parts. Now, nobody but an underground filmmaker would claim that such a structure could be the result of mere chance. For metaphysicians from Plato and Aristotle to eighteenth-century Enlightenment thinkers, enamored of the mechanical symmetry of the universe, and nineteenth-century ones, enamored of the biological complexity of same, the idea that there had to be a Mind behind all this magnificent order seemed pretty obvious. The teleological argument survived for so long partly because the world *is* a pretty amazing place, and partly because the argument's validity never depended on the idea that God is omniscient or omnipotent, only that He's a better planner than the rest of us. However, as Hume, the great debunker, was to point out, even if we could assume the existence of a Cosmic Architect who was marginally better at putting it all together than we are, such a mediocre intelligence, which allowed for so many glitches in the plan, would hardly constitute God. And then along came the mathematicians again, pointing out that, according to theories of chance and probability, the cosmos just might be an accident after all.

POLITICAL
SCIENCE

Contents

Tourists *by Duane Hanson*

What You Need to Know Before Answering a Personals Ad in the International Herald Tribune

A NERVOUS AMERICAN'S GUIDE TO LIVING AND LOVING ON FIVE CONTINENTS

ARGENTINA

HOMENAJE A EVA PERON

THE LAYOUT: South America's second-biggest country (after Brazil), with topography ranging from subtropical forests (the Gran Chaco, near the Paraguayan border) to windblown steppes and melting glaciers (Patagonia, home of some sheep, a lot of oil rigs, and a brand-new outcropping of luxury resorts). Argentina shares the island of Tierra del Fuego, the southernmost tip of the Americas, with Chile, and refuses to relinquish its claim to the little group of islands known as the Falklands (Argentines call them the Malvinas) despite its resounding loss to the British, who'd been occupying and administering the islands for 150 years, in the 1982 Falklands War. Argentina has plenty of rich farmland, mineral deposits galore, and, at its top and bottom, wide-open spaces. That's because most Argentines have gone off to live in the pampa, the central grasslands where the gauchos used to roam, the cattle still graze, the wheat grows, and most of the manufacturing is done. In fact, nearly 40 percent of them have set up housekeeping in a few square miles of the pampa over by the coast, in the present capital, Buenos Aires, Argentina's version of Paris, ditto Miami Beach, where those who are not busy blockading highways or sifting through garbage for food can enjoy the views from their high-rise apartments and dream of Swiss bank accounts waiting beyond the horizon.

THE SYSTEM: Well, it's a federal republic for sure, comprising twenty-three provinces and a federal district; beyond that, it depends on what day of the week this is. Between 1939 and 1983, Argentina went through twenty-four presidents and twenty-six successful military coups (as well as hundreds of unsuccessful ones); during the economic crisis of 2001–2002, five different presidents came and went within two weeks. Stability, as foreign investors have learned, is not among Argentina's many attractive qualities. Argentines, for their part, have become accustomed to having their constitutional rights dictated from above or suspended altogether. With a history of rule by *caudillos*—those legendary Latin strongmen with the long sideburns and the private armies—and by the kind of military junta that shoots first and asks you to state your business later, they've come to regard a little repression as almost reassuring; it's taken as a sign that, at least, someone is in charge. Argentina is currently governed by a president and vice president elected for four-year terms. At the moment, they are still reasonably popular with the citizenry. Stay tuned.

WHAT YOU NEED TO KNOW TO READ THE NEWSPAPERS: That the key question is: What's a nice middle-class country like you doing in a mess like this? Up until about twenty-five years ago Argentina was the poster child for Latin American prosperity. Blessed with abundant natural resources, a large middle class, and an educated workforce, the country had the seventh-largest economy in the world. And indeed, throughout much of the 1990s, Armani suits and Vuitton bags blossomed like wildflowers among the sidewalk cafés of Buenos Aires. Argentines will tell you that what happened was something called the "Washington Consensus," an economic policy strongly encouraged by the IMF that called for removing trade barriers, privatizing major industries, opening the country to foreign investors, and pegging the peso to the dollar. By the end of the decade, local industries were bankrupt, Argentina's exports had priced themselves out of the global marketplace, and more than 20 percent of the country's workforce was collecting unemployment. Meanwhile, the peso was on life support, battered by recession in the United States and the sheer unsustainability of pretending to be a dollar when you're really a peso. Much of Argentina's once-robust working class had spent the last few years lining up at soup kitchens, and now the middle class crowded in behind them; more than half the population of Argentina was living below the poverty level. In the winter of 2001, things came to a head when the government froze bank accounts and people heading to their ATMs found "Sorry" notices instead of cash. Thousands of people took to the streets banging pots and pans, a couple dozen people were killed, and the government collapsed. Two weeks and five presidents later, the ruckus finally began to settle after the former governor of Patagonia, Néstor Kirchner, assumed office and inherited, along with a country in the midst of a nervous breakdown, the largest sovereign debt default in the history of the world.

By the way, expect to be confused by the frequent, contradictory references to Peronism, named for the ultimate caudillo, Juan Domingo Perón, and to the Peronist Party, which dominated Argentine politics and defined a version of the Argentine dream from the 1940s through the 1970s and which is represented today, however unfaithfully, by the current president. Even in Perón's day, Peronism was an incoherent muddle of nationalism, socialism, fascism, anti-imperialism, and ferocious anti-Americanism supported by an unlikely mix of social cadres—factory workers, church leaders, army officers, right-wingers of various persuasions—that normally wouldn't allow their kids to run on the same playground. What held Peronism together was the personal charisma of Juan Domingo and especially of his wife Eva, a.k.a. Evita, who was a sort of cross between Marlene Dietrich, Edith Piaf, and Eleanor Roosevelt. The movement drastically increased the power of labor unions and other special interests, bankrupted the country, and gave rise to Argentina's large and perennially discontented middle class. "Peronism" is still the vague umbrella term for the nation's power elite, though there is not much alignment among them on issues of national concern, and the party has now been renamed the Justicialista Party.

WHAT YOU NEED TO KNOW IF YOU'RE DATING AN ARGENTINE: Does your date live in Buenos Aires? Would that be the city proper or the surrounds? It makes a difference. If your date lives in the city, you might want to bring along all the clothes you don't wear anymore to trade for bedlinens or motor oil at the city's ubiquitous barter clubs, after which you might stop in for a light supper at one of the many local soup kitchens. Working-class Argentines began to band together for sustenance when the job market went south, and middle-class Argentines joined them when the peso did the same. The result was an enormous grassroots movement of barter, neighborhood associations, and worker takeovers of abandoned factories that led to euphoria among Latin American left-wingers, who believed they were witnessing the dawn of a new utopian society. Dream on, dudes. Nowadays, you can still leave your American Express card home and barter for just about everything you need—including a haircut or a session with one of Buenos Aires' gazillion psychotherapists—and most neighborhoods still run their own soup kitchens, but with the economy showing signs of improvement and the president talking tough to Argentina's creditors, daily life has settled into a somewhat threadbare version of its old self. In fact, whether your date is rich or semi-broke, you can expect to spend a night or two at one of the tango palaces that are booming in Buenos Aires these days.

However, if your date's address is somewhere in the city's vast outlying areas, bring nothing, unless you're willing to risk outshining your date, and plan to spend most of your time building roadblocks and burning tires along with the other *piqueteros*—the great unemployed masses—on the city's major thoroughfares. Three times the number of residents of Buenos Aires proper live in the *villas miserias* on the outskirts of town. Once the frontline of mass protest, they have now been reduced to a national nuisance by a government that's been cunning enough to use spin rather than shooting to overcome its opposition.

Of course, your date may be one of the lucky—or better yet, well-connected—Argentines who stashed an estimated $100 billion in overseas banks before the recession hit. In that case, pack your favorite Guccis and Chanels and plan on partying like it's, um, 1994.

WHAT YOU NEED TO KNOW TO MEET YOUR DATE'S PARENTS: If your date happens to be the scion of one of Argentina's fine old ranching families, who once owned the pampa, were rich as sheiks, and fancied themselves European aristocracy, pack a copy of Emily Post, not necessarily a recent edition. Your date's parents, broke now and possibly a little loco from twenty-five years of military brutality, government corruption, and financial catastrophe, will still judge you by your manners—the more Old World the better. Otherwise, your date's parents may be activists; in fact, if your date's mom disappears for a couple of hours every Sunday afternoon, she's probably one of the former Mothers, now Grandmothers, of the Plaza de Mayo, who still march weekly to commemorate the 9,000–15,000 original *desaparecidos* tossed into mass graves during the government's "dirty war" of the 1970s. Those old wounds were not exactly healed by the immunity laws that protected former junta members from prosecution until they were finally repealed in 2003. Nor does it help that mass graves are still being uncovered throughout the country three decades later. You might want to prepare some kind of statement regarding the release of documents purportedly showing that Henry Kissinger gave his blessing to the junta's tactics. On second thought, better not to go there at all. Instead, try to keep the conversation focused on soccer, Argentina's national passion, avoiding any mention of drug use by Diego Maradona, the country's legendary soccer hero. Or reminisce about your college backpacking trips through Spain and Italy—whence much of the country's population emigrated a century ago. It's also possible, however, that your date's parents will greet you with thick German accents, and you'll have to spend the rest of your visit wondering if they were among the thousands of Nazi war criminals who were warmly welcomed by the Argentine government after World War II; in this case, you'll definitely want to stick to soccer.

CAMBODIA

THE LAYOUT: A heart-shaped rice paddy the size of Missouri, surrounded by mountains and tropical forests, watered by monsoons and the Mekong River, just right for nurturing a peaceful farming nation. But location is everything, and the neighbors here are a nightmare: The Vietnamese, on one side, and the Thais, on the other, have been sneaking into the backyard to steal vegetables, dump trash, and poison the family pets for centuries. (Laos, to the north, tends its own rice paddies and doesn't bother the Cambodians or anyone else.) Meanwhile, tourism is on the upswing in the seaside resort of Sihanoukville, and Phnom Penh, the country's charming, corrupt, French-built capital, parties on, apparently oblivious to the starved and ravaged countryside over which it is supposed to preside.

THE SYSTEM: Since 1993, Cambodia has officially been "a multiparty democracy under a constitutional monarchy"—which translates roughly as "a nest of vipers." There's a legislative branch that doesn't matter and a judicial branch that doesn't function. Power rests with the executive branch, and more specifically, with the prime minister, Hun Sen, and his political cronies in the ruling Cambodian People's Party (CPP). Hun Sen is a former Khmer Rouge who prudently defected to the resistance when his radical-Maoist/homicidal-maniac comrades-in-arms began purging their own ranks with the same gusto they had previously brought to the slaughter of their countrymen. Despised by many Cambodians as a Vietnamese lackey, he has, over the past couple of decades, proven himself quite capable of masterminding his own foul deeds, thank you. After losing the UN-sponsored elections of 1993, he refused to leave office, and since the CPP controls the police and the military, he ended up in a power-sharing deal with the rival National United Front for a Neutral, Peaceful, Cooperative, and Independent Cambodia (FUNCINPEC), the royalist party headed by King Sihanouk's son, Prince Ranariddh—who, title notwithstanding, is no prince of a fellow himself. Four years later, Hun Sen ousted Ranariddh in a bloody coup, earning frowns from the Western powers until, a year later, he negotiated the surrender of several thousand die-hard Khmer Rouge, thus allowing Cambodia its first peace in thirty years. Ever since Hun Sen won—sort of—the 2001 elections but failed to win the two-thirds majority needed to run the country, he has remained in power while the government has remained in deadlock. Meanwhile, Cambodia is perennially clucked and fretted over—these days, in absentia—by former King Norodom Sihanouk, the eccentric, unpredictable octogenarian who finally abdicated the throne in 2004 in favor of one of his sons, Sihamoni, who, in accordance with the new constitution, "reigns but does not rule."

WHAT YOU NEED TO KNOW TO READ THE NEWSPAPERS: Don't believe anything you read, including body counts. Cambodian policy and politics are so Byzantine that few Westerners would be crafty enough to discern the truth even if they actually cared what happens to Cambodia, which they've shown little evidence of doing thus far. Certainly, Cambodia's highest officials know enough to appear inscrutable to the United States, whose aid and UN vote they need and whose intentions they deeply mistrust, and to neighboring Thailand and Vietnam, with whom there's always been bad blood despite the current trend of smiling and handshaking. Islamic extremists kicking up a fuss in southern Thailand aren't likely to improve relations with the overwhelmingly Buddhist Cambodia, either. In fact, Cambodia's only "friend" to date has been China, which sends vast amounts of aid and encouragement—this, despite the fact that the hated Khmer Rouge were, after all, Maoists funded largely by China.

But then, all alliances (including the WTO, which Cambodia joined in 2004) are likely to be unholy in a country where anyone who owns much more than a few chickens is liable to have skeletons hidden not only in the closet but out in the yard and under the floorboards as well. It's been thirty years since the Khmer Rouge executed, starved, and worked to death upward of a million and a half of their countrymen, yet the government is in no hurry to launch war-crime trials that will be at best embarrassing for those who allied themselves with the Khmer Rouge (including not only Hun Sen but the Sihanouks *père et fils*) and at worst incendiary among the many remaining Khmer Rouge who, after turning themselves in to the government in 1998, are now raising families and shooting up saloons in the wild western region of the country.

WHAT YOU NEED TO KNOW IF YOU'RE DATING A CAMBODIAN: If your date looks awfully young for eighteen, shame on you. Now that sex tourism is a main attraction in Phnom Penh, forced child prostitution is epidemic. Don't come whining to us if you get more than you bargained for; it's no secret that Cambodia has the highest rate of HIV infection in Southeast Asia. Anyway, there's plenty of sightseeing you could be doing, from the temples of Angkor Wat, currently being restored by the French and Japanese governments, to the killing fields of Sien Reap and, we hear, the jungle camp where the infamous Pol Pot is said to have died, which has been turned into a tourist attraction. As a rich foreigner, you'll also have access to fancy restaurants, nightclubs, and taxi-dance halls, and to every variety of luxury goods, from silk scarves to AK-47s. Want to lease a sumptuous villa or a former ministry building? You should have no problem finding helpful officials who will be only too happy to evict the current residents and pocket the rent themselves. No one will get into trouble for it, either, because any private-property records that escaped destruction by the Khmer Rouge were voided by the succeeding Vietnamese-backed government, so nobody can prove ownership of anything anymore.

If your date lives out in the countryside, however, it's strictly BYOE, bring your own everything, because the peasants have nothing, many of them not even a full set of limbs. Thirty years of overwhelming mayhem have left the country utterly devoid of infrastructure but rich in amputees, thanks to the millions of buried land mines and tons of unexploded ordnance that pepper the entire country. If you should get a part blown off, forget about finding a doctor, nearly all of whom were murdered or driven out of the country by the Khmer Rouge; you're better off cutting a deal with some local official willing to sell you a bottle of antibiotics or a bag of blood plasma from the tons of supplies donated by the International Red Cross.

WHAT YOU NEED TO KNOW TO MEET YOUR DATE'S PARENTS: Brush up on your high-school French. True, the Cambodians were only too happy to break away from the French Union half a century ago, but they'd barely waved good-bye to the last boatload of Brie-eating bureaucrats when all these hostile neighbors started marching into the country. At least the French, who were around for a century, had shown some appreciation for Cambodia's rich heritage—in fact, it was French scholars who began the restoration of Angkor Wat. The Vietnamese occupiers, on the other hand, who got their ideas of civilization from China, acted as though Cambodia's culture were some kind of embarrassment, which was pretty much how Cambodians felt about Vietnamese culture, too. Your date's parents may get nostalgic about former King Sihanouk, whom many older Cambodians still view as a god-king, or, at the very least, as a reminder of the good old days when Cambodia belonged, more or less, to Cambodians. Your date probably won't share their nostalgia; the younger generation, outraged by repression and the government's shameless corruption, have no great love for the Sihanouks, whom they see as only slightly less loathsome than Hun Sen. None of this really matters. Ex-king Norodom Sihanouk, who has been kicking around—often in exile or under house arrest—since the French installed him on the throne in 1943, has proven himself to be both a patriot and a slippery character. Purportedly dying for at least the last decade, he spends most of his time being treated for cancer at his palaces in Pyongyang and Beijing, where he posts daily blogs on his Web site, www.norodomsihanouk.info, lamenting the poisonous atmosphere pervading his homeland.

CANADA

THE LAYOUT: The second-biggest country in the world (after Russia, Canada's *other* larger-than-life neighbor), but with fewer people than California. Indeed, space, sheer space, is the salient feature here, with cold a close second: The latter, not better television reception, explains why three-quarters of the population huddles within a hundred miles of the U.S. border. Ontario is the most populous, most prosperous, most powerful, most urban, and most industrialized (also, most resented) of the ten provinces and three Arctic territories that make up the country; it also has the capital, Ottawa, and the biggest, most cosmopolitan city, Toronto. Quebec is the largest and second most populous province, with what used to be the biggest, most cosmopolitan city, Montreal, plus the bulk of the 23 percent French-Canadian minority. The concept of the Pacific Rim has been a real shot in the arm for British Columbia (and Vancouver is clearly aiming for the "Most Cosmopolitan" title). Neighboring Alberta has most of the world's second-largest oil reserve (after Saudi Arabia) and therefore all the money, and is the province that winds up providing big subsidies—equalization payments, they call them—to all but one of the other provinces, grudgingly. Very grudgingly.

Saskatchewan and Manitoba are the prairie. The Maritimes, northeast of New England, cast their nets and work their mines, and hope that today's the day the equalization-payment check arrives.

THE SYSTEM: A federal union, a very loose federal union, in which the prime minister tries to convince his countrymen that Canada's future is as a strong, united nation rather than a confederation of shopping centers and smallmouth-bass fishermen, while the ten provincial premiers plump for priorities—and identities—that are, in a word, provincial, and tell the prime minister to keep his goldarned hands off their oil, uranium, nickel, asbestos, natural gas, and/or newsprint. Also in the picture: a governor-general who represents Queen Elizabeth II, the official head of state, but she—and, for that matter, the queen—is purely a figurehead. Plenty of political parties up here, though no one knows quite what to make of them since until recently politics was dominated by the moderately liberal Liberals and the moderately conservative Progressive Democrats. The irrepressible Pierre Trudeau was a Liberal, as is the current prime minister. The Progressive Democrats (or "red Tories," as they're known up there) virtually self-destructed back in the 1993 elections; they are currently being replaced by the Canadian Alliance, formed by a merger between the right-wing populist Reform Party and an assortment of former Progressive Democrats. Left of the Liberals is the New Democratic Party, popular in the provinces but never quite a national contender, and the Bloc Québécois, now busy *not* declaring independence, though still nursing its resentments. There's a two-house legislature, modeled on Britain's Parliament, of which the important half is the elected House of Commons; the Senate is merely appointed, and by the governor-general, at that.

WHAT YOU NEED TO KNOW TO READ THE NEWSPAPERS: That a lot of the action is in the provinces-vs.-Ottawa tension. It's the goad (also the high) in Canadian politics and it helps to explain why Quebec got to hold referenda on whether or not to secede from the rest of the country and why Alberta gets to claim that not only her oil but her oil revenues, oil-development program, and oil-marketing strategy are her own business. In general, resource-rich western Canada feels exploited by the slick and populous east—a perception that's only been strengthened by the ongoing political scandals that have rocked the Liberal Party. A lot of the problem is that modern Canada was created in the mid-1860s not from within, by pigheaded patriots, but from without, by a jittery Britain, worried about containing the volatile United States, and that there's never been a revolution or a civil war—or even an after-school project—to help forge a Canadian identity. The other part of the problem is that Canada's federal government possesses only those powers not already accorded the provinces (the reverse of the states'-rights setup in effect south of the border); as a result, the provinces are in control of health, education (a big deal in a bicultural country), natural resources, interprovince commerce, etc. As for the long-standing ethnic hostility between Anglophones and Francophones, which for decades was the one thing you could count on to generate sparks around a Canadian dinner table, it hasn't gone away, exactly (47 percent of Québécois still say they want their own state), but bicultural animosities are beginning to seem a bit passé now that Canada—good old white-bread Canada, which, to its credit, just wants to be nice to everybody and take them in and hand them a lager, and which has some of the most liberal immigration laws this side of Australia—has been transformed into an unlikely-looking nation of Ukrainian women in brightly colored babushkas hanging out the wash, Hong Kong–born execs in sapphire cufflinks trading whole blocks of Vancouver, and ramrod-straight Canadian Mounties wearing turbans. Anyway, there are more pressing matters to deal with at the moment—health care, for instance. That universal coverage of which Canadians have long been proud and Yankees envious has begun to buckle under the weight of an aging population. These days, your average sick Canadian—whether Anglophone or Francophone—can expect to wait about eighteen weeks just to get a *referral* to see a specialist.

WHAT YOU NEED TO KNOW TO DATE A CANADIAN: A joke should break the ice— and it is mighty cold up this way, eh? Sorry. The joke every journalist works into his Canada piece: How Canada could have had French culture, British government, and American know-how but for some reason wound up with . . . we think you can take it from here. And how about the time *Maclean's*, Canada's *Time*, ran a contest and invited its readers to complete the phrase "As Canadian as . . . ," and the winning entry was "As Canadian as possible under the circumstances." OK, OK, no, really, thanks, well, all right, one more. "How do you get sixty Canadians out of a swimming pool on the hottest day of the summer?" Answer (this is actually what Canadians call a *riddle*): "Yell, 'Everybody out of the pool.'" Actually, real-life Canadians truly *are* obedient, glum, shy, repressed, and painfully decent, with an unflagging go-for-the-bronze streak. Largely, that's the result of living in a country where the government does almost everything for everybody just as, over a century ago, it built the transcontinental railroad—no whip-cracking robber barons racing for the Pacific here—and treated all settlers equitably, thereby avoiding land rushes, Indian massacres, people shouting "Dance!" at each other, and all other forms of survival-of-the-fittest, Wild West–style bravado. Do let your date know that you know that *all* the cultural currents don't flow from south to north; say thanks to him/her for John Kenneth Galbraith, the late Marshall McLuhan, ditto Northrop Frye and Saul Bellow, Joni Mitchell, Dan Aykroyd, Mike Myers, Martin Short, Jim Carrey, Morley Safer, Peter Jennings (but not Diane Sawyer, who just *seems* Canadian), and of course both Pamela Anderson and Wayne Gretzky.

WHAT YOU NEED TO KNOW TO MEET YOUR DATE'S PARENTS: First, that although you may still get tea and biscuits when you visit them, Canada is inching closer and closer to coffee and apple pie, and, in our opinion, everybody's the loser. Nevertheless, Elizabeth is definitely still head of state, Canada is definitely still in the Commonwealth, and people still celebrate Queen Victoria's birthday every May, which even the English have stopped bothering with. It's all about a healthy respect for the past (and an educational system that hasn't broken down yet), and don't be surprised, either, if the parents remind you how it was Wolfe's defeat of Montcalm on the Plains of Abraham in 1759 that first got things moving, establishing the—appropriately condescending facial expression on your part, please—natural superiority of the English, on the battlefield as off, or, let's try to see both points of view here, *s'il vous plaît*, the braying, bullying ways of the English, *maintenant et pour toujours*. That English-speaking Canada and French-speaking Canada never really got along should come as no surprise, even though the English had made, in 1774, one of the all-time most enlightened decisions in the history of colonial administration—at least that's what Henry Steele Commager says—with regard to their French neighbors: Let 'em speak French and let 'em be Catholics. (Later, unfortunately, it would lead to what the English see as a lot of endless whining about "special rights," although the French would argue it's the only way to keep the Limeys from rolling over them completely.) Anyway, in 1867 Parliament passed the British North America Act, which made Canada a self-governing dominion and served as a makeshift first constitution, kept in some file cabinet over in the mother country, who alone had the right to amend it. Canada didn't become independent until 1931, and it wasn't until 1982 that she became *completely* independent—unbelievable, isn't it?—when Trudeau "brought home" that constitution, presumably in a perfectly normal-looking briefcase. Careful/*en garde*: Acid rain and NAFTA may not be quite the sore points they were ten years ago (although NAFTA still isn't much more popular than acid rain, despite the boost it's given to the local economy), but there are a few new topics you'll want to approach delicately and with—dare we say?—a modicum of humility. Take, for starters, the U.S. invasion of Iraq, in which Canada refused to participate (although that hasn't stopped the Canadians from pouring tons of money into Iraq's reconstruction), its support for the UN-sponsored International Criminal Court for war crimes (which the United States opposes), and its strong support for the Mine Ban Treaty (which the United States refuses to sign). As for its willingness to consider legalizing both gay marriage and marijuana use, don't expect your date's parents to beat their breast in horror. Social liberalism is nothing new in Canada, even if it does stand out in greater relief (and we do mean *relief*) now that the United States is up to its eyeballs in every kind of conservatism. Besides, tourism is big business up here, and when last we checked, even Yankee gays and dopers were still allowed to take vacations.

CONGO, DEMOCRATIC REPUBLIC OF THE

THE LAYOUT: First, let's be clear: There are two African Congos. The smaller, sleepier Republic of Congo (RC), a.k.a. Congo-Brazzaville, was formerly the French colony known as Middle Congo, a part of French Equatorial Africa. To the southeast, just across the Congo River, lies the larger, relatively more hellish, and quite laughably named Democratic Republic of the Congo (DRC), a.k.a. Congo-Kinshasa, formerly known as Zaire and before that as the Belgian Congo. Occupying the heart of central Africa and the belly of the continent, the DRC is what everybody thinks of when they think "darkest Africa." It straddles the equator in the north and is full of the kinds of terrain familiar from old Tarzan movies—mile after mile of steamy tropical rain forest at the center, swampy grasslands in the north, high savannahs in the south, and in the far eastern regions volcanoes and jungle-covered mountains that rise majestically through the mists, providing a picturesque home for the world's remaining mountain gorillas and a home away from home for guerrillas from neighboring Rwanda, Uganda, and Burundi. The land is crisscrossed by many muddy, croc-filled rivers, all tributaries of the 2,733-mile-long Congo River, which, though dangerous and frequently unnavigable, is the closest thing DRC has to a super-highway. Although the country is loaded with natural resources above ground and vast mineral wealth below, fifty-six million Congolese live near the very bottom of the world's misery indices.

THE SYSTEM: Dictatorship supposedly in transition to representative government, but don't hold your breath. The interim government stitched together by President Joseph Kabila in 2003 is an uneasy power-sharing arrangement between former combat enemies, none of whom is dim-witted enough to trust the others. Since elections are planned for the summer of 2006, in a vast, dysfunctional country that lacks roads, railways, functioning laws, basic services, and a voting public (the last election was back in 1960, and anyway, these days a substantial number of Congolese are too busy foraging for edible roots and fighting off plague to vote) but is well stocked with armed profiteers who would prefer that elections not take place at all, what currently passes for Congo's "system" may have morphed into something worse or simply been blasted out of existence by the time you read this. For the moment, at least some of the DRC is governed by the president, who shares power, sort of, with four vice presidents—including one from each of the two main rebel movements, the Rally for Congolese Democracy (RCD), backed by Rwanda, and the Movement for the Liberation of Congo (MLC), backed by Uganda, and one from the civilian opposition. A thirty-five-member transitional cabinet is meticulously if not productively divided among the leaders of the country's many factions. The eastern region of the DRC is still controlled by whichever rebel group or tribal militia gets lucky on a given day. Ten provinces and the capital of Kinshasa have their own governors. There are about 250 known ethnic groups: The official language is French, but Swahili, Lingala, Kikongo, and at least seven hundred local dialects are also spoken here.

WHAT YOU NEED TO KNOW TO READ THE NEWSPAPERS: That the conflict known as "Africa's world war" broke out in the DRC in 1998, sucked in six neighboring African countries, killed a conservatively estimated 3.8 million Congolese, and is still causing about a thousand civilian deaths a day in the eastern regions, despite an official end to hostilities in 2003. The war has been aptly summarized as being "partly about ethnic hatreds but mostly about loot." Don't be surprised if you have trouble keeping the combatants straight—even the ones who *don't* go into battle wearing dresses have complex agendas and serious identity issues. There are, for instance, the Interahamwe, the Hutu militias blamed for the 1994 genocide against the Tutsis next door in Rwanda. The Interahamwe are said to have sparked the Congolese war when they escaped across the border into the DRC, indistinguishable from a million and a half more or less innocent Hutu refugees who fled the advancing Tutsi army. In 1998, Rwanda and Uganda invaded the DRC with help from Burundi, ostensibly to stop the Interahamwe from launching attacks from inside Congolese territory but also, as it turned out, to massacre as many Hutu refugees as possible and install a Tutsi-friendly regime in the DRC. The Western powers, feeling sheepish about their failure to stop the Rwandan genocide, bent over backward to support the Tutsis, even after it became clear that the latter were out for revenge and a genocide of their own. Finally, the governments of Angola, Namibia, and Zimbabwe jumped in to defend the Congolese regime, partly because the DRC is critical to the stability of the entire region, but also, in the case of the Zimbabweans, because engagement gave them—along with the Rwandans, Ugandans, Burundians, Congolese warlords, government ministers, and at least eighty-five known multinational corporations—a chance to plunder the DRC's vast resources at their leisure.

Oh and by the way, if you're reading English-language newspapers, brace yourself for the inevitable allusions to Joseph Conrad's *Heart of Darkness*.

WHAT YOU NEED TO KNOW IF YOU'RE DATING A CONGOLESE: How to party down with someone who's suffering from disease, malnutrition, and post-traumatic stress disorder. Try a little tenderness. If your date is a woman, she may have been gang-raped by rebel soldiers on her way to meet you, especially if you've arranged a rendezvous outside one of the squalid refugee camps where some of the two million or so internally displaced Congolese huddle in tents, waiting for supplies that never arrive. If your date's a man, congratulations on having found a live one!

Let's hope he's younger than forty, which is the average life expectancy of a Congolese man these days. Keep an eye on your guy. If he shows up wearing a piece of garden hose as a necklace, he's probably a Mai-Mai. They're the rabidly anti-Rwandan teenage militia fighters who are still tearing it up all over Ituri province, near the Rwandan border. The Mai-Mai are convinced that magic water protects them from bullets and allows them to fly. They also like to pump up for the next round by cannibalizing their enemies, but around here, who doesn't?

If you date a civilian, he might work as forced labor in the mines, illegally extracting diamonds, gold, or the ever-more-valuable coltan, a mineral used in cell phones, to be smuggled out of the country. Other than that, employment opportunities are pretty much limited to raising cassava behind your hut or selling plastic flip-flops from a bicycle. The average Congolese who earns money at all earns about a dollar a day in the better neighborhoods, eighteen cents a day in the war-torn east. Don't expect big meals, but do expect to party, no matter how wretched your date's condition. Congolese music is legendary, and although the war destroyed Kinshasa's music industry, wildly popular *ndombolo* is still played and danced everywhere.

Do you need to be reminded to practice safe sex? You're in AIDS country. We'd shock you with the dizzying HIV rates but, what with the ubiquity of rape these days and the fact that so much of the populace is already out sick with polio, malaria, and plague or just terminally run down, most humanitarian organizations won't even hazard a guess.

WHAT YOU NEED TO KNOW TO MEET YOUR DATE'S PARENTS: If you're American, you may be called upon to explain why the CIA backed Joseph Mobutu's (later known as Mobutu Sese Seko) overthrow of Patrice Lumumba a year after Lumumba won Congo's first national elections. That one's easy. It was the Cold War, the DRC was strategically positioned, and we couldn't let a suspected Commie sympathizer like Lumumba run the country, could we? And why did we spend the next thirty years propping up the kleptocracy of Mobutu, despite his questionable taste in hats and the unbridled enthusiasm with which he pursued the World's Most Corrupt and Repressive Dictator award? That's a no-brainer: He was on our side. Remind your date's parents that once the Cold War was over, we began to feel uncomfortable with Mobutu's international image and in 1997, when rebel armies were about to march on Kinshasa, we made it clear to him that he no longer had our support. It wasn't our fault that Laurent Desiré Kabila, the thuggish, Rwandan-backed rebel leader whom we helped put in his place, turned out to be just as bad. Anyway, no harm done—or not that much; Kabila was assassinated just a year later.

Point out to your date's parents (trying not to sound *too* patronizing) that Congo's troubles really started back in 1885, when Belgium's King Leopold II tricked the European powers carving up the African continent into letting him claim most of the Congo River basin as his personal property. Having convinced them that he was on a humanitarian mission to halt slavery in the region and make the heart of Africa safe for Christianity and capitalism, Leopold turned his Congo Free State into a forced-labor camp from which he extracted a fortune in wild rubber. His agents raped, murdered, and routinely cut off the hands of those who failed to meet their daily rubber quotas; an estimated ten million Africans died under his rule. (But surely your date's parents can be proud of the fact that Leopold's brutality gave rise to the world's first mass human rights movement!) In 1907, faced with international scandal, the Belgian state took over. It renamed the country the Belgian Congo and ran it as a colony until 1960, when riots and unrest caused the Belgian government to hurriedly grant Congo independence and head for the airport.

Now, as you squat together in the dense jungle underbrush, sharing stories instead of food, keeping an eye out for boys carrying AK-47s, and soothing the brows of plague-ridden relatives, you can remind your date's parents that, here in the Congo, things could be worse.

ETHIOPIA

THE LAYOUT: Ethiopia used to stand tall, even without shoes. Located in the Horn of Africa, just across the Red Sea from Saudi Arabia and Yemen, it was a venerable Christian stronghold flanked by Muslim states, with its feet planted firmly in black Africa and its face turned toward the Middle East. Later, it became a militant Marxist outpost in spine-tingling proximity to the Suez Canal. Then the country's sense of geographical identity, already under stress from its loss of strategic importance at the end of the Cold War, took a further hammering in 1993, when Eritrea, the northern coastal province that provided Ethiopia's only access to the sea, formally won its thirty-year battle for independence. Now all one can safely say about Ethiopia is that it's got a lot of mountains. Ethiopia is one of only two black African countries—Liberia is the other—that largely escaped colonial rule in the nineteenth and twentieth centuries. (Italy invaded in 1895 but, having been thoroughly trounced in the ensuing war with the locals, was forced to content itself with colonizing Eritrea.) But in this case, owning your own country hasn't turned out to be all that much fun. Primarily a high central plateau seamed with deep valleys and fringed by semi-desert, Ethiopia is, as one freaked-out traveler put it, "a terrain of crag and precipice, where Nature seems to have lost her temper with the landscape or to have become demented." It is, at any rate, the kind of radically divisive topography that makes tribal warfare seem like a sensible alternative to recipe-swapping among the nation's eighty or so different ethnic groups. It has also encouraged Ethiopians to lose touch with the outside world—and their leaders to lose touch with reality—for centuries at a time.

THE SYSTEM: As of when the constitution was adopted in 1994, a federal republic (officially, the Federal Democratic Republic of Ethiopia) comprising nine ethnically based regions, each of which has considerable autonomy and the right to secede. At the federal level, there are a president elected for six years, a prime minister who heads the government and selects the Council of Ministers, a bicameral parliament, a supreme court, and enough political parties to grind every ax in a spectacularly fractious land. It all looks promising on paper, but of course, none of it actually works. And really, why should it? Ethiopia, formerly known as Abyssinia, was just your average biblical empire until 1974. That was when Emperor Haile Selassie (whose name, reggae fans, was Ras Tafari up until his 1930 coronation), who claimed royal descent from King Solomon and the Queen of Sheba, was deposed (and later strangled in his bed) by the Provisional Military Administrative Council, better known as the Dergue. For the next few years, the Dergue busied itself replacing Selassie's feudal state with "scientific socialism," a one-party Marxist system complete with collective farms, nationalized property, and a government stranglehold on the economy. Bitter infighting among the Dergue's 120 members led, in 1977, to a shoot-out from which Colonel Mengistu Mariam emerged as the country's leader. Mengistu's rule, characterized by militant Marxist-Leninist orthodoxy coupled with a short-man complex, lasted for seventeen years and earned him the nickname "the black Stalin." During this period, he managed to build the largest standing army in black Africa, which, with the help of Soviet weapons and Cuban troops, allowed him to keep a lid on the rebellions percolating in virtually every Ethiopian province. Finally, in 1991, with the Soviet Union no longer around to back him up, Mengistu was routed by a loose coalition of rebel groups calling itself the Ethiopian People's Revolutionary Democratic Front (EPRDF) and forced to catch the next flight to Zimbabwe, where he'd been scouting real estate for some time. Since then the EPRDF, which took over a country that, oops, suddenly lacked an army, navy, air force, police department, money, or anything resembling an infrastructure, has been struggling—with limited success and a questionable human-rights record—to keep Ethiopia from splintering into warring ethnic groups. Of course, all this may have changed by the time you read this; the the EPRDF's claim that it won the 2005 election, amid charges of election fraud, brought violent protests and a brutal clampdown by the government. So it may be back to the old brutally-repressive-government cauldron for a nation that, for a little while, seemed to have to cope with only famine, extreme poverty, centuries-old ethnic resentments, and fallout from violence in nearly every neighboring country.

WHAT YOU NEED TO KNOW TO READ THE NEWSPAPERS: That from the end of the Cold War, which destroyed the country's standing as the Western powers' strategic outpost in the Horn of Africa, to the massive violence that followed the 2005 elections, you had to turn to at least page sixty in the major newspapers (forget about your local ones) to find out whether there even *was* an Ethiopia anymore. In the absence of accessible oil or mineral reserves, only the threat of another world-class famine, as there was in 2003, seemed sufficient to attract the attention of the Western press—and even then, journalists seemed less interested in the potential starvation of millions than in the possibility of a sequel to 1984's Live Aid concert. Things have picked up, however, since we became obsessed with violent Islamic fundamentalism. Ethiopia's surrounded by it.

It's true that, since the overthrow of Mengistu, hundreds of newspapers have come into print. Unfortunately, hundreds of journalists have also been killed, jailed, or exiled for writing about the EPRDF's stunningly unsuccessful relocation program, in which thousands of subsistence farmers were transported from the deforested, eroded soil of the central plateau to the outlying mosquito- and tsetse-fly-infested lowlands near the Sudan border, where hardly any of the promised resources awaited them and from which they were quickly bused back home again, weighing even less than before. Nor will you see many accounts of the battles raging in the western Gambella region, where the indigenous Anuak have been ambushing the more recently arrived Highlanders and are being, observers say, ethnically cleansed in return. Meanwhile, on the (entirely government-controlled) radio and TV (and yes, there are plenty of TV antennas flying above those decrepit huts) you may be treated to reports of the new landscaping in Addis Ababa, part of the city's ongoing bid to be the capital of Pan-Africanism and of Ethiopia's never-ending struggle to attract foreign development funds instead of just emergency ones.

By the way, should you decide to turn to the Arab or Muslim African newspapers for global awareness, you will, sooner or later, learn of the dastardly Israeli/Ethiopian plot to steal the life-giving waters of the Nile. As the story goes, the two governments have for some time been conspiring to build dams that will divert the water currently shared with Egypt and Sudan. Expect this paranoid thread to appear as a hard news "account" every time an Israeli minister, diplomat, or grandmother (remember all those Ethiopian Jews who were airlifted to Israel during the war with Eritrea) gets off a plane in Addis Ababa.

WHAT YOU NEED TO KNOW IF YOU'RE DATING AN ETHIOPIAN: Don't bother to write; your date can't read. Despite a couple of decades of hand-wringing and a few actual attempts at school construction, Ethiopia's literacy rate still hovers around 43 percent—that is, pretty much where it was a couple of decades ago. To be fair, educating the populace has its challenges. Even where there are schools, there are likely to be no roads leading to them, no teachers to run them, and certainly no hot lunch to fortify anyone for an afternoon's slog through some donated textbook about the songbirds of eastern Maine. Nevertheless, in rural areas, Ethiopian kids who do attend school tend to view the experience favorably, since getting there each day offers them the opportunity to practice marathon running, which is something of a national sport.

If your date's a girl, of course, literacy will be less of an issue than sex. You'll both have plenty to think about before you jump into bed, such as Ethiopia's dizzying HIV infection rate; an absence of birth control so widespread that, despite an average life expectancy of forty, the population has nearly doubled since the famine of 1984; and certain complications resulting from your date's personal experience with genital mutilation.

Oh well, every relationship has its difficulties. You will at least be able to enjoy a good cup of coffee together. (And who needs food when you're in love?) Ethiopia, as every Starbucks regular can tell you, is famous for producing the world's best coffee. However, since the bottom dropped out of the world coffee market, your date may, like many others, have turned to raising the narcotic khat instead, which yields at least three times the profit. Either way, you'll be buzzin'.

WHAT YOU NEED TO KNOW TO MEET YOUR DATE'S PARENTS: First, don't bother trying to make small talk, unless you're fluent in Amharic (the official language), Galligna, Tigrigna, or one of nearly a hundred local dialects. Second, do get your prejudices straight: the Ethiopians resent the Eritreans, who consider themselves Arabs and who, after a really, really long civil war, finally won the right to secede from the Ethiopian Republic in 1993. They left, taking with them Ethiopia's only access to the sea, but the divorce seems to have left neither party feeling freer or happier. Landlocked Ethiopia no longer has access to shipping routes, Eritrea has the seaport but lacks anything to ship, and an unresolved border dispute between the two countries perennially threatens the uneasy peace. Ethiopians look down on the local Somalis (the Muslim residents of Somaliland, a southeastern province, which you have every right to confuse with Muslim Somalia next door), whom their nineteenth-century Emperor Menelik labeled "the cattlekeepers for the Ethiopians." The Amhara, light-skinned aristocrats from the northern highlands, feel superior to all other Ethiopians and resentful of their perennial rivals, the Tigreans. The Tigreans, also from the north, feel underappreciated; they were the ones who led the final assault on Mengistu, yet their efforts at peaceful, pluralistic nation-building are drawing fire from all sides. The southern Oromo, who comprise about 40 percent of the population, have been poor and powerless for centuries; now they're mad as hell and they're not going to take it anymore, although as far as anyone can tell, they have no agenda. If your date's parents are among the Amhara or Tigrean elite, you might try currying favor with stories of your days as an altar boy. Christianity, in the form of the ancient, powerful, and once staggeringly rich Ethiopian Orthodox Church, was the official state religion and, for sixteen centuries, the foundation of upper-class Ethiopian life, right up until Selassie's downfall. Proceed with caution, however: Mengistu did a pretty good job of discrediting the Church by nationalizing its vast land holdings and killing, cowing, or co-opting most of its priests. And if your date's parents are peasants, they're probably Muslim converts anyway. Don't expect to win any points by gushing about Mengistu's defeat or rhapsodizing about the prospect—however dim—of democratic rule. If you really want to make a good impression, just bring lunch.

FRANCE

THE LAYOUT: The location's lovely—friendly neighbors, water views on three sides—but of course, the facilities are hardly modern. The five famous rivers, for instance (the Seine, Loire, Rhine, Rhône, and Garonne), aren't the great commercial waterways they were back when boats were smaller, and despite recent efforts at decentralization, all roads still lead, culturally and administratively, to Paris. Still, the place has character. And it has undergone extensive renovation: It's now officially divided into twenty-two regions, ninety-six administrative *départements*, and 36,000 communes, although mentally everyone continues to carve it into the same geographically distinct *anciens provinces* (Normandy, Brittany, Burgundy, Gascony, etc.) they were pledging fealty to back in the Middle Ages. (When chatting up the waiter at your local bistro, remember that Provence is the name of a particular province—the one with the Riviera in it—and that, to a Frenchman, everything that isn't Paris is *"les provinces."*). In addition to the main property, a wide variety of time-shares are available in exotic locales—on the island of Corsica, for instance, which is officially a region of France, and in any number of former possessions that still maintain administrative ties to the mother country, from Guadeloupe and Martinique to New Caledonia, French Polynesia, and Adélie Land. The latter, by the way, is located in Antarctica and usually has openings even in high season.

THE SYSTEM: France is now on its fifth republic. The four earlier republics, dating from the French Revolution, were ended by Napoleons I and III, the collaborationist Vichy government during World War II, and Charles de Gaulle, respectively. Each had its own constitution and a somewhat different internal organization. Given that only de Gaulle, with his imperious personality, his incessant talk of *"la gloire de la France,"* and his intimidating height, was able to make any of these republics take root, you may be right in suspecting that, however much the French liked the idea of a republic, some part of them still hankered for a king. France is headed by a president elected for five-year terms, who is invested with greater powers than just about any other elected head of state (except for an American president or two who have apparently believed they ruled by Divine Right). Among these are the right to dissolve the National Assembly, to challenge existing laws, and to handpick his prime minister, thus presumably ensuring the latter's loyalty. However, the major political parties can regroup to form complicated and potent opposition alliances that pit president and prime minister against each other in a hostile "cohabitation," causing the whole system to strain at its seams.

Throughout most of the Fifth Republic, political power has been divided—though, heaven knows, never neatly—among four major forces: the conservative neo-Gaullists, the non-Gaullist right, the Socialists, and the Communists. Lately however, things have become messier. The neo-Gaullists and most of their former conservative allies have joined forces as the Union for Popular Movement (UMP), a coalition that was formed to win elections but is so fractious and full of rivalries that it may well have the opposite effect. The Communists haven't had much clout since at least the 1980s, and the Socialists, who, under François Mitterrand, ran the country from 1981 to 1995, have been leading a not-ready-for-prime-time coalition of leftist parties whose agenda, in the midst of major social upheaval, has been largely confined to debating the wisdom of gay marriage. Even the party of the far right, Jean-Marie Le Pen's stridently xenophobic National Front, which has never been known for the complexity of its platform (Down with Muslims! Down with Jews! Send all the immigrants back where they came from!), has split into two rival factions. Wait for the dust to settle before casting your vote.

WHAT YOU NEED TO KNOW TO READ THE NEWSPAPERS: It would certainly help to know what a neo-Gaullist is. Unfortunately, no one really does (although we can help with the prefix; see page 638). Gaullism was the political ideology defined by Charles de Gaulle's presidency (1959–69), but since so much of de Gaulle's presidency was a matter of personal charisma, being a Gaullist didn't necessarily mean you subscribed to all of his policies. The heart of Gaullism was and is, however, the insistence that France be able to survive on her own, without depending on—or taking orders from—any foreign power. The practical effect: Since the end of World War II, France has hardly been what you'd call a team player. Determined, throughout the Cold War, to take what it saw as its rightful place among the superpowers (third on the dais next to the United States and the Soviet Union), it adopted a foreign policy aimed at asserting its independence from both American and Soviet influence and at creating a strong Europe with itself at the helm. It fought for the creation of the Common Market (and fought to keep Britain out); exploded its own atomic bomb back in 1960; withdrew militarily from NATO in 1966, kicking U.S. and NATO forces out of the country; was one of the first to recognize the government of mainland China, long before the United States did; and made a point of maintaining a "special relationship" with—which usually meant selling arms or plutonium to—whichever radical Middle Eastern country nobody else was speaking to at the moment. Merely by saying *non* to whatever the superpowers wanted, France was able to position itself as a country that stood on principle (which, in a self-serving, self-aggrandizing, semisincere way, it did) and was the champion of nonaligned nations everywhere. The end of the Cold War, however, left France without a fence to sit on and worse, without a cause. (For a brief period in 2003, fierce opposition to the U.S. invasion of Iraq provided the French with an exhilarating sense of national unity, but it couldn't last. Sure, the French knew they were right—the French are always right—but was it God or Allah who was on their side?)

Meanwhile, the task of uniting Europe has turned out to be remarkably annoying, requiring all sorts of risks and sacrifices—of jobs, prestige, market shares—the French hadn't counted on and which further divided public opinion. Look for shifting alliances—particularly with her old nemesis Germany—as France struggles to get a grip on geopolitical reality and jockeys for position in the new balance-of-power game.

WHAT YOU NEED TO KNOW IF YOU'RE DATING A FRENCH PERSON: Be prepared to discuss, for hours and hours on end, politics, philosophy, foreign policy, the politics of philosophy, the philosophy of politics, the politics and philosophy of the French film industry (be sure to let your date take the lead on that one), and that hardy perennial, what's wrong with America. Be conversant with trendy intellectual theories (see page 337 for some tips on deconstruction), keeping in mind that intellectuals are to the French what NASCAR drivers are to your brother-in-law. If you're lucky, your date will be a student at, or a graduate of, one of the *grandes écoles*—the elite universities that turn out virtually all of France's political and industrial leaders—and you'll do your endless debating over foie gras at some four-star restaurant (but brace yourself for a diatribe against affirmative action in the universities—which your date will cite as another heinous example of Americanization eroding the French way of life). If your date isn't one of the chosen few, he or she will either attend one of the overcrowded, underfunded schools that constitute the rest of France's university system (be sure to tuck that headscarf or yarmulke away in your backpack before entering the classroom) or spend his days boning up on the Koran at one of the country's many madrassas (nearly 10 percent of France's population is now Arab and Muslim). Given France's unemployment rate, which is the highest in Europe, your date may not be one of the lucky ones to have landed some low-level office job. In that case, wear comfortable shoes; you'll be spending a lot of time in the streets, protesting the government's attempts at reforming the social welfare system.

WHAT YOU NEED TO KNOW TO MEET YOUR DATE'S PARENTS: That almost anything you say is going to precipitate a history lesson. The French can recall the succession of kings in the Merovingian dynasty or the events that led up to the

Third Empire at least as clearly as you can remember your last love affair, and they're likely to be a good deal more entertaining on the subject; in fact, nothing will give them more pleasure than to share their illustrious past with an ignorant American who hasn't got one of his or her own. Relax, enjoy your *boeuf bourguignon*, and hope that the talk doesn't turn to current events. This will inevitably lead to an anti-American harangue revolving around what your hosts regard as America's criminally misguided foreign policy and "the serious threat of Anglo-American hegemonism," as exemplified by Euro Disney, McDonald's, American television shows (although they may grudgingly appreciate those *Golden Girls* reruns), and the mess in the Middle East. It will be difficult, but try to have a little compassion. Remember that your date's parents are struggling with the disconnect between the quasi-mythical France they grew up in—the birthplace of democracy, the most civilized country in the world, a role model for everyone unfortunate enough not to be French—and the present-day reality of chronic unemployment, rising crime rates, and a failing economy. Why, France herself isn't even French anymore. To be sure, immigrants have been arriving by the hordes for a hundred years, but it was always understood that the main job of the new arrivals was to assimilate, to become true Frenchmen—even if they did end up living in ghettos and working as street sweepers. Today many of the *beurs* (the country's six million or so immigrants of Arab descent) are demanding the right to be different; they flatly refuse to eat charcuterie and don't even bother to learn the language. The whole thing has been a terrible blow to your hosts' self-image. Try to cheer them up. Engage them in a passionate discussion of French literature, during which, the one time you do manage to get your two centimes in, everyone at the table will gleefully leap to correct your grammar.

GERMANY

THE LAYOUT: Even before reunification, in the fall of 1990, West Germany alone had more people (sixty-two million), more neighbors (nine), and a bigger gross national product (well over a trillion dollars) than any other European country except the Soviet Union, at the time still a player, thanks for asking. The merger—funny how corporate-takeover language seems right at home here—added eighteen million enthusiastic, if famously careworn, East Germans to the mix, as well as a long border with Poland and what had been by far the second biggest economy in the Soviet bloc. Flat and Protestant up north, hilly and Catholic down south (the latter tendencies culminate in the Alps of Bavaria), Germany, like Italy, is crawling with cities, including dirndled Munich, pinstriped Frankfurt, minked-out Düsseldorf, and chicly understated Hamburg, all of which have long competed for German cultural, financial, and/or industrial primacy. In 1999, Berlin (she's the one in the leather miniskirt) became Germany's capital again, taking over from longtime stand-in Bonn (in something from a mail-order cata-log). Meanwhile, in the east, make a note of Leipzig, in a shiny new jogging out-fit and a babushka, and Dresden, in a gas mask, the only sensible response to all those industrial fumes from the Czech Republic billowing northward en route to the Baltic Sea. The Ruhr Valley, practically in Holland, is the manufacturing heart of the country; the Rhine flows right through it, carrying cars, chemicals, and automatic coffeemakers to the rest of Europe and the world.

THE SYSTEM: Federal republic, made up of thirteen *Länder*, or lands, and three Freistaaten, or free states, all with powers similar to those of American states (no accident, this; the United States was *the* postwar influence in West Germany), and a two-house legislature, the important—and elected—half of which is the Bundestag. There's a president, but the big deal is to be chancellor (like Konrad Adenauer; Willy Brandt; and the two Helmuts, Schmidt and Kohl; and, as of this writing, Angela Merkel, the first woman, and the first former citizen of East Germany, to lead the country). As in so many European countries, the vicissi-tudes of coalition—rather than the reversals of head-to-head elections—are the basis for the shifts in political power. Here the major players are the moderate, leftward-drifting Social Democrats, the conservative, pro-Atlantic Christian Democrats (who, allied with the far-right Christian Socialists of Bavaria, held power from the early 1980s to 1997), plus the liberal Free Democrats and the Greens (both fewer in number but with the power to make or break elections). Also to be factored in: a whole slew of ultra-nationalist parties, of which the neo-fascist skinheads are only the most photogenic.

WHAT YOU NEED TO KNOW TO READ THE NEWSPAPERS: That Germany turns out to be a lot less Western than we'd all been thinking it was. In fact, it's only since 1945 and the three-power Allied occupation that anybody's been lumping it to-gether with its Atlantic-looking neighbors and assuming that the Germans want roughly what the English, French, Dutch, etc. do. Before that, the country seemed merely "other," neither Western (all craft guilds and splashing fountains) nor Eastern (all onion domes and howling wolves). Granted, Germany has done itself proud with its imitation of the American model in matters of government and industry; its close collaboration with traditional-enemy France in matters of culture and commerce; and its integration into the European Union, in the course of which it became somebody you could once more invite to family gatherings. Moreover, its long-standing policy of *Ostpolitik* (*ost* means "east," by the way), of attempting to take the pulse of and preserve the dialogue with its other traditional enemy, Russia, may actually have paid off; when the Wall came down and the bor-ders were opened, the two countries were already practiced schmoozers. In fact, with a constitution that specifically forbids military involvement beyond the boundaries of NATO, those are the only foreign affairs the Germans, lacking

France's nuclear capability, blue-water navy, long-standing African and Mideast interests, and silver tongue, *could* legally conduct. Today, all that's changing. It was Germany who blew its allies' minds by waking up one morning and deciding to recognize Slovenia and Croatia, and it was Germany who pressed for a broadening of NATO and the European Union to take in Poles, Czechs, Slovaks, Hungarians, and so on, thereby shoring up its security, as well as winning points, and customers, throughout Mitteleuropa. And it was Germany who first spoke out in opposition to the U.S. invasion of Iraq—although she then stood prudently at the back of the room while the French hogged the spotlight and took the heat. Even the pacifism the Germans have embraced with near-religious fervor since the end of World War II has begun to give a little, with German forces participating in NATO's 1995 intervention in Bosnia and later in Afghanistan. Paranoiacs take heart: The need to underwrite all those reunification costs, resettle all those Balkan asylum seekers, and deal with a huge and increasingly restive jobless population should suffice to keep Germany busy—and homebound—for the foreseeable future.

WHAT YOU NEED TO KNOW IF YOU'RE DATING A GERMAN: Essentially, there are two easy-to-distinguish models, the Wessis and the Ossis. (The Stasi were the East German secret police.) The Wessis are the relatively well-to-do former West Germans, with their pigskin bags and BMWs, plus all those rules and laws and habits for which their country has long been notorious; the Ossis—there's that *ost* again—are stuck with the polyester and the simulated leather and the rattletrap Wartburgs and Trabis they drove over from Thuringia in. Ossis complain that the Wessis are hostile and patronizing; Wessis insist that it was never made clear just how expensive, inconveniencing, and endless this reunification business was going to be, and note that the Ossis are gauche and slow and have obviously forgotten how to work. As resentments continue to simmer, Germany's skinheads—with their Doc Martens and baseball bats—are on the march, with their signature chants of "What do they want here, anyway?" and the eloquent "Oi, oi, oi," but they're being forced to share the headlines (though not yet the photo ops) with a rising number of alienated teenage immigrants from Turkey and Uzbekistan, who fill their empty after-school hours by playing video games and bashing in the heads of their German-born classmates.

WHAT YOU NEED TO KNOW TO MEET YOUR DATE'S PARENTS: Ach. It's not that your date's parents don't like Americans, it's just that there are so many potential conversational land mines, of which the Holocaust is only the most obvious. Also try to avoid too many references to reunification—a triumph, yes, but a high-priced one. Even if Vati and Mutti *have* managed to keep their jobs at the Porsche factory and the little beer brewery down the road, the postwar German standard of living (the envy of the entire industrialized world) has been heading south for a while now and, given all the tax increases meant to defray the costs of reunification and make sure the hordes of refugees and their kids have somewhere to curl up for the night, they've had to say good-bye to those fabulous month-long holidays and big unemployment checks everybody got so accustomed to. You could talk culture: German was, after all, the language of that intellectual holy trinity, Marx, Freud, and Einstein, nor is there any ignoring Kant and Hegel and Goethe and Nietzsche, not to mention all the composers, but even that will backfire if someone in the group wonders aloud where all that dark, heavy, unrelenting stuff ever *got* Germany. Which reminds us, try not to compare Germany to other countries, and especially don't compare her to France. While it's true they remain ostensibly the best of friends, too much talk of her more glamorous neighbor may remind Germany how (1) she doesn't have twelve centuries of consolidated national identity to fall back on, and (2) nobody ever watched her with envy and admiration when she took to the dance floor.

INDONESIA

THE LAYOUT: Wins the most-fragmented-nation award: more than seventeen thousand islands, about six thousand of which are inhabited, strung necklace-style along the equator, just south of Indochina. (Java's the most important of them, but you've heard of Sumatra, Bali, Borneo, and New Guinea, too). Lushly tropical, with torrential rains, machete-proof jungles, snakes, tigers, elephants, crocodiles, etc. Also volcanic, fertile, and full of Asia's most enticing assortment of natural resources, including oil. The fourth most populous country in the world (after China, India, and the United States) and the most populous Muslim one, with more people than Egypt, Iran, Turkey, and the Arabian Peninsula combined. Ethnically complex, with over three hundred mutually unintelligible languages and dialects; fortunately, everybody's agreed to speak something called Bahasa Indonesia, much touted locally as the purest form of Malay.

THE SYSTEM: A former soldier state struggling to survive as a baby democracy. The president is the major power player here. Previously, the presidency was decided by a thousand-member People's Consultative Assembly (MPR), 60 percent of whom were appointed by the president—which made this a great country in which to be the incumbent. In 2004, the president was elected by popular vote for the first time. New rules also dictated a maximum of two five-year terms (Suharto, Indonesia's last strongman, had just begun his seventh term when he was forced to step down in 1998). There is now a 550-member House of Representatives and a restructured MPR comprising the members of the House plus four reps from each of the country's thirty-two provinces. The governing ethos here is Pancasila, the five principles—literally—on which modern Indonesia was founded: belief in a single supreme god (almost any god will do), concern for one's neighbors (all 210 million of them), nationalism, democracy, and social justice, all of which add up to a sort of live-and-let-live, unity-in-diversity, shades-of-Woodstock thing. (In practice, government here has traditionally been an exercise in enriching oneself and one's circle of friends at the country's expense.) Although the armed forces have, for the first time, been officially excused from political duty, Indonesia's military, which has served as the ruling party's power base since independence, remains the only thing in the country resembling a national institution, so don't expect the generals to retire to little fishing villages anytime soon.

WHAT YOU NEED TO KNOW TO READ THE NEWSPAPERS: That it will be at least ten years before the country recovers from the effects of the 2004 tsunami. With that in mind, a little modern history might also help. From the end of World War II, when first the Japanese and then the Dutch were kicked out, until 1998, Indonesia's history revolved around two men and two men only: Sukarno and Suharto. (One-word names are common in Indonesia, especially in Java.) The former, flamboyant and charismatic (with an adman's gift for slogan-making, e.g., among many others, both "Pancasila" and "the year of living dangerously"), fought for its independence, guided it to nationhood, became, in 1949, its first president, and went on to take his place, with Nehru, Nasser, Tito, and Nkrumah, in the pantheon of "nonaligned" leaders. At home, he adopted the authoritarian system he called "guided democracy," dissolved existing political parties and ruled by decree, and left the inflationary economy pretty much to fend for itself. Abroad, he flirted with the Chinese Communists, set out to crush neighbor Malaysia (that was in 1963, the "dangerous" year), grabbed the western half of New Guinea from the Dutch, and withdrew in a snit from the United Nations. An abortive pro-Communist coup against the anti-Communist military in 1965 gave strongman Suharto his chance: He removed Sukarno (implicated as an engineer of the coup, though, thirty years later, nobody really knows what happened), slaughtered somewhere between 100,000 and a million Indonesian Communists plus anybody else who got in the way, turned his back on Peking, made nice with such pro-West neighbors as Thailand, Malaysia, Singapore, and the Philippines, dug for oil, rejoined the United Nations, fixed his attention on such matters as national identity, agricultural self-sufficiency, and industrial growth, and called the whole program the "New Order." His two big PR blunders: gobbling up the miniscule adjacent Portuguese colony of East Timor and treating its population—already ragged and run-down—even worse than Portugal had; and rewarding his wife, children, and old friends with lucrative business deals worth, conservatively, hundreds of millions of dollars. Still, Suharto managed to hang on to power until the late Nineties, when Indonesia was battered, more or less simultaneously, by the Asian economic crisis, the worst drought in fifty years, and the results of a lot of un-helpful advice from the International Monetary Fund. When Arabs joined Chris-tians and workers teamed with students in mass protests, even Suharto's best buddies knew it was time for him to resign. From 1998 until the elections of 2004, three successive presidents did their uninspired best to stabilize the economy and lure back foreign investors while the poverty rate tripled, Islamic extremist groups made headlines with bombings in Bali and Jakarta, and separatist violence—including the slaughter of 1,200 people by government-backed militias in newly independent East Timor—raged from one end of the archipelago to the other. By the time of the 2004 elections, Indonesia's moderate Muslim majority was waxing nostalgic for the law-and-order days of the generals and showed a new willingness to contemplate the return of a father figure in uniform. Which is what they got.

WHAT YOU NEED TO KNOW IF YOU'RE DATING AN INDONESIAN: Let's begin by as-suming that your date is a *pribumi*, a "son of the earth," i.e., an ethnic Malay, from a family that's been in Indonesia forever. More likely than not, he or she re-ally does work the land, growing rice or cloves or peanuts or sisal, or sweating on a rubber plantation, or in a bauxite mine, or cutting down giant teak or ma-hogany trees—Indonesia's got it all. Alternatively, your date may work in a fac-tory shelling shrimp or making shoes or rolling cigarettes, working ten to twelve hours a day for a fraction of the $2.50 minimum hourly wage (especially if your date's a woman, like the majority of Indonesia's factory workers, or a nine-year-old child). Labor laws, like most other laws of the land, are rarely enforced. Of course, some *pribumi* have managed to get themselves educated; in fact, there's a cadre of technocrats who are famous locally for all having studied economics at Berkeley, and a wave of trendy thirtysomethings whose racy chick-lit evocations of sex and the city (known locally as *wang sastra* or "fragrant literature") are top-ping the bestseller lists (admittedly not a great challenge, given how little In-donesians, as a whole, read; still, it is taken as encouraging evidence that this is no Saudi Arabia—yet). By the way, how open-minded are you about religion? Indonesia is an impressively mixed bag. Besides all those Muslims (88 percent of the population, most of them moderates, though the number of fundamentalists keeps growing), keep an eye out for a considerable Christian minority, Hindus,

Buddhists, the mystics of Java, and the volcano- (or soybean-) worshipping animists of the outer islands. Now, let's think about where you and your date will live (sorry, don't mean to rush you). The odds favor your settling in Java, which boasts all the big-city excitement—video arcades, supper clubs, gay bars, etc.—and most of the picturesque courtly refinements you're likely to find in Indonesia, not to mention 60 percent of the country's population in 7 percent of its area. Also a possibility: Bali, predominantly Hindu and one of the world's long-standing vacation destinations—that is, until Jemaah Islamiyah, a homegrown Islamic terrorist group, bombed a packed nightclub in 2002, bringing the entire Bali tourist industry to a halt. You'll want to think twice before buying real estate in the devastated, mostly Muslim province of Aceh, on the northwestern tip of Sumatra, where, even before the tsunami hit on December 26, 2004, leaving 170,000 people dead and missing and another half a million homeless, thousands of civilians had been killed in the crossfire between separatists and government troops since the mid-Seventies; or on Sulawesi, Indonesia's fourth-largest island, where Muslims and Christians have been snuffing each other quite efficiently with homemade bombs, guns, and bows and arrows; or in Papua, currently in a state of emergency and bleeding both from decades-old secessionist battles and from clashes between the region's Muslims and its Christian and animist populations; or in Kalimantan, the Indonesian part of the island of Borneo, where the indigenous Dayak people, enraged by the influx of outsiders brought in under Suharto's massive transmigration program, killed a couple hundred migrants and chased thousands more right off the island; or even in the Moluccas, the chain once known as the Spice Islands, where Muslims and Christians lived peacefully together until about 1999, when they began slaughtering each other by the thousands. Peace accords brokered in some of these areas over the last couple of years have reduced the violence to sporadic skirmishes and occasional church bombings, but separatist sentiment, religious conflict, widespread unemployment, mind-boggling government corruption, and the fear of another tsunami, coupled with the growing influence of Jemaah Islamiyah, Laskar Jihad, and other Al Qaeda wannabes are likely to keep property values low throughout the archipelago for some time to come.

WHAT YOU NEED TO KNOW TO MEET YOUR DATE'S PARENTS: You may find your prospective in-laws almost surreally laid-back; try to remember that they, like most Indonesians their age, were brought up to eschew confrontation and displays of ambition. For fifty years, they managed to avoid *our* worst-case scenarios for them—Communism in the 1960s, Islamic militancy in the 1980s—as well as separatism, Indonesia's worst-case scenario for itself. So there's no telling how they feel now that the last two, unleashed in the laissez-faire atmosphere of the post-Suharto years, are today's in-your-face realities of life. At least the flight of foreign investors has meant that your date's parents no longer have to sit by and watch as the rice paddies of their childhoods are turned into golf courses. (Although they still have to watch all their quality topsoil rush by during the rainy season as a result of out-of-control logging practices.) Most likely, they still take solace in the islands' arts-and-crafts, sarongs-and-amulets traditions: *wayang,* the famous shadow-puppet shows, featuring elaborately painted buffalo-hide puppets, and occasionally humans, that you watch from either side of a screen, depending on whether you want to monitor the figures or—illusion and reality, illusion and reality—their shadows, is the one no Winnetka tourist would miss, and for no extra charge it's often backed up by a *gamelan,* an up-to-forty-piece percussion orchestra that should satisfy your craving for gongs well into the next century. Don't ruin a pleasant evening by bringing up your hosts' recent colonial past. Yes, we know, back in college you spent an idyllic three days exploring the museums and canals of Amsterdam, but the Dutch still aren't likely to be on your date's parents' list of favorite people. From the seventeenth century on, when they established control over Java, the Dutch were famous for their lack of a sense of fair play (also of humor), and they showed their absolute worst side in the late 1940s, when they refused to get out even after the war for independence had largely been won. As for the Japanese, just remember that Indonesia (then still the Dutch East Indies) spent most of World War II as the centerpiece of Tokyo's "Greater Co-Prosperity Sphere."

ITALY

THE LAYOUT: Unlike Orion's Belt or the Great Bear, Italy actually resembles the thing it's supposed to look like: an old boot, high-heeled and in need of resoling, trying to kick Sicily across the Mediterranean. You can, for convenience's sake, pinpoint Rome just behind the kneecap and Florence at about mid-thigh. You'll run into trouble when you hit northern Italy, though, where a cloud of smoke seems to be issuing from the top of the boot. Don't let it throw you; northern Italians would just as soon not share an image with the backward Mezzogiorno (i.e., everything south of Rome; pronounced "METSO-jyorno"), and smoke is a perfectly appropriate symbol for the industrial heart of the country. The way the smoke seems to be disappearing into the rest of Europe makes sense, too, given northern Italy's historical ties with France and Austria. Across the top of the country stretch the Alps, nice for skiing but never very effective at discouraging foreign invaders. The Apennines, running the length of the country, served for centuries to keep Italy region- rather than nation-minded and to make it virtually ungovernable (remember that Italy, like Germany, came together as a country only in the last century). To the west, in mid-Mediterranean, lies the big, barren, mineral-rich vacationland of Sardinia, which is not only an integral part of Italy but a reminder of how times have changed in this part of the world; Sardinia has belonged, in various periods, to Genoa, Pisa, Spain, and Austria, and was a kingdom on its own for a while, encompassing Turin. Just above Sardinia is the island of Corsica, which, though Italian by culture and temperament, belongs, uneasily, to France. And on 100-plus acres within Rome, the Pope holds court as absolute monarch of the Vatican City.

THE SYSTEM: On the surface, the world's most fluid parliamentary democracy, with a president elected every seven years and a new prime minister appointed, it often seems, weekly. There have been fifty-nine governments (quite possibly more by the time you read this) since the end of World War II, when Italy ceased to be a chaotic monarchy. Lots of political parties to choose from, but for forty-five years, the inevitable winners were the center-right Christian Democrats; keeping them in power was Italy's way of ensuring that the PCI, the strongest Communist Party in the West, would never get its foot in the door (the front door, at any rate; ever pragmatic, the Christian Democrats usually hustled the PCI in through the service entrance). This formula held from the beginning of the Cold War, when Italy decided to cast its lot with Western rather than Eastern Europe, to its end, when, the "Communist threat" having disappeared (and the PCI having changed its name to the Democratic Party of the Left), the system began showing signs of dry rot. In the early 1990s, a series of corruption scandals finally laid low the Christian Democrats, discrediting, along the way, just about everyone who was anyone in politics and industry and prompting a lot of people to wonder if this whole Italy idea belonged in the recycle bin. But, not for the first time, the country demonstrated the miraculous regenerative powers of a steamrollered cartoon cat. In 2001, media mogul Silvio Berlusconi, the richest man in Italy, became prime minister, heading a right-wing coalition led by his party, Forza Italia ("Go Italy!" after a soccer chant), and managed to remain in power longer than any head of government since Mussolini. (How'd he do it? It certainly helped that he controlled, directly or indirectly, nearly all of Italy's mass media, including 90 percent of its television networks; that he personally employed a hefty portion of the country's electorate; and that, by tinkering with the judicial system, he successfully avoided prosecution on charges of accounting fraud, bribery, money laundering, conflict of interest, and other equally colorful misdeeds.) Meanwhile, back in the real world, each of Italy's twenty regions has its own bicameral government, a situation that, on one hand, tends to keep business humming on the homefront whenever the national leadership falls apart and, on the other, adds to the bureaucratic red tape, the opportunities for graft, and the general impossibility of getting any real work done.

WHAT YOU NEED TO KNOW TO READ THE NEWSPAPERS: That after *Tangentopoli* (rough translation: "bribe city"), the nickname for the cataclysmic political scandals that swept the country in the early 1990s, Italians seemed ready to usher in a new era of squeaky-clean government. But this was still Italy, after all, so they elected Berlusconi. *Tangenti,* which refers specifically to the big-bucks, high-level corruption practiced regularly by politicians, business tycoons, and organized crime, as opposed to the nickel-and-dime *mazzetta* everyone else specializes in, flourishes throughout Italy thanks to a vast state-controlled economy and a thoroughly entrenched system of political patronage in which all state jobs and contracts are treated as spoils of war by the dominant parties. Outraged as your average Italian citizen was by the extent of *Tangentopoli,* the fact is that most Italians, including many who are officially unemployed or disabled, habitually make their rent through the country's hugely profitable "submerged economy," made up of (1) businesses small enough to avoid taxes and union restraints and (2) businesses that don't legally exist at all. This two-tiered system of criminality makes for a society that runs rather smoothly on the private level, thank you, and not at all on the public one. Keep the faith; a history of nearly continuous warfare and of domination by every variety of despot seems to have strengthened the country's resistance to disaster and heightened its appreciation for crisis.

WHAT YOU NEED TO KNOW IF YOU'RE DATING AN ITALIAN: It all depends on where your date lives. In Milan, you may have an easier time getting reservations at fancy restaurants now than you would have back in the booming 1980s, when all northerners seemed to be rich and Italy became the West's fifth-largest economy. But don't count on it: Statistics that look grim for the country as a whole tend to ignore the huge disparity between Italy's still-prosperous, industrialized, yuppified north and its largely unemployed, agricultural, donkey-riding south. The divergence of lifestyles is so extreme that the separatist Northern League, a party whose platform for many years centered on making northern Italy into an independent nation called Padini, is a political force none dare snicker at. (Since the adoption of the euro, the Northern League has shifted its focus from separatism to xenophobia and its targets from the thousands of southern Italian workers who migrate to the north in search of factory jobs to the thousands of Albanians and North Africans who do the same.) If your date lives in central Italy—in the regions of Tuscany or Emilia-Romagna—he or she will probably remain loyal to what's left of the PCI, Italy's Communist Party, now renamed the Democratic Party of the Left. Don't start lecturing your date on the evils of Communism—the Italian version always functioned more as the workers' rich uncle than as anyone's Big Brother, and the PCI was virtually excommunicated from Moscow for failing to toe the party line. In the Mezzogiorno you can skip politics—or for that matter, conversation—altogether, provided you drive a fancy car. It might pay, however, to memorize the names of the local organized-crime branches—Cosa Nostra in Sicily, Camorra in Naples, 'Ndrangheta in Calabria, Sacra Corona Unita in Puglia—to one of which your date probably owes his current job parking cars or making pizzas.

WHAT YOU NEED TO KNOW TO MEET YOUR DATE'S PARENTS: Well, again, that will depend. In the north you should know something about Italian history, for instance, how to pronounce *risorgimento* (the *s* sounds like a *z*, the *g* is soft), the nineteenth-century struggle to get out from under foreign rule, overcome regionalism, and unify the country. You should know that Venice wasn't always a mecca for honeymooners: Back when it was the trade link to the Orient, it was one of the world's richest states and one of the few in these parts to resist enemy invasion. You should know a little something about Renaissance art, of course, especially if your date's folks are Florentines, and you ought to be able to tell your Guelphs (supporters of the popes) from your Ghibellines (supporters of the Holy Roman Emperors). In other words, you may have to crack a few textbooks. In the south, relax. Italians on the whole read fewer newspapers than other Europeans, and the illiteracy rate in the Mezzogiorno still hovers between 20 and 30 percent. Here, however, you'd better learn to love your date's family because you'll be seeing a lot of them. For one thing, your date will almost certainly live at home, thanks to the chronic housing shortage. For another, *familismo* is still strong around here; a lot of people insist it's what really holds the country together. But even *familismo* may be doomed: Thanks to those snooty northerners with their big-shot careers divorce is on the rise (although it's still about a third of the U.S. rate), and Italy now has the lowest birthrate in the world.

MEXICO

THE LAYOUT: South of the border—and no border separates, however laxly, two more contrasting standards of living than the U.S.-Mexico one. There's a lot of contrast within Mexico, too: between tropical coastal lowlands and chilly inland mountain ranges; between a few huge, unmanageable cities (most notably Mexico City, the capital and, at close to twenty million people, the third-largest metropolis in the world, after Tokyo and New York) and tens of thousands of remote rural communities, still waiting for running water, electricity, and sewers; between a hard-nosed, entrepreneurial, sure-we-know-what-Prada-is elite, and a hard-pressed, blanket-wearing, maize- (or poppy-, where the drug cartels have taken over) planting Indian population larger than that of any other Latin American country. The Yucatán Peninsula, complete with Mayan pyramids and Hyatt hotels doing bad imitations of them, juts out into the Caribbean from Mexico's southeast. Nearly all the oil—and Mexico has the world's seventh-largest reserves of it—lies along the southern Gulf, not far away. Chiapas, the country's poorest state, where, on New Year's Day of 1994, perennially exploited Mayan Indians traded in their sombreros for wool ski masks and their guitars for submachine guns, nestles up against Guatemala. On the U.S. border are towns that, over the last couple of decades, have become cities, thanks largely to the assembly plants called *maquiladoras*. The two biggest, each with an adjacent U.S. partner: Tijuana (San Diego) and Ciudad Juárez (El Paso).

THE SYSTEM: Don't be fooled: Until the elections of 2000, Mexico was about as much of a democracy as one of those West African soldier states. In fact, with the Soviet Union's demise, the country's Institutional Revolutionary Party, or PRI, became the longest-governing (since 1928), most entrenched (the "revolutionary" part of the name has been, in some circles, a reliable laugh-getter since at least the 1930s) political party in the world, never losing a national election and, until the 1990s, never losing an election at any level at all. Being perpetually assured of a solid majority in both houses of Congress and the backing of nearly all of the country's thirty-one governors endowed Mexican presidents with almost mystical powers, in the tradition of Aztec emperors, Spanish viceroys, and Latin American strongmen everywhere. One difference: The president has to step down after six years. That was never a problem for the PRI, thanks to a quaint local custom known as the *dedazo*, translated as both "the pointing of the finger" and "the tap on the shoulder," which allows the incumbent president to name his party's candidate to succeed him. In July of 2000, however, a confluence of bad vibes inside and outside the PRI caused the system to break down, giving a narrow but wildly celebrated victory to Vicente Fox of the opposition Alliance for Change. Fox's election prompted much dancing in the streets and euphoric promises of reform but, blocked at every turn by the PRI, which still dominates both houses of Congress and numerous states, the president hasn't been able to get much real work done. The framers of the 1917 constitution weren't thinking in terms of checks and balances. As of this writing, PRI hard-liners look good to make a comeback in the presidential election of 2006.

WHAT YOU NEED TO KNOW TO READ THE NEWSPAPERS: That the jury's still out on whether hopes for genuine democracy—whatever *that* is—are sinking because of the ho-hum performance of a president who was expected to spin maize into gold overnight or because Mexico's constitutional structure is not especially democracy-friendly. It certainly isn't set up to turbocharge an economy that's still crawling toward first-world status on its knees, carrying a blanket and a basket of flowers on its back. (One example economists invariably cite: the fact that Mexico sits on huge oil and natural gas reserves but has to import energy from the United States because the law restricts private investment in the energy sector and the government can't afford to finance exploration.) Keep in mind that Mexico is desperately dependent on foreign trade, especially on trade with the United States, which buys close to 90 percent of its exports. It takes about five minutes for a downturn in the U.S. economy to shut down factories throughout Mexico's industrial north and send foreign capitalists running in search of better-fortified accommodations. Unfortunately for the government, that's just what happened in 2001, less than a year after the new administration took over. Meanwhile, the proliferation of little "Made in China" labels on everything from binoculars to bobble-head dolls strikes fear in Mexican hearts, and somehow the knowledge that if they *had* managed to keep their jobs they'd be making three times the hourly wage of their Chinese-peasant counterparts hasn't sufficed to keep a quarter of a million unemployed factory workers happy.

Keep an eye on the left-wing mayor of Mexico City, Andrés Manuel López Obrador, whose popularity and staunch opposition to just about everything the current administration stands for make him a promising contender in the next presidential elections. Another force to contend with: the Chiapas-based Zapatistas, most often represented by the charismatic Subcomandante Marcos, still looking good in that ski mask, who fiercely opposes globalization, privatization, commercialization, and the tendency of the country's elite to treat its indigenous peoples like pack animals.

WHAT YOU NEED TO KNOW IF YOU'RE DATING A MEXICAN: If you're hanging in Mexico City, where intellectuals—and worse, economists—are still sought-after dinner-party guests, the terrain will seem familiar enough: a semiformal business of dark suits for the men and regular visits to the colorist for the women, against a backdrop of your date and all his colleagues jockeying for a seat next to your date's boss when they bring out the brandy and cigars. On your way home, watch out for cars with dark-tinted windows cruising close to the curb, and don't stop to give directions to anyone wearing a lot of gold chains. Kidnapping is big business these days, with the number of abductions annually nearly rivaling that in

Colombia, and you don't even have to be rich to be snatched and held for ransom anymore. We won't get into how to behave if your date is living in a cardboard box somewhere outside the city proper, but we *will* mention that Mexico City—where oxygen-starved motorists have fatal heart attacks sitting in highway underpasses at rush hour, and not only ozone and sulfur dioxide and other industrial pollutants but microscopic particles of fecal matter often hang suspended in the air—is no longer the destination of choice for many poverty-stricken but optimistic migrants, who may head instead for a provincial city like Guadalajara or Aguascalientes to avail themselves of the state agencies the government relocated there in a desperate attempt to keep at least a few Mexicans out of the capital. Or they might still try the cities of the border, of which Tijuana is just the biggest, where, in the *maquiladoras* owned by GE and Xerox and Sony and Panasonic, electronic components and a lot of other stuff arrive duty-free from the States and are assembled by sweet, and single, young girls from all over Mexico (girls are held to be more docile, more dexterous, and more willing to work for eighty-five cents or so an hour without feeling a compulsion to join the union), then shipped back, again duty-free, to whichever humongous transnational sent them down in the first place. For a while the system made everybody money and employed *señoritas,* even if it was grinding, no-future work. But the big companies soon discovered that labor was even cheaper down in the Mexican boonies or, worse, in China, and moved their operations accordingly. Meanwhile, there are the hundreds of girls, some from *maquiladoras,* others waitresses or students or flower sellers, but all poor and powerless, whose murders have gone unsolved in the border state of Chihuahua for so long that by now everyone assumes that the state government—or at least the local police—must be involved. So when you meet your date, treat her nicely.

WHAT YOU NEED TO KNOW TO MEET YOUR DATE'S PARENTS: We're going to assume your date's parents are Indians, or at least *mestizos* (of mixed-blood, Indian-and-Spanish descent), if only because virtually all of Mexico is—30 percent simply Indian, 60 percent *mestizo.* As a rule of thumb, the more purely Indian someone is, the more likely to live in Mexico's so called Deep South—though there are also plenty of Indians in the valleys around Mexico City—and the more likely to be living in poverty. *Attención:* Race is a shifting category, more about culture than color, in much of Latin America and both *mestizos* and purebred Indians may be, exhausting as it sounds, attempting to pass for European, speaking Spanish rather than, say, Nahuatl, wearing shoes instead of sandals, and living in the capital, where they make a show of preferring tortellini to tortillas. But back to the *milpas,* the cornfields the real Indians have been endowing with magical powers for centuries (*they* wouldn't be caught dead growing the wheat the Spaniards brought to the New World). Landownership is a whole thing with a long history all over Mexico, a country where there's far too little of it and where you either live grandee-style on tens of thousands of acres or you take your humble *ejido*, the plot the government—finally, after years of promises and some real whoppers—handed you to farm, collectively, alongside Pedro and Pablo and Luz, a plot so dry and rocky you could break your hoe, and perched on the kind of nearly vertical hillside even goats regard with skepticism. Under the circumstances, it's a big challenge to feed yourself and your eleven children, which is precisely why everybody, quite possibly including your date's ancient-looking-even-though-not-yet-forty parents, is always leaving home for a few months to tidy up a kitchen in Beverly Hills or harvest a few dozen acres of tomatoes just outside Fresno, then hurry home with a wad of greenbacks just in time to get in the maize and the beans. Speaking of north-of-the-border matters, your date's parents aren't likely to have forgotten how, in the Texas and Mexican-American Wars, the United States grabbed half of what was then Mexico; it doesn't help that, in the intervening century and a half, the land has only gotten primer. Try to make an end run around the entire nineteenth century, and extol the 1910–1917 revolution, which wasn't, as it's so frequently portrayed, an entirely good thing, but it did break the power of the old aristocracy, produce a constitution, and get the Church more or less off people's backs. You can also try praising Mexico's cultural record, beginning with the Aztecs and the Mayans and the Toltecs and—a slight gap here—segueing into the famous twentieth-century muralists, most notably the revolutionary Diego Rivera; also, his cult-figure wife, the surrealist painter Frida Kahlo. Since it's unlikely that your date's parents can read, you won't get very far trying to launch a discussion of Carlos Fuentes and Octavio Paz, but the parents have quite possibly caught a glimpse of local-hero architect Luis Barragán's huge three-faced multicolored concrete towers in the middle of the highway outside Mexico City while they were hitching a ride north to the border.

NICARAGUA

THE LAYOUT: The biggest country in Central America, with plenty of variety to the landscape—mountains, lowlands, virgin forests, two huge lakes, and a torrid, swampy Caribbean coast. Most of the human action, however, takes place on a little volcano-studded strip of land between the mountains and the Pacific. (The Miskito Indians, who consider themselves a nation apart from Spanish-speaking Nicaraguans, have traditionally claimed a big chunk of the Caribbean coast as their turf, but even many of them were forced, in the early 1980s, to pack up and resettle on collective farms in the west.) Nicaragua is one of four Central American countries—the others are Honduras, El Salvador, and Guatemala; Panama and Costa Rica have their own problems—that are so bound together by climate, history, social conditions, and the fact that they all share an isthmus trapped between two culturally distinct continental giants, that what happens to one can't help rattling the others. As a result, observers, both inside and out, have had reason to view the area as prime domino-theory territory. During the 1980s, it was Honduras, Nicaragua's northern neighbor and the only Latin American nation even poorer than it is, that became the main staging area for the CIA-directed *contra* war against the Sandinista government. On the other hand, in the late Nineties it was the president of Costa Rica, Nicaragua's relatively prosperous, demilitarized neighbor to the south, who initiated the peace process that finally ended the war.

THE SYSTEM: A struggling democracy. To appreciate the current system, you'll need the backstory, and it is, as your grandmother might say, a doozy. In 1933, when the U.S. Marines finally pulled out, after hanging around for a decade protecting U.S. commercial interests, they left Anastasio Somoza in charge of the National Guard. Before you could say "Latin American dictatorship," Somoza had turned the Guard into his personal militia, arranged for the assassination of his rival, General Sandino (the guerrilla leader for whom the Sandinistas were named), and made himself president. For the next forty-five years, the Somoza clan ran Nicaragua more like a shady family business than a country. Finally, in 1979, after much guerrilla fighting, Sandinista revolutionaries managed to overthrow the Somoza dynasty. Elections held—and, according to some admittedly cranky Western observers, rigged—in 1984 put the revolutionary hero (later known as revolutionary strongman) Daniel Ortega in the presidency, sharing leadership with a nine-member Sandinista directorate. Things would have been tough enough even without interference from the north, given the fact that a bunch of underage guerrilla fighters were suddenly faced with turning the Somozas' family-owned sweatshop into a functioning economy. Given, too, the uneasy marriage that had made the revolution in the first place: middle-class professionals and businessmen hoping for moderate reform on the one hand, Marxist ideologues vowing a radical transformation of society on the other. Add to that a decade of virtual embargo by the United States and of ferocious, unrelenting attacks by U.S.-backed *contra* rebels, and you have the mess that is Nicaragua today. In 1990, an electorate fed up with civil war as a lifestyle—and convinced the United States would never take its foot off Nicaragua's neck as long as the Sandinistas remained in power—voted to replace Ortega with a hybrid right-centrist government headed by Violeta de Chamorro, widow of a (what else?) martyred newspaper publisher. Chamorro's administration, which included a weird mix of political elements ranging from former National Guardsmen to former Sandinistas, soon lost nearly all of its original supporters and has, paradoxically, been propped up for some time by Ortega's defeated Sandinistas, who still controlled the army and police and who remain to this day Nicaragua's strongest political force, despite the fact that no two Sandinistas have agreed on anything for years. Two subsequent elected presidents, both from the Somoza family's old political party, also failed to accomplish much (although one managed to become the first Latin American ex-president ever to be jailed for corruption), and as of this writing, Ortega's hat is in the ring again for the next presidential election. Everyone agrees that the country is a mess. The good news is that it's a *democratic* mess. The voting age is sixteen.

WHAT YOU NEED TO KNOW TO READ THE NEWSPAPERS: Although blaming the other side is practically a national pastime here, take all accusations with a grain of salt. Neither Sandinistas nor *contras, recompas* (ex-Sandinistas who refused to stop fighting after the war was officially over) nor *recontras* (ex-*contras,* ditto) are entirely to blame for the sorry state Nicaragua's in today. None is blameless either, of course. Like all good Marxists, the minute they took office the Sandinistas began holding compulsory pep rallies, punishing incorrect thinking, and pressuring reluctant peasants to leave their homes and move to prefab farming cooperatives. Like any young adults who've spent their formative years holed up in the mountains with their AK-47s, they weren't above looting confiscated estates or spending the money earmarked for farm machinery on the girls up at the hotel, either. (Let's not forget, however, their education crusade, which virtually eliminated adult illiteracy in a year.) The *contras,* on the other hand, were, as every good liberal knew at the time, mere pawns of the CIA. Disgruntled peasants and Indians manipulated by sadistic former National Guardsmen, they spent a decade terrorizing women and children and sabotaging every Sandinista reform effort. While we're pointing fingers, how about that U.S. government, which showed itself to be the world's sorest loser after the Sandinistas' victory and which was quite prepared, throughout the 1980s, to disgrace itself (remember the Iran-*contra* Affair? remember Oliver North?) while scuttling the entire country plus most of the rest of Central America, in order to assuage its Cold War paranoia? How about Arnoldo Alemán, Nicaragua's president from 1997 to 2002, currently under house arrest for stealing something like $100 million from the national kitty? And how about Daniel Ortega, who's been willing to play all sides against each other—and to use his considerable influence with poor Nicaraguans to disrupt the reform efforts of his successors—in order to hang on to political power? Well, nobody's perfect. At least everybody seems to agree on one thing: The country is *jojido*—all screwed up.

WHAT YOU NEED TO KNOW TO DATE A NICARAGUAN: You'll be spending a lot of time together, since your date is almost certainly unemployed or underemployed, like about 60 percent of the workforce. That doesn't mean he or she will do nothing, though. If your date lives in Managua, you might spend your days together selling candy or oranges at traffic lights, washing the windshields of the new SUVs owned by members of the government, or scrubbing laundry for friends of the administration. You'll also enjoy taking in the sights. Former mayor Arnoldo Alemán, accused of looting the treasury when he became president, spent a lot of tax money beautifying the capital, which was once considered to be among Latin America's ugliest. You'll be able to stroll the broad boulevards, admiring the splashing fountains, the luxury hotels, and the new malls you can't afford to shop in. If your date lives out in the countryside, bring your gardening gloves! If you're lucky, you might make half a dollar a day picking coffee beans, bananas, sugarcane, or cotton. Many of the big estates that were confiscated during the revolution are now being reclaimed by their former owners, while land that was redistributed to peasant farmers during the 1980s, or promised to the *contras* in return for demobilizing after 1990, lies fallow, its ownership still in legal limbo.

WHAT YOU NEED TO KNOW TO MEET YOUR DATE'S PARENTS: That they're probably *mestizos*, like nearly 70 percent of the population, and that they've spent their whole lives picking cotton, bananas, or coffee beans and being treated like dumb animals by the folks up at the hacienda. They may have had high hopes for the revolution at some point (or they may not have known it was going on), but by now they're beginning to feel nostalgic for the old Somoza days, when they could still afford tortillas to wrap their beans in. And you may be sharing meager dinners with your date's uncles and their families rather frequently. Many families were split during Nicaragua's civil war, with one sibling fighting for the Sandinistas while the other fought with the *contras,* and estrangements lasted long after the *contras* demobilized (partly because the Sandinistas never did). Now, however, many Sandinistas and *contras* have been reconciled by the realization that not much has changed for the better, no matter which side has been in power. In fact, the only person your date's family is likely to have a good word for is the local priest. Nicaragua's Catholic Church, one of the most radical in Latin America, played a key role in mobilizing the *campesinos* in the early days of the Sandinistas' rebellion, though it later became as politically divided as everyone else in the country. In the end, the bishops opted for moderation, and the Church helped pave the way for the elections of 1990. At the 2003 celebration of the revolution, the Church gave its blessing to the Sandinistas for the first time since 1980, which many people on both sides see as a sign that the Sandinistas know exactly what it's going to take to get back in power by the next presidential election.

NIGERIA

THE LAYOUT: It's the biggest, fanciest house on the block, but the block's in a shantytown—nine ramshackle converted colonies crowded together in a row, looking as though their stilts are about to give way. Not surprising, since they were all carved out of the mangrove swamp a century ago by imperialists who were thinking more about administrative convenience for their respective motherlands than about sensible zoning, with the result that nearly all of them are having to struggle to remain upright. Nigeria's the one at the far end, before you leave West Africa and turn the corner into Equatorial Africa. A former British colony surrounded by former French ones, it's much bigger than its neighbors and has, topographically, a lot more going on: swamps and tropical forests in the south, grasslands and savannas in the middle, semidesert in the far north. With around 130 million inhabitants, it's also the most populous country on the continent and growing fast. According to the United Nations, Lagos, the former capital, could be one of the world's five largest cities by the year 2010. Even the new capital, Abuja, an oasis of plate glass and polished marble set in the dead center of the country to avoid any taint of regional favoritism, is beginning to experience traffic jams. Designed to reflect Nigeria's high-roller image of the Seventies and early Eighties, when the country dreamed of becoming Africa's first global superpower, Abuja was also meant to serve local and international VIPs as an escape from the continuously escalating crime, congestion, and chaos of

Lagos, which, aside from active combat zones, is one of the world's least relaxing travel destinations.

THE SYSTEM: A U.S.-style presidential democracy has been struggling to take root since 1979; unfortunately, the gardeners keep stealing the seedlings, and guys in army boots periodically trample the flowerbed. Currently, there's a president, now in his second four-year term, and a two-house assembly. The question is, how can they get 250 mostly impoverished and frequently hostile ethnic groups to function democratically in a sacked and gutted country? Well, you could start by rigging elections, as President Olusegun Obasanji, a former army general, is accused of having done. And you could carry on Nigeria's time-honored tradition of dispensing favors—e.g., contracts, jobs, and cash—to your supporters while disenfranchising the opposition. Still, it's risky business to run a potentially rich country with a dirt-poor but feisty population and a military perennially itching for a coup. Soon after gaining independence in 1960, Nigeria became a federal republic comprising four more or less self-governing territories—North, West, and East Nigeria (a.k.a. Biafra) and the federal Territory of Lagos—loosely bound together under a weak central government. When north-south hostilities broke out in 1966, the Supreme Military Council took over and held things together—through a couple of attempted coups and an assassination—until 1979, when the American model of government was adopted and the country was reorganized into nineteen states in an effort to defuse regional antagonisms. (That number has since grown to thirty-six plus the capital territory, though nobody seems to get along any better for it.) After four years of corruption and mismanagement, the military put the civilian government out of its misery. General followed general, all of them interchangeably larcenous, as far as your average Nigerian could tell, until 1994, when General Sani Abacha took over. Abacha promptly dismantled whatever democratic structures his predecessors had established, took greed and larceny to a new level, and in a refreshing change of pace did *not* immediately set a date for handing power back to civilians. Civilian rule was finally reinstated soon after Abacha graciously died of a heart attack in 1998. A new constitution was introduced in 1999, but it's been a tough sell to the many Nigerians who are still agitating for a return to weak central government and a loose federation of states.

WHAT YOU NEED TO KNOW TO READ THE NEWSPAPERS: That Nigeria is the world's sixth-leading exporter of oil—a particularly pure, particularly desirable variety of oil—and was, in the 1970s, a Cinderella state for which sudden wealth created more problems than it solved (e.g., an unstable, overspecialized economy; a boomtown atmosphere of high inflation, widespread corruption, and unrealistic expectations; and a government that, when faced with a depressed oil market, was left holding a bag of unfulfilled promises it could no longer afford to keep).

Also, that Nigeria has long ranked high on lists of the world's most corrupt countries (where it usually ties for first place with Haiti and Bangladesh).

Along with oil, Nigeria's got unification headaches: 250 ethnic groups that can't understand each other's lingo, including three big ones that actively dislike each other, and a north-south split that led to civil war back in the Sixties, when the Igbos (pronounced "EE-boze") of the southeast tried to secede and form the Republic of Biafra, only to be blockaded inside their own barren (but oil-rich) land, where more than a million of them starved to death. The country is still recovering from five years of devil-may-care brutality and treasury-looting by General Abacha, who managed to drive an already shaky economy into the dirt and frighten one of Africa's boldest, most confident peoples into something resembling submission. Nigeria was suspended from the British Commonwealth in 1995 after Abacha, ignoring international outrage, executed the prominent playwright and activist Ken Saro-Wiwa, who had campaigned against oil-company exploitation.

WHAT YOU NEED TO KNOW IF YOU'RE DATING A NIGERIAN: Still sitting by the phone, waiting for your date to call? Don't take it personally. There are plenty of telephones in Nigeria, but they hardly ever work. (A cell phone would make a great gift. Everyone—that is, everyone who can afford to eat—is getting them.) When you do finally get together, at least you won't spend many boring nights in front of the TV, since the few TVs around are usually missing parts nobody can afford to import anymore. Besides, you'll only have electricity if you're in one of the bigger cities, like Lagos, and even there the two of you will spend most evenings cuddled in the dark because of power outages. If you *are* in Lagos, going to the movies—or anywhere else—will be a hassle. Your date may have a car, but even if you're lucky enough to pay scalpers' prices for a few liters of gas, you'll spend hours sitting in traffic jams, or "go-slows," during which you'll want to stay on your guard against carjackers. Should you decide to walk, beware of kidnappers, robbers, muggers, rioters, and car drivers—the talk about drivers who don't bother to stop when they've run over a pedestrian is not mere urban legend. Out in the country, things are not that much safer, just less crowded. Since most people are subsistence farmers who, despite the billions of dollars in oil revenues that have been stolen or squandered by corrupt politicians over the last fifty years, have less to eat today than they did back at independence, you may notice signs of irritability, not to say psychosis, in your date. And if you're down around the Niger Delta, where violent conflict between major oil companies, gangs of thugs, and local militias kill about a thousand people a year, be advised that the bandolier your date is wearing is not a mere fashion statement.

WHAT YOU NEED TO KNOW TO MEET YOUR DATE'S PARENTS: If they live in one of Nigeria's many cities, they'll probably speak English, but out in the bush, anything goes. It's just as well: Communicating through sign language will minimize your chances of putting your foot in your mouth. The air is thick with ethnic antagonisms left over from colonial days, when the country was divided administratively into north and south and the southerners, who were mostly Christians, benefited from the best educations and fastest economic development. Remember that while it's standard practice to think of the country as three ethnically separate regions dominated by Nigeria's three largest ethnic groups, in reality no region is anything like homogeneous anymore. Still, some general guidelines might come in handy when meeting your date's parents. If they live in the north (and are wearing turbans) they're probably Hausas—conservative, traditional, and solidly Muslim. The Hausas once ruled empires (you might still see a sultan or two in full regalia), are now the largest ethnic group in Nigeria (which has one of the biggest Muslim communities in the world, although Muslims and Christians come out about even in countrywide head counts), and wield a lot of political influence, to the dismay of non-Hausas. If your date's parents live in the west (and are wearing flowing robes, matching headpieces, and three or four tribal scars on each cheek), congratulations! They're probably sophisticated Yorubas, known for their lavish hospitality. Well-educated, thoroughly Westernized (except for the robes, headpieces, and scars) and about half Christians, the Yorubas are the Nigerians most likely to be doctors, lawyers, writers, or presidents of the country. They might be feeling a little tense, though. When sharia (Islamic law) was introduced in northern Nigeria in 2000, Christians living in the north interpreted it as part of a Muslim takeover and a couple thousand people were killed in the ensuing protests. You might try calming your date's parents by pointing out that their fears were exaggerated, stoked by political factions hoping to destabilize the civilian government. (Or you might just keep your mouth shut and enjoy your dinner.) Finally, if your date's parents call one of the southeast territories home, you can assume they're activist Christian Igbos, who feel chronically put-upon because, despite the fact that most of Nigeria's oil is dug out of their land, they've never, they insist, been given more than a tiny sliver of the profits. Don't mention Biafra, whomever you're talking to; the very name still provokes anxiety attacks in a country so ethnically inflammable that even a minor intertribal snub is likely to be seen as a threat to national security. And while you're tiptoeing through the conversational minefields, remember that ethnic resentments here are not some principle-of-the-thing abstraction. They're a reaction to the fact that tribal loyalties still so thoroughly outweigh any concept of national interest that a politician who *didn't* funnel all the plum jobs, government contracts, and kickbacks-worth-mentioning to his own tribe would be shunned as a turncoat.

PAKISTAN

THE LAYOUT: Say hello to the subcontinent (make sure there are no Pakistanis in the room before you go calling it the Indian subcontinent), where anything can happen and something unimaginably gruesome usually does. Pakistan, the slab to the west, angling down from the Hindu Kush and the Himalayas to the Arabian Sea, marks the spot at which the Muslim and Hindu worlds collide. West of Pakistan are the rich relations: Iran and the Middle Eastern gang, all reassuringly Muslim, if a bit unbalanced. Eastward yawns the gaping maw of India, Pakistan's Mommie Dearest. Travel northwest or due north and you've got your pick of death traps: Afghanistan, happy campground for warlords, militants, and opium smugglers, especially along its notoriously porous 1,500-mile border with Pakistan, and the chronically inflamed territory of Kashmir, partitioned, to no one's satisfaction, between India and Pakistan. Just beyond Kashmir, China, which has a history of bad blood with both India and the former Soviet Union, blows kisses and sends weapons to Pakistan across some of the world's most impassable mountains. All in all, Pakistan comprises four provinces (Northwest Frontier, Punjab, Sindh, and Baluchistan) and a territory (Federally Administered Tribal Areas), each with a mind—and weapons—of its own, and a clutch of colorful cities and towns, including rich, conservative Islamabad, the capital; raunchy, dangerous Karachi, the major seaport; Rawalpindi, home of the military; and Peshawar, the wild frontier town that's become the unofficial convention center for Islamic holy warriors from around the world.

THE SYSTEM: Parliamentary pseudo-democracy in uniform. Back in 1947, when Pakistan was carved out of old British India as a homeland for South Asia's Muslims, India inherited the colonial bureaucracy more or less intact, while Pakistan got bad memories and a lot of soldiers trained in the Indian army. As a result, government here has been very much in the Argentine mold—a few years of civilian floundering habitually culminating in a military takeover. In 1977, it was Prime Minister Zulfikar Ali Bhutto, a Perón-like populist demagogue, who got bumped (and later hanged) by his chief of staff, General Muhammad Zia ul-Haq. Zia, who'd claimed he'd only be around for ninety days, appointed himself president, twisted the constitution around to inflate presidential power, and began to enforce Islamic law. In 1988, Zia was killed in a mysterious airplane crash. A succession of shaky civilian governments followed, all remarkably similar in their corruption, incompetence, and let-them-eat-cake attitudes toward their countrymen, who, with the exception of a few wealthy landowners given to shopping in Paris, tend to be mud-hut dwellers, well near the bottom of the poverty scale. Twice, these administrations were led by Benazir Bhutto, the Radcliffe-educated daughter of the former prime minister, who became the first woman ever to head a Muslim country and the first to be dismissed, twice, for corruption. In 1999 General Pervez Musharraf staged a bloodless coup that put the country back under military rule, causing much international finger-wagging and Pakistan's suspension from the British Commonwealth. Ho hum. In 2001, Musharraf declared himself president. In 2002, he announced that elections would be held that year, then declared himself the winner of a controversial and probably unconstitutional referendum that gave him the presidency on a platter for another five years while allowing him to remain head of the army. He then amended the constitution to grant himself many wonderful new powers, including the right to pick whomever he wants to be Supreme Court judges and military commanders and to dismiss an elected parliament. He also created a National Security Council, dominated by the military, that has power over the civilian government. However, the four provincial administrations retain considerable power of their own and aren't shy about blowing raspberries at the central government. And after surviving four assassination attempts in two years, Musharraf really ought to be the only person in the country who *wants* his job. Pakistan's president must be a Muslim, by the way, and the legal system is a combination of sharia (Islamic law) and British common law.

WHAT YOU NEED TO KNOW TO READ THE NEWSPAPERS: That the end of the Cold War meant that Pakistan, whose frontline position in the defense against the Communist March on Asia no longer mattered, was suddenly dropped from Washington's A-list. The White House kept Islamabad on speed-dial, however, for a couple of reasons. One, it saw the wisdom of maintaining ties with a moderate Islamic state in a part of the world increasingly given to wild-eyed Koranbrandishing and the slaughter of infidels. Two, there was that nasty, ongoing dispute over the largely Muslim state of Kashmir and Jammu, which India refused to relinquish and which Pakistan insisted should join "free"—read Pakistani-controlled—Kashmir next door. (For the record, the Kashmiri insurgents themselves would prefer to be independent of both countries, but who cares what they want?) The West finds this conflict riveting because both India and Pakistan have nuclear weapons and a make-my-day attitude toward using them. Things turned around, sort of, after September 11, 2001. Given a choice between acting as Washington's point man in the "war on terror" (and receiving tons of financial aid, plus U.S. support for his regime), on one hand, and placating Pakistan's growing number of radical Islamist groups (but ending up like Afghanistan, with heaps of rubble where towns used to be), on the other, Musharraf prudently chose both sides. Ignoring threats and dodging bullets, he manages one of the word's trickiest juggling acts (in addition to disgruntled mullahs and radical groups both domestic and global, the president must mollify the powerful Pakistani army, which is packed with high-level, hard-line Islamists). Note, too, Pakistan's new willingness to dance with India, after nervously watching her flirt with both the United States and China.

WHAT YOU NEED TO KNOW IF YOU'RE DATING A PAKISTANI: Sorry, you haven't given us enough information. "Pakistani" doesn't mean much unless you're in New York, London, or one of the Gulf states, where a couple million remittance men work to support their wives and families back home (sorry, sweetheart, your date's just using you to get a green card). Within Pakistan, more than half a century after partition, the concept of nationhood is still not much more prevalent—or deeply rooted—than cable TV. So who's your date? A tenant farmer from Punjab? A little gardening experience should go a long way; in this agriculturally based economy, most farms consist of only five or six acres of land. A rug merchant from Sindh? He or she may be a *muhajir,* one of the millions of refugees (or their descendants) who fled India at the time of partition and who, being better-educated than the locals, soon controlled the country's industry and commerce, but were never entirely accepted by the neighborhood. A tribal leader from Baluchistan? Make sure your life insurance premiums are paid; you may well spend thrilling Saturday nights blowing up pipelines to protest the way the government reaps all the rewards from gas that's pumped out of your date's ancestral lands. A mullah from the Northwest Frontier Province? That's double jeopardy. Until the Saudis began opening the religious schools, or madrassas, that educated a generation of Taliban, mullahs, the lowest-ranking of local Islamic clerics, were usually considered ignorant and bigoted even by village standards—which is saying something in a country with a literacy rate of 50 percent, max (much, much lower if you count girls, which no one in these parts does). To further strain your relationship, Pashtuns, as the northwesterners are called, have Pakistan's most male-dominated society. This is the kind of place where they like to tell you a dozen times a day that "women have no place but the home and the grave." A note to dopers: Exercise extreme caution, if you're still capable of that sort of thing. Marijuana, both wild and cultivated, grows all over Pakistan, and the opium that's been produced for centuries along both sides of the northwest border accounts for a large percentage of the country's real GDP, but that doesn't necessarily mean that your date's going to want to fire up the old bong with you in the evenings. The Islamic injunction against alcohol has been stretched to include all types of intoxication. (Your date may or may not take this seriously.) Of course, you can ignore many of these warnings if your date is very rich.

WHAT YOU NEED TO KNOW TO MEET YOUR DATE'S PARENTS: That they're probably not having a ball in their golden years. So many divisive elements and so much violence! Sure, there have always been splits in society—fundamentalists vs. modernists, English-speakers vs. Urdu-speakers, the army vs. civilian administrators, the native-born vs. the *mujahirs,* various tribes and clans vs. the central government—but they were usually held below the boiling point. The ongoing tension between majority Sunnis and minority Shi'ites, for instance, used to be fodder for scholarly debate, not, as it is today, a pretext for bombing each other's mosques. This surely wasn't what your date's folks had in mind back at the beginning, when they dreamed of creating a Muslim homeland. But religion, especially a religion as loosely interpreted as Islam, has so far turned out to be a poor substitute for a common nationality, shared culture, or established democratic institutions. Things started to go sour in 1971, when East Pakistan, a thousand miles away, rebelled against long-distance government from West Pakistan and made a bid to secede. After being ruthlessly suppressed, the East Pakistanis were backed by India, which launched an offensive that forced the Pakistani army to its knees and allowed for the creation of an independent Bangladesh. Traumatized and humiliated, with its very raison d'être suddenly in doubt, Pakistan went into an emotional tailspin from which your date's parents, among others, still haven't fully recovered. Try boosting your date's parents' self-esteem; smile broadly when they brag about Abdul Qadeer Khan, Pakistan's top nuclear scientist, who secretly helped Libya, North Korea, and Iran develop nuclear weapons programs. Despite the outrage of the international community, Khan, who claims he acted alone (do *not* mutter "Yeah, right") was quickly pardoned by the Pakistani government and remains a national hero to his compatriots.

SAUDI ARABIA

THE LAYOUT: 830,000 square miles of stupefying desert, with temperatures routinely in excess of 118 degrees and nary a river, stream, or hotel bar in sight. The oil fields are in the east, over near the Persian Gulf; the Muslim holy cities of Mecca and Medina, along with Jeddah, the leading port, are in the west, over near the Red Sea; Riyadh, the capital, is in the big middle chunk, the traditional preserve of the Sauds, the country's ruling family; and to the south is the bone-dry, Texas-sized Rub al Khali, the Empty Quarter, which even the Bedouins avoid. In fact, only 2 percent of the country is suitable for growing so much as a date palm.

THE SYSTEM: A feudalistic monarchy, even if the country is only a little over seven decades old. The royal family, consisting of something like five thousand princes and an equal number of princesses, is descended from Abdul Aziz ibn Saud, the man who back in 1932 established a kingdom out of a patchwork of rival desert tribes and a couple of shards of the former Ottoman Empire. Ever since, he and a succession of four of the oldest of his forty-four sons (until fairly recently kingship always passed through the first king, rather than the current one) have ruled with absolute authority. Today's king (and prime minister) is named Abdullah, and all the ranking cabinet ministers and ambassadors, as well as every one of the thirteen regional governors, are his brothers, half-brothers, sons, sons-in-law, or nephews. (Not for nothing do the Israelis grumble, "It's not a country, it's a family.") In 1992 then-king Fahd presented the country with the Basic Law of Government, the closest thing it's ever had to a written constitution, and rejuvenated the royal talent pool by including *grandsons* of Ibn Saud, too. The following year he established the Majlis Al Shura, an advisory council now made up of 150 prominent Saudi citizens. True, the king appoints its members and can, at any point, dismiss them and appoint new ones, but at least now there is an established forum where nonroyals can talk things over. Meanwhile, the crown prince and virtually every other royal functionary continue to hold regularly scheduled *majlis*es, somewhere between an audience and an open house, at which they hear all gripes anybody in the kingdom cares, and dares, to make. The other authority in this patriarchal, puritanical nation: the *ulama*, the religious scholars and priests, who function not only as clergy but also as the national judicial system (sharia rules), meting out punishments Koran-style and on occasion even overriding the monarch. In 2004 Saudi Arabia held its first-ever national elections—a big deal here, even though only half the seats on municipal councils were at stake, women were not allowed to vote, and most of the winners came from lists preapproved by fundamentalist clerics.

WHAT YOU NEED TO KNOW TO READ THE NEWSPAPERS: That the Saudis are sitting on more than a quarter of the world's proven oil reserves and are, by a long shot, its largest oil exporters (the United States and Russia pump more, but they're using, not selling, most of it and they're going to run out of the stuff much sooner). That this, and not some pietistic resolve to keep the Persian Gulf safe for feudalistic monarchies, was why we were so willing to put American lives on the line back in 1990. And that, in addition to a bill for $55 billion, the Gulf War left Saudi Arabia with a lot of seriously upset religious leaders for whom the hundreds of thousands of infidel American soldiers, some of whom were *women*, camped out along their pipelines—this, in an isolationist, fundamentalist state that sees itself as the world center of Islam and guardian of the Holy Cities— were a sacrilege. Feeling unwelcome, the Americans finally moved next door to Qatar in 2003, but that didn't stop any number of by now wildly enraged radical groups from bombing the Saudi capital, Riyadh, soon afterward. And *that* finally lit a fire, so to speak, under the notoriously slow-moving monarchy, prompting it to crack down on terrorist types, despite the fact that the royal family is itself split between traditionalists and modernists and is feeling the pain of being squeezed between its close ties to the United States and the virulent anti-Americanism pervading the Middle East.

WHAT YOU NEED TO KNOW IF YOU'RE DATING A SAUDI: If your date's a woman, she'll be a teacher, a nurse, a social worker, a princess, or unemployed; there still aren't many professional options for Saudi women—and they still aren't allowed to drive—though a lot of them do go to college, where they listen to the lectures on closed-circuit TV so that they won't breathe the same air as the guys. She'll most likely be veiled and covered head to toe by a loose-fitting black *abaya* (only men get to wear white in this heat). The really good news: In 2005, the country's top religious leader banned forced marriages—but don't count on anyone's actually eschewing them out in the boonies. If you're dating a man, things will be that much easier, especially if he's a member of, friend of, or supplier to the royal family, in which case he's making plenty of money again after a few relatively lean years in which he may have had to pass on that fifth Rolls-Royce Corniche Turbo. If he's not well connected, he'll probably be unemployed. Millions of guest workers do the menial jobs to which Saudi men refuse to stoop, as well as most of the demanding high-level ones that require knowledge never acquired by your average university graduate, who majored in theology and studied only Wahhabism, the particularly austere brand of Islam that is the country's official religion. In any event, you won't be hard up for creature comforts. Most families own an air conditioner, a washing machine, a radio, a television, and, if they live in town, four or five DVD players. Do stay on your toes, however. The *mutawin*, or religious police, keep an eye round the clock on everything from drinking, drug use, gambling, begging, and homosexuality to the strands of hair straying out from under a woman's veil; to dating couples sitting together in the "family area" of the snack bar out at the new shopping mall; to satellite dishes, hidden in rooftop water tanks, capable of beaming CNN—or worse, *Desperate Housewives*—into Saudi homes from neighboring Bahrain. Most Saudis manage to avoid the big-deal offenses of murder, adultery, and heresy if they're paying attention at all. Nevertheless, keep Fridays free for public beheadings and/or stonings.

WHAT YOU NEED TO KNOW TO MEET YOUR DATE'S PARENTS: A couple of Arabic words will prove that your heart's in the right place. To *majlis* and *ulama* and *mutawin*, which you've already learned, add *hajj*, the pilgrimage to Mecca, Muhammad's birthplace, which every Muslim is enjoined to make once in his life (or he'd better have a damn good excuse), and *salat al-fajr*, or dawn prayers, one of five compulsory prayer sessions in the course of the day. Old Abdul Aziz may still be talked of, and how he united Saudi Arabia "by the will of Allah and the strength of his right hand." Don't, however, allude to his oldest son, Saud (who was deposed in 1964 for wantonness and incompetence), and be respectful if the name Faisal comes up (he returned the country to moral rectitude and fiscal responsibility, and was assassinated by a nephew in 1975 in the middle of an otherwise routine *majlis*). You might lament the passing of the Bedouins, those proud nomads of yore, falcons perched on their wrists and salukis prancing at their sides, who are now down to a population somewhere between Sacramento's and Hartford's. Or you might simply gape at the modernization—car dealerships, Tower-of-Babel construction crews (all those guest workers), and at least three major airports that claim to be the world's largest.

SWITZERLAND

THE LAYOUT: Small, landlocked nation of central Europe, sealed off top and bottom by mountain ranges (the Jura and the Alps) and on either side by lakes (Geneva and Constance), and full of edelweiss, brass cowbells, fondue pots, rushing streams, hiking trails, snow-capped peaks, ski resorts, and, it turns out, among the highest heroin-addiction, youth suicide, and HIV-infection rates in Europe. Derives its languages and cultural preferences from its neighbors: The western sector (focused on Geneva) speaks French; the central and eastern sectors (focused on Zurich and constituting the bulk of the country) speak German; and the south gesticulates in Italian.

THE SYSTEM: Federal republic, officially known as the Swiss Confederation. Still the most direct and most genuine democracy going anywhere, with lots of referenda ("Should we decriminalize abortion?" "Should we have four car-free Sundays a year?" "Should we shut down our nuclear power plants?"), citizens' initiatives, and gung-ho government at the state and local levels. (The states here are called cantons, and there are twenty-six of them, including six half-cantons—don't ask—each with its own constitution, budget, and laws.) It's true that in general, not that many Swiss actually know what any given election is about, but this, pundits point out, only prevents a tyranny of the majority, since any minority with something at stake in a given election can usually make itself heard over the bewildered mutterings of the 40-something percent of voters who actually turn out to vote. There is no prime minister, and the federal council, Switzerland's executive branch, chooses annually, from among its own seven members, a new president and vice president, who'll spend most of their time greeting foreign dignitaries and toasting visiting dance troupes. Each council member represents one of the leading political parties and heads a cabinet ministry. Real power, however, both political and economic (not that it's easy to tell the difference in Switzerland), has traditionally been concentrated in the hands of a few hundred industrialists, farmers, bankers, trade union leaders, and the like, who hammer out consensuses in "preparliamentary commissions." Political parties and a two-house legislature exist but have agreed to agree on most issues.

WHAT YOU NEED TO KNOW TO READ THE NEWSPAPERS: That while Switzerland is devoutly neutral and has been for centuries, it's not the least bit pacifist. Not only does it have a long history of supplying mercenaries to the rest of the world (of which the Swiss Guards in the Vatican are the last vestige), it maintained, throughout the Cold War, Europe's second-largest army (after Germany) and a reserve system that kept every able-bodied man in the country on twenty-four-hour call until he turned fifty—all to defend a population of six million. Today, the Alps are alive with the fifteen thousand or so armed bunkers and secret tunnel systems built throughout the twentieth century, major cities are still ringed by underground hangars ready to disgorge fighter jets at the first alarm, and it wasn't until 2002 that voters finally ditched the law that had, for half a century, required every Swiss home and business to have its own fallout shelter—although these had already been doing interim duty as laundry rooms and wine cellars for decades.

Also, that the exponential growth of the right-wing Swiss People's Party (SVP) and the election of its billionaire industrialist leader to a seat on the federal council in 2003 (the party's second) finally upset the genteel power-brokering arrangement known as the "Magic Formula," which had, for forty-four years, put collegiality above partisanship and allowed differing political viewpoints to coalesce into a remarkably stable federal government. The rising influence of the nationalist SVP has encouraged the Swiss to shelve—yet again—any nascent idea of joining the EU and prompted Swiss banks to resist increasing international pressure to loosen the secrecy laws that have made Switzerland a money-laundering Shangri-la for corrupt dictators, drug cartels, and terrorist groups worldwide.

WHAT YOU NEED TO KNOW IF YOU'RE DATING A SWISS: That all that materialism, conservatism, claustrophobia, and early-to-bed-early-to-rise stuff can get a person down. Who, after all, really enjoys feeling as if he's permanently on sedatives and confined to his bed in the local sanitarium? (And who could *really* take much pride in the fact that he's a citizen of the one European country that might never be mentioned in a college-level European-history textbook and not even be missed? Ditto that, apart from Jean-Jacques Rousseau—see page 594—its literary tradition is pretty much summed up by William Tell, *Heidi*, and *The Swiss Family Robinson*?) Even if your date seems content to follow Papa in the watchmaking, banking, or pharmaceuticals business, he or she may seem a little down—just like the Swiss economy, which recently discovered that even putting your currency and trade laws in perpetual quarantine won't keep you from catching a global recession. Try to cheer up your date with a stimulating debate over why it took women until 1971 to get the vote in Switzerland (at least in most of Switzerland; women in one German-speaking canton weren't allowed to vote on local issues for another twenty years). If that doesn't work, excuse yourself and discreetly search the house for a military rifle and a *locked* box of ammunition. Until recently, these were required gear for every man in the army reserve. U.S. opponents of gun control love to point to the heavily armed Swiss citizenry as the ne plus ultra of homeland security (and to gloat over the country's low gun-crime rate), but the Swiss themselves recently decided differently, given that astronomical suicide rate.

WHAT YOU NEED TO KNOW TO MEET YOUR DATE'S PARENTS: Well, Switzerland is Europe's oldest republic, and that's nice. Also, it's been officially neutral in every conflict since 1815, and that's nice, too, provided you don't get hung up on how, as a neutral, it sold corn, wheat, and armaments to the Nazis and made a bundle shipping all of the above on its strategically located Germany-to-Italy railways. On second thought, best not to rock the boat at Sunday dinner. So before you get going on the morality of isolationism (Switzerland didn't decide to join the United Nations until 2002), compliment your hosts on running such a well-ordered country and on their reputation as a haven for émigrés, of both the rich and fashionable and the dissident and brooding varieties. (Visitors during the twentieth century included Thomas Mann, James Joyce, Aleksandr Solzhenitsyn, Lenin, and Tristan Tzara plus, in the former category, various deposed royals and overreaching fashion designers.) Don't expect necessarily to be taken to your date's parents' bosom, however: Many a Swiss mother to this day advises her daughter not to marry "foreign"—a category that includes not only the world beyond the Alps but those areas within them that don't speak the same language she does.

TAIWAN

THE LAYOUT: Small, teardrop-shaped island—a.k.a. Formosa, Taipei (after its capital), and, officially, the Republic of China—located less than a hundred miles off the southern coast of the *other* China. One of the most crowded countries in the world, and, because of the rugged and heavily forested Chungyang mountain range running spinelike down its middle, things are even more congested than they sound: 23 million people eat, sleep, love, plow (less and less of this, as farmland is converted into industrial parks), tool around on their motorbikes, and make laptop computers in an area considerably smaller than Connecticut.

THE SYSTEM: A wildly successful capitalist-style democracy (the democracy part only since 2000). Was under strict martial law for four decades, with local legend

Generalissimo Chiang Kai-shek, followed by his son, the panda-like Chiang Ching-kuo, as president. It was Chiang junior who in 1986, two years before he died, sniffed the Taipei air, realized the middle class wasn't going to put up with repression forever, and got liberalization rolling. Out of the blue, opposition parties were legalized, press restrictions eased, and the imprisonment, torture, and killing of political opponents phased out. He also opened up lines of communication with the mainland. Today there's a multiparty setup, with a president, a national assembly (currently ceding power to a legislative one), and a clutch of *yuans,* or councils. The biggest difference, though, is that now not only can you actually vote for your president and representatives, you don't have to anticipate their being in office for the rest of their, and your, lives.

WHAT YOU NEED TO KNOW TO READ THE NEWSPAPERS: Let's cut to the chase—in this case the 1949 chase by a zillion Red Chinese of two million defeated Chinese Nationalists, the Kuomintang (KMT) of Chiang, who ferried them across the Formosa Strait and set them all down on Taiwan to catch their breath and take a bath before turning around to recapture the four million square miles of territory they'd just lost to Mao. Nearly four decades later, they were still waiting, an increasingly autocratic bunch of very old men—the native Taiwanese referred to them behind their backs as the "old thieves"—who, in the meantime, held office season after season, year after year, because, given that Chiang saw himself and his men as the legitimate government of *all* China, new elections couldn't possibly be held until *all* Chinese, from the Vietnamese border to the Mongolian one, could be gotten to the polls. (Meanwhile the mainland Chinese believed that *they* were the true rulers of all of China, although they didn't waste valuable time worrying about niceties like voting, plus they, at least, really did account for 95 percent of China's area and population.) A couple of additional mad-tea-party touches here: First, as a result of both Taipei's and Peking's claims, talk of the former's simply declaring its independence and moving on to some next thing was, in terms of logic, let alone the gunboats the Reds kept threatening to send over, out of the question and, more than that, proof of sedition. (Yes, you *could* talk about reunification, not that anybody thought it was in the cards.) Second, that for as long as the KMT were camped out on the island, the native Taiwanese, who probably wouldn't have minded hosting Chiang and his men for a couple of months, or even years, were relegated to the status of nonpeople, and on home turf yet. For years, things went Taiwan's way: The West endorsed its we-are-China stance, not only keeping it in the United Nations but preserving its veto power on the Security Council. The trouble started in 1964, when France recognized Mainland China and "derecognized" Taiwan. In less time than it takes to stir-fry bean curd, Taiwan was ousted from the United Nations altogether and the People's Republic installed. In 1972, Nixon visited Beijing; in 1978, Carter severed relations with Taipei and normalized them with the mainland (though pointing out that the United States still wouldn't look favorably on a third party's invading the island). Since the early 1990s, when Taiwan finally declared an end to war with the mainland and gave up its cockamamie claim to be China's legitimate ruler, and the Chinese government, for its part, came up with the ambiguous "one country, two governments" formula to describe what it still sees as an estrangement that must inevitably lead to reunification, cross-Strait business has been booming. In recent years, China has edged out the United States as Taiwan's number-one export customer and Taiwan has become the biggest investor on the mainland, where a million Taiwanese now live and work. Still, the reunification-vs.-independence debate never stops being a cliff-hanger, as the ever richer and more outspoken Taiwanese—who increasingly see themselves as, well, Taiwanese—wonder why they have to keep pretending to be China's prodigal child when they're obviously a grown-up nation with an apartment of their own, and the mainland government, which keeps hundreds of missiles pointed across the Taiwan Strait, sends crystal-clear messages that—with all due respect to family ties—it would rather blow the island off the map than allow it to secede.

WHAT YOU NEED TO KNOW IF YOU'RE DATING A TAIWANESE: It really has been one big Confucius-meets-Horatio-Alger, electricity-comes-to-the-straw-hut, annual-per-capita-income-soars-from-a-postwar-$162-to-$25,000-today-and-still-growing tale. And unlike such fellow "Asian tigers" as Hong Kong and South Korea, with their high-profile multinational corporations, Taiwan made its money largely through hundreds of thousands of mom-and-pop shops and factories, with Mom and Pop working day and night, reinvesting their earnings, and cheating on their taxes (a time-honored custom here, along with accepting bribes on election day). Your date may be too spoiled to want to follow the parental example, but he or she is likely to believe wholeheartedly in ambition, success, and money—and to cheat on his or her taxes. Depending on where he lives and whether his parents were refugees from the mainland or native Taiwanese, your date may be consumed by politics, caught up in the tensions between the old KMT, which favors eventual reunification with China, and the newly powerful Democratic Progressive Party (DPP), which is vociferously pro-independence. Feel free to provide your date with assurances of America's interest in and commitment to Taiwan, but be darned sure you stop short of promising that we'll actually intervene if China ever decides to invade the island. Don't worry, though: Your date, like just about everyone else in the world, would probably just as soon keep matters the way they are—unsettled and relatively copacetic—as long as he or she can be guaranteed a high-paying job.

WHAT YOU NEED TO KNOW TO MEET YOUR DATE'S PARENTS: That long before the economic miracle, long before Chiang Kai-shek and the KMT, there was an island, a beautiful island, called Taiwan, full of people, beautiful people, called

Taiwanese—and that, despite the influx of those millions of Chinese National-ists, they still constitute over 85 percent of the island's population. Long-suffering (and, some say, slightly lacking in imagination), they've had to deal not only with the Nationalists, in the course of whose arrival some ten thousand of them were killed in riots—traumatic, sure, but ultimately less galling than the fact that the Chiang people put on airs, drinking tea and playing chess all day. Before that there was a fifty-year stint under the Japanese, including the tension-filled war years, and before that various snoopy Europeans. Of course, the Taiwanese, who emigrated en masse from the mainland in the sixteenth and seventeenth cen-turies (in an effort to, even then, avoid paying taxes) were originally interlopers themselves, forcing the local Malayo-Polynesian aborigines into the mountains, where most of them, perhaps wisely, have chosen to stay. On a happier note, how about planning a family weekend in the People's Republic? Everybody who can come up with a cousin—or the name of a cousin, or, for that matter, just a name—is free to visit the mainland and take a look around, although you, like any other commodity, have to travel through Hong Kong to do it. When you finally get to, say, Guangzhou, your date's parents will probably be overtly con-temptuous: Mainlanders still spit on the street and even today, most don't own any mode of transportation more upscale than a bicycle.

TURKEY

THE LAYOUT: East meets West—or tries to. Most of Turkey's in Asia, where it takes the form of a bulbous peninsula known to geographers and 70 million Turks as Anatolia, and where it's located next to several Neighbors from Hell: Syria and Iraq to the south, Iran to the east, and to the northeast the onetime So-viet republics of Georgia and Armenia, both engaged, with varying degrees of enthusiasm, in ethnic feuding. Note, too, that European snippet, which, in addi-tion to poignantly recalling how the Ottomans used to run the whole Balkan peninsula, also keeps Turkey in touch with traditional enemies Greece and Bul-garia. Istanbul (originally Byzantium, then Constantinople) sits on the crack, the Bosporus Strait, which controls traffic from the Black Sea to the Mediter-ranean—a passage lusted after for centuries by Russia. Inland you'll find Ankara, the capital, at which point fertile plains turn into rugged mountains and, if you hang a ralph, Turks give way to longtime Turk-hating Kurds.

THE SYSTEM: The *other* Middle Eastern democracy. In theory a republic ever since 1923, when a defeated Ottoman Empire, severely retrenched by the victo-rious Allies at the end of World War I, suddenly and against all odds, began to behave as if it had been Western for years, with a president, a prime minister, and a parliament you actually got to vote for. Even so, until 1947 Turkey had only a single political party, and for at least a decade after that the incumbent government was inclined to announce who'd won at the polls before bothering actually to count the votes. Today, Turkey's all grown up, with nearly fifty political parties that tend to be as mutable as the political weather. In the parliamentary elections of 2002, nearly all of the ten or so significant ones were swept out of the National Assembly by the landslide victory of the Islamist—but apparently West-leaning—Justice and Development Party (AKP), headed by the current prime minister, Recep Tayyip "Whose Side Is He Really On?" Erdogan (pronounced "AIR-dow-an"). Two political influences worth noting: the Kongra-Gel, made up of former members of the Kurdish Workers Party (PKK), which was known for its demands for a freestanding Kurdistan and its willingness to shoot schoolteachers as well as Turkish security officers; and the adamantly secular Turkish army, which is currently docile enough but has seized power three times in three decades.

WHAT YOU NEED TO KNOW TO READ THE NEWSPAPERS: That exoticism (minarets, opium, a non-Indo-European language, and *falaka,* the custom of beating political prisoners on the soles of their feet) notwithstanding, Turkey has done everything it can think of to become a full-fledged member of the Western family, and it's beginning to lose patience with the ongoing rejections. Not out-and-out rejections, necessarily. Turkey does belong to NATO, after all, and in fact fields its second-largest army. And after a few years of big-deal legislative reforms—including the abandonment of the death penalty (which is more than you can say for Texas) and of its traditionally tolerant, Turks-will-be-Turks attitude toward marital rape and police-station torture—Turkey finally got the European Union to stop misplacing pages 4 through 11 of its membership application and get down to serious negotiations, even if the talks *will* take ten years and may not really lead to membership. It's the little things: the way some other EU members seem quite ready to call off the whole party rather than have Turkey invited in. The way Turkish guest workers in Germany and other white-bread countries are made to feel that their seams are crooked (when, that is, they're not being firebombed in their sleep). The way the West still seems to side with Greece in the perennial Greco-Turk rivalry, dating back to the Trojan War and currently being played out on the island of Cyprus, where Turkey gave in and did everything Brussels demanded of it, only to have its offer to kiss and make up scorned by the Greek Cypriots. And *then* there's the war in Iraq. As if Turkey hadn't gotten into enough trouble with its neighbors when it helped the United States during the first Gulf War, now it's being treated like some kind of pariah (and being cut no slack on its sizable foreign debt) for refusing to serve as home base for the U.S. invasion of Baghdad—which 90 percent of the Turkish population ferociously opposed, occasionally with car bombs. Meanwhile, the United States hasn't lifted a finger to stop the PKK, happily hunkered down in the shelter of northern Iraq, from launching raids on Turks. It's all been enough to en-rage the local Islamists—who, like fundamentalists everywhere, have a louder voice now than they did even a decade ago—and drive secular Turks to start wav-ing their fists and singing the national anthem.

WHAT YOU NEED TO KNOW IF YOU'RE DATING A TURK: First of all, that there's a good chance he's in the army. This is not a bad thing. The military plays a unique role in Turkey: It's a political force, it's a major employer, it's the single most co-hesive element in Turkish life (many of whose other elements carry bombs and machine guns in their briefcases), and it's a time-honored way for a young man to get ahead. So if your date gets a little overheated when he talks about who his all-time favorite general is, don't roll your eyes: This military is best viewed as a progressive force, the obvious heir to Kemalism, the secular, pro-Western spin given the new nation by its soldier-founder (see below). Women don't serve in the army—or, for that matter, in restaurants—but they do work in offices and have made inroads in law, medicine, education, journalism, and telecommunica-tions. In 2002, women were finally given full legal equality with men, although women's rights had been sanctioned by Mustafa Kemal Atatürk, who got West-ernization rolling in Turkey more than half a century earlier. Feminism, it's true, is still a bit of a dirty word, at least among Turkish men, and a girl would have to be crazy even to utter the words "sexual harassment suit." Virginity is still prized, at least by the men, and honor killings (avenging illicit sex) weren't outlawed until 2004. Read about all of the above in the Turkish version of *Cosmo*. Male or female, your date will certainly be Muslim, like 99 percent of the population, though whether or not she wears a headscarf or he actually answers the call to prayer that comes crackling over public loudspeakers five times a day has a lot to do with geography and social class. Does your date live in the richer, more devel-oped western region of the country or the poorer, more traditional eastern part? Are the two of you strolling through downtown Ankara, the capital, where you'll be hard-pressed to find a single mosque, or in the outlying *gecekondu*, one of the shantytowns (literally, "built in a night") that surround all of Turkey's big cities, where yesterday's peasant farmers, having traded the endless tedium of the coun-tryside for urban squalor, struggle to maintain some sense of identity? Either way, if you decide to stop for a glass of tea you'll have to sit in separate rooms. Don't make a big deal about the Muslim thing; most Turks don't. It's true that Is-lamist fervor is on the rise, but then, what can you expect after it was suppressed for at least seventy years? Even for most secular Turks, the idea of religious free-dom implies the freedom to be religious if you want to.

WHAT YOU NEED TO KNOW TO MEET YOUR DATE'S PARENTS: Forget piercing and/or sentimental questions on the subject of the old Ottoman Empire; the Turks are themselves ambivalent about it at best (assuming they remember it at all). Besides, its every vestige was obliterated by Atatürk. (Secularists still love Atatürk, as you'll see from the photographs of him in white tie on top of your date's parents' television.) By his death in 1938, he'd rallied the army and prevented Turkey's asphyxiation at the hands of Greece, who'd had the sense to side with the Allies in World War I; established state industries; changed the written form of Turkish from Arabic to Latin; broken the stranglehold of the Muslim religion; abolished the wearing of turban, fez, and veil; given women the right to vote; and insisted that everyone come up with a last name (e.g., Atatürk), just like the ones they used on the other side of the Bosporus. Consequently, Turkey has been that rarity, a Westward-minded Muslim—although, and this is important, *not* Arab—nation. As for the Kurds, just hope the subject doesn't come up. After fighting a fifteen-year war for Kurdish autonomy in southeastern Turkey, the PKK finally declared a cease-fire in 1999, and its leader, Abdullah Öcalan, was captured. A couple of years later the Turkish government, making nice in order to impress the European Union, finally acknowledged its fifteen million resident Kurds—whom it had always insisted on calling "mountain Turks" instead—by legalizing, on paper at least, limited Kurdish-language education and media broadcasts. But the Kurds want more, causing steam to rise from the collars of Turkish nationalists. Meanwhile, after calling off its cease-fire in 2004, the PKK has been misbehaving again, launching attacks from its new digs in northern Iraq. Of course, the Turks are past masters at what we today call ethnic cleansing, but given current sensitivities, you're better off *not* asking what happened, back in 1915, to the eight hundred thousand or so Armenians who used to live up by the Black Sea.

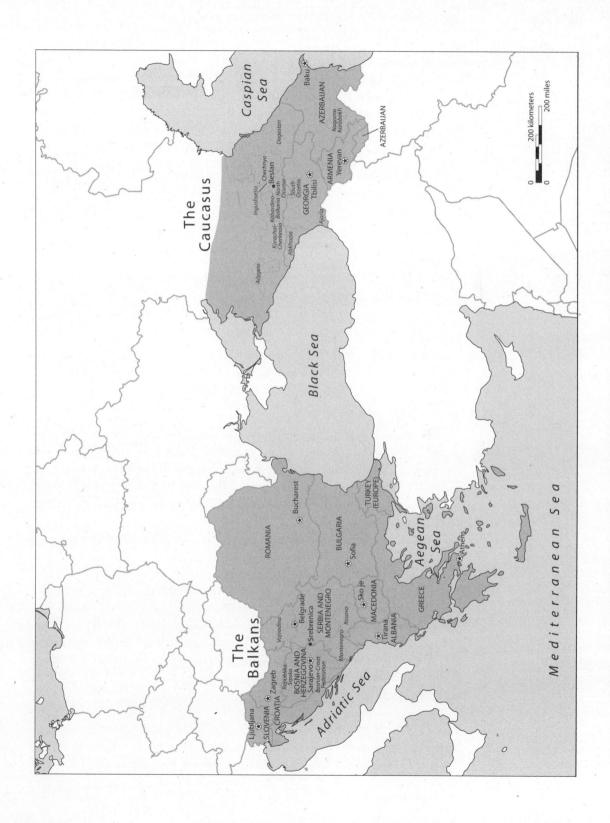

The Caucasus

Caspian Sea

Baku

AZERBAIJAN

Dogestan

Nagorno Karabakh

AZERBAIJAN

Chechnya

Beslan

ARMENIA Yerevan

Ingushetia Kabardino- North
Balkaria Ossetia

South
Ossetia

Karachai- Tbilisi
Cherkessia GEORGIA

Abkhazia

Ajaria

Adygeia

Black Sea

The Balkans

TURKEY
(EUROPE)

Bucharest

ROMANIA

BULGARIA

Sofia

Aegean
Sea

Athens

Vojvodina

Belgrade

Srebrenica

SERBIA AND
MONTENEGRO

Skoje

Kosovo

MACEDONIA

GREECE

Montenegro

Tirana

ALBANIA

Republika
Srpska

BOSNIA AND
HERZEGOVINA

Sarajevo

Bosnian-Croat
Federation

Zagreb

CROATIA

Ljubljana

SLOVENIA

Adriatic Sea

Mediterranean Sea

200 kilometers

200 miles

0

0

Separated at Creation?

HOW TO TELL THE BALKANS FROM THE CAUCASUS

Two bullet-riddled, bombed-out mountain regions whose residents are notorious for serious issues with authority and an inability to stop fighting among themselves. Both straddle classic East-West fault lines and have the kind of strategic importance that attracts foreign interference. Both turned psycho in the early 1990s, when the Communist regimes that had kept them, since World War II, sedated or straitjacketed, finally collapsed. Both have been boosting evening news ratings with assorted atrocities for more than a decade. The problems plaguing these two geographic powder kegs are centuries old, multilayered, and devilishly complex, but let's face it, the hardest part, for many of us, is just remembering which is which. The following pages may help.

THE BALKANS

WHAT ARE THEY?

A mountain range and peninsula in southeastern Europe. The term "Balkan states" refers to the countries of the peninsula: Slovenia, Croatia, Bosnia and Herzegovina, Macedonia (a.k.a. the former Yugoslav Republic of Macedonia), Serbia and Montenegro, Albania, Greece, Bulgaria, part of Romania, and the European piece of Turkey. Not to be confused with the Baltics—Estonia, Latvia, and Lithuania—up near Sweden.

Forms an unofficial border area between Western and Eastern Europe.

WHAT WERE THEY?

From 1945 to 1991, the republics of the west-central Balkans—now the independent states of Slovenia, Croatia, Bosnia and Herzegovina, Macedonia, and Serbia and Montenegro—constituted the Socialist Federal Republic of Yugoslavia. What was left of Yugoslavia after the secessions and civil wars of the 1990s became, in 2003, a loose two-part federation that was formally renamed Serbia and Montenegro. By the time you read this, however, Montenegro may have reluctantly packed up and left.

WHAT'S THE PROBLEM (in 250 words or less)?

Well, you can't entirely discount basic personality disorders, but centuries of subjugation by one conqueror after another have left the diverse peoples of the

Balkans, especially of the western Balkans, with a tangle of conflicting customs and divided loyalties, ample reason to mistrust each other, and a predilection for the kind of gung-ho nationalism that's easily manipulated by outside powers with hidden agendas. For thirty-five years, Josip Tito managed to hold together Yugoslavia, a crazy quilt of eight nationalities, five languages (written in two different alphabets), and three major religions, by raising living standards and promoting pride in its status as the only Communist state not under Moscow's thumb. But when the economy crumbled after Tito's death in 1980, ethnic Serbs, Croats, Bosnians, and Albanians who'd been living next door to each other, sharing the same factory lavatories, and dancing—albeit warily—at each other's weddings for years suddenly took to murdering each other's mothers and raping each other's kids. Some may have been more enthusiastically homicidal than others—the Serbs certainly come to mind—but every group committed atrocities and engaged in some degree of "ethnic cleansing." Although the worst of the infighting was over by 1995, NATO's 1998–1999 invasion and bombing of Serbia didn't improve the general quality of life. Blood feuds, a demolished infrastructure, widespread poverty, massive unemployment, huge displaced populations, political corruption, organized crime, occupation by foreign "peacekeepers," and the consumption of copious quantities of slivovitz combine to keep regional stress levels high.

MAJOR HOTSPOTS
Kosovo, a Serbian province bordering Albania and Macedonia. The Serbs, who consider it their historic heartland, refuse to give it up, while its 90-percent-ethnic-Albanian population will settle for nothing less than complete independence. A UN protectorate since 1999, when NATO bombs finally drove out the Serbs, it remains in a political limbo while organized crime takes over and foreign mujahideen set up shop. Albanian Kosovans, who are powerless and nearly all unemployed, take out their frustrations on the few remaining Serbian residents.

Macedonia, scene of a six-month civil war between ethnic Albanians and Macedonians in 2001.

NEXT UP
Albania, 70 percent Muslim, which dreams of a "greater Albania" that would include the sizable ethnic Albanian populations of neighboring countries.

THE CAUCASUS

WHAT IS IT?
A region of rugged mountains and surrounding lowlands between the Black Sea and the Caspian Sea. Geographically part of Asia, but full of historical and cul-

tural ties with Europe. Think of it as a kind of wild frontier between the two. The northern slopes of the Caucasus are occupied by seven autonomous republics of the Russian Federation. (For the record, these are Adygeya, Chechnya, Dagestan, Ingushetia, Kabardino-Balkaria, Karachai-Cherkessia, and North Ossetia, but you're not likely to remember them without writing them on your hand.) The southern section of the Caucasus, called the Transcaucasus, includes the newly independent nations of Georgia, Azerbaijan, and Armenia. Don't confuse the Caucasus with the Carpathians, the relatively peaceful European mountain range that links the Alps with the Balkans.

WHAT WAS IT?
Until 1991, the whole area was part of the USSR.

WHAT'S THE PROBLEM (in 250 words or less)?
For starters, there's the Tower of Babel effect resulting from more than fifty different languages being spoken in an area roughly the size of California. This means that the Caucasian equivalents of the residents of Berkeley and those of Oakland, for instance, can't understand each other. Not that there are such equivalents in the Caucasus, of course. Instead there are more tribes, clans, and complex kinship alliances than your average central government could effectively list, much less manage. The manageability issue is especially thorny in the North Caucasus, one of the most ethnically and linguistically diverse regions on the planet and the source, if not always the site, of most of the violence over the last fifteen years. Nearly all the republics of the North Caucasus are Muslim, dirt-poor, and ticked off, either at the government or at each other. Most of them loathe the Russians, to whose empire they've had to pretend to pledge allegiance for a couple of centuries while muttering ancient curses under their breath. The two exceptions: North Ossetia, an enclave of mostly Christian people who have traditionally supported Moscow and tend to be a little better off than their neighbors (Beslan, where three hundred hostages, most of them children, were killed during a terrorist attack on a school in 2004, is in North Ossetia), and Chechnya (see following), whose residents have always shouted their curses, preferably while spraying Russian soldiers with bullets or blowing up tourists in Moscow. That's just for starters, though. Throw in a few thousand radical Islamists; a motley assortment of bandits, warlords, and crooked politicians; every imaginable variety of underworld activity; Russian security forces at least as out of control as the people they're sent to repress; and a widespread belief in the cheapness of human life, and you begin to get the flavor of the North Caucasus today.

MAJOR HOTSPOTS
It would be simpler to list the places that *aren't* inflamed, if we could think of any. Certainly, the least promising candidate to host a Winter Olympics would have to

be Chechnya, which has been struggling to break free from Russia's hammerlock since the days of the tsars. The Chechens haven't forgotten the way they, along with the citizens of four other republics, were marched off in the snow by Stalin during World War II, on the pretext that they were Nazi sympathizers. When they were finally allowed to return in the 1950s, those who'd managed to survive came back mean, mad, and loaded, as it were, for bear. Chechnya declared itself independent in 1991 and a few years later the Russian tanks rolled in, intending to crush the Chechen regime like a pesky mosquito. Almost two years and many thousands of corpses later, Chechen guerrillas succeeded in driving the Russians out. The republic was de facto independent until 1999—although the place was no more peaceful or law-abiding then than it had been during the war—when the Russians invaded again. Now, with a puppet government in place and thousands of locals "disappearing" every year, those Chechens who aren't busy taking potshots at Russian soldiers from their own village rooftops are crossing borders, looking to stir up a little jihad in neighboring republics and the newly minted countries to the south.

NEXT UP
Possibly, the Russian Federation itself. The instability of the North Caucasus could, it's predicted, strain the central government to the point of collapse, as the war in Afghanistan did to the Soviet Union. Oh, and then there are those Caspian Sea oil reserves. Still largely untapped, they raise the stakes in the region, both for Soviet-era apparatchiks hoping to make a comeback and for foreign power players such as the United States, which has, for the first time, established military bases in the Caucasus—as, you know, outposts in the "war on terror."

Dead-Letter Department

ACRONYMS—AND ACRIMONY—
FROM MAASTRICHT TO MOGADISHU

While military alliances—expedient and temporary—had been going strong for centuries, it wasn't until the League of Nations took shape, shortly after World War I, that a lot of people began to think ongoing participation in some larger order might be a good idea in and of itself. And for fifteen years or so, the League really did seem to make for a less scary world, a world with an agreed-upon place to talk things over, however stupidly or insincerely. Today, the United Nations, successor to the League, is by far the most comprehensive of the world organizations that matter: Only Taiwan (ruefully, see page 396), the Vatican (fondling its gold brocades), and a handful of South Pacific island nations (presumably saving those tourist dollars and coconut revenues for something more appealing than a membership fee and a Manhattan brownstone rental) don't belong. Beyond that teem economic unions, trade organizations, ethnic orders, and social and charitable societies; you pacifists will be happy to learn there aren't a lot of military alliances left. Here's a look at some among them that tend to do business under their initials alone.

NATO (NORTH ATLANTIC TREATY ORGANIZATION)

Formed in 1949, with Berlin under Soviet blockade and the Communist world looking downright monolithic, by the usual suspects: the United States, Canada, and ten European nations (Britain, France, Italy, Belgium, the Netherlands, Luxembourg, Norway, Denmark, Iceland, and Portugal). The West's bottom line in the old days, when war and rubble-strewn residential neighborhoods were still front-and-center in most people's minds, NATO was a military-defense treaty providing for mutual assistance and collective action in the event any member of the alliance was attacked—"an armed attack against one or more of them in Europe or North America shall be considered an attack against them all" is how the treaty reads—as well as a way of letting the world know what side of the geopolitical fence you were on. Greece and Turkey joined in 1952, vouchsafing the "free world" 's southern flank; West Germany signed on in 1955, Spain in 1982. France, in a move that had all the earmarks of a bad attack of PMS, withdrew its armed forces from joint military command in 1966, though sticking by the alliance in spirit, and headquarters were moved from Fontainebleau to Brussels.

NATO was, to its credit, an alliance that actually *worked*: It kept the Russkies at bay and made them think twice about trying any funny business; naturally, they had their own alliance, the Warsaw Pact. In 1991, a reunified Germany pledged allegiance to NATO and the Warsaw Pact closed up shop. Then, in one of those ironic, *Days of Our Lives* reversals that were a hallmark of the post–Cold War era, four former Warsaw Pact members (Poland, Hungary, the Czech Republic, and Slovakia), craving security just like anybody else, applied for full NATO membership. In 1999 they were invited to join. By that time the question was: With the Soviets gone, who, exactly, was the enemy and what were all those supreme NATO commanders supposed to be doing to earn their keep? Regional conflicts (the Gulf War, for example), terrorist organizations, and natural disasters had never been NATO's idea of a good time. Yet, after dithering through a long and tortured midlife crisis, NATO undertook the biggest military action in its history—and its first-ever use of force against a sovereign state without UN approval—in 1999, when it bombed Yugoslavia for eleven weeks in an effort to stop "ethnic cleansing" in Kosovo. The operation led to a truce in the Balkan war, despite the fact that the rusty NATO air command apparently missed more targets than it hit. Since then, it has been up to NATO troops to keep the peace, such as it is, in the region. But it was the bombing of the World Trade Center on September 11, 2001, that finally took NATO off the endangered-species list. Suddenly, even Russia agreed that something ought to be done to maintain world peace. So the NATO-Russia Council was born, giving Russia an equal say with NATO members on policies to deal with terrorists and other security threats. NATO has made the most of its new role; in 2003, its troops left European boundaries for the first time to assume command of UN-mandated peacekeeping forces in Afghanistan, and not long afterward the alliance launched a rapid-reaction force that would allow it to respond to threats anywhere in the world. The U.S. invasion of Iraq, which was bitterly opposed by France and Germany, provoked a NATO crisis in 2003, since several alliance members took part, even though the alliance itself did not. In 2004, Slovakia, Bulgaria, Romania, Slovenia, and the former Soviet republics of Estonia, Latvia, and Lithuania all became full NATO members. Nowadays NATO doesn't have to worry about a shortage of enemies to defend against—its secretary general lists political convulsions in adjacent regions, jihad terrorism, failed states, and the proliferation of weapons of mass destruction, just for starters. But it still has a couple of kinks to work out. For one thing, Europe doesn't have all that much to contribute to NATO, militarily speaking, since it's gotten used to depending on the United States for protection, and NATO's forces are already stretched thin. For another, the tendency of the current U.S. administration to bomb first and build consensus later doesn't strike some NATO members as what they mean by the term "alliance." Stay tuned for further developments. Or not.

EU (EUROPEAN UNION)

A simple trade pact that grew and grew over the space of four decades, the EU integrated and replaced at least two previous European bonding experiences, including the so called Common Market.

It all began modestly enough in 1952, when six industrialized if somewhat battered nations of Western Europe—France, West Germany, Italy, and the Benelux countries (Belgium, the Netherlands, and Luxembourg)—pooled their coal and steel resources and abandoned protective tariffs on them in the European Coal and Steel Community (ECSC), thus permitting the ready flow of those two commodities across their borders, under the direction of a "high authority" to which each nation surrendered a little of its sovereignty. Soon enough the group had eliminated all shared tariff barriers and facilitated the free movement of workers and money among themselves, as well as hit upon a unified trade policy with regard to the rest of the world. By 1992, the ECSC—which in the interim had done business as the European Economic Community (EEC, nicknamed the Common Market and nick-nicknamed the Inner Six) and the European Community (EC)—was finally the European Union (EU), committed to nothing less than the exploration of complete economic and, even more amazing, political union (although citizens of member nations would presumably still be permitted to hum their own favorite folk songs). Now there were twelve countries aboard, with the addition of Britain, Ireland, Denmark, Greece, Spain, and Portugal, stretching from the Atlantic to the Aegean, containing close to 350 million people, and accounting for an annual output considerably bigger than that of the United States and double that of Japan. Three more countries—Austria, Sweden, and Finland—signed on the dotted line in 1995 (three others—Norway, Sweden, and Iceland—said no thanks), and in 2004, the EU underwent its biggest expansion yet when it took in ten new states—the Eastern European nations of Hungary, Poland, the Czech Republic, Slovakia, Slovenia, Estonia, Latvia, and Lithuania, all formerly Communist, plus Malta and Cyprus—bringing the total number of members to twenty-five. Bulgaria and Romania are up for membership in 2007, while Turkey, which has been waiting in the wings forever, tries to content itself with membership talks that could take another decade.

If that seems like a lot to wrap your mind around, wait till we get to the EU's setup: a parliament (elected by the voters back home), a high court, a council of ministers, an executive commission, and a presidency that rotates among member countries every six months, plus more agencies, advisory bodies, and preparliamentary committees than almost anybody can keep track of, divided among Brussels, Luxembourg, and Strasbourg, and attempting to adjudicate, legislate, or just keep an eye on everything from women's rights to immigration policy, the freedoms of college students to the standards for air conditioners, telecommunications practices to wine prices. And a single currency, the euro.

Sounds a bit dull, and is almost parodistically bureaucratic—but it did seem, at the time, to be a brilliant idea, even better than NATO. With a series of voluntary suturings by several no-longer-great European nations, a new economic power was born to the west of the Soviet Union and the east of the United States. At the same time, in a succession of bold strokes, any number of old European rivalries, suspicions, and scratch-one-another's-eyes-out traditions of centuries' standing were smoothed over. Moreover, Germany got to feel respectable again. France (who hadn't exactly distinguished herself in World War II and was about to lose an empire) got to feel like the very heart and soul of something again, smiling to herself as she vetoed Britain's first application for membership.

Have there been tensions among the members? Don't get them started. Agricultural policy, in particular, can be counted on to provoke tag-team wrestling matches, with, for instance, the poorer southern countries demanding subsidies for their olive oil and tomatoes and the northern ones getting tired of being treated like easy touches. More significantly, Germany and France have long been bent on "deepening" the relationship, pushing the single currency, a common military, a unified foreign policy. Britain—an island after all, and not sure it's even really European—wants instead to "broaden" it, to take in as many new members as quickly as possible; at Maastricht, the small Dutch town where in December 1991 the EC became the EU, Britain opted out of the currency and made help-me-I'm-being-strangled noises at the idea of the other two. Six months later, Danish voters balked at approving the Maastricht treaty at all, which left everybody wondering where it—and European federation—*really* stood. The EU pressed on, but ran into an even bigger snag in 2005, when the citizens of France and the Netherlands voted a big thumbs-down on the proposed EU constitution and the governments of several member countries nearly came to blows over the budget. At this point, nobody thinks the EU is going to fall apart, exactly, but nobody knows what's to become of it, either.

OECD (ORGANIZATION FOR ECONOMIC COOPERATION AND DEVELOPMENT)

Created in 1948, under a slightly different name, to help administer the Marshall Plan, that postwar American effort to get Europe back on her feet and keep her out of the arms of the Communists. Originally made up exclusively of European countries, it expanded in 1960 to include the United States and Canada, then Japan, Finland, Australia, and finally, in 1973, New Zealand. In 1994, after intense U.S. lobbying, Mexico became the twenty-fifth member, the first addition in twenty years. During the period from 1995 to 2000, the OECD opened up to Eastern Europe, inviting in the Czech Republic, Poland, Hungary, and Slovakia; it also took in South Korea along the way.

Fancily set up in Paris, the OECD was, until the mid-1990s, considered a "rich man's club," made up of twenty-four countries accounting for 16 percent of the world's population and two-thirds of its output. With its low-profile, think-tank image, it monitored and predicted and recommended and then went out to lunch. Now, since the advent of high-kicking Asian economies and bent-double former Communist ones, a single European market and the proliferation of regional trading blocs, there's been pressure on the OECD to get a little more hands-on, actually emerging from its tony headquarters long enough to set some policy on, say—and this is just a suggestion, guys—unemployment, investment, the environment, that sort of thing. In the meantime, try not to confuse it with the *OED,* the *Oxford English Dictionary,* that other monument to the ways of the wonk.

G7/G8 (GROUP OF SEVEN/ GROUP OF EIGHT)

Formed in 1975 by the six biggest industrial democracies—the United States, Japan, Germany, France, Britain, and Italy—and joined by Canada a year later. Starting in 1991, the USSR, then Russia, began dropping by for postsummit conferences. In 1994 Russia became a regular visitor, and in 1998 it became a full participant in what now became the G8, although the G7 has continued to function alongside the formal summits, presumably just to confuse the average newspaper reader. These days, the G8 meets annually, and by turns, in the capital, another big-deal city (Montreal, Florence), or a jewel-like historic landmark or golf resort (Versailles, Williamsburg, Gleneagles) of the host nation, with everyone's finance minister (our Treasury secretary) and all the prime ministers (our president) in attendance, at which point it considers, and attempts to bring into line, matters of economic policy and planning, then schmoozes, often managing to work out an intractable problem or two over one of the six-course dinners prepared by the host country to show off the national cuisine. With old-style Kennedy-and-Khrushchev-type summit meetings largely a thing of the past, the G8 get-togethers have become some of the most important meetings in the world, real pileups of power and money at which issues as broad as terrorism and the environment are hashed out, often leading to the creation or resuscitation of some new international organization to "handle" the problem.

OAS (ORGANIZATION OF AMERICAN STATES)

A Pan American "arrangement," formed in 1948 to promote "peace, security, and hemispheric solidarity" and continuing at least some of the traditions of the Pan American Union, founded in 1910, in whose former marble monument in Washington, D.C., the OAS is headquartered. Every country in the hemisphere belongs (although Cuba was expelled in 1962 and Canada didn't join until 1990). Long considered a major do-nothing (and a rubber stamp for U.S. interests in Central America) whose delegates pull up in their limos at two in the afternoon for that ten-in-the-morning session, the OAS has lately become a little more assertive, monitoring elections and vowing to stay on top of military coups; but intervention is prohibited by the terms of the OAS charter, there's no money to give out, and even trade sanctions have to be imposed back home, in the national legislatures, member by member. Meanwhile, genuine crises wind up being taken to the United Nations. In a way, it's just another one of those Latin American initiatives—the Good Neighbor Policy and the Alliance for Progress also come to mind—that gets a lot of press at the outset, then seems to fade away (although the Monroe Doctrine manages to keep a high profile). Still, democracy is today a given in most Latin and Caribbean nations, and small-scale trade pacts (Caricom in the Caribbean; the Andean Pact; Mercosur, among Brazil, Argentina, Paraguay, Uruguay, Chile, and Bolivia) are all thriving, and if the OAS is even 5 percent responsible for any of it, who are we to be looking down our noses? By the by, if you haven't read a newspaper in forty years, this is not the *other* OAS—l'Organisation de l'Armée Secrète, the terrorist military group out to gun down de Gaulle during the Algerian War for Independence.

OPEC (ORGANIZATION OF PETROLEUM EXPORTING COUNTRIES)

Founded in 1960 by Saudi Arabia, Iran, Iraq, Kuwait, and Venezuela and later joined by Qatar, Ecuador (which dropped out in 1992), Indonesia, Gabon (dropped out in 1994), Algeria, Libya, the United Arab Emirates, and Nigeria. Its eleven current members account for about half the world's oil supply. They attempt to maintain stable oil prices by controlling production, a notoriously difficult task that's made even more problematic by the members' habitual failure to agree on anything and the tendency of at least a couple of them to cheat on quotas. The international cartel began striking fear in Western hearts back in 1973, when, in retaliation for U.S. support of Israel in the Yom Kippur war, it embargoed oil supplies to the United States and yanked worldwide prices from around $3 up to $12 a barrel (about $10 to $40 a barrel in today's dollars). Prices have been fluctuating wildly ever since—in response to turmoil in the Middle East throughout the Seventies and Eighties and to the Asian economic downturn of the Nineties, among other things. These days, prices are peaking at well over $60 a barrel, but economists say the reason is simply the increased, and apparently insatiable, demand caused by all those Americans driving around in Moby Dick–sized SUVs and all those Chinese trading in their bicycles for subcompacts.

OAU (ORGANIZATION OF AFRICAN UNITY)

Established in 1963 by thirty-two African nations, it's since grown to fifty-three members, including every independent country on the continent and island just

Clockwise from top left: The European Community (EC), a.k.a. the Common Market, and today the European Union (EU); the Association of Southeast Asian Nations (ASEAN); the Organization of African Unity (OAU); and the Organization of Petroleum Exporting Countries (OPEC)

off it, black and Arab both. South Africa joined in 1994, which was, at the time, another of those mind-blowing events, like former Soviet republics applying for membership in NATO (see page 408). The OAU sets itself the task of promoting unity and development, defending sovereignty and territorial integrity, eradicating colonialism, and coordinating economic, diplomatic, educational, defense, etc., etc. policies. There are no colonies left to speak of—though connoisseurs will immediately bring up the Western Sahara, just south of Morocco, which has spent thirty years trying to absorb it—so this goal can be judged a success, although not particularly thanks to the OAU. As a·result of Africa's having been divided up so cavalierly, arbitrarily, and ineptly by the colonial landlords at the end of the nineteenth century, border disputes and secessionist provinces get a lot of attention at OAU meetings, although members, each of whom is afraid some tribe or neighbor of his own is planning a civil war or an invasion and needs only a little encouragement to actually try it, are inclined to support the status quo, even when appalled by it. A further complication: Arab Africans and black Africans have little in common and, worse, don't seem to like each other much; consider Sudan, with a lot of each and a particularly nasty civil war.

ASEAN (ASSOCIATION OF SOUTHEAST ASIAN NATIONS)

Formed in 1967, when the Vietnam War was in full swing, by Thailand, Malaysia, Singapore, the Philippines, and Indonesia, five countries in search of a little regional security. But the organization didn't meet, not even once, until 1976, by which time the United States had pulled out of Vietnam, leaving a vacuum in the area. The five then decided to create "a zone of peace, freedom, and neutrality," although for years they seemed interested only in containing Communism. Since the breakup of the Soviet Union, ASEAN's been an economic union. It describes itself as mellow and consensus-seeking, "in the manner of a traditional local village," but gosh, its members sure buy a lot of weapons. Granted, it's been forced to deal with everything from terrorists to tsunamis lately. Actually, ASEAN began to come alive in the early 1990s, when it began shifting its focus to security matters and taking a broader view of its own region. In 1993 it came up with the idea for the Asian Regional Forum (ARF; ASEAN's member states plus their "dialogue partners," the United States, Canada, Australia, New Zealand, the EU, Japan, North and South Korea, Russia, China, and India, and also Papua New Guinea, whose observer status does not really mean it has to sit on a folding chair at the back of the conference room). The tiny, oil-rich sultanate of Brunei became a full member of ASEAN in 1994, and Vietnam, Laos, Myanmar, and Cambodia all came aboard between 1955 and 1999. Claiming to be sick of the old bilateral arrangements of the Cold War—the

United States and Japan, the United States and South Korea, the United States and the Philippines, and so on—ASEAN says it wants to think multilaterally, which seems like a reasonable enough idea. At a meeting in Bali in 2003, the member nations agreed to create an "ASEAN community" with a population of five hundred million, annual trade of $720 billion, and a free-trade area, by 2020. They are also working toward a trade agreement with China that would create the world's most populous market, with 1.7 billion consumers. Lick your chops, eBayers.

CIS (COMMONWEALTH OF INDEPENDENT STATES)

Founded in December 1991 by Russia, Ukraine, and Belarus, the Slavic heartland of the former USSR; eight other of the republics that made up the ex-Soviet Union—what Russia calls its "near abroad"—joined soon after. In 1993, Georgia committed itself to joining (it had been slow to join the United Nations, too). The Baltics weren't interested; from the beginning they had their eye on EU membership. Well, the Russians had to do something, if only to coordinate policies on all those leftover nuclear missiles, and this was it. It's hard to be too specific here, but the goals outlined in the charter include the prevention of inter-republic warfare (otherwise known as descent into chaos, and bear in mind all the trouble Russia's having keeping even itself and its remaining minorities together), the mediation of disputes, the military in general, and the promotion of trade, among themselves and in the world. The CIS—like the British Commonwealth—is not itself a country, simply a loose confederation of countries, so that all of us other countries have a lot of extra embassies to staff, but it's all for a good cause. Isn't it?

APEC (ASIA-PACIFIC ECONOMIC COOPERATION)

Founded—though to no practical effect—in 1989 by "member economies" of the Pacific Rim: the United States, Canada, Japan, South Korea, China, Taiwan, Hong Kong, the six original ASEAN countries (Indonesia, Malaysia, Singapore, the Philippines, Thailand, Brunei), Australia, and New Zealand. For the United States, the idea was to satisfy (and cash in on) East Asia's dreams of an economic alliance "without drawing a line down the middle of the Pacific Ocean," as then—secretary of state James Baker put it. Papua New Guinea, Mexico, and Chile joined in 1993–1994, the inclusion of the latter two causing some analysts to worry aloud about diverting the group's attention from East Asia with a lot of Latin America stuff. Peru and Russia joined in 1998, although Russia, which had been knocking at the door since the group was born, wasn't sure exactly why it wanted to be a member, since its share in the region's trade was less than 1 percent. Potentially the biggest regional economic grouping in the world, accounting for 40 percent of world trade and most of the world's economic growth, and making the EU and G8 look like pikers, APEC set out to transform the Pacific Rim into something more than a geographical term and could, it was thought, one day turn America's influence, economic and military, 180 degrees away from Europe. Its official mission, stated in 1994, was "free and open trade and investment in the Asia-Pacific by 2010 for industrialized economies and 2020 for developing economies." Although this hardly qualified as a rush job, there hasn't been much progress so far. The Asian economic bust of 1997–1998, which APEC was powerless to stop, considerably dimmed the group's luster, and America's "war on terror" put its members at odds. APEC's recommendations are nonbinding, anyway, so nobody seems too upset by the fact that the member economies haven't been able to agree on trade policy for years. Supporters say APEC works best as a sort of regional trial run for the WTO (see below).

WTO (WORLD TRADE ORGANIZATION)

The only global organization dealing with the rules of the international marketplace, the WTO is, simply put, out to promote free trade. Created in 1995, it is the successor to GATT (General Agreement on Tariffs and Trade), which was established by the United Nations after World War II to keep an eye on world trade in much the same way its sister organizations, the World Bank and the International Monetary Fund, were to oversee investment and currency. GATT, specifically, was charged with preventing the world from falling back into the benighted protectionist practices of the Depression years—quota restrictions, sky-high tariffs, and the like—and to promote David Ricardo's make-what-you-make-best-and-shop-for-the-rest theory of comparative advantage (see page 131), which had long provided the basis for most thinking people's thinking about international free trade. The WTO, which was part of the plan for GATT from the beginning, is much grander and more authoritative than its predecessor. Whereas GATT had 23 members, the WTO has, as of this writing, 148, with another fistful of countries, including Russia, waiting in line for admission. Headquartered in Geneva, the WTO operates both as a forum in which to negotiate international trade rules and as a high court for settling disputes over them. Unlike GATT, it actually has the power to enforce its "agreements," which cover everything from tariffs on manufactured goods to intellectual property rights and food safety standards around the world. Critics of the WTO are legion; in 1999 tens of thousands of protestors famously derailed the organization's summit in Seattle, Washington, and anti-WTO NGOs have been proliferating ever since. They have many complaints: lack of transparency in the WTO's decision-making processes, a structure that allows rich countries to strong-arm poor ones, and a version of globalization that subjugates humanitarian and environmental concerns to commercial interests, to name just a few. On the other side of the police barricades, supporters argue that worldwide prosperity is the best insurance against human rights and environmental abuses and that, since globalization is not only inevitable but well under way, it makes more sense to try to shape its growth through international regulations than simply to step back and let it run wild. It's tricky stuff, pitting, for instance, left-leaning workers'-rights and environmental advocates against hungry third-world countries worried that compliance with rules against, say, factory emissions and sweatshop labor will put them out of business, and at the same time outraging right-leaning politicians who are discovering that, in the WTO's version of globalization, corporate power trumps national and state sovereignty every time, even when that sovereignty is American. We'd love to hear what *you* think about all this, but please don't get in touch until you've read and understood the 23,000-page compendium of international agreements that serves as the WTO's user manual.

NAFTA (NORTH AMERICAN FREE TRADE ASSOCIATION)

The media coverage of this, the trade deal linking the United States, Canada, and Mexico, seemed almost willfully incomprehensible at the time (although perhaps not so willfully incomprehensible as the public debate), both before and after NAFTA actually went into effect on the first day of 1994. Part of the problem was that NAFTA wasn't really news. The United States and Canada had had their own bilateral trade agreement since 1989, and were so heavily invested in each other even before that that NAFTA didn't *really* stand to change a whole lot. Mexico is a little different—we never used to party with them much, and they did seem a little, it hurts us to say this, inclined to the making of brooms—but even here the United States had been treating Mexico like an enormous, if backward, fifty-first state just south of Texas since at least the mid-1980s, when it started endowing all those *maquiladoras* (see pages 376-378). Of course, this didn't, at the time, alter the intellectual perceptions (if you can call them that) of anybody—e.g., the Clinton administration, along with most Democrats (pro), or Ross Perot, Ralph Nader, and the AFL-CIO, leadership and manpower alike (con), with the Republicans having to decide (1) whether NAFTA was the sort of big-business proposition they ought to like and (2) even if it was, whether they still shouldn't vote against Clinton. Then there was the problem of all the different systems all of the above players had devised to count things up, especially jobs—e.g., NAFTA would have created somewhere between 30,000 and 170,000 new jobs in the United States by 1998, a range of estimates that were actually published with a straight face. Jobs were the most roiling of NAFTA issues, especially blue-collar—or, in the case of Mexico, no-collar—jobs, an ongoing trauma for all three countries. In 2004, when NAFTA celebrated its tenth birthday, neither side had moved much from its original position. These days, NAFTA supporters, mostly wearing Armani, will point to the dramatic increase in intra-American trade, which more than doubled in the association's first decade. Investment is way up, too, they beam, bringing with it more and higher-paying jobs as well as lower costs for consumers. Environmental and working conditions have benefited from NAFTA side agreements. And just look at Mexico, which finally has an almost-first-world credit rating and is now seen by corporate boards and venture capitalists as more of a North American country than a Latin American one. "Bull droppings!" shout NAFTA opponents, sporting T-shirts and serapes. "Trade and investment may be up, but the only people who've benefited are the rich shareholders, owners, and executives of multinational corporations." They insist that workers in all three countries have lost jobs or rights or at the very least have seen their wages fall relative to their productivity. Mexico, they point out, is poorer than ever, with manufacturers now moving to China for cheap labor and poor peasant farmers having their livelihoods buried under thousands of tons of subsidized U.S. corn. Statistics show that the number of Mexicans crossing the border to find work has doubled since NAFTA went into effect. And forget about laws protecting workers' health and the environment, say NAFTA-haters; they're subordinated at every turn by the chance to make a buck. Observers trying to maintain neutrality usually conclude that both sides have a point, and that in the end NAFTA may matter most as a lesson in how to, and how not to, stitch together future trade agreements, such as the pending CAFTA (Central American Free Trade Agreement) and the even bigger-deal FTAA (Free Trade Agreement of the Americas) currently being negotiated by 34 countries.

A Trio of Geographical Clarifications for a Nation That, Frankly, Would Rather Skateboard

One way to divide up the Western Hemisphere is to snap it in two just a little below its narrowest point, the Isthmus of Panama. (Not for no reason did they decide to dig the canal there, rather than across, say, Honduras.) This gives you two big pieces: North America, which includes Canada, the United States, Mexico, Central America, the West Indies, and, up top, Greenland, still owned by Denmark; and South America, which includes the continent's twelve independent nations (ranging in size from Brazil, the fifth-largest country in the world, to Suriname, the former Dutch Guiana), plus French Guiana and the notorious Falkland Islands.

On the other hand, there are times when a person wants to speak collectively of his southern neighbors (more and more of whom are, we grant you, trading in the metaphor of neighborhood for a substandard three-room apartment right down the block). Now the term of choice is Latin America, and it takes in everything from Mexico and Cuba all the way to Chile and Argentina. Everything, that is, that speaks a Romance language, which leaves out most current and former British colonies, likewise Dutch ones, as well as the U.S. Virgin Islands; Puerto Rico, though, is Latin American.

South-of-the-border breaks down in other ways, too. Central America is the seven nations stretching from Guatemala and Belize, which you may remember as British Honduras, to Panama. Middle America—however ridiculous the term sounds in light of all those old double-knit-polyester jokes—includes, in addition to Central America, both Mexico and the countries of the Caribbean (a.k.a., more or less, the West Indies; see box), regardless of language and colonial past. Meso-America, which archaeologists and anthropologists like to throw around, designates the area from Mexico to roughly Nicaragua, rich in pre-Columbian architecture and artifacts. South America we've already talked about.

Now, what if you want to point only to those people in Latin America who speak Spanish—i.e., the Mexicans, the Central Americans, the residents of Cuba, Puerto Rico, and the Dominican Republic (*not* Haiti, next door, which speaks a free-form version of French), plus almost everybody in South America except the various Guianans and the Brazilians (the last of whom speak Portuguese)? Then you'll say Spanish America, or better, given that the United States kicked Spain out of Cuba and Puerto Rico, its last New World holdings, in 1898, Hispanic America.

ISLANDS IN THE STREAM

A few nice distinctions for revolutionaries and winter vacation-goers. First, don't think that *Caribbean* and *West Indian* are exact synonyms. The West Indies (which disappointed Columbus by not turning out to be the East Indies, that is, present-day Indonesia) includes all the Caribbean Islands (from the Carib Indians whom Columbus found living there, the source, also, of our word *cannibal*) *plus* the Bahamas, which aren't any more in the Caribbean than Fort Lauderdale is. The Caribbean Islands themselves break down into two big groups: the Greater Antilles (Cuba, Jamaica, Hispaniola, which is shared by Haiti and the Dominican Republic, and Puerto Rico; called "Greater" simply because they're big), and the Lesser Antilles (everything else, none of it with much heft). The Lesser Antilles break down, in turn, into the Leeward Islands (e.g., the Virgins, Antigua, Guadeloupe) and the Windward Islands (e.g., Grenada, Martinique), plus Barbados, Trinidad and Tobago, and Curaçao and the rest of the Dutch Antilles. Bermuda, by the way, is not a West Indian island at all, but a flyspeck of a British colony a few hundred miles off the coast of North Carolina, all pink stucco houses and Shetland sweaters. If you're heading there for a February vacation (or a revolution), you've made a terrible mistake.

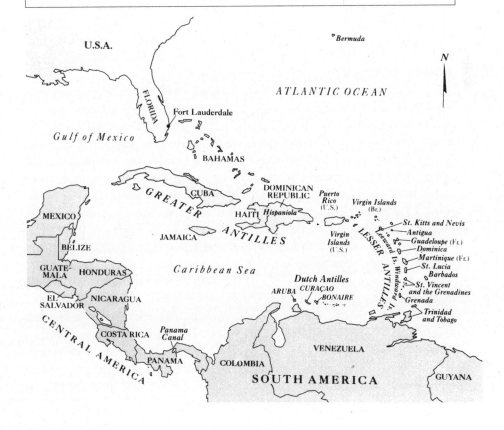

WHY ENGLAND, WHILE ADMITTEDLY A ROYAL THRONE OF KINGS AND A LITTLE WORLD, IS NOT EXACTLY A SCEPTERED ISLE OR A PRECIOUS STONE SET IN THE SILVER SEA

It isn't a sceptered isle or a precious stone set in the silver sea because it's only a *part* of that isle and that stone. The other parts are called Wales (to the West) and Scotland (to the north), and together the three have made up a single country since the 1707 Act of Union between England (which had already swallowed up Wales) and Scotland. It was called "Great" less out of copywriter's overkill than to distinguish it from "Little Britain," better known as Brittany, across the channel in France, which had been named and settled by Celts driven out of "historic" Britain by the Germanic Angles and Saxons in the fifth and sixth centuries. Not to be outdone, evidently, the Angles came up with "England."

No, we're not finished. The British Isles is the name for the islands of Britain and Ireland taken together, along with such outlying island groups as the Shetlands and the Orkneys and the British possessions of the Isle of Man and the Channel Islands. The United Kingdom is the formal name for the nation you now won't be referring to as England; its full name is the United Kingdom of Great Britain and Northern Ireland. (It was known as the United Kingdom of Great Britain and Ireland from 1801 until southern Ireland—a.k.a. the Irish Free State, a.k.a. Eire—pulled out in 1922.) Today, both "Britain" and "the UK" are accepted shorthand forms for "United Kingdom."

No, we're not finished. The British Empire, which at its height, just after World War I, took in 450 million people spread over 14 million square miles (a quarter of the earth's population and land surface), from Canada to Ceylon, Ireland to Iraq, Australia to Antigua, and which the sun was supposed never to set on, hasn't existed since 1947, when India and Pakistan became independent, and when "British Commonwealth" seemed like a more diplomatic heading under which to be bearing what remained of "the white man's burden." Now, unless you're a reactionary yourself, you'd do well to call it "the Commonwealth," more formally "the Commonwealth of Nations," no "British" about it.

No, we're not quite finished. British—the adjective—can be used of the island of Britain and the people who live on it, assuming you don't want to be more specific and say English, Welsh, or Scottish (which, for what it's worth, is preferred by most Scots to "Scotch," unless it's broth or whiskey you're talking about); the Northern Irish are Irish, not British, but begorrah, and we'd best not be opening that one up. A person who lives in Britain is a Briton, as opposed to a Breton, which is a person who lives in Brittany (or Bretagne, as the French like to say). "Britishers" is what Americans sometimes call Britons, who find the word mildly funny. Be all that as it may, you'll still probably choose, with most Britons, to refer to Prince Philip's wife not as "Her Britannic Majesty" but as "the Queen of England."

WHY THE ORIENT EXPRESS
NEVER GOT TO TOKYO

Nobody uses "Near East" much anymore as a way of indicating Turkey, Cyprus, Syria, Lebanon, Israel, Jordan, and Egypt, and usually Iraq and the countries of the Arabian Peninsula. (Earlier, in the nineteenth century, it had been used exclusively of the Balkans, Greece, and Turkey, "near" with regard to "civilized" Europe.) "Middle East"—or, more folksily, "Mideast"—is still going strong, however, and takes in all of the above, from Turkey on down, as well as Libya and the Maghreb (see below); the Sudan; Ethiopia and Somalia (the so called Horn of Africa: think rhinoceros), plus Iran and Afghanistan. And if you're nostalgic for Days of Empire, India, Pakistan, Sri Lanka (then Ceylon), Bangladesh (formerly East Pakistan), Burma (now Myanmar), and even Nepal, today usually lumped together as the Indian Subcontinent, although Burma has lately been sliding into the lap of Southeast Asia, over to its right.

"Arab world," an expression that varies in popularity according to whether the Arabs are speaking to one another at the time, leaves out Israel, obviously; it also leaves out Iran (which is Muslim but not Arab), Ethiopia (which is full of Christian blacks), Turkey (which is full of Turks, who, incidentally, in the days of the Ottoman Empire, played landlord to the entire neighborhood), and all points beyond. On the other hand, "Arab world" very definitely includes Tunisia, Algeria, and Morocco, which together with Libya form a strictly regional grouping called the Maghreb, from the Arabic word for "west," which is where they lie with regard to Egypt and Arabia, secular and spiritual Arab headquarters, respectively. "Arab League" is the loose twenty-two-nation political association of Arab states throughout the region, Morocco to Iraq, Lebanon to Somalia, with Arab nationalism its raison d'être; "United Arab Republic," you may remember, was the short-lived union of Egypt and Syria.

So much for now. There's also a sizable backlist of geographical names, any of which can pop up without much warning. "Palestine" got a new lease on life with the PLO; historically, it describes the territory defined roughly by present-day Israel, from biblical times to its British mandate following World War I, with bits of Jordan (formerly Transjordan, "across the Jordan [River]") and Egypt thrown in. "Asia Minor" ("Little Asia") is essentially Turkey, at least the 95 percent of it that's not in Europe and that's also today known as Anatolia. "The Fertile Crescent" arches from the Mediterranean coast of Syria in the west to Iraq and the Persian Gulf in the east; like the Nile Valley, it's a famous Cradle of Civilization, especially the Mesopotamian portion of it, centered on the plain

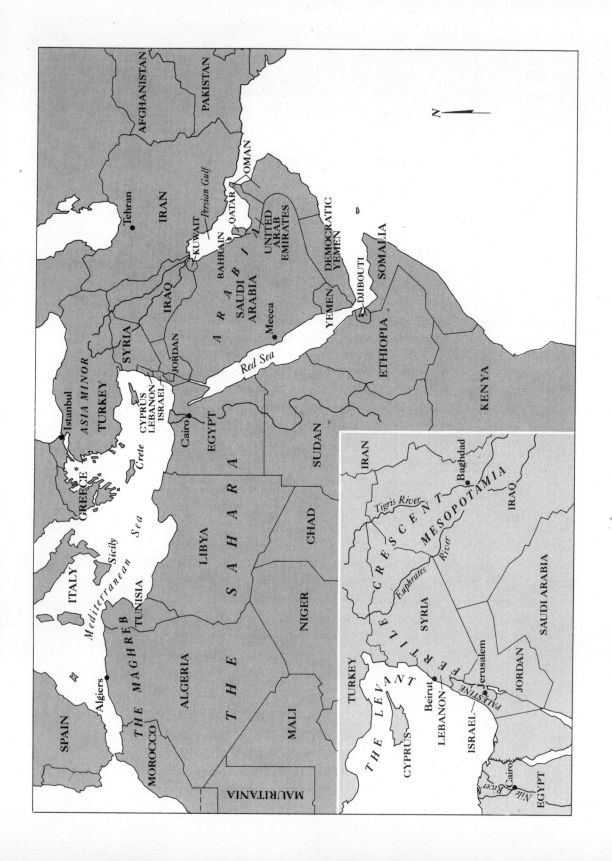

bounded by the Tigris and Euphrates rivers. "The Levant" (from the French word for "rise," which the French enjoyed thinking the sun did there) is the eastern tier of the Mediterranean, Greece to Egypt, but especially the Syria-Lebanon portion of it, which the French got as *their* mandate following World War I.

Which brings us to the term "Orient" itself, from the *Latin* word for "rise," a term that, until this century, was used invariably to designate Turkey, Arabia, Egypt, Persia (our Iran), Palestine, etc., *not* China, Japan, Korea, and the Philippines, which were known then, as they still are today, as the Far East. This shouldn't come as a surprise: The fellows in whose honor "We Three Kings of Orient Are" was written weren't, after all, shoguns.

PSYCHOLOGY

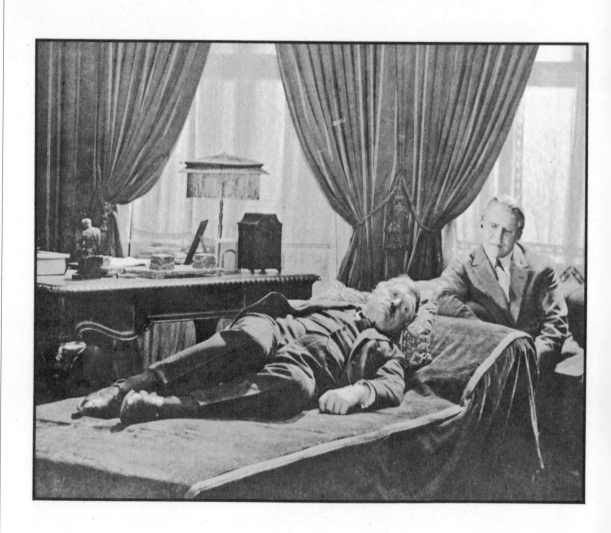

Contents

Undergoing an analysis, Hollywood-style, in the early talkie Secrets of a Soul

Herr Doktor, What's Wrong with Me?

A GUIDE TO NEUROSIS, PSYCHOSIS, AND PMS

Somebody—was it Freud or one's freshman-year roommate?—defined a "neurotic" as a person who could neither love nor work, but who was still, nine days out of ten, able to get around. In other words, whatever trouble he or she may be having with unresolved anxiety, guilt, or revulsion, a neurotic remains capable of coherent speech, good manners, tasteful outfits, and what psychologists—or was it one's freshman-year roommate?—call reality-testing.

The neurotic (unlike the psychotic, about whom more in a minute) is not out of his mind. If anything, he's too much in it, condemned to try to use his neurotic symptom (the obsessive-compulsive's ritual hand-washing, for instance) as an outlet for the least objectionable part of an objectionable impulse and, usually, as a barrier against the enactment of the rest of that impulse as well. Where do these objectionable impulses come from? Childhood sexual wishes, mostly, some as early as in-crib masturbation and feces smearing, some later and directed against one's parents, nearly all of which proved painful or unwieldy and were repressed, that is, chased out of consciousness and "forgotten." As if all that weren't enough, the fledgling neurotic's libido—his sex drive and primary energy source, lying inside him, as Freud pointed out, like so much crude oil—regresses, finding safer, more manageable satisfactions in an earlier, less intimidating stage of sexual development.

Don't take it personally. This one-two punch is the fate of almost everybody, and it generally connects with us in mid-Oedipus complex, just when we're trying to catch the bus for kindergarten. But not everybody has to deal with it all over again later. That chore falls to the adult for whom adult-style goings-on—or the lack of them—have become so painful, so unwieldy that he reinstitutes the long-dormant repression-and-regression process. Tied to a period and a pattern in the past, with things going badly now, he repeats, or acts out, over and over and over again, the trauma he can't "remember." As Freud once sighed, "Today, neurosis takes the place of the monasteries, which used to be the refuge of all whom life had disappointed or who felt too weak to face it."

Like cancer and AIDS, the other mythic diseases of the century, neurosis is a grab bag of ailments, syndromes, and prognoses, with a complex causation closely linked to individual susceptibility. Reach in and you're likely to pull out one of the following, quaintly divided here, as they were in Freud's day, between the "transference" and the "narcissistic" varieties.

The transference neuroses, also known as the classical neuroses, were the ones Freud thought psychoanalysis could actually cure. They include:

HYSTERIA: from the Greek word for "womb," used, pre-Freud, to designate only certain female disorders; subsequently applied to any disorder in which anxiety is converted into bodily paralysis or a sensory disturbance like blindness

PHOBIA: in which anxiety is projected onto a single class of things (wide-open spaces, say, or little white mice) that are then scrupulously avoided

OBSESSION: where talismanic doing, fussing, straightening, and sometimes just plain thinking are used to express frustrated sexual energy; ritual hand-washing is the well-worn example here

The reason these are called "transference" neuroses is that the analyst, by roughly re-creating the original childhood conflict and acting as a stand-in for hard-pressed, erratic Mommy and/or Daddy, allows the patient to "transfer" submerged emotions onto him and work through the conflict one more time—this time within the safety and consistency of the analysis.

The good news: The phobic, the hysteric, or the obsessive can usually regain (after several years of analysis and tens of thousands of dollars) all the energy that was formerly at the service of his neurosis.

The bad news: These days, there aren't all that many classic hysterics, phobics, and obsessives around to be cured; seems that sexual liberation pretty much thinned the ranks. However, the era of safe sex (or no sex) may well bring on a resurgence.

The narcissistic neuroses, with considerable shading (and a little fudging) on the part of the psychoanalytic community, correspond to what we think of as psychoses. These tend to manifest themselves not in terms of a single easy-to-identify symptom but rather a diffuse, fugitive "feeling" and include, traditionally (i.e., according to Freud):

MELANCHOLIA: severe depression, with or without its manic counterpart in tow

DEMENTIA PRAECOX: our schizophrenia, called "praecox," or premature, because of its typical onset in postadolescence

PARANOIA: projection (a defense mechanism we'll be getting to in the next session) magnified and embellished to the point of delusion, usually of either the somebody's-out-to-get-me-and-he's-poisoned-the-tap-water or the I-am-the-Red-Queen-off-with-their-heads sort

In all of them, the ego is not merely under siege; it's long gone. And the chances of recovery are not so hot. The person with the narcissistic neurosis—whose sexual wishes had never developed to the point of being attached to Mommy and/or Daddy; who had instead remained, literally, "stuck on himself"—couldn't, according to Freud, be reached by the analyst either. It's true that some analysts, led by a couple of latterday Viennese named Heinz Kohut (see page 443) and Otto Kernberg, shifted the emphasis of their work from Oedipus to Narcissus, from castration anxiety to self-love, and from Victorian-era sexual repression to Me Decade grandiosity, enough so that there's some hope for the narcissist. But he remains a tough cure.

Confidential to all you schizophrenics out there (and you know who you are): Hang tough! Granted, you've been accused of having regressed to the ultimate narcissism, an infantile state in which everything you see, touch, or hear reads as an extension of you. And, yes, your mind is split between a tiny little normal person with a wee small voice who recalls how nice things used to be and the population of ten randomly selected Bosch canvases plus your entire junior high school. In fact, if our century still admits to madness as something certifiable, you've got it. But what can you expect? You've lost gray matter the way middle-aged men lose hair. At least no one can accuse you of having repressed anything. You're living it, baby.

Footnote for fetishists, devotees of S & M, homosexuals, and perverts of all stripes: No, you are not, according to Freud, neurotics. Perversion, while marked by regression to some soft, unchallenging, essentially self-involved state (or occasionally by one's never having moved beyond that state at all), does not involve repression, conflict, or the batting around of the ego by the superego and/or the id. You may be perfectly happy. Probably not, though: Most perverts wind up with their share of independently generated neuroses, too. And that's a little like working double shifts. Or do we mean both sides of the street? We'll think about it while we're washing our hands.

Oh, and we were just kidding about the PMS.

Eleven Ways to Leave a Mother

If Hollywood were to make a movie out of the structure of your mind, they wouldn't be wrong to cast Jim Carrey as the id, Daniel Day-Lewis as the ego, and Alan Rickman as the superego. The id's always going to leer, mug, and try to get its way. The ego's always going to come across with the subtlest (simultaneously most restrained and most inventive) acting, only occasionally exuding false nobility and/or martyrdom. And the superego's always going to register as a bit of a stiff, a sometimes well-intentioned, sometimes despotic outsider.

Whereas you're born with your id, seat of the instincts and repository of libido, in full swing, your ego comes together only gradually. Once in place, it has to integrate sensory perceptions, modulate voluntary movements, keep tabs on the instincts that are penned up in the id next door, and provide for their, as well as its own, pleasure, all without ever losing sight of reality. Sometime in the course of childhood, as early as age five or six, the superego takes shape, incorporating the early influences of parents and teachers; thenceforth, on top of everything else, you're saddled with conscience, morality, and a tendency to come down on yourself at the worst possible moments.

So the ego is up against the id (which wants to disobey it), the superego (which tries to make it feel bad), and the outside world (which, on some days, is enough to make it feel like drowning itself in the tub). To the extent that it is a strong and healthy ego, it attempts to honor the demands of all three. To do so, even the well-endowed ego makes compromises, adopting special techniques called defense mechanisms, so that, when confronted with certain demands, it doesn't have to panic, self-destruct, or assume the fetal position. By actively intervening, the ego thereby transforms what it or the world or the superego views as bad into something neutral or better.

This "armor-plating of character," as Wilhelm Reich (see page 45) described it, is innocent enough in moderation; it is also virtually inescapable. But when defense mechanisms become too powerful, so encumbering character that it can't make it down the hall to the bathroom, problems ensue. You'll get a sense of those problems when you take a look at this rundown of the most celebrated defense mechanisms. The comment on the right reflects how each might be employed by a nine-year-old boy who's angry at his father and who, natch, feels guilty about feeling angry—not that he's necessarily in touch with either the anger or the guilt, let alone the defense mechanism.

1. *Repression*   "Hmm? I don't know what you're talking about."

Whoever represses simply forgets—blissfully (unless, that is, the repressed material resurfaces). Repression may be the most potent defense mechanism of all; certainly it is the best at combatting sexual wishes. Other defense mechanisms, some psychiatrists say, simply do the work it leaves undone.

2. *Regression*   "Goo. Flubba dada?"

To regress is to revert to an earlier, less threatening stage of psychosexual development; it's a basic prerequisite for most neuroses and all perversions. It needn't result in talking baby talk, but it gets you—and your ego—off the hook by taking you back to a time when things were easier, still merely anal, say, and you didn't have to worry about being castrated by Daddy just because you happened to love Mommy.

3. *Projection*   "Oh, no, I'm not mad at Daddy. *Mommy* is
                        mad at Daddy."

The anger is attributed to someone else; guilt and anxiety thus become unnecessary. Projection doesn't alter the nature of the feeling: It gets rid of it by pushing it out into the world, to the same degree that repression would bury it. Projection can be dangerous, though; it's this defense that causes you to hear censuring voices. Those voices are only your super-ego, of course, but *you* don't know that.

4. *Denial*   "You must be crazy. I'm not mad at Daddy."

This is the wholesale falsification of reality, and the flip side of repression. Whereas repression severs the ego from internal pressures, denial severs it from those of the outside world. It's perfectly normal—desirable, even—in children; in adults (for whom full-scale fantasy lives are no longer practical), denial can indicate advanced mental illness.

5. *Reaction formation*   "Mad at Daddy? I *love* Daddy! Where is he
                                 anyway? I want to sit in his lap."

Here you convince yourself that the exact opposite of something awful and unacceptable is, in fact, true, then replay your revised version of it a zillion times a day. A veteran reaction formationer (most often an obsessive-compulsive) becomes excessively solicitous of the person he hates, often instituting elaborate ceremonial acts to keep his true feelings at bay.

6. *Reversal*   "Mad at Daddy? Daddy's mad at *me!*"

This one's as old as the first conflict between ego and instincts; in fact, it, along with repression, was one of the first defense mechanisms your young ego used. (You used it yourself in first grade: It's the "You're dumb" "No, *you're* dumb" of the playground.) Like displacement (below), it is usually invoked as a preliminary to more complicated defensive maneuvers.

7. *Displacement*   "Mad at Daddy? I'm mad at Rags. Bad dog!"

The emotion is transferred from a dangerous object, who can retaliate, to a safe one, who can't. As with reversal, it's usually a first step: The ego, having gone this far, will probably give things at least one more twist—

regression, say, or reaction formation. Otherwise, you might figure out how you really felt.

8. *Isolation*   "Yes, I guess I'm mad at Daddy. It would be fun to shoot him and watch him die. May I have some more milk and cookies, please?"

Recognition minus affect: You don't bother to deny, repress, or reshape the traumatic emotion, you just disconnect from it. You can talk about it without feeling a thing.

9. *Intellectualization*   "Well, yes, I am mad at Daddy. I'm probably wishing him dead so that I can have Mommy all to myself, which, of course, is quite normal at my age."

Isolation for smart people. In this one, also known as "rationalization," you overthink the problem in order to avoid making contact with the emotion or anxiety behind it.

10. *Undoing*   "Uh-oh, I'm very mad at Daddy. I'd better go line up all my teddy bears so they're *exactly* even with the squares on my rug."

Here, an action is meant to expiate an emotion, or an earlier action, that the ego can't bear to deal with. Undoing can involve actually canceling something out (for instance, shopping yourself bankrupt, then returning everything you've bought) or magically doing so, through a compulsive (and apparently unrelated) ritual.

11. *Sublimation*   "Mad at Daddy? Excuse me, I really must get this finger painting finished."

Of all the mechanisms of defense, the only truly desirable one. By the time it's acquired, the superego's well in place, channeling the libido into some useful endeavor, transforming the instinctually gratifying into the socially useful. Artists are alleged to be the biggest sublimaters around, expressing in paint, clay, or guitar riffs what the rest of us take out on our stomach linings. Freud said it best, of course:

> [The artist] opens out to others the way back to the comfort and consolation of their own unconscious sources of pleasure, and so reaps their gratitude and admiration; then he has won—through his phantasy—what before he could only win in phantasy; honour, power, and the love of women.

Return with Us Now to a Quiet Side Street

*in a Working-Class Neighborhood in Turn-of-the-Century Vienna,
Where, in a Darkened Second-Floor Room, a Man with a White Beard
(and a Nosebleed) Beckons You to Lie Down on a Horsehair Sofa. And
Please, Feel Free to Say Whatever Comes into Your Mind . . .*

FREUD AND HIS FOLLOWERS

Freud, like the philosophers who preceded him and the psychoanalysts—and,
for that matter, the physicists—who followed, struggled to formulate a system for solving the mysteries of the soul. What he came up with: a therapeutic
procedure that would, he hoped, help recover those dark, submerged parts of
man's being that force him into a lifetime of repetitive action and ritual discontent. For Freud, this procedure called for the patient (henceforth known as the
analysand) to lie on the couch for fifty-five minutes and relate anything that
came to mind, no matter how silly, shameful, or self-incriminating. If the treatment was often, literally, nightmarish for the analysand, it was no day at the
beach for the analyst, either. As Freud warned, "No one who, like me, conjures
up the most evil of those half-tamed demons that inhabit the human breast and
seeks to wrestle with them, can expect to come through the struggle unscathed."

He didn't. Nor, presumably, did five of his most prominent disciples. All of
whom undergo, on the following pages, short-term treatment with contributor
Barbara Waxenberg, Ph.D.

SIGMUND FREUD (HIMSELF)

In the beginning there was Freud—or as he is universally labeled, Freud himself, with the pronoun wired inextricably to the noun. Not to refer to him this way immediately reveals you to be a parvenu on the psychoanalytic scene. To establish your credentials among the cognoscenti, you must, whenever some arcane metapsychological point is discussed, ask whether the speaker is referring to the early writings (1895–1900) or to the middle phase (roughly 1900–1910); that is, to theories which Freud himself (see how it's done?) revised in his later papers. It also adds a bit of heft to throw in such remarks as "Yes, but in 'On Narcissism' or in 'Analysis Terminable and Interminable,' Freud himself said . . ."

It was in the early period that Freud made some of his most revolutionary contributions: the nature of the unconscious, the mechanisms of repression and resistance, the phenomenon of transference, the significance of dreams ("the royal road to the unconscious," as he put it), and the method of free association. He also developed his seduction theory, the belief that neuroses stemmed from actual sexual assaults on young children, a theory he later abandoned in favor of the belief that such traumas were not real events, but fantasies that stemmed from unconscious wishes. This recasting of seduction, exploitation, and betrayal from an external event to an internal conflict-laden desire was to color Freud's sense of what psychoanalysis was all about; henceforth, he would emphasize the idea of intrapsychic forces over the individual and his environment. This was to remain the dominant bias of psychoanalysis until it was challenged by Otto Rank and Sándor Ferenczi in 1925 and, much more vehemently, by Harry Stack Sullivan a decade later. It tied psychoanalysis to an instinctual-drive theory, rooted in biology and based on sequential phases of infant sexuality. It also laid the groundwork for viewing the Oedipal conflict as a universal experience, pivotal in human development.

The word "metapsychology" has been defined as a psychological theory that cannot be verified or disproved by observation or reasoning. Which is to say, its verifiableness can be eternally argued. The further removed from consensus the theory is, the more easily it remains enshrined in the hearts of its followers. So it is with Freud's instinctual-drive theory. For Freud, the instinctual drive acts as a constant and inescapable force that creates a state of tension that one works at reducing. Although man (and woman, but Freud was notoriously puzzled about what, exactly, women want) is regulated by the pleasure principle, "pleasure" is more or less defined as the absence of excitation. So much for fun and games in turn-of-the-century Vienna. Instincts have a source of excitation within the body, an aim (the removal of excitation), and an object (the means by which the satisfaction of the aim is achieved). In the Freudian model, this object need not be a person, although everyone would probably agree that if the desired "object" turns out to be a statue or a French poodle, one is wasting one's time and libidinal energies or losing one's marbles.

In tracing the stages of human development, Freud postulated that erotic feeling is first experienced in the mouth, the newborn's primary source of pleasure; later shifts to the anus, where enjoyment is derived from the retention and expulsion of feces; and ultimately, at about age three or four, to the genitals, in the so called phallic stage. Under normal conditions, interest in these organs progresses in orderly sequence. Fixation occurs when, as a result of trauma or constitution, libido is bound at a particular developmental stage so that some portion of it never advances beyond this point. When the person gets into trouble later on in life, he is likely to regress to the point of fixation. Adult patterns of behavior take shape according to the way each erotic phase is negotiated. For example, possessiveness, meticulousness, orderliness, and retentiveness are viewed as anal traits, while passivity and helplessness or sadism and exploitation are seen as oral ones.

The phallic period coincides with that of the Oedipus complex, which is central in the Freudian theory of neurotic development and which begins to develop at about age three, when little girls and boys decide that marrying the parent of the opposite sex and killing off the parent of the same one is a neat idea. This is often quite flattering to Mommy or Daddy, who is probably having a hard time with bulges, hair loss, and his spouse and who could do with a bit of stroking. But it can be a bit wearing on the parent rival. "When is Daddy going to die?" goes down poorly with morning coffee. The family romance begins to wear thin at about age five or six when the boy, fearing castration by his father (a bit of talion revenge), turns away from Mom, identifies with Dad, and goes back to watching television instead of primal scenes for the years of the so called latency period, during which sexual interest is in abeyance. The fate of the girl is more complex since she's got nothing to lose, ostensibly because Mommy's already done away with her fancy equipment. And now Mommy has Daddy and Daddy's penis and everything and it's not fair! But eventually she identifies with mother, accepts the feminine role (i.e., her castration and penis envy), adopts a Cabbage Patch doll, and represses her incestuous wishes. Ho hum.

According to Freud, the bases for psychological disorder are laid down between ages one and six and all later learning is an elaboration of early conflict. In structural terms, conflicts exist among id impulses (those unconscious reservoirs of sexual and aggressive impulses constantly seeking discharge), ego defenses (which ward off the direct discharge of the impulse and its access to consciousness), and superego restrictions (the stern conscience which embodies parental and cultural standards). The embattled ego must mediate between the primitive forces of the id and the censoring, guilt-inducing power of the superego. In psychoneuroses, the ego becomes progressively less able to effect satisfactory compromises and is eventually overwhelmed. The ultimate aim of psychoanalysis is to increase the relative strength of the ego so that it can effectively deal with pressures from above and below and with external reality.

Originally, Freud postulated a life-preserving instinct and a sexual instinct. After World War I, he turned his attention more fully to the problem of repressed aggression. This gave rise to his second instinct theory, the conflict between Eros, the life-preserving instinct, and Thanatos, the death force. Both aggression and the compulsion to repeat events are, in complicated ways, related to the death instinct. Since man strives for a homeostasis in which tension is minimal, death would be the ultimate relief of this tension.

Today, while Freud's biomechanical view of human functioning has been seriously (and continually) questioned, his method of psychoanalytic inquiry, his concepts of transference, repetition, and resistance, and his theory of unconscious experience remain the cornerstones of the analytic process.

FIVE FOLLOWERS

Psychoanalysis was—and is—a rigorous undertaking, but its rigors are not exactly what they used to be. Freud saw the same twelve patients every day, six days a week (and then wrote late into the night); present-day psychoanalysts, more pleasure-seeking and self-preservative, will see a patient only three to five times a week (and then sit down to dinner). On the other hand, analyses were more compact in those days, extending from six to twelve months, rather than six to twelve years, perhaps because the array of symptoms, from hysteria to obsessional neurosis to phobia, were more amenable to treatment than today's vague anxieties, characterological issues, and "disorders of the self."

Then there are differences that now exist between analytical schools; between, say, the Interpersonalists, who maintain that they contact the "unique individual" rather than the Freudians' "Oedipal cliché," and the Freudians, who accuse the Interpersonalists of not dealing with unconscious experience. To add to the tension, there are even theorists who point out that only a masochist, a social isolate, or a nut would accept a stranger's invitation to lie down on his couch, turn your back to him, and spill your guts while the stranger says nothing in response.

There's nothing new about such dissension; it's known in science as pluralism, and it's been characteristic of the psychoanalytic movement ever since Alfred Adler challenged Freud in 1910 over the relative importance of the sexual drives. Adler viewed the core problem as man's struggle to overcome feelings of inferiority (he coined the phrase "inferiority complex") and saw the "wish to be a complete man"—in the face of physical handicaps and environmental conflicts—as the guiding fiction behind every neurosis. Moreover, unlike Freud, who regarded society as a limitation on the individual, Adler came to see social interaction as essential to mental health. Freud, never one to take kindly to dissent, showed Adler the door (and would later refer to him cuttingly as "Dr. Alfred Adler, who was formerly an analyst").

Next to exit was Carl Jung, who also objected to Freud's heavy emphasis on sex. He saw man as influenced by higher forces (in his emphasis on a collective unconscious and his heavy use of symbolism, Jung could get pretty mystical), which conflict with his animal nature. Libido was regarded as a general life force, sexual in origin, but no longer reducible, in adulthood, to its sexual components. Jung developed a theory of character based on two fundamental personality types: the introvert who is absorbed in his inner world, and the extrovert who turns outward at the expense of private experience. For Jung, the overriding goal was always the achieving of a harmony between the conscious and the unconscious; that alone could make a person one and whole. Moreover, he argued that neurotic symptoms were not always the residue of an unhappy childhood, as Freud maintained, but were often attempts on the part of the mind to correct its own disequilibrium, and therefore could serve as pointers to a more satisfactory synthesis.

And that was just the first generation. The following pages concentrate on subsequent generations of rebellious, argumentative, and lapsed Freudians who, together, have effectively challenged the Master's view of what psychoanalysis is and what it ought to (and can) accomplish.

Melanie Klein (1882–1960): Hypothesis on Hypothesis

If prospective parents were to read Melanie Klein instead of Benjamin Spock, there would be a lot fewer babies. Klein's writings, if understood, would probably rival the pill as the most effective form of birth control yet devised. For to bear a "Kleinian baby" is to bring a potential cauldron of destructiveness and hate into the nursery, a child whose fantasies rival, in greed, malevolence and envy, those of Stephen King, Edgar Allan Poe, and the Marquis de Sade.

Briefly, Klein subdivided the first year of life into two phases; the paranoid-schizoid, in which the infant relates to anatomical parts of persons, chiefly the breast and penis; and the depressive, in which the mother is recognized as a whole person who can therefore be destroyed by the child's own hatefulness. In essence, the infant is capable of constructing elaborate phantasies (Kleinians use the *ph* spelling to express their extension of the term to the imaginings of the infant) about the good breast, which nourishes and is loved, and the bad breast, which deprives and is consequently destroyed. Don't even ask about bottle-fed babies; things are complicated enough already. Under the impact of anxiety and frustration, the child's desires and phantasies extend to the mother's entire body, which is seen as containing all kinds of goodies, including the father's penis, incorporated during intercourse. Klein writes, "The dominant aim [of the baby] is to possess himself of the contents of the mother's body and to destroy her by means of every weapon which sadism can command."

Meanwhile, the infant tries to incorporate enough good objects and substances to neutralize the bad objects and substances in his own body. There is a Jungian, as well as a Dracula-like, feeling to all this, an acceptance of some primordial, racial unconscious. The newborn enters the world with an innate sense of the existence of the mother and the contents of her body. Klein's babies live in a doggie-eat-doggie world in which punishments for destroying the bad breast or emptying the good one are anxiously anticipated. To survive in this jungle, the child wards off the dangers of the bad objects and feelings by "splitting" or separating their images from the good objects and feelings. As if this weren't bad enough, even the "good" is contaminated by primitive forces of envy, stirred up by the fact that the appearance and disappearance of the milk-laden good breast is controlled by the mother and not by the child. To add insult to injury, bad objects seem even more malevolent because of the hatred projected onto them by the rageful, greedy child whose needs are insatiable.

This takes us up to the second half of the first year (although it might seem that a lifetime has already been lived) when, if all has gone well, the paranoid-schizoid position is superseded by the depressive position. The outstanding feature of this position is the unification of the mother; no longer safely split into good and bad entities, she becomes a single person with both good and bad features. Integration, naturally enough, brings with it despair, since the good features of the mother are now no longer protected from the child's destructiveness.

Klein took Freud's death instinct and his theories of aggression and ran with them, adding her own view of envy as a biological given. The environment contributes little, but, like a mirror, reflects the baby's own conflicts back on him. Klein did not concern herself with parental defects and sufferings; she concentrated solely on the child's destructive urges and regrets. In this, she differed from Sullivan, Karen Horney, Erich Fromm, and Erik Erikson in America, as well as from W. R. D. Fairbairn and Donald Winnicott in England. What she accomplished was to focus attention on the earliest stage of human development, before the Oedipal conflict comes into play. Although she retained Freud's drive model and his id-ego-superego terminology and regarded herself as fundamentally orthodox in approach, there is little of Freud's psychophysiology in her schema. Instead of regarding drives as discrete quantities of energy, she redefined them as passionate feelings of love and hate. She saw human life as an intense dramatic tragedy that has its roots in the infant's constitutional makeup. In this framework, the Oedipal conflict becomes more a wrestling for power and destruction than a struggle with libidinous impulses. Anxiety and guilt stem from aggressive phantasies and fear of retaliation.

Klein's work split the British Psychoanalytic Society into two factions, one loyal to her, the other to Anna Freud. Others, like Winnicott, formed a third, nonaligned group. Although Klein's views are unverifiable, the recent emphasis on the importance of pre-Oedipal life in the understanding of borderline and narcissistic disorders has lent more credence to her theories.

Harry Stack Sullivan (1892–1949): Things Are Often What They Seem

After all this meta-messing, Harry Stack Sullivan, a native American of the what-you-see-is-what-you-get school, comes as a relief. For Sullivan, what you see (and get) is all bound up with how you participate: We can know another person only in terms of how we interact with him. Where Freud concentrated on what went on within the psyche of the individual, Sullivan focused on his relationships with others.

For Sullivan, the data of psychoanalysis—the behavior of the analysand and the analyst's public and private reactions to what the patient says and does—are there to be directly observed; excluded are all hypothetical events occurring in some never-never land "inside" the patient, not to mention the unconscious as an explanatory concept. Thus Sullivan, along with Clara Thompson, Karen Horney, Erich Fromm, and Frieda Fromm-Reichmann, spawned a new psychiatric movement in America, based on how a person makes sense of and responds to what is going on around him, rather than on the biological-drive that is the pillar of Freudian theory. In other words, to understand the individual, one must understand the network of relationships in which he is enmeshed; one must pay attention to the "interactional" rather than the "intrapsychic."

What really interested Sullivan was why people failed so badly at living productive and creative lives and, instead, stereotypically repeated the same unsatisfying actions. Perhaps influenced by the insecurities and privations of the Depression, Sullivan pared down his motivational system to two basic needs: satisfaction (both biological and emotional) and security (which he viewed as the avoidance of anxiety). The search for satisfaction inevitably propels a person toward involvement with others; Sullivan thought loneliness was the most painful of human experiences.

Like Klein's child, Sullivan's develops notions of "good" and "bad," but Sullivan saw these impressions as linked to the actual responses of the mother, not as derivatives of the fantasy life of the child. Sullivan's good mother is the nonanxious mother; his bad is a nervous or timid soul who empathically communicates her distress to the child, who then gradually learns to modify his behavior in order to modulate Mommy's anxiety. Of the child's introduction to the world of malevolence and mystification, Sullivan wrote, "Once upon a time everything was lovely, but that was before I had to deal with people."

Sullivan came up with the Self System, that configuration of traits that have been reinforced by the affirmation of the significant persons in the child's life, and the security operations the child develops in order to avoid anxiety and threats to self-esteem. Three areas are delineated: the "good me" (Mommy's smiling and not all wigged out and I feel pretty good too); the "bad me" (Mommy's feeling anxious and cross and I'm not feeling too cool either); and the "not me" (she's flipping her lid and I'm shaking from head to toe). If Sullivan had raised children instead of cocker spaniels, he might have added the category "who me," as in "Did you glue all your underwear together?" "Who, me?" But he didn't. And he didn't.

The Self System acts as a steering mechanism directing the child toward experiences that are associated with parental approval and freedom from anxiety, and away from ones that have met with disapproval and are subsequently blocked out of awareness. From all of this arises a pattern of I-You interlocking behaviors: If I act weak and helpless, then You, like my parents, must be solicitous and caretaking. If I am adorable, You must be admiring, and so on. Sullivan labeled these pairings "parataxic integrations": They become rigidified and dominate adult life, sometimes almost completely overlaying one's perceptions of the real people in one's life, who, stripped of their individuality, are seen as echoes and shadows of parental figures.

Donald W. Winnicott (1896–1971):
The "Good-Enough Mother" of the Year

Winnicott is every reader's fantasy (with an *f*) of all that a good mother should be. Few practitioners could engage the heart and mind of a child so directly, poignantly, and emphatically as this psychoanalyst, who had spent forty years as a pediatrician. (This nourishing holds true for grown-up children as well.) As for the mystique of psychoanalysis, Winnicott once wrote, "In doing psychoanalysis, I aim at:

> Keeping alive
> Keeping well
> Keeping awake

I aim at being myself and behaving myself." Good advice in any ballpark. Like Spencer Tracy, he knew his lines and didn't bump into the furniture.

From Winnicott's perspective, man's core problem lies in his struggle to arrive at an existence which is his and his alone but which, at the same time, allows for intimate contact with others. Intimacy, however, is an inherently limited affair. "At the center of each person is an incommunicado element, and this is sacred and most worthy of preservation. This core never communicates with or is influenced by the external world."

Life begins not with the infant but with the infant-mother pair, with the crucial developmental factor being the currents of empathic understanding that flow between caretaker and fledgling. It is the responsibility of the former to mediate between the inner world of the child and the environment about him. In plain language, she's got to help him to feel safe, for whether or not the child develops a real self will profoundly affect the nature and state of every problem the adult experiences. The mother must initially be exquisitely attuned to the physical and emotional needs of the infant as if an invisible band stretched between the two of them. She must respond when called and refrain from impinging when not needed. In such an environment, offered continuous nurturance, the infant enjoys a seemingly omnipotent position, in which whatever he imagines for himself is followed by the mother's presentation of the desired object. He is the source of all creation and can, through the magic of hallucinating what he wants, will his own satisfactions. Given this sunlit enchantment, he gradually becomes able to tolerate longer and longer separations from the mother without experiencing the terror of annihilation. Ultimately, he develops the capacity to be alone. Later comes the capacity for concern. Concomitantly, the mother awakens from a period of "maternal preoccupation" and begins to note with some astonishment that the world continues to function beyond the walls of the nursery. Bliss has ended.

Motherhood in this framework of empathic bonding is a hard row to hoe. Myriad pitfalls exist, predominantly linked to failure to respond to the infant's hallucinatory experiences (need to nurse, be caressed, be comforted, etc.) or to too much interference or overstimulation when the child would prefer to be alone, staring at the ceiling. The mother must be able to contain both the child's dependency and the aggressiveness that is an inevitable accompaniment to the process of separation, without becoming overwhelmed or fighting back. She must also be able to respond to his need to play.

In the worst-case scenario, the infant becomes compulsively attuned to the needs of others, primarily the mother, and in order to survive, develops what Winnicott terms a "false self." The "false self" contacts and complies with the directives of others, while his "true self" becomes dissociated, goes underground, and protects itself by remaining hidden. The psychoanalyst must provide what the parents failed to offer, a holding environment that is durable, attentive, and responsive, a *symbolic* re-creation of early mother-child interaction but not an actual regression to the patient's early years. And, like the "good" mother, he must be able to survive the inevitable assaults of the analysand without being annihilated. In this safety, the patient's true self can emerge.

Heinz Kohut (1913–1981):
Mirror, Mirror on the Wall

Over and over the wheel must be invented. Although it is obvious that psychoanalytic theories overlap, they are promulgated as if they have sprung full-blown from the heads of their creators, products of parthenogenesis and not of union.

So it is with the concept of empathy, pretty much derided when touted by Carl Rogers (nondirective counseling) or Franz Alexander (corrective emotional experience). It was viewed then as a surface phenomenon, secondary in the therapeutic bag of tricks, soothing and supportive but hardly such stuff as psychoanalyses are made of. But in the last decade, empathy has had quite a revival; given clout and respectability by a former president of the American Psychoanalytic Association, it now gets star billing.

What has created all this furor is the spread of borderline and narcissistic personality disturbances. Modern patients suffer from wounded self-esteem, shift rapidly from adoration to abhorrence and from grandiosity to despair, and are far more fragmented and eruptive than the hysterics and obsessives for whom the psychoanalytic method was devised. Until recently, they were considered to be beyond the pale of insight-oriented psychoanalytic treatment. But lately there has been a rush to modify technique to embrace this more disturbed population; you can hardly find a conference that does not focus on the problems of treating the "difficult" patient. Cynics might remark that the psychoanalyst had either to widen his scope or take down his shingle since the popularity of other forms of treatment (psychotherapy, behavior modification, encounter groups, and medication—not to mention step aerobics and video rentals) has made the intensity, duration, and cost of psychoanalysis far less appealing. Where psychiatry was once a highly regarded medical specialty, it is now far down on the preference lists of medical students.

And so along came Kohut (the aforementioned president of the distinguished APA) and his "disorders of the self," by which he meant defects in the sense of inner cohesion and continuity. In his 1971 volume *The Analysis of the Self*, Kohut straddled two positions: On the one hand, he maintained his allegiance to Freud by holding to the instinctual drive theory and to the conviction that Oedipal issues were central in tracing the origins of the structural neuroses; on the other, he established a parallel path of narcissistic development that allowed him to concentrate on the relationships established in earlier stages of human evolution. In the system that Kohut eventually constructed, man's search became a struggle to develop a cohesive and integrated self.

With Kohut, we are confronted once again with a baby in need of empathic response, but in this theory, parental figures are referred to as self-objects, signifying that the child is not yet able to differentiate himself from other objects in his world. Like Sullivan, but using different terminology, Kohut saw the child as experiencing the feeling states of these self-objects. The way that self and self-objects interrelate determines whether a cohesive or a fragmented self will emerge.

What the child requires of these self-objects is the mirroring of his capacities; he needs to sense that the self-objects can enjoy his exhibitionistic displays and are present as continuous, nurturing, empathic, and respectful figures. In addition, the growing child needs to be able to idealize at least one of his parents, to feel that the self-object that he's tightly tied up with is a swell human being. Although it seems simplistic in light of the complexity of interfamily relationships, Kohut sees the self as based on these two polarities of experience—admiring and being admired. Failure to develop at least one aspect, either mirroring or idealization, ultimately leads to a defective sense of self and the inability to maintain a consistent sense of self-esteem, that is, to narcissistic pathology.

Thus Self Psychology began with an effort to bring the narcissistic disorders within the purview of psychoanalysis. This widening of the net yielded a different set of data, largely concerned with relational issues and, since the self-systems of these patients were more primitively organized, a different series of transference and countertransference reactions to deal with. Kohut never completely dispensed with drive theory, although he waffled quite a bit on the subject. But his system, unlike Freud's and Klein's, does not rest on a conflict model. Even the Oedipal conflict, the heart of the Freudian matter, is avoidable if the parent-child interaction is a salutary one. Furthermore, Kohut viewed the Oedipal period not in terms of a triad of sexuality, hateful jealousy, and guilt, but as a growth stage in which the child derives joy from exercising new capacities and mastering new challenges. Where Freud saw Guilty Man who fears castration as a consequence of sexual rivalries, Kohut saw Tragic Man whose anxiety lies in the threat of annihilation.

In working with patients who present narcissistic pathology, the analyst initially acts as a self-object, providing the empathic responses that were missing in the patient's early life, and presents him- or herself as a person who can be, and who will allow himself to be, idealized. Like small children preening before their mothers, these patients look to their analysts as one looks in a mirror in order to see one's reflection and to bask in a sense of specialness. Or they may adore and experience themselves as merged with these exalted beings, feeling strong and secure as long as this bonding is maintained. Growth occurs largely through experiencing a relationship that supplies what the parents failed to supply, rather than through the power of verbal interpretation. Ultimately, because an analyst is as flawed and as short-tempered as anyone else, the patient begins to view the deity in a more realistic light and correspondingly sees himself and his own capacities more clearly.

The encouragement of mirroring and idealizing transferences sets Kohutians apart from classical theorists, particularly right-wing Freudians who regard the model as far too supportive and nurturant. Although some of Kohut's theoretical positions resemble Sullivan's (e.g., the emphasis on the self and on early one-on-one patterns of relationships), his definition of the analytic stance differs markedly from that of the Interpersonalists. The latter are far more likely to address themselves to (and sometimes to trample on) the weeds and flowers that are clearly visible in the garden, rather than the fragile shoots that are only beginning to emerge from the ground.

Jacques Lacan (1901–1981): Enfant Terrible

What do you do with the *Écrits* of Jacques Lacan when you've got three years of college French at best and a vocabulary maintained largely from reruns of *Breathless*? While Lacan's confrères nudge one another in the ribs and roll their eyes over such Gallic ticklers as his extended verbal play on *"Le Nom du Père"* (alternatively, God the Father, the father as definer of law, or modestly, Lacan himself as definer of psychoanalysis), its homophone, *"le non du père"* (the father's "No!" or the absent father) and its extension, *"les nonnes du père"* (Lacan's singularly devoted female disciples), you, *mon pauvre petit,* stand outside the charmed circles feeling alienated and perplexed.

Reading Lacan requires, along with your degree in the language, familiarity with Freud, Heidegger, Hegel, Sartre, the structural linguists, and the structural anthropologists. And that's just to *read* him. Understanding requires a good deal more. It is disheartening, however, after wading through his *Stade de Miroir*, ferreting out the true meaning of the Other (not at all what you'd suppose), and distinguishing full from empty speech, to learn from Stuart Schneiderman that since Lacan has emphasized the centrality of the spoken word in the analytic cure, his theories cannot be transmitted through the written one. *"The only way to learn the correct application of Lacan's theories to psychoanalysis is through supervision by a member of the Freudian School of Paris"* (italics his). So it looks like you'll also need an airplane ticket.

Basic to Lacan's theories is his insistence that the unconscious is structured like a language. What exactly Lacan means by this is rather obscure, and his intention is clearly (and this is the only clear thing about Lacan) to keep things that way. It takes a certain amount of chutzpah to take a hypothetical construct and authoritatively define its structure, but Lacan was never famous for diffidence. Any man who can begin the following sentence with the phrase "to put it in a nutshell" is not going to let you off easy:

> To put it in a nutshell, nowhere does it appear more clearly that man's desire finds its meaning in the desire of the other, not so much because the other holds the key to the object desired, as because the first object of desire is to be recognized by the other.

Through his style, Lacan explicates his thesis; that is, through enigmas within conundrums inside rebuses, he demonstrates the quirkiness of the unconscious. Or maybe not.

Lacan highlights the fact, that regardless of the metapsychology of the practitioner, "psychoanalysis has only a single intermediary: the patient's Word." He believes Freud's greatest contribution was an understanding of the way language is structured and a recognition that the unconscious can be reached through the process of free association. But for Lacan, the unconscious is the structure hidden behind the patient's discourse, since in the process of speaking he moves further away from himself. In the act of describing how you think or feel, you no longer experience what you are describing. The unconscious cannot, therefore, be revealed through conscious speech, but can be tapped into only through "gaps" in discourse: forgetting, misuse of words, slips of the tongue, puns, dreams, etc. Lacan returns to the Freud of *The Psychopathology of Everyday Life* and *The Interpretation of Dreams* for the bedrock of his theories.

More poetically, in the words of a follower:

> The unconscious is not the ground which has been prepared to give more sparkle and depth to the painted composition: it is the earlier sketch which has been covered over before the canvas is used for another picture. If we use a comparison of a musical order, the unconscious is not the counterpoint of a fugue or the harmonics of a melodic line: it is the jazz one hears despite oneself behind the Haydn quartet when the radio is badly tuned or not sufficiently selective. The unconscious is not the message, not even the strange or coded message one strives to read on an old parchment: *it is another text written underneath and which must be read by illuminating it from behind or with the help of a developer.*

But what has intrigued Americans about Lacan is not his theoretical formulations, which approach incomprehensibility, but his waiting room, which had something of the flavor of a dentist's. Also of Grand Central Station. Not for Lacan the ordered fifty-minute schedule of the modern psychoanalyst; his practice was of a whimsical character. He was known to throw a patient out after a few minutes of idle associations, to extend a session according to his fancy, or to keep a patient hanging around all day if this seemed appropriate. A depressed patient might be treated with the consulting room door open (so that the man might remain in contact with the other sufferers in the corridor) for ten-minute sessions at intervals spread out over the day until his despair lifted. Lacanians defend their erratic ways in terms of "logical punctuations," that is, sessions defined by the needs of any given analysand on any given day. It makes sense, but it's a hell of a way to run a railroad.

CRUMBS FROM THE MASTER'S TABLE: QUOTATIONS FROM THE WRITINGS OF SIGMUND FREUD

Analysis almost seems to be the third of those "impossible professions" in which one can be quite sure of unsatisfying results. The other two, much older-established, are the bringing-up of children and the government of nations.

Analysis Terminable and Interminable (1937)

I do not think our successes can compete with those of Lourdes. There are so many more people who believe in the miracles of the Blessed Virgin than in the existence of the unconscious.

New Introductory Lectures on Psychoanalysis (1932)

A culture which leaves unsatisfied and drives to rebelliousness so large a number of its members neither has a prospect of continued existence nor deserves it.

Future of an Illusion (1928)

We believe that civilization has been built up, *under the pressure of the struggle for existence*, by sacrifices in gratification of the primitive impulses.

Introductory Lectures on Psychoanalysis (1916–1917)

I then made some short observations upon the *the psychological differences between the conscious and the unconscious*, and upon the fact that everything conscious was subject to a process of wearing-away, while what was unconscious was relatively unchangeable; and I illustrated my remarks by pointing to the antiques standing about in my room. They were, in fact, I said, only objects found in a tomb, and their burial had been their preservation: the destruction of Pompeii was only beginning now that it had been dug up.

Notes Upon a Case of Obsessional Neurosis (1909)

In girls the motive for the demolition of the Oedipus complex is lacking. Castration has already had its effect, which was to force the child into the situation of the Oedipus complex. Thus the Oedipus complex escapes the fate which it meets with in boys: it may be slowly abandoned or dealt with by repression or its effects may persist far into women's normal mental life. I cannot evade the notion (though I hesitate to give it expression) that for women the level of what is ethically normal is different from what it is in men. Their superego is never so inexorable, so impersonal, so independent of its emotional origins as we require it to be in men. Character-traits which critics of every epoch have brought up against women—that they show less sense of justice than men, that they are more often influenced in their judgments by feelings of affection or hostility—all these would be amply accounted for by the modification in the formation of their superego which we have inferred above.

Some Psychical Consequences of the Anatomical Distinction Between the Sexes
(1925)

A man who has been the indisputable favorite of his mother keeps for life the feeling of a conqueror, that confidence of success that often induces real success.

Life and Works of Sigmund Freud, vol. 1, by Ernest Jones (1953)

One might compare the relation of the ego to the id with that between a rider and his horse. The horse provides the locomotor energy, and the rider has the prerogative of determining the goal and of guiding the movements of his powerful mount toward it. But all too often in the relations between the ego and the id we find a picture of the less ideal situation in which the rider is obliged to guide his horse in the direction in which it itself wants to go.

New Introductory Lectures on Psychoanalysis (1932)

Where id was, there shall ego be.

New Introductory Lectures on Psychoanalysis (1932)

A woman who is very anxious to get children always reads *storks* instead of *stocks*.

The Psychopathology of Everyday Life (1901)

Occasionally I have had to admit that the annoying, awkward stepping aside on the street, whereby for some seconds one steps here and there, yet always in the same direction as the other person, until finally both stop facing each other . . . conceals erotic purposes under the mask of awkwardness.

The Psychopathology of Everyday Life (1901)

When a member of my family complains that he or she has bitten his tongue, bruised her finger, and so on, instead of the expected sympathy I put the question, "Why did you do that?"

The Psychopathology of Everyday Life (1901)

FRUITS OF THE MASTER'S LABORS: FIVE FAMOUS FLIPPED-OUT CASES

ANNA O.: A compendium of hysterical symptoms from paralysis to hydrophobia, famous within the profession as a study in the pitfalls of countertransference, the thing that happens when your shrink starts reacting neurotically to *you*. Actually, Anna began as the patient not of Freud, but of his colleague Josef Breuer, who abruptly terminated treatment when his wife became jealous, suspecting that the twenty-one-year-old girl was experiencing more than just catharsis on the couch. Breuer was called to Anna's bedside that same night to find her thrashing about in the throes of false labor, convinced she was pregnant with his child. The next day, Frau Breuer whisked away her guilty, overinvested husband for some extended R & R in New York. Freud later picked up on the "cathartic method" Breuer had been using—more or less successfully—with Anna, and Anna herself went on to become Germany's first social worker (although no one is quite sure what that fact has to do with her treatment).

LITTLE HANS: A five-year-old who wouldn't go out of doors for fear a horse would bite him. The case is remarkable because Freud saw Little Hans only once, and treated the boy by proxy through his father. The trouble had started when Hans was three and a half and his mother tried to discourage him from masturbating by warning him—as mothers did in those days—that if he didn't keep his hands where they belonged she'd send for the doctor to "cut off your widdler and then what will you widdle with?" Little Hans, who was developing quite a fascination with widdlers in general, had not failed to notice that horses had great big widdlers and that his mother had none. Before you knew it, horses, Mommy, and the possibility of castration were all mixed up with his fears of competing with his father. Guided by Freud, Little Hans' father reassured the boy and was eventually able to help him overcome his phobia, thereby becoming, himself, simultaneously part of the problem and part of the solution. What's more, Little Hans grew up to be a musician, just like his dad.

DORA: One of Freud's most famous cases—and reads like a soap opera. Dora, a teenager in the "first blossom of youth," was sent by her father to Dr. Freud for treatment of various hysterical symptoms linked to a dastardly proposition made to her by a neighbor, Herr K., whose wife, it just so happened, was having an affair with Dora's father. To complicate matters further, Dora looked to Frau K. as a surrogate mother, since her own mother was too preoccupied with scrubbing and cleaning to pay attention to her family. Dora's father asked Freud to "bring Dora to reason," by which he meant keep her quiet. Dora, a spirited eighteen-year-old, listened to a lot of talk about her shameful sexual feelings and none whatsoever about the web of deceit she was caught in. After eleven weeks of analysis and two famous dreams, she quit treatment, seriously hurting Freud's feelings. Still, much later, he realized he'd learned two important lessons from the case, namely, that hysterics tended to reveal an awful lot through dreams and free association and that it paid to mistrust what he labeled the patient's "flight into health," a speedy but only temporary improvement in the early stages of analysis. Dora, on the other hand, got considerably less out of her treatment; she grew up to hate men.

THE RAT MAN: Not a sci-fi character, head of rat, body of man, but an army officer who became violently agitated when he heard a fellow officer describing an exotic form of punishment in which a pot of rats was overturned on a man's naked buttocks and left to gnaw their way through the anus. The officer immediately began to imagine this happening to either his father or the woman he loved, and soon he developed a complicated obsessional system to prevent it, despite the fact that his father had been dead for several years and his lady friend was safe at home darning socks. The dénouement of the case involved a lot of wrong turns by both patient and analyst and a good deal of linguistic play on the word "rat," but eventually Freud helped restore the man to health, in time for him to be killed a year later in World War I. Freud used the case to illustrate the mechanism of displacement (see page 432) and the sadistic anal eroticism that he believed underlay most cases of obsessional neurosis.

THE WOLF MAN: A rich young Russian in a state of complete helplessness who could make contact with reality only after he'd emptied the contents of his intestines with an enema. The case is famous because Freud concentrated on little but the child within the man and treated the "infantile neurosis," at the expense, some say, of the adult patient. The nickname derives from a childhood dream in which the patient opened his eyes to see six or seven white wolves with tails like foxes' sitting quite still on the branches of a large walnut tree outside his window. The deciphering of the dream involved catching Mommy and Daddy busily engaged in a primal scene (Freud's term for the sex act as witnessed by a child), with intercourse occurring doggie-style. Freud made considerable progress with the Wolf Man, but when the patient became too enamored of the analytic process, Freud fixed a date for termination: one year, no matter what. Resistance crumbled, analysis proceeded apace, and the Wolf Man went home to Russia, ostensibly cured. He returned to Freud after the revolution, destitute, homeless, and once again a fruitcake, thereby proving that reality counts for something, too.

Hello, Jung Lovers

No, we haven't forgotten you. And yes, you—and Carl Gustav—deserve more than an offhand paragraph or two in a Freudian's tribute to Freud (see page 434). Of course, we can't expect to make up here for decades of benign neglect, second-bananadom, and jokes about flying saucers. But we can arrange to quote your man a little bit, remind you of some of his favorite terms, and say a word or two about what he stood for.

He is, happily, almost as quotable as Freud, although you can't always be sure, when you summon him up, whether it's a lecture hall or a hot tub you'll find yourself sitting in. The lecture-hall Jung sounds something like this:

> The more the critical reason dominates, the more impoverished life becomes; but the more of the unconscious and the more of myth we are capable of making conscious, the more of life we integrate. Overvalued reason has this in common with political absolutism: under its dominion the individual is pauperized.

The hot-tub Jung sounds more like this:

> Somewhere there was once a Flower, a Stone, a Crystal, a Queen, a King, a Palace, a Lover and his Beloved, and this was long ago, on an Island somewhere in the Ocean 5,000 years ago. . . . Such is Love, the Mystic Flower of the Soul. This is the Center, the Self.

Among the terms Jung came up with: "collective unconscious" (the deep, species-wide layer of the psyche underlying the personal unconscious) and "archetypes" (the mythic images and motifs that go to make up the collective unconscious); the "complex" (a group of interrelated, and emotionally charged, ideas or images); "individuation" (not so very different from our self-actualization, and a process that involves coming to terms with the thinking/feeling and intuition/sensation axes that together determine the four psychological "types"); the pairs "extrovert/introvert" and "anima/animus" (the latter pair alluding to the woman-inside-every-man and the man-inside-every-woman); the "active imagination" (by dint of which one writes or paints one's unconscious fantasies, and a staple of Jungian analysis); "synchronicity" (a meaningful coincidence of two casually unrelated events); and the "Self" (the very center of one's being).

If Jung sometimes gets a little trippy, well, that's one of his endearing qualities. To Freud's tight-ass reductionist, always looking for a scientific reason for everything, always talking about repression, always rooting about in the muck of the past, Jung is loose-limbed and open-minded, an expansionist. He's committed to the spirit, to exploring art, religion, philosophy, and borderline phenomena from alchemy to ESP. He believes in the future (even at those moments that he isn't feeling so optimistic about it). And when it does strike him as right to stop and think about what's gone before, he's more interested in construing it as rich mythology than as stifling autobiography.

Getting Straight

A CORNUCOPIA OF CURES, CRAZES, AND QUICK FIXES

Of all the established academic disciplines—the one for which the chapters of this book are named—psychology has made the rockiest transition into the twenty-first century. For this, there are any number of possible explanations. Let's begin with the dawning of the New Age, in which crystals and runes and the state of one's *chakras* began to count for more than memories (or the repression thereof) and the preoccupation with mind-body connections made any party to which the former was invited without the latter seem not only discriminatory but likely to bomb.

Intramurally, too, things got ugly. It didn't help that Freud changed his mind about childhood sexual abuse, first believing it was real, then deciding it was just one more unfulfilled fantasy kids have—a conclusion that wasn't good for sales in a country where, increasingly, everybody seemed determined to cling to his or her victimhood, on *Oprah* as in the shower. And, coming after at least a decade's worth of unflattering media stories in which analysts and therapists were portrayed as pompous, self-righteous, or downright predatory, the endless Janet Malcolm/Jeffrey Masson mud-slinging contest hardly made shrinks (or biographers, for that matter) seem like fit companions for people with life problems.

Perhaps most important, though, was the widespread realization that popping a pill could make you feel better, and more reliably, than several months' (not to mention years') worth of couch-time. The pill cost less, too, and you *certainly* didn't have to pay if you missed a day.

Finally, given that most of us weren't the hysterics, phobics, or compulsive hand-washers that classical analysis had had its biggest successes in treating, but *were* narcissists, who didn't respond very well to it anyway, why not opt instead for a personal trainer, who could pretty much guarantee us firmer thighs and tighter butts?

Nevertheless, psychology was such a big deal in this country for such a long time that it still behooves us to pay our respects. Here, contributor **Helen Epstein** takes a perfectly unjaundiced look at a venerable, if currently somewhat bankrupt, roster of psychological therapies.

You may already know that psychiatrists are licensed physicians who charge as much as $200 for as few as forty-five minutes of their time; that clinical psychologists hold doctorates in psychology but are not M.D.'s; that mental-health social workers hold neither degree and often may not be covered by your health insurance; and that there are thousands of lay therapists in business with no certification whatsoever.

Of course, none of this really helps explain *why* Americans became so obsessed with psychotherapy in the first place. What's the matter with families and friends? Why must we pay strangers to pay attention to us? Are we certifiably crazier than citizens of other nations?

Perhaps it's because the United States is a free country, and a little freedom can be dangerous to mental health. Are the French, after all, routinely called upon to choose among dozens of flavors of ice cream? Are the Japanese constitutionally bound to the pursuit of happiness? Must either consider a panoply of alternatives—graduate school, hang-gliding, etc.—to the allegedly inevitable process of growing up?

Ironically, psychotherapy is a European invention. The word derives from the Greek, means "treatment of the soul," and first achieved prominence in turn-of-the-century Vienna (see page 434). Before World War II, therapy had been deemed appropriate mostly for the bona-fide crazies. But the Sixties underlined the inadequacy of such an absolutist point of view: It was increasingly difficult to determine who was sane for one thing, and, for another, there was a new market for "awareness," "authenticity," and "self-realization." Psychotherapists obligingly opened their doors and created new styles, indeed new schools. Today, as a result, over three hundred types of therapy are available in the United States.

The oldest is *psychoanalysis*, the "talking cure" discovered by Josef Breuer and developed by Sigmund Freud for middle-class Viennese ladies suffering from hysteria (page 429). Whether or not you will be able to transform "hysterical misery into common unhappiness" (as Freud put it) can't be predicted. There are few, and inconclusive, studies of success rates in analysis, although first-person accounts, often disguised as novels, abound. At four times per week and $75 a (bargain) session for eleven (current average) years, the cost comes to $154,000, but with inflation, health insurance, and tax deductions that's not so bad—considering how well you get to know yourself.

Psychoanalytically oriented psychotherapy is psychoanalysis adapted for people who can't take the time and/or won't lie down. In POP, your therapist may shed the "Dr." an analyst insists on in favor of "Don" or "Sue," and may even call you by your given name. Your sessions may occasionally run over fifty minutes; you may not have to pay for sessions you miss; and because sessions are scheduled only one or twice a week, you may ask to have them changed around if you win the lottery and decide to go to Bali.

Instead of allowing you to ramble on uninterrupted (or fall into stony silence) about your emotionally distant mother, the therapist will interrupt you and talk about what you have/haven't said. POPers have all studied Freud but many draw on the work of such defectors from the Master as Alfred Adler (see page 437), Harry Stack Sullivan (page 440), Karen Horney, Wilhelm Reich (page 45), or Carl Jung (page 452), who either disagreed with Freud or abandoned him altogether. Like analysts, POPers decorate their offices with Persian carpets, off-white furniture, and innocuous art. Like analysts, they will be interested in hearing you explore that limitless well of material—your childhood—as well as occasional items from your daily life and the newspapers (an assassination maybe, or a particularly evocative war) *if* it has personal associations and you don't begin to intellectualize as a defense against getting to your true feelings (see page 432). POPers are in general more likely than analysts to tell you exactly what tricks you are using to avoid taking responsibility, such tricks as denying your feelings, resisting your therapist, acting out old patterns, and projecting your state of mind onto the bus driver. In therapy, you "work it through."

Nor does it have to take eleven years to work it through. Lately there has been a strong push toward *short-term dynamic therapy*, which sets firm deadlines and specific goals in an effort to spur the patient's will to be well. With the patient anxious about, say, his upcoming wedding, the STDT therapist will typically not only interrupt and guide, he'll also raise questions calculated to provoke anxiety, e.g., "Is it possible that your mother is jealous of your fiancée? Are you afraid that your father is secretly furious about your wedding?" Thus encouraged to confront his true feelings, simultaneously relating them to past events and working to

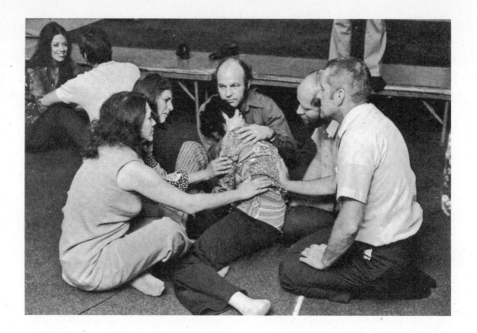

solve the problem at hand, a patient can, while still following Freud, "get it all out" in something like eight or nine sessions, usually in the out-patient clinic of a large hospital or university health service.

Latest wrinkle: *brief therapy*, in which "clients" (not analysands or even patients) achieve "consumer satisfaction" (not a cure) in as few as one or two sessions, and usually no more than ten. "Brief" therapists tend to concentrate on lesser ills—mild depression, work stress, grief—and take a here-and-now approach to problems that pretty much ignores causation and childhood in favor of relief and the future, pointing out that memory is not necessarily accurate, let alone therapeutic, and that solving a problem has a higher priority than ferreting out the root of it. A session probably won't cost you more than $100, and is often considerably cheaper.

If at this point it's sounding as if we all think too much, consider *Gestalt*, which is German for "configuration" and which aims to get around what you say to how you feel. Developed by Fritz Perls, of Esalen Institute fame (yet another apostle gone astray) during the 1940s, Gestalt dismisses Freud's concern with the There and Then in favor of the Here and Now. It throws what we lay people call thinking, dreaming, assuming, guessing, and wishing into one category called Fantasy and disparages it. Instead, the patient (usually called "client" in these precincts) is urged to discover his five senses, the key to Perceptual Reality.

According to Gestalt, simple awareness of one's moment-to-moment sensations is therapeutic. A session involves tuning out the "background" of life and focusing on the distinct "figure" or problem that's bothering you Right Now. One step beyond the POPer, the Gestalt therapist will find out your nickname, will touch as well as talk to you, and may invite you out for coffee later. You will not be allowed to sit back and retell your favorite stories of trial or abandonment. Rather, you will be interrupted after every few words with a question like: "Why are you smiling as you describe your father's funeral?"

When you try to answer, you'll likely be interrupted again by a warning to stay in the Here and Now. Gestalters don't want you to mess things up by using your brain. Instead they provide props on which to act out your feelings. These may include stuffed animals, pillows, and empty chairs to serve as substitutes for other people, other situations, or your other selves. These objects can be stroked, scratched, or pummeled without fear of retaliation. And while you are punching out the ex-lover you have imaginatively placed in the empty chair, your therapist is giving you lots of feedback on what all three of you, him included, are feeling.

Gestalt may be experienced one-on-one or in a group, one or more times a week. Like psychoanalysis and POP, its goal is to make the patient stop repeating "sick" patterns of behavior, get rid of emotional "garbage," and "take responsibility" for his life. Additionally, Gestalt aims to facilitate "fuller living," with regard to which the therapist serves not only as guide but as model. Consequently, a Gestalt shrink can be expected to be warm, open, caring, sensually on the ball, and persuaded of everyone's inherent ability to "grow and change." You may forget such basic skills as where to cross the street and how to eat lobster, but with luck you'll learn to be completely Here Now.

Feeling tense with confusion (or disapproval), sweating, or suffering stomach aches? Then maybe *bioenergetics* and/or *biofeedback* is for you. These therapies focus neither on the Where and When or the Here and Now, but on manipulating physiology to change emotional patterns.

Bioenergetics owes its beginnings to Wilhelm Reich, another Freud dropout, who had begun to work on "character armor" and the "energy economy of the body" in the 1940s. The goal of bioenergetics (as well as of such Reich-influenced therapies as Rolfing and the Alexander technique) is to relax this armor, deepen the patient's breathing, and release his "life force"; the latter entails getting in as many orgasms as possible. Sessions take place once or twice a week, often involving special dress and/or undress as well as intensive patient-therapist interaction. The patient performs special exercises; the therapist questions, comments, and makes physical adjustments designed to "break through" and "unblock" energy. The exercise might be pounding a mattress with a tennis racket (to unleash feelings of rage) or draping

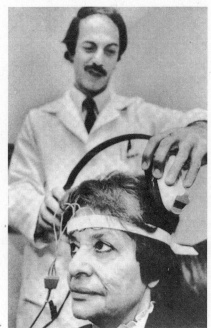

oneself (stomach up) over a padded stool and panting (to get in touch with suppressed pelvic cravings). Patients are required to sing, sigh, hum, laugh, cry, shout, or hiccup in order to specify the kind of energy they are releasing at the moment. They may also talk.

In biofeedback, they often do not talk at all. Once the therapist and patient have discussed the offending physiological problem (breaking out in hives when faced with a date, heading for the washroom when asked a direct question), the patient is hooked up to monitoring machines which translate agitation into quantifiable—and visual—terms. If the patient is suddenly forced to think of unpleasant things, the dial swings to the right; as the patient employs biofeedback relaxation techniques, the dial returns to the safe, low readings. The patient is told to ignore the details of the anxiety-provoking situation and simply work on getting the salient physiological process (blood-vessel, sweat-gland, or stomach-acid activity) back to normal. Whereas bioenergetics teaches the "release" of tension, biofeedback teaches its "control." Usually practiced once a week, it has the distinction of being among the shortest-term therapies (six months on the average). With no audience, there is little incentive for the patient to procrastinate, and while it is not recommended for anybody trying to decide among ice-cream flavors or career choices, it is said to do wonders for migraines.

B. F. Skinner

Behavior therapy is the only major form of psychotherapy in the United States to have developed independently of the Viennese analysts. It draws partly on the work of Ivan Pavlov, whose experiments with dogs and drooling might ring a bell, partly on the work of B. F. Skinner, who examined the cause-and-effect relationship between environment and behavior. Starting from the proposition that all behavior is learned, behaviorists believe that they can fix anything that's wrong with you, provided you follow a special regimen. Such a therapist doesn't care what you call each other. He also has little or no use for "transference" or "energy" or, as far as that goes, any explanation you might offer for your difficulties. According to a behaviorist, neurotic symptoms—especially phobias, obsessions, compulsions, and a wide range of sexual problems—are simply learned bad habits. His job, he believes, is to help you unlearn them and to replace them with new, more productive patterns. And he wants immediate results.

You have trouble riding elevators or airplanes? Crossing bridges? Cracks in the sidewalk? No problem: First they'll "desensitize" you, then reeducate you. Want to stop choosing psychopaths for friends? Lose weight?

Start jogging? The behaviorists have a system, a set of homework assignments, clearly defined "goals," and all the assurance in the world that you can do it.

Behavior therapy has an infinite variety of applications. In sex therapy, partners learn how to express, and reinforce, what each finds pleasurable; in assertiveness training, you may be taught to walk into a coffee shop and ask for a glass of water without ordering so much as a corn muffin. You will be expected to do reading, keep a journal of your homework assignments and their consequences, and, most of all, behave the way the therapist and you have decided you should. How you feel at the moment doesn't matter; whether you've succeeded in changing the way you act does. But, because of the way feelings and behavior tend to dovetail, you're expected to start feeling better, too.

A variant of behavior therapy is *cognitive therapy*, although what it sets out to modify isn't so much behavior as thought and attitude. A relatively short-term (six weeks to three months) treatment developed by Aaron Beck of the University of Pennsylvania, it's based on the premise that a person's thought processes (and the linguistic structures that underlie them) go a long way in determining psychological disturbances. In Beck's view, a depressed person, for instance, through a process of distortion and exaggeration, has misinterpreted reality. The resulting thoughts (e.g., that he has nothing to offer anybody, that he's the lowest of the low) have become automatic and entrenched. Solution: Make the person aware of the automatic—and ultimately the invalid—nature of his "cognitions."

Doubtless you're longing to retreat to a discussion of some less messy subject, such as Art or maybe the Politics of Philosophy. Fine, but don't think that means there's no such thing as *family therapy*, in which whole families allow their actions to be scrutinized, sometimes videotaped and then rearranged. Or *art, music, dance, video,* and *biblio therapies,* in which painting, singing, dancing, watching TV, and reading books, respectively, serve as the catalysts for the releasing of emotion.

Probably, too, you'll want to skip such retro fashions as *transactional analysis,* which involves figuring out what kinds of "scripts" you might be "buying into," and *primal scream therapy,* in which large numbers of screamers congregate on mattresses and throw themselves against padded walls. Instead, focus on the American tradition of self-betterment, the problem of moving into a postindustrial world, and the pragmatic idealism that has in the past produced better can openers, taller basketball players, and more amendments to the Constitution. And, during working hours, anyway, do your best to keep the lid on.

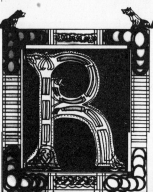ELIGION

Contents

Frontispiece Book I of Milton's Paradise Lost *(see page 190), 4th edition, 1688*

Those Old-Time Religions

DIVINE TO SOME, MERELY FABULOUS TO OTHERS

Have you ever noticed how prophetic revelation seems to give some people a new lease on life at about the same time others their age are gearing up for midlife crisis? Buddha, Jesus, and Zoroaster all got the Message when they were hovering around thirty, a birthday that signals middle age in any culture where people start begetting as teenagers. True, Muhammad was forty when he first chatted with the Angel Gabriel, but then Islam as a whole was a late bloomer. So to those of you who find, after scanning the great faiths outlined here, that the monotheisms of the West and the polytheisms of the East all leave you cold; that you can't really get behind karma, nirvana, yin and yang, the Holy Trinity, or separate dishware for meat and dairy; and that you're as depressed and alienated as ever, our advice is: Stay loose and keep your eyes fixed on the heavens.

JUDAISM

14 million believers, mostly in Israel and the United States.

It's c. 1700 B.C.E. (Before the Common Era, a designation considerably less irritating to Jews than the Christian B.C., Before Christ). Heaven is crowded with divinities of the moon, sun, stars, trees, and irrigation, as well as with various celestial dog-and-pony acts. Enter, below, a Sumerian named Abraham, who insists that there's only one God and all the rest are wannabes. Acting on direct orders from this God, whose name is Yahweh (but for pete's sake, don't say it out loud), Abraham has packed up his kin and his kitchen utensils and relocated to the Promised Land, on the other side of the Euphrates, thereby earning his entourage the name "Hebrews" (from an ancient word meaning "the other side") and establishing an exhausting pattern of Jewish migration that will repeat itself for the next four thousand years. Pleased with Abraham's obedience and general salt-of-the-earth comportment, Yahweh promises him offspring galore (Abraham is ninety-nine at the time), along with rights to the Promised Land—a place called Canaan, later renamed Palestine, after the Philistines, who occupied part of it—in perpetuity. The agreement is oral but binding; it simultaneously marks the debut of monotheism in the world and sows the seeds of future unrest in the Middle East.

But all that's family history. Judaism as a more or less coherent religion didn't really get rolling until Moses led a group of transplanted Hebrews out of slavery in Egypt and trekked with them back to the Promised Land. Moses took his orders directly from Yahweh, who was quite clear about what He expected from His Chosen People, issuing directives on everything from ethical conduct ("Thou shalt not kill," "Thou shalt not covet thy neighbor's wife," etc.) to diet ("Hold the bacon"). The shalts and shalt nots were recorded, along with much divinely revealed history, in the Torah, later compiled and edited into the first five books of the Bible.

If this is beginning to seem like an awfully long story (and we're only up to about 1300 B.C.E.), so much the better. In the absence of a homeland, a strong national identity, or even passably tolerant neighbors, history is about all the Jews had to rely on to keep their traditions alive through the next several millennia of persecution, exile, and general *tsuris*. History, that is, and the law, as embodied in the Torah and buttressed by the scholarly commentaries on same, were later collected in the Mishnah and the Talmud, Judaism's next-most-important books.

Because Jewish law and tradition evolved as a kind of survivor's guide to life on a hostile planet, Judaism is somewhat more practical and here-and-now oriented than many other religions. (The childhood trauma that might explain Judaism's you-only-live-once mentality: the Diaspora, which originally referred to the destruction of the Temple of Jerusalem in 586 B.C.E. and the subsequent exile of the Jews to Babylonia, known as the first Babylonian Captivity, later to the chronic dispersion of the Jews across the face of the earth.) Jews don't believe in the doctrine of original sin, for instance, or in a devil powerful enough to instigate anything worse than a parking violation, and they spend considerably less time fantasizing about a blissful afterlife than planning for a comfortable retirement in Florida. It's true that ethical conduct—especially helping anyone worse off than one is—is an almost obsessively big deal in Judaism (it's no accident that so many liberal Democrats, social workers, and shrinks are Jewish), but morality isn't hitched to a system of rewards and punishments, the way it is in Christianity. A Jew is required to do the right thing, just because. "The right thing," by the way, can be loosely defined as any action that would put a smile on God's face if He should happen to be looking. (And if He had a face; Judaism posits a God who can't be adequately pictured or conceptualized. In this, Jews are a little like physicists.) Such obligatory good deeds are called *mitzvahs* and can range from faithfully lighting the Sabbath candles every Friday night to saving a life or picking up after your dog.

Other key terms: Orthodox, Conservative, Reform, and Reconstructionist, the four branches of modern American Judaism, which differ mainly in the degree to which they adhere to tradition—Orthodox, 100 percent, no excuses; the other three, anywhere from about 75 percent down to about 10 percent, depending on the congregation, the individual, and/or the zeitgeist—although occasionally they'll agree to disagree about a core belief, such as whether God is a personal entity or, as many Reconstructionists insist, a natural force, like gravity. Then there's Zionism, the political movement born in reaction to European anti-Semitism in the nineteenth century (and in particular, to the Dreyfus Affair; see page 626), that aimed at making good Yahweh's original offer of a Jewish homeland in Israel; and Kabbalah, Judaism's complex mystical tradition, based on esoteric reinterpretations of Scripture and currently enjoying a vogue among Hollywood celebrities. Holocaust you already know.

CHRISTIANITY

1.5 billion followers: 1 billion Roman Catholic; 170 million Eastern Orthodox; 370 million Protestant. Dominant in Western Europe and the Americas.

The first Christians weren't Christians at all, of course, but Palestinian Jews who, smitten with Jesus of Nazareth's notions about universal love, the brotherhood of man, and redemption through faith, saw nothing particularly disloyal or disruptive in regarding themselves as Jews for Jesus. It wasn't until Jesus' followers began recruiting non-Jewish converts, who insisted that circumcision was weird and Christ divine, that Christians and Jews started giving each other dirty looks across the bazaar.

Although it's never easy to launch a new world religion, the early Christians had a particularly tough time of it, beset, as they were, by a lot of internal bickering over who, exactly, Jesus was, and by any number of competitive pagan religions bent on co-opting the Savior for their own nefarious purposes—notably the Gnostics, with their salvation-through-revelation occultism and their predisposition to see Good and Evil in very black-and-white terms. In fact, most early Christian doctrine was formulated as a defense against total incoherence; hence its tendency toward dogmatism and the Christian establishment's later habit of excommunicating anyone who didn't toe the party line. There was also the problem of the ruling Romans, who, not in the least obsessed with distinguishing true Christians from false ones, simply declared open season on all of them.

It wasn't until the fourth century, when the Emperor Constantine himself converted to Christianity, that Christians were transformed from persecuted underdogs into imperial pets. After the construction of Constantinople as Christian capital and arts center, a new yuppie constituency began replacing the original slave, peasant, and humble-laborer devotees. In A.D. 325, the church was rich enough to host its first ecumenical council, out of which came the Nicene Creed, which affirmed, mainly, belief in the Holy Trinity and which is still the basic statement of faith for most Christians. By the end of the century, Christians had put together a testament of their own, comprising the four Gospels, the Acts of the Apostles, twenty-one epistles, and the Revelation of St. John the Divine. (They'd already appropriated the entire Hebrew Scriptures, which they renamed the Old Testament, plus the Apocrypha, a collection of writings retrieved from the cutting-room floor, whose authorship was more than ordinarily dubious and which were later rejected as uncanonical by Protestants.)

Success didn't eliminate dissent within the ranks, however. In 1054, after a few centuries of squabbling over such issues as whether or not art was OK (remember the biblical injunction against graven images), the Pope of Rome excommunicated the Patriarch of Constantinople, and the Church was henceforth split into Roman Catholic and Eastern Orthodox divisions. Today, the two Churches differ mainly in decor (the Eastern Orthodox Church got the Byzantine domes and the elaborate mosaics; the Roman Catholics got the Gothic cathedrals and the Renaissance art collection), style (the Eastern Church still goes in for interminable masses, showstopper rituals, and the burning of extravagant amounts of incense), language (Greek and local vernacular in the East; Latin, and lately, local vernacular in the West), their attitudes toward the Immaculate Conception (not bloody likely, according to the EOC), and, of course, the infallibility of the pope.

More fussing and fighting in the West led, in the fourteenth century, to the Great Schism, during which two rival popes ruled simultaneously, one from Rome, one from Avignon; and in the fifteenth century to the Reformation, when Luther, Calvin, Zwingli, et al., fed up with Church corruption, split Western Europe into Catholic and Protestant factions.

Today, Protestant sects (there are about 250 of them) dominate much of northern Europe and the old British Empire, and maintain a slight edge over Catholicism in the United States, while the Catholic Church has pretty much cornered the market in France, Italy, Spain, and Latin America. The modern ecumenical movement hopes, someday, to put all the pieces of the Church back together again. In the meantime, the combined Catholic-Protestant head count still matters, since Christianity, as anyone who has ever opened the door to a Seventh-Day Adventist knows, is one of the great missionary religions of the modern world.

ISLAM

More than 1 billion believers (and growing fast), only about a fifth of whom are Arab. Indonesia is the world's largest Islamic country. Islam is also the dominant religion in Turkey, Iran, Pakistan, and Afghanistan, in addition to the Arab world.

Oops. Did we say it's never easy to launch a new world religion? We overlooked Islam (you can bet it won't happen again), the youngest of the monotheistic megafaiths. In A.D. 622, its official birth year, Islam was little more than a gleam in the prophet Muhammad's eye; less than two hundred years later, it was the power behind an empire that stretched from Spain to India. Of course, Muhammad didn't really start from scratch; as a Bedouin trader (and a direct descendant of the prophet Ishmael, the first son of the prophet Abraham) living on the outskirts of Mecca, he'd already picked up a lot of gossip about Judaism and Christianity by the time he began having divine revelations of his own. As a result, Islam bears an uncanny likeness to its two predecessors, though with variations that, from the beginning, made it highly appealing to the common man (and we do mean *man*) as well as to certain fierce desert tribes prepared to appreciate Muhammad's policy of winning through decapitation.

One of the main attractions of Islam (Arabic for "submission to the will of God") is its practicality. Your average Muslim (Arabic for "one who submits") can get to Heaven not by striving for some quasi-mystical and pretty much unattainable state of grace but simply by honoring the Five Pillars of Islam. First and most important of these is the affirmation of faith, in the words "There is no God but Allah and Muhammad is His prophet." Say this with real feeling just once in your life and no one can accuse you of not being a true Muslim (although only you and Allah will know for sure). Two: Pray five times a day, turning toward Mecca (no need to check your watch; just listen for the call of the *muezzin* and hit the ground when everyone else does). Three: Fast from sunup to sundown throughout the entire month of Ramadan (and, if you're a well-to-do twenty-first-century Muslim, binge-eat into the wee hours). Four: Make the *hajj*, the pilgrimage to Mecca, at least once if you can afford it (luckily, you no longer have to travel on foot or by camel; flights leave daily from most major cities). Five: Give alms, unless you're so poor you have to beg them. And if you want to earn bonus points to ensure a smooth entry into Heaven, simply contrive to die while fighting a holy war.

In case you get confused, you can look up the essentials in the Koran, the one and only sacred text of Islam, which contains the words of Allah as revealed to Muhammad. You may find the going a bit tricky, however, since Muhammad wrote in a rhythmic Arabic that's completely untranslatable. Join the club; three-quarters of the Muslim world is now composed of non-Arabs, and none of them can read their own Scriptures, either. Anyway, most of the Koran is devoted to retelling the stories of the Old and New Testaments from the Muslim—that is, the correct and uncorrupted—point of view. (For instance, the five great early prophets were really Adam, Noah, Abraham—the first Muslim—Moses, and Jesus. Alexander the Great was a prophet, too, and Muhammad was the last to carry Allah's divine word to man; and that's Allah, by the way, not Yahweh, which must have been some sort of typo.) The Koran won't give you much detail about ethical behavior or daily ritual; for that, you'll have to turn to the Hadith, the collected sayings of Muhammad, which, almost everyone acknowledges, are probably not authentic.

The Muslim world (and remember, that's not synonymous with the Arab world) is meant to be a theocracy, and it's in the who's-running-the-show department that Islam splits into its two major sects, Sunni and Shi'a. Sunnis, who make up about 85–90 percent of all Muslims, believe that Muhammad's old friend Abu Bakr, who was elected the first caliph after the Prophet's death, was the latter's legitimate successor. The minority Shi'ites insist that the Prophet chose his nephew and son-in-law Ali to succeed him; they trace the line of succession through Ali and Fatima, Muhammad's daughter. They believe in rule by twelve imams or perfect leaders, under whom the ayatollahs compose a sort of middle-management cadre. Over the years, politics widened the rift between the two camps, which tend to regard each other as heretics, although they agree on most of the religious fundamentals.

From its inception, Islam has had great success in winning converts in hot, arid, impoverished countries where the locals are susceptible to a lot of shouting and sword-brandishing, and to the promise of a Heaven that, unlike home, consists of green meadows and babbling brooks. Another bonus: Traditional Islam is basically egalitarian and flexible; follow the simple rules and nobody is going to torture you for heresy or shun you because of the color of your skin. Feminists, pacifists, and drunk drivers, however, need not apply.

ZOROASTRIANISM

150,000 believers, mostly Parsis living in India.

You pretty much had to be there—Persia, in the sixth century B.C., that is—to get the full flavor of Zoroastrianism as Zoroaster conceived it. (Actually, as he conceived it, it was called Zarathustrianism; Zoroastrianism is the Greek translation.) By the time it became the state religion of Persia, in A.D. 226, Zoroaster's own mother wouldn't have recognized it. But use your imagination. Picture yourself trying to settle down and run a peaceful little ancient farm while surrounded by a zillion nature gods perpetually vying for your attention. You could spend half the day sacrificing to gods of twigs and pebbles and the like just to get in a decent harvest, and you still wouldn't have a clue as to how to behave nicely or raise your kids. Zoroaster eliminated a lot of the time-wasting twig worship while adding a relatively coherent moral dimension to daily life. It's true that Zoroastrianism, in its earliest form, was mainly concerned with increasing the harvest and ensuring the happiness and well-being of various farm animals; nevertheless, it was as subtle and sophisticated an ethical system as anything you'll find in . . . well, wherever you look for ethical systems nowadays.

Zoroaster trimmed the pantheon of Persian gods to two warring ones: Ahura Mazdah, a.k.a. Ormuzd, the Creator and God of Goodness and Light; and Ahriman, God of Evil and Darkness. Ahura Mazdah is attended by six lesser deities, or archangels, or *ahuras*, or abstract qualities, take your pick, who translate roughly into Good Thought, Highest Righteousness, Divine Kingdom, Pious Devotion, Salvation, and Immortality. Ahriman, naturally, has his own entourage of evil spirits, called *divs* or *daevas*. Human beings, by their thoughts and actions, can side with Goodness, Light, and Life or with Evil, Darkness, and Death, and, by doing so, participate in the ultimate destiny of the Universe. Up to a point. The catch—and what makes Zoroastrianism different from the purely dualistic religions that were all the rage in ancient times—is that eventually, Ahura Mazdah is going to win. This makes for a nice, if somewhat complicated, marriage of free will and determinism—and, eventually, for a kind of happy ending.

Daily life for a Zoroastrian was nevertheless a very risky business, with evil spirits lurking everywhere. Near-constant ritual purification was necessary to ward off the forces of corruption, darkness, and death. At the same time, Ahura Mazdah's elements, fire, water, and earth—all of which are reverenced but not, as any modern Zoroastrian would be quick to tell you, worshipped—had to be particularly well protected from contamination; hence the spooky "Towers of Silence" on which Zoroastrians placed their dead so as not to defile the earth. But physical corruption and defilement were also linked to evil mental states, thought being a very powerful force in the Zoroastrian cosmos. At some point, as you can see, it all becomes a bit much for the techno-happy Western mind to grasp. (Although you can bone up on the purification rituals, along with a lot of songs, hymns, and liturgies, in the Zoroastrian scriptures, the *Zend Avesta*, it's so fragmentary, so corrupted, and so old that you still won't know your forces of Light from your forces of Darkness, much less be able to tell who's winning.) The Eastern mind, on the other hand, seems to do very nicely with it. When Persian Zoroastrianism was wiped out by Moslem hordes in the eighth century, a small group of Zoroastrians escaped to India, where incessant ritual purification is never a bad idea. Now known as Parsis and concentrated in and around Bombay, they've become one of the wealthiest, best-educated, and most-respected minority groups in a society that doesn't normally reward strangeness *or* strangers.

HINDUISM

More than 700 million believers, mostly in India.

Very old: predates all other world religions, except Judaism, by centuries at least. Also, very disorganized: has 330 million gods, more than enough for every family to have its own; a couple of dozen sects; a clutch of holy books; plenty of rituals, ceremonies, and spiritual disciplines; and neither a historical founder nor any consensus as to what, exactly, religious practice consists of. In a sense, Hinduism seems easy—tolerant, inclusive, undemanding, with an embarrassment of color, pageantry, and paths to Brahman, the Infinite Being (and ultimate reality) you eventually want to be at one with. Easy, that is, assuming you're not infelicitously placed within the caste system and stuck being a servant or a peasant; or infelicitously placed without it and stuck being an untouchable—or a pig or a mosquito.

The paradox here: You have plenty of time (in fact, as many lifetimes as you need) and plenty of ways to work out the release of your soul from the world and the ultimate rendezvous with Brahman. But there's a real chutes-and-ladders feeling to the game plan and, rather than getting to simply shake the dice, you're always being judged on how nicely you behaved on your last turn. In other words, your karma—literally, "action"; figuratively, a kind of cosmic system of cause-and-effect—determines your rise (and fall) in caste, through life after life, incarnation after incarnation until you finally get to the top of the board and the end of the game.

Along the way, be prepared to deal with the most prominent of the gods (each of whom, incidentally, is a manifestation of Braham, and many of whom have subsidiary manifestations of their own): Shiva the Destroyer, a.k.a. the Cosmic Dancer; Vishnu the Preserver, a.k.a. Krishna, a.k.a. Buddha; and Shakti the Divine Mother. And with a couple of important sets of books: the *Vedas*, those ancient scriptures, written in Sanskrit, that lay the groundwork for Hinduism and culminate in the *Upanishads* or "secret doctrine"; and the *Mahabharata*, the longest poem in the world, containing India's favorite religious text, the *Bhagavad Gita*, a dialogue between the god Krishna and a soldier named Arjuna. And with any and all animals, especially cows, bulls, monkeys, and snakes (each of which you'll be nice to, since it, like you, is probably on its way up or down). Of course you'll visit Benares and bathe in the Ganges. And you may go Tantric, embracing that branch of yoga (from a Sanskrit word meaning "to join" and related to our word "yoke") that seeks enlightenment through, among other procedures, a style of sensual lovemaking in which "each is both." Needless to say, you'll also be on the lookout for gurus, mantras, mandalas (the former chanted, the latter painted), and sutras (treatises on various aspects of the *Vedas*, the Kama Sutra section of which may remind you of Tantric yoga classes).

Not that Hinduism is all easy-listening. You'll also be expected, en route to Brahman, to give some thought to *maya* (originally, "might"), the illusion that the shapes and structures, the things and events we perceive with our senses in some way stand for reality—otherwise known as confusing the map with the territory. Problem is, as long as we're under the spell of *maya* and think we're separate from our environment, we're going to be bound—and pushed around—by karma, and once again find ourselves being issued an end-of-lifetime report card. At which point, according to Hinduism (and for that matter, Buddhism, warming up in the bullpen), the whole business begins again.

BUDDHISM

310 million believers, mostly in Southeast Asia, China, Korea, and Japan.

Take Hinduism. Subtract the caste system, downplay the gods, the ritual, and the Play-Doh colors, and substitute Nirvana for Brahman. Now add the Four Noble Truths, the Noble Eightfold Path, the Three Baskets, and the Great Wheel, and transport the whole business from India to points south (Sri Lanka), east (Burma, Thailand, and Indochina), and north (Nepal, Tibet, China, Mongolia, Korea, and Japan). Refuse to take any questions on the origin of the world or the nature of the divine and insist that everybody in the group work, quietly on his own, toward feeling better about himself through a program of pity, joy, kindliness, and meditation.

It's not that Buddhism is abstemious, exactly (the robes *are* saffron, after all, and representations of the Buddha can be several stories high and made of gold), just that there's a pared-down quality to it and that it comes down hard in all the places where Hinduism is free-form and assimilative. In part this is because Buddhism had a single founder (and hence an indisputable source and role model), Siddhartha Gautama, the so called "historic" Buddha, son of a sixth-century B.C. Indian prince, who proceeded to renounce worldliness in favor of enlightenment, of the middle way (between extremes of self-indulgence and self-denial), and, eventually, of Nirvana itself—a word that means, literally, a "going out," as of a candle when there's no more wick to burn, and, figuratively, liberation from all desires, cravings, and "becomings," from suffering and from the endless round of lifetimes and selves. And in part it's because Buddhism, as a missionary religion (like Christianity and Islam), had to travel light, both to maximize its chances of getting over the mountains and through the rainforests and to leave its converts some room to use their imaginations.

Basically, these converts fall into two camps, roughly established (cf. Catholicism and Protestantism) along north/south lines. The southern camp (Sri Lanka, Southeast Asia) practice a form of Buddhism known as Hinayana (or "Little Vehicle"), characterized by orthodoxy (what the historical Buddha said goes), austerity, and a concept of salvation based on one's own right living. The northern camp (Nepal all the way to Japan) practice Mahayana (or "Great Vehicle"), which postulates that the Buddha is not just historical but divine and that nobody—not even a bodhisattva, two-thirds of the way to being a Buddha himself—is going to enter into Nirvana until every last one of us is ready to enter into Nirvana. Two important subcamps of Buddhism: the Lamaism of Tibet, in which the Dalai Lama called the shots until Communist China threw him out, and the Zen Buddhism of Japan, transplanted from China, in which *satori*—the attainment of enlightenment, plain and simple, through intuition rather than intellect—is the name of the game, prepared for in activities like judo, calligraphy, flower arranging, and so on, and embodied by the *koan*, a paradoxical observation of the sound-of-one-hand-clapping variety.

Careful: It's often hard to remember what's basically Hinduist, what's Buddhist. Not only did Hinduism spawn Buddhism, it then glommed on to a lot of what the Buddhists had gone on to say and think. So you get nirvana, karma, mantra, tantra, and yoga, not to mention Buddha himself, in both packages (though usually not in the same strengths). Do try to remember that there are now almost no Buddhists in India itself. And that whereas the spirit of Hinduism is theatrical and clubby, that of Buddhism is no-nonsense and do-it-yourself.

TAOISM · *and* CONFUCIANISM

Number of believers unknown, but they're mostly in China.

6 million believers, likewise.

Let's begin with yin and yang. You remember yin and yang: the two poles of experience, joined in a symmetric union, a continuous cycle; yang the bright, creative, male, heavenly force, yin the dark, receptive, female, earthly one, each of the two containing the seed of its opposite. Note that we're not talking Western-style opposites here, of the true-false, good-bad variety, but something more like harmony, balance, completeness, fulfillment.

Turns out, that's pretty much how Confucianism and Taoism work. Each founded in the sixth century B.C. (and thus predating the arrival of Buddhism in China by roughly seven hundred years), and each equipped with its own legendary sage, the two together sum up, play to, and care for the Chinese character as we know—or think we know—it. Confucianism is practical, social, ethical, full of advice on how to behave in the world, father to son, husband to wife, ruler to subject, older friend to younger friend, and it's more code than creed, with no churches or clergy in sight. Taoism is mystical, devoted—even more than Buddhism (though probably less than Zen)—to transcending everyday life and finding the *tao*, the path, the way of the natural order. Nor did the Chinese fall into the trap of doing some schematic Type A/Type B thing with the two. Rather, they chose to emphasize Confucianism when they were educating their kids, then convert to Taoism when they got older in the hopes of regaining the spontaneity that had been squelched by a lifetime of honoring social conventions and playing by the rules.

Confucius—K'ung Fu-tse, or Grand Master K'ung, back home in China—was, you don't have to be told, particularly good with the one-liners: "It is only the wisest and the stupidest who cannot change," "The proper man understands equity, the small man profits," "Silence is a friend who will never betray," and so on, enough of them to fill the *Lun Yü*, or *Analects*, Confucianism's basic reference work. Lao-tzu—the "Grand Old Man" (literally) of Taoism, said to have once baffled Confucius in philosophical debate—had a more enigmatic style, as befits a religion determined to transcend: "Without going out of the door, one can know the whole world. Without peeping out the window, one can see the *tao* of heaven. The farther one travels, the less one knows." His collection is called the *Tao Te Ching (The Way of Virtue)*. The *I Ching* (or Book of Changes), by the way, which you once may have been in the habit of consulting on days when the Tarot wasn't working out, and which is as much about yin and yang as everything else in the country is, predates both men; Confucius even based some of his teachings on it.

So, Confucianism is yang: practical, masculine, dominant, active. Taoism is yin: intuitive, feminine, yielding, passive. The Confucians wanted to get the job done, keep the wheels greased, make sure the system held up for another few hundred generations; the Taoists to lead a perfectly balanced life in harmony with the tao and to leave artifice and conformity in the dust.

Not that it stayed so simple. First, threatened by Buddhism, Taoism sacrificed all the understatement to eye appeal and sheer numbers. Buddhism had thirty-three different kinds of heaven, so Taoists came up with eighty-one. Taoism took over some of the Buddhist gods and restored others from the old folk religions it had supplanted (including the City God, the Wealth God, and the Kitchen God), and developed a lively interest in selling charms, reading fortunes, and sponsoring secret societies. Today, it's still sect-and-society mad, a religion of the semiliterate and the eternally hopeful. Confucianism, too, once it had eliminated the examination system it ran to keep those civil-service candidates on their toes, seems to have had an identity crisis. Both are outlawed in the People's Republic today (it especially didn't help Confucianism that Confucius was a feudal aristocrat), but *we* know that's just a phase of the cycle, don't we?

SHINTOISM

3 million believers, mostly in Japan.

The Hammacher-Schlemmer of Eastern religions, full of odd and largely use-less items, as well as old and demographically undesirable shoppers, and, perhaps most important, overshadowed by Bloomingdale's up the street (that would be Buddhism, a sixth-century import from China via Korea; that there are as many Shintoists as there are today is due in part to sheer force of habit and in part to the fact that most of them are practicing Buddhists, too).

The religion of ancient Japan, Shintoism—from *shin-tao*, the later Chinese equivalent of the Japanese *kami-no-michi*, or "way of the gods" (Japan had no written language until it appropriated China's in the fifth century A.D.)—developed out of a combination of nature and ancestor worships, sometime around 700 B.C. The religion had a complex pantheon of *kami*, or gods, led by a Supreme Sun Goddess and including guardian household spirits; presiding tree-, river-, rock-, and village-divinities (including *kamikaze*, the "divine wind"); deified emperors; and miscellaneous national heroes.

A set of customs and rituals rather than a moral or philosophical system, Shin-toism puts a lot of stress on purity, especially bodily cleanliness, and obedience; makes little of life after death and a lot of self-versus-nonself thinking; and fos-ters the belief that, since the Japanese have occupied their island pretty much by themselves for as long as anybody can remember, they are all related to each other, to their royal rulers, and to the Supreme Sun Goddess herself. It's these last planks in the Shintoist platform that had so many Japanese committing harakiri for their emperor in World War II and Douglas MacArthur banning Shintoism as an instrument of the state, while allowing it as a religious sect, shortly thereafter.

The Good Book as Good Read

Sorry; as far as we know, video Scripture hasn't hit the market yet (although audio Scripture has). However, the written Word itself offers some pleasant surprises, especially if you've been avoiding it since Sunday school days. It is, for instance, tailor-made for short attention spans: You can easily absorb a verse or two while waiting for the cash machine and half a dozen psalms on a short bus ride home. It's chock-full of the kind of homespun wisdom and thoughtful advice you'd be lucky to get in a year's subscription to your favorite lifestyle magazine. It puts any number of book and movie titles into perspective. And given a choice between contemplating "Mother Eats Baby in Bizarre Devil-Worship Ritual!" at the supermarket checkout counter or any one of the passages following, we know which *we* think makes for a nicer day. Being sentimentalists at heart, we also opt for the King James version whenever possible, as we've done here.

1. There were giants in the earth in those days; and also after that, when the sons of God came in unto the daughters of men, and they bore children to them, the same became mighty men which were of old, men of renown.*

Genesis 6:4

2. By the rivers of Babylon, there we sat down, yea, we wept when we remembered Zion.**

Psalms 137:1

3. A little sleep, a little slumber, a little folding of the hands to rest, and poverty will come upon you like a vagabond and want like an armed man.

Proverbs 6:10

4. I am a brother to dragons, and a companion to owls. My skin is black upon me, and my bones are burned with heat. My harp also is turned to mourning, and my organ into the voice of them that weep.

Job 30:29–31

---

*For the record, they're talking about the time before the Flood.

**Properly associated not with reggae music, but with the first Babylonian captivity (see pages 464 and 492).

5. I returned, and saw under the sun, that the race is not to the swift, nor the battle to the strong, neither yet bread to the wise, nor yet riches to men of understanding, nor yet favour to men of skill; but time and chance happeneth to them all.*   Ecclesiastes 9:11

6. Or ever the silver cord be loosed, or the golden bowl be broken, or the pitcher be broken at the fountain, or the wheel broken at the cistern.**
                                                           Ecclesiastes 12:6

7. For they have sown the wind, and they shall reap the whirlwind: it hath no stalk: the bud shall yield no meal: if so be it yield, the strangers shall swallow it up.†   Hosea 8:7

8. And why beholdest thou the mote that is in thy brother's eye, but considerest not the beam that is in thine own eye?   Matthew 7:3

9. For we brought nothing into this world and it is certain that we can carry nothing out.   I Timothy 6:7

10. Faith is the substance of things hoped for, the evidence of things not seen.
                                                              Hebrews 11:1

11. Be not forgetful to entertain strangers, for thereby some have entertained angels unawares.   Hebrews 13:2

12. And when he had opened the seventh seal, there was silence in heaven about the space of half an hour.††   Revelation 8:1

---

* Ecclesiastes (Greek for "preacher") is now believed to have been the nom de plume of a wealthy, kindly old cynic who lived around 200 B.C. For a long time he was considered too materialistic, pessimistic, and agnostic to be included in the Bible at all; naturally, he is a big favorite with modern readers.

** The subject here is old age and death, about which Ecclesiastes worried a lot. The rest of the passage is also worth remembering: "Then shall the dust return to the earth as it was: and the spirit shall return unto God who gave it."

† Spoken of the errant people of Israel who were, as usual, off worshipping false idols and wallowing in luxury while the kingdom collapsed into political confusion and Assyrian armies gathered ominously to the north.

†† The seventh seal is the last of those which secure the great book held in God's right hand. It is being opened, at the moment in question, by a lamb with seven eyes and seven horns.

The Good Book as Good Business

We know, if we think about it, that God didn't speak to His biblical scribes in seventeenth-century English prose; that the King James version of the Bible is not carved, Cecil B. DeMille–style, in stone. This allows for considerable diversity of opinion about how He said whatever it was that He said. It also makes for a Bible-publishing industry that has churned out 2,500 English-language versions alone over the past couple of centuries and that continues to ring up an estimated $180 million in sales each year.

Some of the superabundance of Scripture is justified. For one thing, new discoveries of ancient texts and more sophisticated methods of interpreting them have allowed scholars to correct errors in earlier translations. For another, some people sincerely want to get the Word across to a new generation of readers with considerably different literary needs. Then there's simple chauvinism: Every sect and denomination now seems determined to have its own version of things, translated by its own scholars, to present to its own faithful. So, as scrambled eggs and fried-egg sandwiches have been joined by the Egg McMuffin, next to the King James and the Revised Standard versions, we now have such bestsellers as *The Good News Bible* and *The Book*. Here, contributor **David Martin** provides a brief critical guide to ten Bibles, complete with samples of how each handles two familiar biblical passages.

THE KING JAMES BIBLE (a.k.a. the Authorized Version): Retains its popularity more for sentimental than for utilitarian reasons. Despite ongoing revisions, it still presents translation problems, and some of the language, already slightly outdated when it was published in 1611, is now so archaic that it's impossible to decipher without divine guidance. But it's beautiful stuff, whatever it means, and it did help shape the English language for the next couple of centuries. If you have no purist hang-ups, the abridged and heavily annotated collegiate version known as *The Dartmouth Bible* can make the going a whole lot easier.

THE REVISED STANDARD VERSION: An American reworking of the King James Bible, issued between 1946 and 1952. Proponents praised it for cleaning up the King James language and many of its textual errors. Detractors said it still retained too many archaisms, while fundamentalists blamed the Commies for its supposedly weakened stance on the divinity of Jesus, the integrity of the Trinity, and the historicity of the Virgin Birth. Has become, as the name implies, the familiar version of the Bible in the United States and probably throughout the English-speaking world.

THE NEW ENGLISH BIBLE: Published in 1970 by the Oxford and Cambridge University Presses, and a totally new translation from the original texts. Instead of a word-for-word translation, though, which produces what has come to be known as "Bible English," this goes meaning-for-meaning and favors contemporary idiom; as a result, it's clearer than the King James but also wordier. Its Anglicisms—"truckle to no one," "meal-tub," "throw on the stove"—can drive an American crazy.

THE JERUSALEM BIBLE: Brought out in 1966 and heralded as the first Roman Catholic translation into English from the original text rather than from the Latin Vulgate. A formidable piece of scholarship, it includes book-by-book introductions and notes on archeology, geography, theology, and language that are considered by many to be the most complete of those in any one-volume Bible. The doctrine is relatively liberal, although Catholic dogma does creep into the notes (e.g., on I Corinthians 7: "Virginity is a higher calling than marriage, and spirituality more profitable").

THE NEW AMERICAN BIBLE: The first translation from the original texts for *American* Catholics, and a surprisingly undogmatic one. A word-for-word translation, it gets a bit ponderous, but does clean up a lot of archaism.

THE LIVING BIBLE: Completed in 1971, and comes in various versions. (The one for Catholics called *The Way: Catholic Edition*, and for blacks there's—honest—*Soul Food*.) Literally a paraphrase, *The Book*, as it's now called, has been criticized extensively for its careless treatment of the geography, history, and language of the times, as well as for some of the theological conclusions of its author, Kenneth N. Taylor. Some people also take exception to having *The Book* touted on bumper stickers. No beauty here: The Psalms are done in prose, the Song of Solomon as some kind of a dramatic reading among several speakers, and its colloquial style is sitcom-flat: "Hey, who's that girl over there?" "Martha was the jittery type."

THE GOOD NEWS BIBLE (Today's English Version): The American Bible Society's popular illustrated model, designed to be easily understood by absolutely everyone, including newcomers to the English language. The translation is accurate enough, but the style is strictly newspaperese.

THE NEW INTERNATIONAL VERSION: Published in 1978 with a strikingly familiar format. When someone speaks, there are quotation marks; when the speaking voice changes, so does the paragraph—just like in a James Michener novel. The translation itself, neither literal nor paraphrased, is innocuous, and the theology, conservative evangelical.

VERSION	FROM PSALMS 23	FROM ECCLESIASTES
The King James Bible	The Lord is my shepherd; I shall not want. He maketh me to lie down in green pastures: he leadeth me beside still waters. He restoreth my soul . . .	Vanity of vanities, saith the Preacher, vanity of vanities: all is vanity.
The Revised Standard Version	The Lord is my shepherd, I shall not want; he makes me to lie down in green pastures. He leads me beside still waters; he restores my soul.	Vanity of vanities, says the Preacher, vanity of vanities! All is vanity.
The New English Bible	The Lord is my shepherd; I shall want nothing. He makes me lie down in green pastures, and leads me beside the waters of peace; he renews life within me.	Emptiness, emptiness, says the Speaker, emptiness, all is empty.
The Jerusalem Bible	Yahweh is my shepherd, I lack nothing. In meadows of green grass he lets me lie. To the waters of repose he leads me; there he revives my soul.	Vanity of vanities, Qoheleth says. Vanity of vanities. All is vanity!
The New American Bible	The Lord is my shepherd, I shall not want. In verdant pastures he gives me repose: Beside restful waters he leads me; he refreshes my soul.	Vanity of vanities, says Qoheleth, vanity of vanities! All things are vanity!

VERSION	FROM PSALMS 23	FROM ECCLESIASTES
The Holy Scriptures	The Lord is my shepherd; I lack nothing. He makes me lie down in green pastures; He leads me to water in places of repose; He renews my life.	Utter futility!—said Koheleth—Utter futility! All is futile!
The New King James Version	The Lord is my shepherd; I shall not want. He makes me lie down in green pastures; He leads me beside the still waters. He restores my soul . . .	"Vanity of vanities," says the Preacher. "Vanity of vanities, all is vanity."
The Living Bible	Because the Lord is my shepherd, I have everything I need! He lets me rest in the meadow grass and leads me beside the quiet streams. He restores my failing health.	In my opinion, nothing is worthwhile; everything is futile.
The Good News Bible	The Lord is my shepherd; I have everything I need. He lets me rest in fields of green grass and leads me to quiet pools of fresh water. He gives me new strength.	It is useless, useless, said the Philosopher. Life is useless, all useless.
The New International Version	The Lord is my shepherd, I shall lack nothing. He makes me lie down in green pastures, he leads me beside quiet waters, he restores my soul.	"Meaningless! Meaningless!" says the Teacher. "Utterly meaningless! Everything is meaningless."

THE HOLY SCRIPTURES: Completed in 1982, and the first translation from Hebrew by Jewish scholars since the Septuagint, the Hebrew-to-Greek translation of the Old Testament done more than 2,200 years ago (and so called because it was the work of seventy-two scholars). Although more formal than many Christian translations, it's very literal and reads well aloud (the novelist and rabbi Chaim Potok served as literary coordinator).

THE NEW KING JAMES VERSION: An attempt to update the King James. It restored certain parts of the original seventeenth-century text, which had been inadvertently changed, and modernized some of the language—"sheweth" to "show," "thy" to "your," for example. On the whole, though, the translation tends to vulgarize the prose without making it all that much more accessible. Also available in paperback, in a version marketed as *The Bible*, with commentaries on everything from stress to drugs to homosexuality.

Bible Baedeker

A MERCIFULLY BRIEF WHO-WHAT-AND-WHERE GUIDE TO THE HOLY LAND

SIX IMPORTANT PLACES THAT BEGIN WITH THE LETTER G

GILEAD: A fertile, mountainous region east of the Jordan River, between the Sea of Galilee and the Dead Sea. Badlands of a sort, Gilead (with its colonizers, the Gileadites) was both cut off from the rest of the country and open to attack by hostile neighbors. This was the home of the outlaw king Jephthah and of the prophet Elijah. King David fled to Gilead to escape the rebellion led by his son Absalom, and it was here that the Syrian Laban caught up with his fugitive son-in-law Jacob. The region was known for its spices, myrrh, and balm, which prompted the prophet Jeremiah, seeking a cure for the decline of the Hebrew nation, to ask his famous rhetorical question: "Is there no balm in Gilead? Are there no physicians there?" Poe's narrator in "The Raven" was even more skeptical, wondering: "Is there balm in Gilead?"

GAZA: A town that spelled trouble for Israel right from the start. Located on the plain between the Mediterranean Sea and western Israel that is now known as the Gaza Strip, this began as an Egyptian garrison town and was later one of the five great cities of the Philistines. In fact, it's where the Philistines brought Samson to blind him after his betrayal by Delilah (hence the title of Aldous Huxley's novel *Eyeless in Gaza*); Samson retaliated by bringing down the Philistine temple on top of them all. Later, the unlucky town was besieged, first by Alexander the Great, then during the wars of the Maccabees, and again during the Crusades. Although the exact location of ancient Gaza is unknown, modern

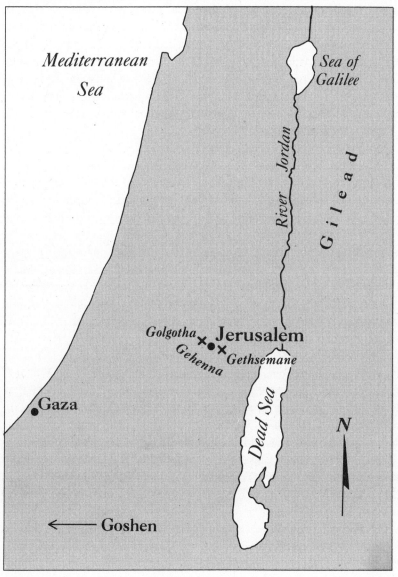

Gaza is the principal city of the Gaza Strip, the impoverished area that, since the 1940s, has been the site of massive Palestinian refugee camps and, despite the removal of Israeli settlements in 2005, the scene of endless clashes between Egyptians, Israelis, and Arab guerrillas.

GEHENNA: A corruption of the Hebrew Ge-Hinnom, the valley outside Jerusalem where, during various periods, the Jews slipped into the pagan rite of human sacrifice. The practice was to burn one's child, usually the firstborn, as an offering to the fire god, Moloch. God was, naturally, appalled by the custom; according to Jeremiah, he laid a curse on the place, changing its name to "the valley of slaughter" and promising: "I will make this city desolate, and a hissing; every one that passeth thereby shall be astonished and hiss, because of all the plagues thereof. And I will cause them to eat the flesh of their sons and the flesh of their daughters, and they shall eat every one the flesh of his friend in the siege and straitness . . ." (Jeremiah 19:8). Later, Gehenna became synonymous with Hell, as in Rudyard Kipling's verse: "Down to Gehenna or up to the throne / He travels fastest who travels alone."

GOSHEN: There have always been too many Goshens to keep track of. One was a region of Egypt, probably located in the northeast part of the Nile Delta, where Joseph settled his brothers and his father, Jacob, after returning from his exile in Egypt. During this period they were under the protection of the Pharaoh, but over the next four centuries the Jews living in Goshen became the slaves of the Egyptians. (When Moses finally came along and delivered them from slavery, they headed directly east, it's thought, to a place called the Sea of Reeds, not, as it says in the Bible, to the Red Sea.) Another Goshen probably refers to the hill country near the Negev, once occupied by Joshua's army; this is the one from which we got the expression land o' goshen. And then, of course, there's Goshen, Indiana, and Goshen, Connecticut.

GETHSEMANE: The olive grove, or garden, on the western slope of the Mount of Olives, east of Jerusalem, where Jesus underwent his "agony" (during which, as he prayed, "his sweat was as it were great drops of blood falling down to the ground," Luke 22:44), where he was visited by an angel, and where, soon afterward, he was betrayed by Judas and arrested. In the Bible, the garden seems to be under a kind of spell, which causes the disciples to fall asleep repeatedly while Jesus struggles with temptation. You've seen the spot as a backdrop in religious paintings.

GOLGOTHA: The same as Calvary; the place where Jesus was crucified. (Golgotha derives from the Hebrew, and Calvary the Latin, word for "skull.") It was somewhere just outside the walls of Jerusalem, although no one knows the exact location. Ever since St. Helena discovered what she believed to be a piece of the cross in the area in A.D. 327, the site has traditionally been placed within what is now the Church of the Holy Sepulchre. There is a hole in the ground inside the church where the cross was supposed to have been set.

FIVE FAMILIAR CHARACTERS WHO WON'T STAY PUT

ABSALOM: King David's handsome third son, who killed his half-brother Amnon to avenge the rape of his sister. He was eventually pardoned by David, who was partial to him and probably overpermissive. Later, Absalom "stole the hearts of the men of Israel" and conspired to overthrow the king. During the decisive battle, Absalom's hair got caught in the branches of an oak tree, and his mule rode out from under him. As he hung there helplessly, one of David's men finished him off, despite the king's orders that his son's life be spared. David's cry upon hearing the news—"O my son Absalom, my son, my son Absalom! Would God I had died for thee, O Absalom, my son, my son!"—is the classic father's lament. Absalom, as a symbol of the son who brings his father grief, was used by Dryden in his satirical "Absalom and Achitophel" and by Faulkner in his novel *Absalom, Absalom!*

ISHMAEL: Son of Abraham, conceived when Abraham's wife Sarah, for years unable to have a child, finally sent her Egyptian maid Hagar in to sleep with her husband. Later, Sarah became pregnant with Isaac and, in a fit of jealousy, had Hagar and Ishmael cast out into the wilderness to die. God came to their rescue, however, by providing a well at Beersheba. Ishmael grew up in the wilderness under God's protection and became the first Arab. (The story is sometimes used to explain the bad feeling between Jews and Arabs.) Ishmael is a symbol of the outcast, because of the line in the Bible that reads: "And he will be a wild man; his hand will be against every man, and everyman's hand against him."

Melville gave the name Ishmael to the narrator of *Moby Dick*, the philosophical schoolmaster who took to the sea every time he soured on the world. Captain Ahab, by the way, also comes directly from the Old Testament: He was Jezebel's husband, a king who succumbed to idol worship.

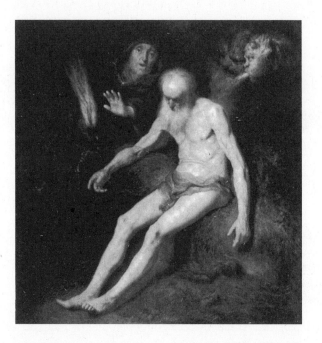

JOB: The most put-upon person in the world; a healthy, happy, prosperous, and godly fellow who, for no apparent reason, suddenly has his family and his possessions wiped out and is himself covered with boils. His wife advises him to "curse God and die," and his friends sit around with him all day urging him to repent for his sins, assuming that he must have done something wrong to bring all this misery down on himself. (The expression "Job's comforters" refers to the kind of friends who, when times are bad, manage to make them worse.) Job never gives in, however; his point is that God doesn't always have to make sense to us, that He doesn't always punish evil and reward righteousness but can do whatever He wants.

God, in the end, decides that Job has passed the test and rewards him handsomely. Writers from Dostoevsky to O'Neill have wrestled with the theme of Job's suffering, and Archibald MacLeish retold the story in modern terms in his play *J.B.*

SUSANNA: The heroine of a famous courtroom drama reported in the Old Testament Apocrypha. A beautiful and virtuous young married woman, she is accused of adultery by two lecherous elders whose advances she's spurned. They claim to have seen her with a young man while she was bathing. She is just about to be found guilty and stoned to death when young Daniel comes to her rescue. Asking to be allowed to cross-examine the elders, he proceeds to demolish their testimony, Perry Mason–style. Justice wins out; Susanna is saved and the elders are stoned. The story was a favorite subject of Renaissance painters, who usually chose to depict the part of the story that takes place in the bath, because that allowed them to produce a religious work and paint a gorgeous nude model at the same time. Susanna reappears as a figure in Wallace Stevens' poem "Peter Quince at the Clavier."

MARY MAGDALEN: An elusive figure, one of several Marys who were devoted to Jesus. She is known to have been possessed by "seven demons," which Jesus exorcised, and to have been present when He was crucified, when He was buried, and again when His tomb was found empty. Beyond that, her story is a series of mix-ups. She may or may not have been the sister of Martha, and she probably wasn't really a harlot; the latter slander came from the fact that she took her name from Magdala, her hometown, which was a seaport with a bad reputation. She may have washed Jesus' feet, but then again, it may have been another Mary who did that. At any rate, she became a saint and a symbol of repentance, and she gave us the word "maudlin," which means "tearful," and the French "Madeleine," the name and the cookie. In paintings, she's usually the one with the red hair.

FOUR PAIRS OF GROUPS WHO KEEP STEPPING ON EACH OTHER'S TOES

Not everybody was alone with his problems, his family, or his God in the Holy Land. The following preferred to travel in packs—packs that, like Democrats and Republicans or Oreo and Hydrox, were not always immediately distinguishable from each other.

APOSTLES AND DISCIPLES: There were twelve of each, but not quite the same twelve. While Judas is always counted as a disciple, he didn't, according to the best sources, make the apostles roster, where he was replaced by somebody

The Sacrament of the Last Supper *by Salvador Dalí*

called Matthias. Strictly speaking, the disciples were *students* of Christ (from the Latin word for "pupil"), the apostles His *envoys* (from the Greek for "send away"). Paul is often added to the list of primary apostles, and Judas sometimes retained, swelling the group to fourteen. Also, the principal missionary to a country is sometimes designated its apostle: St. Patrick is the apostle of Ireland.

SERAPHIM AND CHERUBIM: First of all, they're not those plump babies you see in Renaissance paintings. In the Old Testament, a cherub had anywhere from one to four faces and either one or two pairs of wings, and looked more like a lead guitarist than a toddler; God sat among or just above the cherubim. A seraph, by

A pair of seraphim, one with head, one without—and each with a full complement of wings.

contrast, had three pairs of wings, hovered over the throne of God, had a reputation for zeal and ardor, and was the very highest-ranking of the nine "choirs" of angels. (Or, as the prophet Isaiah once remarked, "I saw the Lord seated on a throne. . . . About him were attendant seraphim, and each had six wings; one pair covered his face and one pair his feet, and one pair was spread in flight.") In art, seraphim are most often red-toned and may carry a candle; cherubim, the second highest-ranking, tend to be blue and sometimes have books. Both are depicted as mere heads, surrounded by the appropriate number of wings. For the record, the nine grades of angel, divided into three hierarchies, are, from highest to lowest: seraphim, cherubim, and thrones, all of which surround God in perpetual adoration; dominions, virtues, and powers, which together govern the stars and elements; principalities, which protect the kingdoms of the earth, and archangels and angels, which carry messages. Angelology, surprisingly, was a fairly exact science.

PHARISEES AND SADDUCEES: The two great Jewish religious sects and political parties in the last two centuries B.C. As far as Jesus was concerned, both were bad news: literal-minded, cold, hypocritical. The Pharisees were the majority party and an intellectual elite—whom we'd probably classify as religious liberals, at least in comparison with the Sadducees—full of learning and piety and consumed with getting their message to the people. That message, while firmly founded on Judaic law, had been much tampered with over the centuries, and its oral form, as practiced by the Pharisees, had come to include belief in institutions like an afterlife, a day of judgment, a resurrection, and the Messiah. The Sadducees were a social elite, supplemented by priests and, as such, deeply conservative; they accepted only the Hebrew Scriptures, rejecting all the oral traditions that had come to encrust it, barnacle-style. They were much stricter than the Pharisees (who themselves were no day at the beach); it didn't enhance their popularity that, not believing in any afterlife or day of judgment down the road, they doled out harsh legal punishments here on earth. The strife between the Pharisees and the Sadducees ended in Roman intervention and domination, but at least the Pharisees made it into the second century A.D.; many of Jesus' sayings find a parallel in the teachings of the Pharisees, and their ideas underlie many aspects of Orthodox Judaism today. (You could do worse than think of the Pharisees as the first rabbis.) Figuratively, of course, a pharisee is a self-righteous hypocrite. There is no such thing as a lowercased Sadducee, a reflection of the fact that they were the minority party, that they'd died out by A.D. 70 (the year the Romans destroyed Jerusalem), and that they left nothing of particular interest, philosophically or stylistically, to either Jew or Christian.

ASSYRIANS AND BABYLONIANS: The bad guys (Mesopotamian division), each of whom was responsible for one especially traumatic dislocation of the Jews. The Assyrians (who predominated during the eighth and seventh centuries B.C., who lived in the mountainous north of the Tigris-Euphrates river valley, whose capital was Nineveh, and who did all those bas-reliefs of winged beasts and heavily bearded humans) were militaristic and wanted nothing more than to fight all day, every day. Their most telling blow against the Jews was the taking captive, in 722 B.C., of the ten northern tribes of Israel, whom they then proceeded to scatter over the Assyrian desert. These so called Lost Tribes have subsequently been identified with the peoples of Ethiopia, Latin America, and Afghanistan, not to mention high-caste Hindus and Japanese, the Indians of the Eastern Seaboard, and, most endearingly, the English. Major Assyrian kings: Sargon, Sennacherib, and Assurbanipal. The Assyrians were eventually defeated by

an alliance of Persians and Babylonians (see below). You can read about them in 2 Kings 16–19.

The Babylonians (who predominated during the sixth century B.C., who lived on the fertile plain in the south of the Tigris-Euphrates valley, whose capital was Babylon, who are sometimes referred to as the New Babylonians—or even the Chaldeans—to distinguish them from a much earlier Babylonian civilization under Hammurabi, and who built the Hanging Gardens), were fighters, too, but they were also fatalists and sensualists, which in the end did them in. Their most devastating move against the Jews is called the Babylonian Captivity (or the first Diaspora), and involved the two tribes of Judah, just south of Israel, tens of thousands of whose members were forced into exile in and around Babylon in 586 B.C. The Babylonian king par excellence: Nebuchadnezzar. His son was defeated by the Persians. You can read about the Babylonians in 2 Kings 20–25, and in Daniel (where Shadrach, Meshach, and Abednego are thrown into the fiery furnace, where Daniel is thrown into the lions' den, where the handwriting shows up on the wall, and where Nebuchadnezzar goes temporarily insane and eats grass, "as oxen").

Seven People Not to Bother Sharing Your Old God-Spelled-Backward Insight With

FIVE ARE GERMANIC PROTESTANTS WHO WON'T THINK IT'S FUNNY, ONE'S AN AUSTRIAN JEW WHO'S ALREADY BEEN STRUCK BY IT HIMSELF, AND ONE'S A FRENCH CATHOLIC WHO MIGHT JUST TRY TO GET YOU TO PUBLISH YOUR FINDINGS

And they're all theologians, engaged in an ages-old attempt to talk rationally about the Word, the Way, and the Messiah, while, like the rest of us, keeping an eye on things down at city hall and out in the 'burbs.

KARL BARTH
(Swiss, Calvinist, 1886–1968)

Not a whole lot of fun. For starters, he'd had it with the liberal Protestant theology of the preceding century, an I'm-OK-thou-art-OK affair that put man and God on roughly the same footing and that burbled a lot about human progress. God, said Barth, is not only totally divine, totally supreme, and totally transcendent (i.e., nothing like the rest of us), He's also totally unknowable except through His revelations, the times and places for which, by the way, He chooses all by Himself. So forget worrying about how you should "talk with God": It's not even an option. Concentrate instead on your own sinfulness, because that—not the goodness and dignity the liberals so liked to emphasize—is man's true nature. You can call all of the above "neo-orthodoxy." Or you can call it "crisis theology," Barth's catchphrase for how faith derives not from front-pew smugness but from front-line peril, in this century specifically from the dislocations and devastations of two world wars. But you'd be smart to let it go at that. The alternative—attempting to dip into Barth's *Church Dogmatics*, twelve volumes' worth of the bottom line on revelation, creation, reconciliation, redemption, and the like—is, as reading experiences go, the equivalent of chewing a mouthful of bubble gum and sand.

PAUL TILLICH
(German Emigrant to the United States, Lutheran, 1886–1965)

Thoroughly modern and more or less human. Tillich viewed theology as a perfectly natural, perfectly personal endeavor, with a built-in man-asks-God-answers format. In many ways the opposite number of Barth, who saw God as wholly other and transcendent, way out there (and not at home anyway), Tillich sees Him as, if maybe still way out there, at least willing and able to make the trip in from time to time. God has presence, not just existence; in fact, He's both the source and the goal of everything—the "Ground of Being," in Tillich's famous phrase—and religion is the "sacred depth," the unifying center of every aspect of life. Drawing on then-trendy existentialism and psychoanalysis as well as on philosophy and theology proper, Tillich attempted to redress Barth's obsession with the "revelatory" pole of Scripture and tradition by dancing round and round the "situational" one of what this century has dealt us. As a result, his work—most notably the three-volume *Systematic Theology* and the chattier, slightly autobiographical *The Boundaries of Our Being*—is full of discussions of culture, society, ethics, and current events. Keep awake especially for raps on Christian socialism and something called theonomy, through which Tillich hoped we could all unite our own beings with the Ground of Being, and in so doing resolve the conflict between the individual and the state. Not that human truth is ultimate—just that the human condition is worth addressing oneself to.

RUDOLF BULTMANN
(German, Lutheran, 1884–1976)

The debunker. Specifically, the man who set out to "demythologize" the New Testament, stripping it of the myths that second- and third-generation Christians had encrusted it with back when Jesus' death was still news and nobody wasn't privy to at least one firsthand account of the Resurrection. Insisting that there was no point in continuing the nineteenth century's search for a "historical" Jesus, yet understandably reluctant to throw the baby (that would be Christ's, and Christianity's, essential "message") out with the bathwater, Bultmann turned to a succession of techniques to get the worshipper-friendly effects he wanted. Among them: form criticism, a biblical-research style that asks, say, why a specific Gospel narrator would choose to relate a miracle when he could equally well have thrown in a parable or a bit of scenic description; hermeneutics, a way of interpretatively updating a text—like the New Testament—so that it bears on and reads for a whole new tribe or generation; and, like Tillich, Christian existentialism, the midcentury movement committed to reassessing religious doctrines and traditions in terms of sheer human interest. A reasonable enough program, you say? Not to Bultmann's critics, who argued that it cut into not only the box-office appeal of Jesus but the big-daddy authority of God.

REINHOLD NIEBUHR
(American, Evangelical, 1892–1971)

Not easy to pigeonhole: A theologian who was able to make the connection between sin and politics and an activist who thought history had more to do with irony than with progress. A pragmatist, certainly, and a Midwesterner, the bulk of whose career was, nevertheless, spent teaching Applied Christianity at Union Theological Seminary in New York City. Also, an aphorist of sorts: The so called Serenity Prayer—"God, give us grace to accept with serenity the things that cannot be changed, courage to change the things which should be changed, and the wisdom to distinguish the one from the other"—is vintage Niebuhr. Nor is it any easier trying to slot the man according to what he opposed: the Babbittry underlying American business life and the American dream; the naïveté of liberal Protestants who thought improving society really brought the Kingdom of God any closer; the emphasis that Barth put on the supernatural; the emphasis that Tillich put on the here-and-now; anybody who thought grace was for Christians only; totalitarianism; unthinking pacifism; pride; and complacency, to name just a few. It's not *wrong* to think of him as a Christian socialist, manning the sociopolitical barricades, meeting power with power, seeing that justice is done, but you should keep in mind that the neoconservatives also claim him as a role model. Anyway, he was a second-generation American (and not all that heavy-duty a theoretician), and he believed that sin is basically a misuse of human freedom; that values and judgments have to be understood in terms of a person's circumstances (Niebuhr is the father of contextual ethics); and that while you have a responsibility to fight for what's right, you don't count on always winning.

DIETRICH BONHOEFFER
(German, Lutheran, 1906–1945)

The martyr. Hanged by the Nazis (but not before he'd smuggled enough letters out of his prison cell to flesh out what would become a transatlantic bestseller), Bonhoeffer knew all about horror, repression, outrage, and the deft turn of phrase. It was the term "cheap grace," an early effort, that first aroused attention; it characterized "comfortable" Christianity, the kind that costs its followers little or nothing in the way of abnegation, hardship, or lack of popularity, and was opposed to the genuine (and expensive) grace that active, exclusive discipleship under Christ entails. Bonhoeffer would later plead for a secular, "religionless" Christianity, directed toward "man come of age," with an emphasis on this world rather than the next, freedom instead of obedience, and "behavior not belief." Such an approach to religion (a word he didn't much go for, by the way) would appeal to men not where they were weak but where they were strong, and in "the marketplace of life" rather than "outside its city limits." (The last turn of phrase is ours, but we think he'd—and maybe He'd—approve.) Not such good ideas, per Bonhoeffer: metaphysics, in which men speculate after God in the interstices of scientific knowledge; psychotherapeutic and existentialist approaches to Christianity; and too much "inwardness," whether on the mystical or the merely pietistic model. All things considered, and despite his premature death, Bonhoeffer has probably had a bigger (and a more international) response than any other modern theologian: Not only are there file cabinets full of "Bonhoeffer literature" consisting mainly of readers' correspondence, with a few scholarly tracts and cult items thrown in, there's also a Bonhoeffer Society that holds regular congresses and keeps those cards and letters coming.

MARTIN BUBER
(Austrian, Jewish, 1878–1965)

This century's most important Jewish religious thinker—for the record, "theologian" is pretty much a Christian label—at least among Protestants and Catholics. (Jews had problems with his iron-out-the-differences, Arab-Israeli-cohabitation approach to Zionism; they also were uncomfortable with his Hasidic tale-teller persona and all that quaint straight-from-the-Kabbalah lore, not to mention the fact that the Christians seemed to like him so much.) The best-known Buber bequest: the "I-Thou" relationship, which can be undertaken only with "the whole being" and "in total openness to the other"; which is opposed to the obviously less desirable "I-It" relationship; and which is how we're meant to get along not only with each other but with God—for Buber not an object of belief, but the subject, the "Eternal Thou." In fact, because, as he saw it, each little daily I-Thou moment, even the shopping-mall ones, had Eternal Thou reverberations (how we behave to each other is how we're behaving toward God), don't be surprised when Buber filibusters about interpersonal relations, public life, politics, community versus society, and life on the kibbutz, all at least as intricately bound up with religion as going to temple ever was. Be prepared, too, for a lot of existentialist imagery: the walk on "the narrow ridge," modern man "at the edge," and a bundle of "abysses," including those between Israel and the Arabs, Jews and Christians, friendship and alienation. Not the scholar's scholar, exactly, but Buber is hands-down the person's person.

PIERRE TEILHARD DE CHARDIN
(French, Catholic, 1881–1955)

Out there—a doer as much as a thinker, and a mystic into the bargain. Trained not only in theology but in paleontology, Teilhard had been in on the discovery of Peking man, then got himself into trouble when he tried to make sense of the find. From most people's point of view, it's hard to see what anyone could dislike about the idea that science and religion aren't irreconcilable, and the notion that human evolution never stopped, just moved indoors, seems like simple common sense. The Catholic Church, though, had other ideas: Teilhard was enjoined from publicizing, in his lifetime, his theory of cosmic evolution—in which, according to him, man has come to have a guiding hand—and his conviction that belief in same does not entail a rejection of Christianity. (He was also packed off to Africa.) Still, nobody can deny that, at least posthumously, Teilhard got off a few good ones, most notably in *The Phenomenon of Man*; among them were the terms "noösphere" (the realm or domain in which the mind does it all, modeled on—and destined to supplant—mere biosphere) and "Omega point" (variously interpreted as the integration of all personal consciousness and as the second coming of Christ). Anyway, turns out you weren't the only one who wondered how come, if all the birds and animals already existed in the Garden of Eden, there could also be dinosaur tracks up the road.

science

Contents

*Miss Helen Richman of Chicago, Illinois, shows models of the crystal
formations of four substances as they would appear under a high-powered
microscope.*

Out of the Cyclotron, into the Streets

Some scientific terms yearn for a notoriety greater than the university community or the industrial complex can provide. Bored with having a precise, agreed-upon meaning known only to a few white-coated old lab technicians, they set their caps at becoming indispensable to David Letterman and Barbara Walters. They may lose a little of their cogency in the process, but they sure do get around.

Catalyst

In chemistry, a catalyst has to satisfy two separate requirements. The first is that it promote, enhance, or speed up a chemical reaction. This it does by combining, on the molecular level, with each of the active ingredients involved, bringing them into certain contact with each other, rather than waiting for their chance collision. The second requirement is that, though it furthers a reaction, it remain itself unchanged, unspent, and unaccounted for afterward. In effect, it simply walks away. (Enzymes, those protein molecules that figure in the chemical reactions of living organisms, meet both these requirements and are hence the body's catalysts.) If you set out to fix up your two best friends, making the restaurant reservation, lubricating the dinner conversation, and paying the bill, you'd be a catalyst. Also a cockeyed optimist, but that's another story.

Centrifugal Force

The "center-fleeing" tendency that comes over a ball when it's being spun at the end of a string, a liquid like blood or milk when it's undergoing separation in a centrifuge, or you when you're taking a curve in a car that's going too fast. Essentially, the effect is one of being pulled away from the center of a specific orbit, to a degree based on the mass of the object in question, the speed at which it's traveling, and the radius of its path. It is the complement of centripetal, or "center-seeking," force, which can be gravitational, mechanical, or electric in nature, and which is what keeps the ball, the blood, the milk, and you from being somewhere over the Atlantic Ocean by now. Both terms pop up all over the place: A historian, for instance, might tell you that Thomas Jefferson's sympathies lay with the centrifugal, not the centripetal, forces of the new nation—with rural life, farming, and the decentralization of powers rather than with urban life, manufacturing, and the centralization of them.

Fission *and* Fusion

They're both nuclear reactions (i.e., they change the structure of an atomic nucleus) and they both represent what happens when Einstein's famous $E = mc^2$ is acted out. In fission, which is behind atomic bombs, nuclear reactors, and radioactivity, the nucleus of a big uranium atom is split into smaller parts when struck by a free neutron. Uranium is the fuel of choice because it "splinters" readily, releasing two or three more neutrons, which in turn strike and splinter neighboring uranium nuclei in a chain reaction. The result: energy; also, Chernobyl.

In fusion, which is behind starlight, sunshine, and the hydrogen (a.k.a. thermonuclear) bomb, and which scientists hope someday to adapt to nuclear-energy production, the nuclei of two little hydrogen atoms are joined together, or fused, at temperatures approaching 50,000,000°C, to form a single, heavy helium nucleus, ejecting high-speed neutrons (and impressively little pollution) in the process. In both fission and fusion, the atoms resulting from the splitting and the joining, respectively, weigh slightly less than the ones that went into the process. It's this difference in mass that has been converted into energy.

So why not forget dangerous, dirty fission and get behind controllable, clean fusion? Because fusion, while it works nicely on the sun, requires temperatures higher than we've in general been able to achieve here on earth except, so far, in the hydrogen bomb, which is triggered by fission—in the form of an atomic bomb—at its core anyway. It's true that in late 1993 an experimental fusion reactor at Princeton produced a few megawatts of power for a fraction of a second; while doing so, though, it used up more power than it produced. Nevertheless, a number of countries, including Japan, China, the United States, Russia, and members of the European Union, are currently collaborating on an International Thermonuclear Experimental Reactor (ITER). Unfortunately, nobody can agree on the site. Experts say economical fusion is still fifty years off, as it has been for decades. (Some scientists are still on the trail of "cold fusion," the alleged result of a 1989 experiment by two researchers in Utah who claimed to have seen nuclear fusion in a room-temperature test tube. Their success has never been duplicated, however, and was widely dismissed as equal parts wishful thinking and sloppy science.) Still, given that fusion, once perfected, could churn out energy equivalent to 300 gallons of gasoline from a gallon of seawater, you can expect the scientists to stay on the case.

In the meantime, bear in mind that fusion is both more natural and more powerful than fission, packing the kind of wallop and carrying with it the degree of conviction that, in life as in the lab, results from putting things together, not tearing them apart.

Half-life

The fixed, invariable amount of time it takes half of an original sample of a radioactive substance like uranium, radium, or carbon-14, to break down, decay, fall to pieces—which all such substances do, nucleus by nucleus. Although scientists can never tell which specific nucleus is going to end it all next, they are surprisingly exact when it comes to predicting the overall rate of change. (It's a little like demographers noting that Buffalo or Detroit is losing population at such-and-such a rate without being able to say which family is going to leave town next.) For instance, the half-life of uranium 238 is 4.5 billion years, which means that at the end of that time a pound will have dwindled to half a pound; the rest will have decayed into thorium. After another 4.5 billion years, there will be a quarter of a pound of the original uranium left; after yet another 4.5 billion years, an eighth of a pound, and so on. Useful to geologists in determining the age of rock specimens (and, by extension, of the planet), half-life also has popular applications: Girls with streaked blonde hair may speak of the half-life of meaningful relationships in their crowd.

Mass

Forget about weight. Forget about volume. Mass—which physicists define as the quantity of matter in a body—is the adult way of coming to grips with the question "How big?" (Weight is simply the measure of the force of gravity acting on that body and, unlike mass, tends to vary, sometimes inconveniently, from place to place. As for volume, some make do without: Electrons, for instance, have mass and no volume at all.) Of course, mass and energy have been shown—by Einstein, in his formula $E = mc^2$—to be roughly the same thing. Which brings us to the dog-eared phrase "critical mass": In a nuclear chain reaction it's the minimum quantity of fissionable material (see previous page) necessary to keep those neutrons popping and those nuclei alert. In *Business Week*, by analogy, it's the minimum level of potency or density you have to be at if you're really going to perform. Thus marketing types might pinpoint a magazine's critical mass at the moment its circulation becomes large enough to attract national advertisers.

Matrix

From a Latin word that meant first "pregnant animal" and later "womb," a matrix (plural, "matrices") is the place where something is generated, contained, and/or developed. The word is used of, among other things, the rock that a fossil or gemstone is found embedded in; the band of formative cells in your nails and teeth; an industrial mold; and, in mathematics, a rectangular array of elements, for example,

$$
\begin{array}{ccc}
2 & 4 & 11 \\
5 & 5 & -3,
\end{array}
$$

where those elements are shorthand for some larger picture (they may, for instance, be the coefficients in a pair of linear equations that are meant to be considered together), and where they are less significant taken one by one than as a composite. Eventually, computer nerds picked up on the word, too, applying it to the point at which input and output leads intersect. It was only a matter of time before ambitious younger persons started using it as a verb, a kind of fancy synonym for networking, for example the woman who declares at a party, "I'm not here to meet men, just to do a little matrixing." From here to the malevolent cyberintelligence that's out to get Neo, Trinity, Morpheus, et al. is, however, a bit of a leap.

Osmosis

When fluid passes through a membrane from one side, where there's a lower concentration of a particular particle, to the other, where there's a higher concentration of the same particle, that's osmosis. Essentially, it's an attempt to reach equilibrium, which biological systems, not unlike yourself, find to be a highly desirable state; in this case, equilibrium will ensure the identical number of particles per cubic whatever of fluid on both sides of that semipermeable (but selective) membrane without any of the particles having to move a muscle. "Learning by osmosis" is likewise automatic, imperceptible, effortless.

Parameter

In mathematics—economics, too—a quantity that varies with the conditions under which it recurs, but that is, for the time being and within the context of the current problem, both constant and knowable. In life, a parameter is the measuring stick we have at hand, whose own length isn't exactly set (it may be a yardstick today and a foot-rule tomorrow) but which nevertheless helps us define, estimate, or describe the totally unknown quantity in the next room. Take the queuing consultant called in by the Museum of Modern Art to help with "flow" during a Picasso retrospective. "Using parametric analysis of the number of people per painting and square feet per person," he explained, "I advised the museum on queuing line layouts and admissions-per-hour." A good use of the word: The parameters here were the existing estimates of how many people could, at a major museum exhibit, look at a painting at the same time and how much space they needed to do it; those guidelines, however, were understood to be subject to change (the mark of a good parameter), depending on canvas size, hanging technique, desirability of standing close to or away from the work, intrinsic interest of a particular painting or roomful of them, etc. Not everybody does so well with the word, however: Press secretaries, for instance, tend to speak of the "parameters" of a problem when all they mean is that problem's distinguishing features. And even careful speakers sometimes use it as a substitute for "outer limit," when the word they really want may be "perimeter."

Quantum

Originally, anything that could be counted or measured (from a Latin word meaning "how much"). In physics, quanta—the plural form—came to refer to the discontinuous series of little packets in which light sometimes travels. Quantum theory, which dates from 1900, when Max Planck (see page 566) proposed it as a way of accounting for the emission of light by a body so hot that it's luminous (a poker thrust into a fire, for instance), and which underlies quantum mechanics (see page 516), was in complete contradiction to the then-prevailing wave theory of light. Later, both theories would prove to be right, neither alone sufficing to explain light, which sometimes travels in waves (like a river) and sometimes travels in quanta (like raindrops), but never does both at the same time; think of it as the difference between a solid line and a dotted one. As for the phrase "quantum leap," it's an abrupt, usually unpredictable change or step—as with an electron's sudden transition from one fixed orbit to another as it circles an atom's nucleus—but it's not necessarily an enormous one. Properly, a quantum leap (or jump) in, say, the number of terrorist incidents is not about size but suddenness.

Quark

Of the over two hundred subatomic particles out of which physicists tell us all matter is made, the quark is the most evasive, the most piquing, and the most basic—so small as to have no size, so simple as to have no internal structure. Of course, nobody's managed to shake a quark loose for closer inspection (the most they've been able to do is hit a few over the head with beams of electrons), but that hasn't stopped scientists from insisting that quarks, like Charlie's Angels, usually travel in threes; from positing that they carry electrical charges that are multiples of one-third; from attributing to them properties they call "color" and "flavor"; from giving them such first names as "up," "down," "strange," "charm," "bottom," and "top"; or from positing the existence of mirror-image, or anti-, quarks. Quarks bond with other quarks in such standard combinations as protons (two up quarks and a down quark), neutrons (two down quarks and an up quark), mesons, baryons, kaons, and so on(s)—all the other subatomic particles, in fact, except leptons (a category that includes electrons, muons, and neutrinos), which are themselves so "elementary" as not to be able to be further broken down. Despite the whimsicality (the word itself is borrowed from a song in Joyce's *Finnegan's Wake*, "Three quarks for Muster Mark," where it may refer to the squawking of birds, their excrement, or both), quarks pack a mean intellectual wallop. They imply that nature is three-sided, and that such dualist constructions as time/space, mind/body, and either/or miss the point. Specks of infinity on the one hand, building blocks of the universe on the other, quarks represent science at its most ambitious—also its coyest.

Symbiosis

The perfect relationship—assuming you're not all that interested in relating to whomever it is you've chosen to settle down with. Take, for instance, the case of the rhinoceros and the yellow tickbird. The tickbird dines on parasites infesting the rhinoceros' horny skin; the rhinoceros itches less and is warned of danger when the tickbird, sharp-eyed and skittish, abandons him for the nearest tree. Or the lichen, that exemplary union of alga, which brings home the bacon (it knows how to photosynthesize), and fungus, which keeps the house (it stores moisture the alga needs and scoops out the rock they're living on to make a bungalow). In such classic instances of

symbiosis ("life together"), both parties benefit but in very different ways, each compensating for the other's shortcomings, rather than duplicating his talents. Although it's tempting to apply the word to, say, the S & M relationship being worked out nightly in the apartment down the hall, you weaken its meaning when you do so. The sadist and the masochist complement each other, all right, but they're deriving too much the same benefit—sexual gratification—from their joint undertaking to qualify as a bona-fide symbiosis, a label that should be saved for arrangements between partners with widely divergent priorities.

Synapse

It's the junction—a microscopic gap, actually—of two neighboring neurons, or nerve cells. And there are loads of them: An average neuron in the human brain has somewhere between one thousand and ten thousand synapses with nearby neurons, some of which are responsible for thinking, some of which are responsible for moving, and some of which are, for better or for worse, simply blank. When a nerve impulse reaches the synapse, there to jump across to the adjacent nerve cell, it's given a nudge along by an electrically triggered squirt of a chemical. Some chemicals enhance, others inhibit; ditto painkillers, tranquilizers, and recreational drugs. The adjacent nerve cell reacts accordingly, either getting all excited itself and relaying the message to a muscle, a gland, or yet a third nerve cell, or giving it the cold shoulder. Caution when using the word: A synapse is properly a place, at most a transaction. It is not in itself a full-scale neural event, and it is even less a good synonym for what is portrayed in comic books as a little lightbulb going off over somebody's head.

Synergy

Like Gestalt (see page 456), another the-whole-is-greater-than-the-sum-of-its-parts manifesto. But at least this one is backed up by lab reports and an etymology you can understand: the Greek *syn-* + *ergos*, "together working." At its most scientific, synergy refers, in biology, to the relationship between "agents" whose combined physiological clout outweighs the sum of their individual jabs; thus booze and barbiturates, ingested together, will knock you out faster and more totally than can be predicted by adding up what each of them does to you on its own. From biology, it's a short step to the boardroom, where executives decide that, by merging with the like-minded types across town, they can pull in a market share in excess of their two individual ones put together.

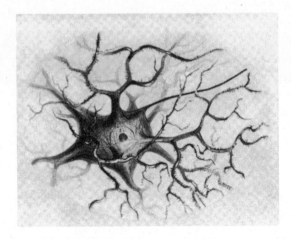

Valence

In chemistry, a measure of the combining power of a specific element, equal to the number of different chemical bonds one atom of that element can form at any given time. All atoms feel most secure when they have a complete outermost electron shell, and they'll go to great lengths to achieve one, borrowing elements from or sharing them with other atoms. For this reason neon, with an outer shell that's full-up at birth, is highly unreactive—so chemically aloof, in fact, that, along with helium and argon (among others), it's been dubbed one of the "noble gases." Carbon, by contrast, with an outer shell of eight electrons only half filled, is a born joiner and an unabashed swinger, almost always requiring more than a single relationship to feel safe and provided for. It's largely as a result of this capacity for interaction that you hear so much about carbon in chemistry circles. As for your valence, broadly speaking it's your capacity—or tendency—to interact with the others out there. Just remember, you don't *have* to go to bed with them.

Keeping Up with Cosmology

In the second century a.d., Ptolemy, a Greek working out of Alexandria, Egypt, codified all ancient astronomical beliefs and made a momentous pronouncement: The earth was the center of the universe, around which the sun, the planets, and the stars all revolved, and beyond the orbit of the most distant star lay the empyrean, the place where angels and immortal spirits dwelled. Rigorously mathematical and highly persuasive, the Ptolemaic system was accepted by virtually all educated Europeans until Copernicus' treatise On the Revolution of the Heavenly Spheres (published posthumously in 1543) broke the news that, far from nestling cozily at the center of things, it was the earth that was doing the revolving, a theory that was soon to be embroidered and enlarged upon by Tycho Brahe (see page 567), Kepler, Galileo, and Newton. Exit angels and immortal spirits. Enter uncertainty, relativity, quarks, leptons, gluons, the strong and weak forces, the Big Bang, and the search for our cosmic roots. Here, with an update: contributor **James Trefil.**

Since the late 1920s, we've known that other galaxies are moving away from our own. The obvious explanation for this is that the universe as a whole is expanding. Because every expansion has to start somewhere, it's also obvious that if we reverse the expansion and follow the galaxies backward in time, to the tune of some fifteen billion years, there will come a point at which all the matter in the universe is crammed into a very tiny space. The appearance of the universe from a single infinitely dense point of matter is what we call the Big Bang.

Astrophysicists tend to dislike obvious explanations like this, which is why, throughout the Fifties and Sixties, there were all sorts of theories that attempted to explain expansion without the Big Bang scenario. But new evidence came in,

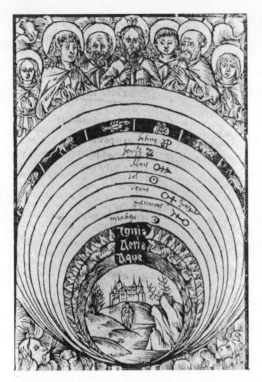

The Ptolemaic concept of the universe.

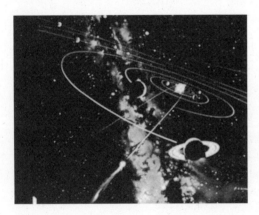

A twentieth-century view of the solar system.

these alternate theories bit the dust, one by one, and today hardly anyone disputes the Big Bang.

The thing about the Big Bang as far as modern physics is concerned is that when the universe was younger, it must have been hotter. Compressing matter always makes it heat up (try touching the barrel of a tire pump after it's been used). Higher temperatures also mean that the building blocks of matter, such as atoms, move faster and collide more violently. Thus, when the universe was younger, its constituent parts were bumping into each other with much higher energy than they do in our own relatively frigid era.

When matter is subjected to high temperatures, two important things happen. First, it changes form. Heat an ice cube and you get water; heat the water and you get steam. If you heat a collection of atoms enough, the collision will become so violent that their electrons will be torn loose and you'll have a new form of matter—a collection of negatively charged electrons and positively charged nuclei. The sun is made up of this sort of matter.

The second important temperature-induced change has to do with the creation of new particles via Einstein's famous formula, $E = mc^2$. The theory of relativity tells us that matter and energy are interchangeable—given enough of one, you can convert it into the other. Thus, when a bit of uranium nucleus is converted into energy in a nuclear reactor, the end result is sufficient electrical current to run your house. Conversely, every day, in giant particle accelerators throughout the world protons and electrons are brought up to almost the speed of light and allowed to collide with a target. The result: The energy of the particle is converted into mass and new particles are created in the collision.

In this early, high-temperature universe, then, we expect two things to happen: Existing forms of matter will change form and exotic new forms of matter will be created from the available energy. But there's one other result we might also expect: that the fundamental forces—the way bits of matter interact with one another—will also change.

The Early Universe

One way of measuring the extent of our knowledge about the universe is to ask how close to the beginning we can get in our description of the events that formed it. In the 1920s, for example, we knew enough about atoms to get to within half a million years of creation. By the Fifties, the development of nuclear physics had allowed us to come within three minutes. Today, thanks to our understanding of elementary particles, we can get to within a fraction of a second—a fraction so small we need a different way of writing numbers to describe it. We can talk about time between 10^{-36} (that's a decimal point followed by thirty-five zeros and a one) and 10^{-43} (forty-two zeros and a one) seconds after the Big Bang. In fact, only one hurdle remains before we get to the moment of creation itself.

The best way to picture the evolution of the universe is to think of a cloud of highly compressed steam. If you let it go, it will expand, cooling off as it does so. When it cools to 212°F it will condense into droplets of water. If it continues to expand and cool it will reach another critical temperature—32°F—at which point the water will freeze into ice. The same thing happened with the universe as would happen with the steam, except that the transitions that correspond to condensation and freezing are both more numerous and more complicated.

Although a few intrepid theorists have speculated on how the initial collection of matter that eventually became the universe came into existence, there is no firm scientific opinion on this subject; right now the question is simply beyond our knowledge. With regard to the first 10^{-43} seconds of the universe—the time elapsed before the first major "freezing"—we're in a little better shape. Although there is no generally accepted theory that describes matter at the temperatures that existed then, we can still make out some of its salient features. Most striking was a tremendous simplicity. Instead of the large number of basic particles we see in matter today, there was just one kind—the so called superparticle. Instead of the four basic interactions (more on this later), there was only one way for matter to interact. Everything was as economical and as elegant as it could be. It's been downhill ever since.

At 10^{-43} seconds, the first "freezing" occurred. Two broad classes of particles appeared—one group similar to the electron, the other similar to the photon (the "particle" which makes up visible light); quarks (see page 506) first appeared at this time as well. The force of gravity became distinguishable from the other forces. During the period from this freezing down to 10^{-36} seconds, the universe may or may not have conformed to something called the grand unification theory (GUT). This theory, first developed in the mid-Seventies, is being subjected to intensive experimentation right now. (More on it later, too.)

During freezings at 10^{-36} and 10^{-12} seconds, respectively, the universe became steadily more differentiated and more complex. At around 10^{-5} seconds (a tenth of a millisecond), the free quarks that had been roaming the universe condensed into the elementary particles that are the building blocks of matter as we know it. At three minutes, these elementary particles started to collect to form the nuclei of atoms. Finally, at five hundred thousand years, the final major transition occurred. The first electrons attached themselves to those nuclei to form simple atoms. In each of these cases, the transition to a new form of matter occurred as soon as the temperature had dropped to the point at which the interparticle collisions no longer had sufficient energy to disrupt the fragile new structure.

The fifteen billion years that have elapsed since then have seen the formation of galaxies and stars and the development of life. During this period, all of the chemical elements heavier than helium, including the iron in your blood and the carbon in your DNA, were made in stars that later died, returning their contents to the interstellar medium, where they were taken into the nascent solar system. Still, from the point of view of fundamental physics, all of the interesting events in the history of the universe were over by the time it was a few minutes old. In fact, it takes longer to describe what happened than it took the universe to undergo the actions described.

What Matter Is Made Of

The best analogy for how we are coming to understand matter is the peeling of an onion. We peel off one layer and penetrate to a deeper one, only to discover that there is yet another to work on. The first layer was peeled off our onion in 1805, when British chemist John Dalton published the modern atomic theory of matter. He showed that the enormous variety of substances that surround us is made up of only a few different chemical elements, each of which has its own type of atom. In the early twentieth century the second layer was peeled off when the structure of the atom was revealed. All of the different kinds of atoms, it was argued, were made up of only three kinds of elementary particles—protons and neutrons in the nucleus and electrons orbiting the nucleus; this picture of the atom would become more or less standard. For a while, its inherent simplicity seemed to be clouded when it was found that there were not just two types of particles inside the nucleus, but hundreds. Most of these appeared and disappeared too quickly to be seen, but they could be produced independently in accelerators.

In the mid-1960s, yet another layer was peeled off. It was pointed out that the myriad elementary particles are actually made up of a small number of still more basic entities called quarks. Quarks are held together by particles called gluons—they're the Elmer's that keeps the three quarks of a proton or neutron together.

Scientists believe that these particles derive from an even more basic form of matter called quark-gluon plasma, a primordial soup that made up the universe ten millionths of a second after the Big Bang. As things cooled down, this liquid went through "hadronization," hardening into protons and neutrons, which in turn coalesced first into nuclei, then into atoms. After that, the atoms came together to form molecules, which eventually transformed into you, this book, and the easy chair you're sitting in. At least, that's the theory.

The Fundamental Forces

Physics is the study of matter and motion. Thus the quest for the fundamental building blocks of matter that led to the quarks is only half the picture. The other half has to do with the way that matter in all stages behaves, i.e., interacts with itself. Up until the beginning of the twentieth century, physicists had been able to find only two fundamental forces in nature—the force of gravity and the force associated with electricity and magnetism. Since then, studies of the nuclear and subnuclear world have produced two more fundamental forces, neither of which is part of our everyday experience. One of these, the strong force, is what holds all the elementary particles together in a nucleus. The other, the weak force, operates in many situations in nature, the most familiar being the slow radioactive decay of some unstable nuclei and particles. These four forces are a varied lot. Some, like electromagnetism and gravity, act over long distances. Others, like the two nuclear forces, act only over distances about the width of a nucleus or less. They also differ markedly in strength, with the strong being the most powerful, followed by the electromagnetic, weak, and gravitational forces.

Despite these apparent differences among the forces, the great advances in physics over the last few decades have been made by theorists who believe that the differences are only apparent, and that the forces are actually *identical*. There are important historical precedents for this view. Isaac Newton gave us the first in the seventeenth century, when he showed that the same force which, in your backyard, causes an apple to fall to the ground also holds the moon and planets in their orbits. In so doing, he reversed two millennia of Western thought, during which scientists had seen no resemblance between earthly and celestial gravity. Yet Newton's Theory of Universal Gravitation, which attributes the motions of both planets and apples to a mutual attraction that exists between all objects possessing mass, says that despite apparent differences, the two forces are, at bottom, the same. We say that Newton unified the two forces of gravity and, because of the term "gravitational field," we say that Newtonian gravity is an example of a "unified field theory."

In 1968, Steven Weinberg (then at MIT) took an important step toward the unification of the forces when he theorized that the weak and electrical forces were unified (i.e., essentially identical), and that apparent differences between them were due more to the present low temperature of the universe than to anything fundamental to their natures. The result was a reduction in the number of basic interactions in nature from four to three. Since 1968, enough predictions of this particular unified theory have been confirmed that it is now accepted by everyone.

The new idea that made this particular advance possible is called the gauge principle. In essence, this principle states that the correct theory of nature must be one in which it is not significant if different observers come up with different definitions of things. For example, the principle suggests that the correct theory of gravity is one in which the amount of energy you expend getting to the top of a cliff is the same whether you go straight up its side or take a more gradual, winding path. Theories like that of the electroweak interaction, which incorporates the gauge principle, are said to be gauge theories.

Gauge theories and unification go hand in hand, and once Weinberg had shown the way, a further unification was not long in coming. This was the grand unification theory mentioned above. In the GUT, the electromagnetic and the strong and weak nuclear forces are all considered to be fundamentally the same. In addition to allowing us to retrace the history of the beginnings of the universe, the GUT predicts the end of it. That is, most GUTs hinge on the idea that the proton, hitherto thought to be the absolutely stable building block of the nucleus, actually decays. And if one proton can decay, *all* of them can—that means no more atoms, no more molecules, no more DNA, no more CNN, no more KFC, no more anything.

The good news—for most laypeople, if not for scientists and prophets of doom—is that after almost three decades of research, not a single proton has decayed. Until that happens, any proof of a grand unification theory is still elusive.

Gravity: Odd Man Out

Given this history, it would seem that the next step is obvious. All we have to do is use the same techniques to bring gravity into the fold and we'll have the ultimate theory, in which all forces of nature are brought together under the same roof. Such a theory would be called the Theory of Everything (TOE).

Unfortunately, this is one of those easier-said-than-done things. Our current concept of gravity centers on Einstein's General Theory of Relativity, and the concept of force used in this theory is radically different from the concepts used to describe the other three forces. To understand the frontier problem in theoretical physics these days, then, we have to know something about relativity.

The first thing to realize is that there are actually two theories of relativity.

The simplest, called the special theory, was published in 1905. It is not a theory of gravitation, but most of the other effects associated with relativity are incorporated into it. The equivalence of mass and energy, the twin paradox (which stated that a twin who went on a long space journey at high velocity would be much younger when he returned than his brother who stayed home), and the increase of mass with speed were all predicted by this theory. It is well verified experimentally; in fact, every time an accelerator delivers a burst of particles, every time a reactor produces a kilowatt of energy, the theory is verified anew.

The general theory was published in 1916. It is anomalous in science because it was accepted with only a few experimental tests, the most familiar being the bending of starlight as it passes the edge of the sun.

Both theories are based on a single principle, called, appropriately enough, the principle of relativity. It states that any two observers will discover the same laws of physics in action, regardless of their relative motion, no matter how different the picture may *look* to the two of them. The special theory is restricted in that the two observers can't be accelerating, whereas the general theory holds for any observers, accelerating or not. Since gravity produces acceleration, it can be treated only in the context of the general theory.

To grasp the picture of the gravitational interaction that arises we need another analogy. Imagine a rubber sheet held taut at the edges. (This is the image most often used to discuss Einstein's curved, four-dimensional space-time continuum.) If we drop a heavy weight on the sheet, the sheet will deform, developing a depression in the area of the weight. If we shoot a marble across the sheet, it could well become trapped in this depression, circling round and round the heavier weight. In general relativity, a large object (such as the earth) distorts the fabric of space and time in just the same way that the heavy weight distorts the sheet. Other objects (such as the moon) react to this distortion by going into orbit. The important point about this view of gravity is that it is purely geometrical—it does not involve any dynamic concept of force. It's this difference between gravity and the other fundamental forces that makes the development of a truly unified field theory so difficult.

There's one more thing to say about relativity. Not only does it *not* imply that "everything is relative," in fact, the whole point is that, even though different observers may see events differently, there is still a firm and unchanging bedrock in nature—a bedrock made up of the laws of physics.

CHECKING IN WITH QUANTUM MECHANICS

Quantum mechanics is the name given to the theory, developed in the 1920s, which describes the behavior of matter on the atomic and subatomic level. It has been the subject of a spate of books and articles, each purporting to show that accepting quantum mechanics requires some basic change in our thinking about the world. Some authors tell us that we have to turn to Eastern mysticism because of it, others that it teaches that the presence of consciousness is required for the world to function. One writer has claimed that quantum mechanics demands the downfall of patriarchal societies.

There's no question that the world of the electron is different from our own. For starters, in our everyday experience, we're accustomed to being able to observe something without changing it. We can watch a bowling ball roll along, confident in the knowledge that the light beams bouncing off it and hitting our eyes won't deflect it from its path. In our everyday world, the possibility of continuous observation allows us to assume that the ball moves smoothly from one point to the next.

In the subatomic world, things are different. The only way to observe a particle is to bounce another particle off it, and this must necessarily disturb the original particle. It's as if the only way we could determine the position of a bowling ball was by bouncing another bowling ball off it. In that case, its smooth, continuous, predictable motion toward the pins could not take place.

In the subatomic world, the act of measurement changes the system being measured, giving rise to what is known as the Heisenberg Uncertainty Principle. The principle tells us that if we choose to measure one quantity (e.g., the position of an electron), we inevitably alter the system itself and therefore can't be certain about other quantities (e.g., how fast the electron is moving). Since an interaction is involved in every measurement, and since measurements are involved in observations, physicists sometimes say that the act of observation changes the system. This is a reasonable statement, provided you realize that it's the interaction of particles, not the conscious observer, that is important. Consciousness has nothing to do with quantum mechanics, although there are plenty of people who misinterpret the principle to suggest that it does.

That probing matter affects its form and behavior is only part of the weirdness inherent in quantum mechanics. Equally bizarre: that some particles exist so briefly that they are not real but "virtual," and that the universe as we know it is based on chance and randomness at the subatomic level.

Hot Science: Two Trendy Theories That May Revolutionize Our Worldview—or May Not Make Much Difference at All

Chaos Theory

A Paradigm Shift

Superstring Theory

The Theory of Everything

Billed as the Storyline

Part One: That even an eensy change in input can make certain kinds of supposedly simple dynamic systems—e.g., weather, heart function, the stock market—go haywire. Therefore, since eensy changes in input are unavoidable, such systems have to be considered inherently unpredictable; that is, a certain amount of chaos is built into them. Part Two: That there's order lurking beneath the disorder; chaotic behavior itself follows simple rules and forms recognizable patterns. What's more, when you translate that behavior into mathematical models, then plot the models on the computer, you get the kind of visuals people used to have to drop acid to see.

The universe is composed not of subatomic particles that are shaped like pencil points— quarks, leptons, neutrinos, etc.—but of tiny strings tied together at the ends to form loops. These strings exist in a ten-dimensional universe that, sometime before the Big Bang, cracked into two pieces, a four-dimensional universe (ours; that's three dimensions plus time) and a six-dimensional universe that condensed and curled up into a ball so small we haven't been able to see it. What physicists have been thinking of as subatomic particles are actually vibrations of the strings, like notes played on a violin. The universe, in fact, could be compared to a symphony of superstrings vibrating at gazillions of different frequencies.

The Time Frame

Meteorologist Edward Lorenz (see following) started tracking chaotic weather patterns on his computer back in the 1960s, and throughout the 1970s, scientists working in various fields felt the urge to study random behavior. Eventually, they started talking to each other. Chaos theory really took off for the rest of us, though, in 1987, when the bestselling book *Chaos* (see following) brought science to the talk-show circuit.

An early, go-nowhere version of string theory—which proposed that quarks were not particles but the ends of pieces of string—first made the rounds in 1968, and a few mathematically inclined physicists continued to play with the idea of strings throughout the 1970s. Superstring theory, with its ten dimensions, supersymmetry (see following), and promises of imminent glory came along in 1984 and kept physicists on the edge of their seats for the next few years. But by the early 1990s, there were five different versions of string theory and it was clear that there were still a few technical problems that might take, oh, another ten, twenty, or maybe fifty years to work out.

	Chaos Theory	**Superstring and M Theory**
The Big Breakthrough	Forced scientists to trash cherished notion of an ultimately predictable, clocklike universe and get in touch with the real, Barnum & Bailey world. Has given everyone a new way to look at data; suddenly, a system's glitches seem as telltale and worthy of study as its stable, law-abiding behavior.	The first theory that manages to link gravity with the three other fundamental forces (strong, weak, and electromagnetic), thereby reconciling Einstein's general theory of relativity (which governs the big stuff: stars, planets, galaxies) with quantum mechanics (which governs the subatomic world). The apparently total incompatibility of these two bases of modern physics has been the biggest stumbling block on the road to a Theory of Everything and has been driving physicists crazy for half a century. In 1995, physicist Edward Witten got everyone excited again when he introduced what's come to be known as M Theory (a.k.a. the Second Superstring Revolution). We won't make your head ache with the specifics; just remember Witten's general idea, which is that the various versions of string theory and the apparently incompatible relationships they contain are, in fact, all connected, but they don't seem to mesh because they are only *approximations* of some other underlying theory. Witten hypothesized that the standard ten dimensions were also an approximation and that actually there are eleven. Mathematically, many pesky pieces of the puzzle, including gravity, suddenly seemed to fit. Not everyone cheered and jumped on the bandwagon, however, since Witten also noted that until more advanced mathematical tools are invented, physicists will have no way of proving, disproving, or even understanding M Theory.
The Box-Office Appeal	Suits the Zeitgeist. Seems true to reality as we know it. Allows ordinary people to feel better about their aptitude for science since, at least, they recognize the word "chaos." Also comforting; implies that even snipers' bullets, terrorist bombings, rapidly mutating viruses,	For theoretical physicists, the sheer elegance of the theory itself, plus the possibility of explaining everything in the entire universe and winning a Nobel Prize. For the rest of us, apart from a vague sense of validation ("Just as we thought, there's more going on in this

	Chaos Theory	**Superstring and M Theory**
	and teenage drivers are part of some cosmic order, subject to natural laws and therefore, presumably, amenable to control.	cockeyed world than what the politicians are telling us"), pure entertainment.
The Critics Complain	What's the big deal? All the study of non-linear dynamics (doesn't seem quite as thrilling without the catchy name, does it?) did was correct a mistaken assumption: that the Newtonian world was predictable. Which makes it a step in the right direction all right, but hardly a revolutionary idea.	"Vibrating strings," how ridiculous. There aren't any strings in nature. Besides, this theory is so complicated that it can never be tested, even mathematically. And any theory that can't be tested is pure sci-fi; it belongs on the trash heap.
The Fans Parry	What do you mean, "*All* it did was correct a mistaken assumption . . . "? That mistaken assumption's been distorting science for two hundred years! You might as well say, "*All* Newton did was correct a few mistaken assumptions about how the universe worked." Or "*All* Einstein did was correct some mistaken assumptions about energy and mass."	Oh really? What about DNA, that's a string, isn't it? And in case you've forgotten, Newton couldn't test his universal law of gravitation when he first discovered it, either; seventeenth-century mathematics was too primitive to handle it. So he went home and invented calculus. You'll be laughing on the other side of your face when somebody comes up with a math sophisticated enough to confirm superstring theory—maybe sometime in the next century.
The Real Problem, If You Ask Us	Everyone's dying to interpret chaos theory to suit the occasion and/or his or her personal agenda (from the Anglican priest who points to it as evidence that the world is a work-in-progress by God to the fashion editor who uses it to explain why some people are wearing ballgowns this fall while others are wearing leather chaps), making it hard to remember what the scientists' original point was.	It's too complex and bizarre even for most physicists to wrap their minds around. So who could possibly direct the movie version?
So What Good Is It?	Has lots of technological applications, from predicting nuclear meltdowns, heart attacks, and stock market fluctuations to making kerosene heaters, "smart" computers, and groovy light-show attachments for home stereo systems.	None whatsoever, unless you believe it really is the fabled Theory of Everything, the Holy Grail of physics—a science whose goal, after all, is not to make better kerosene heaters but, as Einstein put it, "to know the mind of God."

	Chaos Theory	**Superstring Theory**
Celebrities in the Field	Mitchell Feigenbaum (a.k.a. "Mr. Chaos," physicist who constructed much of the mathematics and methodology of chaos theory); Edward Lorenz (meteorologist who gave us the Butterfly Effect, and whom we *will* get to eventually); Benoit Mandelbrot (mathematician who gave us fractals, ditto); James Yorke (mathematician who gave us the term "chaos"); James Gleick (*New York Times* reporter who wrote the bestselling book *Chaos: Making a New Science*, which got so much publicity that a lot of people now think Gleick invented the theory).	John Schwarz and Michael Green (early, preserving proponents of various string and superstring theories, see following); David Gross, Jeffrey Harvey, Emil Martinec, and Ryan Rohm (team of Princeton physicists responsible for a promising version of superstring theory; hence, their nickname, the Princeton String Quartet); Edward Witten (genius leader of the superstring-theory pack, frequently hailed as the new Einstein).
Related Ideas with Market Potential	*The Butterfly Effect:* Edward Lorenz's 1960 observation, vis-à-vis the unpredictability of weather, that a butterfly flapping its wings in Brazil today can cause a tornado in Texas three weeks from now. This illustrates the basic chaos-theory principle of "extreme sensitivity to initial conditions," i.e., even a slight alteration in input can cause wild variations in outcome. *Strange Attractor:* A computer image made up of points of data that form a pattern, a visual model of the chaotic behavior of a particular dynamic system. The very fact that the behavior seems compelled to form such patterns hints at some structure or law guiding the apparent chaos. A strange attractor could illustrate, for example, the population growth of giraffes in Kenya or a week's worth of traffic jams on the Santa Monica Freeway, expressing the results in strange attractors that could look like anything from doughnuts to looped-over ribbons to spooky pairs of eyes.	*Hyperspace:* Higher-dimensional space. String theory, for instance, posits a universe with twenty-six dimensions, sixteen of which are rolled up, geometrically, to leave the ten of superstring theory. All sorts of bizarre things exist in hyperspace, from wormholes (tears in the fabric of space) to parallel universes. *Flatland:* Edwin Abbott's 1884 social satire about the narrow-minded inhabitants of a two-dimensional world who refuse to accept the possibility of a third dimension; the hero is Mr. Square, a Flatlander who's forced to broaden his outlook when he's hurled into the third dimension by Lord Sphere. *Flatland* is frequently evoked by proponents of superstring theory to illustrate their predicament.

Chaos Theory

Fractal: Benoit Mandelbrot's word for an irregular pattern that's self-similar in scale—which means any part of it looks remarkably like the whole. We like to think of the way broccoli florets look, each one of them, just like little heads of broccoli, but the classic example is the coastline of England, which, we've been assured, exhibits the same type and degree of twists and turns whether it's measured in miles from a satellite or in inches under a magnifying glass.

Superstring Theory

Spin-Off

Complexity theory, which tries to understand how simple elements give rise to complex systems (e.g., how did your brain cells ever get together to form your brain?) and how, contrary to the second law of thermodynamics (see Entropy, page 556), chaos, like the chaotic soup of the early universe, manages to organize itself into things as awesomely complex as stars, galaxies, and planets.

Supersymmetry, the perfect mathematical symmetry of higher-dimensional space. Yet another umbrella step toward the unification of absolutely everything, supersymmetry would allow for the interchange, impossible in quantum theory, of bosons, the subatomic packets in which forces travel (think of them as energy particles) and fermions, the parts of atoms (think of them as matter particles). In supersymmetry, a boson could be mathematically "spun" along a dimensional axis in such a way as to turn into a corresponding, though strictly hypothetical, fermion, and vice versa; for instance, a photon would turn into something called a photino and an electron into a "selectron." The generic name for these alter egos of particles is—and here physicists' imaginations seem, for once, to have failed them—"sparticles." According to the mythology of supersymmetry, particles and their sparticles were once identical, in the halcyon nanoseconds immediately following the Big Bang.

Riding Herd on the Life Sciences

They're an ornery lot and skittish to boot, always fighting among themselves, wandering off into the chaparral, grazing near precipices, or popping up unexpectedly with a brood of wacky hybrid offspring in tow. Nobody warned you back in Biology 101 that once you took them on, you'd never be able to turn your back on them again for a minute. (Or that everything you'd learn about them would turn out to be wrong, or at least outdated, just when you needed it most.) Here contributors **Judith Stone** and **Karen Houppert** wrestle a few of bio-sci's meanest subjects to the ground, in an effort to restore some sense—possibly illusory and definitely fleeting—of mastery and control.

ALL IN THE FAMILY

"Descended from monkeys?" the Bishop of Worcester's wife is said to have cried after hearing about Darwin's startling new theory of evolution. "My dear, let us hope it isn't true! But if it is, let us pray it doesn't become widely known!"

Well, the skeleton's been out of the closet for almost 150 years now, and today anthropologists have a fairly clear, though unfinished, picture of the human family tree, based on fossil remains. Like all mammals, we ultimately trace our roots back to a tiny, shrewlike creature that inherited the earth after the dinosaurs disappeared abruptly and mysteriously 65 million years ago. As the shrew's progeny diversified, tree dwellers developed such dandy gimmicks as binocular vision, hands that could grasp, and brains efficient enough to handle all that swinging. This ape line seems to have forked between 10 and 4.5 million years ago; one group stayed apes, the other eventually became us.

About 15 million years ago, the planet's climate cooled; steamy forests gave way to grassy savanna. Those tree dwellers who came down for a look eventually became the family Hominidae, of which our subspecies, *Homo sapiens sapiens*, is the only remaining member. A hominid family album would feature the venerable ancestors following, including Toumai, the oldest—and most human-like—hominid fossil found to date (a nearly complete cranium discovered in Chad in 2001); the controversial, Hobbit-like LB1 (found on an Indonesian island in 2003); Turkana Boy (a nearly complete skeleton discovered in Kenya in 1984); and, of course, Lucy, the 3.2-to-3.6-million-year-old grand dame of the hominid fossils, who achieved celebrity status back in 1974.

Trouble is, the hominid family tree is starting to look less and less like a tall, dignified elm and more like a squat forsythia with branches shooting wildly in all directions. That's because a lot of scientists working in the field of paleontology—the study of ancient life-forms—keep (literally) digging up new discoveries: new species, new genera, some of them overlapping, or coming very close. (Ten of the species listed following were not known to exist a decade ago.) What's more, the dating of the new species is controversial, with some competing scientists basing their claims on limited information and using the skeletons to settle old scores. In the meantime, information continues to trickle in. Who knows? By the time you read this, *Fredus flintstoniensis* may have turned up.

NAME: ***Sahelanthropus tchadensis*** (from Sahel, a region in Africa bordering the Sahara Desert, where the fossils were discovered)

TIME FRAME: Lived 6 to 7 million years ago.

VITAL STATS: Apelike braincase suggests very small brain size (approximately 350 cubic centimeters). But its relatively short and flat face, browridges (the bony structures above the eye sockets), and small canines are typical of later hominids. Lots of debate about whether or not it stood upright.

COMMENTS: A fossil cranium discovered by an undergraduate fossil hunter in 2001 and later identified by Michel Brunet and associates, who nicknamed him—they *think* he's a male—"Toumai," which, in the local Goran language, means "hope of life." Toumai was important for a couple of reasons. First, he was discovered more than a thousand miles from the sites in East Africa where paleontologists have been focusing most of their work. Second, his age and hominid status throw into question the age of the "missing link"—that elusive common ancestor we share with chimps. He does bolster the argument of scientists who suggest that hominid evolution was way messier than originally thought. In fact, it's hard to know whether Toumai lies directly in our evolutionary line or if he belongs to a separate branch of the hominid family tree. Or even if he's a hominid at all; critics insist that Toumai is just a female gorilla in hominid drag. Recently,

one of the leaders of the Toumai expedition added fuel to this fire when he accused Brunet of surreptitiously gluing a wisdom tooth to the jawbone.

NAME: ***Orrorin turenensis*** (*orrorin,* "original man" in Tugen, the language spoken where the fossils were discovered)
TIME FRAME: Lived c. 6 million years ago.
VITAL STATS: Hard to say, since there's not much there. (Fossils consist of fragmentary arms and thigh bones, lower jaws and teeth.) Back teeth are similar to those of *Homo sapiens.* Limb bones are about one and a half times bigger than Lucy's (*A. afarensis,* see following), which suggests that *O. turenensis* was about the size of a female chimpanzee. Grooves in the femurs suggest that the species was bipedal and also adapted to tree climbing, but don't hold us to that.
COMMENTS: Another *really* old possible ancestor; these fossils were found in western Kenya by Brigitte Senut and Martin Pickford in 2001. For more, see following.

NAME: ***Ardipithecus ramidus*** (*ardi,* "ground" or "floor" in the Afar language, and *ramid,* the word for "root"); also ***Ardipithecus kadabba*** (*kadabba,* "progenitor" in Afar)
TIME FRAME: Originally dated at 4.4 million years, but recent analysis of *A. kadabba* dates that species back to 5.2 to 5.8 million years ago.
VITAL STATS: Stood approximately four feet tall and weighed about eighty pounds; could walk upright, but probably spent a lot of its time in the trees; marked by humanlike diamond-shaped canine upper teeth (rather than the V-shaped canines of chimpanzees). But generally pretty chimpy-looking.
COMMENTS: OK, take a deep breath. The competition between *Orrorin turenensis* and *Ardipithecus ramidus,* not to mention the latter's older cousin, *A. kadabba,* is a paleontologist's version of a barroom brawl—it's wild, it's messy, and you never know what they'll find to slug each other with.

A. ramidus appeared first in 1994, when Tim White, Gen Suwa, and Berhane Asfaw came across its fossils in the Middle Awash region of Ethiopia. The team initially believed that their discovery was part of the *Australopithecus* genus but then decided that it belonged in its own category. *A. ramidus* was important for three reasons: First, it was considerably older than the previous discoveries. Second, it lived in a rain forest, which threw into disarray the then-prevalent idea that the hominid's bipedal adaptation was a result of the expansion of savanna habitats. Finally, because it was not part of the *Australopithecus* clan, it meant that it was not actually an ancestor of the later species, but was a "sister taxon" with a common (undiscovered) ancestor. All of this meant that *A. ramidus* wasn't necessarily the infamous missing link—but it was awfully close.

Then, in 2001, just when everyone was getting comfortable with *A. ramidus,* anatomist Brigitte Senut and paleontologist Martin Pickford announced that they had discovered a completely new—and older—species, which they called *Orrorin turenensis,* in Kenya of all places. (Up to that point, anthropologists usually conducted their digs in Ethiopia.) There wasn't much of this specimen left— thirteen fossils, including a partial femur, parts of a lower jaw, and several teeth—but the age of the fossils demonstrated that if this was indeed a hominid, it was the oldest on record. (At least, at that point; Toumai hadn't shown up yet.) Not only did the discovery rain on *A. ramidus'* parade, but the fact that *O. turenensis* may have been bipedal and had a certain size of molars and thick enamel on its teeth showed that it could be a closer relation to *Homo sapiens* than the *Australopithecus.* This suggested that Lucy and her gang may have actually been an evolutionary dead end.

As if this weren't controversial enough, a turf war erupted over excavation rights in the area where Pickford and Senut made their discovery. A Yale anthropologist, Andrew Hill, who'd had a thing against Pickford since their graduate school days at the University of London, leveled the charge. Unfortunately for Senut, Hill had the support of Richard Leakey, part of the famed Leakey family dynasty of anthropologists. (Pickford and Leakey had their own turbulent history, of which we'll spare you the details.) Things got so nasty that the Kenyan authorities (on Leakey's suggestion) arrested Pickford and threw him into prison for a few days. Since then, *Orrorin turenensis* has been treated with at best suspicion and, at worst, contempt by much of the paleontological community.

Now, another fly in the ointment: In 1997 and 2001 more fragmentary fossils were discovered in Ethiopia that were similar to—but a wee bit older (at about 5.8 million years ago) and more apelike—than the 4.4-million-year-old *A. ramidus.* These were initially named *Ardipithecus ramidus kadabba,* but scientists eventually decided that these new fossils were not a subspecies at all and were likely the direct ancestor of *A. ramidus.* As a result, these fossils were categorized as a new species in their own right: *Ardipithecus kadabba.* And if your head isn't swimming yet, there are *other* scientists who claim that *Orrorin turenensis* and *Sahelanthropus tchadensis* are not really separate genera at all, but should be included in the *Ardipithecus* family.

NAME: ***Australopithecus anamensis*** (*anam* means "lake" in the Turkana language)
TIME FRAME: Something like 4 million years ago.
VITAL STATS: Most definitely a biped. Still a very primitive cranium, but a more advanced, humanlike body. An interesting mix of the chimp (big canines, little brain) and the genus *Homo* (strolling about on two legs, thick enamel on its teeth).
COMMENTS: Odd history on this one. The initial find of *A. anamensis*—part of an upper left arm—was actually discovered by a Harvard University expedition way back in 1965. Then, except for a single molar in 1982, nothing else was found until a team organized by Maeve Leakey (wife of Richard Leakey) made a

number of fossil discoveries in the late Eighties and early Nineties in the Kanapoi region in Kenya. Interestingly enough, there are certain physical components of *A. anamensis* that seem to be closer to the *Homo* genus than the later *Australopithecus afarensis* (see below). Perhaps yet another argument for the "branch" theory of hominid development . . .

NAME: *Australopithecus afarensis* (from Afar, a region in Ethiopia)
TIME FRAME: Between 3 and 3.9 million years ago.
VITAL STATS: Brain of about 400 cubic centimeters in a very apelike skull (though with more humanlike teeth). Certainly walked upright, but even so could probably be confused with a chimp in the dark, especially given those long hairy arms. Stood only about three or four feet tall.
COMMENTS: In 1974, in Ethiopia, anthropologist Donald Johanson found a female skeleton he dubbed Lucy, after the Beatles song "Lucy in the Sky with Diamonds." Scientists figure she was about twenty-five years old when she died. Lucy captured the imagination of journalists for a long time, until she was overshadowed by older fossils in the 1990s. Part of her appeal lies in her completeness; unlike many other fossilized discoveries, more than 40 percent of Lucy's remains were found.

NAME: *Australopithecus africanus*
TIME FRAME: Between 2 and 3 million years ago.
VITAL STATS: Similar to *A. afarensis,* but with a slightly bigger body. Cranium is a bit bigger, too—between 420 and 500 cubic centimeters. Though this is bigger than a chimp's brain and could suggest some analytical skills, nobody really thinks that *A. africanus* was reciting the Gettysburg Address.
COMMENTS: One of the earlier paleontological finds, this one was the result of an arduous seventy-three-day dig by the famous anthropologist Raymond Dart in 1924 in South Africa. Named the Taung Child after the area where he was discovered, this three-year-old specimen caught the world's attention because he was so obviously somewhere between an ape and a human. He also blew apart the idea—commonly held up until that point—that Asia was the home of the origins of man.

NAME: *Australopithecus garhi* (*garhi,* "surprise" in the Afar language)
TIME FRAME: 2.5 million years ago
VITAL STATS: Still has a pretty teeny brain. However, *A. garhi*'s teeth, which are really quite large, along with its humanoid humerus and femur, suggest that it could be a middle mark between the gracile and robust *Australopithecus* families (just as you fear, we're going to explain that in a moment) or even a link between its cousin *A. afarensis* and early members of the *Homo* genus. But don't quote us on that.
COMMENTS: Calling this one a surprise is an understatement; *garhi* is quite controversial, since its existence throws into disarray a lot of previously held as-

sumptions about the other members of the *Australopithecus* group (especially *A. africanus,* which could be an evolutionary dead end). Biggest debate stems from the fact that fossils of animal bones discovered nearby bore cuts from stone tools. This would mean that *A. garhi* is the first tool user and also that such behavior predated increases in brain size. (The oldest stone tools, thought to be about 2.6 million years old, were also discovered nearby.)

NAME: ***Australopithecus aethiopicus***
TIME FRAME: Somewhere between 2.6 and 2.3 million years ago.
VITAL STATS: Interesting mix of the primitive and the advanced. Small brain size (410 cubic centimeters) and other parts of the skull are reminiscent of *A. afarensis.* Large, flat face with no forehead. Huge teeth, along with evidence of powerful chewing muscles suggests that this species ate grains and other tough foods.
COMMENTS: Known mostly by the "Black Skull," a fossil discovered in 1984 in the Lake Turkana area of Kenya. Scientists generally can't make up their minds whether to classify this in the *Australopithecus* or *Paranthropus* genus, since it is clearly on the border between the gracile species described previously (known for their lighter build, particularly in the skull and teeth) and the more robust (heavier-skulled, with larger teeth) species following, which many researchers classify as *Paranthropus.*

NAME: ***Paranthropus*** or ***Australopithecus robustus*** (Take your pick.)
TIME FRAME: About 2 to 1.5 million years ago.
VITAL STATS: Similar body to *A. africanus* (see previously), but the brain's definitely getting bigger (530 cubic centimeters). Considerable difference in body size between females and males, with males standing about four feet four inches tall and weighing about ninety-two pounds, and females standing three feet seven inches and coming in at a svelte seventy-one pounds.
COMMENTS: Nobody's sure of the exact relationship between the robust species. This one was discovered in South Africa by Robert Broom in 1938. Along with "Nutcracker Man" (below), it is assigned to the genus *Paranthropus* by some researchers, and to *Australopithecus* by others. Once again, this species demonstrates a powerful chewing mechanism, made for eating tough and coarse foods, which suggests these guys might have been the first vegetarians. This would make sense, since at this point we're on the verge of an ice age, so certain kinds of food might have been getting scarce. There is some speculation that the species may have been using tools as well, since animal bones found with the fossils might have been used for digging, and *P. robustus'* hand bones are developed enough to suggest some fine motor skills.

NAME: ***Paranthropus*** or ***Australopithecus boisei*** ("super robust")
TIME FRAME: 2.1 to 1.1 million years ago.

VITAL STATS: Similar in many ways to *P. robustus*, but beefier, standing as tall as five and a half feet and weighing as much as 150 pounds. Had even bigger teeth (he was known as the "Nutcracker Man"), with some molars measuring two centimeters from front to back. This suggests that these guys were still vegetarians, specializing in nuts, roots, and tasty tubers.

COMMENTS: The first *P. boisei* specimen was discovered in 1959 in Tanzania—a first for that area—by Mary Leakey. (Yes, that would be Richard's mom—are you seeing a pattern here?)

NAME: ***Homo habilis*** ("handy man")
TIME FRAME: Somewhere between 2.4 and 1.5 million years ago.
VITAL STATS: Four and a half to five feet tall, 64 to 100 pounds, brain volume about 750 cubic centimeters. Higher forehead indicates developed frontal and temporal lobes, and thus greater reasoning powers. Possibly capable of basic speech.
COMMENTS: Handy man clearly used tools—thus his name. Was generally smaller than his australopithecine cousins and had smaller teeth, so he ate just about anything he could get hold of, including meat. However, *H. habilis* was too small to take on big game, so his bigger brain came in handy to outsmart leopards.

NAME: ***Homo georgicus*** (named after Georgia, the ex-Soviet country where it was found)
TIME FRAME: About 1.8 million years ago.
VITAL STATS: A transitional species between *H. habilis* and *H. erectus*.
COMMENTS: Discovered in 2002, this specimen challenges the "out of Africa" mind-set. Before *H. georgicus*, hominids—specifically, the highly intelligent (comparatively speaking) *H. erectus*—were thought to have ventured into Europe no earlier than 1 million years ago. *H. georgicus* blows that theory out of the water.

NAME: ***Homo erectus*** ("erect man")
TIME FRAME: From 1.8 million to 300,000 years ago.
VITAL STATS: Nearly our size, with smaller jaw and larger brain (varying between 750 and 1225 cubic centimeters) than its predecessors. Probably stronger than modern humans. Despite its name, not the first to stand upright, but a more graceful walker than modern humans, whose frames have had to compensate for big-brained infants.
COMMENTS: A very Atkins-like protein-rich diet meant a larger brain and a smaller gut than the species that came before it. The good news: *H. erectus* produced the first hand axes, and was the first to make use of fire and shelter—the rude beginnings of culture. The bad news: Some of the skull fossils discovered

revealed that the brains had been removed prior to death, suggesting that *H. erectus* might have been a cannibal.

NAME: ***Homo ergaster*** ("work man")
TIME FRAME: 1.7 to 1.5 million years ago.
VITAL STATS: Despite differences (different-shaped brows, smaller brains), this African species is pretty much the same as the Eurasian *erectus*. In fact, some scientists classify *H. ergaster* as an earlier version of *H. erectus*, but it's a bit of a chicken-and-egg situation.
COMMENTS: As the name suggests, this species had a pretty extensive toolbox. Notable for the 1984 find of Turkana Boy, an almost complete skeleton of a lanky eleven-year-old adolescent. Considered the first hominid with a conscience, since a female *H. ergaster* was found to be in the advanced stages of a nasty bone disease, meaning that other members of the tribe must have looked after her.

NAME: ***Homo sapiens*** ("wise man")
TIME FRAME: From about 600,000 to 100,000 years ago.
VITAL STATS: Flatter faces, bigger brains (about 83 percent the size of ours), but still had bulging browridges.
COMMENTS: Also known as *Homo heidelbergensis*, from Heidelberg, Germany, where the first fossils were found back in 1907. No miracle makeovers here—*H. erectus* segued slowly into *H. sapiens*. He hunted, cooked his food, made wooden tools, and may have launched language. (The word *sauté* did not appear for several hundred millennia, however.)

NAME: ***Homo sapiens neanderthalensis*** (after the Neander Thal—or "valley"—of Germany, where they were first discovered)
TIME FRAME: From about 250,000 to 30,000 years ago.
VITAL STATS: Not hunched brutes, as popularly believed; the first skeleton, found in 1856, just happened to be that of a big, arthritic specimen. They were actually powerfully built, short (average male height was five feet six inches) and very solid; probably an adaptation to the nasty Ice Age climate.
COMMENTS: Generally accepted as a subspecies of *H. sapiens*, though believed by some to be a separate species, *Homo neanderthalensis*. Probably the first humans to conduct funerals, as evidenced by remains of flower pollen at a Neanderthal gravesite. The Neanderthals disappeared mysteriously about 35,000 years ago, to be replaced by Cro-Magnons, a hipper subspecies of *H. sapiens* responsible for the celebrated cave paintings in Lascaux, France. Nobody is sure whether the Neanderthals died out, were killed, or simply intermarried themselves into oblivion. Or maybe we all have a trace of Neanderthal in us and just don't know it.

NAME: ***Homo floresiensis*** (from Flores, the Indonesian island where they were discovered)

TIME FRAME: 94,000 to 12,000 years ago.

VITAL STATS: Nicknamed the Hobbits, and for good reason; these were wee creatures. The most complete skeleton was from a thirty-year-old female who stood a little taller than three feet and weighed a slight fifty-five pounds. Their brains were only about as big as grapefruits. Still, they made a variety of tools and clearly used fire.

COMMENTS: The Hobbits have put a lot of scientists into a quandary. Traditional paleontology has it that hominid intellect is directly correlated with brain size. So, what to make of these guys, who existed at the same time as modern *Homo sapiens* and were clearly smart enough to make weapons to hunt a variety of wildlife (including their favorite prey, a rat the size of a small golden retriever)? Even weirder, local Indonesian myths mention hairy little creatures called Ebu Gogo, who had a reputation as the worst sort of dinner guests, eating everything from the serving plates to the village infants.

NAME: ***Homo sapiens sapiens*** ("wise, wise man")

TIME FRAME: From about 195,000 years ago to today and perhaps even tomorrow.

VITAL STATS: Look in the mirror. Your brain probably logs in at about 1,350 cubic centimeters and you wouldn't kick yourself out of bed.

COMMENTS: Our subspecies, right or wrong. Its members were hunter-gatherers until relatively recently; they domesticated animals 18,000 years ago, invented agriculture 12,000 years ago, founded cities only about 5,000 years ago, and didn't invent the Slinky until the mid-twentieth century.

THE SPLICE OF LIFE

Genetic engineering is the process that inserts genes from one living organism into the cells of another, thereby custom-tailoring them to do work they weren't designed for. (But they still won't do windows.) For example, thanks to genetic engineering, or recombinant-DNA technique, millions of bacteria are kept busy churning out precious human insulin. Scientists built the microfactories by slipping the human gene responsible for the creation of insulin into *E. coli*, a mild-mannered bacterium found in our intestinal tract. (It beat waiting around until a pig died, then harvesting its pancreas.) So far, genetic engineering has been most successful with microorganisms, plants, mice (whose immune systems have been made to mimic those of human beings), and—Stephen King, take note—live-stock: pigs that gain weight faster, cows that give more milk. Science is still working on the problem of getting genetically altered DNA back into a human cell and, we're told, isn't even close to a solution. Someday, however, we may be able to replace or repair bad genes, like the ones responsible for such diseases as cystic fibrosis, sickle-cell anemia, and perhaps even cancer.

To understand how genetic engineering works, you've got to know about deoxyribonucleic acid, or DNA, three letters even more important than MTV. First, go back to the days when you were a single cell—a fertilized egg, or embryo, whose nucleus contained forty-six packages called chromosomes, twenty-three from each parent, carrying the coded information for all your inherited characteristics, from hair color to susceptibility to stress to, some would argue, sexual orientation and propensity for violence. As your cells divided, each new cell was issued forty-six identical chromosomes (except for your reproductive cells, which, in anticipation of future mating, have only twenty-three apiece). The strandlike chromosomes are made up of several thousand genes, each responsible for a particular trait. And the genes are composed of DNA, the chemical that runs the show, programming and operating all life processes. All living things have DNA in every cell. (The exception: Some viruses contain only a chemical cousin of DNA called RNA.) Indeed, it has been said that if the instructions coded in one person's DNA were written out, they would fill one thousand encyclopedia-sized volumes. You might want to wait for the movie.

In 1953 Francis Crick and James Watson earned a Nobel Prize for discovering that DNA is shaped like a spiral staircase, the famous double helix. Phosphates and sugars form the railing of the staircase, and pairs of four nitrogen bases in various combinations form the steps—up to about three billion of them in human DNA. The order of the base pairs determines the particular characteristics of any shrub, egret, or stand-up comic.

Twenty years after this discovery, two California researchers, Stanley Cohen and Herbert Boyer, found a way to perform DNA transplants. For example, it was they who turned bacteria into human-insulin factories, removing DNA from a human cell and cutting it with special enzymes at the spot where the needed gene is found. Then, using more enzymes, the human gene was snapped into a plasmid, a strand of extra DNA, found in bacteria. When that bacterium reproduces, it creates millions of copies of itself, each with the new gene. In this way scientists produce not only insulin but growth hormone and cancer-fighting interferon.

There's plenty of controversy and intrigue in the world of genetically altered organisms. In 1985, such an organism was tested for the first time outside the lab—semiofficially. A vaccine made by genetically altering a herpes virus was injected into 250 piglets. The test may have launched a golden age of agriculture—or a regulatory nightmare. What if the gene-altered vaccine goes wild, mutates, affects humans? And, not to slip into anticlimax or anything, will small family farmers be able to afford the new technology? You see the problem: legislators who have a hard time formulating a policy on Haiti set loose on something like this.

Gene splicing is not to be confused with cloning (see page 540). And don't get genetic engineering mixed up with in-vitro fertilization, the creation of test-tube babies. In that case, an ovum (more likely, several ova, to maximize the chances for success) are removed from the mother, fertilized in a petri dish by sperm from the father, and returned to the mother's womb. Today there are more than a million in-vitro children in the world; in fact, the first, Louise Brown of England, is now all grown up. And the term is unfair: The kid spends only a couple of days in a dish, as an egg $1/25$ of an inch in diameter.

Dr. James Watson, left, and Dr. Francis Crick with their Nobel Prize–winning model of the DNA molecule

In a newer procedure, so called prenatal adoption, a woman needn't even produce her own egg. Rather, the fertilized ova of another woman, who has been artificially inseminated with sperm from the first woman's mate, can be implanted in the womb of the first woman and the resulting fetus carried to term.

Yet another technique allows the freezing of eggs, sperm, and full-fledged embryos for future use. A woman might deposit a fertilized egg, meant to be reimplanted later, once she's sown her wild oats or launched her career. Or she could rent a womb, paying someone else to carry her child.

But mightn't that lead to the creation of a class of drone-moms, employed by people who want to buy their way out of morning sickness? Ah, that's just one of the ethical problems of biotechnology, the blanket term for all this fiddling around with Life Itself. Other sticklers: What if the wrong people start tampering with characteristics like physique, building a brave new world of superjocks and ultrawimps? What if a genetically engineered microbe escapes from the lab or the test area? There are still some eensy bugs to be worked out.

MANY ARE COLD BUT FEW ARE FROZEN

Yes, the Big Chill is coming, but you won't need your industrial-strength thermal underwear for another 3,000 to 20,000 years.

Over the past billion years, the earth has experienced three long periods during which ice built up at its poles, each period made up of several 100,000-year "ice ages," when glaciers advanced to cover much of the world. These ice ages were punctuated by 10,000-year "interglacials," warm spells marked by the melting of the vast ice sheets. We live at the end of such a temperate time-out; the last great ice age wound down about 7,000 years ago. At its peak, 20,000 years ago, glaciers encased much of North America, Europe, and Asia. Days were about eleven degrees colder than they are now, forcing humans and animals southward.

It's not hard to see how an ice age is caused by a temperature drop, creating summers cool enough that the previous winter's snow never melts. Several seasons' snows accumulate and compact to form glaciers. But what turns down the thermostat? The cold facts have been hotly debated, but the theory most widely accepted—the "astronomical" theory—states that three periodic changes in the earth's position relative to the sun seem to have launched ice ages by influencing the amount of solar radiation the earth receives.

Because of the gravitational pull of the sun and moon on the equator, the earth wobbles on its axis like a toy top slowing down. Every 22,000 years or so, it describes a circle in space. The axis also tilts, causing the seasons. When the North Pole tips away from the sun, it's winter in the Northern Hemisphere. Today, the angle of tilt is 23½°, but every 41,000 years it moves from 22° to 24° and back again. Perhaps the most important cycle is a change in the shape of the earth's orbit—from nearly circular to highly elliptical and back to circular—every 100,000 years due to the gravitational tug of fellow planets. The combined effect of these three cycles is to place the earth farther away from the sun at certain times, cooling the planet into an ice age.

If the astronomical theory makes sense to most scientists, why do some of them get all worked up about an imminent ice age? They insist that a veil of dust thrown up by man-made pollution and increased volcanic activity, together with thicker cloud cover generated by jet vapor, will lessen the amount of heat we get from the sun. (As so often happens in the wacky world of science, other people worry that some of these very same problems will make the earth too hot, not too cold.) Even if pollution and volcanoes do kick up enough dust to cause a slight drop in temperature (and we did find ourselves wearing sweaters a lot in the summer of 1991, right after Mount Pinatubo erupted in the Philippines) most scientists agree that this will not alter the primordial rhythms of the cosmos. It'll be thousands of years before the ice age gathers steam, to mix a metaphor. In the meantime, ours may ultimately be the warmest interglacial in history—dangerously warm, thanks to the greenhouse effect, up next.

SOME LIKE IT HOT

Leave your car parked all day in the sun with the windows rolled up and you'll return to an interior much hotter than the air outside. That's because window glass admits sunlight but traps heat. Carbon dioxide (CO_2), the gas we exhale, has a similar physical property; it is permeable to solar radiation (sunlight) but opaque to infrared radiation (heat). We need *some* CO_2 to act as insulation, along with water vapor and ozone, an unstable form of oxygen. No sweat, as long as CO_2 stays in its current proportions, i.e., only about .03 percent of the total atmosphere.

In the last 100 years, however, the amount of atmospheric CO_2 has increased about 15 percent, thanks to the burning of coal, oil, and natural gas and to widespread deforestation, which has eliminated plants that would have photosynthesized thousands of tons of CO_2 into oxygen and carbohydrates. The more CO_2 in the atmosphere, the hotter we get. A rise in the global temperature of a mere 2°C to 4°C (3.6°F to 7.2°F), which some climatologists and a brace of computers think could happen by this century, would melt polar ice caps, causing seas to rise and submerge coastal cities; upset weather patterns, triggering droughts and floods; and decrease wind circulation, playing havoc with ocean currents and depleting the fish supply. Already global average temperatures are 1.1°F warmer than they were a century ago, and virtually all the hottest years on record have taken place in the last two decades.

As is usual in the apocalypse biz, a few people see the greenhouse effect as a boon, not a bane. First of all, they insist, it won't get all *that* hot, and since CO_2 stimulates photosynthesis and increases plant yields, agricultural productivity could soar. Others think the warming trend could extend our interglacial period (see preceding entry) and even stave off the next ice age. More people, however, side with the British scientific journal *Nature*, which observed some time ago that the release of CO_2 from all those fossil fuels we've been burning may be the most important environmental issue in the world today.

Don't confuse the greenhouse effect with deodorant doom, the notion that such man-made chemical compounds as jet exhaust and chlorofluorocarbons used as spray-can propellants and in air-conditioning (and now being phased out in the United States and much of Europe but not in most of the rest of the world) will destroy the ozone layer (ten miles up and twenty miles thick) that protects the planet from deadly ultraviolet and other high-energy radiation and you from skin cancer and cataracts. But feel free to fret. In 1985, scientists reported a large, mysterious hole in the ozone layer over the South Pole. The hole, which has appeared every winter since, is as big as the continental United States and growing. It could be a transient, fluky weather phenomenon, a previously unnoticed cyclical event—or the awful thing everyone said would happen if we overdid the Aquanet.

ONE SINGS, THE OTHER DOESN'T

As the host said, rolling his eyes at the departing couple, "I don't know how they stay together. She's so left hemisphere, and he's so right hemisphere." He meant not that one of them's from Peshawar and the other's from Pittsburgh, but that their personalities epitomize the different ways the two halves of our brain seem to deal with the world. The left hemisphere, which controls the right half of the body, is responsible for language and logic; the right hemisphere, which controls the left half of the body, handles such intuitive, nonverbal processes as emotions and spatial relationships.

Uncovering this dichotomy earned a 1981 Nobel Prize for Roger Sperry, the Caltech psychobiologist who has experimented with people whose hemispheres had stopped speaking to each other. Ordinarily, the two halves of the brain are connected by a bundle of millions of nerve fibers, the corpus callosum, that allows signals to pass between the hemispheres and enables us to function as an integrated unit. By observing epileptics whose corpora callosa had been severed to prevent the spread of seizures, Sperry learned how the hemispheres divvy up the chores. In one classic experiment, he showed a different picture to each hemisphere simultaneously. (What the right eye sees is processed in the left hemisphere, and vice versa.) The left, verbal hemisphere was shown a picture of a knife and the right, nonverbal hemisphere was shown a picture of a spoon. Asked to *name* what he saw (to use language, a left hemisphere skill), the subject said knife. Asked to feel about with his left hand (a spiral spatial skill, controlled by the right hemisphere) and pick up what was in the picture, the subject chose a spoon from a group of objects. The right brain didn't know what the left brain was doing.

Until recently, the division of labor between left and right seemed fairly clearcut and accounted for a variety of functions: intellect versus intuition, concrete versus abstract thinking, objective versus subjective understanding, linear versus holistic perception. But now the head honchos themselves are split on a number of issues. Most agree that in 95 percent of right-handers and 67 percent of left-handers, the left hemisphere is specialized for language. But new evidence suggests that the right brain handles some important language functions: recognizing narrative and humor (storyline and punchline), interpreting tone of voice, making metaphors. Scientists also thought that the rational left brain was definitely boss, relinquishing control to the right only during sleep and dreams. Now it appears that there may be complementary dominance: Each hemisphere has a specialty and kicks in when duty calls.

The specialization may have less to do with what the task is than with how it's done. The right hemisphere seems to be a creative generalist, trying lots of solutions until one works. The left brain seems to be a plodding specialist, good at problems that are already familiar. Physical differences between the hemispheres support this hypothesis: The right hemisphere has long fibers plugging into many different areas of the brain, so it can schmooze and tune into the grapevine to solve a problem. The left brain contains shorter fibers tapping a smaller space, allowing it to do more detailed work. Still more studies (don't these neurologists ever go to the movies?) show that the right

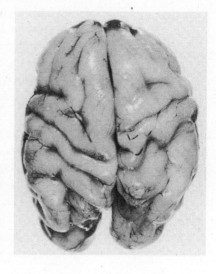

brain handles novelty, the left brain what's old hat. Unfamiliar faces are registered with the right hemisphere, familiar faces recognized with the left. Seasoned telegraphers interpret Morse code with the left brain, young whippersnappers, the right. Nonmusicians recognize melodies with the right hemisphere, but musicians use the left.

One interesting bit of conjecture to come from split-brain theory: the idea that *déjà vu*—the feeling that what's happening now has already happened in the past—may be nothing more than a neurological glitch that causes information to reach one hemisphere a split second before it reaches the other, so that a single event is processed twice.

STATE OF SIEGE

In the last thirty years, researchers have pieced together a picture of what happens when a foreign invader (e.g., a virus, bacterium, or parasite) enters the body. First, the army—our trillion white blood cells, born in the bone marrow—is alerted. These cells are of two major kinds: phagocytes ("cell eaters") that constantly patrol the body looking for intruders to devour, and lymphocytes, little commandos called T and B cells (T is for thymus, a small gland in the neck where T cells mature, B for bone marrow, the birthplace of B cells).

The soldiers in this army communicate via special proteins called cytokines. (Yes, of course, the military metaphor is tired, but "the body's bowling team" just doesn't cut it.) At the first sign of attack, special phagocytes called macrophages begin to swallow up the enemy, taking from each the equivalent of its dog tag—a tiny piece called the antigen, which a macrophage then displays on its own surface to attract helper T cells trained to recognize that particular antigen. (The thymus apparently has on hand a T cell able to recognize each of nature's hundreds of millions of antigens.) The macrophage secretes a cytokine called interleukin-1, which stimulates the helper T cells to reproduce. The helper Ts in turn secrete interleukin-2, which causes the creation of still more helper T cells and of *killer* T cells, whose job it is to clobber body cells already taken over by the invader. The new helper T cells release a lymphokine that orders the production of B cells in the spleen and lymph nodes. (Gives a whole new meaning to the term "sick day," doesn't it?)

Helper T cells then produce yet another lymphokine that tells B cells it's time to stop reproducing and start making antibodies, proteins tailored to fight specific antigens. The B cells are capable of creating millions of different antibodies, which either fight the invaders or flag them so phagocytes can recognize and devour them. The helper Ts, bless 'em, also secrete gamma interferon, a lymphokine that boosts T cell activation, assists B cells in producing antibodies, and helps macrophages digest the enemy.

When the invaders are vanquished, suppressor T cells tell the rest of the immune system to call it quits. Turning off the immune response is as important as launching it; some forms of blood cancer seem to be the result of T and B cells gone wild. And the immune system can mistakenly attack the body's own cells, as in such autoimmune diseases as rheumatoid arthritis and systemic lupus erythematosus. (Allergies are basically an immune-system overreaction to harmless invaders like dust and pollen.)

After the battle's over, phagocytes clean up the debris—dead cells, spilled protein fragments. Certain B and T cells, called memory cells, remain in the blood and the lymphatic system, on guard against renewed attack by the same antigen. Vaccination is a sort of basic training for memory cells; it introduces dead or weakened disease-causing substances into the body, priming memory cells so that they'll recognize the invader should it ever appear again in full force.

The good guys don't always win, of course. Cold viruses, for example, are constantly mutating to escape detection, and chemicals like asbestos overwhelm macrophages, which can't digest them. But for every bout with flu or herpes you suffer, thousands of sneak attacks have been thwarted.

There's one attacker against which the body seems to be powerless. HIV, the virus that causes AIDS, enters the body hidden inside helper T cells and macrophages in blood, semen, or vaginal fluid from an infected person. The virus apparently hijacks the victim's helper T cells when they come to investigate the intrusion. It keeps more or less quiet for months or years in these hostage T cells until they begin to divide, perhaps in response to some subsequent infection. Not only do the helper T cells fail to sound the alarm that would activate killer T and B cells, but they are themselves spreading the disease. Second-wave invaders, in the form of opportunistic infections, meet no opposition when they march in for the kill.

There is, however, good news on other fronts. Researchers are harnessing the arsenal of the immune system to fight cancer. Crossing spleen and cancer cells, they've cloned the resulting hybrid to produce antibodies that scout the body for incipient tumors. These so called monoclonal antibodies may someday be routinely used to deliver drugs or radiation to a specific diseased site in the body, bypassing healthy tissue.

Perhaps the most dramatic advances come from the relatively new field of psychoneuroimmunology, the study of interactions between the mind and the nervous, endocrine, and immune systems. Scientists have found, for example, that a body under stress produces an excess of the steroid cortisol. Because macrophages coping with all that cortisol can't seem to handle other infections, we catch more colds when we're stressed out. We know that exercise seems to stimulate the brain to produce natural painkillers, called endorphins and enkephalins, and that it might even affect T cell production. Why? And how do the brain and immune system communicate? It looks as though the brain may speak to the white blood cells through the cytokines, the protein messengers—and the white blood cells may talk back. The immune system may ultimately be found to work not just as an army, but as part of an elaborate feedback loop. Is it the body's discussion group? Its town meeting? Stand by for new metaphors.

GENES "R" US

OK, here's a quiz: The Human Genome Project was (a) a vast government-funded science project that began in 1990 and ended in 2000 with a fancy joint press conference hosted by then-president Bill Clinton and British prime minister Tony Blair; (b) a vast government-funded science project that began in 1990 and ended in April 2003, when the National Institutes of Health decided that it had closed many gaps in the previous calculations; (c) a vast government-funded science project that began in 1990 and ended in October 2004 when the journal *Nature* published what it called the most complete sequence of the human genome; or (d) all of the above.

You guessed it: d. And that's the beauty—and complexity—of the Human Genome Project. Its mission, essence, and conclusion are all in the eyes of the beholder.

But let's back up. You've read, or at least we've talked, about genes and DNA already (see page 530) and how there are thousands of genes in each of us, crammed along a tightly coiled strand of DNA in the nucleus of every one of the one hundred trillion cells that make up the human body, including hair and nails (but not red blood cells, which have no nucleus). And as we've mentioned, the information contained in that strand equals the data in a thousand encyclopedia volumes or, if you prefer, 125 Manhattan phone books. It programs the birth, development, growth, and death of each of us. And like any good computer program, it's relentlessly binary: Three billion pairs of chemical code letters form the railings of the famous spiral staircase, a.k.a. the double helix, and are responsible for making proteins, the basic building blocks of life.

The Human Genome Project (HGP) was originally set up in 1990 by the U.S. Department of Energy and the U.S. National Institutes of Health to identify the thousands of human genes and map the exact sequence of the three billion base pairs (or nucleotides) that make them up. (It's worth noting that about 97 percent of the nucleotides are "junk"—that is, they don't correspond to protein coding.) It was a complicated job, and in some ways a humbling experience. For one thing, as scientists got closer to completing the sequence, they realized that the number of genes humans have is considerably lower than original estimates: from upward of a hundred thousand back in the mid-1990s to a (more or less) final count of twenty-five thousand, which puts us on par with the puffer fish and the mustard weed. As Dr. Francis Collins, director of the HGP, put it: "If we wanted to claim our special attributes on this planet come from the gene count, we've taken a serious hit." (Since this discovery, scientists hoping to explain what makes humans different from other living creatures have begun focusing on the aforementioned "junk" parts of the genome, which, many believe, might turn out to be some kind of complicated genetic circuitry. If so, it could mean that human complexity arises not from the basic building blocks themselves but from the way those proteins are wired together.)

For a government agency, the HGP did a pretty good job. Regardless of which of the aforementioned dates count as the completion, it came in ahead of schedule (the project had been slated to take at least fifteen years) and, depending on your accounting system, probably under budget.

The mapping of the human genome is seen as the first step in tracking information on, among other things, four thousand genetically linked diseases. Theoretically, identifying the specific gene for a disease could lead to new therapies, which in turn could lead to cures for everything from Lyme disease to Alzheimer's to ALS (Lou Gehrig's disease) to severe combined immunodeficiency—the so called boy-in-the-bubble syndrome (all of which, and many others, have in fact been identified, thanks to the HGP). It could also give doctors a leg up in devising treatment plans for particular individuals. According to its proponents, someday your personal genome might be interpreted and the information transferred to a smart card. Then, when you got sick, you could walk into any hospital and hand over the card; doctors would be able to see all the glitches in your code (don't take it personally, we all have them), identify precisely what the problem is, and prescribe just the right treatment for your specific genetic makeup.

But as you may have guessed, we're still a long way from such a scenario. Yes, there *have* been major advances in the number of disease genes identified (from about 150 in 1990 to about 1,500 in 2002), and even in their application to cancer research (in 2004, scientists located a region of genes that increase a person's risk of getting lung cancer). But once you've discovered the elusive gene, the next steps—understanding the pathogenesis of the disease, then treating, and eventually, preventing it—are difficult, time-consuming, and costly.

There are also ethical complications, which tend to multiply, not disappear, as the science evolves. Do you really want to be in on that biggest of secrets, your biological fate? What would happen to unborn babies who were found to have the gene for, say, Huntington's chorea or cystic fibrosis? Would their parents decide to abort? What if you were told that your fetus had a better-than-50-percent chance of developing breast cancer or Alzheimer's in middle age? That's an awful lot of good years to decide to cut off in the name of a mere probability. And there are legions of parents who wouldn't be happy to hear that their child carried the gene for obesity—or homosexuality.

Granted, we've calmed down about some of these issues. For one thing, scientists have explained that it's rarely a single gene that makes Jimmy gay. Instead, they believe it has to do with how numerous genes interact with each other, how that genome "junk" works—and how closely the prepubescent Jimmy identifies with Judy Garland. Meanwhile, the focus has been shifting from the genes themselves to the *proteins* they make. (We may have the same number of genes as a field mouse, but our superior protein production means we're the ones exploiting Stuart Little and Mickey, not vice versa.) In any case, current thinking leans toward the conclusion that it's neither nature nor nurture that decides our fate, but rather some of both. After all, we know that cultural and economic factors—not to mention the dearth or glut of fast-food chains—have as much to do with obesity as the fat gene.

Nowadays, the ethical debate over genetic research revolves around more mundane questions; for instance, how will we keep personal genetic information from being used against us by employers and insurance companies? (It wouldn't be hard for them to obtain, given how it's all right there, in blood, fingernail clippings, and the hair on the barbershop floor.) Some U.S. politicians have tried to push a Genetic Nondiscrimination Act through Congress, but so far it has failed to gain passage.

On a more philosophical level, all of this genetic scrutiny has made one thing clear: Genetically speaking, people are a lot more alike than they are different. Scientists now say that 99.9 percent of human beings' DNA sequencing is identical. Not only that, but 50 percent of our genes are the same as a banana's. And we're even *closer* to the genetic makeup of a fruit fly. You might want to think about that the next time you reach for the flyswatter.

CLONING AND THE STEM CELL DEBATE

It all started with a little lamb named Dolly. Born on July 5, 1996, the ewe caught the world's attention as the first mammal to be cloned from the adult body cells of another. Until then, most scientists didn't believe that cloning from adult cells was possible. But Dolly, named after country singer Dolly Parton, opened up a whole new scientific realm—and a big can of worms.

But we should back up here. For all its cutting-edge, sci-fi associations, "cloning" is actually a pretty old term. Coined by a horticulturalist in 1903, it originally described an exact genetic copy of an individual organism, asexually produced, such as when a strawberry plant sends out clones to take root at an appropriate distance from the parent plant. Cloning took on new connotations in 1952 when biologists made a new frog from the DNA in the nucleus of an intestinal epithelial cell of a tadpole. After that, the floodgates opened, and within two decades scientists had cloned mice, pigs, sheep, and cattle. All of these clones were cultured from embryo cells. Dolly, however, was in a class by herself, since she was cloned from an adult cell—and her birth decimated the then-generally accepted theory that once cells reached adulthood, they were no longer totipotent (that is, able to develop into a complete organism).

Somatic cell nuclear transfer—the fancy name for cloning—is pretty simple, at least in theory. A cell is taken from an adult animal. The nucleus, along with the DNA inside it, is pulled out and placed beside an empty egg cell without a nucleus. (Think of it as sort of a blind date in a petri dish.) The egg and the nucleus are then nudged together by a mild electrical current and bathed in a kind of chemical love potion. The egg is essentially duped into thinking it has been fertilized, and in the best-case scenario it starts dividing like crazy. Although we like to think of clones being a mad-scientist experiment exclusively created in a test tube, the fact is that only the very beginnings of the process actually happen in vitro. Soon after its creation, the blastocyst (the ball of dividing cells that develops after conception) is transferred to the womb of a surrogate mom. (Dolly—or her cellular beginnings, anyway—were only "grown" in the lab for seven days before they were inserted into a blackface ewe's womb. The surrogate then carried her to term.)

As simple as all this sounds, cloning is notoriously ineffective. For every happy clone that survives beyond birth, there have been, according to some estimates, as many as a thousand unsuccessful ones. Obviously, those aren't great numbers. There are also questions about whether clones are genetically dysfunctional. Many cloned animals were born ill or deformed, or have died prematurely. This includes, alas, our friend Dolly, who developed lung disease along with a number of other ailments, and had to be put down in 2003 at the relatively young age (for a sheep) of six. Some scientists suggested that the genetic blueprint actually wears out, meaning that cloning has less in common with a Xerox copier than with the old ditto machine in the office of your junior high. Still, that hasn't stopped enterprising entrepreneurs from cloning other animals including, notably, champion racehorses. And as of this writing, one company, Genetic Savings and Clone (don't look at *us*), will create a carbon copy of your cat for only $32,000.

All these precedents have made it clear that the reproductive cloning of human beings is now within the realm of the possible. Whether or not it is desirable is another story, and a hot topic. Duplicating humans in the laboratory has an unnerving, *Frankenstein* (or at the very least *Boys from Brazil*) aspect to it that makes many people queasy. Though there have been no successful births of cloned humans (despite a number of unsubstantiated claims), in 2004 an alarmed United Nations General Assembly adopted a largely symbolic, nonbinding resolution to prohibit all forms of human cloning.

But cloning isn't only, or even chiefly, for reproductive purposes. Many scientists are far more interested in the fact that cloning can be used to create stem cells, the jacks-of-all-trades of the cell world. Stem cells are part of the body's repair system, dividing without limit and replenishing other cells in the organism. These remarkable creatures can either stay as they are or morph into something more specialized, such as a muscle cell, a brain cell, or a red blood cell. Advances in this kind of technology—called therapeutic cloning—may hold the key to curing diseases such as Alzheimer's, Parkinson's, and diabetes.

Unfortunately, therapeutic cloning and reproductive cloning are often collapsed in the public debate—particularly by those who believe that life begins at conception. (To the latter, extracting stem cells from cloned embryos—which destroys the embryo in the process—is simply high-tech abortion.) The moral complexities have resulted in restrictions in many countries, including Japan, where there is a mandatory ten-year sentence for anyone found guilty of attempting to clone human beings, and the United States, where federal funding for the creation or manipulation of embryos is prohibited. These restrictions have frustrated many scientists and their supporters (including former First Lady Nancy Reagan, who became an outspoken advocate of stem cell research when her husband succumbed to Alzheimer's), who see embryonic stem cell research as the key to future advancements in medicine. But even advocates urge caution.

One popular scenario warns of the experimental procedure in which human stem cells are inserted into an animal embryo to see how they divide and change in a living system. The research may be necessary—you would probably want to test the technology on lab rats before you tried it on a human friend—but what do we make of the chimera (named after the creature in Greek mythology that is part lion, part goat, and part serpent) that has been created? Since it possesses human qualities (at least on a cellular level), does that mean it has human rights? And what happens if a male lab-created mouse with human cells mates with a female lab-created mouse that also has human cells? As one science writer put it, there is the chance we could have "a sort of Stuart Little scenario, but in reverse and not so cute."

Making a Name for Yourself in Science

ARCHIMEDES' PRINCIPLE

Holds that buoyancy is the loss of weight an object seems to incur when it is placed in a liquid, and that that loss is equal to the weight of the liquid it displaces. Takes off from (but is not restricted to) the "Eureka!" business.

To recap, it's the third century B.C.; we're in Syracuse, in Sicily (for centuries an important Greek outpost); and the local king, Hiero II, has reason to suspect that the royal jeweler has sneaked some silver into the new, and supposedly 100 percent gold, royal crown. Hiero calls in Archimedes, who for a while is stumped. He knows that gold weighs more than silver and consequently has less volume and that the volume of a piece of pure gold and of a crown of pure gold weighing the same amount would be the same. But how to measure the volume of a strange-shaped thing like a crown? Then, pondering the problem one day in

the tub, Archimedes realizes that a body immersed in liquid displaces exactly its own volume of that liquid. Measure the volume of the water that's spilled over the side of the tub and you've got the volume of the thing *in* the tub. At which point, Archimedes shouts "Eureka!" and runs home naked, where he puts first the piece of pure gold, then the crown said to be of pure gold, in a basin of water. The crown causes the water to rise higher, revealing itself to have a greater volume (and hence to be less dense, i.e., *not* pure gold). And revealing the jeweler to be guilty.

The story told, bear in mind that Archimedes' principle, as opposed to Archimedes' bath, applies not only to bodies immersed in water but to bodies floating on it, and not only to solids but to liquids and gases. It explains, in addition to why ships float, why balloons rise, and it warns that in determining what will and what won't sink, float, or fly away, both weight and volume must be considered, not to mention shape and position. If you can manage to remember anything here beyond "Eureka!" you might go for "specific gravity," the ratio of a given density of a solid or a liquid to the density of water (and of a gas to air), and a term that, while unknown to Archimedes, pretty much sums up what his principle winds up being all about.

FIBONACCI SERIES

He started with 1, as who among us wouldn't? Then he repeated it: 1, 1. Then he added the two: 1, 1, 2. And he kept on adding, always the concluding pair of what was now, unmistakably, a series: 1, 1, 2, 3; 1, 1, 2, 3, 5; 1, 1, 2, 3, 5, 8. And so on, all the way to 1, 1, 2, 3, 5, 8, 13, 21, 34, 55, 89, 144. And why stop there? So . . . 233, 377, 610, 987, 1,597, but you get the picture. Now, if you're wondering what, apart from the lack of late-night television in thirteenth-century Pisa, accounts for Fibonacci's perseverance, we can report that he was working out the solution to the problem of how many pairs of rabbits can be produced from a single pair of rabbits, if every month every pair begets a new pair, which from the second month on is itself productive, assuming that none of the rabbits die (or become bored) and each pair consists of a male and a female.

Wait, it gets interesting. Turns out that the Fibonacci series not only connects with controlled population growth, it also keeps popping up on nature walks. For instance, the ratio of scales distributed in opposing spirals around a pine cone is 5:8; of bumps around a pineapple, 8:13; of seeds in the center of a sunflower, 21:34. All of which are *adjacent Fibonacci pairs*. If nature doesn't do it for you, try culture. Seems the ratio between any two adjacent Fibonacci numbers (after 3) is roughly 1:1.618—none other than the ratio behind the celebrated Golden Section, in mathematics the division of a line segment into two parts such that the whole segment is to the larger part as the larger part is to the smaller. The Golden Rectangle, whose length and width are the two parts of a line segment divided Golden Section–style, is a big deal in art and architecture because its proportions are so satisfying to the eye, incorporating, to hear the aestheticians tell it, both static unity and dynamic variety. The classic example here is the façade of the Parthenon, but Golden Rectangles have also been found in paintings by everybody from Leonardo to Mondrian.

THE LINNAEAN SYSTEM OF
TAXONOMIC CLASSIFICATION

What's it to you whether or not we have an orderly, scientifically sound method for cataloguing plants and animals? Not much. But it comes in awfully handy for scientists who, up until the middle of the eighteenth century, had to say something like "that little yellow flower with the spots on its petals" every time they wanted to compare notes. It was the Swedish botanist Carolus Linnaeus who came up with the idea, shocking in its day, of dividing plants into twenty-four "classes" distinguished by their sex (for which he has been called "the Freud of the botanical world"), that is, according to the length and number of stamens and pistils in their flowers, then subdividing those classes into "orders" based on the number of pistils. The sexual approach made sense in light of the then-novel idea of dividing God's creatures into broad categories, called "species," according to their individual characteristics; Linnaeus grouped his species by their ability to reproduce the same characteristics, generation after generation.

Besides coming up with a game plan, Linnaeus hit on the idea of using binomial nomenclature—that is, two names, one for the genus (as in "*Homo*"), one for the species (as in "*sapiens*")—as a shorthand labeling system to replace the cumbersome and confusing descriptive names botanists were using at the time. Then he got everyone he knew to run around frantically naming plants and animals as fast as they could, hoping to get absolutely everything in creation named before some unsuspecting botanist or zoologist somewhere used the same name for a different species, thereby messing up the system. As a result, many of these names were arbitrary, spur-of-the-moment affairs that may, today, strike us as unsystematic and not all that helpful.

Modern naturalists also disagree with certain of Linnaeus' categories, and, to the old "kingdoms" of Plantae (plants) and Animalia (animals) they've added a third, Protista, to cover single-celled amoebas, bacteria, slime molds, and the like. Nevertheless, the Linnaean system, arbitrary and artificial as it may be, is still the best we've got.

BROWNIAN MOVEMENT

The zigzag, irregular dance done by minute particles of matter when suspended in a liquid; named for Robert Brown, the botanist who established its existence in 1827, while watching microscopic pollen grains float around in water. Brown noticed that although the direction any particular pollen grain would take was unpredictable, all the grains moved faster when the water got hotter and slowed down as it cooled. Einstein later did a paper on Brownian movement, theorizing that the grains were always in motion because they were being batted around by water molecules; the hotter the water, the faster the water molecules moved, and the more direct hits to the pollen grains. Eventually, Brownian movement became an important substantiating factor of the kinetic molecular theory of matter, which states that matter is composed of tiny particles (a.k.a. molecules) that are constantly in motion.

THE DOPPLER EFFECT

The change in the frequency of a wave (whether of sound or of light) that occurs whenever there is a change in the distance between the source and the receiver; named for the early nineteenth-century Austrian physicist Christian Doppler. If the source of the waves and the receiver are approaching each other (or one is approaching the other), Doppler observed, the frequency of the wavelengths increases and the waves get shorter, producing high-pitched sounds and bluish light. If the source and receiver are moving farther apart, sound waves are pitched lower and light appears reddish. (The most commonly cited example of the Doppler effect: the train whistle that screeches in the distance, dropping in pitch as it approaches the platform where you're standing.) Used in radar to track the velocity of a moving object; in astronomy to measure distances between and rotations of stars, planets, and entire galaxies; also to track satellites. When, in 1929, the astronomer Edwin Hubble noticed that the light from distant stars was becoming redder, he took this "Doppler shift" or "red shift" to mean that the stars were rushing away from earth. His conclusion, known as Hubble's Law and now generally accepted, was that the universe is expanding.

BOOLEAN ALGEBRA

Ever since Aristotle—as George Boole, the nineteenth-century English mathematician, would have been the first to tell you—language has been getting in the way of truth. That is, the way we talk, with all its inaccuracy, ambiguity, and potential for hysteria, tends to mess up the way we think.

Boole's solution: Get rid of the words altogether, instead letting symbols (*a* and *b*, *x* and *y*, *P* and *Q*, whatever; it doesn't matter that they're arbitrary as long as they're precise) stand for the components of thought, which, not entirely coincidentally, often turn out also to be the elements of formal logic. Then, manipulate the symbols mathematically, in a kind of mental algebra that's based on such simple operations as negation (corresponding roughly to what you and I mean by "not"), conjunction (our "and"), and alternation ("or"); and that—here's where you're supposed to stand up and applaud—always reduces things, no matter how complicated or abstruse, to either a "1" (standing for "all" or "true") or a "0" (standing for "nothing" or "false"). Thus was not only Boolean algebra born, but also the device known as the truth table (which lists all possible combinations of true and false values that can accrue in the interplay of two or more statements) and the intellectual specialty known as symbolic logic (which succeeded in wresting logic from the philosophers and delivering it over to the mathematicians).

For fifty years nobody but Lewis Carroll seems to have gotten all that turned on by Boole's "laws of thought," but those laws did, shortly before World War I, knock the socks off Alfred North Whitehead (see page 328) and Bertrand Russell, who relied on them to establish more or less persuasively that not only was logic the proper domain of mathematics, it was indeed where the latter's roots lay. Since then there's been no stemming the Boolean tide. First lawyers took to constructing truth tables in the courtroom. Then telephone-company engineers began thinking of parallel "on/off" switches and "open/closed" circuitry in 0-vs.-1 terms. To the point that today it's the rare computer that doesn't proceed along the relentlessly binary lines first laid down by Boole—as stunning an example as the atom bomb of how theory, and the wackier the better, fuels technology.

MÖBIUS STRIP

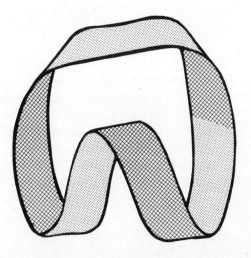

Take an ordinary flat strip of paper. Give it a half-twist. Now Scotch-tape the two ends together to form a loop. OK, ready? Take a red Magic Marker and color in one side of the loop, and a green Magic Marker and color in the other. Whoops! That's right: The strip has only one "side"—or do we mean "one" side? Easy to construct and hard to imagine, the so called Möbius strip (named after the nineteenth-century German mathematician and astronomer who first described it) also reacts strangely to scissors: Cut it along a line drawn lengthwise down its middle and you'll get not two Möbius strips but a normal two-sided strip twice as long as the one you started with. (The mathematicians' explanation for this: A Möbius strip has only one edge; the cut adds a second edge and with it a second side.) Now try cutting a new strip along a line one-third of the way in from its edge; we won't tell you what you'll wind up with, but it's pretty weird, too.

As to what's *really* going on here: The subject is geometric transformations undertaken in space, collectively known as topology. Superficially a series of exercises in paradox reminiscent of all those old M. C. Escher drawings, topology nevertheless crystallizes a bunch of the century's top issues. For instance, in the case of the Möbius strip, what does it purport that something that appears at a given point to be two-sided, when traced round its continuum, is in fact one-sided? One theory: that life is holistic, not reductionistic; that persisting in trying to consider everything in terms of its component parts (the brain as a collection of neurons, say) risks missing the whole (the brain as mind).

GÖDEL'S INCOMPLETENESS THEOREM

The problem here—if you, unlike most twentieth-century theoreticians, still want to look at it as a problem—is self-reference, a historic stumbling block for logicians. In 1931, the Czech-born mathematician Kurt Gödel demonstrated that within any given branch of mathematics, there would always be some propositions that couldn't be proven either true or false using the rules and axioms (statements like 1 = 1 that are accepted without proof) of that mathematical branch itself. You might be able to prove every conceivable statement about numbers within a system by going *outside* the system in order to come up with new rules and axioms, but by doing so, you'll only create a larger system with its own unprovable statements. The implication is that *all* logical systems of any complexity are, by definition, incomplete; each of them contains, at any given time, more true statements than it can possibly prove according to its own defining set of rules.

Gödel's theorem has been used to argue that a computer can never be as smart as a human being because the extent of its knowledge is limited by a fixed set of axioms, whereas people can discover unexpected truths. (Maybe, but we've met pocket *calculators* that are smarter than some of the people we went to high school with.) It plays a part in modern linguistic theories, which emphasize the power of language to come up with new ways to express new ideas. And it has been taken to imply that you'll never entirely understand yourself, since your mind, like any other closed system, can only be sure of what it knows about itself by relying on what it knows.

Fun—or at Least a Few Minutes—with Numbers

Either mathematics is poetry, all density and precision, or it's the most flagrant type of entrepreneurship, in which nobody's satisfied until his headquarters is taller than anybody else's headquarters. Exhibit A: Numbers—the symbols we use to count up all the things around us that aren't unique or continuous—an area where mathematicians have gotten either more lyrical or more rapacious over the years, depending on how you look at it. Below, some of the number "types" they've managed to corner and/or construct for themselves.

The Number System

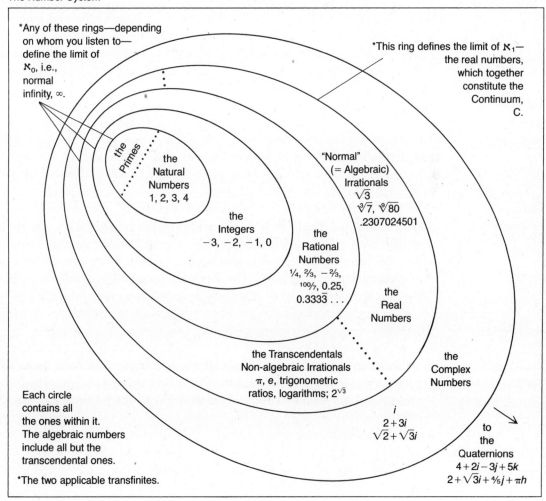

*Any of these rings—depending on whom you listen to—define the limit of $\aleph_0$, i.e., normal infinity, ∞.

*This ring defines the limit of $\aleph_1$—the real numbers, which together constitute the Continuum, C.

the Primes

the Natural Numbers
1, 2, 3, 4

the Integers
−3, −2, −1, 0

"Normal" (= Algebraic) Irrationals
$\sqrt{3}$
$\sqrt[3]{7}$, $\sqrt[9]{80}$
.2307024501

the Rational Numbers
¼, ⅔, −⅔,
¹⁰⁰⁄₇, 0.25,
0.3333 . . .

the Real Numbers

the Complex Numbers

the Transcendentals
Non-algebraic Irrationals
π, e, trigonometric
ratios, logarithms; $2^{\sqrt{3}}$

i
$2 + 3i$
$\sqrt{2} + \sqrt{3}i$

to the Quaternions
$4 + 2i - 3j + 5k$
$2 + \sqrt{3}i + \frac{4}{5}j + \pi h$

Each circle contains all the ones within it. The algebraic numbers include all but the transcendental ones.

*The two applicable transfinites.

NATURAL

NATURE:	The counting numbers.
EXAMPLES:	1, 2, 3, 4, . . .
HISTORY:	In use since man first felt a need to know how many of something—goats, pots, issues of *Penthouse*—he owned. Some primitive societies still make do with "one," "two," and "many."
PRACTICAL USES:	Conducting censuses, scoring basketball games, seating people at dinner parties.
MATHEMATICAL RESONANCES:	One of the first creative highs. The sense among early "numbers" types that they were on to something big, something real *and* abstract. Also, the inevitability of distinctions between "odd" and "even," and "cardinal" (1, 2, 3; the counting numbers) and "ordinal" (1st, 2nd, 3rd; the ranking numbers). Ditto, of considerations of "infinity," the quality of endlessness, symbolized as ∞, toward which the natural numbers were seen to progress.

PRIME

NATURE:	Those natural numbers higher than 1 that can't be evenly divided by any number other than themselves and 1. (Opposed to the *composite* numbers.)
EXAMPLES:	2, 3, 5, 7, 11, 13, 17, . . .
HISTORY:	Arduous. Also, odd. Euclid proved there was no end to the primes. Somebody else constructed a "sieve" to isolate them. Any number of Renaissance-and-later men tried to devise a formula that would generate all possible ones: no dice. Then there's the Goldbach conjecture of 1,742. The largest known prime (as of this writing) has 7,816,230 digits; needless to say, they now have the computers on the case.
PRACTICAL USES:	None whatsoever, unless you find yourself at a mathematicians' convention.
MATHEMATICAL RESONANCES:	A thorn in the side. Mathematicians can't bear that they still don't know why primes fall where they do, or, for that matter, how many there are. Then, too, primes are just one example of sets of numbers having special properties that the Greeks and others managed to isolate. Another time we'll tell you about the perfects and the amicables.

INTEGER

NATURE: The natural numbers, plus 0 and all the negative numbers. Also called the whole numbers.

EXAMPLES: $\dots, -4, -3, -2, -1, 0, 1, 2, 3, 4, \dots$

HISTORY: Zero, an ancient Hindu innovation, arrived in Europe in Roman times, along with the Arabic numerals; it was an instant hit. Negative numbers (from the Latin *negare*, "to deny") had a harder time: If the root of an equation was less than 0, the Greeks, so flexible in other respects, called it "fictitious" and threw it out. Only in the sixteenth century did an Italian, Cardano, systematically use negative numbers, pointing out that there *can* be less than nothing—a debt, for instance.

PRACTICAL USES: Negative numbers make debit-heavy bookkeeping elegant. Zero makes 37 different from 307 or 3,700.

MATHEMATICAL RESONANCES: Now there was a genuine number line, stretching infinitely to both left and right. Also, all equations of the $A + x = 0$ variety could be solved. And, there was 0, with all its inherent weirdness, to think about.

RATIONAL

NATURE: The integers, plus all fractions (or their decimal representations), positive and negative, a fraction being defined as the ratio of two integers, a/b, where $b \neq 0$.

EXAMPLES: $1/2, 7/5, -2/3, .25, .\overline{3333}, \dots$

HISTORY: The Egyptians and the Babylonians could handle fractions, though (a) they didn't know what they were doing, and (b) conservatives of the day sneered at the idea of a number like $7^1/2$, which was neither 7 nor 8. As usual, it took the Greeks to dignify, codify, and promote the idea. Since then, second nature to everybody.

PRACTICAL USES: Measuring (as opposed to counting), dealing with continuous quantities like age, Brie, and drapery material, which don't always break into convenient pieces. Also, sharing.

MATHEMATICAL RESONANCES: A flush of pleasure: Rationals *felt* good. Besides, all linear (or first-degree) equations, of the $Ax + B = 0$ variety, now had one—and only one—solution. Geometrically speaking, all you needed was a straightedge.

REAL

NATURE: The rational numbers, plus the zillions of irrational ones, which can't be expressed in fraction form: imperfect square, cube, and higher roots; decimals that neither terminate nor repeat; the transcendentals.

EXAMPLES: $\sqrt{2}, \sqrt[3]{7}, \sqrt[19]{311}; .2302030020000732\ldots; \pi, e$

HISTORY: $\sqrt{2}$, the first irrational, was discovered by Pythagoras, c. 500 B.C., when he constructed a right angle, each of whose sides was one unit long, and measured its hypotenuse. His proof that it couldn't be put into fractional form was very upsetting, and resulted in the immediate sacrifice of a hundred oxen. π, the ratio of a circle's circumference to its diameter, wasn't proved to be irrational until 1761. In between, it was discovered that there are a whole lot more irrational numbers than rational ones.

PRACTICAL USES: With the exception of π and e, few if any, despite all the brouhaha. On the other hand, square roots are as much a part of the collective consciousness as asparagus or the march from *Carmen*.

MATHEMATICAL RESONANCES: Like arriving at your surprise party with a 102° fever: elation tempered by shakiness. But, the real numbers could be shown to correspond in a perfect, one-to-one way with all the points on a line (regardless of its length); this endless series of points was termed the Continuum (abbreviated C), and proved to be much more endless than the mere ∞ formed by the natural numbers. Also, you could now solve any quadratic (or second-degree) equation of the $Ax^2 + Bx + C = 0$ variety.

TRANSCENDENTAL

NATURE: A special category of irrational numbers: They're real, all right, but they're not algebraic.

EXAMPLES: π, e, plus all the trigonometric ratios and logarithms they give rise to; also any quantity (except 0 and 1) raised "radically," e.g., $2^{\sqrt{3}}$.

HISTORY: In 1844 the Frenchman Joseph Liouville proved the existence of transcendentals—irrationals that would not serve as solutions to any of the infinite number of polynomial equations in any of the infinite number of degrees possible—but couldn't come up with an example. In 1873 somebody else showed that e, the base of the so called "natural" logarithms, was transcendental. In 1882 still another somebody showed the same of π. Since then, so many transcendentals have turned up that a lot of us have simply stopped answering the doorbell.

PRACTICAL USES: π (or pi, from the first letter of *perimetron*, Greek for "measurement around") is indispensable in carpentry and construction. e figures in statistics and nuclear physics, and, in the days before slide rules and pocket calculators put logarithms out of business, enjoyed a certain vogue. They tell us that trigonometric functions allow you to gauge the height of a telephone pole from the length of its shadow, but where we live all the phone lines are underground.

| MATHEMATICAL RESONANCES: | The transcendental numbers constitute an infinity even greater than the algebraic ones. Also, since π is transcendental, nobody has to try to "square the circle" using only a straightedge and compass anymore. Flash: $e^{\pi i} = -1$. |

COMPLEX

| NATURE: | The real numbers, plus all the *imaginary* ones, based on i, defined as $\sqrt{-1}$. But especially, these numbers when seen to consist of both real and imaginary components. |

| EXAMPLES: | $3 + 2i$, $3 - \sqrt{2}i$, $0 + \sqrt{2}i$, $3 + 0i$ |

| HISTORY: | What *do* you do with an equation like $x^2 + 1 = 0$? In 1777, Leonhard Euler, the most prolific mathematician of all time, introduced the symbol i (for "imaginary") to stand for the $\sqrt{-1}$. Like the X in "X-ray," it was both a shriek of victory and an admission of perplexity. But imaginary numbers, like negative numbers, caught on. |

| PRACTICAL USES: | The description and handling of vector quantities, which have not only magnitude but direction. |

| MATHEMATICAL RESONANCES: | The complex numbers constitute a plane and correspond in a perfect one-to-one way with the points in it (cf. the *line* of real numbers). Also, with them on board, you'll always have the solutions to polynomial equations of the $Ax^n + Bx^{n-1} + Cx^{n-2} + \ldots + Z = 0$ variety, no matter how high n gets, and you'll always have exactly the same number of solutions as the degree of n. With the complexes, man can solve any such polynomial, providing it has rational coefficients. In general, mathematicians were so excited by all of this that they couldn't not push their luck: The result was quaternions (see next page). |

ALGEBRAIC

| NATURE: | So called because they turn up as the solutions of algebra-style equations. Which means all of the above numbers except the transcendental ones. |

| EXAMPLES: | To reprise: 2, 0, −2, $\frac{1}{2}$, $-\frac{3}{4}$, .3333 . . . , .2302030020000732 . . . , $\sqrt[3]{7}$, 3 + 2i, 0.5 − 3i |

| HISTORY: | The nineteenth century was the big one here: Gauss, Kummer, and Dedekind. Ideals, unique factorization, and Abelian number fields. |

| PRACTICAL USES: | There were repercussions in mathematical physics, but we admit that's not rewiring the living-room lamp. Frankly, lingering over this category is probably a mistake. |

| MATHEMATICAL RESONANCES: | First and foremost, a way of gathering all of the above together so that they make sense and can breathe a bit. However, what was originally a scheme for investigating the solution of problems had now become a whole *thing*, an end in itself. The beat goes on. |

TRANSFINITE

NATURE: "Styles" of infinity. And the sky's the limit.

EXAMPLES: $\aleph_0$, $\aleph_1$, $\aleph_2$, $\aleph_3$, . . . , $\aleph_n$ (The letter is aleph, first of the Hebrew alphabet. Say "aleph-null," "aleph-one," "aleph-two," and so on. Or maintain a discreet silence.)

HISTORY: In 1895, the German mathematician Georg Cantor worked out "the arithmetics of infinity," a whole series of endlessnesses. Aleph-null is simple infinity: the familiar ∞, roughly equivalent to the endlessness of the natural numbers (or, in some systems, the integers or even the rationals). Aleph-one is the infinity of the Continuum, C, roughly all the real numbers or, depending on how you look at it, all the points in a line (or a square or a cube). Aleph-two may or may not be the endlessness of all curves. And nobody has been able to figure out what aleph-three, let alone aleph-thirty, might stand for.

PRACTICAL USES: Hmmm?

MATHEMATICAL RESONANCES: The mathematical imagination rents the video of *Yellow Submarine*, then goes out for Indian food. While everybody continues to talk about this one, it was really Cantor's baby, and he's with his alephs now; a kind of dead end.

QUATERNION

NATURE: The complex number concept extended from two dimensions to four.

EXAMPLES: $4 - 2i - 3j + 5k, 2 + \sqrt{3}\,i + \frac{4}{5}j - \pi k$

HISTORY: First suggested by William Hamilton in 1843 in response to his personal successes with complex numbers. Subsequently taken into even more dimensions—just as you suspected they would be.

PRACTICAL USES: Engineers get into them. But you're up past your bedtime.

MATHEMATICAL RESONANCES: The feeling that, once having learned to walk, one can run. Also fly. The lesson here is that when you extend numbers beyond the complex stage, you do so at the expense of something called permanence; one by one, properties you took for granted fall away. For instance, with quaternions, you have to give up either the role 0 plays *or* multiplicative commutativity (i.e., x times y no longer equals y times x). Say good night, Gracie.

Double Whammy

A s it happens, two of the biggest deals in modern science start with the letter *e*: entropy and evolution. Each spans two centuries (plus this one), and each has the kind of reverberations that can't really be done justice to on restroom walls. These are their stories.

ENTROPY, THE LAWS OF THERMODYNAMICS, AND WHY YOU MAY HAVE BEEN FEELING TIRED AND LISTLESS LATELY

Entropy is what the Second Law of Thermodynamics is all about. Unfortunately, most of us seem to have gotten bogged down shortly after the First Law. Nothing surprising about that—understanding the First Law doesn't demand much in the way of concentration or stamina. The basic principle of thermodynamics, the branch of physics dealing with the transformation of heat into work and other forms of energy, it simply states that "energy is conserved"; that is, it's indestructible—there is always the same total amount of it in the universe. The First Law of Thermodynamics was a big deal back when people were trying to build better steam engines; today, it serves chiefly as the solid platform from which scientists and philosophers like to hurl themselves into the abyss of the Second Law.

The latter states, with deceptive simplicity, that "the entropy of the universe tends to a maximum." Already, whether you know it or not, you're in trouble. Entropy is a measure of the total disorder, randomness, or chaos in a system. In thermodynamics, it crops up every time any work gets done, since the only way work *ever* gets done is through heat transfers—hot water coming into contact with cool air, for instance, to produce the steam that drives a steam engine. At the outset, the system is said to be at a low level of entropy: The fast-moving water molecules are distinct from the slow-moving air molecules, and the whole thing has a kind of order to it. But as the heat flows into the cooler medium—as heat naturally does—the fast-moving molecules begin to spend themselves, mixing with the slow ones until eventually all the molecules are moving at approximately the same speed. At this point, we're at maximum entropy; everything is at the same temperature, all the molecules are milling about without any particular order, and nothing more can be accomplished—the system has, literally and figuratively, run out of steam. The energy within the system is still there, but unless you separate the molecules again, returning them to a state of tension by heating some and chilling others, it can't be used to make things happen anymore.

Not your problem, you think, since your car runs on gas? Guess again, mush-for-brains. Outside thermodynamics, increased entropy—things going from a state of relative order to one of disorder—is the upshot of all natural actions. It's what happens when you let your vodka on the rocks sit around for a while and before you know it the ice cubes have melted into the vodka and the only thing worth dealing with is the lemon twist. It's what happens when you move into a nice neighborhood and within a few years it turns into the South Bronx. It's what happens to your body from about age thirty on. And, as scientists predicted back in the nineteenth century, it's what's going to happen to the universe—or at least, to our galaxy—in the scenario known as the "heat death" of the universe: Solar energy, the product of a hot sun turning in cold space, will inevitably run out, molecular chaos will prevail, and we'll all be left sitting in a lukewarm cosmic bath watching our toes decay.

You can see why the concept of entropy made the Victorians, already obsessed with keeping their corset stays in place, rather sad. Today, however, we prefer to brood about our weight and take a more objective approach to the Second Law, which has all sorts of interesting ramifications. It has, for instance, given us the "arrow of time," a metaphor that expresses the purely physical distinction between past and present; the fact that time is an observable, one-way progression from order to disorder, and not just a figment of our imaginations. If you look at two still photos of eggs, one showing them in their unbroken shells, the other, scrambled in a frying pan, you immediately know which came first; reverse the order and you know something's screwy. Time flows in one direction only. Another thing about progressive disorder: It's synonymous with increasing complexity. The picture of the eggs in their shells is neater, simpler, and easier to make sense of than the one showing a gloppy mess in the pan. These two concepts—the arrow of time and the increased complexity of high-entropy states—helped convince scientists earlier in this century that the universe did, in fact, have a beginning, and encouraged them to come up with the idea of the Big Bang (see page 509).

Entropy is also a hot topic among information theorists, who point out that increased complexity seems to add up to more, not less, order; and anyway, if it leads to richness of thought and communication, more power to it. Besides, according to the Second Law, the world should be falling apart by now, and it's not. But maybe that's because the universe is expanding; who's to say that the apparent order we see in our corner of it isn't balanced by total chaos at some other extremity? Then there's the whole business of probability, with which entropy is embroiled in a way that's enough, in itself, to make your brains hurt: There is no law that states absolutely that entropy *can't* be reversed, that the scrambled eggs can't re-form into their shells or your body revert to a state of adolescent glory—only that the probability of any of that happening is so small as to be virtually nil. At least in the universe as we know it. But what do we know? Maybe what looks like disorder to us is really order. And then there's the fact (don't slow down now or you're lost) that the Second Law doesn't seem to operate the same way on the subatomic level, where time flows in at least two directions, if it flows at all. Oh, there's a lot more to think about, including, yes, the Third Law of Thermodynamics, but by now, you're probably mulling over the First Law again. As for us, we're smart enough to know maximum entropy once we're up to our eyeballs in it.

EVOLUTION, THE LAW OF NATURAL SELECTION, AND WHY YOU MAY HAVE BEEN FEELING STRESSED OUT AND PARANOID LATELY

Evolution—literally, "unrolling"—wasn't Charles Darwin's invention, much less his personal property (see page 564). In fact, the Enlightenment, a whole century before, had celebrated the notion of progress, a basically upbeat take on the inevitability of gradual human change. Hegel had introduced evolution into philosophy, and Marx brought it into politics. Even scientists—geologists and biologists—had been speculating, since 1800 or so, on the evolutionary development of the earth and of the things that lived on it. What Darwin did was to make evolution come off as science—first, in his *Origin of Species*, published in 1859; later, in his *Descent of Man*, published in 1871.

By evolution Darwin meant that all plant and animal species are by their very nature mutable, able (and, more than that, under some pressure) to undergo small changes in their makeup; and that all existing plants and animals have developed in such a fashion from others that went before them. Also, that all life is interrelated and subject to the same laws; and that the history of living things is a unified one, unfolding continuously over millions and millions of years.

Here is how Darwin said evolution worked: Given that nature is competitive, that more daisies and starfish and foxes are "produced than can possibly survive, there must in every case be a struggle for existence, either one individual with another of the same species, or with the individuals of distinct species, or with the physical conditions of life." Constantly embroiled in fights to the finish, nature is thus, in Tennyson's famous formulation, "red in tooth and claw." Nor is it about to provide any "artificial increase in food" or "prudential restraint from marriage." Darwin's conclusion: "Any being, if it vary however slightly in any manner profitable to itself, under the complex and sometimes varying conditions of life, will have a better chance of surviving, and thus be *naturally selected*." There's more:

"From the . . . principle of inheritance, any selected variety will tend to propagate its new and modified form." Let such a process go on long enough, even randomly, and not just new species, but new genera, new families, and even whole new orders will be evolved.

About this thing called "natural selection." First off, it has nothing to do with conscious, intelligent, or purposeful behavior on the part of an organism; in that sense, nobody's "selecting" anything. A species changes, not through choice or will, but through chance, through the "play" of heredity. Inherit a useful characteristic—speed if you're a cheetah, strength if you're an oak tree, turn-on-a-dime savvy if you're a virus or a human being—and you'll be better set up to eat, compete, and mate; in short, to pass that characteristic along. Thus useful traits tend, more than useless ones, to be successfully passed on to the next generation, which profits from them in turn, until, in time, a whole species takes a slight turn to the right or left, *adapting* itself better to its environment, not through careful planning but through the cumulative luck of the draw. This is survival-of-the-fittest stuff; the "natural" simply points up that it's without self-consciousness on the part of the species, or intervention on the part of God.

About Darwinism. It's true that Darwin couldn't prove his theory since, as he put it, the great span of evolutionary time was simply unrecoverable. But that was OK, the circumstantial evidence—in the form of fossils, species distributions, plant and animal structure, embryology—was pretty good. And, except to the religious fundamentalists of the day, the basic setup *felt* right, just as the theory that the earth was round had felt right. What was upsetting were evolution's vibes: that nature had gone from being a sun-kissed harmony to being a tag-team wrestling match; that everything was always in flux, always on its way to becoming something else; that there was no such thing as virtue, just more and more adaptation; and that there were greater rewards for being "fit" than for being good or even for being right.

Darwinian evolution steamed intact into the twentieth century, alongside psychoanalysis and socialism, an intellectual tall ship that had made it through the straits of Victorian England and would make it over the shoals of Scopes-trial America. In fact, in the Twenties and Thirties, it was to be both bolstered and refurbished (but not structurally altered) by the new science of genetics. You remember genetics. Derived initially from the nineteenth-century work of Gregor Mendel, the pea-planting monk who first came up with the laws of genetic inheritance, it crystallized around the discovery of the first gene (or unit of heredity), which, within fifty years, would be shown to make up each chromosome and itself to be made up of DNA.

Fitted out with genetics, Darwinism passed into Neo-Darwinism. It still couldn't "prove" the theory of evolution, but now it could at least demonstrate exactly how evolution worked. Neo-Darwinism is considered a scientific up for two reasons: First, it gracefully ushered evolution into the twentieth century; second, it showed that the Master's basic hypothesis had stood the test not only of time but technology. After genetics, as before it, natural selection was *still* the name of the evolution game.

Ten Burning Questions in the History of Science

POSED AND FIELDED BY CONTRIBUTOR MARK ZUSSMAN

WERE THE ANCIENTS REALLY SCIENTISTS OR DID THEY JUST MAKE SOME LUCKY GUESSES?

Unlike the Scholastic Aptitude Test and the Graduate Record Exam, science gives credit not just for the right answers but for the method, as in "scientific method," by which the right answers are arrived at. Science, in other words, wants to see your worksheet. And by worksheet standards, the lowest grades go to the same ancient scientists who appear to have been the most on the ball: Democritus, who articulated an atomic theory, and Empedocles, who believed that something more or less like evolution occurred by a process more or less comparable to the survival of the fittest. Face-to-face with poetic insight, real science throws up its hands.

Now, Aristotle rarely made a good guess. Aristotle believed in spontaneous generation (e.g., that a fly might arise out of a dung heap, no help from Mom and Dad). He believed that heavenly bodies were attached to rotating mechanical spheres. (Think clear plastic). He believed that terrestrial motion was regulated by a principle of inertia such that all bodies desired to be at rest at the center of the earth. He believed that the chemistry of things could be explained in terms of the four elements: earth, air, fire, and water. By worksheet standards, however, Aristotle gets reasonably high grades for empirical observation in zoology (he classified some 540 animal species, at least 50 of which he'd dissected) and particularly for his chicken embryology.

If you want to speak well of an ancient scientist, though, the one always to go with is Archimedes, whose virtues include not just the formulation of the principles of buoyancy (see page 543) and the lever and the finest mathematical mind before Newton but a whole lot of method in the absence of any system or metaphysics.

IS IT TRUE THAT THE ARABS KEPT SCIENCE ALIVE DURING THE MIDDLE AGES, WHILE EUROPE SLUMBERED?

Strictly speaking, this is not true. It wasn't the Arabs who kept science alive: it was the Arabic language, which played the same role in the vast spaces from Spain to India that Latin played farther to the north. Arabic was in effect the great switching station—or to put it another way, Islam made science international. Here's what the medieval Muslims did: They translated Galen, Ptolemy, Aristotle, Euclid, Hippocrates, and Dioscorides. Al-Razi, a Persian physician, wrote *The Comprehensive Book*, whose title suggests the overall range of the effort: It summed up everything that had been known of medicine in Greece, India, and the Middle East and some of what had been known of medicine in China.

At the battle of Samarkand in A.D. 704, the Muslims got their hands on some Chinese papermakers. They then built paper mills of their own at Samarkand and at Baghdad, and they passed the process along to Europe by way of Spain, another medieval switching station. Al-Khwarazmi, a Baghdad mathematician, borrowed our numeral system from the Hindus and then went on to develop algebra, without which the complex weight distribution of Gothic cathedrals probably couldn't have been pulled off. Someone called Leonardo of Pisa introduced Arabic numerals into Europe in 1202.

Europe, meanwhile, sat on its thumbs only in the universities. Away from the gownies, things were cracking; even before the Renaissance happened along, Northerners had substituted trousers for the Roman toga. They had invented skis and the stirrup and the spinning wheel and the heavy-duty plough and mechanical clocks, and they had figured out how to cast iron and harness horses and make a barrel. This was the practical, nonacademic tradition that would sooner or later give the world the Connecticut Yankee, the Wizard of Menlo Park, and better living through chemistry.

DID GALILEO REALLY DROP A COUPLE OF LEAD WEIGHTS FROM THE LEANING TOWER OF PISA, THEREBY PROVING SOMETHING OR OTHER?

By common consent, this most famous of all experiments (or, more properly, demonstrations) was a nice one, if it occurred. Aristotle had claimed that objects of different weights fall at different speeds—so, anyway, the sixteenth-century Aristotelians believed he'd claimed; and anyone with a little equipment at the top of the Leaning Tower could have shown that the Aristotelians were wrong as usual. Whether or not Galileo did drop the weights, however, has been in dispute for most of this century.

The story was first told by Galileo's last pupil, Vincenzo Viviani, who said that Galileo dropped the weights in front of an audience of the entire faculty and student body of Pisa University. But if Galileo had done so and if Aristotelian mechanics had been shown up for the fantasy it was, why isn't there a single independent account of the event in university records or in letters or memoirs? This is the question as modern scholarship puts it.

Galileo

And it leads to a corollary question. If Galileo didn't drop weights from the Leaning Tower, what did he do? What he did was propagandize for the Copernican view that the earth voyages around the sun, not vice versa, and, what was worse, he did so in modern Italian, not in Latin, thereby stirring up trouble. In *The Dialogue Concerning the Two Chief Systems of the World, the Ptolemaic and the Copernican*, moreover, he made the Ptolemaic lunkhead Simplicius sound suspiciously like Pope Urban VIII.

As it happens, Galileo also constructed a telescope through which he discovered spots on the sun, mountains on the moon, satellites in the orbit of

Jupiter, and phases of Venus; and he laid the groundwork for a modern mechanics. But if you want to remember just one thing about Galileo, remember that he was the first scientist-philosopher who routinely approached problems mathematically, by quantifying them—and also the first to get a bad case of the creeps at the thought of colors, tastes, odors, and anything else he believed to be nonquantifiable.

DID NEWTON REALLY WATCH AN APPLE FALL—AND IF SO, SO WHAT? (AND IF NOT, SO WHAT?)

Isaac Newton

Here, obviously, we are onto another one of those Galileo-and-the-lead-weight questions. Sir David Brewster, one of Newton's nineteenth-century biographers, claims actually to have visited the tree the apple fell from and to have walked away with a piece of the root. Brewster also claims that in 1820, six years after his pilgrimage, the tree had decayed to such an extent that it was chopped down, the wood, however, like any other holy relic, being "carefully preserved"—in this case, by a Mr. Turnor of Stoke Rocheford. The story of course is that it was the falling apple that suggested to Newton the theory of universal gravitation, and the story, as Brewster acknowledges, was spread by Voltaire, who got it from Newton's niece, Catherine Barton. Voltaire, who wrote about Newton in detail, in fact never got to see the elderly mathematician-physicist, though, like any good journalist assigned to a palace press room, he did spend a lot of time hanging out in his subject's antechambers gathering scabrous anecdotes. The net of it is that the apple story is probably false and that the apple itself belongs in a barrel along with the one that Eve gave to Adam and the one that William Tell shot off his son's head and the golden one, inscribed "For the fairest," that Eris, the goddess of discord, tossed in the direction of Juno, Venus, and Minerva. On the other hand, how important is it whether he did or didn't watch an apple fall? Plenty of people other than Newton watched apples fall, and the theory of universal gravitation didn't occur to *them*.

The theory of gravitation, by the way, however obvious it may seem to every seven-year-old today, is on the face of it no less implausible than the much earlier theory that the planets and the stars are attached to clear rotating spheres that make music (if only we could hear it); and, when you think about it, it's not really a lot less occult. You know, what is this spooky stuff called gravity that holds everything in place without glue, paste, screws, nails, or even spit? Newton himself said:

> That gravity should be innate, inherent, essential to matter, so that one body may act upon another at a distance through a *vacuum*, without the mediation of anything else, by and through which the action and force may be conveyed from one to another, is to me so great an absurdity that I believe no man who has in philosophical matters a competent faculty of thinking can ever fall into it.

Newton's $F = G \dfrac{mM}{d^2}$ was nevertheless the $E = mc^2$ of its day. What it says is that the force of attraction between any two bodies will be directly proportional to the product of their masses and inversely proportional to the square of the distance between them.

HOW COME CHEMISTRY TOOK SO LONG TO COME UP FROM THE DARK AGES?

Chemistry took so long to come up from the Dark Ages because even after physics and astronomy and anatomy had assumed something vaguely like their modern contours, instruments didn't exist to isolate gases and no one troubled much to weigh or measure anything. Then a German named Stahl came along and carried the science down the dark, lonely dead-end road of the phlogiston theory. This theory held that all combustible substances had a physical component—namely, phlogiston—that was released on burning; new findings were wrenched about to fit the theory (for example, the discovery that the ash of a piece of firewood weighed more than the unburnt firewood led to the conclusion not that oxygen had been absorbed, but that phlogiston had

An eighteenth-century chemistry lab

negative weight). Which is to say that at the time of the American Revolution, chemists still believed that of the four elements of the ancients—earth, air, fire, and water—all but earth were irreducible. H_2O? Not yet. Water.

It was Antoine Lavoisier who got chemistry out of the fix. Lavoisier saw the implications of the findings of other men and worked them into a unified system. Both Joseph Priestley, an Englishman, and Karl Scheele, a Swede, had already isolated oxygen, but they failed to get straight the relationship between oxygen and either fire or water (Priestley, in fact, never gave up on phlogiston). Lavoisier saw that air was made up of two elements of which one contributed to combustion and one, nitrogen, did not. Henry Cavendish, an Englishman, combined hydrogen and oxygen to get water but concluded that water was hydrogen minus phlogiston. Lavoisier came up with the conclusion that satisfied your high-school chemistry teacher.

WHO GOT TO THE EVOLUTION THEORY FIRST, DARWIN OR THIS ALFRED RUSSEL WALLACE? AND ONCE YOU'VE ANSWERED THAT ONE, WHAT'S AN ENLIGHTENED MODERN PERSON SUPPOSED TO THINK OF POOR VILIFIED LAMARCK?

Darwin

Wallace

The first of these questions was somewhat baffling to Darwin himself. Darwin kind of thought that the evolution theory was his own intellectual property, but at home one day in June 1858, tinkering away at the future *Origin of Species*, he received from Wallace (who was in Malaya, recovering from malaria) a paper setting forth not just a theory of evolution but a theory of evolution by natural selection. And talk about spooky: The evolutionary process had been suggested to both men in exactly the same way. They had both read Malthus' *Essay on Population*, according to which an expanding human population is always pressing on food supply with the result that poverty and death are inevitable (see page 133). N.B.: It was neither Darwin nor Wallace but the philosopher Herbert Spencer who coined the Victorian catchphrase "survival of the fittest," and Alfred Tennyson, the poet laureate, who added the cheerful chorus, "For nature is one with rapine, a harm no preacher can heal."

Actually, what was at issue between the two naturalists was not who got to the theory first, but who had title to it. Darwin had started keeping his *Notebook on Transmutation of Species* in 1837. He had a first intimation of the role of adaptation in early 1838, and he added Malthus to his stewpot later that year. Wallace didn't begin to think of the transmutation of species until 1845, after he'd read Chambers' *Vestiges of the Natural History of Creation*. Wallace, however, *announced* his theory to Darwin before Darwin had published anything on evolution anywhere. This, then, would probably have been one for the lawyers, had both men not done honor to science by behaving like gentlemen. They actually praised each other.

As for poor Jean-Baptiste-Pierre-Antoine de Monet, chevalier de Lamarck, the pity is he's remembered for his zany ideas about how an animal that stretches its neck often enough to get at leaves on high branches will sooner or later become a giraffe and—why stop there?—the acquired characteristic of longneckedness will be passed along to its offspring. In fact, Lamarck not only got the idea of evolution out into the intellectual atmosphere, he also invented the categories "vertebrate" and "invertebrate" and he turned "biology" into an early-nineteenth-century buzzword.

HONEST, NOW, WAS LOBACHEVSKY THE GREATEST MATHEMATICIAN EVER TO GET CHALK ON HIS COAT?

This, to be sure, is what Tom Lehrer alleged of Lobachevsky in the famous song that also advises, "Plagiarize, plagiarize, why do you think the good Lord made your eyes?" Nikolai Lobachevsky not only ran the University of Kazan, he also found time to squeak through Euclid's undefended window of vulnerability,

Nikolai Ivanovitch Lobachevsky

namely, the fifth axiom, which states that through a point P, not on a given line l, only one line l' can be drawn so that l and l' are parallel and so that they will never meet no matter how far they are extended in either direction.

Lobachevsky demonstrated that if you throw out the fifth axiom, which was never proven, even by Euclid, who didn't try, you can construct a non-Euclidian geometry in which more than one parallel line will pass through the point P and all the angles of a triangle will add up to less than 180°. Lobachevsky did not apparently mean his geometry as a description of the real universe, yet it is not only as internally consistent as Euclid's, it also has implications for geodesics and great circle navigation. In any case, as Einstein was later to demonstrate, the real universe *is* both weird and non-Euclidean, regardless of what Lobachevsky thought.

There is just one problem with naming Lobachevsky the greatest mathematician, etc. Carl Gauss had gotten to non-Euclidean geometry before him, concluding that geometry, "the theory of space," was no longer on a level with arithmetic, the latter being exclusively a product of mind, the former, empirical. Most people, in fact, will tell you that not only was Gauss greater, so was Newton, who invented calculus, and Archimedes, who almost invented calculus with less to go on. Archimedes, though, doesn't pass the chalk-on-his-coat test. Archimedes didn't work in chalk. He worked in sand, ash, or, occasionally, olive oil.

WHAT DOES PLANCK'S CONSTANT HAVE TO DO WITH HEISENBERG'S UNCERTAINTY?

In a mutable world where yesterday's $1-a-slice pizza parlor becomes tomorrow's $13-a-radicchio-salad watering hole, a constant is always a nice thing to happen on; and Planck's, though it was scoffed at when it was first offered to the scientific public in 1900, has turned out over the years to be one of those rare harborages that you can tie up at with confidence. Its numerical value, always represented by the letter h, is 0.00000000000000000000000006547—a mite of a thing, to be sure; but it has been confirmed by many hundreds of methods, and in a world like this one, you take what constants you can get and you put your arms around them. What Max Planck discovered is that radiant energy is given off in particles or, as he called them, quanta; it is not given off continuously. You want to find the energy quantum of light, for example—namely, the photon? You multiply h by the frequency of the radiation, represented by the letter v, and voilà—there you've got it. Historians have taken the quantum theory to be the dividing line between "classical" and "modern" physics.

Now, constancy is a lot less modern than uncertainty, so it's not surprising that, come 1927, Werner Heisenberg took Planck's constant and used it to elevate uncertainty beyond mere pose: Heisenberg made uncertainty into a basic principle of the cosmos. He observed that the closer you get to observing the velocity of a particle, the further you inevitably get from measuring its position, and vice versa. Indeterminacy of velocity times indeterminacy of position will equal roughly—you guessed it—the famous h. For this, Heisenberg won the 1932 Nobel Prize. But, because it seemed like a mockery of the law of cause and effect, even Einstein didn't like it much, and he went on record with the remark: "I shall never believe that God plays dice with the universe."

WAIT, YOU'RE FORGETTING THE DANES. DIDN'T THEY CONTRIBUTE ANYTHING?

It's hard to know exactly how you mean this, but let's assume you're serious. In fact, the Danes are *not* just blue cheese and breakfast pastries. Denmark may even have been the first country to have something like a national science policy. King Frederick II, in order to avoid brain drain to Germany, set up the astronomer Tycho Brahe as feudal lord of the island of Hveen and provided him with the wherewithal to establish what in effect was the world's first observatory and think tank. Brahe spent twenty-odd years there making the most complete and precise survey of the heavens since the Greeks closed up shop. But when the new administration of Christian IV came along and cut off funding, he migrated anyway, to Bohemia, where he made his greatest contribution: He provided the data on the basis of which Johannes Kepler, a German and his successor as Imperial Mathematician, calculated the elliptical orbits of the planets.

Let's raise a tankard to the memory of Olaus Roemer. Roemer, in the Tycho tradition, traced the path of the planet Jupiter carefully, then used his results to calculate the speed of light, thereby beating out Aristotle, who thought that the speed of light was infinite, and Galileo, who tried to calculate a finite speed by trading lantern signals with an assistant on a nearby hilltop.

Hoist another tankard for Thomas Bartholin, who discovered the lymphatic system, and one more for his brother Erasmus, who discovered the double refraction of light through a piece of Icelandic crystal. And "skoal" to Hans Christian Oersted, who brought a compass needle close to an electrical wire, thereby stumbling on electromagnetism.

Niels Bohr won the Nobel Prize in 1922 for developing a new model for the hydrogen atom. Then—another forward march in the evolution of Danish science policy—he opened the Copenhagen Institute for atomic studies and drew theoretical physicists from all over the world, as Tycho had once drawn astronomers. Whereas Tycho's operation had been bankrolled by the Crown, however, the Bohr Institute was funded by the Carlsberg brewery.

IS SCIENCE WORTH DYING FOR?

This is a good question, and though the evidence is inconclusive, the answer is probably no. Life is sweet, and over the long haul the truth outs anyway. You can't kill a good idea whose time has come, etc. Be that as it may, the evidence strongly suggests that the average ecclesiastic does enjoy getting his hands on a scientist with a good idea (this is particularly true if the idea is expressed in such a way that laymen can understand it) and wringing the life out of it or, better yet, him.

In favor of dying for science, partidans of martyrdom used to invoke Giordano Bruno. The Inquisition gave him a chance to recant, but he wound up burning at the stake anyway. Since Socrates, no man had fought less to save his own life. Or at least that's the way Victorian press agentry told the story. Bruno had been an adherent of Copernicanism (the earth moved; the universe was infinite) but he was also of a mystical stripe (other worlds were inhabited; infinite universe was indistinguishable from infinite God). As a case for martyrdom for science, therefore, this can be thrown out on technical grounds: By modern criteria, Bruno wasn't a scientist at all. Rather, he used scientific ideas to dress up a system of hermetic magic. And, in any case, the Inquisition didn't indict him for Copernicanism; they indicted him for his lukewarm acceptance of the doctrine of the Trinity.

In 1633, thirty-three years after Bruno took the torch, Galileo was invited to have a look at the Inquisition's instruments of torture, and abjured. According to legend, he also said in an aside, *Eppur si muove*: It—that is, the earth—moves, even if you and I say it doesn't. But this doesn't make Galileo a martyr, only a brinkman. When it came to actually dying for ideas, Galileo wasn't having any.

As for Lavoisier, his head did roll in Robespierre's terror, but the case against him wasn't that he had invented modern chemistry, only that he had been a tax collector under the *ancien régime*. Like Galileo, Lavoisier believed that ideas were worth living for, not dying for, and so informed his accusers, thereby evoking the famous response, "The Republic has no need of scientists." But this, by and large, has not been the view of scientists themselves.

WORLD HISTORY

Contents

The old history-as-cosmic-juggling-act theory, illustrated here by the
nineteenth-century French caricaturist Grandville

The World According to Whom?

Gosh, so much has happened over the years. Wars and revolutions, edicts and referendums, dynasties and one-night stands, rebuffs and embraces. You'd think we'd have learned something from the whole business by now; after all, as the turn-of-the-century Harvard philosopher George Santayana admonished, "Those who cannot remember the past are condemned to repeat it." But how do you decide whose version of things you're going to buy? Well, you should begin by realizing that there's history (or, more formally, historiography), which is the writing down of everything that ever happened, and then there's the philosophy of history, which attempts to say what, exactly, that act of writing down accomplishes and/or where, eventually, the historical process itself leads; and that most "historians" do one or the other, although some wind up doing both. Beyond that, don't look at us: We've just examined everybody's celebrated account of one or more of the world's great moments and it seems perfectly obvious that everybody's lying.

SPOKESPERSONS

Ten guys, two each from five different history-minded civilizations; listen to them and you'll find out how the world—and the history biz—has been going for the past 2,500 years.

The Greeks: Herodotus and Thucydides

The Greeks got history—from their word *histor*, "learned man"—started, the same way they got philosophy and drama started, and their history, like their philosophy and drama, hits the ground running. Suddenly, it seemed obvious that events accumulated and that the past connected not only to the present but to the future. For the Greeks, the big deal was war, with a tip of the hat to revolution, and it was to wars that the two great Greek historians addressed themselves: Herodotus (c. 484–c. 425 B.C.) to the Persian ones (see page 606), which were still going on when he was growing up; Thucydides (c. 460–c. 400 B.C.) to the Peloponnesian one (likewise), which ended in 404 B.C., shortly before he died.

Both men are clear-eyed, go-with-your-instincts observers, but there the re-

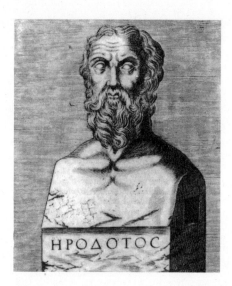 

Herodotus (left)
and Thucydides

semblance ends. Although only a generation older, Herodotus has less in common with Thucydides than he does with Homer, who'd been dead for five centuries already. Expansive, digressive, myth-minded, insatiably curious, and gossipy, capable of repeating anything anybody tells him (not that he necessarily believes it himself), with, as Macaulay put it, "an insinuating eloquence in his lisp," Herodotus comes across like Truman Capote. Thucydides, on the other hand, is Gore Vidal: concentrated, critical, clinical, obsessed with his own methodology and limited in his interests, cold, aristocratic, grave. Of the two, Herodotus, who claimed in his *History* to want only "to preserve the great and wonderful actions of the Greeks and the Barbarians from losing their due meed of glory," is the good read—the one you could get into on a cross-country bus trip, where his anthropologist's impulses would seem right at home. Thucydides, who was more the political-scientist type and who hoped his *The Peloponnesian War* "would be judged useful by those inquirers who desire an exact knowledge of the past as an aid to the interpretation of the future," is the choice of assistant professors, junior senators, op-ed-page writers, and anybody else who requires a little status along with his relevance.

The Romans: Livy and Tacitus

It was one thing after another in that burg, and getting it all down on papyrus took priority over figuring out what the hell it meant. The top stories invariably concerned the state and the men who ran it, and they went from being exercises in glorification and myth-making in the days when Rome was still getting started (and still smelling like a rose), to displays of outrage and breast-beating a mere hundred years later. Livy (c. 59 B.C.– c. A.D. 17), who was reportedly employed by various government agencies, winds up sounding like the PR person with the Ancient Rome account: From Aeneas and "the founding of this great city," through Romulus and Remus, the Sabine women, Cincinnatus, Hannibal, et al., up to his own Augustan Age and "the establishment of an empire which is now, in power, next to the immortal gods," his *History of Rome* is historiography at the disposal of patriotism, even more full of drum rolls than the *Aeneid* of his contemporary, Virgil—also, it turns out, on the imperial payroll. (For what it's worth, the only other history with as many plugs for divine providence, manifest destiny, tradition, election, and generation is the Old Testament.)

Tacitus (c. A.D. 55– c. 117), the most readable as well as the most reliable of the Roman historians, gives us just as one-sided a view. His Rome is well into its decline, without a scrap of *fides*, *pietas*, or *clementia* to its name, a city that's part bordello, part reign of terror, and part George Romero movie. (It's Tacitus who, in the *Annals*, provides us with the lowdown on Tiberius, Claudius, Nero, and Agrippina, complete with poisoned mushrooms and ships that fall apart in the night.) Against a background of evil like you wouldn't believe, Tacitus—doing his last-moral-man routine—inveighs, exposes, and pours on the lurid details. "This I regard as history's highest function," he says, "to let no worthy action go uncommemorated, and to hold out the reprobation of posterity as a terror to evil words and deeds." With the emphasis on the latter.

The Germans: Ranke and Mommsen

Not exactly household names. Still, if anyone turned history around—made it rigorous and new—and pointed it roughly in the direction it's still moving in today, it was the Germans, who, beginning around 1800, left the Enlightenment (so glib, so self-involved, so French) doing its nails and marched purposefully off to the university library and the archeological dig. Leopold von Ranke (1795–1886) is not only the most important of these German historians, he may be the most important of all nineteenth-century historians. Determined to see every epoch in its own terms (as opposed to the terms dictated by *his* epoch), he searched for the "ideas" and "tendencies" that ruled it, comprehending rather than passing judgment, applying "scientific" principles where, before, murky humanistic ones had prevailed—a methodology he summed up in the somewhat memorable phrase *"wie es eigentlich gewesen,"* how it really was. Not that the old boy was as clinical and impartial as he'd have you think: An archconservative, who depended on the support first of Metternich, then of Bismarck, and who believed that Germany had a mission to develop a culture and a political system all its own; a Lutheran who, in his *History of the Reformation in Germany*, gave Luther the benefit of every doubt; a mystic who claimed to see "God's finger" in human affairs—he didn't travel light or bias-free.

Theodor Mommsen (1817–1903), his colleague and chief among his legatees, is, by contrast, one of those inspiration-to-us-all people. Like Ranke a practitioner of the new objective history, he was a model of professionalism, of scholarship, and of saying what he meant. His *History of Rome* is based, not on old legends and myths, but on coins, inscriptions, and artifacts, many of which Mommsen literally dug up himself. Modest, wise, and good, he sought "to bring a more vivid knowledge of classical antiquity to wider circles." And he's the flip side to Ranke on the Days-of-Prussia LP: a frustrated liberal who had sided with the protesters in 1848, who deeply resented Bismarck, who deplored the beginnings of anti-Semitism in Germany, and who, when awarded the Nobel Prize for Literature in 1902, asked everyone not to clap. The times, he said, were too grave.

The Victorians: Macaulay and Carlyle

Don't make the mistake of writing Victorian England off as simply self-satisfied, all eight-course dinners and back-slapping conversations about how well things were going in the Punjab. In fact, the place was schizophrenic, divided down the middle by issues as unwieldy and unsettling as economic reform, Darwinism, industrialization (already run amok), and what to do about women. Which means, before you read any historian of the era, you'd better know which team he's playing on. Thomas Babington Macaulay (1800–1859) is self-satisfied, at peace with his age (though an outspoken critic of its culture), an influential politician, and in favor of peace, liberty, property, applied science, progress, and the Industrial Revolution. He's in sympathy with the Whigs of the previous century and their descendants, the Liberals of his own day. He announces to a nation of Englishmen that they are "the greatest and most highly civilized people that ever the world saw"—and that things are only going to get better. (A lot of them listened: His *History of England from the Accession of James II* has gone through more printings than any other book in English but the Bible.) And if he's a little philistine, a little too much the bellow of the Establishment, he could still tell the kind of good story—upbeat, well-paced, easy to read—that made his constituents feel better about the wacky times they were living through.

Not so Thomas Carlyle (1795–1881), a Scot with a sense of mystery, a fetish

Macaulay (left)
and Carlyle

for imagination, and the conviction that Macaulay's *History* was "a book to which 400 editions could not lend any permanent value." Carlyle was the era's self-appointed prophet, also its scourge, the sworn enemy of the Establishment, the Spirit of Progress, and the looking-out-for-number-one middle class. His French Revolution—"A wild savage Book, itself a kind of French Revolution," as he put it—which features an imaginary reporter as its narrator, has a you-are-there, docudrama quality that is as riveting, and as off-the-wall, as history, of whatever century, gets. Here, as in his biographies of Cromwell (whom he rehabilitated) and Frederick the Great (whom he adored), Carlyle's central thesis—which would be shared by Nietzsche, Shaw, D. H. Lawrence, and Wagner, and which would, rightly, be cited as a contributing factor in the rise of Fascism—was that the Hero, not the Establishment or the State, causes things to evolve, that "Universal History . . . is at bottom the History of the Great Men who have worked here."

Meanwhile, Back at the Ranch: Turner and Beard

You realize, of course, that there's an ocean between us and them, and that they're stunted and jaded and on their way out. Frederick Jackson Turner (1861–1932) realized it, and singlehandedly wrested American history not only from the Old World but from New England too, relocating it smack-dab in the middle of his own upper Mississippi Valley. For Turner, the frontier was "the cutting edge of American civilization," and American democracy and the American character the products of "the existence of an area of free land, its continuous recession, and the advance of American settlement westward." Part Walt Whitman, part Mr. Chips, Turner now stands for the turn-of-the-century national and regional values he swore by. If modern historians have long since stopped subscribing, they still remove their hats.

Charles A. Beard (1874–1948) is a tougher nut, less influential than Turner (who established a whole school of history) and more controversial. Irreverent and nonconformist, even before he studied his Marx he'd arrived at an economic interpretation of American history: The Constitution was "an economic document drawn with superb skill by men whose property interests were immediately at stake" and there was something hokey about its ratification; the Civil War had nothing to do with slavery or states' rights, but was instead the collision of the old agrarian culture with the new industrial one. All very stimulating. And, it turned out, most unsound: Beard had manipulated facts and deliberately overlooked evidence in order to prove his theory. It didn't help, either, that he preached isolationism during World War II—"American continentalism" was his term—and accused FDR of staging Pearl Harbor. Still, he got everybody thinking, he was a useful prototype for young activist intellectuals, and he obviously loved what he did. "The history of a civilization, if intelligently conceived," he says in the introduction to a bestselling textbook he wrote with his wife, Mary, "may be an instrument of civilization."

THINK TANKERS

You know the type—reclusive but bossy. These are the historians who couldn't care less about documents, artifacts, and eyewitness accounts. They're not out to reconstruct the past, but to let us in on what it, plus the present and the future, *mean*.

ST. AUGUSTINE (354–430): Forget the Persian Wars and the founding of Rome: The big events in human history have been the Fall, the Incarnation, and the Resurrection, with the Second Coming next on the agenda. History is not cyclical (Christ died only *once* for our sins), but a glorious unfolding, "the great melody of some ineffable composer." The earth is merely the footstool on which History rests her feet, the existence of man a subplot in the Divine Comedy. And, through thirteen centuries and a succession of anchorpersons as persuasive as Dante and Milton, that's simply the way it was—night after night after night.

VICO (1668–1744): A poor scholar in dusty, provincial Naples, he announced to anybody who'd listen that history was not a succession of great men, a wrap-up of the millennium's top stories, or a grade-school pageant with God as director, box-office manager, or even prompter. It was, rather, the work—and the reflection—of men, men like you and me, men who can love and understand history (unlike nature, which will always remain a mystery to us) precisely because we've created it. Not content with one bombshell, Vico dropped another: Nations, like human intelligence, undergo an ordered and predictable progression, from an initial primitive stage through divine (or childish), heroic (or adolescent), and finally civil (or adult) ones. Then they die, and the process begins somewhere else. History is not a great unfolding; it is, rather, cyclical.

VOLTAIRE (1694–1778): Fed up with Augustine, with their own bishop Bossuet (whose *Histoire Universelle* parroted him), and with God, the *philosophes* made faces at, and attempted to refute, all three. Voltaire, the most unstoppable of them, in his *Essay on the Customs and the Spirit of Nations*, rejected Providence, thanks just the same; opined that events have more to do with chance than with design; and proposed a new kind of *histoire universelle* (note the lowercase letters), based on the notion that men are alike, no matter what country they live in, endowed with the same natural rights and faculties, destined to proceed along the same path of reason and enlightenment. It's a small world, after all! And mainstream history is, for the first time, worldly in spirit.

HERDER (1744–1803): The first wave in the German intellectual tide that would wash over the nineteenth century. According to this earnest Protestant pastor, the world isn't all that small, or people all that much alike. Rather, true civilization arises from native roots: It is the common people, the *Volk*, who engender a national character, the *Volksgeist*. German ways are different from French or English ones—not necessarily better, just different—and nationalism is inevitable. And one more thing: It's a mistake to treat the past as if it were the present's slightly retarded older brother, even if it does dress funny.

HEGEL (1770–1831): Not only are German ways different, they're a whole lot better. They're also the next sure thing, how history will be carried through the upcoming stage in its development from Pure Being (that was China) all the way to the Absolute Idea (the highest unity of thought, all integration and harmony, and obviously Prussia). World-Historical Individuals—heroic types who seem to embody the very nature of the transition to come—count for something, but the State is the important thing; in his *Philosophy of History*, Hegel invites it to fill the tall-and-big-men's shoes recently vacated by the Church. As you may already have heard, the mechanism underlying the whole historical process he outlined is called the dialectic, and it, at least, isn't hard to grasp: The dominant idea, or "truth," of an epoch (its thesis), brings with it its precise negation (its antithesis); out of their sparring emerges a brand new, more or less hybrid "truth," or synthesis. (This was Marx's favorite part; see page 616). Thus the very disunity of Germany, the fact of its being fragmented into all those little principalities and duchies, summons up the idea of unity, and *must* ultimately bring about the creation of a German state. That is, State—according to Hegel, the institutional embodiment of reason and liberty, "the march of God through the world."

SPENGLER (1880–1936): Surprise! The state isn't that big a deal, after all. In fact, the real action is all in the "culture," which passes through four historical phases (just like Vico said), eventually falling into complete, irreversible decay. And we're no exception, according to Spengler, who, in *The Decline of the West*, foresaw imminent Asiatic domination. Doom, gloom, and the dubious comfort that it's always been and always will be thus. Toynbee (see page 581) would agree. So, in a way, would the Nazis, to whom all this pessimism looked like a welcome mat. In fact, as early as 1918, Spengler was claiming to hear their "quiet firm step."

LEGENDS

Two major reputations—one still in vogue, one already in mothballs—you simply have to deal with.

Edward Gibbon (1737–1794)

It was at Rome, on the 15th of October, 1764, as I sat musing amidst the ruins of the Capitol, while the barefooted friars were singing vespers in the Temple of Jupiter, that the idea of writing the decline and fall of the city first started to my mind.

from *Memoirs*

The various modes of worship, which prevailed in the Roman world, were all considered by the people as equally true; by the philosopher, as equally false; and by the magistrate, as equally useful.

from The Decline and Fall of the Roman Empire

I have described the triumph of barbarism and religion.

from The Decline and Fall of the Roman Empire

Six volumes. Three thousand pages. A million and a quarter words. Accounting for fourteen hundred years (from "the Age of the Antonines," in the first century A.D., to the stirrings of the Renaissance) in the lives of three continents, Britain to Palestine, including both halves of the Empire and all the nations that border on it, with special attention to the rise of Christianity *and* of Islam and to the eventual "fall" of Rome into the "superstitious" Middle Ages. Considered the greatest history ever written in the English language, a glorious melding of heavy-duty scholarship and high style.

Be that—be *all* that—as it may, there are really only three things you've got to keep in mind about *The History of the Decline and Fall of the Roman Empire.* First, that Gibbon believed Christianity was the central destructive force in the collapse of Roman civilization. (Watch him excoriate it in the infamous fifteenth and sixteenth chapters.) By offering a lot of non-self-starters—"useless multitudes who could only plead the merits of abstinence and chastity" is how he puts it—the promise of a life after death, Christianity undermined the rational pursuit of both virtue and reward, thereby weakening the Empire's defenses against the barbarians, who took a more pragmatic, now-or-never approach to life. There were compounding factors, of course—imperial corruption, for instance—but it's Christianity that Gibbon nabs, tries, and sends up the river.

Second, that the book really *reads.* Granted, it proved a bit much for some people, even at the time; as the then Duke of Gloucester remarked, "Another damned, thick, square book! Always scribble, scribble, scribble! Eh, Mr. Gibbon?" For most everybody else, though, *Decline and Fall* is a great story told against a big backdrop, with a cast of characters who make ethnic sitcoms look subtle by comparison; a model of balance, precision, wit, and malice, veined with irony and spiced with innuendo. (Check out, especially, Gibbon's footnotes, where, somebody once remarked, it was clear he lived out most of his sex life.) And if it's sheer sonority you're after, there's at least as much of it here as in the speeches of Winston Churchill—himself a Gibbon freak.

Third, that there are implications. Gibbon believed that there existed a special connection between Rome at its height and his own England (which had, after all, just passed through *its* Augustan Age and which was about to enter its imperial heyday), and that everybody would surely like to see that connection analyzed, complete with it-can-happen-here overtones. Of course, it now seems clear—as far as ancient-modern analogies go—that the role Britain really played was Greece, leaving to America the somewhat thankless and totally grandiose role of Rome. Which is precisely why *The Portable Gibbon* deserves a place on the old bookshelf right next to *Animal Farm* and *1984*.

Arnold Toynbee (1889–1975)

Civilization is a movement and not a condition, a voyage and not a harbor.

Reader's Digest, October 1955

Successive Occurrences of the War-and-Peace Cycle in Modern & Post-Modern Western History: Premonitory Wars (the Prelude), The General War, The Breathing-space, Supplementary Wars (the Epilogue), The General Peace—Overture and four Regular Cycles, 1494–1945

Title of chart, with column headings, *A Study of History*, Vol. 9

In London, in the southern section of the Buckingham Palace Road, walking southward along the pavement skirting the west wall of Victoria Station, the writer, once, one afternoon not long after the end of the First World War . . . , found himself in communion, not just with this or that episode in History, but with all that had been, and was, and was to come. In that instant he was directly aware of the passage of History flowing through him in a mighty current, and of his own life welling like a wave in the flow of this vast tide.

from *A Study of History*, Vol. 10

The historian as vicar, out to provide a little comfort (admittedly, cold comfort), in the face of a couple of world wars, the demise of the doctrine of social progress, and a universe gone all relative and weak-in-the-knees. Toynbee sets out to solace his reader with his own special combination of cosmic rhythm, faith-of-our-fathers piety, and three-ring erudition. The one-volume abridgment of his twelve-volume *A Study of History* (1934–1961) is, evidently as a result, the only theory of history ever to hit the mass-market racks. And if you come away from the enterprise less reassured than filled with a sense of impending doom, there's always the Durants.

History, per Toynbee, is not the great upward climb (as orchestrated by either God or Darwin) but a series of pulsations, pendulum swings, seasonal cycles, in which civilizations—of which our Western one is but the most recent of exactly twenty-one—rise, flourish, break down, and fall apart, the victims not only of external attacks, but also of internal failures of nerve. The basic mechanism in all this Toynbee calls "challenge and response," and he proceeds to illustrate how, from Egyptian and Sumerian times down to the present, every civilization has gradually lost its ability to cope, inevitably succumbing to such unhappiness as the "time of troubles" and, finally, the "universal state," which sounds good, but isn't (Hitler was out to create ours). Toynbee's system draws heavily on Spengler (see page 579), but for the latter's love of violence and pagan pessimism it substitutes mildness and the hope of religious salvation.

There's a lot of Toynbee to be impressed by: sweep, scope, breadth of knowledge, wealth of detail, boldness, conviction, energy, the determination to see a pattern in the tea leaves. And a lot to roll your eyes at: didacticism, long-windedness, and the determination to see the same pattern in the tea leaves in the bottom of every cup in the tearoom. Professional historians bring additional charges: twisting of the evidence, procrustean-bed methodology, untestable conclusions, "pernicious determinism." (They're especially annoyed at how, along about Volume 9, Toynbee announces that it is religion, not civilization, that is "the serious business of the human race.") And nobody, professional or passerby, knows quite how to behave when Toynbee takes time out from his system and lets fly with another of those trippy insights of his. Still, no other twentieth-century historian has known as much about as many different ages, peoples, and cultures; has made such a determined effort to see the forest even as he's counting and recounting the trees; or has been able to make history seem like quite such a big deal.

THE PARIS BUREAU

Frog historiography is a clubby affair. Even the radicals and the firebrands, once they've sat down at the old écritoire, start to behave as if they're contributing to a single grand enterprise, consolidating a single grand reputation, both of which, in case you were wondering, begin with *F*. Still, what other country can boast fifteen years of revolution, another eleven of Napoleon, plus major shakeups in both 1830 and 1848 *and* a humiliating defeat at the hands of the Prussians in

1870? With action like that, *mon cher*, you don't have to send your best minds off to sift through the debris of ancient Rome just so they'll have something to do.

The great national historian of France is Jules Michelet (1798–1874), who liked to think of himself as a child of the Revolution and of the masses who made it; who singlehandedly "resurrected" medieval France (complete with Jeanne d'Arc), intuiting and emoting what he couldn't piece together from the archives; and who bit by bit extended the story through his own day, becoming more and more bitter, and more and more biased, as he went along. His *L'Histoire de France*, in six volumes, is kind

Delacroix's Liberty Leading the People

of like a magic-carpet ride (he'd bought Montesquieu's old theory that geography and climate determine, among other things, form of government, and he insists on detailing every last hectare of La Belle France), kind of like a D. W. Griffith movie (he'd fortified himself with Vico's belief that it was the man in the street who made history), and—at its best—kind of like a salmon swimming upstream, trying to get back to the essence of what *was* by ignoring, as much as possible, the overwhelmingness of what *is*. He won't shut up, but the man has heart.

Not so most of his colleagues, who tend to be of an aggressively theoretical, even clinical turn of mind. There's Henri de Saint-Simon (1760–1825), the grand-nephew of the acid-tongued duke who'd skewered Louis XIV and his court, who distinguished between "critical" and "organic" phases of civilization; who plumped for the reorganization of society under a governing elite of scientists, financiers, and industrialists, with artists in place of clergymen; and who had a big influence on Marx and on John Stuart Mill. There's his disciple, Auguste Comte (1798–1857), arrogant, dogmatic, and a bit crazy, who divided history into three stages—the theological, in which God's will was how people explained things away, lasting until Martin Luther made the world safe for atheism; the metaphysical, in which natural laws accounted for everything, lasting from Luther until the French Revolution and the rise of the machine; and the scientific, in which you reject sweeping generalizations, unquestioned assumptions, and wishful thinking in general for the elegance of the observable fact and the verifiable law, meant to go on forever. Comte called this "scientific," eyes-on-the-road attitude positivism, and he promoted it nonstop; he also came up with the word for and the discipline of sociology, the study of man in society.

And there's that second-half-of-the-century duo, Hippolyte Taine (1828–1893) and Ernest Renan (1823–1892), each devoted to cleaning out as many national bureau drawers as possible. Taine, a disciple of Comte, thought of history as "mechanics applied to psychology" and believed that if you assembled enough facts, and then were very, very on the ball, you'd be able to come up with all the laws that operated on them. He really wasn't *that* interested in counting and measuring, but that didn't stop Taine from feeding all of history, plus literature and art, into his fact processor, then setting it on "mince"; from announcing that culture is a matter of race, milieu, and moment, which together determine something called *la faculté maîtresse*; or from positing that vice and virtue are no less chemically analyzable than sulfuric acid and sugar. Renan, who was less pedantic than Taine and who wrote better besides, yoked science and religion, *raison* and *sensibilité*, attempting to explain, among other things, Christ's Resurrection without resorting to words like "divinity" and "miracle."

Are we forgetting anybody? Well, Alexis de Tocqueville (1805–1859), of course, who was more political thinker than historian, and who had the good sense to get out of France for a few years. Having set up shop in America, he drew a line between liberty and democracy, worried aloud about "the tyranny of the majority" and the distrust of excellence, and predicted, just as Comte was telling everybody about positivism for the second or third time, that, within a century, the United States would have a hundred million people and would, along with Russia, be one of the world's two leading powers.

Then there are Braudel and Foucault; we'll get to them in a minute.

ROLE MODELS

A century's worth of them for the historians of tomorrow.

JACOB BURCKHARDT (1818–1897): The master craftsman. And still seminal after all these years. True, his *Civilization of the Renaissance in Italy* ignored economics, scanted the peasants, and kicked the Middle Ages while they were down, but it also came up with the understanding of the period we call "Renaissance"—of man just turning modern, learning to function as an individual, painting pictures and practicing statecraft and *knowing* that he's painting pictures and practicing statecraft—that scholars have been going on ever since. A cool, collected Swiss, with no particular ax to grind, Burckhardt took the Italy of the fourteenth through sixteenth centuries and distilled and bottled it, Borgias, *condottieri*, Michelangelo, and all.

BENEDETTO CROCE (1866–1952): The godfather. Exercised something like a benevolent intellectual dictatorship over Italy for half a century, during which he told Italians what to read and what not to read in literature, philosophy, and history. (Some of them still haven't gotten over it.) Transcendental, intuitive, and just this side of mystical, Croce wanted to defend history against the incursions of science—and to give it a nudge in the direction of fellow-feeling. Or, as he put it in his *History: Its Theory and Practice,* "The deed of which the history is told must vibrate in the soul of the historian." Himself equally the historian of aesthetic theories and of Italy, especially Naples; a fervent anti-Fascist before and throughout the War; with the shrewdest, sweetest (think Jiminy Cricket) kind of common sense: Croce is hard to resist. And even harder to read.

PIETER GEYL (1887–1966): The voice of reason. In Holland, the crossroads of Europe, where tolerance and sturdy ankles are a way of life, men make a point of taking the long and balanced view, of assessing what their larger, more ambitious neighbors are up to. Of course, Geyl can't refrain from invoking, in the same breath with Michelet, Ranke, and Macaulay, a Dutch historian named Groen van Prinsterer, but at least he quotes Agatha Christie, too. Measured, penetrating, the upholder of the standards of historical scholarship, with a style someone once likened to a "douche of cold water," Geyl rolled his eyes and delivered four lectures at the mention of Toynbee's name.

FERNAND BRAUDEL (1902–1985): Had the common touch. Heir to the so called *Annales* school of French historiography—which said, "Enough, already, with the kings and the popes and the generals; let's see what the rest of us used to be up to," and which tried to bring to history some of the methods of the social sciences. In the end Braudel cared less about, say, the Peace of Westphalia than about the fact that wolves were attacking Parisians well into the 1400s; that tea is popular only in countries where there are no vineyards; and that even rich people ate with their hands until the late eighteenth century, which, coincidentally, is also when the idea of privacy was invented. If anthropology is your idea of history, if you like minute observation against a sweeping backdrop, and if you don't care if you ever hear another *theory* of history in your life, then Braudel—either his two-volume *The Mediterranean and the Mediterranean World in the Age of Philip II* or his three-volume *Civilization and Capitalism, 15th–18th Century*—is for you.

A. J. P. TAYLOR (1906–1990): A smart Alistair Cooke. Dubbed "the pyrotechnician of history," presumably because of his ability to hold millions of Brits spellbound while lecturing on various complex historical issues of the last few hundred years, and on the telly no less. Then there are his (at last count) twenty-six books, including *English History: 1914–1945*, sometimes said to be his masterpiece; *The Trouble Makers*, about dissent and foreign policy; and *The Origins of the Second World War*, a scandal in its day inasmuch as it portrayed Hitler as a traditional German statesman rather than a ravening warmonger, and laid a lot of blame at the doorsteps of Britain and France. All of which suffices to make him the most widely known British historian since Macaulay. Industry gossip: Even with the popularity *and* the productivity, Taylor in 1957 lost out on Oxford's Regius Professorship of Modern History to Hugh Trevor-Roper, the *other* British historian of our times, nicknamed "the sleuth of Oxford," who'd been one of the front-liners in the attack on Taylor's *Origins*. You can bet Taylor cackled to himself, though, when Trevor-Roper made the mistake, in 1983, of certifying as genuine the sixty Hitler diaries for which *Stern* and *Newsweek* had paid a forger several million dollars.

ISAIAH BERLIN (1909–   ): Mister—make that Sir—Sagacity. Born in Latvia, raised in England, and canonized at Oxford, he's all for choices (the harder the better) and "the painful conflicts and perplexities of the disordered freedom of the world beyond the [prison] walls." Once just another philosopher, now a historian "of ideas," of thinking about thinking, Berlin is a thorough-going liberal, a dyed-in-the-wool pluralist, and a fearless crusader against determinism and "historical inevitability" (he rolls his eyes at the mention of Toynbee's name but is above discussing him as an individual case). Naturally, he's also a champion of the intellectual underdog, the thinker (Vico is his favorite) who is out of synch with, because ahead of, his time. Caution: While he's been positioned as "the don who can't write a dull essay," be on your guard against sentences as long as freight trains and the creepily casual dropping of the biggest names of the last couple of millennia, Plato to Pasternak and Newton to Nijinsky.

BARBARA TUCHMAN (1912–1989): Twenty-twenty hindsight. Not only does Tuchman see both doom and folly everywhere—in France's wrongheaded strategy during the opening days of World War I in *The Guns of August*; in the primed-to-explode energies of fin-de-siècle Europe and America in *The Proud Tower*; in the chaos of the disaster-ridden fourteenth century in *A Distant Mirror*—she can't wait to rub everybody's nose in it. Though she's a pretty good storyteller (she's been compared with Gibbon in terms of clarity and conviction) with a knowledge of how to excite public—as opposed to merely academic—outrage and debate on behalf of her field, Tuchman's character-is-fate expositions of morality can get on a person's nerves. A bigger problem (but don't let on we're the ones who told you): She usually doesn't wind up proving, after seven hundred or so pages, the thesis she posited with such elegance way back in chapter one.

RICHARD HOFSTADTER (1916–1970): Good buddy. The first major American historian who didn't come from either a small town in the Midwest or a long line of Bostonians, Hofstadter's the product of New York City, and he never stopped thinking in the cultural and political—and faintly radical—terms he learned there. Interested in such contemporary phenomena as the New Deal, McCarthyism, paranoia, the plight of the American intellectual, and Barry Goldwater; easygoing and personable (he wore clip-on bow ties and hitched up his trousers a lot); willing to admit that the picture he'd painted was subject to change without official notice ("I offer trial models of historical interpretation"): Hofstadter wrote to figure out what he really thought—and to share it with you, bro.

MICHEL FOUCAULT (1926–1984): Velvet fist in an iron glove. Tended to ask, but usually didn't stick around to answer, the bravest, vaguest, and thorniest kinds of questions: What are the "discourses" that inform, say, our attitudes toward sexuality or our treatment of the insane? How do the "discourses" emerge? What rules do they obey? How and why do they change? Foucault, who has been claimed by both the structuralists and the poststructuralists (see page 334) and who described himself as a "historian of systems of thought," kept two generations of Parisian Marxists and American graduate students guessing as to what the correct answers were, without himself ever being pinned down—like a particularly outrageous drag queen (as one insider's simile has it) foiling the arrest attempts of a whole squad of policemen. While it seems clear that Foucault never did a whole lot of library research into madness, sexuality, prison, hospitals, or anything else, and while some of his insights seem like plain showing off, you'll want to pay attention to his notion of the *episteme*—from the Greek word for "knowledge," a sharp break between one historical period and another, marked by the end of one intellectual framework and the beginning of a new one, as when the Age of Reason, reviewing the differences between what was normal and what wasn't, decided to reclass the insane (who in the Middle Ages had been thought

of as divinely inspired), this time behind bars. Ditto to his belief (heartfelt, incidentally) that the subtlest problem in the world, and the one most worth studying, is the relationship between liberty and social coercion, or, stated the way Foucault used to state it, between truth and power.

Fun Couples

JUSTINIAN AND THEODORA (married A.D. 525): The team that made the Byzantine Empire what it isn't today. A couple of climbers (he came from peasant stock and worked his way up to the throne; she was the daughter of a bearkeeper at the Hippodrome), they're a classic example of what the right woman can do for a man. Justinian had energy (he was the one about whom it was first said "The emperor never sleeps"), personal appeal, and a knack for recognizing talent when he saw it. He was, however, an unstable egomaniac and an intellectual lightweight. Theodora was a troublemaker, but she had the requisite brains and nerve to keep Justinian in the imperial driver's seat. While she was alive, he consolidated the empire, drove out pesky barbarians, established the famous Justinian Code, and initiated most of the architectural feats associated with Byzantine glory. After she died (of cancer, in 548), he spent the rest of his reign tinkering.

HELOISE AND ABELARD (married c. 1118): What a tearjerker! Peter Abelard was the most celebrated logician,
theologian, and teacher of his day, and the biggest ego in
medieval France. Taking a shine to young Heloise, the brilliant seventeen-year-old niece of a canon at the university,
he finagled a job as her tutor and promptly seduced her.
After she gave birth to a son named Astrolabe (don't look at
us, we weren't consulted), the couple were married, but secretly, to avoid damaging Abelard's career. Heloise went
home to live with her uncle, who became increasingly
freaked out over the whole affair. He took to slapping
Heloise around on general principle, and finally hired a
couple of thugs to sneak into Abelard's room at night and
castrate him. This hurt Abelard's pride. He crept off to become a famous teacher somewhere else, write controversial
scholarly treatises, and establish an order of literary nuns, of
which Heloise eventually became the abbess. Poor Heloise,
who was forced to take the veil, never got to spend more
than five minutes with her husband after that fateful night
in Paris, but she and Abelard did publish the love letters
that substituted for sex for the rest of their lives; centuries
later, these inspired the epistolary novel, if that's any consolation.

HENRY II AND ELEANOR OF AQUITAINE (married 1152):
Not only did they form the most potent concentration of
forces in feudal Europe, but their relationship contained
enough sex, power, and ambition to fuel a Broadway play
and a Hollywood movie. Eleanor was thirty, Henry nineteen when they met. She saw in him a lusty young adventurer, the future King of England. He saw in her the
chance for a brilliant political alliance (England was no
prize in those days and she did happen to own—personally—more than half of France). Two towering egos, they
spent the next twenty years intimidating the neighbors and
trying to dominate each other. He turned England into a
respectable kingdom; she ran Aquitaine. He fought the
Church; she patronized the arts. He ran around with other
women; she sponsored young troubadors. Finally, she
talked her sons into making war on their father; he won
and had her thrown in jail for fifteen years. She had the last
laugh, though; she outlived him.

FERDINAND AND ISABELLA (married 1469): It was a Catholic ceremony. The bride, Isabella of Castile, was the product of a Gothic-novel childhood— gloomy castle, demented mother, sexually depraved half-brother and all—but she didn't let that stand in her way when the throne of Castile was up for grabs. The groom, Ferdinand of Aragon, was dashing, dynamic, and due to inherit the province next door, plus Sicily, Sardinia, Naples, and the Balearic Islands. They were a perfect match, a couple of high-stakes players sitting on a lot of undeveloped real estate. To tame the local nobles and instill a sense of family loyalty, the couple decided to start the Spanish Inquisition. This, combined with the expulsion of the Jews and Moors, the conquest of Grenada, and the high returns on Isabella's investment in Christopher Columbus (with whom she was almost certainly *not* having an affair), did the trick. Spain became the most fearsomely Catholic country in the world and the most ironclad monarchy in Europe, and Ferdinand and Isabella, "the Catholic kings," became the best argument for or against marrying within your own faith, depending on your point of view.

WILLIAM AND MARY (married 1677): Now here's a boring couple. Paragons of Protestant restraint, they nevertheless managed to undermine the whole concept of absolute monarchy. William (that's William of Orange) was a stolid, sensible Dutchman; fatherless, childless, humorless, and utterly devoid of table manners, he seemed incapable of any passion except a rabid hatred of the French. He was imported by the English Parliament to unseat Mary's father, the Catholic James II, which he did in a bloodless victory of political maneuvering over divine right known as the Glorious Revolution. Thanks in part to the obedient Mary, who was merely William's safe-conduct to the English throne, Parliament gained supremacy over the crown, England became securely Protestant again, and William, who didn't care a fig for the crown, for England, or for Mary, got to pursue his impossible dream: eliminating all things French from the face of the earth.

NAPOLEON AND JOSEPHINE (married 1796): An unlikely match, but it seemed to work. He was a short
Corsican soldier six years her junior with minimal connections, few social graces, and no money in the bank.
She was a seductive Creole from Martinique with two
children, expensive tastes, and one of the most fashionable salons in Paris. His family loathed her. She
wasn't impressed with him, either, but her politically
prominent lover encouraged the match. Two days after
the wedding he marched off to conquer Italy. She
stayed home, shopped, and had affairs with younger
men. He put up with her infidelities and her laziness
and found comfort in the vast empty spaces of her
mind. She put up with his rages and his round-the-
clock workdays and worshipped him from across the
room. For thirteen years they lived happily in the fast
lane. He conquered most of Europe, rearranged the
rest, and had himself crowned emperor. She took to
wearing Empire-waist dresses and bought more hats.
He never did manage to get her pregnant, though, and
in the end he annulled the marriage to hitch up with
an eighteen-year-old Austrian princess who bore him
an heir. Too bad; it broke Josephine's heart and, as it
turned out, he needn't have bothered.

FRANKLIN AND ELEANOR ROOSEVELT (married 1905):
The closest we ever had to a king and a queen. Or to
a pair of kings, but let's leave Eleanor's sexual preferences out of this, shall we? FDR *did* have a dictatorial
streak, what with the New Deal, the way he tried to
butt into the Supreme Court's business, and his getting us into the war. But don't forget that dema-
goguery was in flower in those days and it could've
been worse: We could've had Huey Long. Besides,
Franklin gave us Eleanor, who was a great lady in spite
of those sensible shoes. Not content with planting
memorial shrubs, she was even more of a reformer

than he was; in fact, some people called her a Communist—an understandable
mistake, given her holier-than-thou attitudes and the fact that she didn't see anything intrinsically wrong with "Negroes." This was more a partnership than a
marriage, really, and sometimes it seemed more like a rivalry than either. But isn't
that, after all, the American Way?

MAO ZEDONG AND JIANG QING (married c. 1938, if ever). They showed the West that Chinese Communists can have marital problems, too. He was already on his third wife when he met her; she was an ambitious Shanghai actress who'd been through one husband and several, well, mentors. For nearly thirty years she had to be content with typing his lecture notes and occasionally outraging his comrades by daring to appear in public as Madame Mao. Then, in 1966, she suddenly emerged as first deputy leader and chief witch-hunter of the Great Proletarian Cultural Revolution. For the next ten years she publicly purged bourgeois reactionism from the arts while privately screening Greta Garbo movies for her friends. Mao, who lived (and, more particularly, slept) elsewhere, kept in touch by sending her cryptic notes and right-thinking poems. Almost immediately after his death in 1976, she was arrested as one of the "Gang of Four," charged, in a show trial, with plotting to become "the new empress," and expelled from the Party as a "bourgeois careerist, conspirator, counterrevolutionary, double-dealer, and renegade." Her famous retort: "I was Chairman Mao's dog. When he said 'Bite,' I bit." She spent the next fourteen years in a Chinese jail, where, according to the official version, she hanged herself from her bedframe in 1991.

Vintage Years

1453

The Hundred Years' War (actually the Hundred and Sixteen Years' War, but who's counting?), between England and France, is over. So are: chivalry (the armor couldn't stand up to the new English longbow, plus most of the knights had come to seem more greedy than valiant); Joan of Arc (burned at the stake, but she really *had* singlehandedly saved France); and the illusion that England, the loser, sort of, and France, the winner, sort of (even though the former, an underpopulated little island, had, in the course of the war, managed to win possession of most of the latter, the biggest, fattest country in Europe, only to be routed at the end) were destined to be a single nation. By war's end, too, kings are firmly back in the saddle after two centuries of cagey maneuvering on the part of the nobility and its parliaments (and of their own royal ineptitude). And the Middle Ages are teetering on the brink of Modern Times.

Joan of Arc at Prayer *by Rubens*

1598

Henry IV of France issues the Edict of Nantes, promising French Protestants, or Huguenots, the same civil and religious rights that French Catholics had. Unlike England, where the Catholic minority had no rights at all, and Germany, where religion was all about grabbing a free city or a principality and imposing your own creed on it, France was suddenly, and out of the blue, behaving like a grown-up. For this, there is Henry to thank, a former Huguenot (and a particularly savvy one), who, having been crowned king, realized that if he wanted to be let inside the gates of heavily Catholic Paris, he was going to have to make a few concessions—the occasion for his religious conversion and for his famous obser-

The Peace of Westphalia

vation, "Paris is well worth a Mass." Make a note of Henry IV (born Henry of Navarre): He's the most popular and most fondly remembered of all the French kings (except maybe for St. Louis, back in the Middle Ages), he was the first politician ever to make use of the slogan "a chicken in every pot," and he was the founder of the Bourbon dynasty, laying the foundations for the absolutism of the Louis (see page 598) who followed him. Unfortunately, Henry was assassinated in 1610; the Huguenots would get theirs, too, in 1685, when Louis XIV revoked the Edict of Nantes and France started to pretend it had never even heard of religious tolerance.

1648

The Peace of Westphalia ends the Thirty Years' War, the most destructive war yet. Wave good-bye to the medieval worldview, the Counter-Reformation, wars of religion, the Holy Roman Empire, Germany's prospects for the next two hundred years, and Spain's prospects, period. Brace yourself for the triumph of secular thinking, the ascendancy of France (in the person of Louis XIV), and a new age of pluralism, in which nobody will even pretend Europe has any overriding unity, spiritual, political, or other, and in which states will behave like the discrete, self-interested entities they are.

1762

Jean-Jacques Rousseau publishes his *Social Contract*. His glorification of the common man, the "noble savage," had already managed to make breast-feeding

Rousseau, center, ventures into society

fashionable again (and would later encourage Marie Antoinette to dress up as a milkmaid). Now Rousseau, feeling alienated as ever—he was Swiss, Protestant, and paranoid, among other things, and nobody wanted to play milkmaid with *him*—describes a society in which he thinks men, himself included, could be happy: Individuals would surrender their natural liberty to one another, fusing their individual wills into a General Will, which, rather than a king or even a parliament, would be the true sovereign power. With his *Social Contract*, Rousseau becomes the prophet of both democracy and nationalism; in just a few years, the ideas he set forth in it will help to bring about the French Revolution. The book is not, however, a bestseller.

1815

The Congress of Vienna puts its stamp on Europe. The four great powers—England, Russia, Prussia, and Austria—having finally managed to write *finis* to Napoleon's plan for a France that stretched from Madrid to Moscow, now sit down and work out a "balance of power" that will pretty much prevail until the First World War. Not that the diplomats who gathered in Austria's capital—the shifty Prince Metternich, the crafty Baron Talleyrand, and so on—were all that forward-looking; in fact, most of them, intent on squashing the liberalism and nationalism and democracy that had sprouted in the aftermath of the French Revolution, were downright reactionary. But neither were the diplomats dopes: The Treaty of Vienna wisely let France off fairly easy (applause here for Talleyrand, who knew an opening when he saw one), deeded over to Britain the

*The Paris
barricades, 1848*

best and the brightest colonial empire, smoothed over the rivalry between Prussia and Austria for domination of the German-speaking world, and resolved the issue (for at least the next couple of generations) of who'd push Poland around. And, for a hundred years after the incredible (and exhausting) brouhaha of the French Revolution and Napoleon, there was—if you leave aside the insurrections of 1830 and 1848 (see below) and a few eensy localized conflicts like the Franco-Prussian War of 1870—peace.

1848

Barricades and cobblestones, radicalism and the June Days. All over Europe—Paris to Budapest, Copenhagen to Palermo—the existing order is challenged, and sometimes overturned, only to be back still pretty much on top a few months later. (Britain and Russia alone missed out on the chaos.) The issues: nationalism, constitutional government, broadened suffrage, the abolition of serfdom in the Balkans. The enemy: the ruling classes, the Catholic Church, the farflung Hapsburg influence. The result: a basic misfiring—serfs are freed, all right, but dreams of liberalism and good government bite the dust. The legacy: class hatred and national jealousy, a new toughness of mind (which the Germans, whose day is at hand, will call *Realpolitik*), and the setting of the stage for Marxism. In fact, *The Communist Manifesto* had appeared that January.

1854

Commodore Perry, an American, opens Japan. He finds there an elaborately civilized nation, much given to city life, novels, the theater, the contemplation of landscape, lacquer work, and fans. None of which stops him from threatening to open fire if the Japanese don't accede to his demands to trade with America, and on terms hugely advantageous to the latter. Ditto, to trade with everybody else in a gunboat and a cocked hat. Japan, sealed off tight little-island-style from the rest of the world since 1640, when it had kicked out all of an earlier generation of Europeans except for a handful of Dutch merchants in Nagasaki, will soon find itself undergoing Westernization in everything from the codification of its laws to the delivery of its mail. The Japanese wind up getting what they soon realize they'd really been needing all along—science, technology, bureaucracy. And they get it real fast. In fact, never have so many people undergone so profound a transformation in so few years. Or, a short century later, so succeeded in upstaging their teachers.

1945

Churchill, Roosevelt, and Stalin take another meeting, this one at Yalta, an old czarist summer resort on the Black Sea. Victory over Germany and Japan is in sight: But how are the Allied powers to deal with the defeated? Likewise, each other? Roosevelt miscalculates, choosing to trust Stalin too much, listen to Churchill—a past master at the old spheres-of-influence, keep-your-distance style of diplomacy—too little. Russia not only gets most of Eastern Europe (not that it doesn't have one big furry boot on it already) plus parts of Japan (who it hasn't even been at war with), it gets the West's seal of approval, too. And all in the name of, talk about irony, international friendship.

Churchill, Roosevelt, and Stalin at Yalta

Louis, Louis

I t's hard enough trying to keep track of the English Henrys and Richards; what is one to do with the crazy French monarchs who, for centuries, insisted on naming their eldest sons Louis? Our advice: Start small. Here, the four Louises to remember, and a few things to remember them by.

THE MAN: LOUIS XIII
(1601–1643)

Timid, sickly, and depressed, he spent most of his life trying to assert himself; first toward his mother, the fat, silly, overbearing regent Marie de' Medici; then toward his minister, Richelieu, on the one hand, and toward Richelieu's innumerable enemies, on the other. Despite his personal problems, Louis wanted very much to be a great king. History has only recently begun to do him justice, noting that he had the sense to recognize his own limitations and the guts to play second fiddle to a minister he hated for what seemed, at the time, to be the good of France.

HIS MATE

Anne of Austria: The daughter of the King of Spain (Spain was then under Hapsburg rule), she was selected by Louis' mother, who hoped to cement an alliance between the two countries. Louis responded by ignoring Anne; it took four years for him to consummate the marriage, and twenty to father their first child. Anne had a strange life, but not the worst imaginable for a French queen; although she was perpetually at loggerheads with Richelieu, who was both arrogant and vehemently anti-Hapsburg, her husband, at least, lacked the energy to be actively unfaithful to her. She became regent once the king and his minister were dead.

HIS MINISTER

Cardinal Richelieu: The proud, ruthless power behind the throne, whom you may best remember as the villain in Dumas's *The Three Musketeers*. Any French schoolchild would be able to recite Richelieu's famous three-point program for consolidating the power of the monarchy and the French state: Suppress the Protestants, curb the nobles, and humble the House of Austria. "Red Robe," as the Cardinal was known, succeeded, up to a point—he had a knack for crushing conspiracies and, importantly, he had the support of the king—but he nearly bankrupted the state through sheer financial ineptitude.

HIS MOTTO

"Now I am king."

HIS CHAIR:

THE MAN: LOUIS XIV
(1638–1715)

This little man, believe it or not, ruled the France that produced Corneille, Racine, Molière, and Pascal, and was himself the greatest repository of personal power in an age that was crawling with absolutist, divine-right monarchs. Short (which is why you'll always see him in heels and a mile-high wig), not pretty (that hooked nose and receding chin were the trademarks of the Bourbon dynasty), harsh, egotistical, and only moderately intelligent, he succeeded in getting himself nicknamed "The Sun King" largely because France was ripe for a leader. He did, however, have certain qualifications for the job: common sense, an ability to recognize talent, stand-out style, a strong feeling for the state, and an absolute delight in the day-to-day business of being king. Under his rule (which lasted seventy-two years, making him the longest-running monarch in French history) France became the most powerful and prestigious country in Europe, although it was financially ruined in the process.

HIS MATES

Marie Thérèse of Spain: Louis' small, swarthy, somewhat insipid queen, whom he married to fulfill a treaty agreement. She played little part in his life, produced several children who died in infancy and one rather mediocre prince, the Grand Dauphin, who died before he could become king.

The Duchesse de la Vallière: She loved him, bore him children, and retired, heartbroken, to a nunnery when he abandoned her.

Mme. de Montespan: An intriguer who, after replacing the Duchesse de la Vallière, managed to hang on for twelve years, and to bear the king eight illegitimate children. She fell into disgrace during the Affair of the Poisons, a court scandal involving the mysterious deaths of various nobles, among them the woman Louis had recently chosen to replace her.

Mme. de Maintenon: A pious widow in her forties, renowned for her successful literary salon. Louis gave her the task of raising his children by Mme. de Montespan. These two were friends before they were lovers; Louis, an aging libertine, admired Mme. de Maintenon's intelligence and austerity. After the death of the queen, they were married secretly. She played an important role in politics, caused a major change in the king's lifestyle, and transformed the later years of his reign—making them, some thought, slightly depressing.

HIS MINISTERS

Cardinal Mazarin: An Italian, inherited from Louis' mother, Anne of Austria, to whom, it was rumored, he was secretly married. Mazarin's aims and policies were much the same as Richelieu's, although his style leaned more toward subtlety and unscrupulousness than open ruthlessness. His ongoing attempts to center power in the crown led to the open rebellion known as La Fronde, in which nobles and bourgeoisie nearly succeeded in toppling the monarchy, but ended by turning on each other instead. Mazarin ran the country while he lived, but after his death, the young Louis dispensed with the office of chief minister altogether and held the reins himself.

Colbert: Louis' finance minister for twenty years, he was one of the great practitioners of mercantilism, the system of building national wealth by exporting goods in exchange for gold and other precious metals. Hoping to make France economically self-sufficient, he encouraged industry, built roads, began construction of a navy, and patronized the arts, but in the end most of his programs—and his reputation—collapsed under the weight of Louis' personal extravagance.

HIS MOTTO

"L'état c'est moi." ("I am the state.")

HIS CHAIR:

THE MAN: LOUIS XV
(1710–1774)

Handsome and frail, he was dubbed "le Bien-Aimé" (the Well-Beloved) by his adoring subjects early in his reign; before long, the epithet was purely ironical. Louis wasn't stupid, but he was spoiled rotten; an incorrigible débauché, he chose to flirt rather than rule. His method of governing consisted of fomenting gossip and intrigue at court and setting up an elaborate spy network, known as "le Secret du Roi," abroad. By the end of his reign, royal authority at home and French influence in Europe were just pleasant memories and Louis was, personally, the most hated man in France.

HIS MATES

Maria Leszcynska: The daughter of a dethroned Polish king, and considerably older than Louis, she was the best that could be found in a hurry. They were married when he was fifteen, and for a while they got along fine; she was modest, sweet, and able to produce ten children in ten years. Eventually, however, she refused to sleep with the king for the sake of her health, after which she had to resign herself to being a good sport while Louis threw sexual discretion to the wind.

Mme. de Pompadour: Her bourgeois background scandalized the court more than loose morals ever could. Louis made her a marquise, and she did whatever was necessary to hang on to power for the next nineteen years. This was no small feat since, according to the history books, Louis was sexually insatiable and Mme. de Pompadour was "frigid"; she solved the problem by procuring beautiful mistresses for him. An inveterate schemer, she had a genius for stirring up trouble at court, and she helped Louis shape his disastrous foreign policy. On the plus side, she had taste and wit and was committed to encouraging artists. She provided Voltaire with support and protection and Paris with the Place de la Concorde.

Mme. du Barry: She played Lolita to Louis' Humbert Humbert. His last official favorite, la du Barry was a pretty, vivacious, rather vulgar courtesan who got on many people's nerves, but apparently meant no harm. She was, at least, an aristocrat. She reportedly sat on the arm of the royal chair during council meetings, making faces at the minsters like a pet monkey.

HIS MINISTER

Cardinal Fleury: Already seventy when he took office, he ran the state honestly, economically, and cautiously. But he couldn't live forever; when he died in office, at the age of ninety, Louis decided not to appoint another minister in his place.

HIS MOTTO

"Après moi, le déluge." (Louis never really said this; it was a measure of his unpopularity that everyone believed he had.)

HIS CHAIR:

THE MAN: LOUIS XVI
(1754–1793)

Flabby, sluggish, humble, and shy, he was probably cut out for something, but it wasn't being king. He read slowly, danced poorly, made conversation barely at all, and always looked a mess, no matter how much trouble his valets took. Even if his piety and basic good-heartedness had been leadership qualities, Louis lacked the will to put them to work. The only things he really cared about were food, his wife, and the hunt, in ascending order. To him, a day without hunting was a day not really lived. On July 14, 1789, he wrote in his diary, "Nothing."

HIS MATE

Marie Antoinette: She'd been the Archduchess of Austria and she was everything Louis wasn't: majestic, charming, sophisticated, proud, and frivolous. He adored her; she despised him. The fact that a genital malformation kept Louis from consummating their marriage for eight years didn't do much to keep her home at night or to make her treat him kindly. Still, rumors that she was unfaithful were probably false; she was more interested in shopping than in sex. Although her extravagance earned her the nickname "Madame Déficit," it was her Austrian background that the French found really unforgivable. In fact, letters discovered after her death revealed that the queen's mother, Maria Theresa, had had every intention of using her daughter as a tool of the Austrian government (and her meddling in politics certainly shooed the Revolution along its way), but the French had no way of knowing that at the time.

HIS MINISTERS

Maurepas: An old courtier intent on offending no one, he missed his chance to squelch lethal court factions and refused to support the financial reforms proposed by the liberal minister Turgot because he was jealous. By the time he died, the Revolution was only eight years away.

Necker: A conservative financier who came into prominence largely because of his ambitious wife, who presided over a brilliant literary salon. He ran afoul of Marie Antoinette, and by the time he'd regained power, his orthodox financial policies were too little, too late.

HIS MOTTO

"Let them eat cake." Not his, of course; hers.

HIS CHAIR:

Special Souvenir-Program Section

YOU CAN'T TELL THE PLAYERS—OR, IN SOME CASES, THE INNINGS—WITHOUT ONE

Persian Wars, Peloponnesian War, Punic Wars

In the *Persian Wars* (500–499 B.C.), the Greeks—most notably Athens and Sparta—defeated the greatest empire the world had up to then known, an empire that embraced not only Persia, but Asia Minor, Mesopotamia, Egypt, and much of what is today Afghanistan. The wars began in Ionia, on the Turkish coast, as a colonial revolt against the "barbarian" landlord; Athens stepped in on the colonists' side, and won a big victory at Marathon. The Spartans got involved and, with the Athenians, suffered a famous (though they'd been very brave) defeat at Thermopylae; but the same year (480) the Greeks had a big naval victory at Salamis. Eventually they destroyed the Persian fleet—it was Xerxes I who suffered the defeat, his father (Darius I) having started the war—then pushed the Persians inland (where Alexander the Great would zap them a century later) and opened the entire Aegean to Greek shipping. Herodotus (see page 572) tells the story of the Persian Wars, which mark the coming of age of Greek nationalism and sense of superiority to the "Orient," as well as the ascendancy of Athens.

In the *Peloponnesian War* (431–404 B.C.), greedy, cocksure Athens, now the preeminent Greek city-state, and its allies, the so called Delian League, took on spiteful, jealous Sparta and her allies, the so called Peloponnesian League (from the Peloponnese, the southernmost Greek peninsula, which Sparta dominated). Athens, which was all about democracy and high culture and maritime trading, initially tried to wear down the resistance of Sparta, which was all about oligarchy and military discipline and living off the land. (The Persians, happy enough to see their rivals fighting, funded both sides, first one, then the other.) Ultimately, the war ruined Athens, which made a lot of miscalculations (and wasn't helped by a plague, in which Pericles, its leader, died, or by the revolt of several allies). Sparta, triumphant, took over the Athenian empire, where it did away with voting and playwriting; though it wasn't able to control Athens for long, Sparta remained the dominant power in ancient Greece for another thirty years. Thucydides, who wrote about it (see page 572), calls the Peloponnesian War the worst disturbance in Greek history, but then he hadn't met the Romans.

In the *Punic Wars* (three of them: 264–241 B.C., 218–201 B.C., and 149–146 B.C.), those Romans were able to finish off their "hated city," Carthage, in present-day Tunisia, a rival for trade and empire throughout the western Mediterranean. ("Punic" is from the Roman word for Phoenician, Carthage having been settled by the Phoenicians in the ninth century B.C.) In the first Punic War, Rome, which had just succeeded in showing the rest of the Italian peninsula who was boss, kicked Carthage out of Sicily (then grabbed Sardinia and Corsica while nobody was looking), and came to appreciate the value of naval power. In the second Punic War, Hannibal, a Carthaginian, invaded Rome from Carthaginian Spain by crossing the Alps, but wound up getting wedged into the toe of Italy's boot. Rome relieved Carthage not only of Spain but also of its fleet, then invaded the city itself. This was the end of Carthaginian commercial and imperial greatness, though the place didn't go down the tubes completely. Didn't, that is, until the third Punic War, in which Rome—incited by Cato the Elder's famous *Delenda est Carthago* ("Carthage must be destroyed") speech—first blockaded, then conquered the city, taking it apart house by house and stone by stone, and finally ploughing the whole place under. The survivors became slaves and the surrounding lands the Roman province of Africa. That same year (146 B.C.), Greece was annexed. Rome was off and running.

Middle Ages, Dark Ages, Medieval Times, Feudalism

The *Middle Ages* are the thousand years that elapsed between the fall of the Roman Empire in the West in A.D. 476 and the onset of the Renaissance in Italy in about 1500. Scholars subdivide the Middle Ages into the Early Middle Ages (476 to 900 or 1000, the central figure of which is Charlemagne), the High Middle Ages (900 or 1000 to around 1300), and the Late Middle Ages (1300 to 1500); together the three periods account for the millennium that separates the Ancient world from the Modern one.

The Dark Ages is what Renaissance people, looking down their aquiline noses, called the whole of the Middle Ages. Scholars, however, stepping in once again, preempted the term for the Early Middle Ages only, arguing that the five centuries after the year 1000 weren't, give or take the Hundred Years' War, the Crusades, the Spanish Inquisition, and the Great Plague, really as bad as all that.

Medieval times—or the medieval era, or whatever—is simply, and literally, a Latinate way of saying "Middle Ages," from the Latin *medius*, "middle," plus *aevum*, "age." And *feudalism* describes not a period of time but a political system that prevailed during it, in which vassals (the ancestors of our nobles) pledge fealty (our loyalty) to their liege lord (our king) exchanging their service in time of war for inheritable fiefs (our real estate). As it happens, feudalism was in effect in most of Europe from about the tenth century until the end of the fourteenth. But while it coincides with much of the Middle Ages, that doesn't mean you get to substitute one term for the other.

Thomas Aquinas, Thomas à Becket, Thomas à Kempis, Thomas More

All four are saints. Think of them as the scholastic, the martyr, the mystic, and the humanist, respectively. But let's do this in chronological order.

Thomas à Becket, a twelfth-century Englishman, is the martyr. After a somewhat loose-living youth, during which he gave his friend King Henry II (see page 589) every reason to think he'd make an easygoing enough Archbishop of Canterbury, Becket fooled everybody, including himself, by either, depending on whom you talk to, getting religion or going on a power trip. Anyway, he interfered enough with Henry's attempts to consolidate national power at the expense of the Church that he wound up being assassinated in 1170 in Canterbury Cathedral. Thus began a martyrdom that would see immediate baronial rebellion (and the consequent withering of royal power), subsequent canonization, an enormous and centuries-long tourist industry (it's Thomas' shrine that Chaucer's pilgrims are headed for), plus all those plays (by Tennyson, Eliot, and Anouilh) and movies (with Richard Burton and Peter O'Toole).

Thomas Aquinas, a thirteenth-century Italian, is the scholastic, one of that breed of philosophers who liked to argue about how many angels could dance on the head of a pin and, regardless of *that* answer, whether or not they had navels. In a sense, he transcended the genre (see page 312), managing to channel some of that endless Q&A energy into arguing with the real dopes about how faith couldn't be endangered by reason, which meant it wasn't a sin to go on thinking. Known to some as the Angelic Doctor, to others—the result of the slowness of his delivery—as the Dumb Ox.

Thomas à Kempis, a fourteenth-century German, is the mystic. Purported author of something called *The Imitation of Christ*, which charted the progress of the individual soul up to and including its union with God, in fact he spelled big trouble for the Catholic Church. After all, emphasize enough how we can all commune directly with God in perfect solitude, without need of words, worship, or sacraments, let alone church property, and a few of us are going to stop showing up on Sunday. This wasn't Kempis' intention (he still honored the Church's pattern of salvation), but it got Martin Luther, among others, thinking.

With *Thomas More*, we're back in England and it's the sixteenth century. A northern humanist, like the Dutchman Erasmus and the Frenchman John Calvin (see below), he took Renaissance energy—which tended to be employed down in Italy to make beautiful things and explore the infinite riches of the human personality—and applied it to thinking about God, society, science, and human nature. A statesman (and the author of *Utopia*, his version of which was a severe and snobbish agricultural community with plenty of slaves to take care of the degrading stuff), he, like Becket, was put to death for refusing to do his king's bidding. Required by Henry VIII to sign the 1534 Act of Supremacy, which declared the English monarch to be the "Protector and Only Supreme Head of the Church and Clergy of England," thereby getting England out from under the thumb of the Pope *and* allowing Henry to get his divorce from Catherine of Aragon, More demurred. He was offed the following year and canonized four centuries later.

John Wyclif, John Huss, John Calvin, John Knox

Another group who, basically, gave the Catholic Church a bad time. *John Wyclif*, an Englishman teaching at Oxford, had noticed, like Thomas à Kempis, that it was possible to do without the elaborate possessions of a church and, if you were devout by nature, even without priests. The difference is that in 1380 or so, he, unlike Kempis, said as much, furthermore recommending that everybody simply go home and read the Bible, which he just happened to have translated into English.

John Huss, a Bohemian from central Europe who lived at about the same time, took things one step further by turning his ritual-resistant Hussites from a religious group into a Czech national movement in protest of German supremacy in the area. Both Wyclif and Huss were branded as heretics.

John Calvin, a Frenchman who lived from 1509 to 1564, is a much bigger deal. A generation younger than Luther, he experienced a sudden conversion at the age of twenty-four, joined forces with the religious revolutionaries, and published his *Institutes of the Christian Religion*, addressed—unlike Luther's writings—not just to Germans but to everybody who was dissatisfied with the existing Roman setup. Because Calvin did so much with the idea of predestination (God had chosen some people to be saved, others to be damned; you knew who you were, and that was that, don't even bother to struggle), Calvinists tended to be militant, uncompromising, self-righteous—i.e., Puritans. They also refused to recognize the subordination of church to state or the laying down of rules by any king or parliament. Rather, Christians should, according to Calvin, Christianize the state, as Oliver Cromwell would do a century later in

England. In the meantime, Calvinism took root in France (the Huguenots were Calvinists) and spread not only to England and Germany, but to the Netherlands, Poland, and Hungary, too.

In Scotland, *John Knox*, a particularly sober-sided type who would give Mary, Queen of Scots, a bad case of the shakes, made Calvinism—later called Presbyterianism—the established Scottish religion.

Jacobean, Jacobite, Jacobin, Jacquerie

All four come from the Latin given name "Jacobus," the ancestor of our "James" (and the Frenchman's "Jacques"). *Jacobean* describes the period—rich, exuberant, and increasingly cynical—during which the Stuart king James I ruled Britain, right after Elizabeth. More a cultural term than a historical one, it evokes the late, great tragedies and romances of Shakespeare; the grisly, overwrought drama of his contemporaries John *The Duchess of Malfi* Webster and John *Tis Pity She's a Whore* Ford; the poetry of Donne and the Metaphysicals; and, natch, the King James version of the Bible.

Jacobite describes those Brits who, several decades and an expulsion or two later, were trying to get James I's Stuart descendants—Scottish, Catholic, and firm adherents of the divine right of kings—back on the English throne. Even with a lot of collaboration on the part of the French and a couple of out-and-out invasion attempts, via Scotland, in 1715 and 1745, the Jacobites, who'd hoped to turn the clock back by a century or so, didn't so much as get the minute hand moving. The net impact of their scheming was the stripping down of the traditional Scottish Highlands clans and the banning of kilts and bagpipes for thirty years.

Today, "Jacobite" is pretty much relegated to the history books (except when used, impishly, of Henry James fans). *Jacobin*, by contrast, still shows up in the odd George Will or Mary McGrory column. Originally, it signified the most radical of the essentially well-educated, middle-class revolutionaries during the French Revolution (who'd met in an old Jacobin, or Dominican, monastery in Paris); it embraced such subgroups as the Girondists and the "Mountain"; and it included almost every French revolutionary leader you ever heard of: Robespierre, Marat, Danton, Condorcet, St. Just, etc. Eventually, the Jacobins were found—by the rabble, the *popular* revolutionaries like the sans-culottes (so called because they went around not in knee breeches but in trousers)—to be insufficiently militant, and most of them wound up, like the royalists before them, at the guillotine. Today, "Jacobin" is used to describe radicals, or extreme leftists, who are determined to carry on the revolution at any cost; who like to talk political theory into the wee hours; and who, in general, have contempt for the will of the majority, the persons-in-the-street, believing that it's *they*, the intelligentsia, who are best equipped to call the shots. The Bolsheviks, behind Russia's 1917 revolution, are this century's most famous Jacobins.

Oldest of all is *jacquerie*, from "Jacques," the generic French nickname for a peasant, used to describe an insurrection of peasants, such as was first set off in France in 1358, a response to the economic hardships brought about by the Black Death and the Hundred Years' War (see page 593). Similar massive uprisings took place in England, most notably Wat Tyler's rebellion of 1381, during which, shaking their pitchforks, peasant spokesmen wondered aloud why some people were rich and fancy, others poor and drab—or as they put it in a famous couplet, "When Adam delved and Eve span / Who was then a gentleman?"

Puritans, Pilgrims, Dissenters, Roundheads

The *Puritans* were the extreme, Calvinistic Protestants—as opposed to the moderate, Church of England ones—in seventeenth-century England. The *Pilgrims* were those Puritans who left England for Holland in 1608, and eventually arrived at Plymouth Rock in 1620. The *Roundheads* (so called because of their close-cropped hair) were the Puritan followers of Oliver Cromwell in the 1640s war between the forces of Parliament (spearheaded by Cromwell) and those of the king, Charles I, whose followers had long hair, wore too much lace and cologne, and were known as Cavaliers. By the 1650s, *Dissenters*, a broader term that took in a variety of anti–Church of England nonconformists, was how you would have designated the fellows you used to think of as Puritans.

Diggers, Levellers, Luddites, Chartists

British antiestablishmentarians, all. The *Levellers* (many of whom were, for the record, Puritans) and the *Diggers* were both fixtures in Cromwellian England. The former pushed for almost-universal male suffrage, a written constitution, subordination of Parliament to the will of the voters, and other things it would take the American and French Revolutions (and another century) to get a real taste of. The latter thumbed their noses at the idea of private property and went around occupying and occasionally cultivating other people's land.

The *Luddites* were rioters who took to destroying machinery in the factories of northern England between 1811 and 1816; especially averse to textile machines, they blamed the impact of the Industrial Revolution for their unemployment and misery. Their leader was Ned Ludd.

The *Chartists* were a working-class group, named after the People's Charter they'd drafted in 1838, advocating, among other things, universal adult male suffrage, the secret ballot, equal electoral districts, the annual election of the members of the House of Commons, and the payment of salaries to those members so that you wouldn't have to be independently wealthy to be able to spend your days in session there. The Chartist movement died down as the result of opposition from the government and from businessmen, as well as from internal dissension. But, unlike the Diggers, the Levellers, and the Luddites, the Chartists had at least gotten a lot of smart, influential people to listen. Their full program would be in place shortly after World War I.

Whigs, Tories

Both arose in seventeenth-century England in response to the controversy surrounding the pro-French, pro-Catholic policies of Charles II. The *Whigs*—also known as the Country Party, made up of the biggest-deal aristocrats, always eager to weaken a king since it automatically strengthened *them*, and backed by the middle class and the merchants of London—wanted to see Charles II (not to mention his even more Catholic brother, James II, due to succeed him) checked. They stood for the supremacy of Parliament and for religious toleration. The *Tories*—also known as the Court Party, consisting of the lesser aristocracy, the country squires, and the Anglican clergy—supported Charles and were suspicious of the Whigs' commercial leanings, among other things.

Of course, neither the Whigs nor the Tories were anything like an organized political party back then (even taken together, there were only a few thousand of them), but by the next century they would be the two leading parties of the country, and would remain so right through the nineteenth century, when the Tories renamed themselves Conservatives and the Whigs renamed themselves Liberals.

Both terms were less than complimentary in origin, and were in each case first used by the opponents of the faction in question. A "whig" was originally a Scottish cattle rustler, a "tory" an Irish plunderer. You don't hear much about Whigs these days, but even now, in England, a Tory is a mildly hostile name for a conservative, especially a right-wing one.

Colony, Protectorate, Dominion, Territory, Mandate, Trusteeship, Dependency, Possession

Enjoy them while you can; the era of imperialism is winding to a stop. The familiar word here is *colony*, but it has an edge: A colony, strictly speaking, consists of a company of people transplanted somewhere for the purpose of settling it; as a result, a colony should have a fair sprinkling of faces that remind you of what folks look like back in the Mother Country. (Canada was a colony of Great Britain's, whereas in China—except for Hong Kong, another colony—Britain just had a lot of treaties and trading concessions in effect.) In a *protectorate*, an imperial power doesn't claim to be settling anything; it just strides in and takes over in the name of the existing ruler, presumably to save him and his subjects from other, less noble-minded imperial powers. A *dominion* is a specifically British concept, used of a particularly well-regarded colony that, while still tied to the mother country, was largely self-governing—Canada, Australia, and New Zealand, for example; today, the dominions are independent (which is not to say the queen isn't still constantly popping by). *Territory* applies to a portion of a country—usually remote and undeveloped, like Canada's Yukon and Northwest Territories—that's not deemed ready to become a full-fledged state or province.

A *mandate* is what the victorious Allied powers handed out to themselves from the former empires of the defeated Central Powers after World War I. Thus Britain got Palestine and Transjordan; France, Syria and Lebanon; Japan, some of Germany's former holdings in the Pacific; and—abbreviating the list somewhat—South Africa got the former German colony of Southwest Africa, a.k.a. Namibia, which finally achieved independence in 1990. The same thing happened after World War II, except this time the United Nations supervised the doling out of former Italian and Japanese possessions, plus assumed responsibility for the mandates. The Trust Territory of the Pacific Islands, administered by the United States (which, just between us, seems very reluctant to let go of it completely, though it's granted varying degrees of independence to its component parts), was the last remaining trusteeship, officially dissolved in 1986.

A *dependency* could be any of the above, plus the little sheikdom or sultanate whose foreign affairs you're helping to handle even though you don't claim to own it. If you did, it—like colonies, protectorates, dominions, etc.—would be a *possession*, and you would be both occupying and controlling it.

The Boer War, the Boxer Rebellion

We know you think you know—and you're probably right. But today's Boer War and Boxer Rebellion are tomorrow's Persian and Punic Wars, so let's run through them just to make sure.

The Boers (from the Dutch word for "farmer") were the descendants of the Dutchmen who'd originally settled the Cape of Good Hope, the southern tip of Africa, in the seventeenth century. After 1815, when England annexed the Cape according to the terms of the Congress of Vienna (see page 595), the Boers, simple, old-fashioned folk, made the "great trek" inland and cleared the Transvaal and the Orange Free State in an effort to get away from the British. They didn't think much of slavery or miners or adventurers or fortune-hunting Englishmen. Unfortunately, the English, in the course of their planning for a Cape-to-Cairo railway, now found themselves confronted by two little Boer republics just where a few hundred miles of track were supposed to go down. The discovery of gold and diamonds in the Transvaal pressurized matters further. Brits poured in, the Transvaal refused to pass the bills that would allow the Brits to build their mines, the Brits started to terrorize the Boers, and Europe started screaming about British bullying. (The German emperor, William II, even sent a telegram to the president of the Transvaal congratulating him on having staved off the British raiders "without having to call for the support of friendly powers.") Three years later England went to war with the two Boer republics, and over the course of the next three years, conquered them in the *Boer War* (1899–1902). Incorporated into the British Empire, but with various of their institutions (including their language, Afrikaans) pretty much intact, the Boers soon found themselves a part of the Union of South Africa, today's Republic of South Africa, about which we'll not get going here. Britain, for her part, found herself the least popular nation in Europe—which encouraged her to rethink matters enough to present herself as an acceptable potential ally for a war that, it would turn out, was only a decade away.

The *Boxer Rebellion* also broke out in 1899 and also involved Britain, along with every other Western power with a stake in China—formerly a proud empire, now weakened, demoralized, and on her last legs. Seems a Chinese secret society bent on revolution and named something like the Order of Righteous Harmonious Fists (the Westerners doubled over with laughter at the nickname "Boxers") had besieged all the Western legations—French, Russian, and German, as well as British—in northern China, killing missionaries and railway workers, as well as Chinese converts to Christianity. The European powers, joined by Japan and the United States, sent an international force against the Boxers, squashing them in very short order. The victors made things even harder on the Chinese, hitting them with, among other things, a bill for $330 million. The upshot: The Chinese government decided it was high time to join its neighbor Japan in a Westernization program. And younger Chinese, deciding it was high time to get rid of both the foreigners *and* the government, rallied to a fellow named Sun Yat-sen. It was the beginning of a Chinese revolution that, with time out for World War II, would go on for half a century.

Redshirts, Brownshirts, Blackshirts, Black and Tans

The *Redshirts* were Garibaldi's (he'd gotten the wool for them cheap from the government of Uruguay, whose independence he'd helped secure), and with them he helped achieve the unification of the modern nation of Italy in the early 1860s. The *Brownshirts* were Hitler's; they constituted the *Sturmabteilung*, or SA, the Nazi "stormtroopers." The *Blackshirts* were also Hitler's, in the persons of his elite *Schutzstaffel*, or SS, the "security echelon," but he'd gotten the idea from Mussolini, who'd first come up with the notion of color-coded private militias. The *Black and Tans* were Britain's, recruited to fill vacancies in the Royal Irish Constabulary caused by the killing or intimidation of its native-Irish members during the Troubles of 1919–1923; themselves given to terrorist tactics (and named after a local breed of hound), the Black and Tans wore khaki uniforms and black belts.

Epoch, Era, Period, Age, Eon

"Epoch" and "era" present the big stumbling block here, because almost nobody uses them anymore the way the historians meant them to be used. Which is: An *epoch* is the date of an occurrence that starts things going in a new direction or under new conditions (i.e., a point in time). An *era* is the time during which what started as an epoch continues, building steam, gaining momentum, becoming established—at which point you've got a *period*, an era that's run its course and is ready for another epoch-making event. An *age* is pretty much an era (the Age of Reason, the Era of Good Feeling: both have a sense of center to them); an *eon* any immeasurably, even infinitely long time. Anything else? Well, a *cycle* is a succession of periods followed by another, similar succession. And your *birthday* is the day you were born, celebrated with a cake in most Western countries.

Note to geology majors: You shouldn't have to be reminded—and no one else cares—that the geologic time scale's largest division is the eon (one or more eras), followed by the era (one or more periods), the period (one or more epochs), and the epoch. Thus, one—that is, you—speaks of the Pliocene epoch of the Tertiary period of the Cenozoic era. Right?

Reds

Contributor **Michael Sorkin** casts a cold eye on the men—and the woman—who took Karl Marx's more or less straightforward theory of history and did so much thinking, rethinking, second-guessing, and arguing among themselves as to what he really meant, didn't mean, might have meant, and ought to have meant that poor Marx had no choice but to confess, famously and fairly early on, "Je ne suis pas un Marxiste." But first, a look at the old boy, Marxist or not, himself.

KARL MARX (GERMAN, 1818–1883)

Marx, and Marxism, didn't simply happen. A German, born in 1818, Karl Marx was influenced by the social ideas that came out of the French Revolution, the economic ideas that came out of the British Industrial Revolution, and, especially, by the philosophical ideas that were now coming—and coming and coming—out of Germany as it emerged into the European high noon. In fact, Marx can himself be thought of as one in an ever-lengthening line of German philosophers, the most notable of whom was Hegel (see page 321), to whom he—along with other "Young Hegelians" like Engels—was much devoted in his youth and from whom he picked up the very useful dialectical method. Like any philosopher, Marx was interested in the big questions, and the one his system "solves" is that most basic quandary of history; namely, what makes it go, and where. Marx answers the question by taking dialectics (Hegel's thesis-antithesis-synthesis dynamic) and combining it with materialism, the half of philosophy that says matter constitutes, and has precedence over, mind. The result, as if you didn't know: dialectical materialism.

In a nutshell, Marx's argument is that economic relationships are the basic forces in history and that it is only around them that the whole complex of social relationships arises. Marx called these two interrelated aspects the economic "base" and the social "superstructure." As a materialist, he felt that the "relations of production"—the basic setup and reciprocal interaction among those people or classes who are doing the work and making (or not making) the money—defined by the "base" decreed the "general character of the social, political, and spiritual processes of life. It is not the consciousness of men that determines their existence, but, on the contrary, their existence that determines their con-

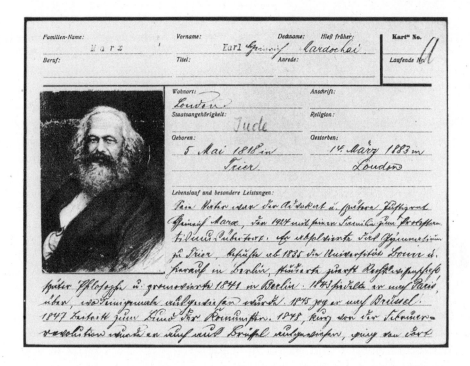

Familien-Name:	Vorname:	Deckname:	Hieß früher:	Kart. No.
Marx	*Karl Heinrich*		*Mardochai*	
Beruf:	Titel:	Anrede:		Laufende No.

Wohnort: *London*

Anschrift:

Staatsangehörigkeit: *Jude*

Religion:

Geboren: *5 Mai 1818 in Trier*

Gestorben: *14 März 1883 in London*

Lebenslauf und besondere Leistungen:

[handwritten German text]

sciousness." (Those who really know their Marxism like to observe along about now how Marx has found Hegel "standing on his head" and—by insisting that actualities come before ideas, that the mind doesn't conceive of freedom, then decide to go out and found a Greek city-state, but the other way around—is here "setting him on his feet again.")

There's one more very big issue: As with all dialectics, change is part of the very nature of things; a force necessarily calls its opposite into being. For Marx, the social system—the superstructure, as it were—contains within itself the seeds of "contradiction," leading to a disequilibrium with the economic base and, eventually, to the overthrow of the whole business—in other words, revolution; also progress. Watch how it works: Material conditions (agrarian, industrial, whatever) spawn economic classes. Thus, at some point, there'd been a feudal, or landholding, class, which, according to the theory, got top-heavy and overwhelmed by a bourgeois, or commercial, class. Now, in plain sight of Marx and anybody else whose eyes were open, that bourgeoisie was calling into being *its* dialectical antithesis, the proletariat. In fact, the more bourgeois a country was, the more it was going to become proletarian: The busier the factories, the bigger the laboring class. Eventually, with all these bourgeois types devouring each other in their race to get ahead, the proletariat will see its chance and take over, "expropriating the expropriators," "seizing the levers of production," and abolishing private property. Marx thinks he sees this coming in 1848, but he's wrong; society isn't quite ready to become classless, the state to "wither away," or religion—"the opiate of the people," the only thing that keeps them from protesting the grimness of their lives by promising all of them another one later—to pack its bags and leave town.

Of course, the theory is much more complicated than that. (Simplified descriptions like the foregoing are the basis for what is commonly called "vulgar Marxism.") In fact, Marx devoted his life to elaborations on all of the above, producing a vast body of work, vastly documented and vastly ramified. But Marx knew that he couldn't change the destiny of the world just by hanging out in the library. He was also a revolutionary who held that theory must be joined with practice. "Philosophers have studied the world," as he put it, "but the problem is to change it." So Marx organized. He lectured and made speeches. He went to meetings and debates. Eventually, he went west, to London and Paris, more evolved than any German city was and hence that much closer to the inevitable revolt. He wrote newspaper articles (Marx was for a time the European correspondent for the New York *Tribune*). He, with his family, starved and got deported. And he, with his friend Engels, wrote *The Communist Manifesto*—perhaps the most stirring and incendiary document ever. "The proletarians have nothing to lose but their chains," it concludes. "They have a world to win. Workers of the world, unite."

Marx had a lot of faith in these proletarians, the class of wage earners capitalism was, in effect, fleecing. Not only were they destined to rise up and overthrow the system, they were the harbingers of everything Marx was working toward—initially a new socialist order in which the oppressed would be freed and wealth would be distributed on the principle of "to each according to his needs, from each according to his ability." Ultimately, even this workers' state would "wither away," leaving no oppressive institutions to mediate among people; in the meantime, it was to be governed, in Marx's phrase, by a "dictatorship of the proletariat."

But while Marx was probably just trying to describe the class content of the regime, many subsequent self-avowed Marxists have seen it otherwise, warming especially to the possibilities of that first word, "dictatorship." Such, as with so many other great thinkers, has been the fate of Marx: He has been interpreted. As his work attained the stature of holy writ, his disciples—and his exegetes—multiplied. Marx became a dogmatist's dream. His work (enormous, changing, and incomplete: *Das Kapital*, his magnum opus, was never finished) has been battled over by countless factions, each of which claims to know the "real" Marx. As a result, the first thing most Marxists want to know about other Marxists is which side they're on. The following may provide some clues.

FRIEDRICH ENGELS (GERMAN, 1820–1895)

Friedrich Engels was the perfect collaborator: patient, intelligent, articulate, enthusiastic, and rich. The son of a wealthy textile manufacturer, he was, for many years, in charge of the Manchester branch of his family's factory. This not only enabled him to send regular checks to Marx (often the one thing standing between the Marx family and destitution), it also gave him a fine vantage point from which to survey the course of mid-nineteenth century capitalism, providing grist for such works as *The Condition of the Working Class in England*. In truth, Engels' work is inseparable from that of Marx (they wrote successive drafts of *The Communist Manifesto*, and Engels ghosted many of Marx's *Tribune* articles), and he proved Marx's staunchest defender in the years after his death. Largely self-educated, Engels was not as deep a thinker as Marx but he was a brilliant polemicist, and his ongoing fascination with science, particularly Darwinism, made him even more adamant than his colleague about the inevitability of capitalism's downfall. Perhaps his most enduring contribution, however, is the elaboration of the idea of the "relative autonomy" of the superstructure, the notion that it could interact with the base, sometimes actually pushing it along a bit, if only for a limited period. Through such subtle divergences as these Engels started a trend toward revisionism—the customary pejorative for any and all tampering with Marx—that would soon become standard operating procedure.

VLADIMIR ILYICH LENIN
(RUSSIAN, 1870–1924)

With Lenin, as with college freshmen, the key word is party—in this case, the Communist Party. Lenin (né Ulyanov) was the revolutionary's revolutionary. He wed Marxism—up to that point, don't forget, a Western doctrine—to a strong, and absolutely Russian, tradition of false names, forged passports, and invisible ink. Then, incredibly single-minded, he proceeded to put everything through the sieve of revolutionary practice in the belief that any issue could be resolved in response to the query: "Is it good for the revolution?" Tireless as a propagandist, prolific as a writer, incomparable as an agitator, and merciless as an adversary, Lenin emerged as the leader of the Bolshevik (or "majority") faction of the

Russian Communists, and became, after the October 1917 revolution, the first head of state of the new Russia. His version of the dictatorship of the proletariat tended to emphasize the dictatorship. As he saw it, authority was to be exercised not by the unwieldy mass of proletarians but by a surrogate: the Communist Party proper, composed of dedicated and knowledgeable people who could both understand the proletarian worldview and act as its instrument. In fact, according to Lenin, there couldn't be any revolution at all without such a powerful vanguard party to get things organized. There was, needless to say, disagreement on this, which Lenin, who died on the job, never saw resolved. Even so, his heirs had him embalmed and placed on display in Red Square, where he remains an object of necrophiliac admiration for what's left of the masses and a source of continuing embarrassment to the post-Communist Russian government, which can't quite make up its mind how to dispose of him.

ROSA LUXEMBURG (POLISH, 1871–1919)

Rosa Luxemburg ("Red Rosa," as she came to be known) was the great champion of revolutionary orthodoxy. Considerably more leftist than Lenin and the Bolsheviks, she vigorously assailed their revisionism, most notably over the issue of party organization. Luxemburg pushed for what she called "spontaneity," the kind of worker-originated impulse that resulted in things like general strikes and that upbraided Lenin for his opportunistic advocacy of "ultra-centralism," arguing that "revolutionary tactics cannot be invented by leaders, they must develop spontaneously—history comes first, leaders' consciousness second." And "We must frankly admit to ourselves that errors made by a truly revolutionary labor movement are infinitely more fruitful and more valuable than the infallibility of the best of all possible central committees."

Luxemburg's major theoretical work is *The Accumulation of Capital*, which attempts to supplement Marx by establishing a precise economic argument for the inevitability of the collapse of capitalism. To make a long story short, she contends that the contradiction between capitalism's reliance on noncapitalist markets and its tendency to destroy its noncapitalist environment can only lead to its ruin. The Leninist camp attacked her for this theory, which they twisted into the "automatic collapse of capitalism" and branded as "fatalistic." Luxemburg would not live to see her reputation totally besmirched—by Stalin—since she and her friend Karl Liebknecht (with whom she founded the Spartacus League, predecessor of the German Communist Party) were murdered while under arrest by the German authorities.

JOSEF STALIN (RUSSIAN, 1879–1953)

What can you say about Stalin except that he was one of the worst pieces of bad news since the Flood? Born Josef Dzhugashvili, he soon changed his name to Stalin ("Man of Steel"), which you'd think would have given someone a clue to his mettle. On assuming power, Stalin's interpretation of the dictatorship of the proletariat turned out to be even simpler than Lenin's: dictatorship by Stalin. His legacy includes the gulag, the cult of personality, the show trials, the purges, mass starvation, a police state, and the industrialization of the Soviet Union. It is to this last that Stalinists tend to point when citing his achievements. Except among the three of them, however, "Stalinist" is considered a term of abuse. When Stalin died, he was put on display next to Lenin until people had second thoughts some years later and removed his corpse to less high-toned surroundings.

LEON TROTSKY (RUSSIAN, 1879–1940)

Like Lenin and Stalin, Leon Trotsky (né Bronstein) changed his name. On other points they had less in common. One of the revolutionary "old boys" (though a relatively late joiner of the party, for which he was given much grief), Trotsky organized the Red Army after the revolution and led it to success in the ensuing civil war. Energetic and smart, he was one of the key men around Lenin, despite differences over the role of the Party. Under Stalin, he was not only not key, he was not even around very long, sent into exile by the jealous despot. The issue over which they nominally came to blows was Trotsky's theory of "permanent revolution," which was in conflict with Stalin's espousal of "socialism in one country." Trotsky had what might be called a "process" view of rev-

olution. He felt that the success of the revolution that Russia was having depended on its continuous expansion, both within Russia and in other European nations. "Socialism in one country," as you may have guessed, held that nurturing the revolution at home was the top priority. The question was finally resolved by one of Stalin's agents, who tracked Trotsky to Mexico and put an ice ax (almost certainly not an ice pick) through his skull. Like so many other things, though, "Trotskyism" was mainly a fiction invented by Stalin (though fervently believed by Trotsky and a few others) out of sheer paranoia. Not that Trotsky was such a prize, either, being rigid, doctrinaire, and even brutal, although he *was* a fine writer and the author of the definitive account of the 1917 revolution. Should someone call you a "Trot," however, it's to the former attributes that he or she is probably alluding. Remember also that a "Trotskyite" is a "Trotskyist" to a Stalinist.

MAO ZEDONG (CHINESE, 1893–1976)

Mao Zedong's was the last truly great cult of personality. Beside him, such upstarts as Tito, Khaddafi, and Barbra Streisand pale into insignificance. Indeed, among Marxists, Mao's was the last of the great isms. Mao surely helped all of this along by being as brilliant an aphorist as he was a revolutionary, stirring untold billions of Chinese with lines like "The world is progressing, the future is bright, and no one can change the general trend of history," "We know the pear only by eating it and we know society only by participating in the class struggle," and "Some play the piano well and some badly, and there is a great difference in the melodies they produce."

What makes it all so special? To start with the obvious, Mao's Marxism is uniquely Chinese, with dialectics as much indebted to Taoist yin and yang as to Hegel. But Mao's major contribution is the idea of peasant revolution. In the late 1920s Mao broke with the orthodox view that the proletariat was the only revolutionary class and proposed, to the consternation of the Soviets, that the peasantry play the leading role—a strikingly apt idea in a country that had jillions of oppressed peasants and scarcely a prole. Mao also departed from theoretical orthodoxy by emphasizing the importance of the superstructure. Later, this was to lead to the so called Hundred Flowers Campaign (which encouraged people to criticize the Party and which rapidly got out of hand) and to the so called Cultural Revolution (which encouraged people to criticize the Party and which rapidly got out of hand). In the West, nobody much is a Maoist anymore, probably because you can only say "The revolutionary is like a fish swimming in the sea of the people" so many times before beginning to feel a little silly.

GEORG LUKÁCS (HUNGARIAN, 1885–1971)

If you're determined to go after bourgeois culture with a Marxist cleaver, the work of Georg Lukács is indispensable. Lukács (that's pronounced "LOO-kahsh") provided the first serious evaluation of Hegel's role in Marx's thought, revising then-current views of dialectics. No intellectual lightweight, he argued that the historical interaction of subject and object is the basic form of dialectics, insisting in *History and Class Consciousness*, his major work, that a developed class consciousness would impel the proletariat to become both the subject and the object of history. As he put it, proletarian dialectics implies an idea of consciousness which "is not the knowledge of an opposed object but is the self-consciousness of the object *the act of consciousness overthrows*, the objective form of the object."

Another riveting concept of Lukács' is "totality." Bourgeois society, he insisted, tends to destroy the possibility of images of the whole, forest-for-the-trees-style, preventing proletarians (among others) from acquiring true knowledge of reality. Dialectics is the answer, because "only in this context which sees the isolated facts of social life as aspects of the historical process and integrates them in a totality, can knowledge of facts hope to become knowledge of reality." Which brings us to the idea of *reification*, the one thing to remember about Lukács should you choose to remember anything at all. Reification (a concept Marx had introduced in his discussion of the fetishism of commodities in *Das Kapital*) is the process by which bourgeois society transforms social relations into commodity relations, the process by which people become mere objects, and it's the real culprit behind our inability to grasp the totality of things.

ANTONIO GRAMSCI (ITALIAN, 1891–1937)

Antonio Gramsci is everyone's favorite Marxist, as poignant and congenial a figure as the movement has spawned. A hunchbacked scholar and man of action who was in on the founding of the Italian Communist Party, he spent the last ten years of his brief life in a Fascist prison, where he managed to write the appropriately named *Prison Notebooks*, his major legacy. A lengthy sentence allowed him to focus his attention on theoretical questions and, over the years, he constructed a Marxist philosophy of culture, in the process becoming the great theoretician of the superstructure.

Perhaps one of the reasons for Gramsci's current popularity in academic footnotes is the great emphasis he places on the significance of intellectuals, whom he saw as the leading agents of ideology, an indispensable (and heretofore counterrevolutionary) force in preserving the dominance of the ruling class. This ideological ascendancy he called "hegemony," the central Gramscian cocktail-party concept. The danger of hegemony lies in the way it sneaks in everywhere, so much so that the *Weltanschauung* of the ruling class comes to seem like simple common sense. To combat this, Gramsci urged proletarians and other progressive elements to struggle to create a counterculture (sound familiar?) that would challenge the hegemonic domination of the prevailing ideology. In opposition to Lenin—obsessed with the seizure of governmental control—Gramsci envisioned a cultural, educational role for the Party. In the Sixties in the United States, however, Gramsci's countercultural ideas wound up resulting less in Party than in partying.

HERBERT MARCUSE
(GERMAN-BORN AMERICAN, 1898–1979)

Marcuse is one of ours, local hero to a generation whose Marxism tended to be closer to Groucho's than Karl's. Never mind his early work on Hegel—Marcuse's great contribution was the joining of politics with sex, a conjunction that would come to be virtually synonymous with the Sixties. Abandoning Freud's pessimistic view of society (with so much labor-saving technology everywhere you looked, who needed the repression and sublimation that used to get us all to the factory on time?), Marcuse held that we could finally afford to liberate Eros, to eroticize all human relations. This sounded good.

Marcuse was also popular around the campus because of his implacable opposition to positivism, empiricism, and formal logic, the ABCs of your typical college curriculum. He stood for the union of Logos, more or less "reason," with Eros, again, which, rather than the union of subject and object à la Lukács, he saw as the main job of dialectics and which he felt would make for freedom and happiness. Marcuse was a Meher Baba among Marxists, a utopian apostle of good times. He was also keen on pointing out who was keeping whom from having any fun—the reified, "one-dimensional" society which, with its pluralist "repressive tolerance," tried to make it look as if we had options but which really only offered the terrors of conformity. You needed violence to overthrow this, violence which Marcuse believed would be wielded not by the industrial proletariat (which had been bought off) but by people who were *really* outside the system, like racial minorities and students. No wonder the kids loved him.

LOUIS ALTHUSSER (FRENCH, 1918–1990)

Of contemporary Marxist theorists, the hardest one to read is Althusser, which may account for his recent vogue. Althusser is the main proponent of a hybrid of structuralism (see page 334) and Marxism, a combo he opposes to old-fashioned Hegelo-Marxism as well as to more recent Marxist humanism. Basically, Althusser focuses on Marx's later work (the humanists celebrate "the young Marx," Marx the "poet" and the utopian, the messianic and "hip" Marx), citing an "epistemological break" between the early writings, hopelessly mired in our old friend the "subject," and the mature ones, in which Marx was finally able to get down to something that might be the basis of a real *science*.

After explaining how to give Marx the properly "symptomatic" reading (paying attention, like the psychoanalyst, to both what is said and what gets left out), Althusser explains how the object of knowledge is different from the *real* object. This process—equivalent to knowledge working on *its* object—he calls "theoretical practice." Such theoretical practice, when applied to society, leads inevitably to a view of society as a totality (you remember "totality"), which can, however, be broken down—not into a vulgar base/superstructure scheme, but into a tripartite division of economy, politics, and ideology, each of the three relatively autonomous but all of them united in a larger "structure of structures." Or, as Althusser says, "The whole existence of structure consists of its effects."

As you may have gathered, these structures are very complex and have very complex relationships. Althusser calls particular relationships among them *conjunctures*, and reasons that any specific conjuncture is likely to be, in his memorable term, "overdetermined." Which is to say, complex—also, slightly redundant. This is the one Althusserian concept you may actually be able to use: If you are late to work because your mother called, you couldn't find your contact lenses, *and* the bus broke down, your lateness might be said to be overdetermined.

Otherwise, should you actually meet an Althusserian, there's not much you can do. In a pinch, try asking by what criterion he or she *knows* historical materialism is scientific. Failing that, the charge of Stalinism may prove useful. In any case, Althusser proves our basic point as well as the next Marxist: Nobody really understands Marx any better than you do.

Four Cautionary Tales

*EACH OF THEM CONSIDERABLY MORE
SOBERING THAN THE ONES
MAURY POVICH AND JERRY SPRINGER
TRY TO SCARE YOU WITH*

THE DREYFUS AFFAIR

A landmark in the history of modern France and a national disgrace. In 1894, Captain Alfred Dreyfus, a wealthy Jewish officer in the French artillery, was accused of having betrayed secrets to the Germans. Although the evidence against him was slim, rabid anti-Semitism in the military prompted a court-martial to convict him of treason and sentence him to life imprisonment on Devil's Island. Great applause from the public. Two years later, Colonel Georges Picquart, chief of army intelligence, discovered new evidence pointing to the innocence of Dreyfus and the guilt of one Ferdinand Esterhazy, a major in the army and a notorious adventurer. The military, however, was unwilling to admit its error and opted for a cover-up. Picquart was silenced and the authorities refused to reopen the case. But Dreyfus' brother made a few discoveries of his own, and soon the whole affair turned into a major political issue, with all France divided into two factions: the Dreyfusards and the anti-Dreyfusards (for which read pro-republic, anticlerical liberals, and royalist, militarist conservatives, respectively). The former group included a number of intellectual—and a scattering of polit-ical—big guns, including Émile Zola, Georges Clemenceau, and Anatole France, who, although determined to redress the injustice, were actually less con-cerned with the plight of Dreyfus himself, who was still languishing on Devil's Island, than with discrediting the rightist government. The anti-Dreyfusards, who included no small number of reactionaries and out-and-out bigots, felt obliged to resort to perjury and intimidation to protect their idea of patriotism.

The plot continued to thicken. Major Esterhazy was finally tried and acquit-ted by a court-martial. An outraged Zola wrote his famous open letter begin-ning "*J'accuse*," for which he was promptly sentenced to jail. He escaped to England. Major Henry, an army intelligence officer who, it now turned out, had forged much of the evidence used against Dreyfus, committed suicide. Ester-hazy followed Zola's lead and escaped to England. A Dreyfusard became pre-mier. Dreyfus was retried, convicted again by a military court—this time, found "guilty with extenuating circumstances." Great hue and cry from the public. The President of France finally stepped in and pardoned Dreyfus, but by this time, pardon wasn't good enough. The public was still up in arms, and demands for Dreyfus' complete exoneration were coming in from all over the world. Fi-nally, in 1906, he was cleared, and, in 1930, his innocence was proven by the publication of secret German papers showing that Esterhazy had, in fact, been the culprit.

The repercussions of "*l'affaire Dreyfus*" were enormous. It discredited the roy-alist elements in France, brought the left wing to political power, gave rise to a period of rabid antimilitarism and anticlericalism, hastened the separation of church and state, and exposed the extent and depth of French anti-Semitism. And for at least a decade, the country remained split between die-hard anti-Dreyfusards and righteous Dreyfusards, many of whom were neighbors or mem-bers of the same family, who would no longer sip a *vin du pays* together. As for poor old Dreyfus, he was promoted to the rank of major and decorated with the Legion of Honor, but he had a hard time readjusting to army life. He died in ob-scurity in Paris in 1935.

THE SARAJEVO ASSASSINATION

June 28, 1914: The visiting Archduke Francis Ferdinand, heir to the Austrian throne, and his wife, Sophie, are shot dead in the streets of Sarajevo, the capital of Bosnia, for centuries under Turkish rule but since 1878 a part of the Austro-Hungarian Empire. The assassin is a young Bosnian revolutionary named Gavrilo Princip, member of the Black Hand, a secret society headquartered in the kingdom of Serbia, just next door. The murder has the characteristic irony of many political assassinations, since the Archduke was, himself, something of a Serbian-rights activist. One month later, Austria, delivering an outrageous ultimatum to the Serbian government, demands to be allowed to participate in suppressing anti-Austrian feeling in Serbia and in punishing any conspirators in what has turned out to be an assassination plot involving officials of the Serbian government. When the Serbs tactfully rebuff the ultimatum, Austria declares war. As a result of the elaborate, if somewhat tenuous network of alliances in effect, Germany declares war on Russia, and France and Great Britain declare war on Germany, all within a week. By the end of the month, Japan is engaged against Germany, too, and three months later, Turkey jumps in on the side of the Germans and Austrians, an alliance known as the Central Powers. World War I is in full swing, and all because a fanatic from some weird little country nobody ever heard of blew away a man who wasn't even a monarch yet.

Obviously, blaming World War I on what happened at Sarajevo is like blaming Norman Bates' slasher impulses on Janet Leigh's turning on the hot water. Europe had been on the verge of a nervous breakdown since at least the turn of the century as a result of both family and personality problems dating back to the 1870s. That was when Germany, having just trounced the French in the Franco-Prussian War, started angling for its own place in the sun among the powers of Europe. In order to consolidate the new German position and forestall any thoughts of revenge on the part of the French, Bismarck, then Germany's chancellor, ran around forging secret alliances with anyone who'd let him in the door—specifically, the Hapsburgs, who were looking for an ally against the Russians in their attempt to grab a bigger piece of the Balkans, and the Italians, who liked the idea of siding with a winner. Virtually everyone else was offended by the Germans, who struck them not only as parvenus, but as too ambitious, truculent, and devious to make acceptable neighbors. Bismarck's Triple Alliance turned an undercurrent of resentment into out-and-out paranoia. Pretty soon France, Russia, and Great Britain had formed the Triple Entente—not anything as formal as an alliance (Britain was too determinedly isolationist for that), but an *entente cordiale*, whereby each would pitch in to help out if either of the others was attacked by members of the Triple Alliance. This didn't make the Germans, who now saw themselves surrounded by potential enemies, any easier to get along with. By the early 1900s, every major power had armed itself to the teeth, and Europe was divided into two camps, each nervously waiting for the other to draw first.

In such a high-stress situation, a German unexpectedly scratching his ear might have been enough to set things off, but there was a better catalyst: the Balkans. A cluster of wild, backward countries that had only recently gotten out from under the thumb of the crumbling Ottoman Empire, the Balkans were the object of perpetual rivalry between the Russians and the Austro-Hungarians, both of whom were on their last legs without realizing it, and were, therefore, semi-hysterical much of the time. The Austrians, in particular, had to be a little crazy to keep trying to throw their weight around the Balkan peninsula (see page 404), much of which was inhabited by angry Slavs—Serbs, Croats, Bosnians, Montenegrins, and Slovenes—who, believe it or not, saw themselves as a single nationality and who, being quasi-Orientals who still depended on garlic to ward off vampire attacks, felt closer to the Russians than to the Austrians, who looked down on them as ethnically inferior.

Thanks largely to the Serbs, who had a tendency to register discontent by forming secret societies and committing terrorist acts, both rival empires were, by 1914, ready to be driven around the bend. An assassination was just the ticket. It was also the chance the Germans had been waiting for. Fed up with being treated, as they saw it, as second cousins, and convinced that the Russians, who had been notoriously unreliable allies up to that point, wouldn't fight, they gave full rein to their ambitions—and to the military strategy they'd had ready for ten years. As for Great Britain, it felt honor-bound to declare war on Germany when German troops invaded Belgium on their way to smash the French. At this point, no one was thinking clearly and everyone was wishing the whole business would just go away. But, as the British historian A. J. P. Taylor noted, politicians and generals had a hard time keeping up with each other's point of view in those days, and before they knew it, the heads of state had lost control. "Their sensations, when diplomacy collapsed," writes Taylor, "were those of a train passenger who sees the express thundering through the station at which he intended to alight."

And that's only what was happening on the surface. Behind all these global neuroses was the newfound conviction, born out of the traumatic effects of Darwinism (see page 557) on human consciousness, that Nature was a struggle for survival of the fittest; that, in the case of people, the fittest meant the best-armed;

and that, under the circumstances, war was inevitable anyway. Those who still hoped this wasn't true tended to believe that enormous military strength on all sides would act as a deterrent, and that common sense would surely prevail. Wrong again. Not only was World War I out of control virtually from the beginning, it went on for four years, and it wound up ending European domination of the world.

THE SPANISH CIVIL WAR

World War II broke out officially on September 1, 1939, when the Nazis overran Poland, but it had really been going on for the better part of a decade. Germany had already, you may recall, invaded Austria and Czechoslovakia, adding a few million additional Germans—some happy about it, some not, and some not even exactly German—to her empire, as Britain and France stood huffily by. Italy was entrenched in Ethiopia and Albania, and Japan in China's Manchuria. The League of Nations protested from time to time, but, puhleez, who cared what the League of Nations thought? The saddest, most wrenching events of the proto-War period, though, took place in Spain—for over a century Europe's backwater, self-contained, aloof, apathetic with regard to the rest of the continent, unenviable, even contemptible, in its eyes.

Civil war didn't start until 1936, but for the preceding five years, since King Alfonso XIII was driven out in a fairly uneventful revolution, Spain had been feeling shaky. The new republican government, pledged to economic and social reform and determined to propel the country out of the eighteenth century and into the twentieth, moved against the Church (separating it from the State, which it had been pushing around since at least the Inquisition); broke up a few of the big landed estates, redistributing the acreage among the peasants; and gave a degree of local autonomy to the Catalans, in and around Barcelona, as well as to the Basques. Frankly, it was all a case of too-little-too-late, at least in the eyes of the extremists (anarchists and Communists, mostly). But it was more than enough to infuriate the priests and the landowners, not to mention the former royalists, who were upset anyway. In 1933, the government fell into the hands of the rightists, who themselves proved both ineffectual and inflammatory: A simple miners' strike was put down with more than your average brutality, and the Catalans were sent to their rooms without any supper.

Okay, now it's 1936. New general elections. All the leftist types (republicans, socialists, communists, anarchists, trade-union members) join in a Popular Front against all the rightist types (monarchists, priests, landowners, army officers, and Fascists, known locally as Falangists). The leftists beat the rightists at the polls—but it's *very* close. Even so, the leftists push ahead with their vision of the new Spain, figuring that reconciliation was a luxury, or an impossibility, or that it damn well could wait—this part isn't so clear.

Next thing you know, the military (never a factor to be discounted in Spain) has acted; revolts at Spanish army bases in Morocco, led by General Francisco Franco, result in what amounts to an invasion of Spain, with almost all the soldiers siding with their officers—and the rightists. Thus the battle lines are drawn: the leftists, or Republicans, sometimes called the Loyalists, are concentrated in the south, which tends to be poor, in the industrial region around Barcelona, and in Madrid, the capital; the rightists, or Nationalists, sometimes called the Rebels (even though they're the Establishment types), are strongest in the ancient—read strongly Catholic—heartland of Spain, plus Galicia, in the northwest corner.

Even without the foreign intervention, which we'll be getting to in a minute, it would have been an especially appalling civil war. Neither side behaved itself particularly well; the Republicans, at their worst, raped nuns, cut off the ears of priests, and fought savagely and treacherously among themselves. The Nationalists came in the night and shot in the dark, with the result that whole villages weren't around in the morning; their most famous victim was the Spanish poet García Lorca. In the end, some six hundred thousand Spaniards would die, with many more permanently crippled; still others were in exile, never to return.

But it was the Great Powers—Hitler and Mussolini on the side of the Nationalists, Stalin on the side of the Republicans—who, by taking a local amateur production and turning it into a dress rehearsal for bigger things, made sure the civil war turned into chapter-length world-history-book stuff. The Germans and Italians sent troops (the Italians over fifty thousand); the Soviets technicians and military advisors; both sides as much equipment—tanks, planes, guns—as they could pack up, with the emphasis on those items that still needed to be tested on the battlefield. The British and French, again, hung back, though plenty of Brits, French, Americans, and others went to Spain as volunteers, usually on the Republican side.

A lot more happened in the course of the Spanish Civil War, which lasted until 1939, by which time the Nationalists, led by Franco, had crushed the Republicans. Guernica, in the Basque country, was bombed by the Nationalists, or at least by the Germans (Picasso got it down on canvas); General Mola tossed off his famous "fifth column" line (about how he had four columns of soldiers encircling Madrid, and a fifth column infiltrating and undermining it from within); and Ernest Hemingway completed his research for *For Whom the Bell Tolls*.

But what really mattered was what the war had crystallized: the splitting of the world into Fascist and anti-Fascist camps; the proof that Germany and Italy could work nicely together in a Rome-Berlin Axis; the general belief that not just war, but War, was inevitable. Also to be noted: the arrival on the world scene of Generalissimo Franco, a brilliant military strategist and so-so politician, who, far from attempting to conduct Spain into the twentieth century, would, over the course of the next forty years, insulate her from the rest of the world and immunize her to the present.

DIEN BIEN PHU

Years later, nearly everyone would agree that France's colonial ambitions in Indochina had been doomed from the start, that her seven-and-a-half-year war in the region had been a series of disastrous misjudgments and miscalculations, and that her empire had been little more than a grand illusion since at least the end of World War II. But it wasn't until the total defeat of its forces at the North Vietnamese garrison of Dien Bien Phu in May 1954 that the French government was forced to drop its blindfold and admit that the game was over. And no sooner had the smoke cleared than the American government crept back to the battlefield, retrieved the blindfold, and tied it securely over its own eyes.

The area now called Vietnam had always been the biggest headache in France's Indochinese empire. The territory was divided, geographically and culturally, into two native kingdoms, Tonkin and Annan, in the north, and a colony, Cochin China, in the south, a fragmentation that made communication difficult and administration awkward. What was worse, the peoples of the north, the center of Viet culture, were proud, feisty, and subversive by nature; they had never been ones to bow and smile when outsiders tried to take over their turf. By the time Japan invaded Indochina in 1940, the French had already spent a couple of decades putting down village rebellions, scattered resistance groups had begun to coalesce into a Communist-dominated nationalist underground, and Ho Chi Minh had learned some valuable lessons in organization and strategy. When the Japanese took the keys to the country away from the French, who were too busy keeping up with the war in Europe to put up much of a fight, and turned them over to the Vietnamese, the struggle for control in the north was effectively over, although none of the major powers realized it at the time.

The nationalist Communists, by then known as the Viet Minh, didn't waste any time. Keeping discreetly out of the way of the Japanese, they spread the faith in the villages and fortified their positions in the countryside. When Japan surrendered in 1945, Ho Chi Minh had consolidated enough power to declare himself head of the Democratic Republic of Vietnam.

This, however, was not what the Allies had in mind. Determined to restore European equilibrium by boosting France's fractured self-esteem, they decided to give her back her colonies, sending the British to take over Saigon and Chinese troops to recapture the north. Enter, at this point, General Vo Nguyen Giap, soon-to-be hero, from the nationalists' point of view, of two Vietnamese wars. Giap raided the local arsenals for the weapons left behind by the French and Japanese and made as much trouble as he could for the occupying French and Chinese forces. For the next few years the war in Vietnam consisted of inconclusive skirmishes and lots of military bungling on both sides, with the Viet Minh learning the hard way that conventional warfare was not their strong suit and the French continually trying to launch surprise raids on an enemy they couldn't see.

The nature of the enterprise began to change in 1949, when the Reds took over China. Ho Chi Minh suddenly found himself with an ally at his back and a steady supply of artillery pouring in from both China and the Soviet Union. The United States began to talk about keeping the Communist threat within safe perimeters. Vietnam was suddenly everyone's business. General Giap, for one, was heartened. Ho had long ago declared himself ready to lose ten men for every one of the invaders, and Giap made good the promise, launching a series of ferocious assaults that decimated his own forces but did, at least, have the effect of setting French nerves on edge and driving French troops back to fortified positions. Eventually, it also led them to make their fatal mistake.

Hoping to draw enough fire to exhaust the Viet Minh's resources and weaken their position in the rest of the country, the French decided to play on the enemy's aggressiveness by setting up fifteen thousand men in a defensive position at Dien Bien Phu, near the Laotian border of North Vietnam. Although the men stationed at the fortress could be supplied only by air, the French, who, by this time, were being heavily backed by the United States, were confident that they could hold out indefinitely. What they didn't count on could, and did, fill volumes; for instance, the amount of Russian and Chinese heavy artillery that had gotten through to the Viet Minh, and the Viet Minh's ability to use it; the dense vegetation surrounding the fortress, which made it impossible to see the enemy, much less destroy its supply lines from the air; and the United States' refusal to respond to France's last-ditch appeals for help by sending its own air power to the rescue. Dien Bien Phu was besieged for fifty-five days, beginning in

March 1954; on May 7, the French surrendered completely. Although the Viet Minh had suffered more casualties, they had won the war. The French defeat led directly to the Geneva Conference, at which France was forced to grant independence to Laos, Cambodia, and Vietnam, thereby ending her empire in Indochina.

In hindsight, the lessons of Dien Bien Phu seemed pretty clear, at least to some people. On the military level, it demonstrated the futility of depending on superior manpower and technology to overcome a well-armed, thoroughly entrenched guerrilla force fighting on difficult terrain and prepared to make outrageous sacrifices to defend a homeland. In terms of global politics, it showed just how much trouble a country could make for itself when it confused grandiosity with ideology.

The United States seemed, for a minute or two, to get the message. President Eisenhower had, after all, refused to get directly involved in the Vietnam conflict without the approval of Congress, and the Chiefs of Staff had already declared the whole territory of Indochina to be "without decisive military objectives." But U.S. policy in the region had never been characterized by clear thinking or consistent action. Pretty soon Eisenhower was focusing more on his "falling dominoes" speech and the Red Terror than on what had just happened at Dien Bien Phu—this despite the fact that the Russians and Chinese had already stopped speaking to each other and it was unclear just where the Red Terror would be emanating from. When the Geneva Conference partitioned Vietnam into North and South along the 17th parallel, with the promise of free elections in two years to decide on possible reunification, Eisenhower decided to fight rather than let the Vietnamese, who were solidly behind Ho Chi Minh in the north and simply confused in the south, vote. JFK compounded the error when he started looking around for a way to reaffirm U.S. prestige in the wake of Sputnik and save face personally after the Bay of Pigs, and somebody happened to mention that things were not going well in Saigon. By the time Lyndon Johnson got into office, we were headed for Dien Bien Phu all over again. History repeats itself, some people like to point out—and not just in Vietnam.

LEXICON

A Few Hours' Worth of Remedial Work in Vocabulary, Spelling, Pronunciation, and Foreign Expressions

Contents

The Confusion of Tongues, *by Gustave Doré*

In the Beginning Was the Prefix

Go ahead: Amaze your doorman, dazzle your periodontist, shut your prospective brother-in-law up for good with your dextrous and inventive handling of such mind-clouding prefixes as demi-, crypto-, and, yes, even meta-. After all, you mastered re-, pre-, and dis-, didn't you?

WHO'S ON TOP?

arch-
vice-
co-
para-
sub-

Highest up is the man with *arch-* before his title, be it duke, bishop, or angel, each of whom towers over mere dukes, bishops, and angels, respectively; likewise your archrival gives you more trouble than all your regular rivals put together. The *vice-*person—president, admiral, -consul, or, the only common such word written solid, viceroy—is next on the list; he's the stand-in, the understudy, the one who is ready to fill in in an emergency or to succeed in the event of death. The *co-* fellow, whether author or conspirator, is all for common cause (and/or shared culpability); sometimes his partner will be in the ascendancy (as with a copilot, who always has Dana Andrews playing him when the pilot is Burt Lancaster), but more often power and responsibility are evenly divided, just as it was between the cocaptains of your high school football team. The *para*legal, the *para*medic, the *para*professional in general—from a Greek preposition meaning "alongside of"—are not full-fledged, licensed, or in charge, nor, at the rate they're going, will they ever be. But then some people thrive in the glorified-assistant role. (For the record, paratroopers have a different prefix to thank for their job

title, the same one you see in parachute and parasol, a Latin verb stem meaning "protect, ward off.") And don't let's even consider dealing with the guys who are *sub*, as in subaltern and sublieutenant: Obviously, they don't know who *you* are or they'd never even suggest it.

WHO'S FOR REAL?

crypto-
quasi-
neo-
pseudo-

When Gore Vidal made media history by calling William Buckley a "*crypto*-Nazi" in front of millions of television viewers during the 1968 Democratic convention, he presumably meant that beneath Buckley's conservative facade lurked a fascist trying to keep the public—or himself—from seeing his true colors. At least, that's the way Buckley took it; Vidal later pointed out that what'd he'd actually called his archenemy was a "*pro*-crypto-Nazi," in reference to Buckley's defense of the Chicago police, who were at that moment battering demonstrators with gleeful abandon in the streets outside. This version would make the cops the Nazis-in-law-enforcement-officers'-clothing; Buckley merely a sympathizer and, possibly, only a *quasi*-Nazi himself. (This "less-than-a-full-fledged-Nazi" interpretation is bolstered by Vidal's adding that, in fact, he hadn't meant to use the term "Nazi" at all; had he not blown his cool, he said, he would have called his opponent merely "Fascist-minded.") Because a crypto-Nazi has something to gain by keeping his real feelings hidden, and a quasi-Nazi probably isn't sure just what his real feelings are, you don't have to get out of the way of either of them quite as fast as you do some of those *neo*-Nazi organizations, whose members like to parade up and down Midwestern streets in modified Luftwaffe surplus, paint swastikas on synagogues, and bash the heads of whichever minority groups they feel are polluting the race these days. In other words, the neo-Nazi is, or likes to think he is, the real thing, updated. Last and certainly least, don't worry at all about those fifteen-year-old *pseudo*-Nazi rockers who like to affect combat boots and Iron Crosses and who go around spouting a lot of racist rhetoric they picked up at the last heavy-metal concert; unlike *neo*-Nazi skinheads, who tend to have more frown lines and fewer teeth, these kids are just out to scare you in the hopes of being taken seriously for a change.

WHICH CAME FIRST?

> proto-
> archaeo-
> *Ur-*

The thing that boasts *proto-* (from a Greek word meaning "first") before its name, whether protozoan, protoplasm, Proto-Germanic (linguists' jargon for the earliest form of a language, in this case German, that they've managed to reconstruct), or prototype. Vying with proto- for deftness at conferring precedence is another Greek word, *archaeo-*, which, while it's not particularly active in spur-of-the-moment word formation, does manage to connote not only "beginning," but "chief, ruler," as well

(cf. arch-, above), as in archaeology and archetype.

(To split hairs for a moment, while a prototype is an early form or instance of something that then goes on to serve as a model for a whole string of subsequent somethings, the thing that came *first*, an archetype, is all that and more: It's not only as old as the hills, it's ageless. Thus, as Macaulay (see page 573 pointed out, England's Parliament is the archetype of representative assemblies; he could just as easily have said "prototype," but his point was that Parliament's still sitting there next to the Thames, a bit gray around the temples, perhaps, but a lady with no intention of retiring, and, what's more, immediately recognizable from pictures of herself as a girl. Gutenberg's printing press, on the other hand, is the prototype of the modern printing press—an early model that served and inspired an entire hemisphere—but it's not the archetype of it: Few people would see a resemblance between the two, and no printer in his right mind would want to use the original.)

Those annoyed with this Greek jockeying for position will wish to make the acquaintance of *Ur-*, like "echt" (see page 672) a German traveler who occasionally puts up at the Connaught or the Harvard Club. *Ur-* means "original, earliest, primitive," as in *Ur*text (also spell "urtext," no cap, no italics, no hyphen, which lets you know the prefix is in the process of being naturalized), a text reconstructed from extant later texts. Thus, to present a symphony of Beethoven's in urtext and in urperformance is to do it with obvious mistakes unrectified and with an orchestra of the size and proportions Beethoven wrote it for. As for everything that's not proto-, archaeo-, or Ur-, consign it to oblivion with a toss of the head, a raised eyebrow, and a prefixed *neo*-: From Neo-Platonists to Neo-Nazis, who needs 'em?

HOW BIG?

> mega-
> megalo-
> macro-
> micro-
> mini-

The key prefix here is *mega-*, which, back in Greece, meant literally "million." Thus a megaton bomb has a force equivalent to a million tons of TNT and megabuck is somebody's idea of a funny way to say million dollars. (The related *megalo-*, indicating greatness or strength, without a specific numerical value, is what you get in megalomaniac and megalopolis.) Also worth noting: The opposing prefixes *macro-* (denoting largeness, length, or overdevelopment, as in macroeconomics, see page 129; macrocosm, a.k.a. the universe; and macrobiotics) and *micro-* (denoting the reverse, as in microeconomics, microcosm, and microfilm). The former is still little enough known that the doorman may be impressed; the latter's debased by centuries of overuse—though it still beats *mini-*.

WHICH HALF?

> bi-
> semi-
> demi-
> hemi-
> half-

All right, is a *bi*monthly magazine one that comes twice a month or one that comes every other month? There's no real consensus out there, but take our advice and use bimonthly for the every-other-month one, and call the twice-a-month

a semimonthly. *Semi-*, derived from the Latin, means "half," or sometimes a bit less—but then so do *demi-*, from the French, as in demitasse and demimonde; and *hemi-*, from the Greek, as in hemisphere. If you're indulging in creative prefixing, purists would have you choose, in any given situation, the prefix of the same nationality as the root you're attaching it to, but that doesn't account for demigod, among others. Of the three, semi- combines most freely, and when in doubt you can always fall back on good old native *half-*, as in half-wit, half-portion, and half-gainer. Note to absurdists and Anglophiles everywhere: The British word for a musical sixty-fourth note (and you knew they'd have one) is hemidemisemiquaver.

TO WHAT DEGREE?

> hyper-
> hypo-

The stupidest mnemonic is all you need here, so voilà: *hyper-* has more letters, and it's the one that means "over, too much," as in hyperactive, hypertension, hyperbole, and just plain hyper. *Hypo-*, with only four letters, means "under, too little," as in hypoglycemia (too little blood sugar), hypodermic (literally, "under the skin"), and hype (from the old slang for the kind of hypodermic injection we now call a fix). Both began life as Greek prepositions, and both traveled well. Hyper-, in particular, is an industrious, even promiscuous prefix. Which means that hypo- —less seen, less understood—may be a better one to be able to throw around.

WHERE DO WE GO FROM HERE?

meta-

Not all Greek prepositional prefixes are as graspable as hyper- and hypo-. For instance, we wanted to hold forth here on *ana-* and *cata-*, but forget it: While you can point out that they mean roughly "up" and "down," that really doesn't equip a person to savor "catalogue" or "Anabaptist." Besides, as prefixes go they're dead; only a scientist would use one to make a new word these days. Not so *meta-*, which currently is a hotter linguistic ticket than ever, our candidate for the prefixer's prefix. While it has two "flat" meanings as a simple preposition—"with, among" (cognate with English "mid" and German "mit") and "after, behind"—it's come to be equated with pursuit, quest, and change, with the person, object, or idea that transcends all existing forms, with the restless and the ineffable. Actually, this grandeur on the part of meta- is the result of a little philological misunderstanding: Aristotlecalled the book he wrote on transcendental philosophy *Ta meta ta phusika* ("the things after physics") because it followed his work on that subject, thereby ensuring that metaphysics would forever be equated with the transcendental, even though it was just a simple sequel. Not that that's stopped anybody from devoting his life— or his ego—to such pursuits as metahistory ("A historian writes the history of a period, a metahistorian compares different periods in order to derive an essence," as one scholar recently put it), metalinguistics, and even metaculture. With meta- in your pocket, you don't ever have to feel stagnant, flaccid, or middle-aged.

Distinctions Worth Making

(OR AT LEAST BEING IN A POSITION TO MAKE)

affect *and* effect

Promise to get this one down and we'll spare you "lie" and "lay." "Affect" is the verb most of the time; it implies influence: "Smoking can affect one's health; how has it affected yours?" "Effect" is the equivalent noun: "Smoking has had an effect on me and on my health." Sometimes, though (and here's where the trouble comes in) "effect" is the verb. When it is, it brings a sense not of mere influence, but of purpose, even impact: "I must effect my plan to stop smoking"; "By not smoking, I have succeeded in effecting my complete recovery." Of course, not drinking may also have *a*ffected your recovery—may have contributed to it, may have hastened it along—but here you're claiming that stopping smoking was what really turned things around.

Two little problems: (1) the way one *a*ffects a jaunty air or an English accent; and (2) the so-called affect (watch that noun) in psychology: all the emotional stuff surrounding a particular state or situation. But don't worry too much about them; concentrate on the difference in meaning above, which is where you stand to blow it if you're going to blow it at all.

anxious *and* eager

Famous last stand of the language purists: You're not anxious to spend a languorous evening with your oldest married friends, you're eager to spend it. Unless, that is, you've been sleeping with one of them for the past three months. Then you *are* anxious.

assume *and* presume

When you presume, you take for granted that something is true; when you assume, you postulate that it's true in order to go on to argue or to act. Presuming has tied up in it the idea of anticipation, of jumping the gun, of taking liberties;

hence the adjective presumptuous. Assuming isn't necessarily a swell thing, either (hence the adjective self-assuming), but at least it's up-front about the fact that it has a chip on its shoulder. So, was Stanley being rude when he said, "Dr. Livingstone, I presume?" No, not really; after all, he'd been trailing the Scottish missionary and explorer for months, on assignment for a New York newspaper, and they must have at least furnished him with a photograph. On the other hand, had it turned out that the distinguished stranger standing on the shore of Lake Tanganyika was not Dr. Livingstone, but Dr. Doolittle, it's possible Stanley might have wished he'd said "assume" instead.

authentic *and* genuine

Something that's genuine hasn't been forged; something that's authentic tells the truth about its subject. In other words, you might, one Friday morning, regale your coworkers with the details of your Thursday night at the latest East Village nightspot, when you'd really stayed home and watched television again; such an account would be genuine (you *are* the author of it) but not authentic (you weren't even in the East Village). Conversely, you might that same morning have been lucky enough to overhear, on the Madison Avenue bus, the account of somebody who had been at the club in question the night before, then repeated it verbatim to your coworkers; *that* account would be authentic (assuming the person on the bus was telling the truth himself) but not genuine, because you'd be passing off somebody else's good time as your own.

canonical, catholic, ecclesiastical, ecumenical, evangelical, *and* liturgical

The central word here is "ecclesiastical," which means pertaining to the church or its clergy. "Canonical" means pertaining to church law, binding on all its members. "Evangelical" means pertaining to the teachings of Christ, especially the Four Gospels; easy to get from there to hitting the road for Jesus. "Liturgical" means pertaining to the liturgy, the whole ritual of public worship. (The litany is a form of prayer in which the clergyman and the congregation alternate responses.) "Catholic" and "ecumenical" are the hard ones: They both mean universal. "Ecumenical" derives from a Greek word meaning "of the inhabited earth," and most often refers to councils or regulations that govern the entire church, or all of any one branch of it, or the spirit behind such councils and regulations. "Catholic," from a Greek phrase meaning "in general," "in respect of the whole," has an additional sense of inclusiveness, of tastes, sympathies, interests that are all-embracing. (That's with a lowercase *c*, though; uppercase, and it's the old Popes and Hail Marys business.) Both "ecumenical," a term Protestants seem understandably to prefer, and "catholic" are the opposite of parochial, "of the parish."

compleat *and* complete

The first form is simply archaic; in a just world, no one would ever have to deal with it again. Unfortunately, the world's not just, and for a few centuries now, editors, publishers, and copywriters have found "compleat" to be a word that jazzed up titles and boosted sales. Isaak Walton did it first and best, back in 1653, with his *The Compleat Angler* (subtitled *Or the Contemplative Man's Recreation*), a discourse on fishing liberally laced with rural wisdom and unshakable Christian faith. Now look for, at your corner bookstore, the likes of *The Compleat Werewolf*, *The Compleat Belly Dancer*, and *The Compleat Nevada Traveler*. Used to describe a person, as in any of the foregoing examples, the word—however you spell it—is best defined as "perfectly skilled or equipped; consummate, accomplished."

compose *and* comprise

The wolves compose the pack; the pack comprises the wolves. (If you want to get passive about it, the pack is composed of the wolves, and the wolves are comprised by the pack.) In short, "comprise" is sort of an uptown synonym for "include"—except that a pack that comprises wolves is all-wolf, while one that merely includes them may have two hyenas and a German shepherd in it, too.

continual *and* continuous

"Continuous" is uncompromising: A continuous slope or vigil or downpour is steady, unbroken, invariable, without even a temporary reversal or a tiny interruption. "Continual," on the other hand, allows for gaps, and suggests, in fact, that something recurs at regular intervals, with time out in between: Continual showings are what you get at the movies, and continual setbacks may crop up at the rate of only half a dozen a year. Now, try to remember that "continu*ous*" is, in general, more seri*ous*—not to mention scientific, as in the mathematician's continuous function, the physicist's continuous wave, the astronomer's theory of continuous creation. Continu*al* is what you us*ual*ly mean; it's more figurative, describes how things seem, feel, strike an onlooker, as in Swift's "These people are under continual disquietudes, never enjoying a minute's peace of mind."

converse *and* inverse

"Converse" is a matter of simple transposition: "He hit me" is the converse of "I hit him"; "He had glamour but no money" is the converse of "He had money but no glamour." "Inverse" is a more extreme—and a more ambiguous—business; it entails turning something inside out or standing it on its head. Thus, when two quantities vary inversely, one gets bigger as the other gets smaller; the inverse of a mathematical operation is the one that will nullify it (e.g., division is the inverse of multiplication). In logic, the inverse of a statement is attained by negating both its hypothesis *and* its conclusion: The inverse of "If Alice is drinking J&B, then she's drinking scotch" would be "If Alice isn't drinking J&B, then she's not drinking scotch"—as it happens, a logically defective, or "false," statement. (So is the converse: "If Alice is drinking scotch, then she's drinking J&B." Don't feel bad, though; the woods are full of defective inverses and converses.)

deprecate *and* depreciate

In terms of etymology, "deprecate" is the opposite of "pray for"; "depreciate" is the opposite of "praise." If you put yourself down a little, you make a self-depre*ciat*ing remark; if you really let yourself have it (and you know how bad you've been being lately), the remark might then, but only then, be self-depre*cat*ing. Don't expect anybody to applaud, though—either the flagellation or the preciseness of your language; this is a distinction almost nobody knows he's even supposed to be making.

discreet *and* discrete

"Discreet"—prudent, circumspect, just this side of walking on eggs—is what you should be when you're having an illicit love affair. "Discrete" (which, for what it's worth, comes from the same Latin word, *discretus*, "sifted through") means distinct, discontinuous, separate, as in "discrete entities," "discrete particles," "discrete elements," and should probably be reserved for dress-up occasions.

dock *and* pier

Don't try to walk on a dock: It's the space where a ship comes to rest and it's full of water. ("Drydock" makes the point nicely: Picture the space with all the water drained out of it so that the repairs can start.) The pier is what you *can* walk on; it's the structure on which the passengers stand and onto which the cargo is unloaded. Assuming, that is, the structure runs out into the water, away from the shore, preferably at a right angle to it. If it runs *along* the shore, it's technically not a pier but a wharf. P.S.: Don't mention any of this to Otis Redding.

egotist, egoist, solipsist, *and* narcissist

They're all stuck on themselves, but only two of them could tell you why. The egotist (from the Latin word for "I") couldn't: He just wants to fill you in on the details of his life, even if you have heard them all several times before. (Think of that *t* as standing for "talk.") The egoist, by contrast, might explain that self-interest is the foundation of all morality, and that it's therefore not just silly but downright antisocial *not* to put oneself first. The solipsist (from the Latin word for "alone"), who took even more philosophy courses as an undergraduate than the egoist did, would maintain that no person has any proof that anything exists outside his own mind, that each of us, like him, is totally alone with our own thoughts, and not just on rainy April afternoons, either. (As it happens, while no major philosopher has ever accepted solipsism, neither has any ever been able to refute it; Schopenhauer—see page 322—for his part dubbed it "theoretical egoism" and hoped we wouldn't worry about it too much.) The "narcissist," a term of Freud's devising (see page 434), after the Greek youth who couldn't stop looking at his reflection in a pool of water, is basically going steady with himself and may not want to talk to you at all. If he does, his goal will not be to expound on the nature of his belief system, but to charm you into joining his fan club.

enormity *and* enormousness

Straightforward enough. "Enormousness" is the one that's a synonym for immensity: the enormousness of the cosmos. "Enormity" refers to something so far outside the moral *norm* (the root in both words) that it's monstrously wicked, unthinkable, the lowest of the low: the enormity of his crimes. Of course you can talk about the enormousness of somebody's crimes, too, if all you mean is they're big. But do try not to refer to the enormity of the cosmos—unless you know something we don't.

epidemic *and* endemic

An epidemic disease breaks out somewhere and eventually goes away again; an endemic disease breaks out and is still there centuries later. Cholera is endemic in parts of Asia; when it broke out in Europe, it was epidemic. (Think of it as the difference between *epi-*, "over," and *en-*, "in.") Which means that the AIDS epidemic is looking more and more like the AIDS endemic. Make that pandemic, given that it's shaping up to be in residence pretty much everywhere at once.

epigram *and* epigraph

Both words derive from the Greek preposition *epi,* meaning "upon" or "over," plus the familiar Greek word for "write," and both began by designating the kind of inscription you find on a monument or statue. "Epig*raph*" still does mean that—sometimes. More often, it refers to a motto or quotation set at the beginning, or "over," the body of a book, chapter, or poem, intended to set the tone for or provide an entrée to the work to come (for instance, the snatch from Dante at the head of Eliot's "Prufrock," the "If I thought I were talking to anybody but a dead man" business). "Epig*ram*" never refers to an inscription anymore; it occasionally is used of a super-short poem expressing a single acidulous thought, but usually it refers to a concise, cleverly worded, essentially antithetical statement, with a sting or twist at the end (e.g., Dorothy Parker's "If all the young ladies who attended the Yale promenade were laid end to end, no one would be the least surprised").

To complete the picture, an *epitaph* is an inscription, always on a tombstone; an *epilogue* the little speech or poem that concludes a play, or the short section at the end of a book sketching the future of its characters—in short, the structural opposite of the epigraph.

ethics *and* morals

In early English scholarship, the two words were treated as synonyms, deriving from Greek *ethos* ("nature or disposition") and Latin *mos* (genitive form, *moris*; "custom"), respectively. Gradually, though, ethics came to be viewed as the science or philosophy of morals (see page 306), morals as the practice or enactment of ethics; as often happened in those days, the Latin-derived word was used for the real, tangible, everyday doing of something, the Greek-derived one reserved for the idealized, theoretical understanding of that doing. Today some people say "ethics" even when they mean "morals," simply because the word is that much less common. Don't pay any attention to them. Instead, save your strength to make the distinction between the adjective forms, "ethical" and "moral." Here, "moral" has been tainted by the association of its opposite, "immoral," with *sexual* misconduct, and as a result lost much of its range. "Ethical" has been left to describe all kinds of recognizable, day-to-day behavior that is, for whatever reason, proper, admirable, or just plain honest.

farther *and* further

The deal is this: "Farther," etymologically, means "more far; further, more to the fore, more forth." So, it's farther from Miami to Palm Beach than it is from Miami to Fort Lauderdale; plus, if you hate Florida's Gold Coast, you'll want to move farther away still—Daytona, maybe. Once you're settled in Daytona, no further steps (note the shift from literal to figurative) should be necessary. A couple of additional qualifications here. First, "farther" can apply as easily to time as to space: you may have packed up and left Miami farther back than you can remember. Second, there are so many cases where trying to decide which is right—farther to go or further? more far (in terms of sheer distance) or more forth (in terms of effort or visibility or prominence)?—that thinking *too* hard about the distinction, while it may help you get a grip on what you really mean, will also slow you down to the point that you never make it out the front door.

flaunt *and* flout

Don't try to tell us you were appalled—or, for that matter, listening—back when President Carter declaimed at the height of crisis, "The Government of Iran must realize that it cannot flaunt, with impunity, the expressed will and law of the world community." After all, using "flaunt" (of unknown origin; meaning to parade oneself ostentatiously, to be gaudily in evidence, to wave proudly, and to generally show off) when what you mean is "flout" (probably akin to the Old French word for flute, an instrument whose whistling noises can sometimes sound derisive; meaning to be scornful of, to show contempt for, to fly in the face of) is a problem for everybody. The confusion is understandable: Both words bespeak behavior that's excessive, inappropriate, and potentially disruptive. But remember that flaunting and flouting are, when push comes to shove, virtual opposites—acts typical of the chauvinist and the seditionist, respectively.

heathen *and* pagan

Neither's partaking in the great Judeo-Christian tradition—yet. "Pagan," though, with its classical background (from a Latin word meaning "country district"), often refers specifically to the ancient Greeks and Romans, whom it was hard even for nineteenth-century Christians to hold in total contempt; "heathen" is simply a slam term, directed at some poor benighted creature not yet one of us. Thus Christian missionaries go out to convert the heathens, all loincloths and pulsating jungle rhythms, while the pagans hold orgies and debate the relative merits of red and white wine and the connection between pain and pleasure. The infidel, unlike the pagan or the heathen, had a religion the European at least felt threatened by, most often Muhammadanism, well supplied with scimitars and minarets. Today, it denotes, among Roman Catholics, any unbaptized person, from heathen to Protestant.

infer *and* imply

It's a matter of where you stand, of whether you're transmitting or receiving. You imply something in a remark to a friend, who infers something from that remark. Anybody who goes around saying "What are you inferring?" is, unless he's addressing a philosopher, almost certain to be pretentious, and not all that smart.

insidious *and* invidious

The thing that's insidious (from the Latin word for "ambush") sneaks up on you; it's not only undesirable, it's stealthy and it's treacherous, like cancer. The thing that's invidious (from the Latin word for "envy") isn't subtle or sneaky, just repugnant and certain to cause trouble, in the form of ill will, resentment, or envy itself, generally directed against whoever said or did it. When Jesse Jackson called New York "Hymietown," in the mid-Eighties, he made an invidious (and a politically not very savvy) remark.

jealousy *and* envy

Envy is the simple one, and—along with wrath, gluttony, and the rest—one of the seven deadly and absolutely unmistakable sins. Implying both resentment and greed, it's when you first begrudge your neighbor the possession of something (ox, ass, VCR), then covet it for yourself. Jealousy is much subtler and less materialistic. At its classiest, it implies principled protectiveness, as when a father is "jealous for" his daughter's welfare, or principled intolerance, as in "a jealous God." More often, it has to do with ongoing personal rivalry, known or suspected, frequently of a sexual nature, coupled with a fear of loss or supplantation. Envy may make us behave badly, even turn us green, but it doesn't necessarily cloud our minds; jealousy always does.

mean, median, mode, *and* average

The umbrella term here is "average"; all the others are types of it, employed mainly by schoolchildren, sportswriters, and statisticians. Take the following numbers: 2, 4, 6, 7, 7, 8, 8, 8, 13. What you think of as the average (add them all up, divide by the number of terms you added) is, technically speaking, the arithmetic mean, here 63 divided by 9, or 7. The median is also 7, but for a different reason: 7 is the center term in the sequence, with four terms to either side of it. Statistically, the median can sometimes give a more reliable picture than the mean, for instance, when three people get a 60 on a test and one gets 100: Here, the mean—70—might make you think a successful learning experience had been going on, when in fact three-quarters of the class hadn't learned much of anything, as revealed by the median—60. The mode is the least used of the three kinds of average: It's simply the term that crops up more frequently than any other, in the sequence given not 7, but 8.

mutual *and* common

Just remember that *Our Mutual Friend*, the Dickens title, is a famous solecism, that is, a language-use blunder of a particularly blatant sort. More precisely, "mutual" implies exchange, interaction, reciprocity, none of which occurs when you simply share a friend with somebody else—when you have a friend in common. "Mutual admirers," on the other hand, makes perfect sense: I admire you and you admire me. We're reciprocating, we're interacting. We're provided for. We're happy. Note, though, that if somebody admires both of us, he is our common admirer—unless, of course, each of us is willing to admire him back, thereby making the admiration mutual. Careful here: Some people think they can tell how educated you are on the basis of how you handle the one word "mutual."

objective *and* subjective

If you're objective, you sacrifice your personality, your mood, and your need for attention to some higher (or at least bigger) goal: You become, say, a reporter for the *Washington Post* and you vow just to give the facts. If you're subjective, it's how you feel, where you're coming from, and what you make of the situation in Beirut, not to mention the fact that you're getting older, that your wallet was stolen last week, and that country music is big, that counts: So you angle to take over Andy Rooney's spot on *60 Minutes*. Simple enough, we grant you, but you should know that "objective" and "subjective" are fighting words for (a) literary critics, who can't decide which of them good criticism, or, since you ask, good literature should be, let alone how to tell the difference; and (b) philosophers, who've been arguing about the subject (the active mind, the thinking agent) and the object (everything else, further analyzable into several dozen categories), the seer and the seen, the thought and the thing, ever since Aristotle.

oral *and* verbal

Quick: How do you describe a contract that two people strike over the phone? Well, sure, it's verbal. But so's any contract that uses words. The right answer is oral—spoken, as opposed to written. And don't confuse "oral" (from the Latin word for "mouth") with "aural" (from the Latin word for "ear") even if they are almost always pronounced alike.

pathos *and* bathos

Pathos, which in Greek means "suffering" or "passion," is the quality in literature or art that stimulates pity or compassion in the onlooker. Bathos, which in Greek means "depth," is a downward (and an unintentional) slide into the maudlin or the banal. Alexander Pope (see page 191) named it, in 1727, in a mock-critical treatise called "Peri-Bathous, or, Of the Art of Sinking in Poetry." One of his favorite examples, from a contemporary poem: "Ye Gods! annihilate but Space and Time, / And make two lovers happy." Equally bathetic: the description of the death of Little Nell in Dickens' *The Old Curiosity Shop* (of which Oscar Wilde remarked, famously, that only a man with a heart of stone could read it without laughing) and the motto "For God, for Country, and for Yale." The *a* is long in both words, by the way.

redundancy, tautology, *and* pleonasm

Deadwood. "Redundancy" is the blanket term here, describing any instance of the other two (as well as language that's merely verbose, that uses too many words even if they don't all mean the same thing). "Tautology" and "pleonasm" are both more specialized. The first, from the Greek *tauto-*, "same," repeats what is explicit in a way that suggests the speaker isn't entirely up to using the words he's chosen, and it's widely held to be indefensible. Examples: bibliography of books, visible to the eye, consensus of opinion. (It's also used in logic of the kind of assertion that sets out to prove itself through simple restatement: "This is the best poem that Sylvia Plath ever wrote; after all, none of the others is nearly so good.") The second, from the Greek *ple(i)on*, "more," is an established rhetorical device. It repeats what is already implicit by adding a word or phrase that is not, strictly speaking, necessary, although it may contribute to overall clarity, empha sis, or effect. Examples: fall down, to see something with one's own eyes, only just begun. Too much pleonasm can get on a person's nerves, but sometimes it's the point of the exercise: The Bible, for instance, is built on it.

sensuous *and* sensual

In both cases, it's the senses, not the mind, that're being gratified; sensations, not ideas, that you wind up having. Coined by Milton ("[Poetry is] more simple, sensuous, and passionate [than rhetoric]," he wrote), "sensuous" is today a more or less uncharged term and applies to the kind of pleasure you get from art, music, scented candles, and seedless grapes. "Sensual" has more to do with erotic pleasure, with the indulgence of the appetites, with gluttony, lust, and motives that aren't all they should be. Make the "sensual"/"sexual" connection, and the pair won't give you any trouble.

sententious *and* tendentious

You don't want to be either of these, if you can help it. The first is all about affectation and pompous moralizing, the second about the relentless proselytizing of the tract writer.

specious *and* spurious

Good debunking words, these, possessed of an Oxford-debates-Cambridge rarefaction and spleen. Both mean "lacking authenticity or validity, counterfeit, false." "Spurious" also has overtones of bastardy, illegitimacy, and tends to pop up in gutsy phrases like "spurious brood." (Which isn't to say that a document or a bit of financial advice can't equally well prove spurious.) To the basic sense of rotten at the core, "specious" adds a veneer of charm, seductiveness, plausibility. From the Latin *species*, "outward appearance," it describes the thing that seems fair, sound, or true, but that, on closer inspection, is anything but. Specious evidence is not only false evidence, but evidence presented with intent to deceive—and, implicitly, evidence that almost succeeds in doing so.

sybarite, hedonist, *and* epicurean

The ancient Greeks are behind all three. Of the kinds of pleasure-lover they designate, the sybarite is the most blatant and unredeemed. Unlike the other two—both of whom had ancestors with Ph.D.'s—he doesn't have a thought in his head: *His* folks, wealthy Greek colonists in the southern Italian town of Sybaris, simply knew how to have a good time. A hedonist, by contrast, has an elaborate justification for his pursuit of pleasure (*hedone*, in Greek): He believes that it is, simply, the chief good, though he'll probably have his hand on your leg as he's telling you why. An epicurean may or may not be hedonistic. If he is, he'll at least yoke gratification with tastefulness, and probably put ease before orgasm. If he isn't—if he's a bona fide follower of the Greek philosopher Epicurus—you'd better not even offer him a drink. A true Epicurean (note cap), while he accepts the primacy of pleasure in life, tends to equate it with the avoidance of pain, the rational control of one's desires, and the practice of virtue, and to seek it in intellectual rather than bodily hiding places.

sympathy *and* empathy

For centuries, we English-speakers made do perfectly nicely with "sympathy," "feeling with," the power to share another person's emotions, to be affected by his experiences, to walk a mile—or simply a few yards—in his shoes. No big deal: Just a little compassion, is all, and the chance every so often to cry at a movie. "Empathy," "feeling into," originated in 1912 as a pseudo-Greek translation of the German psychoanalytic term *Einfühlung*, the ability to project one's personality into someone in order to understand him better. Several questions here: Is empathy a bigger deal than sympathy? Is it somehow "heavier," or just more self-conscious? Does one require special imagination or training to feel it? To use it? Should one be content feeling sympathy for Elizabeth Bennet and Holden Caulfield or have the stakes been raised to the point that sympathy is no longer enough? Is one in trouble if one's shrink has sympathy but no empathy? Empathy but no sympathy? What's it all about, Alfie? Write to us care of our publisher. Goodbye.

synecdoche *and* metonymy

Both are highly specialized forms of metaphor. Synecdoche (sin-EK-duh-kee) uses an appropriate part of something to signify the whole; thus "ten hired hands" means "ten hired workmen," and "wheels" were your father's car. Metonymy (muh-TAHN-uh-mee; literally, "name-changing") includes, technically, all synecdoche, but most often denotes the use of an associated or outside attribute for the object or institution under discussion; thus journalists are spoken of as "the press," one steps on "the gas" as routinely as on the accelerator pedal, and an idea comes to you out of "the blue" rather than the sky. Literary critics and classical linguists still make a lot of this pair, but don't spend too much time on rhetorical devices; these days, you'll get more mileage out of being able to distinguish between Verizon and Cingular.

turgid, turbid, *and* tumid

In botany, turgor (from a Latin verb meaning "to swell") is cellular rigidity as the result of a plant's having taken in too much water. By extension, "turgid" means swollen, inflated, enlarged; and, by further extension, pompous, bombastic. "Turgid" does not mean "tur*b*id," which derives from the Latin word for "crowd," and means "muddy, impenetrable, opaque; confused, disordered." (You can remember it from "turbulent.") For better or for worse, "turgid" *does* mean "tu*m*id," which is related to the word "tumor" (from another Latin verb meaning to swell), and which means "swollen, inflated, enlarged," as well as "pompous, bombastic." The one difference we can make out: "Turgid" can imply normal or healthy distention (a branch turgid with sap) and the kind of rant that at least doesn't put you to sleep. "Tumid" almost always has overtones of morbidity: a starvation victim's tumid stomach, a cow's tumid ulcer; figuratively, it bespeaks sheer bloat.

uninterested *and* disinterested

The former means "indifferent, uncaring," the latter "impartial." It's that simple.

venal *and* venial

The two have nothing to do with each other, etymologically or conceptually. "Venal" (from the Latin word for "sale") means "open or susceptible to bribery, capable of betraying one's honor or duty for a price, obtainable by purchase rather than by merit." "Venial" (from the Latin word for "forgiveness") means "pardonable, easily excused, minor in nature"; thus "venial sin" (as opposed to the mortal variety). Suggested mnemonic: "Venal" rhymes with "penal," and prison is where bribe-takers wind up; "venial" rhymes with "genial," which you can afford to be, given that you're not going to be taken to task for your mistake.

Twenty-Five Words Not to Say Wrong

Ten where you have no choice:

1.	flaccid:	FLAK-sid
2.	heinous:	HAY-ness
3.	scion:	SIGH-en
4.	segue:	SEG-way
5.	ague:	AY-gyoo
6.	caste:	KAST
7.	dais:	DAY-is
8.	inchoate:	in-KOH-it
9.	quay:	KEY
10.	ribald:	RIB-uld

Eight where you have to choose between being unimpeachably correct (and risk sounding pretentious) or disarmingly casual (and risk sounding uneducated):

		Correct	*Casual*
11.	dour:	Rhymes with "poor"	Rhymes with "power"
12.	err:	Rhymes with "fur"	Rhymes with "fair"
13.	grimace:	Accent on second syllable: gri-MACE	Accent on first syllable: GRIM-us
14.	harass:	Accent on first syllable: HAR-ass	Accent on second syllable: huh-RASS
15.	impious:	Accent on prefix: IM-pee-ous	Accent on root: im-PIE-ous
16.	schism:	SIZZ-em	SKIZZ-em
17.	extant:	Accent on first syllable: EKS-tunt	Accent on second syllable: eks-TANT
18.	long-lived:	Long *i* (as in "life")	Short *i* (as in "live")

Four where you have to know what you mean before you open your mouth:

19. forte: It's one syllable (ignore the *e*) when it means strong point; two (FOR-tay) when it's the musical direction meaning loudly.

20. bases: More than one base? Say BAYS-es. More than one basis? Say BAYS-ees.

21. slough: In America, SLOO (rhymes with "goo") is preferred for the actual mire, swamp, bayou, or backwater; SLOU (rhymes with "cow") for the deep despair figuratively akin to it; SLUF is the only acceptable pronunciation when you're shedding dead skin.

22. prophecy/prophesy: The former's the noun and you say PRAH-fuh-see; the latter's the verb and you say PRAH-fuh-sigh.

Plus three more where which side you're on counts for more than simply being right:

23. junta: It's the Spaniards' word for "council," and they're going to want you to say HOON-ta. The British (and most of our anchorpersons) prefer JUN-ta.

24. sheik: The Brits *and* the Arabs say SHAKE, and the anchorpersons, slowly but surely, seem to be coming round. The rest of us seem more at home with SHEEK, as of Araby.

25. Celtic: The Greeks (who made up the word Celtic) and the Bretons (who *are* Celtic) both spelled this with a *k*; and purists, including many British speakers, continue to make that *c* hard: KELT-ic. But then, *you* have the Boston Celtics to think about.

Twenty-Six Words Not to Write Wrong

We'll assume that you mastered "necessary" and "separate" back in the eighth grade, and that you remember "all right" on the grounds that it's the opposite of "all wrong." Beyond such basics, here are the twenty-six words you're most likely to go wrong on in your next business letter, interoffice memo, or screenplay. To make things just a bit more galvanizing, we've listed them in ascending order of difficulty (our criteria included rarefaction—see #20—as well as trickiness). And we've provided commentary.

1. trav*e*ler   The English do it with two *l*s, but America doesn't double-up except in accented syllables, e.g., controlled, propeller, referral.

2. princip*le*/princip*al*   They offered this one in eighth grade, too, but we were putting on Clearasil at the time. Briefly, a princip*le* is a ru*le*, and the princip*al* (the most *important* person in your school) is your *pal*.

3. station*a*ry/station*e*ry   With the first, you're st*a*nding in one place; with the second, you're on your way to what the English still call the station*e*r's.

4. coo*lly*   First it looks right, then it looks wrong. The fact is, you're simply adding that familiar suffix, with its *l*, to the root. Likewise the double *n* in drunkenness, the double *s* in misspelling (it works with prefixes, too).

5. emba*rrass*   Two *r*s two *s*s. But "ha*ra*ss."

6. unpa*rallel*ed   The archetypal trick word.

7. *sei*ze   Forget "i before e except after c," which works for the English derivatives of the Latin *capio* ("I take") family: "deceive," "receipt," "conceit," etc., plus

others like "ceiling." But: "weird," "sheik," "inveigle." And, to muddy the waters, there's "siege."

8. pre*ced*ing

Okay: There are three verbs in *-ceed*: "succeed," "proceed," "exceed." Of course, there's "supersede." All the rest are *-cede*, including "precede," whose present participle is therefore spelled thus.

9. nick*el*

Maybe it's just us.

10. fo*r*go/fo*re*go

The first, meaning "relinquish," uses *for-*, an old Anglo-Saxon word indicating abstention or prohibition, as in "forbid," "forsake," "forbear." *Fore-* you know: It refers to what's gone before, as in "forewarn," "forebode," "foregone conclusion."

11. superintend*e*nt

Likewise, "correspond*e*nt," "independ*e*nt." You have to memorize which are *e* and which *a*: Even knowing the Latin conjugations and their stems won't help (e.g., "attend*a*nt").

12. mo*cc*asin

Those use-what's-at-hand Indians. Likewise, "ra*cc*oon."

13. glam*ou*r

So far, so good. But it's "glam*o*rous."

14. impost*o*r

The single hardest case of "*-er* or *-or*?" In general, learned, Latinate words take *-or*, simple Anglo-Saxon ones, *-er* (e.g., "perpetrat*or*" and "do*er*"), but watch out for exceptions (e.g., "actor" and "executioner").

15. de*si*ccate

If you use an adult word you can't afford to misspell it. Note the single first interior consonant, the doubled second one; it's a pattern, too, in titillate, vacillate, flagellate. But: "di*ss*i*p*ate," "exa*gg*e*r*ate."

16. re*su*scitate

Your move.

17. i*n*oculate

Nothing to do with pain or injury (as in "in*n*ocuous"). From the Latin *in* plus *oculus* ("eye"), referring to the little eye the needle makes in your skin. For analogous reasons, which we won't go into here, it's "a*n*oint."

18. sacr*i*legious

The relationship is with "sacr*i*lege," not "religious." Now try to remember how to spell "sacrilege." (Hint: It's like "privilege." Now try to remember how to spell *that*.)

19. con*s*ensus

Not a head-counting, but a coming together of feeling.

20. rar*e*fy

Also: "liqu*e*fy," "stup*e*fy," "putr*e*fy," and their noun forms—"rar*e*faction," etc.

21. prophe*s*y

The verb, which you pronounce "-sigh." The noun is with a *c*.

22. gene*a*logy

With "miner*a*logy" and "an*a*logy," one of a handful of words that don't end in "-*o*logy."

23. pav*i*lion

Not helped by the French word from which it's derived, *pavillon*. Or by "cotillion," its equally high-living cousin. Also: "verm*i*lion."

24. dy*s*function

This prefix is Greek for "disease," not the familiar Latin one. While we're talking medicine (and *ys*), a swollen blood vessel is an aneur*ys*m.

25. bragga*d*ocio

The double *g* (as in "braggart") is easy enough; the problem's with the single *c*, which imitates neither the Italian suffix *-occio*, or the Spenserian character—Braggado*chi*o—from which the word derives.

26. autar*ky*   Here's a prestige distinction, and if you're ambitious you'll contrive to make it this week. Autar*chy* is absolute sovereignty, total self-control; autar*ky* (from a different Greek stem) is self-sufficiency, especially of an economic, damn-the-imports nature.

PLUS, AS AN EXTRA ADDED BONUS, SIX PHRASES YOU MAY NOT EVEN KNOW YOU WRITE WRONG

---

b*at*ed breath   That is, shortened—as in "abate." No entrapment here.

p*ore* over   What you do to a manuscript. It's not the same as what you do to a stack of pancakes.

hare*brained   Ditto "harelip."

test your met*tle   Unless you're at the pig-iron auction.

chaise lo*ngue*   You still want one poolside, but it's a "long chair," not a lounge.

to the man*ner* born   It's all in the execution, not in the family real estate.

Mistaken Identities

ADJECTIVES WHOSE LOOKS ARE DECEPTIVE

CAPTIOUS: Perversely hard to please, given to fault-finding and petty criticism. Like your boss on a bad day. Or invalid wives in the kind of movie where the husband ends up burying the body in the basement and everyone in the audience hopes he'll get away with it.

FRACTIOUS: Peevish, irritable, cranky, or, in a more general sense, inclined to cause trouble. Often used to describe children or people who behave like them. Fractious derives from fraction; breaking or dividing is, after all, what a fractious individual is after. Not to be confused with "factious," from the noun "faction," which also can mean "divisive"—but for different reasons.

NOISOME: Has nothing to do with noise, quite a bit to do with smell. Means "disgusting, unwholesome, unpleasant," as in "a noisome gas," or "downright harmful," as in "noisome prison conditions."

FULSOME: Originally meant what you'd think it would mean: "full, rich, plentiful." But eventually some people became uncomfortable with hedonism, and the "too much of a good thing" connotation crept in. Today, "fulsome" means offensively excessive or insincere. Fulsome praise, for instance, is the kind you get from someone who doesn't like you much but hopes you've got a job for his brother-in-law.

RESTIVE: Impatient or nervous as the result of restraint or delay. The way you used to feel when your mother said you couldn't go out with your friends, you had to stay home and clean your room. Often used to describe balky animals and mutinous crowds. Unlike "restless," "restive" implies resistance to outside control.

TORTUOUS: Full of twists and turns (but not necessarily excruciating ones), like the road to Shangri-la, or Madonna's career path, or foreign policy as practiced by Henry Kissinger.

PARLOUS: Simply a medieval contraction of "perilous," which is, more or less, what it means: "dangerous, precarious, risky." Archaic, but it still crops up regularly in political discussions, the sports section, and the phrase "parlous times."

PASSIBLE: Capable of feeling or suffering; impressionable. Comes from the Latin *passus*, past particle of the verb "to suffer," and is hence related to both passion and patience. Women were once considered passible creatures.

FECKLESS: Just remember that "feck" is a Scottish shortening of "effect"; "feckless," therefore, means weak, ineffective, or, more commonly, childishly careless and irresponsible.

DILATORY: Has to do not with dilation but with delay; means tending to procrastinate. Can refer to a deliberate attempt to stall or simply to a bad habit. Don't confuse with "desultory," disconnected, haphazard, rambling.

MERETRICIOUS: Originally meant "like a harlot"; hence, the current meaning: "attracting by false charms, gaudy, flashy, or tacky," like the meretricious appeal of the *National Enquirer*, or "falsely persuasive, not to be trusted," like the meretricious promises of a Don Juan.

FORTUITOUS: Accidental, happening by chance. Not to be confused with "fortunate": If you and Moby Dick both pick the same spot to swim in, your meeting will be fortuitous (neither of you planned it) but not, from your point of view, fortunate.

ENERVATING: The opposite of "energizing," i.e., sapping, debilitating, depriving of strength or vitality. Lying on the beach in the hot sun all day is enervating; the cold shower you take afterward is energizing.

GNOMIC: Means wise and pithy, full of aphorisms. But there's no way you'll ever not think of a wrinkled little guy with turned-up toes; OK, picture him saying, "Freedom's just another word for nothing left to lose." That's an example of a gnome making a gnomic statement.

Unknown Quantities

ADJECTIVES WHOSE LOOKS ARE TOTALLY INSCRUTABLE

LAMBENT: Flickering lightly over a surface, as a light or a flame; having a gentle glow, luminous. By extension, effortlessly brilliant, as in "a lambent wit." From a Latin verb meaning "to lick."

PLANGENT: Striking with a deep, reverbating sound, as waves against the shore. By extension, plaintive, as in "the plangent notes of a saxophone." From a Latin verb meaning "to lament."

INCHOATE: Just begun, undeveloped, immature, imperfect. From a Latin verb meaning "to begin." Pronounced "in-KOH-it."

JEJUNE: A word with too wide a range of meanings, from "meagre, scanty, barren" to "weak, insubstantial, unfortifying" and "dull, insipid, childish, unsophisticated." Solution: remembering that "jejune" comes from the Latin word for "fasting," i.e., having no food in your stomach, and that it's thus centered on a lack of nourishment. (It's also related to "jejunum," the part of the small intestine that the ancient Roman medical man Galen kept finding empty when he performed autopsies, and to the French *déjeuner*, literally "to break the fast.") Pronounced "juh-JOON."

ATAVISTIC: Resembling one's ancestors, especially one's remote ancestors, rather than one's parents; reverting to ancestral type, as in "atavistic tendencies." From the Latin word for "great-grandfather's grandfather."

HEURISTIC: Concerned with ways of finding things out or of solving problems; proceeding by trial and error; using hypotheses not to come to an immediate conclusion but to eliminate irrelevancies and modify one's take on things as one goes along, with any luck arriving at a theretofore unknown goal. Used of certain computer programs and educational philosophies; the "heuristic method" trains a student to find things out for himself. From the Greek verb meaning "to find," and related to Archimedes' "Eureka!" ("I have found it").

DEMOTIC: Originally, relating to the simplified form of ancient Egyptian writing, the one most people at least stood a chance of understanding. (As such, opposed to "hieratic," "of the priests.") By extension, "popular, in common use." Today, also designates the colloquial form of Modern Greek. From the Greek word for "the people."

FUSTIAN: The base meaning is a coarse, thick cloth usually dyed a dark color to resemble velveteen. By extension, a derogatory term (noun as well as adjective) for an overblown, pompous, padded, and ultimately empty style of speaking or writing. From Fostat, the Cairo suburb where the cloth was first made.

HERMETIC: Pertaining to alchemy or the occult; hence esoteric. Also, airtight (as in "hermetic seal," a process developed by alchemists), protected from outside influences, hidden from view, cloistered. From Hermes Trismegistus, "Thrice-Great Hermes," author of ancient books about magic, equated with both the Greek god Hermes and the older Egyptian god Thoth.

NUMINOUS: Dedicated to or hallowed by a deity, especially a local one, as in "a numinous wood." By extension, holy, awe-inspiring, appealing to the spirit. From the Latin word for "presiding deity."

PROTEAN: Changing form easily; variable, versatile. From the Greek sea-god Proteus, who knew everything but could not be pinned down and made to answer questions because he kept changing his shape, from fire to snake to water, etc. Not to be confused with two other myth-derived adjectives, "promethean" (from the Greek hero Prometheus; see page 257) and "procrustean" (from the Greek robber and villain Procrustes, of the one-size-fits-all bed).

PRIAPIC: Suffering from a persistent, and usually painful, hard-on. By extension, phallic; obsessed with masculinity or virility, generally one's own. From Priapos, the Greek god of procreation.

INEFFABLE: Unutterable, either because you can't (it's too overwhelming) or you shouldn't (it's too sacred); unable to be described in words. From the negative of the Latin verb meaning "to speak out."

INELUCTABLE: Inescapable, inevitable, as in "the ineluctable modalities of the visible and the audible" with which Stephen Dedalus was obsessed in *Ulysses* (see page 250). From the negative of the Latin verb meaning "to struggle against."

ALEATORY: Depending on chance (literally, on the throw of a die, *alea* in Latin, as in Caesar's *Alea jacta est*, "The die is cast"). By extension, involving random choice by an artist or a musician, as when John Cage (see page 283) used to throw the I Ching to determine which notes to play next.

OTIOSE: Originally, indolent, lazy. Today, ineffective, serving no purpose, futile. From the Latin word for "leisure."

EIDETIC: Very vivid, but not real; said of images that are perceived, wrongly, to be outside the head, experienced most often in childhood. The person with an eidetic memory summons up an image, as if on a mental screen, without necessarily comprehending it. From the same Greek word for "form" that gave us "idea" and "idol." Conceptually related word: "oneiric," having to do with dreams, from the Greek word for "dream."

VISCOUS: Having high viscosity, yes. But does that mean it flows fast, like gasoline, or slow, like molasses? Answer: slow. A viscous substance is only semifluid; it's sticky, glutinous. From the Latin word for "bird-lime," a substance used to catch birds.

Six Mnemonic Devices

MEMORIES ARE MADE OF THESE

1. The order of the planets from the sun outward: My very earnest mother just served us nine pickles (Mercury, Venus, Earth, Mars, Jupiter, Saturn, Uranus, Neptune, Pluto).

2. The seven hills of Rome: Poor Queen Victoria eats crow at Christmas (Palatine, Quirinal, Viminal, Esquiline, Capitoline, Aventine, Caelian).

3. The twelve cranial nerves: On old Olympus' towering top, a fat-assed German viewed a hop (olfactory, optic, oculomotor, trochlear, trigeminal, abducens, facial, acoustic, glossopharyngeal, vagus, accessory, hypoglossal).

4. The Linnaean system of classification: King Peter came over from Germany seeking fortune (kingdom, phylum, class, order, family, genus, species, form).

5. Ranking order of the British peerage (see page 224): Do men ever visit Boston? (duke, marquess, earl, viscount, baron).

6. The names of the departments in the president's Cabinet: See the dog jump in a circle; leave her home to entertain editors vivaciously (State, Treasury, Defense, Justice, Interior, Agriculture, Commerce, Labor, Health and Human Services, Housing and Urban Development, Transportation, Energy, Education, Veterans Affairs).

"How Do You Say in Your Country 'Yearning for the Mud'?"

A STAY-AT-HOME'S GUIDE TO WORDS AND PHRASES IN THREE LANGUAGES

LATIN QUARTER: A COUPLE DOZEN DOUBLE-BARRELED PHRASES AND AN EQUAL NUMBER OF SAWED-OFF WORDS AND ABBREVIATIONS

Now that nobody even thinks about taking Greek anymore, it's Latin, actually a more or less businesslike language, that comes off as the height of erudition. And not just among lawyers, doctors, cardinals, and botanists, either. Here, all the shorthand forms (*re* to *qua*, *e.g.* to *i.e.*, *viz.* to *vide*) you'll ever need, plus our selection of the best of the big-deal phrases.

Sawed-Off Latin Words and Abbreviations

c: Used to show that a date is approximate: "Died c. 1850." Short for *circa*, around. Also sometimes *ca.* Pronounced "SIR-ka."

RE: Shorthand (and memorandumese) for "about," "concerning": "Re your comment yesterday." From *in re*, in this matter. Pronounced "ray."

CF.: Meant to get you to compare something to something else: "cf. page 20," that is, look at it with an eye to the issue at hand. From the Latin *confer*, meaning "consult." If you pronounce it, say the letters, " 'cee eff' page twenty."

FL.: From *floruit*, "he (or she) flourished." Shows up on the brass nameplates of old paintings when it's known when an artist worked but not when he was born (for the record, *n.*, from *natus*) or died (*ob.*, from *obiit*, literally "went to meet"). And while we're on the subject, note also: *aet.*, from *aetatis*, "at the age of," for when they know how old the artist was when he did it but not the calendar year it was done, or want to emphasize the former.

MS.:   The abbreviation for *manuscriptum*, manuscript, in a footnote or bibliography. Not to be confused with *Ms.*, the magazine and form of address. More than one manuscript? MSS.

OP.:   The abbreviation for *opus*, work, used in cataloguing musical works, and designating either a single composition or a group of them that stand as a unit.

VS.:   Against, in the courtroom as the stadium. From "versus," also abbreviated *v.*

D.V.:   God willing, from *Deo volente*. Admittedly not much seen these days, though show-offs of an antiquarian bent use it to mean "if nothing gets in our way."

E.G.:   For when you're about to give (or be given) a bunch of examples: "citrus fruits, e.g., orange, lemon, lime." Does not guarantee completeness of list (no grapefruit, for instance, above). Short for *exempli gratia*, "for the sake of example."

I.E.:   For when you're about to explain (or have explained to you) the nature of something: "citrus fruits, i.e., those from trees of the family *Citrus*, with an inedible rind, juicy flesh, usually in segments, and a high vitamin C content." Short for *id est*, "that is." More authoritative, less chatty than *e.g.*

N.B.:   For *nota bene*, "note well." Calls your attention to something the writer thinks you might miss or not see the, in his opinion, enormous significance of.

QUA.:   "In the capacity of," "considered as," as in "the film qua film"—the film not as a story or an evening's entertainment, but as an act of moviemaking, as cinema, as art. Pronounced "kway" or "kwah." From a Latin relative-pronoun form. Caution: User stands to reveal self as pretentious.

SIC: A nudge, usually parenthetical, often gloating, pointing out how a third party got something wrong or gave himself away: "In his review of the new Sylvester Stallione (*sic*) movie. . . ." From *sic*, "thus." Caution: User stands to reveal self as smug.

VIZ.: Used after a word or expression clearly requiring itemization. Equivalent to our "namely" or "to wit": "The citrus fruits, viz., orange, lemon, lime, grapefruit, tangerine, kumquat." (No mention of tangelo, unfortunately, but you get the point.) An abbreviation of *videlicet*, "it is permitted to see." Likewise, *sc.* or *scil.*, from *scilicet*, "it is permitted to know." Both *viz.* and *sc.*, unlike *e.g.*, guarantee they're giving you a complete rundown.

Q.E.D.: The capital letters printed triumphantly by a person who thinks he's convincingly proven what he set out to prove a paragraph—or a chapter, or a lifetime—ago. Short for *quod erat demonstrandum*, "which was to be shown." A favorite of geometry teachers and miscellaneous pedants.

R.I.P.: Right, on all the old tombstones. But it's short for *Requiescat in pace*, "May he (or she) rest in peace," *not* "Rest in peace," which is why you might see it on an old French or German tombstone, too.

ERGO: "Therefore," "hence." Unforgettable in Descartes' formulation *Cogito, ergo sum*, "I think, therefore I am" (see page 314) and unavoidable in various mathematical proofs.

PACE: "With all due respect to" or "with the permission of," as in "Pace Mies, there are times when more is more." Used to express polite, or ironically polite, disagreement. Pronounced "PAY-see" (preferred by academicians) or "PAH-chay" (less correct, but more common).

STET: "Let it stand," "ignore all previous instructions to alter or correct," "this is, after all, how we want it." A printer's term, but one useful to anybody in a position to make—or not make—final changes. From a form of *stare*, "to stand." The opposite: *dele*, from the Latin word for "delete."

VIDE: In reference to a passage in a book, means "see" or "consult." A shortened version of *quod vide*, "which see," sometimes also abbreviated as *q.v.*

IBID.: One of the old term-paper nightmares. "In the same book, chapter, or passage" (i.e., the one referred to in the note immediately preceding).

Short for *ibidem*, "in the same place." Doesn't, unlike *op. cit.*, short for *opere citato*, "in the work cited," require an author's name, just a page number, and doesn't send you scrolling up through the 150 preceding footnotes.

ET AL.:   "And others," short for both *et alia*, "and other things," and *et alii*, "and other people." More specific than *etc.*, short for *et cetera*, "and the rest," "and so forth," and can, unlike *etc.*, be used of people.

AD HOC: "For this thing," said of something impromptu, improvised, for the matter at hand and that matter only. An ad hoc committee will probably last out only the season (or the problem); an ad hoc solution implies that somebody is—or ought to be—working on a permanent one. Cf. *pro tem*, short for *pro tempore*, "for the time being."

AD LIB.:   "To the desire"; in music, a sign that somebody can play a passage, or an entire piece, as loud and as fast as he wants. In show business, and without the period, a sign that somebody forgot his lines.

PER SE: "Through itself"; intrinsically, by dint of its very nature.

PASSIM: Scattered, occurring throughout. Applied to a word, passage, or reference occurring here and there, over and over, in a specific book or author.

Double-Barreled Latin Phrases

BONA FIDE (BOH-na-FIDE or BOH-na-FIE-deh): Done or made "in good faith"; sincere, genuine.

CASUS BELLI (KAH-sus-BELL-ee): "Occasion of war." An event that justifies or precipitates war.

CUI BONO (KWEE-BOH-noh): "For whom (is it) good?" Question first posed by a Roman magistrate to make the point that one way to approach a crime is to determine who stood to gain from it. Often wrongly used to mean "For what purpose?"

DE FACTO (deh-FAK-toh): "From the fact." In reality; actual, actually in power. A de facto government is not formally elected or installed, but is firmly in control; cf. *de jure*, following.

DE JURE (deh-YOO-reh): "From the law." According to law; in principle. A de jure government is duly elected and installed, but exercises no real power; cf. *de facto*, previously.

EX POST FACTO (EKS-post-FAK-toh): "From what is done afterward." Formulated, enacted, or operating retroactively.

IN MEDIAS RES (in-MAY-dee-ahs-RACE): "Into the midst of things." Into the middle of a story or narrative; without background or preamble. A convention of the classical epic, first formulated by the poet Horace. The opposite approach is *ab ovo*, "from the egg."

MEMENTO MORI (meh-MEN-toh-MOR-ee): "Remember you must die." A reminder or warning of death; a death's head.

MUTATIS MUTANDIS (moo-TAH-tees-moo-TAHN-dees): "The things that ought to have been changed having been changed." With the necessary substitutions having been made, the indicated variances considered.

NE PLUS ULTRA (nay-ploos-UL-trah): "Not further beyond," said to have been inscribed on the Pillars of Hercules (today's Strait of Gibraltar), as a warning to ships. A farthest point, a highest pitch, a culmination; an impassable obstacle; and, implicitly, a suggestion to stay put or, better yet, turn back.

OBITER DICTUM (OH-buh-ter-DIK-tum): "Thing said by the way." Any incidental or parenthetical remark. In law, something the judge says in arguing a point, but that has no bearing on his decision. Plural: *obiter dicta*.

PARI PASSU (PAH-ree-PAH-soo): "With equal pace." Simultaneously, equally, proceeding alongside.

PERSONA NON GRATA (per-SOH-na-nohn-GRAH-ta): "Person not pleasing." Someone unacceptable within a given context.

QUID PRO QUO (kwid-proh-KWOH): "Something for something." A compensation, an even exchange; tit for tat.

SINE QUA NON (sin-neh-kwah-NOHN): "Without which not." The indispensable element, condition, or quality.

SUB ROSA (sub-ROH-sah): "Under the rose," though debate rages as to whether it was the rose Cupid gave someone as a bribe not to gossip about the affairs of

Venus, or a rose carried by the Egyptian god Horus in a statue that also showed him with his finger to his lips, or some other rose altogether. Anyway, "sub rosa" means "in confidence," with secrecy expressed or implied; "clandestinely."

SUI GENERIS (SOO-ee-JEN-er-is): "Of its own kind." Peculiar, unique, not to be analyzed or catalogued along standard lines.

TU QUOQUE (TOO-KWOH-kweh): "You also." The ancient Roman version of "So are you." A response to an accusation directed personally.

ULTRA VIRES (UL-trah-VEER-ayz): "Beyond (one's) authority." Also, outside one's jurisdiction. It's well known that several successive administrations behaved *ultra vires* in Vietnam.

FOUR LATIN PHRASES FOR YOUR DAY IN COURT

CORPUS DELICTI (KOR-pus-de-LIK-tee): "The body of the crime." Tangible evidence of wrongdoing, including (but hardly restricted to) the body of a murder victim.

HABEAS CORPUS (HAY-bee-as-KOR-pus): "You have the body." A writ requiring that a person being detained be brought before a judge; meant to guard against unfair imprisonment, it constitutes one of the most celebrated features of both the British and the American legal systems.

NOLLE PROSEQUI (NOL-leh-proh-SEK-wee): "To not wish to proceed." Statement that the prosecution doesn't want to pursue matters further; the writ ending court proceedings. Shortened to "nol-pros" by fast-talking lawyers.

NOLO CONTENDERE (NOH-loh-kon-TEN-der-eh): "I don't want to fight." Plea made by a defendant that's equivalent to an admission of guilt (and that leaves him subject to punishment), but that allows him the legal option of denying the charges later.

AND FOUR FOR YOUR DAY OF JUDGMENT

DE PROFUNDIS (deh-pro-FUN-dees): "Out of the depths" of sorrow and despair, the first two words of Psalms 130 (and the title of a confessional essay by Oscar Wilde). An especially bitter cry of wretchedness.

ECCE HOMO (ek-keh-HOH-moh): "Behold the man," the words first spoken by Pilate (John 19:5) when he showed Jesus, crowned with thorns, to the mob. A name given to paintings showing Christ thus, also to an essay by Nietzsche in which he announces that he's the Antichrist.

NOLI ME TANGERE (NOH-lee-meh-TAN-geh-reh): "Touch me not," the words spoken by Christ to Mary Magdalen (see page 489) after his Resurrection (John 20:17). A name given to paintings showing Christ *thus*; also, a person or thing that can't be touched; a warning against getting involved or in the way.

NUNC DIMITTIS (nunk-deh-MIT-us): "Now lettest Thou (thy servant) depart," the words Simeon speaks to Jesus, satisfied that he'd finally seen the Messiah (Luke 2:29). A name for that canticle, the "Song of Simeon"; by extension, any permission to go. To "sing nunc dimittis" is to express one's readiness to depart or die.

FROM PRUSSIA WITH LOVE

We promise: There simply aren't that many German expressions for you—or any other non-German—to worry about. Of course, the ones that you do have to worry about tend to be a mouthful. Also, a skullful.

BILDUNGSROMAN (bil-DOONGS-row-MON): Literally, education novel. Tells the story of how somebody came of age, à la Pip in Dickens' *Great Expectations*, Stephen Dedalus in Joyce's *A Portrait of the Artist As a Young Man*, or Hans Castorp in Mann's *The Magic Mountain* (see page 253).

DOPPELGÄNGER (DOP-pul-GENG-er): "Double-goer," the ghostly double, the spiritual (or sometimes flesh-and-blood) counterpart of a living person; as in the Poe story "William Wilson."

GEMÜTLICHKEIT (guh-MOOT-lik-kite): From *Gemüt*, temperament, feeling. Implies geniality, coziness, a sense of shared well-being. The adjective form is *gemütlich*. Use sparingly: Can make you sound like your great-uncle Arthur.

GÖTTERDÄMMERUNG (GUH-ter-DEHM-er-oong): "Twilight of the gods." The last opera in Wagner's four-part *Ring* cycle (see page 287). Also, any terminal breakdown or tragic end, the louder the better.

LEBENSRAUM (LAY-bens-ROWM): "Living space." A big part of Germany's justification for its periodic invasions of its neighbors. Only slightly less convincing than our "manifest destiny."

SCHADENFREUDE (SHAH-den-FROY-duh): "Harm joy." You'll enjoy this one; God knows, you've already enjoyed the feeling—the slightly malicious, slightly guilty pleasure you register at the news of someone else's, and especially a friend's, misfortune.

STURM UND DRANG (SHTURM-und-DRAHNG): "Storm and stress." From a late-eighteenth-century German literary movement (centered on drama and involving, like so much else, Goethe and Schiller), a beat-your-breast, tear-your-hair-out reaction to pussyfooting French classicism. Now, any great emotional turmoil.

WELTANSCHAUUNG (VELT-ahn-SHAU-oong): "Worldview." A philosophy of life, a comprehensive version of the whole enchilada, and how it works.

WELTSCHMERZ (VELT-schmertz): "World pain." Ranges from a kind of sentimental pessimism or world-weariness to full-fledged distress and angst (a German noun so assimilated you don't even have to capitalize it anymore).

WUNDERKIND (VOON-der-kind): "Wonder child." The child prodigy, whether still a child (like Mozart when he first attracted serious attention), or already an adolescent (like Orson Welles when he made *Citizen Kane*). The *Wunderkind*, whatever his age, really does compose, direct, or appear on talk shows brilliantly—unlike the *enfant terrible* (see page 674), who's too busy making trouble to pay much attention to the quality of his performance.

ZEITGEIST (TSITE-guyst): "Time ghost." The spirit of the age, the taste and outlook of a period or a generation.

The Germans shot their wad with the nouns; their adjectives, by contrast, are short, to the point, and appealingly lowercase.

ECHT (EKKKT): Genuine, typical, the real thing. *Echt* Schwarzenegger would be, depending on your point of view, either *Conan* or *Terminator*.

ERSATZ (EHR-zahts): Substitute, artificial, not real. Ersatz Schwarzenegger might be Steven Seagal. (No need to set italic; now at home in English.)

VERBOTEN (fehr-BOHT-en): Forbidden, prohibited, don't even think it. In a roomful of Schwarzenegger fans, it's not crazy to assume that Merchant-Ivory would be verboten (no italics).

Enjoy these German words and phrases? Well, no need to pine for more. Instead, just turn to the following pages and find: Bauhaus (page 105), Realpolitik (page 596), Leitmotif (page 287), Ding-an-sich (page 320), Übermensch (page 325), Ostpolitik (page 366), Gestalt (page 456) and Ur- (page 639).

A LIFETIME SUPPLY OF JE NE SAIS QUOI

The good news is, not as many French phrases have made it into Webster's and the OED as Latin phrases. The bad news is, there are a lot more French than Latin ones that you—and everybody else with an ax to grind or an impression to make—are going to want in on. Following, organized into categories (and getting harder as you read on), our favorites among the still-numerous contenders, each of which was selected because it (a) has no easy and/or economical equivalent in English, and hence isn't merely pretentious; (b) provides a glimpse of the notoriously agile, notoriously devious French mind at work, and hence isn't merely academic; and (c) is more or less tricky in its meaning, form, or use, and hence isn't merely self-evident, in which case we'd all have mastered it already, n'est-ce pas?

For the Freshman

BÊTE NOIRE (bet-NWAR): Literally, black beast; someone or something that one fears, dislikes, or characteristically avoids. Stronger than "pet peeve," more graceful than "bugbear." Note the *e* on *noire*.

DE RIGUEUR (de-ree-GUHR): Absolutely necessary; required by good form if nothing else. Two *u*s in *rigueur*, a relative of our "rigor."

FAIT ACCOMPLI (fet-a-kom-PLEE): Literally, accomplished fact; a thing already consummated, so that fighting it is useless, and changing it impossible.

PAR EXCELLENCE (par-ek-sel-AHNSE): Above all others of the same type; literally, by (virtue of its) excellence. Paris is the European capital *par excellence*.

RAISON D'ÊTRE (ray-zohn-DETR): "Reason for being." Justification for one's existence.

For the Sophomore

BON MOT (bohn-MOH): Not just a "good word," but a witty remark, a memorable comment, an aphorism even. Come junior year, you'll want to take on *mot juste*, the "just word," the word that conveys what's meant more precisely than any word anybody else in the dorm could come up with.

CARTE BLANCHE (kart-BLAHNSH): "White paper," a sheet that's blank except for a signature, with the implication that its bearer can write his own deal. A blank check, yes, but also blanket permission.

COUP DE GRÂCE (koo-de-GRAHS): Literally, stroke of mercy; the death blow, delivered to someone mortally wounded. By extension, any finishing or decisive act. Watch that word *coup*, by the way; it's a favorite of the French, and it shows up again in *coup d'état*, the sudden, and often violent, overthrow of a government, and *coup de foudre*, literally, lightning bolt; figuratively, love at first sight.

ENFANT TERRIBLE (ahn-fahnt-teh-REE-bl): "Terrible child"; can refer to your standard-issue brat or to anybody, typically a young artist or writer, who causes trouble and calls attention to himself through unconventional and boat-rocking behavior. Note: Not to be confused with *Wunderkind* (see page 672).

PIÈCE DE RÉSISTANCE (pee-ess-de-ray-zee-STAHNS): From the sense of "resistance" as staying-power, endurance. By extension, something of substance, toughness, or strength. *Not*, as a lot of people seem to think, the crowning glory, the "capper" in a can-you-top-this sequence of items. At the dinner table, it's the saddle of lamb—not the cherries jubilee—that is, or ought to be, the *pièce de résistance*.

For the Literature Major

BELLES LETTRES (bel-LET-re): Serious literary writings—"beautiful letters"—more "artistic" than "intellectual," especially essays and criticism, but including fiction, poetry, and drama. Today, tends to have connotations of the artificial, the effete, the old-fashioned, of Henry James as opposed to Henry Miller.

FIN DE SIÈCLE (fahn-de-see-EH-kl): "End of century," specifically, the end of the nineteenth century, a period celebrated for its decadence in France (Verlaine, Mallarmé, Huysman, et al.) as in England (Wilde, Beardsley, et al.). Not surprisingly, the phrase is now being applied to the end of the twentieth century, too.

ROMAN À CLEF (roh-mahn-ah-KLAY): "Novel with key," in which people and events have been fictionalized, with any luck tantalizingly.

SUCCÈS D'ESTIME (sook-say-des-TEEM): A success based on reviews (or, sometimes, respect for the author's—or performer's—reputation) rather than on sales, on "esteem" rather than popular enthusiasm. Cf. *succès de scandale*, where the scandalousness, rather than the excellence, of the material is the come-on. Also, *succès fou*, a "mad" success, a smash hit.

TOUR DE FORCE (toor-de-FORS): "Turn of force," a display of virtuosity, an exhibition of skill, often undertaken by an artist in a field not his own just to prove he can do it.

For the History Major

AGENT PROVOCATEUR (ah-ZHEN-proh-voh-ka-TUHR): For example: The undercover agent who infiltrates the trade union or political party, pretending sympathy with its aims, and gets the members to do precisely those things that they can be punished or put away for.

CORDON SANITAIRE (kor-DOHN-san-ee-TAYR): The line, generally heavily guarded, between an infected area and an adjacent, as-yet uninfected one. Applies likewise to the isolating of politically sensitive subject matter or of a state its neighbors consider dangerous.

ÉMINENCE GRISE (ay-mee-NEHNZ-GREEZ): The power behind the throne, the person who exercises his authority unofficially. Literally, "gray cardinal," after Cardinal Richelieu's private secretary, Père Joseph. Éminence, in case you're wondering, is a cardinal's honorific.

LÈSE-MAJESTÉ (lez-mah-zhes-TAY): An offense or crime against one's ruler or sovereign; treason. More commonly, any presumptuous conduct or overstepping of authority. And that's the same *les-* you see in "lesion," ultimately from a Latin word meaning "to injure."

NOBLESSE OBLIGE (noh-BLESS-oh-BLEEZH): "Noble birth obligates," privilege entails responsibility. Point of honor (and *raison d'être*) for aristocrats and other *ancien régime*—or pre-Revolutionary, "former administration"—types.

At the Buffet Dinner

COMME IL FAUT (kohme-eel-FOH): "As is necessary"; used, sometimes slightly sarcastically, of behavior that is socially up to snuff. In introductions that are *comme il faut*, older people are introduced to younger ones and women to men, a little something or other said about each of them to the other, and all the rest of it.

DOUBLE ENTENDRE (DOO-bl-ahn-TAHN-dr): Literally, "to hear or to understand double"; in practice, a remark with a racy, spicy, off-color undertone as well as a flat, seemingly innocent surface meaning. Actually, the French themselves say *double entente*, but that's their problem.

D'UN CERTAIN AGE (duhn-sayr-tehn-AHJ): Not as imprecise as "of a certain age"; means, in fact, middle-aged at least. Used euphemistically, but that doesn't mean that a *femme d'un certain age* is, in the eyes of a Frenchman, necessarily over the hill.

FAUTE DE MIEUX (FOHT-de-MEEUH): "For want of something better"; for lack of a workable alternative, ideal, or guiding philosophy. Cf. *tant mieux*, "so much the better," and, for that matter, *tant pis*, "so much the worse," expressions of cynical resignation in the face of yet another new—and questionable—development.

PLUS ÇA CHANGE (ploo-sa-SHAHN-zhe): "The more it changes," the beginning of (and a recognized abbreviation for) the expression that is concluded by *plus c'est la même chose*, "the more it's the same thing." A worldly, even world-weary way of saying that there's nothing new under the sun, and even if there were, it wouldn't surprise *you*.

At the Black-Tie Dinner

ACTE GRATUIT (ahkt-grah-TWEE): The gratuitous act, sudden, enigmatic, and often disruptive, undertaken on impulse. So dubbed by the novelist André Gide at a time when the Surrealists (along with Gide's characters) were turning out a lot of them. Shooting a gun into a crowd with no particular goal in mind would be an *acte gratuit*; so were many of the Sixties "happenings."

FORCE MAJEURE (fors-mah-ZHUR): Literally, "superior strength." The irresistible force, totally out of your control, generally unexpected, and, most important, serving to release you from your obligations. Includes what English-speaking insurance companies call "acts of God," as well as various forms of strictly human negligence and bad judgment.

HOMME MOYEN SENSUEL (OHME-mwoy-EHN-sehn-soo-EL): The average sensual man, or, as the critic Matthew Arnold put it, introducing the phrase into English in the 1880s, the fellow "whose city is Paris, and whose ideal is the free, gay, pleasurable life of Paris." In other words, anyone who lives the life of the senses and doesn't let moral and intellectual considerations push him around. Today, though, a lot of people use it to mean not much more than "the typical man," "the man of average desires," "the man in the street."

TRAHISON DES CLERCS (trah-ee-ZOHN-day-KLAYRK): The critic and essayist Julien Benda's term (and his 1927 book title); literally, "treason of the clerks," a reference to how intellectuals—writers, artists, and thinkers—had in that century betrayed themselves and each other by allowing their beliefs to be fired by political passions rather than guided by philosophical principles. To be directed at anybody who keeps losing sight of the big picture, the ultimate aim, in his desire to win this evening's argument.

ESPRIT DE L'ESCALIER (es-PREE-de-less-kahl-YEH): Not the spirit, but the wit of the staircase; the slicing, but also rather wise, retort to somebody else's fatuousness that you thought of only as you were on your way downstairs to the street (or upstairs to your room) after the party had ended.

And So to Bed

AMOUR-PROPRE (ah-MOOR-PROH-pr): An old phrase—literally, "self-love"—with an even wider range of meaning than the now-trendy narcissism, from simple self-esteem, to a need for admiration by others, to out-and-out conceit, to neurotic self-involvement. Don't be pleased if someone tells you you're a paragon (*un parangon*) of it.

ARRIÈRE-PENSÉE (ah-ree-AYR-pahn-SAY): Literally, "behind-thought." A famous old trap: Does not mean afterthought or hindsight. Does mean an idea or intention that is concealed, an ulterior motive, a hidden agenda.

CRIME PASSIONNEL (kreem-pah-see-oh-NELL): Crime of passion, sure, but especially murder, and especially when sexual jealousy is the motive. Two *s*s, two *n*s.

DROIT DU SEIGNEUR (dwah-de-sehn-YUHR): The right of the feudal lord, just as you'd expect, but specifically his right to sleep with the bride of any of his vassals on her wedding night.

NOSTALGIE DE LA BOUE (naws-tahl-ZHEE-de-la-BOO): "Yearning for the mud," for degradation, depravity, and your basic wallow, particularly by a person we'd all have thought was above such things, and particularly in a guess-who's-sleeping-with-whom context. Coined by a popular nineteenth-century French dramatist, it's a phrase at this point more familiar to us English-speakers than to the French, some of whom will look at you admiringly when you use it, as if you'd made it up yourself.

INDEX

ILLUSTRATION CREDITS

Museum der Stadt, Vienna; 330 Wide World Photos; 336 Henri Cartier-Bresson/Magnum; 337 Susan Meiselas/Magnum; 339 Library of Congress

CHAPTER 8: 342 Duane Hanson, "Tourists," O.K. Harris Works of Art; 344 UPI/Bettmann Newsphotos; 348, 368 Wide World Photos; 375, 383, 387, 391, 396 Reuters Bettmann; 414 (top left), 414 (top right), 414 (bottom right) UPI/Bettmann Newsphotos; 414 (middle left) Wide World Photos; 421, 424 © David Lindroth, Inc.

CHAPTER 9: 426 Museum of Modern Art/Film Stills Archive; 434, 438, 440 National Library of Medicine; 452 UPI/Bettmann Newsphotos; 456 Richard Kalvar/Magnum; 457 Wide World Photos; 458 Dr. B.F. Skinner, Harvard University.

CHAPTER 10: 460 Michael Burgess, "Frontispiece to Book I of *Paradise Lost*," Metropolitan Museum of Art. Elisha Whittelsey Collection; 463 Picture People; 465, 467 UPI/Bettmann Newsphotos; 469 Bruno Barbey/Magnum; 473 Burry/Magnum; 475 (left) AP/Worldwide Photos; 475 (right) Culver Picture; 477 UPI/Bettmann Newsphotos; 485 © David Lindroth, Inc.; 487 (top) New York Public Library; 487 (bottom) Nicolaes Maes, "Abraham Dismissing Hagar and Ishmael," Museum of Modern Art. Gift of Mrs. Edward Brayton; 488 Jan Lievans, "Job," National Gallery of Canada, Ottawa; 489 (top) Thomas Hart Benton, "Susanna and the Elders," The Fine Arts Museums of San Francisco; 489 (bottom) Mary Evans Picture Library/Photo Researchers, Inc.; 490 National Gallery of Art, Washington, D.C.; 491 New York Public Library Picture Collection; 493 Mary Evans Picture Library/Photo Researchers, Inc.; 494, 498 UPI/Bettmann Newsphotos; 499 Wide World Photos.

CHAPTER 11: 500 Library of Congress; 504 Picture People; 508 Rapho/Photo Researchers, Inc.; 508 American Museum of Natural History; 510 (top) Library of Congress; 510 (bottom) American Museum of Natural History; 515 UPI/Bettmann Newsphotos; 523 American Museum of Natural History; 532, 535 Photo Researchers, Inc. 543, 545, 561, 562 New York Public Library Picture Collection; 563, 564 (left) Library of Congress; 564 (right), 566 New York Public Library Picture Collection.

CHAPTER 12: 570, 573 New York Public Library Picture Collection; 576 (left) National Portrait Gallery, London; 576 (right), 579, 581 Library of Congress; 583 Giraudon/Art Resources N.Y.; 586 Jerry Bauer; 587 (top) Wide World Photos; 587 (bottom) UPI/Bettmann Newsphotos; 588 Metropolitan Museum of Art, Fletcher Fund; 589 (top) Culver Pictures; 589 (bottom) Bettmann Archive; 590 (top) New York Public Library Picture Collection; 590 (bottom) Metropolitan Museum of Art; 591 (top) Picture People; 591 (bottom) Library of Congress; 592 Wide World Photos; 593 North Carolina Museum of Art; 594 Mary Evans Picture Library/Photo Researchers, Inc.; 595 Archive/Photo Researchers, Inc.; 596 Mary Evans Picture Library/Photo Researchers, Inc.; 597 UPI/Bettmann Newsphotos; 598 Mary Evans Picture Library/Photo Researchers, Inc; 599 Museum of Modern Art; 600 Library of Congress; 601 Metropolitan Museum of Art; 602 Mary Evans Picture Library/Photo Researchers, Inc.; 603 Metropolitan Museum of Art; 604 Mary Evans Picture Library/Photo Researchers, Inc.; 605 Metropolitan Museum of Art; 617 Library of Congress; 619 Mary Evans Picture Library/Photo Researchers, Inc.; 620 Archive/Photo Researchers, Inc.; 621, 624 UPI/Bettmann Newsphotos; 626, 628 Culver Pictures; 630 Robert Capa/Magnum; 633 UPI/Bettmann Newsphotos.

ABOUT THE AUTHORS

Judy Jones is a freelance writer who lives in Princeton, New Jersey. William Wilson was also a freelance writer. Wilson went to Yale and Jones to Smith, but both have maintained that they got their real educations in the process of writing this book. William Wilson died in 1999.